Health Psychology

Health Psychology: A Critical Introduction aims to provide students with a stimulating alternative to the textbooks currently available by placing the discipline within the context of the social world and encouraging them to question some of the assumptions and values underlying much current research. A comprehensive survey of the discipline is provided, framed within a lifespan approach, and emphasising social-cultural factors such as gender, ethnicity and social-economic status. All major topics are covered, including health behaviours, health promotion, coping strategies, stress, biomedical and biopsychosocial models of health and illness, chronic illnesses, psychoneuroimmunology, disability, pain and patient-provider communication. Each topic is situated within its social and cultural context and constantly linked back to real-world experience. Chapters include valuable features such as research updates, learning objectives and recommended readings. This book will be an invaluable resource for students of health psychology across a range of disciplines including psychology, anthropology and health studies.

ANTONIA C. LYONS is Senior Lecturer in the School of Psychology, Massey University, New Zealand. She was a founding member of the International Society of Critical Health Psychology and has published numerous articles and book chapters in this field.

KERRY CHAMBERLAIN is Professor of Health Psychology at Massey University, New Zealand. He has published widely in international journals on health and research methods and authored several book chapters. He is co-editor of *Qualitative Health Psychology* and *Exploring Existential Meaning*.

Health Psychology

A Critical Introduction

ANTONIA C. LYONS
and
KERRY CHAMBERLAIN

CAMBRIDGE
UNIVERSITY PRESS

CAMBRIDGE UNIVERSITY PRESS

Cambridge, New York, Melbourne, Madrid, Cape Town, Singapore, São Paulo, Delhi

Cambridge University Press
The Edinburgh Building, Cambridge CB2 8RU, UK

Published in the United States of America by Cambridge University Press, New York

www.cambridge.org
Information on this title: www.cambridge.org/9780521005265

© Antonia C. Lyons and Kerry Chamberlain 2006

First published 2006
Third printing 2009

Printed in the United Kingdom at the University Press, Cambridge

A catalogue record for this publication is available from the British Library

ISBN 978-0-521-80898-9 hardback
ISBN 978-0-521-00526-5 paperback

For Callum with love [AL]

For Vivienne of course [KC]

Contents

Acknowledgements

I would like to gratefully thank the School of Psychology at the University of Birmingham, England (particularly Professor Glyn Thomas) and the School of Psychology at Massey University, New Zealand, for their support of this work. I would also like to thank my teacher (and mentor), Dr John Spicer, for his insight, integrity and clarity in teaching health psychology. Thanks also to my very supportive friends (you know who you are), colleagues and students (especially Gareth Treharne, for being so positive of my own health psychology teaching). Special thanks and love to Ian, whose unceasing encouragement has been very welcome! Finally, enormous thanks must go to the two editors we worked with at Cambridge University Press, Sarah Caro and Juliet Davis-Berry. Sarah, thanks for the opportunity, encouragement and advice; Juliet, it has been a real pleasure to work with you (I'll miss your emails). [AL]

My grateful thanks to all those colleagues and students, past and present, scattered around the world and too numerous to list, who have challenged and informed me through their conversations and friendships over the years, and contributed greatly to enhancing my understanding of health and health psychology – their contributions are generally invisible but definitely substantial. Thanks also to the School of Psychology at Massey University for support of various kinds along the way. Last, but certainly not least, my thanks to Sarah Caro and Juliet Davis-Berry for their support, encouragement and good humour over the course of this project – it has been greatly appreciated. [KC]

We both thank Alan Pearson for his generous consent to the use of his artwork for the cover.

Setting out: using this book

There are many reasons why we feel that a book like this is overdue. We have both been teaching health psychology and searching for a text that takes a more critical approach to notions of health and illness, without success. Although there are many health psychology texts available, and more keep appearing, none seems to us to be suitable for the ways in which we want to approach health psychology, either as researchers or as teachers. Existing health psychology texts do not reflect the changes in this field, where increasingly a variety of methods and approaches, qualitative and critical, are being employed to examine health and illness issues from a psychological perspective. For some years we have felt dissatisfied with the ways in which health psychology conducts its research and promulgates its findings. We are critical of the way it unreflexively continues the traditions of mainstream psychology, assuming that psychological factors have a real existence, that they can be meaningfully and accurately measured, that statistical findings have meaning by virtue of their significance levels and that findings (almost) have the status of general laws. We are critical of the lack of consideration in health psychology of the social context within which health and illness are experienced and understood. We are critical of the way in which health psychology all too readily adopts the premises and assumptions of biomedicine, and the ways in which its findings promote biomedical understandings, albeit in the guise of a 'biopsychosocial' approach, a vague rhetorical entity with many meanings. We are critical of the way in which health psychology fails to engage with any serious theorisation of health issues, and the way it confuses and conflates theories and models.

The absence of texts that take a more critical approach, of any sort, to health psychology is a major concern to us as teachers of health psychology. Although one or two critically oriented texts have appeared, the bulk of health psychology texts seem to us to be virtually interchangeable in their approach to the field, and we find them problematic in a number of ways. First and foremost, existing texts overwhelmingly present ideas drawn from mainstream psychology about health and illness, and use only traditional, positivist research as their literature base. This is problematic because it means that health and illness are located at the individual level, and social, structural and cultural perspectives are not taken into account. These texts atomise the individual into physical and cognitive 'parts' and focus on the individual in isolation, dislocating people from their lived social worlds. This concern plagues psychology in general, but is fundamentally more difficult when matters of health and illness are the focus of study. Second, although existing texts cover most areas of health psychology, they commonly present information in a fragmented and disjointed manner. For example, many of these texts present separate chapters on stress, coping and social support, and detach these from other chapters on specific chronic illnesses such as heart disease, diabetes, cancer and so on. Third, existing texts fail to include any critical notions about health psychology work. The values of positivist 'science' and the 'detached' researcher are taken for granted, and there is no attempt to examine the assumptions and values which underlie the research presented in the texts. There is little reflection on the part of authors about the field of health psychology *per se*, and how it operates as a discipline. This works to exclude issues of power and advantage, and marginalises the meanings of health and illness for specific groupings of people, mainly women, children, ethnic minorities, people in lower socioeconomic positions and minority groups such as those with disabilities and older adults. We are also tired of having to go beyond the current boundaries of health psychology, into medical sociology and anthropology and health sciences, to locate other sorts of findings, other ways of working, and for informative learning resources to bring to our students. We believe it is time that health psychology managed this within its own discipline. We thus feel that there is a strong need for a health psychology textbook which takes a very different orientation to health psychology material, integrating mainstream work with more critical and qualitative research (from outside psychology where necessary), providing a broader and more considered approach to the field.

We have several major aims for this book. First, it sets out to present an original and exciting perspective on the health psychology field. Second, it aims to comprehensively cover the major topics of health psychology, but in doing so to provide an alternative look at traditional material. Third, it aims to locate psychological work concerning health and illness among work from other social science disciplines, such as sociology and social anthropology, while retaining a focus on implications for the individual throughout. Fourth, it aims to present material that will challenge readers to think more broadly, and more critically, about notions of health, illness, sickness and disease. Fifth, it aims to highlight the role that health psychology plays in creating our everyday understandings of health and illness.

What, then, is the approach of this book? We do not have all the answers to the best alternatives for working in health psychology. We are not dismissive of mainstream approaches, but we do try to be critical about how we work, how we might work and the potential benefits of changing the ways in which we work. In this text we adopt a critical approach, outlined more fully in ch. 1, which entails being critical about what we do at a number of levels. First, it means being thoughtful and critical, in both negative and positive senses, about the endeavour we are engaged in – the questions we ask, the methods we use, the understandings we bring and so on. Second, it means taking on notions of criticality, and starting to become more informed about the nature and limits of our approaches, methods and findings, who they include and who they exclude, who they might benefit and who they might oppress. Third, and interlinked with these, it means being reflexive about ourselves, our approaches and our field, questioning our own values and assumptions. We try, throughout the book, to include comment which will make readers reflect on these issues, and we take up the issue of what a critical health psychology might be more fully in the final chapter of the book. At that point, we anticipate that readers will have developed a more informed critical perspective on health and illness from the discussions and commentaries within each chapter.

How have we organised the book in order to promote all this? We bracket the body of the book with introductory and closing chapters focused directly on the field of health psychology. In the opening chapter we locate the field, both of health and of health psychology, and discuss a number of potentialities for the latter. We also argue the case for a critical approach to health and illness. In the closing chapter we relocate the field in the light of the material covered and the arguments made within the text, setting out a version of what a critical health psychology could be. In the body of the book we deal specifically with issues of health and illness. We have used a 'journey' or 'passage' metaphor to sequence this material. This begins with a consideration of ideas about health, illness and the body, goes on to discuss staying healthy by choosing lifestyles and controlling the body, and then continues the journey through becoming ill, comprehending bodily experience, interacting with health professionals, treating illness, experiencing and recovering from illness, and closes with dying. This organisation is quite deliberately radically different from other health psychology texts for two reasons. First, it disrupts the common textual arrangement that structures health and illness around bodily systems and specific diseases, so dominant in the field. Second, it facilitates a more general and integrative discussion of issues ranging across bodily systems and diseases, and enhances the viability of our objective to present a more critical and integrative perspective on matters of health and illness. In taking this approach, we retain the sociocultural location of individuals in view by threading and integrating sociocultural issues – gender, ethnicity, socioeconomic status (SES), minority status, disability and sexual orientation – into the topics of each chapter. This avoids social factors being separated from the person and partitioned off into separate chapters.

We have also incorporated several features within the book to promote learning. Each chapter opens with specific learning objectives that can be accomplished from a study of the chapter. Each chapter then provides an overview of content and an orientation to the specific topics under consideration. There are frequent section summaries throughout, and all chapters end with clear (and opinionated) conclusions that identify implications for the field. Readers are left in no doubt of our position in relation to the concerns discussed within the chapters. Each chapter includes topic-relevant research in focus boxes, which provide an overview of a specific research study together with a commentary and critical reflection on the study and issues arising from it. These are used to provoke critical engagement with the field. Chapters also include a range of relevant figures, tables and sidebars to illustrate specific issues in depth and to enhance interest in the topics under discussion. An extensive glossary of key terms is also provided, and a definition for each term is located alongside the relevant text. Finally, the chapters initially address their material from a traditional perspective and then engage with the implications of this as part of a broader critique, leading to consideration of critical alternatives and interpretations of the material. This is also intended to provoke readers to consider the value and limitations of alternative, and more critical, perspectives.

In short, we hope that working through this text changes the way you think about health psychology.

1 Locating the field: introducing health psychology

I hope I have convinced you of some simple but far-reaching truths. That our mental state and physical health are inexorably intertwined. That stress, depression and other psychological factors can alter our vulnerability to many diseases, including bacterial and viral infections, heart disease and cancer. That the relationship between mind and health is mediated both by our behaviour and by biological connections between the brain and immune system. That these connections work in both directions, so our physical health can influence our mental state. That all illnesses have psychological and emotional consequences as well as causes. That there is nothing shameful or weak about the intrusion of thoughts and emotions into illness. That our social relationships with other people are central to health. That our dualist habit of contrasting mind and body, as though they were two fundamentally different entities, is deeply misleading.   (Martin, 1997, p. 314)

The psychology of health, illness and health care needs to be considered in economic, political, ecological, social and cultural context.   (Marks *et al.*, 2000, p. 1)

Learning objectives

This chapter will provide an introduction to health psychology and locate studies of health and illness within their sociohistorical context. By the end of this chapter, you should be able to:

- provide a brief historical overview of dominant Western views on health and disease;
- outline the historical development of psychological approaches to health and illness, and health psychology in particular;
- define and explain the biomedical and biopsychosocial models of health and illness;
- describe what health psychology covers as a field of study;
- outline how health psychology relates to subfields of psychology, and other health-related fields;
- describe variations in health across social categories such as social class, age, gender and ethnicity;
- critically evaluate the assumptions and values that underlie health psychology research and practices.

Health psychology is a diverse and wide-ranging field. It covers questions about what health is through to how people cope with chronic illness (both their own and others'). For example, think about some of the following questions:

- Do you think psychology has anything to do with health? What do you think health actually is? Is it simply the opposite of illness?
- Has psychology got anything to do with staying healthy? Think about whether or not you do anything to stay healthy. Do you get regular exercise to keep healthy? Or do you get regular exercise for fun, not for health? Or can't you be bothered with regular exercise?
- Is behaving in ways to stay healthy the same as behaving in ways to prevent getting ill? Did you give up smoking cigarettes for health reasons? If you do smoke cigarettes, you probably know you 'should' give them up for health reasons.
- Do you think psychological factors influence getting ill? Does stress really make us ill? Think about your own experiences – when you feel stressed, do you also feel as though you are likely to become ill? If so, how do you know you're getting sick?
- Is psychology relevant to how we interpret sensations in our bodies? How do you know when that strange feeling in your throat is actually a 'symptom' that might require you to go to the doctor? Do things like your gender, your personality, what you're doing, what others tell you, what your beliefs about illness are, influence whether or not you notice physical symptoms?
- Do you like going to the doctor? Why? Is the interaction you have with your doctor relevant to your health? Do you take your medications? Why or why not? Do you do what your doctor says? Why or why not? Do you see alternative health practitioners?
- What if your illness is ongoing and affects your life more than you thought it would? How do you cope with this? What effect might it have on you and others? Do you think about dying? What happens when people close to you die? How do people die?

All of these questions fall within the domain of health psychology, and all of them will be covered in this text at some point. They highlight how diverse health psychology is, and the range of issues it covers (and this is not a comprehensive list by any means). In this chapter we describe the field of health psychology, what it is, how it developed and how it fits into other health-related fields. To do this, we locate these fields both historically and academically, stepping back and considering how the study of health and disease has developed over the centuries. We examine how health psychology differs from other approaches to the study of health and illness such as medical sociology, medical anthropology and medicine. We examine traditional models of health and illness based on the biomedical model, and compare this model to the biopsychosocial model put forward as the basis of health psychology.

We also describe how health varies not just across individuals, but across social groupings, such as social class or socioeconomic status (SES), age, gender and ethnicity. Finally, we describe what we mean by taking 'a critical approach' to topics within health psychology.

First, in order to provide a framework for the study of health and disease, we begin with a very brief account of the major views on health and causes of disease throughout Western history. This description highlights how our dominant Western ideas about health and disease are historically specific. Other cultures have developed different conceptions of health and illness over the centuries; an example is shown in sidebar 1.1.

1.1 Māori beliefs about health

Traditional Māori beliefs about health view it as stemming from well-being across four domains: family/community, physical, spiritual and emotional. For example, illness is seen as due to *mate atua* (the spiritual realm) or to *mate tangata* (the people's realm – wounds, injuries, etc.). Breaches of *tapu* (the sacred or divine) are seen to lead to misery, including physical illness. *Tohunga* are expert healers, who treat not just the physical but also the spiritual, emotional and family/community aspects of health. With the colonisation of New Zealand/Aoteoroa by Europeans from the late 1700s onwards, these beliefs about health and illness were suppressed. Indeed, in 1907 the government passed the Tohunga Suppression Act, making it illegal for traditional Māori healers to practise (the Act was repealed in the 1960s). As Durie (1998) has argued, 'early Māori approaches to health and to health care do provide a cultural and social framework . . . that has a continuing relevance to modern times' (p. 23).

A historical view of health and disease

During Western history three different medical models have prevailed, and these coincided with the periods from c. 300 BC to c. AD 400 (the ancient Greeks), from c. AD 400 to c. 1300 (the Middle Ages), and from 1300 onwards.

The ancient Greek civilisation was one of the first to consider health and illness in terms of bodily functioning rather than seeing illness a result of evil spirits invading the body. The mind and body were seen as part of the same thing, a unit working together. This conceptualisation of mind and body is known as **monism**. Subsequent Greek philosophers, most notably Plato, broke with this view, and proposed that the mind (or soul) and the body were actually separate entities. From this perspective, the body was seen as a physical being, and the mind as something else, something more abstract. Viewing the mind and body as separate substances is a position known as **dualism**.

Hippocrates (c. 460–377 BC) was a firm believer in the dualistic nature of mind and body. He made the radical suggestion that disease occurred in the body and that this process was independent of the mind. Hippocrates proposed that the body contained four specific fluids, called humours: blood, black bile, yellow bile and phlegm. According to this 'humoral' theory of health and

The philosophical view that the body and the mind (or soul, or mental processes) are essentially one substance, and are part of one underlying reality.

The philosophical view that the body and the mind (or soul, or mental processes) are fundamentally different substances.

1.2 The mind–body problem

Philosophers have been grappling with the mind–body problem for centuries. Although dualism has been a dominant perspective for many hundreds of years, problems still remain. How can the non-material mind have an influence on the material body? Are the two things connected? The relationship between the mind and the body is fundamental to health psychology.

disease, when these humours were balanced, a person experienced health. However, when the fluids were out of balance, disease occurred. Treatment therefore involved an attempt to restore balance to the four fluids. This conceptualisation of health and disease was radical for its time because previously disease had been thought to occur as a result of demons or spirits possessing bodies. Hippocrates challenged the dominant view and situated health and disease within the individual body. For this work he is often described as the 'father of medicine'. The humoral theory became dominant throughout Greece and Rome, and was developed further by Galen during the second century AD. A prominent physician, Galen demonstrated that disease can occur in a specific part of the body, and that different diseases can have different effects on the body.

Following the collapse of the Roman empire in the fifth century, the advancement of knowledge slowed considerably. Views on health and disease shifted, and illness was again seen as the result of evil spirits, demons or punishment by God. Ideas about the causes of illness were heavily religious, as were forms of treatment, such as torturing the body to drive away evil. Priests replaced physicians as healers and medical knowledge became the domain of the church. As people and animals were seen as possessing souls, they were sacrosanct and therefore dissection was forbidden. Here we also see a return to a monistic view of the mind and body: physical bodies and minds were seen as one, as the soul (or mind) was inherent in all parts of the physical body.

These dominant religious views on health and disease (and the mind–body relationship) remained until the Renaissance (which began around the fourteenth century). During the Renaissance a 're-birth' of inquiry in Europe led to the scientific revolution during the 1600s. René Descartes, a French philosopher and mathematician, proposed novel views on the body. He put forward the notion that the mind and body are completely separate entities, but that they communicate with one another (through the pineal gland). This was a dualistic account of the mind and body, but Descartes went further by specifying that although mind (or soul) and the body were separate substances, they interacted with one another. Such an idea was extremely radical for the time and led to major consequences for the study of health and disease. Essentially, the body could be conceptualised as a physical machine. Descartes proposed that the human soul left the body at death and that animals have no soul – which enabled dissection of bodies to occur. From here knowledge of the body grew quickly, and Van Leeuwenhoek's work on microscopy in the seventeenth century, along with Morgagni's work on autopsy (seventeenth to eighteenth centuries) led to the rejection of the humoral theory of disease.

Over the next three hundred years medical knowledge and knowledge about bodily processes and functions grew tremendously. Physicians reclaimed the realm of medical knowledge and focused on bodily factors, primarily at the cellular level. Diagnosis and treatment of disease was based solely on physical evidence. These views developed into what is called the biomedical model of health and disease, which is the fundamental basis of traditional Western medicine today. Thus, modern Western medicine also employs a dualistic view of mind and body: the body is our physical being and the mind is made up of abstract processes of thoughts, feelings and so on, which are independent of physical disease processes.

Biomedicine and the biomedical model

The biomedical model of health and disease has dominated the field of medicine for over two hundred years, and continues to do so. According to the biomedical model:

- the body is separate from psychological and social processes of the mind;
- all diseases and physical disorders can be explained by disturbances in physiological processes, resulting from injury, biochemical imbalances, bacterial or viral infection and so on;
- health is seen as biochemical or physical in nature.

The biomedical model stimulated an enormous amount of research into identifying the pathogens that cause particular diseases. It also enabled the development of physical treatments for disease, such as medications, vaccines and surgical procedures (Bernard & Krupat, 1994). Medical technology continues to develop at an astounding rate, and more and more technologies are available to diagnose disease (such as computerised axial tomography, ultrasound and magnetic resonance imaging), conduct surgical procedures (such as heart bypass, organ transplantation, fetal surgery, microscopic surgery) and test for the risk of disease (such as some forms of genetic testing – see ch. 4) (Joralemon, 1999).

Despite these technological advances, however, the biomedical model has been heavily criticised. It has been described as (Hardey, 1998a):

- reductionist, and therefore ignoring the complexity of factors involved in health (Bernard & Krupat, 1994);
- mechanistic, and therefore assuming that every disease has a primary biological cause;
- dualistic, and therefore neglecting the social and psychological aspects of the individual (Engel, 1977);
- empirical, and therefore assuming that we can objectively identify biological causes of disease;

- disease oriented, and therefore emphasising illness over health;
- interventionist, and therefore overly intrusive.

If we assume that every disease has a primary biological cause that we can objectively identify, then behavioural, social and psychological factors will not be considered as potential contributors to disease, because these will not be assessed as part of the process of diagnosis (Stroebe, 2000). Thus, from the perspective of the biomedical model it is difficult to value lifestyle and psychosocial factors as affecting health and illness (Engel, 1977). From a more sociological perspective, many of the criticisms levelled at biomedicine throughout the 1970s were premised on an awareness that the values and activities of the medical profession were congruent with a patriarchal and capitalist society (Nettleton, 1995). Medicine was male dominated and sexist in its teaching, research and practice, and also functioned to sustain the capitalist status quo.

Two major changes occurred during the twentieth century in Western societies that led to serious questioning of the value of the biomedical model. First, there were enormous changes in the illnesses and diseases which affected people and caused death. Second, the concept of health became more prominent and reduced the emphasis placed on illness by biomedicine. Health became conceptualised in a much broader way than previously. These changes are outlined briefly below.

Changes in health and disease

Over the twentieth century rates of infectious disease declined dramatically in Western societies. In the early 1900s, people became ill and died primarily

Illness that lasts only a relatively short time. from **acute illness** (such as tuberculosis, pneumonia, influenza). However, over the course of the twentieth century life expectancy increased dramatically, and people became ill and died from chronic rather than acute illnesses (such

Illness that is ongoing and is usually irreversible. as heart disease, cancer, diabetes) (Donaldson, 2000). A **chronic illness** is a degenerative illness which is slow in developing, and which people live with for a long time. Chronic illnesses are not so much cured as 'managed' (Taylor, 1999).

Although it is commonly thought that the increase in life expectancy and decline in infectious illness was the result of advances in medicine, in many cases the decline occurred many years before effective vaccines and medications were available. This was true for tuberculosis, diphtheria, measles, scarlet fever, typhoid, pneumonia and influenza (McKinlay & McKinlay, 1981). The primary reasons for the decline were better hygiene, better nutrition and reduced poverty (McKeown, 1979). For example, public health innovations and engineering allowed the building of sewage treatment and water purification facilities, which had a major impact on health.

Thus, although the biomedical model was a useful framework for infectious disease, it is not sufficient for the diseases of today. Chronic illnesses such as heart disease, cancer, stroke and diabetes are multiply determined disorders and psychological, behavioural and social factors play roles in their development. They are known as **lifestyle diseases**, as everyday behaviour such as diet, exercise and smoking puts people at risk of developing these chronic illnesses. The inadequacy of the biomedical model for diseases of today has been noted by Carroll (1992), who writes: 'to isolate disease and treatment as topics only for the attention of medicine and biology is to misunderstand the nature of most contemporary illness' (p. 2).

Diseases in which a person's everyday behaviours (e.g. diet, exercise, smoking) play roles in their development, such as coronary heart disease, lung cancer, Type II diabetes.

The broadening perspective on health

In 1948 the World Health Organisation (WHO) defined health as 'a complete state of physical, mental and social well-being and not merely the absence of disease or infirmity'. This definition broke ground for three reasons:

- it is a positive definition, rather than a negative one – health is not merely the absence of illness;
- it recognised various dimensions of health status, including mental, physical and social aspects;
- it included political and social considerations, and was therefore inspirational. For example, well-being might require the elimination of poverty and freedom, enabling people to live in a society with social justice.

However, under this definition it is difficult for very many people to be categorised as healthy. Furthermore, it has been criticised because it is idealistic and utopian (Seedhouse, 1986). In summary, disenchantment with the biomedical model, and an increasing focus on social and psychological influences on health, led to the development of the biopsychosocial model (Engel, 1977).

The biopsychosocial model

Essentially the biopsychosocial model states that health and illness arise from the interplay of biological, psychological and social factors (Engel, 1977). For example, biological factors such as genetic predisposition, behavioural factors such as smoking and stress and social conditions such as social support and peer relationships may all contribute to the development of a particular disease (such as cancer). In terms of the mind–body debate, the biopsychosocial model has a holistic approach and sees that the mind and body are both involved in health and illness. Initially proposed by psychiatrist George Engel (1977), this model developed out of a need for medicine to take the patient into account, including her social context and how society deals with her illness. The biopsychosocial model is certainly in accord with the definition of health provided by WHO in 1948.

While the biopsychosocial model has been a major influence in the development of health psychology (Marks *et al.*, 2000) it has received considerable criticism. Researchers have argued that the biopsychosocial model is still essentially biomedical and needs further theoretical work (e.g. Armstrong, 1987; Ogden, 1997). In psychiatry McLaren (1998) has strongly argued that the biopsychosocial model is seriously flawed and should be abandoned. McLaren argues that this model should be seen in its historical context, as a reaction against psychoanalysis (which is woolly and cannot be pinned down for empirical study) and behaviourism (which strips context from the person). Psychologists have put forward similar arguments. Stam (2000) has argued that authors do not discuss the biopsychosocial model as an explicit theory or formal model. He states (p. 276):

> I think it is sufficient to say that it is a clever neologism masquerading as a model and its naïve distribution to undergraduates ought to lead us to urge publishers to place a warning label on textbooks indicating that they are a danger to the health of one's theoretical education.

On the other hand, Spicer and Chamberlain (1996) have argued that the basic perspective of the biopsychosocial model is right, but that the ways in which it is being implemented are inappropriate. According to these authors, the 'social' part of the model is not being captured in health psychology research, and the integration of the social and psychological has yet to be achieved. In a similar vein, Marks (2002) argues that the biopsychosocial model is not a model in the formal sense, but is better understood as a way of thinking about health and illness which functions heuristically to justify and legitimate research. Suls and Rothman (2004) also argue that 'as a guiding framework, the biopsychosocial model has proven remarkably successful as it has enabled health psychologists to be at the forefront of efforts to forge a multilevel, multisystems approach to human functioning' (p. 119). However, they also state that it is best viewed as a 'work in progress', and that for it to be effective five specific issues need to be addressed:

- transforming the biopsychosocial model from a conceptual framework into a formal model which specifies linkages between subsystems;
- recognising and emphasising that relevant constructs can serve multiple roles within a theoretical model (e.g. culture influences all levels of analysis);
- designing and collecting rich data sets which assess people at all relevant levels and across time, to enable an exploration of complex interacting systems;
- focusing on discovery and exploration rather than prematurely on hypothesis testing and explanation;
- ensuring that research findings translate into practice and policy (and vice versa).

The development of health psychology

Disenchantment with the biomedical model of health and illness, and a growing realisation that behavioural and social factors were important in (particularly chronic) diseases, led to a number of social science disciplines becoming involved with issues of health and illness. Health psychology was one of those that developed at this particular time (during the 1970s) and explicitly employed the biopsychosocial model of health and illness.

The classic, and establishing, definition of health psychology was developed in the early 1980s by a group of US researchers, and has been adopted by the American Psychological Association, the British Psychological Society and other professional organisations. It states that health psychology is the:

> aggregate of the specific educational, scientific, and professional contributions of the discipline of psychology to the promotion and maintenance of health, the prevention and treatment of illness, the identification of etiologic and diagnostic correlates of health, illness, and related dysfunction, and the improvement of the health-care system and health policy formation.   (Matarazzo, 1980, p. 815)

This definition gives health psychology a role in four broad areas that essentially cover the realm of physical health. Specifically, health psychology is involved in:

Promoting and maintaining health: through, for example, understanding what health is and what it means to people (see ch. 2), helping people to change their lifestyles for physical health benefit, changing behaviour that affects health (e.g. eating a high fat diet, not getting enough exercise), planning campaigns to reduce smoking and so on (see ch. 3).

Preventing and treating illness: through, for example, examining screening behaviours such as regular **mammograms** (see ch. 4), exploring how people make sense of physical symptoms and what they do about them (see chs. 6 and 8), assisting with adjustment to chronic illness (see ch. 9).

Studying the causes of illness: through, for example, examining whether psychological factors such as negative emotions play any role in the **etiology** of a specific disease (see ch. 5).

Improving health care systems and health policy: through, for example, examining how hospitals and other health institutions affect patients, how communication by health care professionals affects behaviours such as adherence to medical regimes and treatment programmes (see ch. 7).

Health psychology therefore encompasses all of the contributions that psychology can make to physical health and well-being, and these contributions range from the etiological to the therapeutic (Matarazzo, 1980). It concerns itself with physical health rather than mental health (even though these aspects are impossible to separate (Marks *et al.*, 2000)). While some define health psychology

---

X-ray pictures of the breast, used to detect tumours and cysts. One breast at a time is rested on a flat surface that contains the x-ray plate, and a compressor is pressed firmly against the breast to help flatten out the breast tissue. The X-ray pictures are taken from several angles.

The cause or origin of a disease.

Table 1.1 Knowledge contributions made by other areas of psychology to health psychology

Area of psychology	Contributions
Physiological / biological	How the brain and the immune system interact (e.g. psychoneuroimmunology)
Clinical	Treatment approaches for illness or rehabilitation (e.g. changing behaviour following a heart attack); coping with chronic pain
Cognitive	Models of health-related behaviour, models of illness representations
Developmental	Using a lifespan perspective to show how health and illness are influenced by stage of life, growth and ageing
Social	Changing social behaviour, health promotion and education; more recently critical social psychology encourages health psychologists to consider the implications of their work and the field itself
Cross-cultural	How health and illness are viewed in diverse ways in different cultures. Highlights the ethnocentrism of mainstream psychology

Adapted from Bernard & Krupat (1994).

as a multidisciplinary field (e.g. Marks *et al.*, 2000), the location of health psychology as a subfield of psychology makes it distinctive. There are many health-related fields which are explicitly defined as multidisciplinary, such as psychosomatic medicine and behavioural medicine. Furthermore, health psychology draws on many aspects of other subfields of psychology, most notably social psychology, clinical psychology, cognitive psychology and so on, as described in table 1.1.

During the 1980s and 1990s, health psychology grew rapidly and it continues to do so. This rapid growth has been alongside a more general interest in health and behaviour in the media, workplaces, schools and also in medicine (Baum & Posluszny, 1999). It has been attributed to a number of factors in Western societies (Marks *et al.*, 2000; Taylor, 1999), including:

- an awareness of the major role that behaviour plays in many illnesses and deaths;
- an increasing ideology of health as the responsibility of the individual (in line with increasing individualism within Western societies);
- an increase in critiques of the biomedical framework;
- a disenchantment with biomedical health care and the changing face of health care;
- the escalating costs of health care services (with little improvement in basic health indicators).

Academic location of health psychology

Health psychology is a young and dynamic field, and it sits alongside a number of other disciplines which explore health and illness. As Marks and colleagues (2000) have argued, 'without major contributions from other disciplines and fields it seems doubtful that health psychology can provide a meaningful account of the psychological aspects of health, illness and health care' (p. 13). Interdisciplinary approaches to the study of health and illness provide a new, more powerful synthesis (Marks *et al.*, 2000). There is overlap between, for example, some research carried out in medical sociology and health psychology. Furthermore, research conducted in anthropology can be extremely informative for health psychology. For these reasons, throughout the text we draw on research material that is relevant to the topic and, as you will see, this work is not always conducted by health psychologists or published in health psychology journals. Yet it is central, relevant and informative to our work as health psychologists. It is therefore worthwhile exploring some of these approaches in a little more detail.

Psychosomatic medicine, behavioural medicine, behavioural health

Three other disciplines are closely related to health psychology and developed prior to the emergence of health psychology as a subdiscipline: psychosomatic medicine, behavioural medicine and behavioural health. Psychosomatic medicine developed out of Freud's work in the late nineteenth and early twentieth centuries. Freud had a huge influence on views about the mind and the body, which forced health professionals (and later the general public) to take another look at the relationship between the two. His work on **conversion hysteria** concluded that unconscious conflicts in the mind can have physiological effects on the body. According to this view, repressed psychological conflicts become converted into physical symptoms which have no underlying organic cause. The types of physical symptom seen in conversion hysteria included loss of speech, sight or hearing, muscular paralysis, loss of sensation in a hand (or other part of the body) and eating disorders such as anorexia nervosa and bulimia. Freud's work was continued by Alexander (a psychoanalyst) and Dunbar (a psychiatrist) during the 1930s. They were specifically interested in particular personalities (rather than intrapsychic processes) as pathogenic and proposed that anxiety arising from conflicts led to physiological changes in the body via the autonomic nervous system (Taylor, 1999). This work led to the field of **psychosomatic medicine**. Here, particular disorders are believed to be psychosomatic in origin and work in this field examines the psychological profiles of specific disorders. Ulcers, rheumatoid arthritis, **essential hypertension** and bronchial asthma were all believed to result from specific psychological conflict or pathogenic personalities.

> A condition in which patients have physiological symptoms, such as paralysis or blindness, without any apparent physiological cause.

> A multidisciplinary area of study concerned with treating physical symptoms and disease using a holistic approach.

> Consistently elevated blood pressure with no identifiable cause.

Psychosomatic medicine sectioned off a set of diseases that might be caused by psychological factors, restricting the range of problems to which psychological and social factors might be important. This work remained psychoanalytic

A multidisciplinary area of study concerned with applying behavioural principles and techniques to the prevention, diagnosis and treatment of illness and rehabilitation.

A multidisciplinary area of study concerned with enhancing health and preventing illness in healthy individuals.

until the 1960s, when it expanded to take into account a more holistic way of thinking about health and illness (Totman, 1982). Currently psychosomatic medicine is a much broader field which examines psychosocial factors, physiological functioning and the development of illness (Sarafino, 1998) (see sidebar 1.3).

Disenchantment with the biomedical model and the increasing awareness of the importance of behavioural factors in health and illness led to the development of the fields of **behavioural medicine** and **behavioural health** during the 1960s and 1970s (see sidebar 1.3). At this time, behaviourism was a dominant perspective in psychology. According to this perspective, specific behaviours are learned through conditioning (both classical and operant). Behavioural medicine drew on these principles to explore their role in health, illness and physiological functioning. Biofeedback was developed as a therapeutic technique to help people gain control over physiological processes such as blood pressure. Behavioural medicine is explicitly interdisciplinary, integrating behavioural and medical sciences. An important aspect of behavioural medicine is treating people who are ill (Bernard & Krupat, 1994; Chan et al., 2002); this can be contrasted with its subfield of behavioural health, which is similarly explicitly interdisciplinary, but has as its major focus preventing illness and enhancing health.

1.3

The journal *Psychosomatic Medicine* describes itself as publishing

> experimental and clinical studies dealing with various aspects of the relationships among social, psychological, and behavioral factors and bodily processes in humans and animals. It is an international, interdisciplinary journal devoted to experimental and clinical investigation in behavioral biology, psychiatry, psychology, physiology, anthropology, and clinical medicine. (taken from the home-page of the journal, at http://intl.psychosomaticmedicine.org/misc/about.shtml)

The *Journal of Behavioral Medicine* describes itself as a

> broadly conceived interdisciplinary publication devoted to furthering our understanding of physical health and illness through the knowledge and techniques of behavioral science. Application of this knowledge to prevention, treatment, and rehabilitation is also a major function of the journal, which includes papers from all disciplines engaged in behavioral medicine research: psychology, psychiatry, sociology, epidemiology, anthropology, health economics, and biostatistics. (taken from the home-page of the journal, at http://www.kluweronline.com/issn/0160–7715/contents)

Health psychology, psychosomatic medicine and behavioural medicine have similar goals and there is much overlap in the knowledge employed in these fields. The primary distinction to be made between them is the extent to which they are interdisciplinary: psychosomatic medicine is more aligned with medical disciplines, particularly psychiatry; behavioural medicine is diverse and includes practitioners, academics and students from a wide range of disciplines (Chan et al., 2002); health psychology is a subfield of psychology and employs knowledge from many other areas of psychology (see table 1.1). This distinction is seen in the memberships of the professional bodies associated with these disciplines, although there is also overlap in membership and some people are members of all three.

Table 1.2 Some health-related disciplines relevant to health psychology

Perspective	Associated disciplines and subdisciplines
Cultural	Medical anthropology
Societal	Medical sociology
	Sociology of health and illness
	Medical ethics
	Social policy
	Health economics
	Epidemiology
	Public health
Individual	Medicine
	Surgery
	Dentistry
	Nursing
	Physical therapy
	Occupational therapy
	Behavioural medicine
	Behavioural health
	Psychosomatic medicine

Other disciplines relevant to health psychology

A range of other disciplines are also relevant to health psychology (see table 1.2). We can view these disciplines as providing different perspectives on health and illness, ranging from a cultural perspective, through to a social (or societal) perspective, through to an individual perspective.

At the cultural level, medical anthropology examines how both biological and cultural factors may affect health and disease. This perspective also provides insight into how political and economic factors influence health and illness. Studying health and illness across cultures means that particular kinds of questions can be asked, such as how health varies across cultures. Does it mean different things in different cultures? How do people react to specific illnesses in different cultures? How are health care services structured in other cultures? How much does culture influence what is considered biological? Medical anthropologists have demonstrated how behaviour that puts individuals at risk of AIDS (sex without condoms, use of needles for injecting drugs) is related to economic and social disadvantage. For example, economic necessity forces men and women into sex work, and poverty is related to intravenous drug use (Joralemon, 1999). From this perspective, using questionnaires and focusing on behaviour at individual levels is inadequate.

Many disciplines take a more societal perspective on health and illness. In medical sociology and the sociology of health and illness, the social dimensions of both health and illness are examined. Here, the sorts of questions that have been examined include how a person displays illness to others. What impact does taking up the 'sick role' have on a person and relevant others? Is it easier to claim sickness in certain contexts rather than others? What are the social and cultural reactions to illness? How is illness portrayed in the media? What role does SES play in keeping people healthy?

Another discipline that takes a societal perspective is epidemiology, in which the frequency, distribution and causes of disease in a population are examined and documented. Epidemiology considers **morbidity, mortality, prevalence and incidence**, and these terms are also employed in health psychology. Epidemiologists ask questions such as what the rates of particular cancers are in particular geographical locations. Why do cancer rates vary by geographic location? Why is a particular illness distributed differentially across age, ethnic or cultural groups?

Public health also takes a societal perspective on health. This discipline is concerned with protecting, maintaining and improving health through organised effort in the community (Sarafino, 1998). People in public health ask such questions as how we can communicate more effectively to encourage people to change behaviour. What is the most effective way to get people to stop smoking or wear sunscreen? How effective are health education programmes for specific segments of the population? Other disciplines which take a societal perspective on health and illness are shown in table 1.2.

There are also many disciplines that take a much more individual and behavioural perspective on health and illness. Traditional medical disciplines such as medicine, surgery, dentistry, nursing, as well as aligned disciplines such as physical therapy, occupational therapy and rehabilitation studies, can all be included here. And of course this is where traditional psychology approaches fit best as well. People employing an individual perspective ask such questions as how people adapt to life with chronic illness. How can we get individuals to take their medication as directed? How does entering a hospital setting affect the individual? How do we change a person's behaviour to make it more healthy?

In summary, there are many health-related disciplines and subdisciplines which take differing perspectives on the study of health and disease. Many of these are relevant to health psychology, especially as this field itself is rapidly expanding. We turn now to examine some of the approaches and perspectives that are employed within health psychology.

Approaches within health psychology

As we have already noted, health psychology is a broad field covering an increasingly diverse range of issues. According to Smith and Suls (2004), the focus of work within health psychology is changing to include more of a focus on contextual features of health. In the USA this is largely the result of

---

Illness, injury or disability; morbidity rates are the number of people with a particular illness, injury or disability.

Death; mortality rates are the number of deaths that are due to a particular cause.

The number of cases (people) with a particular illness, injury or disability. Refers to the total number of cases, including previously reported and current cases.

The number of new cases (people) with a particular illness, injury or disability reported during a particular time (e.g. over the previous year).

changes in population demographics, with increased diversity of ethnic groups and an older population (Smith & Suls, 2004). More attention is now being paid to the social contexts of health and illness, and health psychologists study and work with individuals, families, groups, communities, organisations and populations (Marks *et al.*, 2000). Four main approaches have been evolving in health psychology in recent years: clinical, public, community and critical health psychology (Marks, 2002). These approaches and a summary of how they differ from one another are set out in table 1.3.

Clinical health psychology

Clinical health psychology is strongly research based and its work is set primarily within health care systems. Knowledge is applied to a wide and diverse range of clinical work with patients. This is the most established and most mainstream of the four approaches in health psychology, and it has been successful in demonstrating the value of psychological perspectives on health, illness and health care (Marks, 2002). It is also the approach that has advanced most strongly in terms of the professionalisation of health psychology.

Public health psychology

Public health psychology is less concerned with individual patients and treatment, and more focused on health promotion and prevention at the population level. A much broader perspective is taken in public health psychology, where health is seen as the outcome of the social, economic and political aspects of people's lives (Marks, 2002). As Albee and Fryer (2003) note, 'successful intervention in particular individuals with particular diseases has no effect on the rate of new cases in the population' (p. 71). Thus public health psychology focuses on primary prevention as the only way to reduce incidence of disease in the population. Prevention is often done at the collective level, which can make it more difficult for it to secure funds and be taken as seriously as individual-level treatment. Prevention work often takes a long time to have an effect, is hard to evaluate in terms of its effectiveness and takes effect before people are aware they needed it. It is also overwhelmingly difficult to tackle such major social problems as an oppressive labour market and poverty (Albee & Fryer, 2003). Public health psychology is more interdisciplinary than other approaches, drawing on research and findings from epidemiology, public health, health communication, health economics and the sociology of health.

Community health psychology

As with public health psychology, community health psychology views health as an outcome of social, economic and political contexts (Marks, 2002). It is also concerned with general health promotion and disease prevention

Table 1.3 The major characteristics of four types of health psychology: clinical, public, community and critical

Characteristic	Clinical health psychology	Public health psychology	Community health psychology	Critical health psychology
Focus	Physical illness and dysfunction	Health promotion and disease prevention	Physical and mental health promotion and development	Power
Theory / philosophy	The biopsychosocial model	No single theory or philosophy; works towards general theories such as employment improves health. Supports public health promotion.	Uses a social and economic model, focusing on the individual and systems levels for health promotion and prevention. Sees individuals and communities as interdependent	Analyses the values, assumptions and practices of psychologists and other health care professionals. Reflexively examines how power operates and whom it benefits
Values	Maintaining the autonomy of the individual through ethical intervention	Tracking the health of populations as a basis for policy and health promotion, communication and interventions	Increasing the autonomy of disadvantaged or oppressed people though social action	Highlighting the political nature of all human existence; freedom of thought and compassion for others
Context	People with illness and patients in the health care system, such as hospitals, clinics, health centres	Schools, work sites, the media	Families, communities, people within their social and cultural context	Social structures, economics, government; people within their social and political context
Objectives	To enhance the effectiveness of treatments, understand psychosocial aspects of treatments	To improve the health of populations	To engender empowerment and social change	To fight for equality of opportunities and resources for health
Research methodologies	Trials to test effectiveness of interventions; correlational, quantitative and quasi-experimental methods	Epidemiological methods, large-scale trials, multivariate statistics, evaluation	Participatory action research, coalitions between researchers, practitioners and communities, multiple methodologies	Critical analysis combined with any of the methods used in the other three approaches

Adapted from Marks (2002).

rather than individual diagnosis and treatment. Community health psychology focuses on communities and groups, working with them together and aiming for 'empowerment' to combat disease, promote health and enable social change to occur (Campbell & Murray, 2004). This approach developed out of concerns regarding the minimal contribution traditional health psychology has made to debates about how health inequalities come about, and how they should be addressed (Campbell & Murray, 2004). Aligned to community psychology more generally, this approach employs an ecological perspective on healthy psychosocial development. Individuals are viewed as embedded within small systems which in turn are embedded within larger systems (Murray *et al.*, 2004). Community psychology is explicit about the collectivist and caring values it employs as a basis of research and application, and makes explicit use of concepts such as oppression, empowerment, social justice, compassion and respect for diversity (Murray *et al.*, 2004). Undertaking **action research** is one of its main aims. Given the ecological nature of community health psychology, collaboration with other social science and health disciplines is viewed as necessary if we are to make progress in understanding and promoting health (Murray *et al.*, 2004). Community health psychologists also have much in common with researchers working within other health-related disciplines who take a critical perspective.

> Research which endeavours to gain understanding and also make change at the same time. It uses different research methodologies, and is usually participative (includes participants in the process of the research as much as possible) and qualitative.

Critical health psychology

There are many differing approaches to critical study. However, critical psychologists, while differing from one another in varying ways, share the view that it is crucial to evaluate theories and practices within psychology, in order to identify how they may maintain an unjust and inequitable status quo (Prilleltensky & Fox, 1997). In critical health psychology the focus is extremely broad, and includes an analysis of how 'power, economics and macrosocial processes influence and/or structure health, health care, health psychology, and society at large' (Marks, 2002, p. 15). Power is an essential concept here, and is examined in terms of how it functions to facilitate or prevent the achievement of health. Critical health psychology examines power in terms of the role of culture and social structures in health, but power analysis is also applied from micro levels (e.g. in individual relationships) through to macro levels (e.g. policy development) (Prilleltensky & Prilleltensky, 2003). As in community health psychology, one of the key values here is respect for diversity. Many of the ideas employed in critical health psychology developed from the 'crisis' that occurred in social psychology and other social sciences during the 1970s and 1980s. These included an examination of what science is, how knowledge is derived and whether psychologists can be objective and value free. Over the past five years this critical perspective has been growing within health psychology. Initially a critical debate surrounding issues of methodology developed, but this spread rapidly to include issues of research assumptions and underlying values (Murray, 2004).

Summary

Although there are tensions between the different approaches emerging within health psychology, there are also many areas of overlap and many areas that could be beneficially shared across approaches. In a young and growing field, overlap does happen in many cases. Some health psychologists work in two or three of these areas simultaneously. However, there is much greater potential for cross-fertilisation of perspectives and knowledge from the different approaches to the benefit of all. For example, Albee and Fryer (2003) have recently identified a current need to develop a critical public health psychology.

Health psychology: a critical introduction

Throughout this text we aim to provide a critical introduction to the discipline of health psychology. What do we mean by this? The text is not located solely within the critical health psychology approach, as discussed above. Rather, the text presents relevant information and material from all four approaches to health psychology. Topics dictate that in some areas some approaches to health psychology will be more relevant than others. However, across all topics we can cast a critical eye on the research and what we know to date. This is why we subtitled the text 'a critical introduction'.

The term 'critical' has a variety of meanings and is used by different people in different ways. Although the notion of a 'critical' introduction may have negative connotations, this is not what we intend when we employ this term in our work. We see being critical as being challenging, at whatever level we are working at. Being critical does not mean being dismissive; rather, it means being more inclusive. To us, being critical does not mean limiting and shutting off different paths; rather it means thinking through implications and embracing diversity.

A more critical approach has been developing within psychology generally over the past three decades. This has been particularly the case within social psychology and, to a lesser extent, within clinical psychology. Within health psychology, these challenges are only just beginning to surface. Debates about the proper methods for research, the effects of professionalisation, the nature of the values and assumptions underlying the field and the role of health psychology in promoting or reproducing inequality and oppression are just beginning to be heard. We can see the start of a turn from the employment of 'traditional' psychological research methods and the 'taken-for-granted' acceptance of underlying assumptions to the adoption of qualitative interpretative methods and a critical examination of assumptions and practices. Some of these issues will be raised throughout the text where we aim to provide a critical introduction to health psychology topics in three broad ways:

1 We will critically discuss previous research across different topics, by asking questions about the methods employed, the people who participated, the research designs used and so on. We will examine whether individuals are considered within their social and cultural worlds (see 'individualism' below).
2 We will use notions of 'criticality' to question the assumptions underlying areas of research, whose interests are best met by the research, which groups in society are ignored/overlooked, how the research or research area functions for different groups and what the implications are for people (see 'questioning research assumptions' below).
3 We will be self-critical of ourselves as health psychologists, and of the field of health psychology, by reflexively questioning our own value stances and the values behind work in the field (see 'reflexivity' below).

In the remainder of this section, we will expand on these three particular issues involved in taking a more critical approach. These will help lay the groundwork for the approach employed throughout the book.

Individualism

Western societies are individualistic. Individualism sees each person as self-contained and as 'requiring minimum levels of sharing, caring and inter-dependency' (Marks *et al.*, 2000, p. 10). Individualism emphasises values such as self-determination and downplays values such as collaboration, caring and social justice (Prilleltensky & Fox, 1997). However, individual behaviour can only be understood within a social context, and in interaction with others. Trying to understand behaviour by focusing exclusively on the individual neglects the importance of the social world (and the important role played by the social institutions in which interactions are embedded) (Prilleltensky & Fox, 1997).

Individualism in Western societies has led to the assumption that individual health is controlled by, and located within, the individual (although this is a feature of health that is peculiar to Western societies, as discussed in ch. 2). Indeed, in her well-known health psychology textbook, Taylor (1999) claims that 'staying well is heavily determined by good health habits, all of which are under one's personal control' (p. 6). As we shall see throughout this book, good health habits (as well as how they are understood and what they mean to people) vary by social and cultural location and are not necessarily always under the individual's control. An ideology of individualism fits well with a discipline whose objective is the understanding of individual behaviour. This ideology neatly reinforces the demands for individual-level interventions to keep us healthy and works to minimise the notions of social context, interconnectedness and interdependence. It obscures from view the role of poverty, race, class and gender as influences on health and illness.

Questioning research assumptions

Some major critiques have been made of social psychology since the 1970s, and many of these critiques are relevant to health psychology. The critiques led to some social psychologists arguing for a different way of doing things, a different way of seeing things, and a different way of studying things (Ibáñez, 1997). Researchers began to question the nature of reality (positing ontological questions), how we can know that reality (positing epistemological questions) and what methods we can use to study that reality (positing methodological questions) (Chamberlain *et al.*, 1997).

Some writers have convincingly argued against the supposedly natural character of certain phenomena, and have described how these phenomena arise from particular historical, discursive, social and cultural realms. This has been achieved on a general level by Michel Foucault (e.g. Foucault, 1975), and on a more specific level for psychology by Kenneth Gergen (e.g. Gergen, 1985; Ibáñez, 1997). Sociologists have challenged the idea that entities such as 'disease' and the 'body' are natural categories, arguing that they are products of social activities and do not simply reflect biological realities (Nettleton, 1995). As Nettleton points out, 'this is not to say that people do not suffer from bodily dysfunctions, nor does it deny the realities of pain and distress; what it does argue is that *all* knowledge (including medical and scientific) is socially contingent' (p. 14). From this perspective, a person with asthma will experience pain and suffering, but how this is interpreted (and treated) will depend on the historical time and place in which it occurs.

The notion that the world we experience, and our understandings of reality and people, comes from social life. Thus, our reality is a product of social life and does not exist in a straightforward, taken-for-granted manner.

This perspective is known as **social constructionism**. Social constructionists argue that we come to understand our reality through our ideas and paradigms. This is in contrast to empiricists, and most medical scientists, who argue that we look at the reality 'out there' and 'simply' develop descriptions about it (Nettleton, 1995). Social constructionism has developed alongside postmodernism. This is set apart from modernism, in which matters are straightforward, reality can be tested, defined, described or at least approximated. In modernism, progress is assumed to be linear, coherent and relatively unified. In postmodernism, however, there is an emphasis on multiple realities, a denial of any one single truth or reality, and 'a loss of faith in a single, coherent, unified, linear and progressive account of the past' (Nettleton, 1995 p. 34).

As with most paradigms, social constructionism does not provide a unified perspective, and debates continue to rage between people who call themselves constructionists. One such debate is the realism–relativism debate. This debate concerns the extent to which an external world exists independently of our representations of it. Realists argue that an external world exists independently of our representations, while relativists argue that there are no grounds to assume a reality which is independent of us and our ways of knowing (Nightingale & Cromby, 2002). Despite this, most social constructionists take a critical realist perspective (Edley, 2001). From this view, the existence of bodies, diseases and poverty is accepted, but how we know them are as socially constructed entities; furthermore, we can only know them in this manner. For example, while no one would deny the reality of the physical constriction and inflammation of the airways during an episode of asthma, the meaning of this event (as an attack, as an illness, as a limitation, as an embarrassment, etc.) will vary according to its context and the perspectives of the people involved.

Knowledge gained in different disciplines highlights how our ideas about health, illness, disease and the body can vary by social, cultural and historical location. Consider some of the following examples:

- Sociologists have demonstrated how medical 'facts' are created through language (e.g. Foucault, 1975).
- Medical anthropologists show how the biomedical model of health and illness is a Western belief system, and only one of many belief systems about health (e.g. Joralemon, 1999).
- Historical analyses have demonstrated how diseases change over time, as do our experiences of our own bodies, as we will see in later chapters. Diseases have been shown to reinforce the particular social structures and political struggles of the time. For example, women in the nineteenth century who wanted to further their education were labelled as suffering from hysteria (Smith-Rosenberg, 1984, cited in Nettleton, 1995).

Such findings reinforce the notion that biomedicine, although authoritative and powerful globally, is culturally specific and that its practices and knowledge are social in origin (Nettleton, 1995).

It is important to note here that saying our knowledge is socially constructed is not at all the same as saying that our knowledge is worthless (Nettleton, 1995). Social constructionists try to put forward different ways of understanding how knowledge comes to be created. This task has been taken up recently in health psychology, and some researchers have begun to study language and discourse as topics in their own right. Such research has a number of aims, and includes consideration of how situations, facts, ideas, knowledge are constructed and used in language and everyday talk. This work has been able to highlight the individualistic roots of mainstream psychology, and to show how various discourses work to legitimise oppressive and unjust social relationships (Murray & Campbell, 2003).

While it has been argued that a focus on language can divert attention from broader material issues (Murray & Campbell, 2003), all our understanding comes about through shared symbols, practices and languages. Our meanings, sense of selves, understandings of health, illness and the body, arise from our social and cultural worlds. They arise from social interaction, through language or other forms of meaning-making. This means that people experiencing different social worlds (people in different cultures, men and women, the elderly and children, gay and heterosexual people) are also likely to experience different meanings and understandings of events, 'facts', health, illness, bodies and so on. Therefore, it follows that any study of health and illness must not assume there is one truth about these constructs that everyone holds; rather, it must explore how experiences, beliefs, knowledges may differ across different social and cultural locations, and what this means for the individual (especially in relation to what we hold as 'normal' or 'mainstream' knowledge).

Reflexiveness

Reflexiveness involves taking an explicit look at the broader consequences of practices within a discipline. Critical examinations of the assumptions and practices of health psychology as a discipline have very recently begun to develop, involving considerations of how it functions to sustain established notions, how its practices limit understanding and how it legitimates or marginalises particular groups or institutions in society. Health psychology is a discipline formed at a particular social and historical moment. Psychology developed out of nineteenth-century individualism and positivism (Murray & Campbell, 2003).

It has been argued that the theoretical assumptions of health psychology have actually hindered attempts to improve health. Waldo and Coates (2000) have argued this point in relation to the control of the spread of AIDS. This has come about, it has been argued, because health psychology directs its attention to an individual level of analysis in terms of health-related behaviour. This masks 'the role of economic, political and symbolic social inequalities in patterns of ill-health, both globally and within countries' (Murray & Campbell, 2003, p. 231). Furthermore, social cognition models used by health psychologists to understand and try to change health behaviour may actually be hindering attempts to improve health (Murray & Campbell, 2003).

By endorsing individualism, health psychology could be said to contribute to the emphasis on individualistic rather than collective values, as has been claimed of psychology more generally (see, for example, Prilleltensky & Fox, 1997). There is little discussion about the implications of individualism in health psychology and little discussion of the implications of the field of health psychology itself. The sorts of questions that could be asked of the discipline are whether it contributes to the status quo. Is health psychology beneficial for health? Whose health does health psychology benefit?

Psychologists need to be fully aware of the broader (and sometimes unintended) impact that their work has on people's lives. Furthermore, as Marks and colleagues (2000) have pointed out, psychologists also need to be fully aware of the social and economic context in which they and other professionals live and work if they are to make genuine improvements to health and health care.

Summary

Theories in health psychology have mostly developed within the English-speaking cultures of the USA, Europe and British commonwealth (Marks *et al.*, 2000). The emphasis on the individual in health psychology has focused primarily on factors within individuals (such as cognitions) and between individuals (such as personality attributes) and rarely on the social worlds of individuals. Ironically, this is apparent in the almost complete absence of theorising around the body and **embodiment** in health psychology: the individual is treated as a thinking, cognitive being, but not one that is (and has) a physical body (see ch. 2 for more on embodiment). At this point it would be useful to review some of the evidence which shows that health is not simply an individual phenomenon: health and illness vary across some major social categories. To highlight how health and illness are intertwined with social life, we outline how they vary across different social groups.

The experience of both being and having a body.

Variations in health by social groups

In this section we provide an introduction to research which has examined how health and illness differ across particular groups of people, such as men and women, and children and adults. We emphasise that although these factors could be considered individual (sex and age, for example) they are also inherently social: what they mean and how we come to understand them is achieved socially. This point will become clearer throughout this section. Variations in health by social group are important as they affect the individual. Health psychology's traditional concern with the individual has tended to overlook the social realm, but as we will argue throughout the rest of this book, the social realm is fundamental to the health and well-being of the person. We focus on four aspects of social life, as each provides a good demonstration of how health is more than simply an individual issue.

SES

A consistent negative relationship between SES and health has been observed for some time now, and continues to be observed (Davey-Smith *et al.*, 1990; Wilkinson, 1996). Health is worst for individuals at the bottom of the SES hierarchy, and best for those at the top. In between, health (and morbidity) improves in a stepwise gradient as SES level increases. There is unequivocal evidence for the effects of income inequality on a number of health outcomes, including morbidity rates, health behaviour, self-reports of health, health care utilisation and mortality rates (McDonough & Walters, 2001). This is not a modern day phenomenon: health variations by socioeconomic position have been evident throughout history (Carroll & Davey Smith, 1997). Thus, the rich live longer and healthier lives than the poor (Coburn, 2004).

When we look at differences in absolute deprivation, that is, between an individual who has very few material resources (money, housing, transport) and an individual who has plenty of material resources, we can easily see how deprivation affects health. However, the evidence has consistently documented that this is not the only difference. Relative deprivation also affects health outcomes, so that even those people at middle SES levels fare worse healthwise than people at higher SES levels. Much research has been undertaken to try and explain these consistent findings. The accumulated evidence suggests that the findings are not the result of statistical bias or social selection (where healthy individuals move up the SES scale and unhealthy individuals move down) (see Williams, 2003).

1.4   SES and health

How does SES affect health? A neo-materialist explanation

Researchers argue that SES affects material conditions, which in turn affect health. Lynch and colleagues (2000) use the metaphor of airline travel for this explanation. People who can afford to fly long-haul distances in a first-class cabin get more space, better food, more comfortable seats which recline into beds, among other advantages. People who fly economy class have a cramped space, uncomfortable seats and often find it difficult to sleep. When the passengers get off the plane, those stepping out of the first-class cabin do so rested and refreshed, while those stepping out from economy class do so weary and often desperate for sleep. The material conditions in which the passengers travelled has affected their well-being, and this is not due to relative deprivation or perceptions of relative disadvantage.

In recent years, explanations for the relationship between SES and health have focused on structural and material factors, such as:

- exposure to toxins and other health-damaging agents, such as hazardous wastes, ambient and indoor air pollutants, ambient noise, air quality, crowding, housing quality, etc. (Evans & Kantrowitz, 2002);
- social integration and social cohesion (Kawachi & Kennedy, 1999).

A nice metaphor for the materialist explanation for SES and health differences is that of airline travel, as illustrated in sidebar 1.4.

The importance of psychosocial explanations of the SES–health findings has also been argued for strongly (e.g. Wilkinson, 1997), and such explanations have included:

- psychological well-being, where low status leads to poor self-esteem and other negative emotions (e.g. shame) or states (e.g. lack of control) which influence psycho-neurobiological pathways, which then affect health;
- the importance of consumption: in Western society consuming goods serves social, psychological and symbolic purposes and expresses (and constructs)

identity, which in turn influences physical well-being (Marmot & Wilkinson, 2001);

- health behaviour such as smoking, drinking, having a poor diet: evidence shows that while behaviour accounts for some of the findings, clear inequalities remain after behaviour has been considered (Blane *et al.*, 1998).

Many researchers now believe that SES inequality is clearly correlated with health, but that this inequality is a proxy for 'a variety of social conditions, operating through individual and collective, material and psycho-social pathways, rather than income inequality being a single main cause of poorer health' (Coburn, 2004, p. 43). An important point here is that SES shapes the life chances and biographies of individuals, in that people have advantages and disadvantages from the time they are children, and these influence what happens to them later in life. Thus, a lifecourse perspective is useful here, particularly if it can identify 'critical periods' at which intervention may be beneficial (Blane *et al.*, 1998).

Despite the emphasis on relative deprivation, it is important not to forget that the worst health outcomes occur at the bottom of the social hierarchy. What this means in real terms depends on the country in which it is experienced. For example, Lynch (2000, p. 1004) points out that:

> In the United States, the most marginalized social groups have no health care, a pitifully low minimum wage, underfunded schools, poor transportation links between where they live and where they work, low levels of neighborhood resources and poor housing. The most marginalized groups in countries like Sweden or Norway experience a different set of neo-material living conditions. It is also true that absolute health inequalities in these countries are smaller and average levels of population health higher than in the US.

As we will see throughout the rest of this section, SES combines with many other social factors to jointly affect health outcomes. For this reason it can be seen to confound research which attempts to isolate the effects of ethnicity and gender on health (McCarthy *et al.*, 2000).

Gender

The physiological differences between the sexes lead to differences in health and illness between men and women. Most obviously, there are sex-specific diseases such as cancer of the cervix in women and cancer of the prostate in men. However, it is increasingly clear that these biological differences extend beyond the reproductive organs and hormones. For example, sex differences have been found to exist in the incidence, symptoms and prognosis of such diseases as HIV/AIDS, tropical infectious diseases, tuberculosis, autoimmune problems and coronary heart disease (Doyal, 2001). Furthermore, biological differences are only one factor influencing differences in men's and women's health. In recent decades, there has been a growing recognition that gender

1.5 Sex versus gender

Sex differences refer to the physiological differences between men and women. When they refer to a person's sex, researchers are identifying whether the person has reproductive organs that define them as woman or man.

Gender differences refer to non-physiological differences between men and women. We learn what it means to be and behave in a manner consistent with being a male or a female in our society. And we learn this very early on in our lives. When referring to a person's gender, researchers are identifying whether a person is a male or a female, both of which are socially constructed roles.

As Lorber (1997) has pointed out, 'it is extremely difficult to isolate basic biological sex differences [from gender differences] because biology, physiology, genetic inheritance, and hormonal input always occur in and are shaped by social and environmental contexts' (p. 6).

differences are also important in the health and illness of men and women (see sidebar 1.5). This work initially focused on women as an underprivileged group, but went on to emphasise the social construction of gender and the relationships between men and women as factors important in health (Doyal, 2000). Thus, research has examined what it is about femininity and female social roles that might negatively influence women's health; more recently attention has also turned to masculinity and how 'being male' may be detrimental to health. Specifically, researchers have examined why women live longer than men yet men appear to experience less ill health than women.

Gender differences in mortality

There is a mass of evidence that women live longer than men. This is true within all modern industrialised societies and there are now few societies in which men live longer than women (Doyal, 2000). At the beginning of the twentieth century, women lived on average two to three years more than men. This difference is now approximately seven years (Lorber, 1997). Furthermore, there is a tendency for men to die earlier than women at every age. More male deaths occur in utero and at birth than female deaths, and more male deaths occur at every age throughout life than female deaths (Waldron, 1995).

Gender differences in morbidity

Although women live longer than men in industrialised societies, evidence has accumulated over recent decades that women experience more illness throughout their lives than men. Indeed, there is a saying in epidemiology that 'women get sicker but men die quicker' (Lorber, 1997, p. 14). Women's higher morbidity rates have been demonstrated in terms of them reporting more illness, having more days off work because of illness, taking more medication, and seeing doctors and other health care workers more often than men (Rodin & Ickovics, 1990; Verbrugge, 1985). Women also have higher rates of acute illnesses and most nonfatal chronic conditions (Rodin & Ickovics, 1990).

However, the broad statement that women experience more ill health than men overall has been questioned by some researchers, who argue that this may be an overgeneralisation. Using two large datasets in the UK, MacIntyre and colleagues (1996) have demonstrated that there are morbidity differences between men and women, but that these are not consistent and depend on the symptom, condition and stage of life. These authors reinforce previous findings which demonstrate that gender differences in health do occur, but vary by age, how a condition or symptom is measured, what is measured and also social context (MacIntyre *et al.*, 1996). A number of studies have since demonstrated that gender differences in morbidity are more complex than previously thought (see McDonough & Walters, 2001, for a review).

Being female: what does it mean for health?

Various explanations have been put forward to explain women's excess morbidity. These range from the biological (e.g. hormones, genetic differences) through to the social and cultural. Gender divisions in social, economic and cultural life have been linked to physical health and well-being, highlighting how gender inequalities affect women's health detrimentally (Doyal, 2001). Furthermore, our social norms regarding who does what in terms of (unpaid) work inside the house as well as (paid and unpaid) work outside the house frequently mean that women shoulder heavy burdens of responsibility (Lee, 1998). Many women must combine employment with domestic work, pregnancy and childrearing (Doyal, 2001). Gender differences in occupations, incomes, work-hours and experience in the workplace often mean that women are disadvantaged compared to men (Annandale & Hunt, 2000). Even though gender-equality laws have been passed in most developed countries, these have had little effect on women's status, quality of life and physical health. National surveys consistently show that women continue to be seriously disadvantaged compared to men. They have less money, less financial security, less desirable employment and less political and social power, and this has a detrimental effect on their physical health (Lee, 1998).

Being male: what does it mean for health?

Previously, concern with gender was concern with women, and men's lives were not seen as gendered at all (Doyal, 2000). Indeed, two medical professionals have noted that when they asked men (both colleagues and patients) what masculinity meant for them, most men were astonished, some made jokes and no consistent answer was given (Kiss & Meryn, 2001). There tends to be little reflection on how men are socialised and act in everyday life. In very recent years, much greater research attention has been devoted to examining male gender, and as part of this, what maleness might mean for health.

While traditional masculinity might seem to provide privileged access to various resources and opportunities (e.g. education, employment, income, access to services), there are aspects of being male that are detrimental for health. As Doyal (2001) writes, 'though the shape of masculinity may vary between communities, the development and maintenance of a heterosexual male identity usually requires the taking of risks that are seriously hazardous to health' (p. 1062). For example, the stereotypical role of the man as 'provider' puts men at much greater risk of occupational accidents (Doyal, 2000). Furthermore, many men often feel that they need to engage in risky behaviour to 'prove' their masculinity (Kimmel & Messner, 1993). Thus, men are more likely to engage in behaviour which is harmful to health, such as drinking excessively and smoking cigarettes (Waldron, 1995). Men are also more likely than women to be murdered, killed in a car accident or killed during a dangerous sporting activity (Doyal, 2000). As we will see later in the book, traditional masculinity is also aligned with not attending to one's body and not seeking help when feeling unwell, with such behaviour being interpreted as signs of weakness. Thus, researchers have begun to highlight how certain versions of masculinity are associated with poor health outcomes, including risk-taking behaviour, assaults on the body and higher male mortality (Annandale, 1998).

Gender differences in health: what else matters?

Like all social categories, gender does not operate in isolation. There are also racial, ethnic, age, occupational, cultural and social class divisions between women and men, and often research into sex or gender differences does not do enough justice to this variation (Lorber, 1997). For example, poverty has a strong negative impact on health for both men and women. However, poverty itself is a gendered phenomenon, with women being especially vulnerable (Doyal, 2000). Cooper (2002) has also strongly argued that ethnicity is a neglected area in studies of gender and health, with ethnic minority women facing multiple discrimination which may have a major impact on health. Furthermore, it has been argued that gender, SES and social integration are all intricately linked, and that SES mediates the relationship between gender and health outcomes (Ballantyne, 1999). As Ballantyne summarises it:

> Women's relationship to the labour market establishes and perpetuates their socioeconomic inequality relative to men, and may produce contradictory influences on women's health. Furthermore, for women, the marital relationship is paradoxical: marriage may at once improve economic and social support opportunities, while diminishing control over paid and unpaid work – potentially increasing *as well as* compromising the health status of women.

Thus, health outcomes for individuals are profoundly influenced not just by gender, but also by factors such as class, race and geopolitical status (Doyal, 2000).

It is also worth noting that there are large similarities between men's and women's health. However, these similarities have been neglected in research, and there has been a call for research to start examining similarities in health and disease between men and women (McDonough & Walters, 2001). Furthermore, large health differences exist within men as a group and within women as a group, and these differences have also been relatively under investigated (Annandale & Hunt, 2000).

Taking a broader perspective and looking globally, life expectancy for women is lower in societies where women's social status is very low than in industrialised societies (Lorber, 1997). This arises from a combination of social factors, including (from Santow, 1995):

- eating last and eating less than everyone else;
- experiencing complications of frequent childbearing and sexually transmitted diseases (women often have no power to demand abstinence or birth control);
- experiencing infections and haemorrhages following genital mutilation;
- neglect of symptoms until they are extremely severe;
- restricted access to modern health care.

Factors such as these clearly have direct and unquestionable effects on the physical health of women, and powerfully demonstrate the impact of social factors on health.

Age

Age is another factor that affects health, but it needs to be understood in social context. The health needs of men and women vary across the lifecycle, as do the resources required to meet these needs (Doyal, 2000). On the face of it age may seem a straightforward concept: it is the number of years people have been alive. However, there is a lack of conceptual refinement of the term 'age', as Arber and Ginn (1998) have pointed out. They argue that often little distinction is made between different meanings of age, including:

- chronological age (the individual's age in years): this is the criterion that is most often employed when making decisions about medical treatment, and it is usually assumed to be closely related to other meanings of age;
- physiological age: a medical concept which is associated with the ageing body, and processes of degeneration of body tissue and functional impairment. However, it is not related to chronological age in a straightforward manner. Men and women aged between 65 and 69 who have previously had manual jobs have been found to display more functional impairment than people of the same age from upper-middle-class jobs (Arber & Ginn, 1993);
- social age: the view that age is socially constructed and heavily gendered. People's perceptions of their age depend heavily on cultural views about ageing (which differ for men and women). There are also social norms about age-appropriate behaviour.

Health outcomes and health issues vary by age, although differences within age groups may be more important than differences between age groups (Arber & Ginn, 1998). There is no particular age at which health deteriorates in a continuous manner, although health is often related to stage of the lifecy-cle and social roles, such as undertaking risky behaviour, having children, raising families, experiencing employment and unemployment and so on. Fur-thermore, decisions made within medicine are often based on age criteria; for example, being denied the opportunity to undergo regular breast cancer screening (which in the UK is not available after the age of 64). An emphasis on preventing 'premature deaths' in the National Health Service in the UK, along with the exclusion of older people from clinical intervention studies, have been argued to be discriminatory (Arber & Ginn, 1998).

Two particular stages of life appear to be relatively absent in much of the research in health psychology. Only recently have researchers started examin-ing children's perceptions and understandings of health and illness, and explor-ing the possibility that children may wish to be actively involved in taking care of their own health (James, 1998). Previously, researchers discussed children's health and illness with adults. Similarly, in interactions between children and health professionals, children have often been excluded from the discussions, with questions directed at the carer rather than the child (see ch. 7). Thus, children's health has been traditionally positioned as an adult problem (James, 1998). This has grown out of a particular view of children and childhood in Western societies. Childhood is seen as a time of innocence, vulnerability, lack of responsibility and naturalness (see James, 1998, for more on the social construction of children and childhood). Indeed, James argues that 'the study of children, health and illness cannot be divorced from an understanding of the ways in which ideas of the child and of childhood are socially constructed' (p. 111).

While the voices of children have been relatively silent in many areas of health research, so too have the voices of older adults. Adults in later life are often viewed as 'older adults' because they have reached some kind of life marker, such as retirement, pension age or a particular chronological age. How-ever, none of these is necessarily related to health status (Arber & Ginn, 1998). Specific concerns face adults in older age, and these in turn influence how they may experience illness, seek health care, or engage in healthy behaviour. These include normative expectations, ageism in society, material resources and the availability of family carers (Arber & Ginn, 1998). Stereotypes of older people as a burden continue to persist, although data from the USA demonstrate that older people now actually have lower levels of disability and fewer chronic conditions than in previous times (Manton et al., 1995).

Finally, like other social factors, age does not operate in isolation and there is diversity of ageing across gender, class, ethnicity, marital status, employment history, fertility history and so on. For example, compared to older men, older women have fewer resources (for basic health needs as well as for accessing health services and care), experience more chronic and disabling illnesses and are more likely to be widowed or live alone (thus having no partner to provide care) (Arber & Ginn, 1998). Furthermore, SES inequalities in health have been found among older adults (aged 60–79) and the oldest-old (over 80) across eleven European countries, highlighting the importance of material, social and cultural resources for health outcomes at all age groups (Huisman *et al.*, 2003).

Ethnicity

There are many terms that describe an individual's cultural background, including race, ethnicity and culture. Race is assumed to refer to biological and genetic differences between groups of people; however, this is a highly problematic conceptualisation. Root (2000) discusses some of the problems with the construct of race, as described in research in focus box 1.1. **Ethnicity** is a broader term which refers to a person's shared cultural background (Julian, 1998). Research in health fields may examine the health of **ethnic minorities** and compare it to the health of the dominant ethnic group in a country. Culture is a term that is broader again; while ethnicity can describe an individual, culture describes the larger social world (norms, roles, understandings, beliefs, ways of doing and being) in which we live.

A term used widely in sociology, referring to a shared cultural background.

An ethnic group which is not the dominant ethnic group in a country or society. The term highlights power differences between different ethnic groups.

However race is defined, evidence shows that there are major health differences across people in different racial categories or from different ethnicities. For example, blacks in the USA have much poorer health outcomes than whites. Newborns of black women are almost twice as likely to have a low birth weight than infants of white women (David & Collins, 1997). Black adults are twice as likely to die of stroke, heart disease and diabetes than white adults (Cooper, 1993). In the UK, morbidity has been found to be worse for many minority ethnic groups, including Pakistanis and Bangladeshis, although Indian adults have been found to have similar health profiles to white adults (Cooper, 2002).

Health outcomes are especially poor for indigenous populations. In Australia non-indigenous women have a life expectancy of over 80 years, and non-indigenous men a life expectancy of 75 years. However, in the indigenous Aboriginal population, life expectancies for women and men are approximately fifteen to twenty years less than their non-indigenous counterparts (Anderson *et al.*, 1996, cited in Gray & Saggers, 1998). Similar findings occur in other countries around the world, including Canada, New Zealand and the USA (Gray & Saggers, 1998; see ch. 10). Gray and Saggers argue that such inequalities in the health of indigenous populations arise from, and reflect, structural inequalities related to dispossession of land and political marginalisation.

So far research attention has largely focused on genetic, biological, cultural and behavioural explanations for ethnic health variations, at the expense of social and environmental factors (Karlsen *et al.*, 2002). Social and environmental factors appear crucial here. Ethnic groups differ not only by cultural background, but also in terms of their social location and where they fit in terms of social inequality (Julian, 1998). Cooper (2002) draws on arguments made previously by Krieger (2000) to state that 'unequal social relations,

1.1 Problems with race in medicine

Root, M. (2000). The problem of race in medicine. *Philosophy of the Social Sciences, 31*, 20–39.

Root argues that although race is used extensively in the biomedical sciences, descriptively and analytically, there are major problems with it as a concept. Six particular problems are identified: three concern problems with definition and three concern explanations of why there might be racial variation in disease.

1. **Reliability:** racial difference studies in epidemiology, pharmacology, etc. are not based on a single definition of race, but many. For example, in the USA racial data are derived mainly from the US National Center of Health Statistics, as well as records of birth and death, and medical records. In terms of birth records, up until 1989 the race of a newborn was decided by the race of both parents: if both were white, the child was classified as white. If one parent was black, the child was classified as black (a 'one-drop' rule). In 1989 the rules changed, and the child was classified as the same race as its mother, whatever her race. Thus for many, race depended on birth date (a black baby born in December 1988 could have been white if he/she had been born a month later). This increased the number of white infants born. The average birth weight of white infants also fell between 1988 and 1989 in the USA: a change due to definition not health. Race at death depends on who completes the death certificate, frequently the funeral director or next of kin. Race as recorded by census is based on self-identification. Therefore, in the USA one 'can be black at birth, American Indian at 40, and white at death' (p. 23).

2. **Validity:** for a race measure to be valid, it must be true to the facts. But what is actual race? Previously it was thought that there were large genetic variations between races. However, biologists now state that while there are heritable differences between people, they do not cluster into the groups we call race. There is as much genetic variation within as between genetic groups. For example, people differ in skin colour and this is heritable, 'but skin color is inherited independent of other biological traits; moreover differences in color are continuous rather than sharp and vary as much within as between racial groups' (p. 24). Others, from Julian Huxley in the 1930s to the American Association of Science more recently, have argued that race is an artificial way to categorise people.

3. **Is race real?** Some argue that racism is real but races are not. However, Root argues that race is real but not a biological classification. Rather, it is

more like marital status, with the divisions due to humans (inventing matrimony) not nature. Thus, racial data are valid if we agree that they do not indicate biological differences.

4. **Explanations for racial variation in disease:** epidemiologists generally see racial differences as arising from social inequalities, including racial discrimination, occupational hazards, environmental toxins, stress, SES differences and so on. Once these social factors are accounted for, any variation remaining is believed to be due to race. However, it is difficult to conclude that all social factors have been accounted for. Race affects a person's prospects through life, and therefore can affect health, disease and death. Root argues that the 'biomedical researcher should consider that race is a master status in matters of health and illness no less than in policing or housing segregation' (p. 27).

5. **Genetic diseases:** how can we explain race differences in genetic diseases, such as sickle-cell disease (an inherited haemoglobin disorder and the result of a single gene)? Sickle-cell disease is much more prevalent in blacks than whites in the USA, although it can occur in whites. Root argues that the sickle-cell gene is most common in areas of the world where malaria is also common, such as East Africa and southern India. Here, children with the gene are more likely to survive than those without it. And here also, sickle-cell disease is as common in whites as blacks. Therefore, more blacks than whites have sickle-cell disease in the USA because they are descendants of people who originated from these malarial areas, and the difference is a result of immigration, not race.

6. **Drug responses:** groups of people vary in how they respond to drugs. For example, Asian Americans are more sensitive to beta-blockers than whites are. While sex differences may be due to genetic differences in the X or Y chromosome, Root argues that there are no race-linked genes as races are not divided by genetic difference. However, there may be differences in social histories across groups that we label as black or Asian that influence drug metabolism.

Reflection

This paper cogently argues that 'there are no biological races, only man-made ones' (p. 30). Such a position emphasises how defining and categorising by race masks the significance of culture and lifestyle; it also highlights how racial differences in health will remain as long as people continue to be socially or economically disadvantaged because of their race.

characterised by discrimination, exclusion and exploitation, are thought to have profound consequences for the economic and social well-being of gender and ethnic groups that may ultimately be expressed as inequalities in health' (Cooper, 2002, p. 694). A recent major review of the differences in chronic health conditions across racial groups concluded that 'the racial gap in health is spread across all domains of health, and . . . socioeconomic conditions, not health risk behaviours, are the primary origins of the racial stratification of health' (Hayward *et al*., 2000, p. 910). This review also emphasised the importance of looking across the lifespan, and including teenagers and older adults in health research.

Summary

Here we have touched on only four particular social groupings that display differences in health outcomes and health and illness experience. We have barely mentioned cultural differences in health, which are phenomenal when health outcomes in Western countries are compared with those in developing countries. For example, children born in 1999 can expect to live until 70 years of age if they are born in one of the twenty-four healthiest countries in the world. If they are born in one of the fifty-one least healthy countries, however, they can expect to live for only 51 years (Subramanian *et al*., 2002; see ch. 10).

   People belong to many social groups, and these groupings, as well as how they intersect, have a direct bearing on our understandings (and experiences) of health and illness. Throughout this book, as far as possible, we identify how findings vary across people in different social groupings. Where appropriate, we will include consideration of the factors outlined in this section, but where research is available, we will also draw on other social groupings that may be relevant, such as people with differing sexual orientations, transgendered people and people with disabilities.

Summary and conclusions

   Health psychology could more accurately be described as 'illness psychology', as it has focused much more on illness behaviour and management than on health (Marks, 1996). In this chapter we have introduced and located health psychology as a field of study, and emphasised the need to focus on both individual and social factors if we are to obtain a fuller and more adequate understanding of health and illness. We have also highlighted the need for consideration of research from other disciplines, ranging from those that are biomedical in perspective, through to those that are inherently cultural (such as medical anthropology). In summary, we would argue (along with others, such as Marks *et al*., 2000; Yali & Revenson, 2004) that for health psychology to be effective it needs a social orientation, a multicultural perspective, a focus on health as well as illness, an emphasis on the individual as a social being living within a social and cultural world, an understanding of the individual as a creator of meanings and some consideration of factors operating at societal and global levels. The remainder of the book will try and incorporate and describe as much relevant research as possible to achieve these aims.

RECOMMENDED READING

Special section on the future of health psychology. *Health Psychology, vol. 23, Issue 2*, 2004. In this special section, researchers and academics reflect on the twenty-five years of progress made in the field of health psychology since the American Psychological Association's Division of Health Psychology was founded. Eight articles consider both the progress of the field and the future of health psychology and make calls for areas, topics and concepts that need further attention. Several areas are covered across the articles, including the biopsychosocial model, changes in demographics and the importance of context, prevention, clinical health psychology interventions, health care financing and new technologies.

Marks, D. F. (2002). Freedom, responsibility, and power: contrasting approaches to health psychology (editorial essay). *Journal of Health Psychology, 7,* 5–19. This editorial provides a solid introduction to the four main approaches which are emerging within health psychology (clinical, public, community and critical). It compares and contrasts the approaches and positions them in a broader framework to assist in our understandings of health, health systems and social care.

Murray, M., Nelson, G., Poland, B., Maticka-Tyndale, E. & Ferris, L. (2004). Assumptions and values of community health psychology. *Journal of Health Psychology, 9,* 323–33. In this article Murray and colleagues provide a good introduction to community health psychology, outlining how it developed and how it is linked to community psychology more generally. As the title suggests, it outlines the values of this approach, and also provides a clear account of the potential contributions this approach to health psychology could make to changing health inequalities and social injustice.

Prilleltensky, I., & Prilleltensky, O. (2003). Towards a critical health psychology practice. *Journal of Health Psychology, 8,* 197–210. This is one of the few articles which has focused on critical health psychology as a specific approach within health psychology. It is a useful and informative introduction. The authors use a critical perspective to review the field of health psychology and outline what a critical health psychology approach entails in terms of values, assumptions and practices.

2 Thinking about health and the body

Health is becoming a normative super-category, with multiple meanings and a multi-dimensional field of action: health is in everything, and everything is in health. It has been said that health is one of the new synonyms for happiness.   (Herzlich, 1995, p. 169)

Talking about health is tantamount to talking about life.   (Pierret, 1995, p. 183)

Learning objectives

This chapter outlines ideas about health and the body, and how people think about these constructs. It will set notions of health and the body within social and cultural contexts. By the end of this chapter, you should be able to:

- describe different definitions of health;
- explain the interrelationship between health and illness;
- compare and contrast 'lay' and 'expert' understandings of health;
- describe how notions of health and the body vary across social categories;
- define embodiment and outline its importance for understanding health;
- discuss the relevance of the body for health psychology;
- consider the ways in which knowledge about health and the body is socially and historically constructed.

What does it mean to you to be healthy? Are you healthy right now? Why or why not? How would you define health? Is your definition likely to be the same as your friends' definitions? What about your grandmother's or father's definitions? Are your ideas about illness related to your definition of health? Are ideas about health important? Before we study health as a topic, we need to be clear about what it means.

This chapter reviews the research on our ideas about health and, by implication, illness. Good health is often understood in relation to illness (Radley & Billig, 1996). The chapter starts by examining traditional biomedical views on health. These ideas are situated historically to show that they are not a given but have arisen within a particular time and place. The chapter then describes some of the research developed later in the twentieth century which began to explore lay ideas about what it means to be healthy. This work demonstrated that our ideas about health and illness are not static, and nor are they necessarily consistent across different groups of people. Finally, we pay some attention to work examining the importance of the body in people's ideas about health, and argue that any consideration of health as an area of study must include a consideration of the body.

The rise of biomedicine

As discussed in ch. 1, we can trace the beginnings of biomedicine back to the period known as the Enlightenment. During this time the overwhelming dominance of the church started to erode due to a growing humanist emphasis on the importance of people's well-being in this life rather than the next. Descartes conceptualised the physical body as separate from the mind (which was viewed as the location of the soul). Separating the physical body from the realm of the soul meant that it was possible to scrutinise and study the body in an objective fashion. Previously, this had been impossible, given religious views about the sanctity of the body as the home of the soul.

Throughout the eighteenth century this distinction between mind and body was reinforced. The church began to have less influence over society and health care than previously, and increasingly the focus was turning towards individual pathology (rather than societal causes of disease). In this milieu physicians and researchers were able to cut up bodies and examine physiology and disease. Illness began to be viewed in a new way, bodies were objectified, diseases identified and then classified (Senior & Viveash, 1998). During the nineteenth century laws were passed to ensure that doctors had official training, and the medical profession was established, along with the biomedical model of health, illness and disease. Over time the profession grew in status, and biomedical views on health and illness became dominant.

According to the biomedical framework, illness is caused by some kind of **pathogen** (such as a virus or bacteria), a gene or an accident, and illnesses can be classified into different types. This classification process is seen as objective, as is diagnosis of illness (Senior & Viveash, 1998). In the biomedical approach, medical professionals have the authority to identify and diagnose illness, and other people's ideas about illness are not given much attention. This is not surprising given the emphasis on a deductive, rational and scientific approach, which makes it difficult to see health and illness from any other view. Focusing on objectivity and rationality obscures the social dimension of health and illness. At times the social dimensions of illness were examined, but only in terms of how these dimensions played a role in causing disease, and then only at certain times in history (Pierret, 1995). For example, in the nineteenth century the 'hygienist' movement examined how specific social dimensions such as housing, the laying out of villages and roads, working conditions and child labour were related to certain illnesses. However, as Pierret (1995) has noted,

A disease-causing agent, such as a virus or bacterium, or other micro-organism.

'in the last quarter of the 19th century, by singling out germs as the cause of illness, the "Pasteur Revolution" was to provide one and only one explanation for illness and social factors were relegated to the background' (p. 177).

One major critique that has been made of the medical model is labelled **iatrogenesis**. Illich (1976) argued that the medical profession, including doctors, pharmaceutical companies, consultants etc., have a vested interest in making sure there is plenty of disease and have medicalised issues that are part of everyday life (Senior & Viveash, 1998). Experiences once viewed as a normal part of human life, such as childbirth, pregnancy, unhappiness, ageing and dying, have now been brought under medical scrutiny and control (Illich, 1976). This has been seen most recently with the definition and classification of 'female sexual dysfunction' (see sidebar 2.1).

Illness caused by doctors and medicine.

The views of health and illness derived from the biomedical model have gained dominance and legitimation in Western societies and are embedded in people's understandings of health. For example, when people are asked about the causes of health and illness, a great deal of agreement has been found between lay people and health professionals (Muncer *et al.*, 2001). However, as we will see throughout this chapter, there are other ways of thinking about health, some of which are fundamentally different from the biomedical approach. Examining these ideas and beliefs demonstrates that the biomedical model is not value free, but is one way of thinking about health and illness among many.

2.1

Moynihan (2003) argues that drug companies have played a major role in constructing female sexual dysfunction from a difficulty, to a dysfunction, to a disease. This leads to 'ever-narrowing definitions of "normal" which help turn the complaints of the healthy into the conditions of the sick' (p. 47). He quotes two professionals working in the area, both of whom have spoken out about the implications of this process (Moynihan, 2003, p. 16):

> The danger of portraying sexual difficulties as a dysfunction is that it is likely to encourage doctors to prescribe drugs to change sexual function – when the attention should be paid to other aspects of the woman's life. It's also likely to make women think they have a malfunction when they do not.
> (Dr Bancroft, Director of the Kinsey Institute at Indiana University)

> Pharmacological research runs the risk of oversimplifying the sexual difficulties of both men and women because it promotes genital function as the centrepiece of sexuality and ignores everything else.
> (Dr Tiefer, Professor of Psychiatry in New York University)

Understandings of health

Why might we be interested in people's views of health? On a practical level, how people view health influences when and why they might seek professional help. Perceptions of health are also closely related to ideas people have about the causes of health and illness, and will therefore influence health-related behaviour such as smoking, exercising and eating well. More than this, however, people's ideas about health can tell us what this concept means for everyday life and social values, and how it may be employed in certain ways for specific ends. Radley and Billig (1996) point out that researchers have examined health beliefs in many ways. For example, studies have investigated:

- how lay people think about health matters compared to professionals;
- how lay people talk about their experiences of illness;
- how people think about avoiding disease;
- how people define health;
- how people from different socioeconomic groups view health and health matters.

There has been a shift in the value placed on 'lay' people's ideas about health (Herzlich & Pierret, 1985). Increasingly, the perspectives of people who use health care services are viewed as important, and it is acknowledged that the perspectives of health professionals cannot represent these patient views (Chapple *et al.*, 2002). Lawton (2003) points out that over the past twenty-five years in the field of sociology there has been a welcome shift from an 'outsider' perspective on health and illness to a more 'insider' and subjective perspective. This has provided understandings of people's experiences of both health and illness which are sensitive to contextual influences. Further, the move from earlier research describing lay beliefs about health and illness, to research describing lay knowledge, highlights the shift in status given to this work (Kangas, 2002). As Prior (2003) points out, 'the concept of beliefs has a far less sturdy status than the concept of knowledge' (p. 44). Now researchers use the concept of the 'lay expert' (people who are experts because they have experience; see Prior, 2003).

In an early influential study on lay health beliefs, Herzlich (1973) interviewed eighty middle-class adults living in Paris or Normandy in France. These people were not 'ill' but from a 'healthy' section of the population. Three distinct dimensions of health were clear in her interviews:

- Health in a vacuum: health is an absence of illness, and is only paid attention when it is lost through illness of some kind. Here health can be viewed as an objective fact.
- Reserve of health: health is seen as a kind of asset which enables a person to resist illness and maintain good health. Thus, it can be spent or renewed. Here health can be viewed as an individual difference, with some people having more of it and others having less. How much health a person has in reserve is viewed as something he or she is born with, but also as something that can change over time.
- Equilibrium: health is defined as dependent on positive feelings and good relationships with others. If life is going well, a state of equilibrium is present. Here, health involves comparison with others to determine whether things are going well and whether life is in balance.

These three views of health are ordered so that we can think about health from absence to presence, from impersonal to personal and from fact to norm (Radley, 1994). Herzlich's study demonstrated that health was more than the absence of illness, and more than the 'opposite of being ill'. It was inherently tied into people's lives, including their social relationships, life events and activities.

The idea that the knowledge individuals hold about the world is a part of broader 'systems of knowledge' that are shared in society.

Herzlich's study was an attempt to gain some insight into **social representations** of health and illness. In social representations theory our everyday ideas of the world are shaped by ideas that come from different parts of society, including science, politics and medicine (Moscovici, 1984). From this perspective, an individual's ideas and beliefs about health are not simply relevant to that individual and his or her experiences. Rather, interviewing individuals and hearing their accounts of health and illness tells us something about wider shared meanings of health and illness, and elicits a more collective view on these constructs.

Blaxter conducted another large and influential study on lay health beliefs in the UK in the late 1980s (Blaxter, 1990). As part of the national Health and Lifestyles Survey in Britain over 9,000 adults were interviewed about their notions of health and illness. In analysing the responses to these interviews, Blaxter showed that people use a variety of concepts of health. She identified nine different categories of health, as shown in table 2.1. People drew on different categories at different times, but importantly health was viewed as much more than simply the absence of illness or disease. People talk about being healthy despite having a number of minor ailments.

2.2

Quotes from Stainton Rogers' (1991) participants about health and illness:

- Illness acts as a reminder that I shouldn't take all the good things in life for granted.
- Health in general boils down to you yourself leading as healthy a life as you can. If you are fat and unfit you are more likely to have illness.
- It is through the Lord Jesus that we are given our health and well-being.
- It's my body, my risk to die young, and I reserve the absolute right to decide, and not be dictated to by a doctor or so-called expert from the Health Education Council.

In a similar manner, Stainton Rogers (1991) used Q-sort methodology to demonstrate how varied beliefs about health are (this is a particular approach to the study of subjectivity which combines both qualitative and quantitative research traditions). She identified eight different accounts of health and illness and her accounts included a focus on the body, such as 'the body as machine' and 'the body under siege'. Other themes identified included 'health promotion', 'robust individualism' and 'willpower'. Quotes from her work highlight the different ways in which people talk about both health and illness.

The few studies outlined here show the diversity of definitions of health in Western societies, although the biomedical framework remains dominant (Marks *et al.*, 2000). Health means different things to different people, and there

Table 2.1 Popular ideas of health in the UK

Health as not-ill	Health means not having illness or symptoms *Health is when you don't have a cold* (man, aged 19)
Health despite disease	Health means not having a disease or disability
Health as reserve	Having something 'extra' *Both parents are alive at 90 so he* [her husband] *belongs to healthy stock* (woman, aged 51)
Health as behaviour	People are defined as healthy because they engage in behaviour such as exercising, having a good diet
Health as physical fitness	Being healthy was talked about as being fit, especially in young men
Health as vitality	Having lots of energy *Health is having lots of wumph* (women, aged 28)
Health as psychosocial well-being	Health was seen in terms of mental state
Health as social relationships	Being healthy meant that people enjoyed other people's company *Generally it's being carefree, you look better, you get on better with other people* (woman, aged 20)
Health as function	Health gave people the ability to perform their duties, such as manual work or household chores *Health is being able to walk around better, and doing more work in the house when my knees let me* (woman, aged 70)

Adapted from Blaxter (1990).

is no definition of health that everybody agrees with (Senior & Viveash, 1998). Furthermore, differences in views about health are likely to be apparent across different social groups, such as age, gender, occupation and, more obviously, culture. It seems commonsense to point out that people who are employed, have families and are able to access health services are likely to have quite different ideas about health from people who are socially isolated, unemployed and homeless (Radley, 1994). Below we review some of these differences in ideas surrounding health.

Illness experiences

Radley (1994) points out how our ideas about health are likely to be shaped and changed by our experiences of illness. As he notes, 'it is one thing to talk about health when hale and hearty, another thing to give one's views when suffering a serious illness' (p. 37). Experiencing illness shapes later ideas about health, as does experience of other people's illnesses, be it directly (partner, relative) or indirectly (on television, in books).

The personal experience of illness, particularly chronic illness, has been given a great deal of attention. Experiencing chronic illness has been argued to constitute a 'biographical disruption', a major experience which can lead to rethinking one's sense of self (Bury, 1982), as well as a 'loss of self' (Charmaz, 1983). An individual who experiences chronic illness is likely to engage in renegotiating and redefining health (see ch. 9). This process is likely to also affect views of health by significant others in the individual's life.

Gender

There is evidence that how we construct health and illness in our cultures and societies is itself gendered. There is a long history of men being associated with culture (the public realm of life, including work, and issues outside the home such as politics, war, science, etc.) and women being associated with nature (the private realm of life, including home, children, domestic duties and caring for the healthy and the sick). Women have therefore been aligned with health and matters of the body, whereas men have traditionally been aligned with the public sphere of work and productivity (Lyons & Willott, 1999). The language of the biomedical sciences over the previous three centuries has been characterised by this discourse linking women with nature and men with culture (Jordanova, 1989). Thus health and taking care of health have been viewed as part of women's social sphere. On the other hand, men have been treated as the normative standard reference point rather than as gendered beings. Over the past twenty-five years a literature has developed on men and masculinity (Connell, 1993), and men's health is now viewed as a timely concern for researchers and policy makers (Sabo & Gordon, 1995).

Herzlich (1973) has argued that health and illness are viewed as oppositional within society – health is seen as active involvement in society, whereas illness is seen as withdrawal from society. The masculine sphere is one that is defined in terms of work, rationality, goals, and the feminine sphere is defined in terms of care and nurturance. Thus, as Radley (1994) has pointed out, if being healthy is linked to masculinity, what does this mean for illness and femininity? We will take a closer look at issues of gender and health when we consider gendered bodies later in this chapter.

Age

Research shows that the ways in which children discuss and conceptualise health is different from the ways in which adults discuss health. Children's views on health have become an important focus of research in recent years, especially with regard to health education and health promotion (Bendelow & Pridmore, 1998). Children's ideas about health alter as they age. For example, Eiser and colleagues demonstrated that in a sample of 6-year-olds in the UK over half could not say what it means to be healthy. By contrast, all of those in an 11-year-old sample could do so (Eiser *et al.*, 1983). Furthermore, children do not generally equate health with social roles in the same way adults do (e.g. as being fit for chores or work), suggesting that these notions are acquired through socialisation (see Radley, 1994). Bendelow and Pridmore (1998) used a novel technique to explore children's concepts of health in two samples of 9–10-year-olds, one in England and one in Botswana. They employed a 'draw-and-write' technique, as detailed in research in focus box 2.1.

A study which examined concepts of health in Brazilian children highlighted strong similarities in children's views of health and illness across cultures. This study showed that as age increased children showed more multidimensional and differentiated concepts of health and illness (Boruchovitch & Mednick, 1997). Health was seen mostly in terms of positive feelings and engaging in healthy preventive practices. Further, children from middle SES groups were more likely to use feeling states in their definitions of health than children from lower SES groups (Boruchovitch & Mednick, 1997).

Concepts of health not only alter as we grow from child to adult, but also change across the lifespan. Lawton (2003) reviewed studies which showed that our views about health and illness depended on when the illness was experienced in the lifecourse. For older people certain kinds of illnesses are accepted as 'normal' and part of their biographies, because in some ways they are anticipated. For older people, illnesses such as strokes are not perceived as hugely disruptive, as their lives have already been restricted by prior illness (see Pound *et al.*, 1998). This suggests that ideas of health, and the impact of illness, depend fully on age and stage of life.

This point is nicely illustrated by a recent study conducted by Flick and colleagues in Germany (2003). They examined the representations of health in old age held by two groups of health professionals, general practitioners and nurses, working with elderly people. Both groups held concepts of health in old age that were much broader and extended than concepts of health seen more generally. These professionals saw health as relevant even in the presence of chronic illness and/or pain, and linked health strongly to the social and environmental situation in which the elderly individual lived. Further, health was seen in the ability to adjust to restrictions and limitations placed on an individual by illness. The three broad categories of health that professionals employed in the interviews are shown in table 2.2. This study addresses a gap in the health psychology literature. The absence of research examining notions of health in old age is somewhat surprising given the increasing number of elderly people in the population in Western societies, and the increasing numbers of old and very old people seen by health professionals (Flick *et al.*, 2003).

It is not just age but also the historical location in which we experience particular life stages that affect our understandings of health. For example, Murray and colleagues (2003) have investigated concepts of health among 'baby-boomers' in eastern Canada. These people were born in the twenty-year period following the Second World War, and came of age during the 1960s, when employment was high and there was unprecedented affluence in Western societies; they were the people proactive in introducing welfare systems. Now, entering their fifties, they are increasingly turning to health

2.1 Children's images of health

Bendelow, G. & Pridmore, P. (1998). Children's images of health. In
A. Petersen & C. Waddell (eds.), *Health matters: a sociology of illness,
prevention and care* (pp. 128–40). Buckingham, UK: Open University
Press.

This study employed a particular technique to explore concepts of
health in children. Specifically, it involved children drawing pictures
of health issues, and then using these pictures to write or discuss the
concepts raised further. Two case studies were employed, with two
groups of 9–10-year-old children, one group in England and one in
Botswana.

Health beliefs in 9–10-year-old children in England

One hundred children across three different primary schools in the
south-east of England took part in the study. Many were from materially
deprived backgrounds. Approval for each child to take part in the study
was given by teachers and parents. The researchers had access to a class
for ninety minutes, during which time children were given pre-prepared
sheets of paper, which were blank except for numbers in which to
respond to the researcher's questions. Children could draw and write
their responses.

   Children were asked to indicate factors which were responsible for
health and ill health. Most children described between two and four
factors. Boys tended to draw more per page than girls, and girls wrote
more than boys. Most children viewed exercise and healthy eating as the
most important factors in keeping healthy, and smoking and bad diet
were seen as unhealthy. Other factors that came up here were pollution,
hygiene and violence.

Health beliefs in 9–10-year-old children in Botswana

One hundred children from primary schools near the capital city of
Botswana, Gabrone, took part in the study, along with an additional
eleven children from an isolated settlement school for Bushmen children.
Parents, teachers and other community members came to a preliminary
meeting about the study programme, and consent for children to
participate was given at this meeting. Again, the exercise was carried out
in the classroom and a teacher at the school helped as facilitator. Only
three Setwswana words were employed, in order to reduce language
influence, namely *tshameka* (healthy), *nwa* (unhealthy) and *swa* (die).

Very few gender or urban-rural differences were found in concepts of health, although differences were apparent between the Botswana schools and the Bushmen school. For the Bushmen children, being healthy was seen to be related to four categories: food, exercise, medicine and hygiene. For the hundred other children, only one category was seen: food. In terms of notions of what makes you unhealthy, many of the Bushmen children drew pictures of unhealthy behaviour such as drinking, smoking, fighting and having accidents. One child drew herself being hungry. Most of the Botswana children drew pictures of sugars and sweets, with a few drawing dirty food or water.

The 'draw and write' technique

This method has both advantages and disadvanatages, as outlined below.

Advantages

allows more subjective and phenomenological input;
children's ideas not forced into pre-conceived adult categories;
allows children to express ideas for which they don't have words;
has the potential to enable all children to participate;
can be used in diverse cultural contexts;
allows the child to take control and develop capabilities.

Disadvantages

children may feel coerced to participate as conducted in classroom settings;
powerful emotions may be expressed, and these need to be handled with
    care and in an appropriate manner;
interpretation of the drawings is important, especially if the researcher takes
    them away;
ownership of the drawings is an important issue, as is confidentiality of the
    responses.

Reflection

The innovative method used in these studies demonstrates an alternative way of exploring children's beliefs about health and the world in which they live. Its bottom-up approach encourages diversity and range in responses, and does not categorise all participants into a homogeneous group of children.

Table 2.2 Professionals' concepts of health in old age

Health category	Details and concepts within categories
The person's living situation	Independence, self-determination, autonomy
	Mobility, vitality, mental activity
	Quality of life, social integration/participation, receiving support
The person's management of disease and complaints	Subjective versus objective health
	Managing with symptoms and restrictions
	Being satisfied despite physical complaints and restrictions
	Having meaning despite physical complaints and restrictions
The disease and complaint situation	No medical problems, no chronic and dramatic diseases, no complaints or pain
	Prevention/prophylaxis, living with normal decline/treatable problems
	Capacity

Adapted from Flick *et al.* (2003).

care systems for help with their own and their parents' health, at a time when there is much debate about the cost of health care and the state's financial involvement. Through group discussions and individual interviews, Murray and colleagues report how baby-boomers tell stories about changing attitudes to health and illness. They talked about how the meaning of health has shifted across the past generation, from something that was not paid much attention to something that is prominent and can be 'achieved' through a healthy lifestyle. This was seen also in participants' definitions of health as lifestyle and health promotion, although health was also seen in terms of attitude to life, social engagement, reserve, functionality and as a vacuum. Thus, both age and the historical location of our lives affect our understandings of health across life.

SES

People from middle-class groups have been found to have more positive definitions of health than people from lower SES groups. A study conducted in France with over 4,000 adults demonstrated that people from different social classes held different ideas about health (d'Houtard & Field, 1984). Those participants from lower SES groups viewed health as a means to an end, and emphasised the physical nature of health in which the body was seen as being able to perform specific social and physical tasks. For participants in higher SES groups, health was viewed as an end in itself, something to strive for, a value that they could aim for through their more hedonistic lifestyles.

Similarly, Chamberlain and O'Neill (1998) found that in New Zealand working-class people defined health in terms of being able to physically do the things required to get through the day, at work or at home. In contrast, middle-class people defined health in terms of being physically able to do the things they wanted to do in their leisure time.

Another study on people's ideas about health in France was conducted by Pierret (1995). In this study, over a hundred people from a range of backgrounds participated in an interview and completed a questionnaire in which they gave information about their health and behaviour related to health. Pierret identified four ways in which people talked about health:

- Health is not being ill: illness is used as a referent for health. This way of talking about health was used by people from all SES backgrounds.
- Health is the most important thing: the yardstick to compare the rest of life with, people's wealth and capital. This concept was employed by a quarter of the participants, primarily those from lower SES groups.
- Health as a product: the view that health depends on behaviour, living conditions, social system, and can be controlled. Health was seen as a value in this way by two out of ten people living in urban areas, primarily by older people from higher SES groups.
- Health as an institution: health was viewed through social structures and medical institutions, which are responsible for collective health. Young educated participants talked about health in this way.

This study again highlighted how people see health in different ways depending on their social situation. Pierret (1995) concludes by commenting that the right to health is being replaced by an obligation to be healthy.

In summary, research has consistently documented that there are large differences in the ways that people from different SES positions understand and experience health (and illness). This work also shows how concerns about health are embedded in day-to-day life (Chamberlain, 1997). Yet while social location influences notions of health so, in a fundamental way, does culture. How people think about both health and illness is inextricably linked to the broader cultural world in which they live.

Culture and ethnicity

In Western individualistic societies, health is a quality of the individual body, although this is a view 'peculiar to biomedicine', as Marks and colleagues note (2000, p. 70). In other societies, health is viewed as a quality not simply of the individual body, but of the mind, of the spirit, of the family, of social relationships, of being in balance with nature and so on. Across Western countries with quite different health care systems, knowledge about health has been found to be quite similar. For example, Mokounkolo and Mullet (1999) found that French and English people held quite similar lay health beliefs (despite the very dissimilar health systems of France and the UK), and concluded that people's ideas about health are not necessarily influenced by specific medical systems.

   American Indian women in the USA have been shown to hold quite different concepts of health from Western medical views. For example, in her study with Native American women, Canales (2004, p. 420) shows how health is viewed as a balance between mind, body and spirit:

> In my opinion, health is like a three legged stool. It's body, mind and spirit. If one is out of balance or not up to par, then the rest follows. And an unhealthy spirit and mind can affect the body.

Following from this, to feel healthy the women highlighted how they must experience well-being in these three realms of their lives (p. 421):

> Having no physical ailments of any kind. Being mentally stable. Having no mental issues. And also spiritually, being in touch with the spirits and all conclusive. It's not just one thing. It's a whole, well-rounded piece.

This view of health and feeling healthy also affected understandings of the body, and these Native women discussed listening to their body, being familiar with it and in touch with it. This attention to their bodies influenced their understandings of what was happening for them not just physically, but mentally and spiritually as well. Taking care of their own health by focusing on the mind, body and spirit was not individualistic for these women, but complemented their role in taking care of others in their family and community (Canales, 2004).

   An American anthropologist who has spent many years working in northern Italy with her family has written about what health means to Italians. Whitaker (2003) points out that for Italians, health is 'not simply an absence of disease but, rather, the fortuitous, fleeting outcome of a struggle for balance between a permeable self and an unpredictable outside world. Consequently, health must be managed personally on a daily basis' (pp. 348–9). Italian ideas about health are pluralistic and are drawn from aspects of biomedicine, as well as spiritual beliefs. Thus, when something goes wrong, this can be seen as the result of transgressing the rules of balance and moderation, or the agency of a spirit or human malice or a biomedical phenomenon (Whitaker, 2003).

   The ways in which Chinese people think about and experience health are strongly influenced by cultural and religious values (Chen, 2001). There are specific philosophies and religions that influence notions of health in China (Chen, 2001):

Yin and yang This tradition has been dominant in ideas about health and illness in Chinese thought. Health is seen as harmony between the forces of yin and yang, within the body as well as the environment. Imbalance leads to ill health.

Confucianism   This provides principles for social interaction and behaviour. There are five important concepts: benevolence (*jen*), righteousness (*yi*), loyalty (*chung*), filial piety (*hsia*) and virtue (*te*). These characteristics lead to happiness and peace, which promote health and prevent illness.

Taoism   This teaches that people should be in harmony with nature, or tao. Being with nature, in the fresh, clean air, promotes peace of mind and health. Death is seen as an extension of life, as part of nature.

Buddhism   The three key characteristics held up in Buddhism are mercy, thriftiness and humility. Cause and effect (*inn* and *ko*) encourage people to do good, and fate, *inn* and *ko* are seen as the main factors influencing health. When people are morally good, they are peaceful with no guilt, and this promotes health.

Studies which have examined the representations of health and illness held by Chinese people living in the UK demonstrate how these cultural beliefs are employed in their notions of health and illness (e.g. Prior *et al.*, 2000). For example, Jovchelovitch and Gervais (1999) show how notions of balance and harmony (through the forces of yin and yang) are central to ideas of health among the Chinese community in England. As demonstrated in the transcript below, one group of young men discussed this balance in relation to the body being too hot or too cold:

> S1: To the Chinese when you're sick it's more than just either you have a virus in there or anything like that. It's got something probably to do with the way you handle yourself, the way you eat, whether you drink enough water and all these sorts of things. I mean, to us, sick is more than just medicine can get rid of it. It's a whole way of life. Chinese always have the idea of like, your body is too heated or too cold.
> S2: Yes.
> S1: This sort of thing can't be explained by Western . . . You don't have the idea of body, whether your body is hot or cold. It's not measured in terms of your temperature. I mean, it wouldn't show up in your thermometer whether your temperature is too high but to a Chinese, this just, it blends into the way of your . . .
> S3: It's just your life.
> S1: . . . the food we take, there are two kinds of food we take. The heating kind and the cooling kind, so when a friend sometimes he might say he had diarrhoea, I say, oh you ate too much cooling stuff, papaya, watermelon, drank too much chrysanthemum tea.   (p. 252)

Somewhat surprisingly, these Chinese notions of health and illness existed alongside concepts of Western biomedicine, which were also drawn on at different times in the interviews. Such coexistence of different forms of knowledge demonstrates struggles over acculturation and identity. The Chinese people in this study were trying to maintain their Chinese heritage and beliefs, and also to integrate into the English way of life. Those who were more acculturated in

English society employed more concepts of biomedicine and biomedical ways of talking about health than those less acculturated (Jovchelovitch & Gervais, 1999).

Views about health have also been explored in a group of Circassians living in Israel (Haron *et al.*, 2004). The Circassians are an ethnic group who arrived in Israel from the Caucasus mountain region over a century ago, and about 3,000 now live in relative cultural isolation in two villages in northern Israel (they have a worldwide population of around 4 million). Haron and colleagues (2004) interviewed twenty-one elderly community leaders (both male and female), as these are the people in the community who are asked to give advice about health and illness matters. The interviews demonstrated six major categories that affected notions of health and illness. These are displayed in table 2.3. Health was directly related to both physical wholeness and social participation. It was seen holistically, as the outcome of 'successful interaction among physical, spiritual, communal and environmental factors' (p. 70).

Other cultural groups also highlight the importance of social ties for health. For example, Greek Cypriots living in London viewed social contact as significantly related to health, and social isolation to stress and ill health (Papadopoulos, 1999). Furthermore, in talking about susceptibility to illness, Aborigines in Australia talk about social connectedness on three specific levels, of family, community and society (Thompson & Gifford, 2000). Processes operating at family and community levels are health protective; through these processes the individual is connected to family, land and past. Aborigines in Melbourne talk about their 'worries', and these worries can be seen as describing disconnection at the societal level. Their worries stem from the social, economic and political situation imposed by white society. They are also seen as outside the control of the Aboriginal individual, family and community (Thompson & Gifford, 2000).

In summary, when we look to other cultures, we find that ideas about health are quite different from Western individualistic notions and often more socially oriented. Such cross-cultural research demonstrates that Western theories of health are also cultural productions, as are Western health care practices (Harkness & Keefer, 2000). While cross-cultural research has provided us with much more understanding of cultural meaning systems with regard to health, Harkness and Keefer (2000) argue that this work must proceed with caution. Specifically, they argue that researchers:

1 must avoid a new kind of ethnocentrism based on non-Western constructs and measures;
2 must avoid oversimplifying constructs such as individualism and collectiveness, which involve much more complexity than initially proposed;
3 must avoid oversimplifying cultural variability;
4 need to build on the intellectual heritage, methods and theories used in both psychology and anthropology.

Table 2.3 Ideas of health among Circassians in Israel

Category (seen to affect health)	Description	Example quotations
Acts of God	The influence of divine power on an individual's health	Life and death are in God's hands, as is everything connected to one's body
The evil eye	The evil eye has its power from another person's envy: looking at something admiringly. Feared by everyone, but can be prevented by reading verses from the Koran	... the man died suddenly the next day because of the evil eye cast upon him by one of the men who was charmed by his strength and manliness
Mental health and community ties	Being constantly worried about things in life is seen to cause physical ill health. People who are alone and not socially active are seen to be more at risk of illness	Bothersome and tragic life events damage one's health, but if you have a supportive family and are involved in the community, you have less stress and your health is preserved
Bodily cleanliness and purity	Physical integrity is expressed in having a clean body, clean home and clean yard	Cleanliness scares the devil and keeps illness away
Eating habits	Food is seen as important for preserving good health. Longevity is linked to eating fresh and natural food. Women are encouraged to develop a 'portly figure' in order that they produce healthy children. Ideas of feminine beauty reflected this	My father lived to the age of 107 and never ate food that was not fresh. He grew his own food without pesticides or fertilisers
Internal bodily resistance kutze	Kutze means the core of the body, and is seen to be the foundation of inner strength. It is believed to develop from birth, especially during infancy. Having enough kutze is related to health	Someone who does not have sufficient kutze will have low resistance to illness both in childhood and as an adult

Adapted from Haron *et al.* (2004).

Such work becomes even more important as international immigration continues to grow, and more and more cross-cultural encounters occur (Harkness & Keefer, 2000).

Summary

Our understanding of the concept of health is not fixed or definite but continually debated and changing. Further, how we understand health depends on our different personal histories, our age, our stage of life, the historical location of our lives and where we fit in society. In thinking about both health and illness, people draw on knowledge that is available in wider society. As Radley (1994) puts it, 'how people think about their health is not something limited to their own bodies or individual experience. Instead, it is affected by the ways in which health is understood as part of a wider representation of society, and the individual's place within it' (p. 42).

It is worth noting here, however, that almost all of the research conducted in this area has used interviews or focus groups, and thus is produced in a particular and unique context. Radley and Billig (1996) have argued that 'health talk' is ideological in nature and is likely to be both persuasive and functional in any discussion with a researcher. They suggest that researchers take this on board and focus more on health 'accounts' (that is, focus on what people say within the context of an interview with a researcher) than health 'beliefs'. A focus on health beliefs assumes that talk unproblematically provides insight into internal and unchanging beliefs. Accounts can be viewed as participants legitimating their position, and the interview can be viewed as a social act that enables this to occur (Radley, 1994).

Thinking about the body

The idea of the body as an object that can be thought of in many different ways is integral to ideas about health. After all, the body is the centre of health and illness experiences (Bekker, 2000). From the biomedical standpoint, the body is a relatively straightforward entity: it is a biological machine that breaks down when it becomes ill and therefore needs repair. The biomedical view separates person from body, and bodies are seen as docile objects which can be surveilled, used, transformed and improved (Foucault, 1975). Biomedical discourses on the body extend into our everyday lives, as people talk about 'body maintenance' and 'body repair'. However, rather than viewing the body as simply a biological and 'natural' phenomenon, the human body can be seen in sociocultural terms. As Lupton (1998) points out, 'the ways in which we understand and experience the body are mediated through social, cultural and political processes' (p. 122). To take a relatively straightforward example, in current Western societies thin bodies are given status as slimness is considered physically attractive. However, in other historical times and in other societies, larger body sizes were given status and were seen as attractive.

It seems somewhat paradoxical to argue that the physical reality which is our bodies is shaped by psychological, social and cultural factors. After all, individuals go through seemingly 'physical', 'natural' and 'objective' phases in life, such as birth, old age, death and the experience of pain and illness (Herzlich, 1995). However, the experience of

> **2.3**
>
> We are not born with ideas about embodiment and how to experience our body. While writing this chapter, I saw my three-year-old son respond to his father's comment that he had a sore nose. My son promptly stood up, walked over, reached up and touched his dad's nose, and seriously commented 'no Dad, it's not sore, it's ok'.

all of these events, and our understandings and beliefs about them, vary across different social and cultural groups, sometimes quite dramatically (Lupton, 1998). Sociologists have argued that this is because we both are and have a body: we are embodied beings. How people understand and experience their **embodiment** is important for studies of health and illness. In a fundamental sense, the body is our main way of being in the world. An individual is an embodied being, not simply someone who possesses a body, as Merleau-Ponty (1962) has argued (Madjar, 1997).

The experience of both *being* and *having* a body.

Anthropology has had a strong interest in researching the body since the nineteenth century. According to Turner (1991) this is primarily because in pre-modern societies the body provided a public marker of social status, family position, age, gender, tribal affiliation and so on. It was not until the 1980s that the body became of central interest in sociological research. This interest developed partly from the influence of feminism, partly from Foucault's work and partly out of developments in social theory (Cunningham-Burley & Backett-Milburn, 2001). Turner was particularly influential in theorising the body in sociology (e.g. Turner, 1984). In psychology humans continue to be theorised largely as disembodied beings.

While medicine presents a picture of a body which is 'objective' and 'scientific', theorists and researchers have strongly argued that medical knowledge is far from neutral and value free (e.g. Armstrong, 1983; Foucault, 1975). For example, in the medical realm, the young, white male body is represented as the healthy body. Thus, bodies that deviate from this view have traditionally been seen as somehow 'other', 'different' and ultimately, abnormal. Martin (1987) has argued that the negative notions of women's bodies as 'other' or 'abnormal' help to shape how women experience their own bodies, and the meanings that are ascribed to bodily changes (particularly hormonal changes such as menopause). Similarly, bodies of people from lower socioeconomic groups, non-white bodies, disabled bodies and homosexual bodies have been seen as deviant from the 'norm' and viewed in negative ways (as diseased, passive, dirty, lacking self-control (Petersen & Lupton, 1996)).

The experience of seemingly 'objective' life stages such as menopause has also been found to vary dramatically, both across time and across cultures. The symptoms women experience during menopause in North America differ from those experienced by women in Japan (who have significantly fewer hot flushes and night sweats). Drawing on anthropological evidence Lock (1998) demonstrates that these are not simply genetic differences, but that 'culturally mediated lifestyles affect both the menopausal experience and the health of women as they age' (p. 410). The pervasive negative representations of menopause (and ageing women) in Western societies have also been argued to influence mid-aged women's bodily experience (Lyons & Griffin, 2003).

Healthy bodies

When we are healthy, we experience our embodiment unselfconsciously, not giving it much attention and taking it for granted. This is similar to Herzlich's (1973) finding that health is experienced as an unawareness of the body. So, when things are going smoothly, we do not consciously think about our body. However, when effort is required (such as climbing up eight flights of stairs) or when we become ill or injured, we become acutely aware of our body and its activities (Madjar, 1997). This view of the body being in the background, so to speak, and not given too much attention unless day-to-day activities are disrupted, does not hold across all social groups. Paradoxically, in affluent societies, particularly in higher SES groups, the body has been pushed to the foreground. Within these groups, a great deal of time, effort, money and attention is being devoted to creating and constructing what are viewed as 'healthy' bodies (through diet, exercise, surgery). In affluent groups in Western societies, as we will see later, healthy bodies are seen as desirable bodies.

Bodies in medicine

Foucault (1975) argued that as the eighteenth century drew to a close, doctors began to engage in clinical examinations to determine diagnosis and treatment for an individual (rather than relying on patients' own accounts of their symptoms) (Lupton, 1998). This signalled a shift in how bodies were represented and conceptualised in medicine, and enabled what Foucault (1975) calls the **clinical gaze**. Doctors are allowed privileged access to patients' bodies (and are able to use whatever instruments or technology possible for closer and more 'direct' access to the body, such as X-rays, blood pressure monitors, etc.; see also MacLachlan, 2004). This legitimated access to patients' bodies is one way in which doctors and other health professionals have so much more power in doctor–patient interactions than do patients themselves.

The direct and unquestioned access a doctor has to a patient's body (which tends to ignore the patient's emotions or psychological state) (from Foucault, 1975).

The point to highlight here is that medical knowledge helps shape how we conceive of the body, but medicine also directly intervenes in the body through medical practice (Lupton, 1998). Furthermore, patients who enter into a health care setting and are experiencing illness may also be experiencing being in the world, and their bodies, in unfamiliar ways (van der Riet, 1997). Within medical care, the body is often seen as an object rather than a subject. The use of various forms of medical technology (such as automatic blood pressure monitors, x-rays and screening devices) frequently means that the body is objectified, losing its personhood (van der Riet, 1997).

Gendered bodies

Gender identity is primarily based on the body, and influences all domains of life (Bekker, 2000). Gender plays a fundamental role in health as well as in our views on the body. Most obviously, some diseases affect only men or only women, occurring in sex-specific parts of the body or because of genetic risk (Bekker, 2000). However, gender also affects daily life and environment, and as we will see throughout this book, these have a direct impact on health. Gender arises from what culture does with the 'raw material' of biological sex (Bekker, 2000; Unger & Crawford, 1996). Bekker puts it succinctly when she states that 'because culture shapes gender and gender shapes body experiences, male and female body experiences vary across cultures' (p. 20). The pervasive and powerful representations of women's bodies in Western culture create normative processes which women constantly confront (and physically struggle with – think about anorexia nervosa and bulimia). As Bordo (1997) comments, the contemporary aesthetic ideal body for women in Western societies has led to 'an ideal whose obsessive pursuit has become the central torment of many women's lives' (p. 92).

The bodies of women have been much more frequently subjected to the clinical gaze than men's bodies. Furthermore, women have received the lion's share of medical and public health attention (Petersen & Lupton, 1996), and have been represented as weak, frail and sick. Compared to men's bodies, historically women's bodies have been much more targeted, technologised, pathologised and medicalised (van der Riet, 1997). For example, menstruation, pregnancy, childbirth and menopause are all aspects of women's lives that have been medicalised over the past century and a half. Notice how these concerns are all directly relevant to women's fertility, which as Broom (1998) notes, 'is arguably the women's health domain of most interest to men' (p. 48).

Caring for sick bodies, and keeping other people's bodies healthy, has also been the realm of women. Women are expected to take responsibility for men's and children's bodies, and for older relatives as well. Public health initiatives often recommend aiming messages at women to improve the health of men, reinforcing this positioning of women. Media representations of men's health have also been found to function to persuade women that it is in their interests to be responsible for men's health, although without taking overt control. In a study conducted in the UK, Lyons and Willott (1999) analysed a series of

Figure 2.1 *Media representations of men's health (for women)*

articles in a major British Sunday newspaper to explore how men, women and health were constructed (see fig. 2.1). Men's health was constructed as 'in crisis' and men tended to be aligned with culture (and work) and women with nature (and health). Such constructions reproduce and sustain unequal social relations, and do little to benefit women or men.

There are plenty of examples of dualisms that have, over the centuries, reflected differences in sex and gender. These are central to thinking about the body. Some of these are given below. In reading through the list, notice how the first term in each pair has traditionally held positive connotations, and has been aligned with men and masculinity. The second term has more negative connotations and values and has therefore aligned women and femininity with negativity (Bayer & Malone, 1996):

- mind–body;
- culture–nature;
- activity–passivity;
- reason–emotion;
- objective–subjective;
- public–private;
- order–chaos;
- independent–dependent;
- hard–soft.

These dualisms have meant that women's subjectivities, how they are thought about and how they think about themselves, have been linked to the body and bodily functions. As men are aligned with objectivity, rationality and the public world of work, women's bodies (and their psychological and sexual lives) have been measured against a male norm (Bayer & Malone, 1996). This oppositional way of thinking has privileged the male body over the female body. In the previous four decades, feminist research on women and the body has brought forth an awareness that the body is not necessarily a simple 'natural' category, but is 'thoroughly entwined with the workings of social, cultural and political life' (Bayer & Malone, 1996, p. 673).

In direct contrast to how women's bodies have been treated and represented culturally in Western societies, men's bodies have been given limited attention in medicine (after all, these are assumed to be the 'normal' healthy bodies). Men's bodies are culturally represented as strong, healthy and invulnerable. As we will see throughout this book, being socialised into forms of masculinity has implications for health and illness: not paying attention to changes in one's body, not heeding physical symptoms, resisting any claim about 'sickness', all reinforce what it means to be male.

The emergence of men's studies over the previous two decades has led to a recognition that striving for various forms of masculinity as it is constructed in Western societies can be socially, psychologically and physically hazardous for men (Newman, 1997). More attention has been paid to men's health in recent years, and the implications of masculinity for physical health (e.g. Lee & Owens, 2002). Despite this increasing attention, we know very little about the lived experience of the male body and how that relates to ideas and experiences of

> **2.4**
>
> Men's and women's bodies are culturally constructed in different ways:
>
> - Women's bodies are constructed as open, fluid, leaky: open to conception and birth, to menses and penetration (usually by a penis). This 'open' body is exemplified in pornographic literature through specific forms of posturing and posing.
> - Men's bodies are constructed as closed, and therefore more complete, strong and invincible. This 'closed' body is exemplified by the difficulty some men have with the concept of anal sex and particularly male–male sex. (Buchbinder, 1994, taken from Newman, 1997)

health and illness (in stark contrast to the attention paid to women's bodies and embodied experiences). It has been argued that two areas of the male body are critical in male embodiment: the head (intellectual power) and the penis (Newman, 1997). (For more on this, see Horrocks, 1994.)

The gendered body influences how we experience health (Bekker, 2000). Differences in how women and men talk about health highlight how differently they experience and think about the body. For example, Saltonstall (1993) interviewed middle-class people in the UK and found that men and women discussed different behaviour undertaken to be healthy. Men talked primarily about the body as 'a medium of action', and they saw the function and capacity of the body as important. Women, on the other hand, were more concerned with the appearance and presentation of their bodies, although they did discuss its function and capacity in terms of 'doing' for other people. Other differences demonstrated that men and women had different bodily symbols of health. Saltonsall suggests that 'the doing of health is a form of doing gender' (p. 12), by which she means that we, as women and men, keep our bodies healthy, and 'do' health in different ways and for different reasons. By behaving in these ways, we are not simply trying to keep healthy or to appear healthy, but also demonstrating and performing gender – showing that we are male or female. Saltonsall concludes by reinforcing the idea that health is not a universal fact, but is constituted socially, 'constructed through the medium of the body using the raw materials of social meaning and symbol' (p. 12). Selfhood, embodiment and health, she argues, are intertwined.

Studies with people who are transgendered (choose to be both male and female) highlight the plasticity of the body in terms of gender. These people are often consciously actively seeking to re-produce their sexed and gendered bodies with body management practices such as using hormones, surgery and clothing (Finn & Dell, 1999). Work with transgendered people highlights how seemingly 'objective' and 'natural' categories such as man/woman can be undermined (Brown Parlee, 1998). Finn and Dell (1999) conducted interviews with transgendered people, and concluded that rather than viewing transgenderism as an individual pathology (as it is constructed in medical discourses), transgenderism can be seen as a choice. Their interviews highlighted how transgender people emphasise the notion of choice, as the quotes below demonstrate:

> I think humans have choice and expressions of gender. The way I view it [i.e. gender] is that I see it like hair colour and it's much less fixed than we're taught it.   (p. 471)

> The increased libido from hormones [testosterone] and the changes in my sexual response cycle made me feel even better about it all . . . I know that getting pregnant and having a kid doesn't change who I am [a male]. It is a thing my body can do, and I'd like to try to do it . . . People will see something incongruous – someone who has a beard who looks pregnant and make up an explanation for themselves.   (p. 473)

> Being transgender in a way does open up a whole other world that ordinary people don't always get.   (p. 473)

This highlights how gender identity can be seen as an activity produced through the body, rather than as stable and fixed (Finn & Dell, 1999). This is consistent with Butler's (1990) idea that gender can be seen as a doing rather than a way of being. Such work also demonstrates the inadequacy of medical binary categories, such as sex and gender, because it highlights that not all people fit neatly into these catgories (Brown Parlee, 1998).

In summary, there are vast differences in how men and women experience their bodies (Bekker, 2000). Further, the clearly defined categories of 'male' and 'female' bodies have now been brought into question. Studies have consistently demonstrated that men and women think about, experience and live their bodies in different ways and hold different meanings of them. These differences are relevant for health, and health care, although the relationships between gendered bodily experience and awareness with health are currently under-investigated.

Disabled bodies

People with physically disabled bodies are treated differently from able-bodied people. They are relegated to the margins, discriminated against or looked away from, as though they were invisible (Davis, 1995, in Lupton, 1998). Ironically, it has been argued that the discipline 'disability studies' has neglected to study the experience of disabled embodiment, but that this was a strategic neglect: it was necessary to get the disabled body away from its grounding in medical cultures and institutions (Snyder & Mitchell, 2001). The main contention of disability studies was that disability was not embedded in defective biologies but in faulty social structures (Snyder & Mitchell, 2001). As MacLachlan (2004, p. 82) has pointed out:

> not to acknowledge a disabled person's disability may be to deny their physicality, yet to define them by this may be to invalidate them in their own eyes and those of society . . . In seeking to distinguish between the disabled body and the able person we seek to disembody the person from 'that body'.

Recently there have been calls for research investigating the phenomenology of the disabled body.

Women with physical disabilities in the USA have been found to define and experience health in a number of ways (Nosek *et al.*, 2004), including:

- health as functional capacity;
- having a positive mental state;
- having good social support;
- health behaviour for health promotion, adapted to functional limitations;
- general practitioners' knowledge (or lack of it).

The women viewed a number of issues as barriers to health, including disability characteristics, stress, societal attitudes and lack of resources (Nosek *et al.*, 2004). These results demonstrate the similarities in notions of health among women with disabilities and other women. The findings resonate strongly with findings on the experience of health from general populations in both France and the UK, as described earlier in the chapter.

Snyder and Mitchell (2001) have argued that the 'normal' and 'able' body is treated as desirable. They go on to make the point that if traditional views of the able body tell us what is 'ideal', what is it that the disabled body tells us? Snyder and Mitchell (p. 377) sum it up thus:

> **2.5**
>
> Mary Duffy is a performance artist who uses her armless body in her work. She challenges the view that her body is incomplete, and that her body should be changed so it is restored to what people think of as normal biology:
>
> > The words you use to describe me are 'congenital malformation'. Those words that the doctor used – they didn't have any that fitted me properly. I felt, even in the face of such opposition, that my body was the way it was supposed to be. It was right for me, as well as being whole, complete and functional. (Duffy, 1997, cited in Snyder & Mitchell, 2001)

> The different body was more than a site for public scapegoating – cognitive and physical aberrancies acted as reminders of Others in our midst who challenged beliefs in a homogenous bodily order.

Breckenridge and Vogler (2001) comment that there is no single figure of disability. They point out that the view of a person with a disability who is healthy, full of vitality and living her life to the fullest throws into sharp relief our assumptions about disability and health (see sidebar 2.5). Furthermore, they argue that able-bodied people are anxious about disability because being able-bodied is always a temporary state.

Summary

Our views on the body are shaped partially by medical notions, but also by social, economic and political issues (Martin, 1987). A compelling example of this point is the children in poverty in poor countries, who are living on the streets and whose only shelter is their bodies (Breckenridge & Vogler, 2001). Our experiences of embodiment are not static, but change over time and across cultures. In Western societies, control over one's body (to keep it fit and healthy) is seen as highly important. This is tied to representations in medical, public health and commercial realms, viewing bodies which are slim, fit, self-disciplined, young and healthy in a strong positive light, but bodies which are overweight, flabby, disabled or sick in a negative light (Lupton, 1998). These 'negative' bodies are thought to arise because people lack personal control and moral fibre. This highlights how views about the body are intertwined with, and embedded within, the social world in which we live.

The body, and embodiment particularly, has not been a major focus of study in psychology (Braun, 2000). The literature on the body and embodiment comes from many different disciplines, and is diverse and confusing. Braun identifies four ways in which the body has been conceptualised across the literature, as shown in table 2.4. Debates about how best to theorise the body continue to take place across and within disciplines.

Barnard (2000) has argued that psychology must engage with theorising the body in its materiality, and that this is particularly important now as biomedical technologies transform how we understand individual subjectivity. In recent years some health psychology work has engaged with theorising the body (e.g. MacLachlan, 2004; Stam, 1998; Yardley, 1997), although generally how we think about and experience our bodies has not been viewed as of major importance for health psychologists. Stam (1998) has argued that 'modern "biopsychosocial" accounts are incapable of dealing with the body' (p. 10). As MacLachlan (2004) has noted, although there has been much excitement concerning conceptualisations of the body in the humanities in recent years, 'much of this has not been grounded in a way that makes it relevant to people in health-related settings' (p. 2). MacLachlan (2004) has provided a stimulating exploration of the notion of embodiment across a range of health psychology (and clinical psychology) contexts, drawing on both critical and cultural perspectives. He emphasises people's understanding of their bodies across

Table 2.4 Conceptualisations of the body in academic literature

Conceptualisation	Description
The implicit body	A body that 'just is', it is taken as a given. In this conceptualisation there is no critical engagement with the meaning of the body, it is just a fact
The natural body	The flesh and blood of the body are seen as central. It is acknowledged the body is constructed and experienced through certain worldviews, and that it is not value-free, but it is a body of flesh, bones, blood and cells nevertheless. Thus how 'natural' the body actually is is disputed
The experienced body	The body is more than biology or discourse, it is lived and animated, it is embodied. We can 'inhabit' the body differently through particular experiences, such as participating in sport and exercise
The body as a surface	The body is constructed, inscribed, disciplined, produced. We construct meaning of the body's surface, such as the invisibility of the white body, or gender-specific inscriptions on the body

Adapted from Braun (2000).

a variety of distressing bodily experiences (including anorexia, amputation, acute and chronic pain, phantom limbs), in addition to explanations of such experiences. He makes the important point that we experience the world as embodied persons, and that we need to understand the world from this first-person perspective rather than from an objective and distant third-person perspective. This has implications for illness and disability, 'for it implies that it is not simply a breakdown in mechanical functioning, but a disordered way of being-in-the-world, of how one relates to one's own body, or to others' (MacLachlan, 2004, p. 5).

If we are to gain understandings of health, theorising and researching the body is central to this task. Saltonstall's (1993) conclusions, made over a decade ago, about theorising health in social psychology apply equally well in health psychology now: 'if social psychological theories of health are to reflect adequately the everyday experience of health, they must begin to take into account the body as individually and socially problematic' (p. 7). However, as with research into ideas about health, most of the research on embodiment has employed text (obtained through interviews, focus groups, diaries, etc.). Studies of embodiment may be particularly valuable if they use methods which do not rely so heavily on text (Willig, 2000), and draw on other methods such as photography, paintings, role play, media images and so on.

Implications of our understandings of health and the body

People's ideas about health and the body can be seen as important in that they shape individual and social action. People use these ideas to locate themselves within their social and cultural context, and also use them to determine how to act within these locations (Popay *et al.*, 1998). Herzlich (1973) proposed that studies into the social representations of health and illness tell us something about the relationship of the individual to society. Health is perceived as belonging to the individual, and is displayed through his or her active involvement in society. Thus, health becomes an individual thing. Activity or inactivity, as well as participation or exclusion, are the ideas that are used to define the healthy person and the sick person (Herzlich, 1995). Being healthy is therefore aligned with being a worthy and responsible citizen within society, and individual states of health become value laden with a moral aspect (Radley, 1994).

The way in which risk and risk calculations are a dominant part of people's lives in Western society today.

However, with the advent of the **risk society** (Beck, 1992), the growing importance of science and technology, and the ongoing dominance of medicine and medical knowledge, there has been a move away from the view that health is solely a matter for the individual. Health, how it is represented, discussed, valued and striven for, has become part of society. This is most evident in studies on embodiment, and the attention now paid to producing the appearance of healthy bodies. Health is becoming a supreme value, and this has serious consequences for people who are seen as unhealthy (Herzlich, 1995).

Furthermore, from a more global perspective, it is also possible to question the extent to which health might be another way of promoting ideas about 'development'. Development has positive connotations; it implies favourable change and growth, evolution and maturation (Esteva, 1992). However, as Sachs (1992) has argued, 'development is much more than just a socio-economic endeavour, it is a perception which models reality, a myth which comforts societies, and a fantasy which unleashes passions' (p. 1). The pursuit of development has resulted in a tremendous loss of diversity and has destroyed various indigenous forms of living. Development also reminds two-thirds of the global population of what they are not (Esteva, 1992). Yet the term 'development' continues to be a positive one, and functions to allow any intervention to be sanctified (Sachs, 1992). In a similar manner, to strive for and pursue health is becoming an ultimate, and extremely positive, goal. We need to ask how this term 'health' functions in a global context. How is it being employed? And for what means? Is it also allowing and enabling interventions without any critical scrutiny of their consequences?

Health is also a moral state, as pointed out recently by Crossley (2003): 'health issues remain inextricably connected with questions of morality and "the good"' (p. 511). People give accounts of health which involve moral justification (see Crossley, 2003). As Radley (1994) has argued, people do not feel responsible for becoming ill, rather they feel guilty about impairing their health. What are the implications of health as a value, tied to morality and goodness?

- First, there are implications for how we judge people who do become ill. As there are moral requirements to stay healthy (Radley, 1994), people who become ill may be viewed negatively as somehow 'immoral', for not managing to protect themselves from illness.
- Second, with health as a norm, people are being taught how to avoid risk, engage in healthy behaviour and present a healthy (and, by implication, desirable) body.
- Third, all of these practices to be healthy, look healthy and stay healthy have implications for how we view, live and manage our lives: by focusing so heavily on risk and avoiding illness, it is as though it is life itself that needs to be cured (Pierret, 1995).

Conclusions

While health used to be seen as a justification for medical intervention and treatment, in recent years health has come to prominence as a core concept in its own right (Pierret, 1995). Health has gradually been given more research attention, which is related to the emergence of health as a key value in western societies (Pierret, 1993). This means that health is no longer seen as a means to an end, but an end it itself (Pierret, 1995). Crawford (1980) has termed this emphasis on health 'healthism' and a 'new health consicousness'.

In examining people's views on their health and their body, the focus has been predominantly on illness compared to health. Illness experiences are tangible and conscious, and much easier to study than the more intangible experience of health. In health psychology the emphasis has also been on notions and representations of illness (e.g. illness cognitions (Leventhal *et al.*, 1980), see ch. 6) rather than of health. Health has arisen as a topic of study in relation to healthy behaviour, but then the focus has been more on specific behaviour (e.g. diet, smoking, exercise) than ideas and social representations of health (Murray *et al.*, 2003). As we have seen in this chapter, ideas about health and the body are important for a study of health psychology. As health psychologists, we are, as Brown (1995) eloquently puts it, 'after all, talking about phenomena which occur in people's bodies' (p. 37). How we think about health and the body varies with social, material and cultural conditions, as does health itself.

In current Western society, health is represented more in terms of its external appearance than in terms of its function (Lawton, 2003). 'Healthy' bodies are increasingly becoming sites of interest for public health and medicine, with the emergence of the 'risk society' (Beck, 1992). Health psychologists have been heavily involved in helping to shape health and illness preventive behaviour (as we will see in chs. 3 and 4), yet have paid relatively little attention to what people think health is about.

To conclude, much more research and attention has been paid to illness and the study of lay knowledges about illness than to health. This is especially so in health psychology. However, in order to gain insight into, and understandings of, such complex but everyday activities as engaging in healthy behaviour, engaging in health-preventive behaviour, engaging in screening behaviour to catch disease early, deciding to go and see a health professional, we must have some insight into health, what it means for people and how it varies across biographies, ages and social and cultural locations. Similarly, in examining the topics throughout the rest of this book, which is about people and their physical health, we must think about those people as embodied. While the individual is a cognitive being, he or she is also an emotional and embodied one. The individual body is central to our work as health psychologists, yet is absent in most theorising in this field.

RECOMMENDED READING

Lawler, J. (ed.) (1997). *The body in nursing*. Melbourne: Churchill Livingstone. This book examines the matter of the body and embodiment from the perspective of nursing, and relates to many of the issues raised in this chapter about the body. It highlights how nurses continually deal with people's bodies in their work, and attempts to provide some thoughts on how patients' bodies (and nurses' bodies) can be thought about, theorised and studied. It covers a wide variety of material (from the body in health, illness and pain through to technology and the body) and is a somewhat diverse but thoughtful collection of chapters.

Lupton, D. (1998). The body, medicine and society. In J. Germov (ed.), *Second opinion: an introduction to health sociology* (2nd edn) (pp. 121–35). Oxford: Oxford University Press. In this chapter Lupton provides a concise but informative account of how the human body can be viewed as a sociocultural (rather than a biological) phenomenon. It is a very useful introduction and a good starting point for further reading in this area.

MacLachlan, M. (2004). *Embodiment: clinical, critical and cultural perspectives on health and illness*. Berkshire, UK: Open University Press. This book provides an excellent introduction to ideas about embodiment and their relevance to health, illness and disability from a psychological perspective. It explores the notion of embodiment across a range of health psychology (and clinical psychology) contexts, drawing on both critical and cultural perspectives. It is an ideal starting point for further reading on embodiment.

Pierret, J. (1995). The social meanings of health: Paris, the Essonne, the Herault. In M. Augé & C. Herzlich (eds.), *The meaning of illness: anthropology, history and sociology* (pp. 175–206). Paris: Harwood Academic Publishers. In this multidisciplinary book. Pierret provides an insightful chapter outlining a brief history of how health has been conceptualised in medicine, and how it developed to play a prominent role in its own right. The chapter also examines the ways in which health is talked about and employed in everyday life; thus, it situates health squarely in the social realm. The concepts and issues are engagingly discussed by drawing on research data as examples.

Stam, H. J. (ed.) (1998). *The body and psychology*. London: Sage. In this edited book a number of contributors from psychology discuss the body in terms of embodiment. The chapters are structured around the topics of social and psychological bodies, sexed and gendered bodies, and sick and healing bodies. This was one of the first books in psychology to draw on social and cultural theory to examine the body (rather than drawing on biological accounts).

3 Choosing lifestyles

Health is indivisible . . . the domain of personal health over which the individual has direct control is very small when compared to the influence of culture, economy and environment. (Hafton Mahler, former Director General of the World Health Organisation, cited in Parish, 1995)

Learning objectives

This chapter focuses on behaviours that are part of an individual's lifestyle, such as eating, smoking, drinking, taking drugs, using condoms and so on. It reviews different approaches to attempts to influence lifestyles (through health promotion efforts) and reviews research on the contextual nature of individual behaviour. By the end of this chapter you should be able to:

- identify and describe social cognition approaches to the study of lifestyle behaviour;
- compare and contrast individual and structural-collective perspectives on improving lifestyles and health;
- outline and explain some of the limitations of traditional approaches to health promotion efforts;
- describe the implications of strategies that have been employed to influence individual lifestyles;
- explain the importance of social situation and cultural context in understanding behaviours that make up individual lifestyles.

What are lifestyles and how do they relate to health?

What kind of lifestyle do you have? Reasonably affluent, relaxed, busy, 'on the edge', chilled out, stressed, fun, sporty? Does your lifestyle affect your health? Will it affect your health one day in the future? Do you ever think about changing your lifestyle for health reasons? What does a 'healthy' lifestyle mean? Does it equate with doing nothing that is exciting or fun? The concept of 'lifestyle' is a slippery one, but it is central to any discussions about the consequences of how people live and behave for their physical health.

The term **lifestyle** has been used in many contexts, and has referred to conditions of living, product brand names and television programming (Davison *et al.*, 1992). Traditionally in social science work, the concept of lifestyle was about the social distribution of wealth, status and power, and how these affected individual subjectivity. Today, however, the concept is vague and seemingly everything can belong to the sphere of 'lifestyle' (O'Brien, 1995). Lifestyle is often linked with individual health and is widely used in the fields of health promotion, preventive medicine and health research (Backett & Davison, 1995). Here we use this concept to denote the idea of specific behaviour and ways of living that may be related to physical health.

> The ways in which an individual lives his/her life, including specific behaviours s/he engages in.

As we have already noted in ch. 1, how we live and what we do affects our health. Public health initiatives such as sanitation and clean drinking water improved the health of populations in the West early in the twentieth century, dramatically reducing deaths from infectious diseases and leading to longer life expectancies. In Western societies today the main causes of illness and death are related to individual lifestyles (McKeown, 1979). For example, smoking cigarettes, drinking excessive amounts of alcohol and eating a poor diet have been linked to heart disease, stroke and cancer (Matarazzo, 1984). As described in research in focus box 3.1, correlational studies explicitly highlight the links between health-related behaviours and later health status and mortality (Belloc & Breslow, 1972; Breslow, 1983).

Another example comes from a recent large, ten-year longitudinal study carried out in seven European countries. This study examined the effect of engaging in three particular kinds of **health behaviours** (non-smoking, being physically active and eating a good diet) on survival in over 1,200 older people aged between 70 and 75 years. Results showed that each of these behaviours was positively related to survival over the ten years, while engaging in all three was even more strongly related to survival. Conversely, people who did not engage in any such behaviour were three to four times more likely to die in the following ten years (Haveman-Nies *et al.*, 2002).

> Any activity that is undertaken by people to enhance or maintain their health.

Recognition of the inextricable link between lifestyle and health has meant that over the past three decades people in governments and academia, as well as commercial and popular arenas, have been focusing heavily on the ways in which people live (Burrows *et al.*, 1995). Indeed, the health and well-being of individuals is viewed by the those in the health promotion field as a product of their lifestyle (O'Brien, 1995). Health psychologists have been particularly interested in the kinds of health behaviours that make up unhealthy lifestyles, not only because they affect people's health, but because they may be amenable to change. They make a distinction between **positive health behaviour**, which is health enhancing, and **negative health behaviour**, which is detrimental to health. If health psychologists (and other health professionals) can influence people to behave in ways that are healthier, then particular forms of illnesses may be able to be prevented, life expectancy may be increased, quality of life enhanced and the onset of chronic illness delayed (Taylor, 1999).

> Behaviour that is beneficial for a person's health.

> Behaviour that is detrimental to a person's health.

3.1 Lifestyle affects mortality almost 10 years later

Breslow, L., & Enstrom, J. E. (1980). Persistence of health habits and their relationship to mortality. *Preventive Medicine*, *9*, 469–83.

In 1965 two researchers (Belloc & Breslow, 1972) began a large study to explore the relationship between people's lifestyles and their health. Almost 7,000 adults (ranging from 20 to over 75 years of age) answered two sets of questions, one about their health over the past twelve months, and another set about their lifestyle. Seven questions about lifestyle were particularly important, and these are given below. Complete these and see how well you score.

> This survey assesses seven aspects of your *usual* lifestyle. For each of the listed behaviours, answer yes if it describes what you usually do.
>
> - I sleep 7 or 8 hours a day
> - I eat breakfast almost every day
> - I rarely eat between meals
> - I am at or near the appropriate weight
> - I never smoke cigarettes
> - I drink alcohol rarely or moderately
> - I regularly get vigorous physical activity

According to Belloc and Breslow's findings, the more of these behaviours that you engage in now, the better your health is likely to be later in life.

Outcomes

Belloc and Breslow's original findings showed that across all age groups, health was typically better among people who reported that they took part in more healthy behaviours. More surprisingly, however, were the results from the follow-up studies. One such follow-up study examined which people had died nine and a half years later (Breslow & Enstrom, 1980). The results showed that the people who had reported practising more healthy behaviours (as measured by the seven questions listed above) had lower mortality rates than those engaging in less healthy behaviour. This relationship held for men and women, and all age groups, but it was strongest among older people and males. These results have also been replicated in other samples (e.g. Brock *et al.*, 1988). This study shows quite starkly how lifestyle is related to people's health and survival.

Reflection

This is a well known and extensively quoted study, which has been replicated by other researchers. It is surprising that such a seemingly simple pen and paper measure can be related to health outcomes so clearly. However, it must be remembered that this was a correlational study, so cause and effect has not been shown. The relationship could be caused by some third, unknown factor, or perhaps people who were not so well (even at subclinical levels) at the start of the study responded differently to these statements from those who were healthy.

Lifestyles have therefore become appropriate targets for health intervention and for health professionals.

Health promotion and attempts to influence lifestyles

Much of the twentieth century was devoted to disease prevention, an approach to **health promotion** stemming from a traditional biomedical view. The medical view of health and illness is reductionist and mechanistic, in that it focuses on physical functioning only (see ch. 1). From this view, there are two major pathways through which disease can be prevented (Kaplan, 2000). **Primary prevention** is the promotion of healthy lifestyles to prevent the development of disease, and is the focus of this chapter. **Secondary prevention** is the detection, diagnosis and treatment of disease as early as possible, a topic discussed in ch. 4.

In contrast, the latter part of the twentieth century saw health promotion focus more broadly on a social concept of health (Kelly & Charlton, 1995). This was reflected in the WHO's concept of health as a complete state of physical, mental and social well-being (WHO, 1946). The WHO has been an influential driving force behind health promotion, first employing the term in 1974 (Richmond, 1998). Health promotion is a way of trying to improve people's health using a variety of strategies, which can range from the individual through to the national and global. The WHO has encouraged the use of diverse strategies to improve health, from educating individuals about health matters through to changing community environments. However, most Western countries have approached health promotion by focusing on individual behaviour and attempting to change individual lifestyles (Richmond, 1998).

Attempting to change what people do and how they behave is difficult, because often behaviour is not simple or straightforward (very few of us would engage in regular, enjoyable behaviours solely for health purposes). Attempts to change behaviour for health reasons are often attempts to change ways of living and being. Therefore we approach the topics of health promotion and primary prevention from the concept of lifestyle. This concept emphasises people living their lives in a social world, and also implies that people have a choice about how they behave (although this is a problematic assumption,

health promotion Interventions designed to promote changes to improve good health in individuals, communities or populations. These interventions can range from the governmental, environmental and legislative through to the behavioural and individual.

The promotion of healthy lifestyles to prevent the development of disease.

Medical-based prevention aiming to identify disease at an early stage and treat it.

Figure 3.1 *Billboard promoting the use of sunscreen in Australia (from the Sun-Screen skin cancer prevention program). From: http://www.sunsmart.com.au/s/media/advertising.htm*

as discussed later in the chapter). For health psychologists, however, a focus on lifestyle should keep us grounded in the realities of people's everyday lives.

There are a huge number of health promotion strategies. These can be usefully conceptualised on a continuum from those with a purely individual focus through to those having a community, legislative and bureaucratic focus. One example of a health promotion programme is the 'Slip, Slop, Slap' campaign in Australia to encourage people to cover up, wear sunscreen and put on a hat and thus prevent skin cancer (and to encourage people to ensure that children wear sunscreen; see fig. 3.1).

For the purposes of this chapter we will follow Richmond (1998), and dichotomise different health promotion strategies into two polar approaches, namely the 'individualist approach' and the 'structural-collective approach'. The major differences in these approaches are outlined in table 3.1. These opposing approaches have generated much debate about the extent to which individuals should be viewed as responsible for their health (individualist approach) and the extent to which health is viewed as a collective responsibility of communities and societies (structural-collective approach).

Influencing lifestyles: individualist approaches

A great deal of research has been conducted in recent years by health psychologists and other allied health researchers to identify factors which influence people's health-related behaviour (see Bennett & Murphy, 1997;

Table 3.1 Two differing approaches to health promotion

Approach	Individualist	Structural-collective
Focal points	Individual, community, nation 'top-down' (giving health education information to individuals which has been developed by 'experts'), authoritative	Community, nation, world 'bottom-up' (gaining health knowledge from and involving individuals in health promotion efforts), participatory
View on disease causation	Illness caused by individual behaviours (e.g. smoking, lack of exercise, poor diet)	Illness caused by structural (social, economic, political) inequities (e.g. poverty, unemployment, working conditions)
Goals	To change individual behaviour through health education and knowledge	To improve people's health through modifying social, economic, political and physical structures
People involved	Health and allied professionals such as doctors, nurses, psychologists, media and marketing experts	Community groups, pressure groups, workers, community health psychologists, governments
Intervention examples	Mass media campaigns to educate people about the health risks of smoking cigarettes	Legislation to restrict cigarette smoking in public places, and to restrict the advertising of tobacco
	Pamphlets and information given to all new parents educating them about the importance of immunising their children	State-run immunisation programmes backed by registers at general practitioners with recall systems in place

Adapted from Richmond (1998).

Conner & Norman, 1995; Rutter & Quine, 2002). This research aims first to further our understanding of why people behave in the way they do and, second, to use this understanding as a basis for designing interventions to change negative health behaviour and promote positive health behaviour and therefore improve health. Often such interventions are aimed at increasing people's knowledge about the health consequences of their behaviour, as they assume that holding the 'correct' knowledge will lead to automatic changes in behaviour. However, this assumption is problematic, as we will see later in this chapter, and knowledge can be taken up in unintended ways (see sidebar 3.1). As would be expected, individualist approaches focus primarily on factors that are intrinsic to the individual, such as personality, learning, socialisation, emotional factors, personal goals, perceptual and cognitive factors.

Social cognition approaches

Without a doubt, perceptual and cognitive factors have received the most attention in research into what determines health behaviour (Taylor, 1999), and many psychologists view cognitive factors as the 'most important proximal determinants' of behaviour (Conner & Norman, 1995, p. 2). Before we begin, however, it is worth noting that research in this area has examined a diverse range of health-related behaviours, from tooth-brushing, condom use and taking the oral contraceptive pill through to smoking, exercise and alcohol consumption. Social cognition approaches have also been employed extensively to examine more medically oriented behaviours, such as visiting physicians, adhering to medical advice, following medical regimens (such as taking medication and changing dietary habits). As will be shown in ch. 4, these approaches have also been extensively applied to efforts to influence preventive and screening behaviour, such as breast and testicular self-examinations, ante-natal screening and genetic screening. Here we review the major social cognition theories and models that have been applied to the health behaviour field.

3.1   Is your glass of wine equivalent to a standard unit of alcohol?

Alcohol consumption is often assessed using standard 'units' of alcohol in the UK, and people are given advice about how many 'units' are safe for men and women in various situations (across a session of drinking, over a week, for drink-driving, etc.). A study conducted in Scotland found that a 'standard unit of alcohol' did not correspond very well to the actual amount of alcohol people poured themselves in their usual drink (of wine or spirits). Specifically, the average amount of alcohol in a wine drink was 1.92 units, while the average amount of alcohol in a spirits drink was 2.3 units! The researchers queried the assumption (held by researchers and lay people) that a 'drink' is equivalent to a standard unit of alcohol. (Gill & Donaghy, 2004)

Health locus of control

Health locus of control is a construct that has been widely applied to research into health behaviour (Wallston, 1992). It is based on the premise that people who believe they have control over their health will be more likely to behave in ways that are health promoting (Norman & Bennett, 1996). Health locus of control has its origins in social learning theory (Rotter, 1954), which posits that whether or not a person will behave in a particular way depends upon two cognitions, one about expectancy and one about value. Thus, the behaviour is dependent upon:

• the individual's expectancy that this behaviour will achieve a certain goal or outcome (if I eat less salt and fewer fatty foods it will be good for my health);
• an individual's positive evaluation of that outcome (I want good health).

Rotter (1966) went on to develop the idea that people can have generalised expectancies about their actions and consequent outcomes. He distinguished between people with an internal locus of control, who believe that events are the result of their own behaviour and therefore under their control, and people with an external locus of control, who believe that events are not related to their behaviour and are therefore outside their control. Two kinds of external control have been posited: control exercised by chance or fate (Rotter, 1966) and control exercised by powerful others (Levenson, 1974).

Health locus of control is measured with the Multidimensional Health Locus of Control Scale (Wallston *et al.*, 1978), which examines the three dimensions of control, specifically applied to physical health. These three dimensions are shown below, with example items from the scale:

- internal health locus of control: 'I am in control of my health';
- powerful others' health locus of control: 'my family has a lot to do with my becoming sick or staying healthy';
- chance locus of control: 'my good health is largely a matter of good fortune'.

Much research has applied health locus of control to a range of health-related behaviour. For example, one large study conducted in eighteen European countries found that young adults with a high internal locus of control were more likely to engage in healthy behaviours (e.g. exercise, smoking, seat belt use, etc.) than those with a low internal locus of control. Young adults with high chance locus of control were less likely to engage in healthy behaviours than others (Steptoe & Wardle, 2001). Similarly, Friis and colleagues (2003) found that among the elderly, those with a higher internal health locus of control were more likely to walk one mile per week than others. Such studies suggest that interventions to increase people's internal health locus of control may be effective in increasing positive health behaviours.

On the whole, however, findings with health locus of control have been inconsistent and conflicting, and this construct has not proved greatly predictive of behaviour (see Norman & Bennett, 1996, for a review). Even when the research includes measures of the value people place on their health (the second part of the theory), this construct lacks predictive utility (e.g. Bennett *et al.*, 1997). The construct itself is also problematic: Wallston (1992) notes that the chance dimension merely mirrors the internal control dimension, while Allison (1991) has argued that there is an inherent assumption that internality is good, whereas this is not always the case (for example, believing in powerful others may be useful if you have a chronic illness). Further, the outcome in health locus of control research is health, yet this may be too general to be useful, especially taking into consideration the different types of behaviour to which it is applied. The inconsistent and negative results in this area are hardly surprising: it would be a great feat indeed for a single construct to be predictive of complex social behaviours.

Self-efficacy

Self-efficacy is similar to health locus of control in that both constructs emphasise the importance of perceptions of control, and both are based on expectancy cognitions. However, self-efficacy has been more successful in predicting health-related behaviour. Self-efficacy is a key construct in social cognitive theory (Bandura, 1977), and posits that behaviour is determined by three types of expectancies:

- situation-outcome expectancies: beliefs people have about what will happen if they take no action;
- action-outcome expectancies: beliefs people hold about what will happen if they behave in a particular way;
- efficacy-expectancies: beliefs people hold about whether they have the competence to perform a particular behaviour to achieve the desired outcome.

Thus, if individuals perceive a link between their smoking cigarettes and lung cancer (situation-outcome expectancy), believe that if they give up smoking they will reduce their risk of getting lung cancer (action-outcome expectancy) and feel they have the necessary skills and willpower to give up smoking (efficacy-expectancies), then they are more likely to attempt quitting smoking.

Self-efficacy and outcome expectancies have been found to be predictive of diverse types of health behaviour (see Schwarzer, 1992; Schwarzer & Fuchs, 1996 for reviews), leading Schwarzer (1994) to suggest that these form the major determinants of many behaviours related to health. However, this theory has been criticised for its failure to incorporate social influences as well as the value component of outcome beliefs (Conner & Norman, 1995). Nevertheless, its consistency in predicting health behaviours has meant that it has been incorporated into a number of other social cognition models, such as the theory of planned behaviour (Ajzen, 1991) and protection motivation theory (Rogers, 1983), and it is likely that it will continue to be a key variable in the social cognition approach (Conner & Norman, 1995).

Attitude models

The relationships between attitudes, beliefs and behaviour have been of particular interest to social psychologists for decades, and more recently to health psychologists. This interest led to the development of specific models which aim to predict behaviour. Some of these models were developed for predicting general behaviour, while others have been developed specifically for health behaviour. All of these models view attitudes, perceptions, knowledge and beliefs as having a central role in determining behaviour. These factors are conceptualised as 'enduring characteristics of the individual which shape behaviour and are acquired through socialization processes' (Conner & Norman, 1995, p. 5) and therefore as open to change. Attitude models are based on the assumption that whether or not a person will act in a certain way depends upon specific types of cognitions. There are many attitude models, and here we consider two that have been widely used in health psychology.

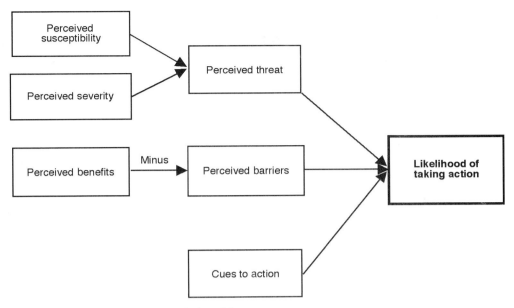

Figure 3.2 *The Health Belief Model*

The Health Belief Model

The Health Belief Model was developed specifically for health education programmes (Rosenstock, 1974) and is probably the oldest and most widely used
model in health psychology (Conner & Norman, 1995). According to this
model, and as outlined in fig. 3.2, whether or not an individual adopts a health-
related behaviour depends upon two kinds of cognitive appraisal, as well as
trigger factors:

- an appraisal of how threatening a health issue is, based on beliefs about
  susceptibility (how susceptible am I to this disease?) and severity (how
  severe would the consequences be if I had this disease?);
- an appraisal which evaluates behaving in ways to reduce the threat of the
  disease, based on perceptions about the costs and benefits of the behaviour
  (what will it cost me to behave in a particular way, how much time, how much
  effort, how much money? Will this behaviour make me healthier, reduce my
  risk of the disease?);
- cues to action are triggers to take part in the behaviour, and they may be internal, such as physical symptoms, or external, such as mass media campaigns,
  advice from others, or the illness of a family member.

Thus, if an individual believed that she might end up with heart disease later
in life (susceptibility), and believed that heart disease was a serious illness
(severity), and also thought that exercise would make her feel good and would
reduce her risk of getting heart disease later on (benefits), and that this would

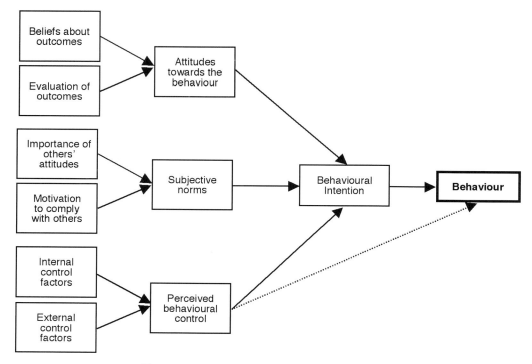

Figure 3.3 *The Theory of Planned Behaviour*

outweigh the cons of taking time and costing money (costs), then she would be more likely to take up some form of regular exercise. Further, media campaigns or other reminders about the importance of regular exercise for health (cues to action) would increase the likelihood that she actually took some action.

As with all of the social cognition models, the health belief model has been applied to a diverse range of behaviours and has been employed in numerous studies. Reviews of such studies highlight the empirical support for this model, and show that the dimensions identified are related to health behaviours (especially beliefs about susceptibility and the costs and benefits of action) (Harrison *et al.*, 1992; Janz & Becker, 1984). However, although associations between the model dimensions and behaviour have been found consistently, these are generally weak (Bennett & Murphy, 1997) and the model has not been so effective in predicting more complex behaviours, such as taking up smoking.

The Theory of Planned Behaviour

The Theory of Planned Behaviour (Ajzen, 1991; an extension of the theory of reasoned action (Ajzen & Fishbein, 1980)) has been applied to a wide variety of general and health-related behaviour. As shown in fig. 3.3, this theory states that the main influence on behaviour is an individual's intention to adopt that behaviour. Intentions, in turn, are influenced by two types of cognitions as well as by perceived control:

- attitudes are the beliefs an individual holds towards the behaviour in question, and these are determined by beliefs about the outcome and whether or not the outcome is valued;
- subjective norms are determined by perceptions of social norms and social pressures (what do other people think I should do?) as well as how motivated the individual is to do as other people say;
- perceived behavioural control is individuals' perception of whether they have the ability to perform the behaviour in question, and this perception can influence both intentions and behaviour directly.

Thus, if an individual believed that cutting down on the amount of fatty foods he ate would be good for his health (attitude to behaviour), believed that other people in his life wanted him to cut down on eating fatty foods and was keen to meet these expectations (subjective norm), and also believed he was capable of changing his diet (perceived control), then this would predict a high intention to change his diet.

There has been much support for the Theory of Planned Behaviour, and it is certainly widely used in a variety of domains within health psychology. According to a review by Ajzen (1991), the three dimensions of the model are reasonably strongly related to intentions (an average multiple correlation of .71), although the relationship of intentions to behaviour is somewhat lower. This last relationship seems to depend greatly on what kind of behaviour is under investigation. A meta-analysis based on 185 studies concluded that the theory of planned behaviour could explain over a third of the variance (39 per cent) in intentions to perform a specific behaviour, and could also explain almost a third of the variance in actual behaviour (27 per cent) (Armitage & Conner, 2001). However, researchers have questioned how much understanding this theory provides, given the temporal closeness between intentions and behaviour. As Leventhal and Hirshman (1982) commented over twenty years ago, 'it is questionable that we greatly advance our understanding . . . by concentrating on the measurement of factors so proximate to action that we are practically using measures at the beginning of the act to predict the action itself'. The understanding we gain from this model, according to Stainton Rogers (1991), is trivial and is applicable only in highly constrained circumstances.

Stage models

The models described thus far are static: they assume that cognitive processes involved in decision making occur about the same time and together (Bennett & Murphy, 1997). However, stage models suggest that people use different cognitions and processes at different times during lifestyle change (Prochaska *et al.*, 1992). The best-known stage model in health psychology is the

Transtheoretical Model (also known as the Stages of Change Model) developed by Prochaska and DiClemente (1984).

In this model, individuals are seen to go through five stages when they are attempting any lifestyle change: pre-contemplation, contemplation, preparation, action and maintenance. For example, to quit smoking an individual would go through the stages as follows:

- pre-contemplation: she is not concerned about her smoking and has no intention of stopping;
- contemplation: she starts to vaguely consider giving up, but is not committed to this change and does not think about how it might happen;
- preparation: she intends to quit and starts planning how she might achieve this;
- action: she actually attempts quitting smoking;
- maintenance: she has abstained for six months and tries to prevent a relapse.

A useful aspect of the model is that it is not linear but cyclical: individuals may move back and forward through different stages, and change may begin at any stage. Further, strategies can be employed to identify people at particular stages and to help them move on to other stages. Other stage models have also been proposed, such as the health action process model (Schwarzer, 1992) and goal setting theory (Bagozzi, 1992). However, these models assume that the pattern of stages and processes seen during one type of lifestyle change (e.g. quitting smoking) can be generalised to other kinds of lifestyle change (e.g. substance abuse); but this may not be the case (Rosen, 2000). Further, the value of these kinds of model is in helping people move from one stage to the next in any lifestyle change, yet the kinds of specific strategies necessary and beliefs to encourage this are not yet well identified (Ewart, 1991; Weinstein *et al.*, 1998).

Criticisms of the social cognition approach to changing lifestyles

The social cognition approach to influencing behaviours and lifestyles has been severely criticised. This is partially because, despite the amount of attention and resources devoted to these theories and models, they have not been very successful at either predicting behaviour or changing it. Health education efforts based on these approaches have seen the failure of many people to take heed of healthy lifestyle advice (Davison *et al.*, 1992). Specifically, these models have been criticised for being too simplistic, thus exaggerating the ease with which behaviour can be changed (Richmond, 1998). More complex models have been developed, such as Ewart's contextual theory of individual action (Ewart, 1991) which sets self-regulation and social learning theory within larger social and environmental systems, although these have not been greatly influential in health psychology. Similarly, although social cognition models aim to identify factors which can be used to change behaviour, they actually tell us nothing about how best to change cognitions (Conner & Norman, 1995). These models also present themselves as value free (but are actually based on a eurocentric view of the individual) and therefore lack culturally appropriate messages.

Ogden (2003b) has recently argued that while social cognition models are pragmatic in terms of guiding research, they are extremely problematic on a conceptual level for three main reasons. First, Ogden argues that negative results with such models are often explained away in terms of methodologies, populations studied and other caveats, and therefore cannot be falsified (and thus tested empirically). Second, Ogden argues that although specific cognitions are distinguished in the models, their operationalisation is similar. For example, perceived behavioural control over snacking has been measured by asking people 'how easy or difficult will it be for you to avoid between-meal intake of sugared snacks and drinks in future?' Behavioural intention is measured by asking people 'how likely or unlikely is it that you will avoid between-meal intake of sugared snacks and drinks in the future?' Ogden points out that the observed high relationship between answers on these questions is unsurprising and would be true by definition. Finally, Ogden also makes the important point that the act of filling in questionnaires about cognitions concerning a particular behaviour may influence (or in some cases create) those cognitions and may also affect the subsequent behaviour. These critiques have been challenged by Ajzen and Fishbein (2004) and the debate continues.

Another major problem identified with social cognition models is their portrayal of a human being as overly rational, like a statistician weighing up various decisions (doing 'cognitive algebra', as Stainton Rogers (1991) calls it). According to these models, if you have the correct knowledge about a behaviour that may have a negative impact (at some distant point) on your health, you would be irrational if you continued engage in this behaviour. However, studies show that people have sensible and rational reasons for engaging in such behaviour, once researchers look further afield to their material and social circumstances. For example, women who are on a low income and are caring for children have accurate knowledge of smoking and its consequences, yet continue to smoke because this provides them with a means of coping, providing physical and emotional distance from the unceasing task of child care (Graham, 1987). Similarly, a study conducted in Wales found that almost all respondents held detailed and accurate knowledge about the risks of unhealthy behaviour for heart disease, yet continued to engage in such behaviours (smoking, eating a high fat diet, not getting any exercise). Their decisions to do so were clearly 'rational' within their wider personal and social context (Davison *et al.*, 1992). Further, such rationality in decision making processes can be questioned in situations

3.2 Choosing to catch HIV and die of AIDS

Tourigny published a study in 1998 which documented how six impoverished African American young people living in Detroit deliberately contracted AIDS so that they were eligible for social services. They viewed AIDS as a terminal illness, but one that took a while to take hold, and which in the meantime entitled them to benefits necessary for their daily lives. A recent editorial (Morse, 2004) highlights how these findings are likely to be generalisable, across cities and across countries. However, because epidemiologists (and others) do not include self-choice as a means of causation of AIDS in surveys, we do not know the extent of such behaviour.

that are loaded with emotion, as is the case for many health behaviours. For example, the process of deciding whether or not to use a condom with someone you have recently met, in the midst of passionate love-making, is not likely to be the same as the process of deciding whether or not you should cut back on the saturated fat in your diet. Our behaviour is embedded in the cultural and moral environment in which we live (Crossley, 2000), and can be seen as rational only within this context. For a tragic example of this point see sidebar 3.2.

Other approaches based on the social cognition approach to changing lifestyles

Attempts to change people's health behaviours have also used other approaches, which are based on social cognition ideas and assumptions. One such approach is **empowerment**, which is 'a process of helping people to assert control over the factors which affect their health' (Airhihenbuwa, 1994, p. 345). Empowerment strategies can be focused on individuals, groups or communities. Self-empowerment is the process of empowering individuals and groups to increase control over their internal (attitudes, knowledge, perceptions, skills) and external (physical and social environments) worlds. This is achieved through various strategies, such as assertiveness and skills training, problem-solving, participatory learning and client-centred counselling (Marks *et al.*, 2000). Self-empowerment has often been used in health education with young adults, to increase assertiveness and resist peer pressure, especially in areas such as sexual health and HIV prevention. Empowerment strategies are also effective in increasing an individual's self-efficacy, which as we have seen is important in forming intentions about health behaviours, as well as behaving in particular ways (Abraham & Sheeran, 1994).

Another approach has been to counsel people to change their health-related behaviour. The women's health movement in particular has employed counselling strategies. In this way information and advice can be provided, individually or in group settings, in a context that encourages sharing and recognises the collective nature of women's health issues (Daykin & Naidoo, 1995).

How effective are individualist approaches to changing lifestyles?

An eminent US health psychologist has argued that 'primary prevention almost always requires behavior change, therefore, successful primary prevention efforts must use behavioral theories and behavioral interventions' (Kaplan, 2000, p. 382). However, behavioural interventions to date have not been greatly successful. Despite decades of work attempting to change behaviours which are harmful to health, the impact of providing knowledge and attempting to change attitudes is disappointing (Frankel *et al.*, 1991). Analysis of survey data has shown that there is rarely a relationship between changes in knowledge and subsequent changes in behaviour (Yoder, 1997).

The theories and models developed within the individualist approach appear insufficient to provide in-depth understandings of behaviours related to health. One review of intervention studies on physical activity concluded that the ability of theory to predict outcomes in this field was very limited (Baranowski *et al.*, 1998). Further, while theories focus on initiating change, few address the issue of maintaining changes in lifestyle. A review examining evidence on maintaining changes in physical activity levels following intervention found little data on this topic (Marcus *et al.*, 2000), leading one commentator to highlight this as a priority for future research (Dubbert, 2002).

Ironically, government campaigns to educate the public about health issues can actually shift perceptions in the opposite direction to that desired (Frankel *et al.*, 1991). Being told what to do and how to live one's life can lead people to react against the advice. (Jokes are made about healthy living, such as asking 'what's your poison?' in relation to the type of alcohol a person wants.) This can be understood partially by examining the theory of psychological reactance (Brehm, 1966), which proposes that individuals see themselves as free to act in realistic ways, either now or in the future. Any threat to this freedom to act, according to reactance theory, generates a motivational state aimed at recapturing the freedom(s) affected. Further, this can affect the value and attractiveness of the threatened freedom, so that, for example, banning smoking can have the reverse effect: it becomes more attractive in and of itself. Also, the stricter the threat to freedom (you MUST change your diet for your own good), the greater the likelihood that it will produce the opposite effect (Fogarty, 1997). Such reactance against health education advice has been found in Danish men's accounts of health behaviour (see Meiller *et al.*, 1996).

Individualist approaches make a number of assumptions about individuals and their behaviours. Four such assumptions (and their counter-arguments) are outlined in table 3.2. Some of these assumptions about individuals and individual behaviour can help to explain their lack of success in changing lifestyles.

Table 3.2 Some assumptions of individualist approaches to health promotion

Assumption	Counter-argument
Individuals have choice and control over their lifestyles	Focusing solely on individuals and their behaviour does not take into account the material disadvantages of people's lives (Nettleton & Bunton, 1995), which severely limit choices about lifestyles
The individual is an independent consumer who can make straightforward choices between various forms of behaviour	Some groups in society (e.g. women, those on low incomes) often do not fit the stereotype of an independent consumer. Strategies may place responsibility for health on women, without taking into account their lack of power to effect change (Daykin & Naidoo, 1995). Women are assumed to be responsible for the health of family members, and to encourage healthy lifestyles (e.g. Lyons & Willott, 1999; Norcross *et al.*, 1996)
Behaviours can be examined separately	Although much of the research from these approaches discusses lifestyles, in reality they almost always examine behaviours separately. However, behaviours go together to make up lifestyles. Qualitative studies show that people talk about behaviours that influence their health as interconnected and making up a complex whole, where there is some kind of homeostatis that will balance out 'good' and 'bad' behaviours (Backett *et al.*, 1994). For example, 'I will eat this piece of pecan pie for dessert only if I go for a run tomorrow'
Individuals do not think in a sophisticated way about their lifestyles and health	People not only consider health behaviours together, but also consider them in relation to the health-promoting benefits of enjoying living life. For example, as one young female recently noted: I think the guilt that people associate with not drinking, not smoking, not eating the wrong things, is actually worse in very many cases than actually committing the sins . . . you're probably getting more benefit from getting enjoyment out of life and your friends than you would if you abstained from everything (from Lawton, 2002)

Implications of the individualist approach

There are several problematic implications of the individualist approach to changing lifestyles. First, its heavy emphasis on cognitive and perceptual factors has meant that many other relevant factors have been little studied and even less theorised. For example, relatively little work has coherently theorised sociodemographic factors (such as age, SES, education), social factors (such as the values of the culture or particular SES group, social norms, social influence) or environmental factors (such as pollution, crowding), all of which are central to individual lifestyles (Winett, 1995).

Second, the individualist approach also implicates people who do become ill as 'responsible' for that illness. If a disease can be prevented by the lifestyle a person lives, then it follows that people who do become ill from that disease are at least partially responsible for their situation (Davison & Davey Smith, 1995). However, some researchers have questioned the scientific basis of attributing some proportion of disease to lifestyle factors. These critiques point out that a focus on individual lifestyle in health promotion overemphasises the role of the individual, and oversimplifies disease causation (Davison & Davey Smith, 1995). For example, not everyone who is at risk of heart disease will die from heart disease. We have all heard of someone who has smoked cigarettes and drunk alcohol all their lives, and yet lived to the grand old age of 94. Health promotion attempts derived from **epidemiology** are based on population statistics (and estimated population risk), and can lead to 'a situation in which many individuals change their lives to no personal end' (Davison *et al.*, 1991, p. 14), because they would not have succumbed to the particular disease anyway. This is known as the 'prevention paradox', in which a prevention programme may provide a lot of benefit to the population, but not much benefit to any specific individual involved (Rose, 1985).

> A discipline of study which examines and documents the frequency, distribution and causes of disease in a population.

Third, this approach can unintentionally be discriminatory, amplifying inequality. Resources, including education and information, may not be equally available or accessible to all people, exacerbating social inequalities. Similarly, the ways in which messages and information are delivered may not be sensitive to different values, expectations and so on, thereby also exacerbating inequalities (Parish, 1995). Fourth, the individualist approach can have unintended consequences for particular groups of people in society. Well-meaning messages may cause inadvertent harm. For example, in trying to convince people not to drink and drive, a poster campaign ran a picture of a wheelchair and the slogan 'Last summer, 1,057 teenagers go so drunk they couldn't stand up. Ever. Don't drink and drive.' Wang (1992) reports that people who are in a wheelchair found such posters devaluing, as they communicated the strong idea that disability was bad, and reinforced the stigma associated with disability. Some of these concerns are highlighted in table 3.3.

It has also been argued that the individualist approach to influencing lifestyles inappropriately targets individuals, rather than tackling important social and economic influences on health (Parish, 1995). According to many sociologists, the individualist approach has been favoured over the more collective model for a variety of reasons: it is favoured by politicians because it is easy, by bureaucrats because it fits the managerialist agenda, by medicine because it furthers medical dominance and by allied health professionals such as health psychologists because this is their starting point (Richmond, 1998).

Table 3.3 Some ethical issues in health promotion strategies

Ethical issue	Description	Example
Individualist approaches to health promotion		
Persuasion	Persuasive strategies may arouse anxieties or fears, be manipulative, impinge on individual rights	Frightening people with terrifying images of people with throat cancer in a media campaign
Targeting	Strategies reach different segments of the population; may widen the gap between those with and without; may be culturally relevant to certain cultural groups and not others	Targeting people in lower socioeconomic groups to change their diet, despite not being able to afford to, while the affluent take heed of the message
Labelling	Inadvertent harm caused by labelling or stigmatising individuals	HIV prevention campaigns using fear appeals which depict people with HIV negatively
Culpability	Inadvertent harm caused by unfairly placing the responsibility and blame on individuals or groups	Individuals with high blood pressure blame themselves for the disease (even though family history is as predictive as behaviour)
Privileging	Influences power in that some individuals are more likely to benefit than others	Labelling a certain level of blood cholesterol as a medical condition means money is provided for its detection and treatment
Structuralist-collective approaches to health promotion		
Coercion	Promotes restrictive policies or regulations to achieve public health goals, impinging on an individual's right to freedom to choose	Regulations on food production in the food industry to reduce saturated fat intake
Harm reduction	Behaviours are supported that are not socially approved	Availability of clean and disposable injection needles to heroin addicts
Depriving	The less privileged are denied pleasures they can afford	Taxing cigarettes so highly denies people in disadvantaged situations their main form of perceived control and relaxation
Exploitation	Individuals may be exploited to achieve health promotion goals	Using a local community organisation to gain voluntary services that should be provided through public funds

Table 3.3 (*cont.*)

Both approaches to health promotion		
Control	May function as a means of social or organisational control	Organisations can require information about employees' outside activities, based on concern for their health
Distraction	The focus on good health distracts people from important social issues	Emphasising diet as crucially important takes attention away from government policies about pollution and environmental waste
Promises	Promises are made that may not be accurate or beneficial	People who live healthy lifestyles can still die from heart disease, despite health information implying that they will not
Health as a value	Promotes a moralism that might not be compatible with other values	Promoting health emphasises individualism at the expense of values such as connectedness and caring

Adapted from Guttman (1997).

Influencing lifestyles: structural-collective approaches

The focus in structural-collective approaches is less on improving individuals' health knowledge and more on improving social and environmental conditions. From this perspective, focusing on 'lifestyle' in health promotion is fundamentally misconceived, because focusing on individuals to change their behaviour does nothing to correct the structural causes of ill health (Waitzkin, 1983). The structural-collective approach employs both small-scale, local interventions as well as broader, legislative ones. Health-related legislation has been successful in many areas. Richmond (1998) points out that legislation in Australia has outlawed industrial pollution, fireworks, flammable nightwear, cigarette advertising, smoking in public places, and has required compulsory car seat belts, water fluoridation and the labelling of poisons. Such legislation has come about through debate within government and political parties, but also through pressure groups, environmental groups and people working outside the conventional political system (Richmond, 1998).

Changing legislation and political practices to improve health are often considered to be outside the realm of health psychology; however, health psychologists have contributed to (and have much to offer) structuralist interventions at the local level. Community psychologists, and community health psychologists, have been particularly important in developing and implementing approaches based on notions around community empowerment and collective action.

Community empowerment

The notion of community empowerment is an attempt to counter the individualism and authoritarianism that emanates from individualist approaches to
changing lifestyles. In this approach, groups of people are encouraged to identify what are the most important health issues for them, to take control of their
destinies and have support to bring about change (Nettleton & Bunton, 1995).
The aim is to facilitate group and community choices about the way people
live. This is achieved by supplementing knowledge acquisition with value clarification and community organising skills, usually by non-traditional means
(Airhihenbuwa, 1994). For example, providing communities with packets of
oral rehydration salts to combat diarrhea may be effective initially, but in the
longer term may create dependency. A more effective solution would be to
empower people by showing them how to prepare their own rehydration mix-
ture, using salt, sugar and water and local implements (Airhihenbuwa, 1994).

The focus within this approach is collaborative, between members of communities and service providers. It opposes the use of 'experts handing down
advice about individuals' adjustment to social realities' (Borg, 2002, p. 346).
Instead, it explicitly recognises that groups within a society hold different levels of power, and also that this power influences individuals' lifestyles and
health, as well as their ability to change both. A recent example of community
empowerment comes from a low-income housing project in south central Los
Angeles in the USA, described in research in focus box 3.2.

The community empowerment approach demands that health psychologists
examine systems of health care, and how appropriate these are for the needs of
individuals and also the contexts of the communities in which those individuals
live (Albee & Gullotta, 1997). This approach sets individual well-being within
a wider social and political context, and as such can be seen as multilevel.
It focuses on strengthening existing resources to encourage the participatory
decision making of community members (Borg, 2002). A key feature of community empowerment is that it is bottom up rather than top down.

However, the effectiveness of community empowerment has been questioned. For example, 'how much "power" do community groups really have?
What kinds of changes can they realistically bring about to improve their
health? To what extent do such groups become absorbed into the political structures of health care?' (Nettleton & Bunton, 1995, p. 45). It seems
that community empowerment can be successful and effective, if it is fully
participatory.

Collective action

The collective action approach focuses on the close relationship between individuals and the socioeconomic and environmental contexts in which they live.
These contexts are seen as the primary causes of ill health, and are therefore

3.2 The Avalon Gardens Men's Association

Borg, Jr., M. (2002). The Avalon Gardens Men's Association: a community health psychology case study. *Journal of Health Psychology, 7,* 345–57.

Following the riots in Los Angeles in 1992, city officials attempted a community empowerment approach to address the community crisis and promote health. This was contracted to the Community Health Realization Institute (CHRI), which aimed to address chronic issues such as endemic health problems, racism, poverty, violence, drug and alcohol abuse, as well as acute problems such as rioting, looting, arson and interracial violence, over a four-year intervention.

The community

Avalon Gardens consists of 161 housing units and 419 residents in south central Los Angeles. It is made up of African American (82 per cent), Latino (17 per cent) and Caucasian (1 per cent) inhabitants. It was a 'distressed community', with high levels of violence, burglaries, poverty and poor health.

The approach

The primary goal of the team was to 'address how the influence of current models of health policy, public health and health care administration had traditionally served to exclude and disempower communities of colour.' Specific initiatives for change were those identified by residents of the community, in a series of workshops run by the CHRI within the community. These were focused initially on the question: 'what is a safe and healthy community?' Empowerment was defined by members of the community.

The men's group

As a result of the participatory intervention, a group of African American and Latino men began meeting regularly, with the community practitioners, to discuss what they could do about the serious health risks faced by members of their community. They called themselves the Avalon Garden's Men's Association. The essential feature of this group was that it was voluntary and initiated by its members.

The weekly meetings

The men discussed the community: its hostile nature, the violence resulting from rival gangs, the 'war zone' they lived within and how these issues had to be addressed before any other health issues could be dealt with. As one member stated: 'It's hard to think about the danger of smoking or eating greasy foods when you're fearing for your life.' They also discussed the stereotypes of men in the community, such as being apathetic and lazy, and talked about how these characteristics function to lessen the danger of standing out and being targeted by gang members and the police.

Collaborations

To address health promotion issues such as drug and alcohol abuse, smoking, HIV/AIDS prevention and diet, the Men's Association began to hold meetings with medical and social service agency providers. This encouraged relationships between residents of the community and health professionals. Members of the men's association also began working closely with a local community-based health care clinic, Unihealth, to foster improved access to health care for community members. Officers from the Los Angeles Police Department were also invited to discuss a partnership with the community which resulted ultimately in a 'community police' initiative.

Outcomes

The residents of Avalon Gardens evaluated their own community at different points over the intervention period. The process of self-assessment allowed people to create their own goals and alliances, and then evaluate their own efforts, leading to the identification of new needs, goals and projects. The intervention produced significant reductions in some behaviours:

Behaviour	Reduced by (%)	Behaviour	Increased by (%)
Reported incidence of violence	43	Health screening	32
Drug- and alcohol-related incidents	38	HIV/AIDS testing	27
Family violence and child abuse	40		
Overall crime rate	35		
Teenage pregnancy	25		
Unemployment	30		

Reflection

Community empowerment is not about measurable goals and objectives, it is about a participatory process. Evaluation of such an approach needs to examine whether people critically engage with the process and evaluate the causes of health problems, and then take community action (de la Cancela *et al.*, 1998). This case study highlights how it is possible for communities to make a difference to their everyday lives, to identify problems and open doors to services and agencies that previously had been inaccessible. It also highlights the importance of social context for any health initiative: if the community in which you live is a dangerous place, who cares whether or not you smoke cigarettes? However, the study also occurred within a distinct political context, and many of the ethical issues raised in table 3.3 are relevant here. For example, how much did this work act as a means of social control? Were inaccurate promises made? Does the focus on health as the primary moral issue distract people from other important social issues?

the target for change. Individuals work together to change social and environmental contexts, rather than changing themselves (Marks *et al.*, 2000). One example of a collective action approach is Raeburn and Rootman's (1998) People-Centred Health Promotion, which is based on the mnenomic PEOPLE:

People-centredness: this approach begins with subjective, everyday experience, and assumes the greatest wisdom is held by ordinary people (rather than experts).

Empowerment is the fundamental philosophical principle of the approach. It involves control over life affairs at the personal, group and community level.

Organisational and community development grounds people in their collectivity, and advocates change in organisational processes to contribute to community development.

Participation involving as many people as possible, recognising diversity and encouraging representativeness will provide more impact and strength in health promotion processes.

Life quality: good health within overall quality of life, where quality of life has a positive orientation and definition, and includes spirituality.

Evaluation is an intrinsic aspect of the approach, where the focus is on the participants involved. Five issues are seen as particularly important are outcome evaluation, process evaluation, cybernetics and self-criticism, accountability and ownership, and the power of data.

There are similar problems with the collective action approach as with other community approaches to health promotion. They may come into conflict with those who have the power in society, such as industry, employers and governments (Marks *et al.*, 2000). There is also the danger that the people who are involved in the initiatives become removed from the grassroots concerns of those they set out to represent (Marks *et al.*, 2000).

How effective are structural-collective approaches to changing lifestyles?

State-level controls have been successful at reducing harmful health behaviour. For example, legislation regarding the wearing of seatbelts has meant that for most people putting on a seatbelt when they get in a car is now second nature. A recent review of tobacco controls in five US states has shown that legislation and efforts to reduce cigarette smoking are effective and produce dramatic declines in smoking in both young people and adults (Siegel, 2002).

Community empowerment approaches have been extremely successful in highlighting the importance of the social and developmental dimensions of health-related behaviour. This is particularly so in the field of HIV prevention, in which empowerment approaches have been effectively used at the individual level with single women in the USA (e.g. Hobfoll *et al.*, 2002), at the local level with the gay community in Australia (e.g. Kinder, 2002) and at the national level with the mining industry in southern Africa (e.g. Campbell & Williams, 1999).

However, structural-collective approaches can also be problematic. It is often very difficult to obtain funding for community development initiatives, as they do not provide easily quantifiable outcome data. Thus they become marginalised and survive only by piecemeal resourcing (Daykin & Naidoo, 1995). The concept of community itself is also extremely problematic. People who live in the same geographical region, or who have the same sexual preference, or age, or social class, are not necessarily homogeneous groups (Marks *et al.*, 2000).

Further, even though many global, national and local health promotion strategies claim that they are employing principles of community involvement and participation, according to Kelly and Charlton (1995) they are in reality technicist, scientific and expert driven. This means that 'communities remain marginalized and invisible – other than in the rhetoric' (p. 81). These researchers also make the point that such strategies reify social systems, constructing them as acting on people in a deterministic way (e.g. unemployment causes ill health). Thus from this approach, too, the individual is not viewed as a thinking and acting human being but becomes an outcome.

Feminist critiques of structural-collective approaches have challenged the way in which women are often constructed as carers in social policy, thereby naturalising gender inequalities. Further, social policies that aim to promote health may end up penalising the most vulnerable (as is the case with women smokers on low incomes when tobacco taxation is increased) (Daykin & Naidoo, 1995).

There are problems with all attempts to alter lifestyles and improve health. Ethical issues are raised by both individualist and structural-collective attempts to influence health. Some of these ethical concerns have been outlined by Guttman (1997) and are summarised in table 3.3. More generally, the critiques we have noted in both the individualist and structural-collective approaches highlight the importance of context. The next section examines individual lifestyle within its social and cultural context.

Influencing lifestyles: the individual in context

In most Western countries, attempts to improve health have been made through trying to get people to change their lifestyles. The theories and models employed by mainstream health psychology focus quite narrowly on cognitive processes and individual behaviour (Crossley, 2000). However, social and cultural issues are very important in the types of behaviour that people engage in (Backett *et al.*, 1994). For example, what would it mean to a 19-year-old in her first year at university to give up drinking alcohol? Would this mean she would become socially isolated, as the new friends she had made continued to go out drinking on Thursday and Friday nights? What if a man who is contemplating giving up smoking has a group of friends and work colleagues who also smoke? Is it more important to smoke and risk one's health than to end up being socially isolated and lonely? Here we consider some of the important contextual factors involved in individual health-related behaviour.

Individuals through the lifecourse

Behaviours are related to social and structural contexts. One important aspect of behavioural context is the individual's position in the lifecourse (Backett & Davison, 1992). Some behaviours are more acceptable and appropriate at different stages. For example, burning the candle at both ends is viewed as life enhancing or career promoting in young adults, but as stressful and damaging to health in older adults (Backett & Davison, 1992). People view a healthy or unhealthy lifestyle differently depending on their stage of life, as research from the UK (Backett & Davison, 1992, 1995) has shown:

Children: young people's bodies are viewed as resilient and able to withstand many 'unhealthy' behaviours (Backett *et al.*, 1994).

Young single adults: the body is viewed as in peak condition, able to deal with toxins and unhealthy living. Healthy lifestyle is achieved by balancing unhealthy (smoking, drinking, eating junk food) with healthy behaviours (exercising regularly, not being stressed, having a young body). Concern about lifestyle and its implications for illness is viewed as boring and middle aged.

Parents of dependent children: new parents change their lifestyles dramatically and change the values they place on their health. This can be paradoxical, in that they may live in unhealthy ways (lack of sleep, overwork) to meet their young children's needs (Backett *et al.*, 1994). At the same time, new parents often report living in healthier ways and thinking more about their health, mortality and their bodies, because 'you couldn't afford to be ill' (Backett & Davison, 1995, p. 636).

Middle age: health behaviours are assessed in terms of current health status. Experience of illness is important in deciding about healthy lifestyles.

Older adults: ideas about healthy behaviour are strongly grounded in personal experiences.

Thus views and motivations about healthy lifestyles need to be located within the lifecourse context. Individuals view what is appropriate and feasible behaviour within the life stage they are at, and it is within this context that engaging in unhealthy behaviour can be viewed as reasonable and rational (Backett & Davison, 1995).

Experience

Lawton (2002) has recently shown that the embodied experience of ill health influences the ways in which adults perceive their future and the possibility of further ill health. In her qualitative study with people living in England, Lawton found that people's motivation to change their lifestyles and behaviour was directly related to how conscious they were of their future morbidity and death. This, in turn, was related to their position in the lifecourse, as well as their experience of ill health. Older participants were more health conscious than younger participants, and were also more likely to perceive their futures as containing ill health and death as certainties. However, Lawton reports two further important findings here:

- the experience of embodied ill health, irrespective of lifecourse position and age, related strongly to perceptions of vulnerability to future morbidity and mortality;
- participants who reported changing their lifestyles for long-term health reasons had done so because they had suffered ill health. Thus their motivation to change was reactive, rather than proactive.

Health was taken for granted by young participants, and in middle- and older-aged participants who had not had health problems. As a 55-year-old male respondent noted: 'Up to forty you don't give a bugger. Do you, you know? You don't really think about it at all.' This study highlights that the people who are likely to change their lifestyles for health reasons are those who are already experiencing embodied ill health.

Experience of previous health promotion strategies may also influence individuals' behaviour. For example, contradictory messages can lead to people ignoring any health advice. Contradictory health messages have been most apparent in relation to diet, where advice about what to eat changes (for example we are now told to turn the classic 'food pyramid' on its head). As participants in studies have noted:

- 'As a child I was always brought up, well you should drink milk and you should eat eggs and you should eat butter otherwise you're not going to be healthy. Well today you're not supposed to do none of them are you? So really who is right?' (from Backett *et al.*, 1994, p. 278).
- 'If you listened to everything they said, you wouldn't eat anything' (from Frankel *et al.*, 1991).

Material disadvantage

The rhetoric of health promotion focused at individuals is that if you know the health risks of a particular form of behaviour, then you have some choice and some power in your life. Yet this vastly exaggerates the options for the poor and economically vulnerable. Individuals in the middle classes may well have some control over their lives, and therefore some capacity to care for their own bodies, but such messages often simply create anxiety for those with fewer material resources (Richmond, 1998).

Further, people who have little choice in their lives as a result of material disadvantage see immediate comforts and pleasures as much more important than what might happen to them later in life (Ritchie *et al.*, 1994). For example, smoking increases with relative disadvantage, so that it is higher among people in lower socioeconomic groups. Efforts to convince people to stop smoking have been most successful with white women in privileged positions. However, it has been argued that explaining the differences in health outcomes between ethnic minorities and the rest of the population in terms of SES reduces health disparities to class and completely ignores (and undermines) the effects of cultural expressions and cultural values (Airhihenbuwa, 1994).

Culture

Much evidence demonstrates that culture is a central feature in health behaviours, perceptions of health behaviours and decisions to alter health behaviours. However, many of the theories and models employed to understand and intervene in health behaviour come from Western cultures, which are characterised by a view of the self as a production of the individual and a view of culture as a man-made part of the environment (Triandis, 1994).

Airhihenbuwa and Obregon (2000, p. 10) have argued that models and theories of health behaviour conceptualise culture as a 'barrier' because of the Western view of culture:

> Controlling one's environment is a central theme in Western conceptions of culture – a conception that eschews other cultural realities such as harmonizing with nature or adapting to one's environment or both. If controlling the environment is the raison d'être of cultures, then the inability to control one's environment suggests retrogression, a barrier to be overcome. Hence 'cultural barriers' (never cultural strength) become a common expression in this discourse.

Models and theories such as the theory of planned behaviour, self-efficacy and health locus of control were developed in an individualistic Western culture and are therefore relevant, meaningful and appropriate here. However, we should not expect these models to be effective in explaining behaviour in other social contexts, where there are different commonsense knowledges of the world (Yoder, 1997). For example, in more collectively oriented societies such as those in Asia, Africa, and Latin America and the Caribbean, family and community are more central to health and well-being than is the individual, and people are less likely to describe themselves in internal terms from the standpoint of 'I'. This means that measuring notions such as health locus of control does not make much sense in such societies. Even in cultures where Western beliefs are dominant, they will not function for some minority groups in which decisions are made in groups, where individual decisions (the key to health behaviour models) go against the grain (Airhihenbuwa & Obregon, 2000). Similarly, the importance of religion and religious beliefs is largely ignored in these models, yet may be primary in affecting people's decisions about health behaviours in non-Western cultures (see sidebar 3.3). These issues can help explain the ineffectiveness of HIV/AIDS prevention strategies based upon social cognitive approaches in Africa, Asia, Latin America and the Caribbean.

3.3 'Born again' young Nigerians and their views on HIV/AIDS

HIV/AIDS has been increasing dramatically in Nigeria in recent years, and it is expected that by 2010 18–26 per cent of the adult population will be infected (Smith, 2004). Many young adults in Nigeria are taking up evangelical and Pentecostal Christianity, and call themselves 'born again' Christians. From this religious perspective they make sense of HIV/AIDS, assess their risk and negotiate their sexual relationships.

Connections between religion, morality and sexuality are complex, with young adult migrants responding in different ways to HIV/AIDS:

- Religious views mean that some young people do not have sex, not just to protect themselves against HIV/AIDS, but also as an ethical choice which may combat the immorality seen to have led to the epidemic.
- Religious views mean that some young people justify certain sexual relationships as more moral than others (e.g. with a girlfriend/boyfriend) and therefore as not putting them at risk and not requiring condom use. Indeed, condom use implies their partner's infidelity.
- Religious views mean that young people rationalise, hide or deny their sexual relationships which would be judged as immoral.

Knowledge of different cultural values is important for the effectiveness of lifestyle interventions, although it is also important to consider the process of communicating health issues. For example, several African countries have an oral tradition in both producing and attaining knowledge. This is not just about speaking or singing, it is also about listening: people are used to learning by hearing. This is why person-to-person home visits have been much more successful in changing particular behaviours in these countries than traditional mass media campaigns (Airhihenbuwa, 1994).

Unfortunately, health promotion efforts in much of Africa have been developed and applied on the basis of Western traditions and values, which may account for why they have not been greatly successful. Health communication campaigns have assumed that if individuals do not gain the 'correct' health information from the campaigns, then they need to learn skills so that they will be able to acquire the correct information (meaning in effect that literacy programmes are necessary for the target population). This places 'all the responsibilities for program failure on the inaction or indifference of people in the target communities' (Airhihenbuwa, 1994, p. 348). This is a classic example of the actor-observer effect, whereby the people observing (health professionals and promoters) attribute the cause of (a lack of change in) behaviour to the actors (targets of health promotion strategies) (MacLachlan, 1997).

In summary, the role of culture is often overlooked in models and theories about health behaviours. Culture is central to the ways in which we live, our values, knowledges and subjectivities. Rather than assuming the global relevance of theories and models developed in social and health psychology, it may be more beneficial and effective for field experience in different cultures and contexts to shape appropriate frameworks (Airhihenbuwa & Obregon, 2000). It is worth remembering here that different contexts and cultures will present opportunities for new and different frameworks, strategies and interventions (MacLachlan, 1997).

Globalisation

Hippert (2002) has recently argued that **globalisation** and the world economy have a major impact on poor health, especially in women. Multinational corporations in Mexico, Malaysia, the Philippines, India and Indonesia have had a serious negative impact on women's health. These corporations do not always provide safe and healthy working environments for their mainly women employees (who have been exposed to toxic chemicals, must endure long work days of over fourteen hours without overtime pay, with no bathroom breaks, with harassment and brutality). However, poverty is the most significant health issue these women face, with the corporations often paying less than the host country's minimum wage requirement (LaBotz, 1993). As Hippert points out, 'these problems could be solved by working against the global economy that keeps developing countries in their place, working for the international accountability of multinational corporations, and working to elevate women's status within local societies and the international community' (p. 866).

To influence people's lifestyles we need to understand not only an individual's ideas and beliefs, but also social structures, how people comprehend these structures, and how these impinge on their lives. As noted by Kelly and Charlton (1995), 'a dynamic and reciprocal analysis of the individual set into context ought to be at the heart of health promotion' (p. 90). Health is related to lifestyle, and lifestyle is set within a personal, social, political, cultural, economic and global context.

Consequences of health promotion efforts to change lifestyles

Researchers have argued that the concept of 'health' has become a key cultural motif in the construction of identity in contemporary societies. According to Radley, health and being healthy are linked to values and morals because they are inseparable from what people believe is good or correct or responsible (Radley, 1994). Crawford makes the case more strongly in arguing that 'the pursuit of health is actually the pursuit of moral personhood' (Crawford, 1994).

3.4　New campaign targets bingeing women's vanity

Lee Glendinning, Thursday 26 August 2004, *The Guardian*

It has reached that stage of the night where the fifth glass of white wine is on offer. Drinking it will almost certainly guarantee that the evening enters that otherworldly domain where there is no place for inhibitions. There could be falling out of the cab after having a good chat to the driver all the way home, thinking it is suddenly OK to send that text message saying how you really feel, and grabbing a kebab from that shop on the corner which is never approached in daylight. Yes, one drink too many can damage your love life, and leave you with a few bruises at the end of the evening, but excessive alcohol is also ruining young women's appearance.

This has prompted the Portman group, a body funded by the drinks industry to tackle the social problems linked with alcohol, to market an anti-binge drinking message as a beauty product to try to reach young women, urging them to consider what alcohol

If healthy behaviours represents all that is morally good and righteous, then the flipside is that unhealthy lifestyles represent what is bad, irresponsible and immoral. Because of this association they take on a value of their own. Thus engaging in risk-taking and unhealthy lifestyles can create a whole new kind of subjectivity, one based on risk and a refusal to attend to 'authority'. Health psychology does not take into account relationships between healthy behaviours and moral identities, and by not doing so may actually be 'instrumental in perpetuating and exacerbating the very behaviours it is trying to reduce, manage and control' (Crossley, 2000, p. 42). It is important to remember that an individual's behaviours are integrated into her sense of self and feelings of belonging to a particular social group (Giddens, 1991).

Further, people now use the language of health promoters and experts to discuss their own experiences and construct their subjectivities. For example, people talk about eating 'five a day' in New Zealand following a health promotion campaign to improve consumption of fruits and vegetables. They discuss whether a glass of orange juice counts as one portion, and engage in social comparison to see who makes the 'five a day' target. Rose (1990) has argued that social institutions and the social sciences produce ways of talking, thinking and being that are fundamental to our subjectivities. These 'technologies of the self' create languages and discourses that shape and create our thoughts and behaviour. Therefore, it has been argued that the efforts of health psychologists and other health promoters may be seen as a form of control, outlining particular social identities that are appropriate in today's culture (Nettleton & Bunton, 1995; see also Giddens, 1991).

Health promotion efforts are also strongly related to consumerism and consumption. Kelly and Charlton (1995) state that 'health is about lifestyle, and lifestyle is about consumption' (p. 88). We live in a consumer culture in which we carve out our identities and subjectivities through purchases and ways of living (see Bordieu, 1984). Our consumption of goods and services contributes to distinct lifestyles (food, cars, clothes, leisure activities).

is doing to their eyes, skin and general smell. They've called it 'masq crème de regret' – a potion to remind women how excess alcohol affects their looks.

Almost inevitable after a big night out are bloodshot eyes, blotchy skin and the smell of alcohol seeping from the pores for much of the following day. But binge drinking can also result in broken capillaries around the nose and cheeks as alcohol dilates blood vessels close to the surface of the skin. Certain drinks dry out the skin, because alcohol blocks the release of the antidiuretic hormone, and causes the kidneys to excrete excess body fluid. And then there are the permanent scars from that odd fall, which didn't hurt at all, at the time.

The mock beauty lotion which is to act as a reminder of these ailments comes in a glass jar with gold labelling and looks just like one of the thousands of other sophisticated beauty products which line department stores. But then, there on the label, is a silver outline of a woman's upper body. Her hands are placed over her eyes, she is leaning over – and throwing up.

It is intended to be a savvy way of driving home an old message which has dulled in the minds of many young women as promotions such as happy hour become more popular.

'We thought this was a nice idea to capture them,' Samantha Jobber of the Portman group explained. 'It looks like any other beauty advertisement until you pick it up and look closer when it lists some of the short term effects of alcohol which a lot of people forget about – which is basically how rough you look the next day.'

The directions for usage of the lotion suggest: 'Put sickening regrets and gruesome skin behind you by allowing your natural moderation to shine through . . .' Pastel coloured posters and postcards advertising the faux cosmetic brand, which look similar to current cosmetic advertisements, will be placed in 250 pubs, clubs and coffee houses around the country next month.

What women will find when they pick up these advertisements is a reminder of the government-recommended daily intake of two to three units. But the question is whether women will be moved to moderate their drinking for the sake of their appearance.

The Portman group says it has tried to appeal to women's vanity, an area of weakness which was likely to have more of an effect than a 'finger wagging' campaign. Ms Jobber said it was important to remind women that the longer they drink each night, although they may feel they look stunning their looks are declining with each glass.

'We decided to target women this year, there's been a lot of press about how much younger women are drinking,' she said. 'Women are having babies later, they have more disposable income to socialise and are more independent. It is acceptable for a woman to be in a pub drinking with the boys now, when it wasn't in the 1950s.'

While drinking habits of men are heavier than women, they have remained steady over the last 20 years, whereas the level at which women are drinking has increased and many will engage in episodic drinking with their male friends. Among women aged 16–24, the proportion drinking more than 35 units a week has more than tripled rising from 3% in 1998 to 10% in 2002.

The Portman Group's chief executive, Jean Coussins, says the pretend beauty lotion has been made to look like something that has been developed by white-coated experts working in a lab, who are trying to hang onto a secret formula.

'In fact, there is no secret', she added. 'Women who want to drink should stick to the government's recommended daily guidelines of three units if they don't want to start running any health risks.'
(Guardian Unlimited © Guardian Newspapers Limited 2004)

Health is constructed as a lifestyle 'choice', and has become part of this consumer culture. In this way, the notion of health is no longer confined to the arena of the hospital or medical professionals, but is now part of our social and commercial lives. There is a blurring between health promotion and commercial literature, so that health can be produced through various products (such as those advertised by fitness, cosmetic and dieting industries) (Nettleton & Bunton, 1995) and marketing techniques (e.g. Maibach *et al.*, 1996). For a good example of this in relation to young women's drinking see sidebar 3.4. Health has become a market commodity: it is fashionable (Kelly & Charlton, 1995). It is trendy to go to the gym, frequent health-food shops, and read about what to eat and not eat in glossy magazines (Nettleton 1997).

This can partially help to explain why health promotion efforts to change lifestyles are more successful with people who are materially advantaged, but have very limited success in changing the lifestyles of the materially disadvantaged (despite the fact that campaigns often target these groups) (Nettleton & Bunton, 1995). If you have no money to spare, you cannot afford to buy extra virgin olive oil or the fresh vegetables that are now available all year around. If you have no money to spare, then buying a takeaway meal for the family will only be possible if it is deep-fried (and cheap) fish and chips rather than stir-fried Chinese food. On the other hand, many goods and services are consumed precisely because they are not healthy, and they become attractive for this very reason. Taking drugs, smoking cigarettes, drinking alcohol can together portray a 'to hell with it' attitude, which in itself can increase social status because of the meanings surrounding such behaviours. Any health professional trying to influence other people's lifestyles must understand the meanings and values that specific health behaviours are accorded.

Conclusions: what do we need in health psychology?

This chapter has further examined the concept of health, which is currently idealised as a self-governed lifestyle choice (Bunton & Burrows, 1995), and is certainly more than the opposite side of disease. Being healthy now represents a fulfilled life with physical, social and mental well-being (Kelly & Charlton, 1995). Aiming to change people's lifestyles to improve health is not the same as changing lifestyles to prevent disease. Health is not merely a neutral idea relating to the absence of illness, but means much more than this and is a value in itself. As a value, it is important to remember that it may not be given high priority by all individuals. Do all people want to be healthy? As we have seen, behaviour that is labelled unhealthy may not be 'health enhancing', but could well be 'life enhancing' (Backett *et al.*, 1994).

This chapter has argued that contextualising health and health behaviours is essential in any attempt to understand and change lifestyles. The mere fact that we focus on individual lifestyles highlights the Euro-American value of individual freedom (MacLachlan, 1997). Generating effective research and theory to guide health promotion practices will only be possible if it takes into account the complex social and cultural meanings of behaviours. People live in social worlds which are 'packed full of value-laden meanings' (Crossley, 2000, p. 40).

The challenge that health psychologists have is to come to terms with the complex relationship between individuals and the collective. Any attempt to change lifestyles needs to focus on the relationship between individuals and the much wider context in which they live (Spicer & Chamberlain, 1996). Thus social systems and the norms and rules of behaviour are key targets for health psychologists. According to Davison and colleagues (1991), the most 'efficient method of mass behavioral change is to change the norms or rules of behaviour – in short to change culture itself' (p. 15). It would be beneficial to examine how different health promotion perspectives might work together. For example, as well as trying to get individuals to change their behaviour in terms of cutting down on the amount of salt they add to their food, it would also be beneficial to change the food processing laws to reduce the salt content of tinned and frozen food (Jamison, 1995). As Richmond has tentatively suggested, 'there may be some ground for convergence . . . health promotion can involve sensitive and culturally appropriate individualistic methods of lifestyle change, coupled with structural and collective methods aimed at producing wider social change' (p. 172).

What can health psychologists do from here? In terms of influencing lifestyles, the research suggests some strategies for the way ahead:

- Be more honest in the depiction of scientific evidence, probabilities and the random nature of illness (Davison *et al.*, 1992). Remember that people's perceptions of health issues are much more sophisticated than health professionals realise (Frankel *et al.*, 1991).

- Do not fragment the study of behaviour, but focus on lifestyles from the perspectives of those creating them.
- Treat social and cultural groups differently but with equal respect.
- See communities as cultures in themselves (MacLachlan, 1997).
- Consider the unintentional consequences of trying to influence lifestyles in particular ways.
- Focus on small improvements in the sociocultural fabric of community life (MacLachlan, 1997).
- Always contextualise behaviour and explore the meaning and value it has for the individual.

Finally, it is worth thinking about the goal of all these efforts to change lifestyles. Is it possible to aim for a world in which everyone is free of disease? Much of the work which attempts to change lifestyles for health benefits assumes that health is a natural state. As Kelly and Charlton (1995, p. 85) remind us, at the same time as health has improved for the Western world, and many diseases have been controlled,

> humans have been devising the most mind-boggling forms of mass destruction, and industrialization has levied a heavy toll on hazards, pollutions and environmental damage. War remains commonplace and famine is endemic throughout much of the world.

RECOMMENDED READING

Backett, K. C., & Davison, C. (1995). Lifecourse and lifestyle: the social and cultural location of health behaviours. *Social Science and Medicine, 40*, 629–38. This paper examines the concept of lifestyle and draws on data from two different qualitative studies to examine how people make sense of their health behaviours in their everyday lives. It provides a good account of why health promoters need to work with, rather than against, cultural norms and values.

Crossley, M. L. (2000). Rethinking psychological approaches to health promotion. In *Rethinking health psychology* (ch. 3, pp. 36–62). Buckingham, UK: Open University Press. This chapter provides a solid overview of some of the problems with mainstream psychological research into health behaviours and health promotion. It places health behaviour in broader personal, moral and cultural contexts and provides excellent examples to demonstrate the points made.

Raeburn, J., & Rootman, I. (1998). *People-centred health promotion*. Chichester, UK: John Wiley. This book provides an inspiring and practical guide to health promotion. It puts people at the centre of health promotion efforts, examining their quality of life and showing how quality of life and well-being can be improved through empowering communities and self-determination.

Richmond, K. (1998). Health promotion dilemmas. In J. Germov (ed.), *Second opinion: an introduction to health sociology* (pp. 156–73). Melbourne: Oxford University Press. This chapter provides a clear and concise overview of different approaches to health promotion and views on health behaviours, and the values and problems associated with each. Written from an Australian perspective, the examples are direct and helpful.

Rutter, D., & Quine, L. (2002). *Changing health behaviour.* Buckingham: Open University Press. This edited book provides a number of chapters outlining specific interventions that have been developed and employed based on social cognition models. A range of different behaviours are examined (e.g. safe sex, smoking, reducing fat intake, vitamin C use, speeding). The final chapter provides a clear discussion of some of the methodological and practical problems involved in devising theory-based interventions.

4   Controlling the body

The physician as lifestyle expert, as wellness adviser, has already begun to appear. And as genetic and other predictive tools improve, the art of prevention will grow far more sophisticated. Physicians will administer tests and, armed with the results, prescribe preventive measures just as precisely as they now dispense medications . . . what all this means is that our present concept of medicine will disappear . . .   (Crichton, 1990, cited in Beck & Beck-Gernsheim, 2001, p. 143)

Learning objectives

This chapter introduces ideas about individuals' understandings and relationships with their bodies, and the body as a site which can be examined and controlled in order to maintain physical health. Thus, behaviours such as breast and testicular self-examination, screening for disease and genetic screening are considered. We discuss the implications of the current pervasive focus on disease risk, self-surveillance and engagement with technological screening programmes. By the end of this chapter you should be able to:

- distinguish between primary, secondary and tertiary prevention efforts;
- describe some of the major forms of secondary prevention of disease;
- evaluate whether screening programmes have a psychological impact;
- outline the costs and benefits of screening programmes;
- identify factors which influence individual uptake of screening services;
- describe the major types of genetic testing currently employed, as well as their psychological and social effects;
- discuss the implications of secondary prevention approaches for the individual;
- examine how secondary prevention practices influence individual perceptions of risk;
- evaluate how morality is embedded within accounts of risk.

What do people do to prevent disease?

As we have seen in ch. 3, one of the ways that disease is prevented is through people's engagement in health behaviours and the uptake of healthy lifestyles. Although stopping an illness taking hold in the first place seems an obvious form of disease prevention, in the realm of public health there are actually three different types of prevention employed to improve the health of populations:

Primary prevention: this aims to reduce the chances that a health problem will ever develop. According to Kaplan (2000), primary prevention almost always requires behaviour change: the modification of individual behaviour to reduce risk factors for disease. The health promotion campaigns we discussed in ch. 3 are forms of primary prevention. Parents who take part in immunisation programmes for their children are also engaging in primary prevention, to ensure that diseases such as diphtheria, polio, whooping cough, measles, mumps and rubella are avoided (and controlled or eliminated). Immunisation is one of the most successful examples of the primary prevention of disease (Woolf, 1996).

Secondary prevention aims to identify a disease in its very early stages, and then to stop its progression through treatment or elimination. Visiting a doctor and seeking medical care for specific symptoms, taking medication, having routine assessments of children's hearing and vision and having blood pressure measured are all examples of secondary prevention of illness. Other forms of secondary prevention involve self-examination of one's own body to detect disease, such as checking for lumps that might indicate breast or testicular cancer. Other forms require medical and technological assessment and employ medical examinations and screening tests, such as **mammograms**, cervical screening, genetic screening and prostate screening.

X-ray pictures of the breast, used to detect tumours and cysts. One breast at a time is rested on a flat surface that contains the x-ray plate, and a compressor is pressed firmly against the breast to help flatten out the breast tissue. The X-ray pictures are taken from several angles (from http://www.nlm.nih. gov/medlineplus/ency/ article/003380.htm# Definition).

Tertiary prevention takes place once a disease has progressed beyond the early stages, and aims to contain or slow the damage of the disease, prevent disability and provide rehabilitation. For example, people with heart disease may take long-term anti-hypertensive medication to reduce blood pressure as well as medication to thin the blood and reduce clotting. Tertiary prevention also involves keeping diseases such as cancer in remission for as long as possible, while heightening a person's comfort and quality of life.

These prevention efforts take place in the context of living in the Western world, where provision of sanitation and clean water is not an issue. Western governments are shifting the health agenda towards disease prevention, and as Price (2002) notes, 'disease prevention is synonymous with health promotion, improved public health and the populist concept of "wellbeing"' (p. 1). In this chapter our focus is on secondary prevention. Secondary prevention approaches rely on individuals engaging in particular kinds of behaviour, such as routinely examining their own bodies, having regular medical check-ups and taking part in national screening programmes. Health psychologists have been involved in researching the factors that influence these behaviours, such as whether or not an individual does engage in self-examination, or does take up and use a particular screening programme. The idea is that if we can identify factors that influence such behaviour, we will be able to modify them and make secondary prevention efforts more effective. If you have already read ch. 3, you should not be surprised that health psychologists have focused on individual attitudes and behaviour in this endeavour.

However, health psychologists and researchers from other disciplines have also examined some of the outcomes of secondary prevention efforts for individuals' physical and psychological well-being. Below we provide an overview of both the benefits and costs of specific secondary prevention approaches for individuals, including two self-examination techniques, four types of cancer population screening techniques, genetic testing, prevention through surgery and prevention through the use of pharmacological drugs. Finally, taking a more critical perspective, this chapter also examines some of the specific ways in which our bodies are routinely scrutinised (by ourselves and others) and come under the medical gaze for the benefit of disease prevention, and the implications this has for individuals.

Self-examination

Breast self-examination

Breast self-examination (BSE) is a simple, non-invasive and inexpensive behaviour that may lead to the early detection of breast cancer. This procedure involves checking the breasts to detect lumps in the underlying tissue. Ideally, BSE should be conducted once a month, approximately ten days into the menstrual cycle. Breast cancer is the third most common cancer in the world, and accounts for 18 per cent of women's cancers worldwide (Hamilton *et al.*, 2003). However, there is a lot of misinformation and misunderstanding about breast cancer and BSE (Salazar & Carter, 1994).

Effectiveness of BSE

As with many screening initiatives, there is debate concerning the efficacy of breast self-examination. The US Preventive Services Task Force (a group of physicians and health care experts who review published studies and make recommendations on the basis of these reviews) concluded that the balance of benefits and potential harm of BSE is not clear, but that BSE is associated with increased risk of false-positive results and unnecessary biopsies (USP-STF, 2002). Green and Taplin (2003) point out that the Canadian Task Force on Preventive Health Care no longer recommends BSE, and their systematic review led to the conclusion that BSE does not increase breast cancer diagnosis or decrease deaths from breast cancer.

Factors influencing BSE behaviour

Few women actually perform monthly BSE. A number of factors have been found to influence women's practice of BSE, including perceptions of breast cancer as the most worrying illness women can have. Factors in the Health Belief Model (HBM; see ch. 3 for a description of this model), particularly beliefs about having a high susceptibility to breast cancer, have been found to be strongly related to the practice of BSE (Jirojwong & MacLennan, 2003). Knowledge and attitudes, performance issues and concerns about others have also been found to influence women's BSE behaviour. Performance issues (e.g. it takes too much time and it is too difficult) seem to have the most negative influence (Salazar & Carter, 1994).

Although research suggests that women say they forget or do not have the time to engage in regular BSE, the plausibility of these responses has been questioned. Press and colleagues (2000) suggest that women find BSE and constant self-surveillance disturbing at some deep embodied level and that the continued 'forgetting' to engage in BSE is actually a form of resistance to such surveillance messages. Discomfort may stem from 'the way in which women performing breast self-examination must objectify their own bodies, approach them entirely from the outside, just as a physician would, and do so in order to search for a disease that most women greatly fear' (Press *et al.*, 2000, p. 246).

Testicular self-examination

Testicular cancer is the most common form of cancer in men aged 15 to 34, with an incidence four times greater in white males than non-white males. It is now possible to treat and cure approximately 95 per cent of testicular cancer which has been detected early (Wohl & Kane, 1997). Early symptoms include a lump in the testicle, painless swelling, a dull ache and a dragging experience (Moore & Topping, 1999). Testicular self-examination (TSE) is a procedure used to check for lumps in the testicles, scrotum and spermatic cord (Wohl & Kane, 1997).

Effectiveness of TSE

Morris (1996) has commented that half a million men between 15 and 35 years of age would have to engage in monthly TSE to prevent one death a year. This level of surveillance may lead to unnecessary anxiety and an increase in unnecessary medical procedures. However, others argue that TSE may not cause, or may actually reduce, anxiety in young men (e.g. Rosella, 1994). Very few studies have evaluated the predictive effectiveness of engaging in regular TSE. One study conducted in Hungary concluded that there is currently not sufficient justification to recommend its widespread use (Geczi *et al.*, 2001).

Factors influencing TSE behaviour

In the USA men who do not practise TSE regularly are reported to be African American or Hispanic; to have less than a college education; to be less satisfied with their job and life in general; to have greater worries in their daily life, more serious family problems and less social support than others

(Wynd, 2002). Further research is required to explore why men, especially men from minority ethnic groups, do not engage in regular TSE.

4.1

Clarke and Robinson (1999) analysed media coverage of testicular cancer and found that it was described through three primary discourses:

a medical discourse which focused on cause and early detection;

a machismo discourse which included masculinity, sexuality, sports, competition, war and battles;

a social support discourse which described emotions, lack of information and lack of support for men.

These discourses have implications for men. For example, describing men in stereotypically masculine ways limits alternative ways of being, and focusing on detection and treatment ignores prevention and cause.

Although men seem to be aware of testicular cancer, they know little about it, such as the age groups it affects and how curable it is (Khandra & Oakeshott, 2002). Lack of knowledge about TSE seems to be an important factor influencing this behaviour. In a study carried out in south London, only 22 per cent of 250 men aged between 18 and 50 attending a GP clinic were practising TSE according to recommendations (Khandra & Oakeshott, 2002). Similarly, a study conducted with undergraduates in the UK demonstrated that again only 22 per cent practised TSE – and only 1 respondent out of 203 was able to recognise the correct procedure (Moore & Topping, 1999). Only 2 per cent of teenage men (15–19-year-olds) in the Netherlands have been found to regularly perform TSE (Lechner *et al.*, 2002).

Undergraduate men in the UK have commented that they would be less embarrassed if they were shown how to perform TSE by a woman rather than a man (Moore & Topping, 1999)! Men obtain information about TSE from the media, pamphlets, friends or medical personnel (Moore & Topping, 1999). Although the media are a primary source of information about testicular cancer, accounts of disease in the media are not usually objective or neutral (Clarke & Robinson, 1999).

Population screening

Population screening is any procedure that is undertaken in healthy and asymptomatic individuals to check for disease. It is a pervasive part of medical practice, and ranges from taking blood pressure, heart rate and cholesterol readings, through to having pre-natal ultrasounds and regular mammography screening to test for breast cancer (Hickman, 2002). A recent review of the evidence on **hypertension** screening showed that hypertension can be identified in a physician's office; the treatment of hypertension can reduce later cardiovascular events (such as heart attacks and strokes); and there are no adverse psychological effects (Sheridan *et al.*, 2003).

High blood pressure (at rest).

However, much of the literature suggests that certain types of screening do not live up to their promise (Hickman, 2002). While screening was originally thought to be a useful, simple and cost-effective way of detecting and preventing further development of disease, the view now is that different screening programmes are complex, their value in terms of reducing mortality rates is questionable, especially for some forms of screening such as mammography, and that their cost-effectiveness is also questioned, with high rates of false-positives leading to quite invasive treatments unnecessarily (e.g. cervical cancer screening; Raffle *et al.*, 2003). In this section we outline four major cancer screening programmes used in many Western countries, namely screening for breast, cervical, prostate and colorectal cancer. We examine the factors that influence screening behaviour and conclude by outlining some of the psychological costs and benefits associated with population screening.

Breast cancer screening

If breast cancer is diagnosed early, survival is claimed to be high (around 95 per cent) (US Department of Health and Human Services, 2000). Mammography is one form of cancer screening which aims to detect breast cancer in its early stages. The US Preventive Services Task Force recommends that for women 40 years of age or older screening mammography should be undertaken every one to two years (USPSTF, 2002). However, uptake of mammography services has not been high, and the goal in the USA that 70 per cent of women over 40 years should have annual mammograms has not been realised (Yarbrough & Braden, 2001). Less than half of US women participate in any kind of breast cancer screening behaviour (Yarbrough & Braden, 2001). Women who are particularly at risk of late diagnosis of breast cancer (and therefore premature death), such as poor women, older women, women of colour and women with less education, do not engage in regular mammography screening (Breen *et al.*, 1996).

Effectiveness of breast cancer screening

A review of the evidence of breast cancer screening estimated that between 1,500 and 2,500 women must undergo screening to prevent one death from breast cancer, and 'mammograms miss approximately 12 per cent to 37 per cent of cancers, generate false-positive results, and cause anxiety while abnormal results are evaluated' (Woolf, 2001, p. 275). A **Cochrane review** on the effectiveness of mammography screening published in the prestigious medical journal *The Lancet* concluded that 'screening for breast cancer with mammography is unjustified' (Gøzsche & Olsen, 2000, p. 129). This produced a storm of controversy and debate in scientific circles and in the media and led at least one commentator to observe that 'at present, there is no reliable evidence from large randomized trials to support screening mammography programmes' (Horton, 2001, p. 1285). Nevertheless, a recent systematic review of the literature concluded that 'the balance of the evidence still favours screening mammography in women aged 40 years and older at least every two years'

A rigorous, well-developed method of reviewing a number of studies (usually in the medical field) on a particular topic.

(Green & Taplin, 2003, p. 233). A similar review conducted in the Netherlands concluded that routine mammography screening was effective in reducing breast cancer mortality rates in women aged between 55 and 74 (Otto *et al.*, 2003), while in the USA reviewers concluded that there is 'fair evidence that mammography screening every 12–33 months significantly reduces mortality for breast cancer', particularly in women aged 50–69, but also in women aged 40–49 (USPSTF, 2002; see http://www.ahrq.gov/clinic/uspstf/uspsbrca.htm). Thus, controversy exists on the effectiveness of breast cancer screening, although overall it seems to be justified. However, as noted below, screening services are not being used by particular sections of the population and more work is required to understand why this is so and how the uptake of services could be improved.

Factors influencing uptake of breast cancer screening

Psychological models have been employed to investigate factors that best predict the uptake of mammography screening programmes. The HBM (see ch. 3) has been the model used most frequently (Yarbrough & Braden, 2001). In an early study of the usefulness of the HBM to predict attendance at a clinic providing mammography, Calnan (1984) found that intention to attend for breast screening was the best predictor of actual attendance, followed by previous use of preventive health services, such as dental check-ups or attendance for cervical screening. Calnan concluded that the HBM provided no coherent theoretical framework for this area of study, and as intention to attend was the strongest predictor of behaviour, his findings actually provided support for Fishbein and Ajzen's Theory of Planned Behaviour.

Yarbrough and Braden (2001) reviewed sixteen studies employing the HBM to predict breast cancer screening behaviour and concluded that this model was not consistently predictive. While factors in the HBM related in expected ways to screening behaviour, these relationships were low to moderate, and the factors did not interact as predicted by the model. Factors in the HBM accounted for between 15 per cent and 27 per cent of breast cancer screening uptake, although this increased to 47 per cent when SES was included. The reviewers concluded that we currently know little about the social, non-health care meaning of breast cancer and breast cancer screening, and that qualitative research may be beneficial in future research, to provide rich descriptions of women's perceptions and choices about their behaviour.

The use of psychological models of behaviour to investigate screening participation has been criticised by minority groups because they do not take cultural concepts into account. As we noted in ch. 3, these models often ignore social context and the influence of social networks on meanings given to illness, as well as the emotional aspects of making important health decisions (Russell *et al.*, 2003). These critiques have been raised particularly in the context of African American women's experience of health and health care (see

Ashing-Giwa, 1999). Compared to white women, African American women are more likely to have breast cancer diagnosed at more advanced stages and they also have poorer prognoses (Royak-Schaler & Rose, 2002). In a review of the literature, Royak-Schaler and Rose (2002) note the lack of information and knowledge regarding uptake of mammography screening programmes in African American women. By moving beyond behavioural models, sociocultural components of health decisions, such as attending for mammography screening, can be captured. However, this requires the use of alternative, more participant-centred, research methods (see research in focus box 4.1).

Results from qualitative studies highlight further factors influencing women's decisions to undergo breast cancer screening. In the UK, women raise pragmatic issues to explain why they do not attend, such as the distance to the hospital or site of screening, difficulties due to a lack of signs and parking, perceived lack of privacy and feelings that staff had no time to deal with them or their questions (Hamilton *et al.*, 2003). In Sweden, women have noted that in the context of mammography screening, they do not feel respected by society or the health care system (Johansson & Berterö, 2003). This feeling of 'getting no respect' was influenced by other factors, such as:

- the equipment used, which was based on a specific template and was unable to take into account variations in women's bodies;
- the impersonalised experience led to women feeling insulted, as though they were on an 'assembly line';
- the compression of mammary glands and tissue during mammography screening which women worried might actually harm their breasts;
- women's diseases not being taken seriously compared to men's: 'if it was a male who should go through this . . . with his fragile parts, I wonder if they should accept it . . . I do not think so' (p. 14);
- the notion that screening may lull women into a false sense of security, because having a negative outcome does not mean that breast cancer will not develop.

The women in this study felt quite strongly that their decisions not to have screening were justified; as one participant noted, 'it is my own private business'.

Another way in which the experience of mammography screening has been communicated by researchers is through photography. Jo Spence was a photographer who explored women's lives in her photography, particularly power relations between women and men, between classes and between patients and doctors. In 1982 Jo Spence was diagnosed with breast cancer, and she decided to use photography to construct photographic narratives of her experiences (Bell, 2002). Figure 4.1 shows Jo Spence having a mammogram. It is available on the world wide web, and has been displayed in exhibitions. The caption Jo Spence put with this photo reads:

Research in focus

4.1 Meanings of mammography screening for African American women

Russell, K. M., Swenson, M. M., Skelton, A. M. & Shedd-Steele, R. (2003). The meaning of health in mammography screening for African American women. *Health Care for Women International, 24,* 27–39.

African American women in the USA have disproportionate breast cancer death rates, and also specific cultural beliefs about breast cancer which are not assessed with traditional health behaviour models. Three focus groups were conducted with a total of thirty African American women (all over 40 years of age) as a way of obtaining a fuller understanding of what health, and the experience of mammography screening, means for them. Seven main categories came out of the group discussions, three about health in general and four about mammography screenings.

Meanings of health

Health was described holistically in terms of the mind, body and spirit; also as enabling women to live their everyday lives; and finally as looking and feeling good: 'If a woman feels that her life is just fine, she looks good, she feels good, she is productive, then as far as I am concerned she is healthy, mentally, physically, and spiritually.' The role of spirituality, talking to God, relationships with family and social networks were all involved in African American women's perceptions of their health.

Mammogram screening and health: a balancing act

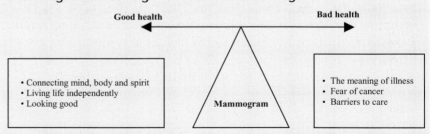

Good health – bad health: having a mammogram was seen as helping woman stay mentally and physically healthy, providing information and easing worry. Media and personal accounts of breast cancer were discussed as influencing screening behaviour.

Prevention–detection confusion: most of the women described the screening as a way to detect cancer, although some thought they prevented breast cancer from occurring. Detection was seen as finding the cancer and slowing the progression of the disease: 'We have been programmed to think that it's prevention . . . [but it's] really a detection tool.'

Being afraid of cancer: fear of cancer, and fear of the unknown, were described as obstacles to screening:

> A lot of people have that fear and don't want to know if it's there. So if they hear the words 'Go to detect whether the cancer is there' they won't go, but if they hear 'Go get your mammogram to prevent cancer', they're going to go.
> For instance, like a car, if there is nothing wrong with it, you don't fix it; you don't go looking for anything.

What gets in the way: mistrusting health care professionals, not having the financial means to obtain health care, and not having enough time were all cited as factors that influenced the women's non-participation in preventive care. Women were seen as losing their identity within the health care system.

Reflection

Having a mammogram was described from both an individual and ethnic group standpoint. Believing that mammograms detect illness, and a cultural belief that pain indicates illness, meant some women thought that mammograms were unnecessary, as they would know themselves if something was wrong. These findings are discussed in terms of assisting in tailoring promotion messages to reflect African American culture, emphasising the holistic nature of health and the positive aspects of having a mammogram. However, it is also noted that if we assume mammography screening is beneficial for this population then financial barriers and health care system obstacles must be addressed. The study constructs mammography as important and its value as a given. This reinforces the view that research should address how to get more people to engage in preventive screening, rather than question whether the screening is beneficial for individuals.

> Passing through the hands of the medical orthodoxy can be terrifying when you have breast cancer. I determined to document for myself what was happening to me. Not to be merely the object of their medical discourse but to be the active subject of my own investigation. Here whilst a mammogram is being done I have persuaded the radiographer to take a picture for me. She was rather unhappy about it, but felt it was preferable to my holding the camera out at arm's length and doing a self portrait.

As shown in the photograph, the breast needs to be separated as far as possible from the rest of the body, and the tissue compressed to enable a good x-ray image. As Bell (2002) argues, this photograph highlights how little control Jo

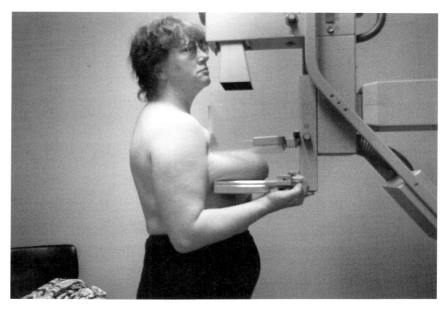

Figure 4.1 *Jo Spence 'Mammogram' (© Jo Spence Terry Dennett by permission)*

Spence has over her body once she becomes a patient, and also how medicine fragments and objectifies women's bodies.

Cervical cancer screening

Cervical screening programmes employ the Papanicolaou test (hence are known as 'pap smears') in which cells are taken from the cervix and sent to a cytology laboratory to be tested. Cells are tested for 'normality' or 'abnormality', and an abnormal result may be indicative of pre-cancerous cells, although to confirm this diagnosis further investigation and testing is required. Women have been found to hold inaccurate beliefs about cervical cancer screening; for example, women undergraduates consistently overestimate the incidence of cervical cancer, underestimate the abnormality rate of screening and overestimate the age at which abnormalities typically occur (Phillips *et al.*, 2003).

Effectiveness of cervical cancer screening

As with other screening programmes, there is debate about the value and effectiveness of cervical screening. In England and Wales, incidence and mortality from cervical cancer have decreased since the mid-1980s and this is most probably due to the cervical cancer screening programmes set up in these countries (Raffle *et al.*, 2003). However, one of the problems with these programmes is overdetection: 'for every death prevented many women have to be screened and many are treated who would not have developed a problem' (Raffle *et al.*, 2003, p. 904). Over 80 per cent of women who are treated for abnormal cervical smear results will not develop invasive cancer. Over 150 women have an abnormal result, over 80 women are referred for further investigation, and over 50 women have treatment for every death avoided (Raffle *et al.*, 2003). This rate of overdetection is important because of the amount of anxiety women experience when they receive an abnormal test result. Raffle and colleagues argue that changing people's perception of the meaning of an abnormal test result is essential. Further, the use of prophylactic treatments based on abnormal results, such as the surgical removal of the ovaries, as well as potentially harmful chemotherapy and radiotherapy treatment, is questionable when these abnormal results may not indicate cancer.

Factors influencing the uptake of cervical cancer screening

A review of research employing the HBM to examine factors influencing both breast and cervical cancer screening behaviours in Hispanic women identified a number of barriers to screening, including fear of cancer, fatalistic views on cancer, linguistic barriers and culturally based embarrassment. Other factors were found to positively influence screening behaviour, including recommendations by physicians, community outreach programmes which use Hispanic lay health leaders, Spanish print material, and the use of culturally specific media (Austin *et al.*, 2002). For Mexican American women, global beliefs about screening have not been found to relate to attendance for cervical screening. However, specific beliefs about pap smears did predict screening behaviour, and to a lesser extent so did demographic characteristics such as age, marital status, level of acculturation and health insurance (Fernández-Esquer *et al.*, 2003). In the UK working-class women have highlighted the problematic nature of getting a positive test result and undergoing further investigations, as well as problems that arise about how their male partners perceive cervical screening (McKie, 1995). The women were concerned that some men perceived cervical screening as a potentially sexual experience which doctors or women might enjoy, and if the person taking the test was a man, male partners were concerned about ownership and control issues.

Prostate cancer screening

The prostate gland is a chestnut-sized organ at the base of the bladder, which maintains proper function of the male reproductive tract. A recent editorial in the *New England Journal of Medicine* claims: 'Prostate cancer is the most common non-skin cancer in the United States, the second leading cause of death from cancer among US men, and the seventh leading cause of death in the United States' (Scardino, 2003, p. 295). Incidence and death rates from prostate cancer increase exponentially with age, and risk factors include family history, black race and a high-fat diet. There is currently no proven method of prevention (Scardino, 2003). Screening for prostate cancer involves testing for prostate specific antigen (PSA), which is associated with clinically diagnosed prostate cancer.

Effectiveness of prostate cancer screening

There is currently uncertainty about whether detecting prostate cancer in its early stages and treating it saves lives. Although prostate screening can detect 80–85 per cent of prostate cancers, there is little evidence that this leads to reduced morbidity or mortality (Woolf, 2001). Furthermore, prostate cancer screening has a high false-positive rate, and following a review of the available evidence, Woolf (2001) concluded that the overall balance of benefits and harm is unclear at present. Harm includes complications of treatment such as incontinence and impotence.

Factors influencing uptake of prostate cancer screening

Although regular PSA testing is not available to all men in the UK, many men continue to request it. Chapple and colleagues (2002) carried out a qualitative study with men who had confirmed or suspected prostate cancer, to explore their views on prostate cancer screening. The men viewed such screening as beneficial: they saw a screening programme for prostate cancer as enabling a better chance of being cured. Further, they mentioned their 'right to know' information about their own health status. The men also commented that a national screening programme for prostate cancer would give them equity with women, who have breast and cervical screening programmes available. The Internet was mentioned as a place where many men had obtained information on prostate cancer screening and the PSA test. Comparing the UK situation on prostate cancer screening with the situation in the USA led to the men specifically requesting PSA testing from their doctor:

> **4.2**
>
> In a recent New Zealand television documentary about Kiwi blokes, men were asked about their attitude to screening for prostate cancer and whether they took part in this initiative. As the commentator noted, one man's response summed up the overall view: 'Why would I go and get another man to stick a finger up my arse voluntarily if I don't need to?'

> I believe that in the Sates, many of the American states, PSA is obligatory or on offer for everyone over 50 . . . in view of the fact that it [cancer] is relatively easy to get rid of if it's caught in time, a PSA test ought to be a requisite for every man over 50. And I'm delighted that many of my friends have gone off and had the PSA test.   (a man who had searched the Internet)

However, not all men are so eager to take part in prostate cancer screening – see sidebar 4.2.

Colorectal cancer screening

The survival rates for colorectal cancer depend greatly on the stage of the disease at diagnosis (Wolf *et al.*, 2001). As with many diseases, people from low-income groups are typically diagnosed and treated at later stages (Steele, 1994), and within these groups black people have higher mortality rates

Table 4.1 Types of colorectal cancer screening procedures

Type	Description
Fecal occult blood testing (FOBT)	Polyps and cancer can cause blood to leak into the stool, so this technique uses a chemical reaction to find traces of blood in stool. Relatively inexpensive
Sigmoidoscopy	A physician uses a flexible tube-shaped instrument to look into the rectum and lower colon to examine it for lesions or polyps, to take samples and to remove polyps. A moderately priced procedure
Colonoscopy	Similar procedure to the one above, but the physician uses a longer instrument in order to examine the entire length of the colon. An expensive procedure
Barium enema	Barium (a material that shows up as white on an x-ray) is put into the colon by enema, then x-rays are taken of the abdomen to examine lesions (if present, a colonoscopy is then required). A moderately priced procedure

Annals of Internal Medicine, Summaries for Patients (2002, p. 138).

than whites (see Wolf *et al.*, 2001). There are several screening methods for colorectal cancer, as outlined in table 4.1. These include periodic examination of stools for occult blood, sometimes with intermittent examination of the bowel. Flexible sigmoidoscopy may also reduce incidence of and mortality from colorectal cancer. However, these methods vary widely in their accuracy, effectiveness of identifying cancerous lesions, potential complications, costs and ease of administration (Anderson, 2000). The best method for early detection is currently uncertain. Further, compliance with colorectal cancer screening programmes is poor (Jänne & Mayer, 2000).

Effectiveness of colorectal cancer screening

There appears to be support for colorectal cancer screening in people over 50, even though there is no agreement on the best procedures and how often screening is best undertaken (Wolf *et al.*, 2001). A recent systematic review of the evidence concerning the benefits of population colorectal cancer screening concluded that the various forms of screening can reduce incidence and mortality, although the evidence does not support one particular test over another (Walsh & Terdiman, 2003). The US Preventive Services Task Force recommends that adults begin screening for colorectal cancer at 50 years of age, and discuss and decide with their doctor the type of screening to be used, which in turn will influence the frequency of testing required (Pignone *et al.*, 2002).

Factors influencing uptake of colorectal cancer screening

Wolf and colleagues (2001) note that our understanding of factors which influence individuals' choices to take part in colorectal cancer screening is relatively poor, especially when it comes to such behaviour in minority populations. A study of 115 urban, working-class, predominantly minority men and women in the USA found that people held many misconceptions about colorectal cancer, including about perceived susceptibility to colorectal cancer, the often asymptomatic nature of the disease, the normative screening behaviour of other people and the accuracy of fecal occult blood testing and flexible sigmoidoscopy tests (Wolf *et al.*, 2001).

Problems with population screening

As seen throughout this section, controversy surrounds population screening, and experts disagree as to the benefits of screening programmes. Further, evaluating the efficacy of such screening can be extremely difficult (Wardle & Pope, 1992). In a recent issue of the *British Medical Journal*, Thornton and Dixon-Woods (2002) describe medical screening programmes as techniques which frequently use imperfect tests, which are sometimes presented to the public in an inappropriate manner, and which discover diseases that we do not fully understand and cannot adequately treat. Kaplan (2000) also identified the following problems associated with population screening programmes:

- According to the disease reservoir hypothesis a huge reservoir of undetected disease exists in the population which can be detected and eliminated through more aggressive intervention. Indeed, large numbers of women over 75 have breast cancer, and nearly 40 per cent of elderly men have prostate cancer. However, these people die from other causes, and by detecting these diseases early, health professionals are actually reducing quality of life with intensive and ongoing treatments.
- While screening places people in diagnostic categories, this does not always lead to better health outcomes, as there is not always effective treatment for the disease diagnosed.
- Diagnoses from screening programmes are not always correct. Some people will be treated for diseases they do not have, and others will not be treated effectively because their diagnosis was incorrect. Further, some cancers may be missed or occur between the screening appointments. A particular problem with incorrect diagnoses is overdetection. Many screening programmes show a high false-positive rate, where individuals are diagnosed with a disease, or with the potential to have a disease, which can lead to unnecessary exploratory procedures and operations. This is particularly a problem for cervical cancer screening (Hallowell, 1998).
- There are risks associated with some screening programmes. For example, the use of x-rays in mammography carries with it a risk of cancer, which may

affect some individuals more than others (Hallowell, 1998). Surprisingly, even the doctor who was largely responsible for setting up British cervical screening programme stated that 'it is absurd to conduct a screening test in such a way that nearly forty women are referred for an expensive and possibly hazardous procedure for every woman who is at risk of developing serious disease' (Smith, 1988, p. 1670).

Psychological costs of population screening

Wardle and Pope (1992) conducted a comprehensive review to examine whether cancer screening has negative psychological effects. They examined four areas in which there may be psychological costs of screening: screening information and invitations to attend for screening; participating in a screening programme; receiving abnormal and false-positive results; and being diagnosed with cancer. Each of these areas will be briefly discussed below; however, it is worth noting in advance that evaluating the benefits and costs of screening can be extremely difficult for a number of reasons. For example, very large sample sizes are required to detect benefits; outcomes such as mortality cannot be evaluated in short-term studies; and people who attend for screening are self-selected, and may be different in various ways from people who do not attend for screening (Wardle & Pope, 1992).

Psychological costs of screening information and invitations to attend

While the 1970s and 1980s saw much research investigating access to screening and factors which influenced participation in cervical screening (particularly barriers), more recent research focuses on explicit and implicit uncertainties about screening participation (Howson, 2001). The sheer amount of public information about risk from cancer, and the messages that individuals receive about the preventive behaviour they should engage in (including participation in screening programmes) leads to uncertainty and anxiety alongside contradictory messages received about the effectiveness of these behaviours. People may attend for screening with a (false) belief that it will prevent them from getting cancer, whereas screening actually enhances treatment effectiveness (Wardle & Pope, 1992). There are uncertainties about risk and risk perception, uncertainties about surveillance of the body, and uncertainties about the technologies employed. Howson (2001) has outlined some of the implications of uncertainties about cervical cancer screening, and these are outlined in table 4.2.

Further, there is a 'moral duty' associated with screening (Oakley, 1998). For example, although there is much uncertainty and unpleasantness about cervical cancer screening, it is represented as a safe, simple, successful and objective test which will reassure women about the absence of cancer or identify cell changes which might develop into cancer (Howson, 2001). Thus, women feel they should comply with such screening programmes (Howson, 1999). The

Table 4.2 Uncertainties in cervical cancer screening

Type of uncertainty	Description	Example responses
Explicit uncertainties	Ambiguity about the purpose of screening	Will it prevent cancer? Will it detect cancer?
	Meaning of an abnormal smear	Have I got cancer?
	Risks of investigation for cervical abnormalities (e.g. a sense of vulnerability, vigilance and being 'more on edge'; concern about future fertility)	What a horrible procedure! What will it mean if I want to have children later? Will it affect my fertility? I am constantly worried now that I'm about to develop cervical cancer. I'll have to be even more vigilant
Implicit uncertainties	Experiences and perceptions of practitioners who carry out screening provision	My GP tells me she's not sure about the reliability of screening
	Ambiguous nature of the practice of cytology	I've even heard that the people who decide whether or not the cells are abnormal – cytologists I think – say this process is subjective

Howson (2001).

converse side of this 'moral duty' is the implication it has for people who choose not to participate in population screening programmes. Women who do not attend for cervical screening are labelled as deviant (see Bush, 2000). Their behaviour not only is not 'normal' (i.e. what every other women does), but it also threatens the success of the screening programme (Gregory & McKie, 1991).

As Wardle and Pope (1992) note, if people take part in screening programmes for reassurance, then this should be capitalised on (without compromising those who receive positive results). The emphasis needs to be on healthy people attending, not on potential patients.

Psychological costs of participating in screening

Attending for screening can be a stressful experience in itself, as we have seen earlier among women going for mammography. People worry about their results and have a strong fear of cancer. Yet it seems that attending for screening has few negative psychological effects on individuals, although there are differences between those who choose to attend or not attend for screening. People who attend are more likely to be middle class, better educated, less anxious and are more likely to have attended screening previously than people who choose not to attend (Wardle & Pope, 1992). However, it has been argued that over a lifetime the cumulative physical and psychological costs of cervical cancer screening are high (McCormick, 1989). Being involved in a number of screening programmes (e.g. cervical and breast cancer screening) means that screening becomes a way of thinking about health, illness and the body.

Diagnostic and screening technologies such as those outlined in this section have enabled public health and preventive medicine to extend their 'clinical gaze' to people who are not ill but who may become ill in the future (Robertson, 2001). This has implications for the regulation of people's bodies. Castel (1991) has argued that this comprehensive ongoing surveillance over our own bodies is actually a way in which whole populations are regulated, as more and more opportunities for intervention based on 'prevention' are developed (see Hogle, 2001). For example, Bush (2000) highlights how cervical screening is built on medical discourses about the need for regulation of women's bodies. Screening programmes that are not one-off instances but require regular uptake, such as breast and cervical screening, mean that the proportion of women's lifespan subject to the medical gaze is extended to cover most of their adult life (Bush, 2000).

Psychological costs of abnormal and false-positive results

People have been found to respond to abnormal results with distress and shock (see Wardle & Pope, 1992). Important concepts involved here are individuals' understandings of risk of disease (remember that abnormal results require further testing to see if they indicate cancer), and how people respond emotionally to risk-related information (Wardle & Pope, 1992). Positive cervical smear results probably represent one of the most common screening abnormalities in the absence of physical symptoms (Wardle & Pope, 1992). For example, once a woman has a positive test result for cervical screening, further investigation is required. Women who receive a positive result have been found to incorrectly assume that because they have an abnormal smear result, they have cancer: 'you either get an all clear or you have got cancer' (Kavanagh & Broom, 1997, p. 1390). Further testing can lead to unpleasant experiences with gynaecologists, confusion and uncertainty. Kavanagh and Broom's study with Australian women showed that, following an abnormal cervical smear result, women were confused by what their doctors told them and felt unable to ask questions in the consultation:

> they didn't give me much information at all. Even as to what they were going to do . . . he told me he was also going to do a biopsy . . . I didn't know what to expect . . . they don't tell you you're going to bleed or have a discharge afterwards. They give you a little sheet of paper and it says do not swim, do not bathe, do not wear tampons, etc . . . but they don't tell you why you can't do these things.   (Kavanagh & Broom, 1997, p. 1389)

The researchers concluded that because of the time pressure of medical practice and its inherent power structure women patients did not receive the detailed information and reassurances they needed to reduce their distress. The experience of further investigation is distressing for women, independent of outcome.

Psychological costs of being diagnosed with cancer

Cancer is probably the most feared disease in the Western world and the uncertainty about outcomes, types of treatment and mortality means that a diagnosis leads to distress. Such a diagnosis may also lead to psychiatric disturbance, suicide or accidents. Research shows that providing people with information about their diagnosis and treatment, and involving them in shared decision making about treatment, can improve psychological autonomy and sense of control (see Wardle & Pope, 1992, for a review). Specific ways of communicating the diagnosis have also been found to reduce negative psychological responses (such as anxiety and depression) (Schofield *et al.*, 2003). The main concern about screening programmes is overdiagnosis, as mentioned earlier. If screening detects cancers which would not have been detected clinically and which are comparatively benign, then the emotional distress associated with this diagnosis must be considered in any calculation of costs and benefits (Wardle & Pope, 1992).

In summary, there are psychological and social implications of screening programmes that require further examination. Compared to the amount of money, time and effort devoted to researching the technological and organisational aspects of screening, relatively little attention has been given to investigating its psychological costs (Wardle & Pope, 1992). This continues to be the case today, and health psychologists are well placed to make a difference in this field.

Genetic screening

Increasingly, genetic tests are being developed and used to detect inherited disorders and risk factors. It is expected that this type of screening will become a common part of medical care (Lerman *et al.*, 2002) and that psychologists will play significant roles in helping individuals undergo and cope with genetic tests and their outcomes (Patenaude *et al.*, 2002). Several different types of genetic tests have been developed and are employed today. These can be divided into pre-natal screening, carrier testing and the more recently developed personal susceptibility testing. These different forms of genetic testing are outlined and described in table 4.3.

Pre-natal testing

Pre-natal testing is offered to pregnant women to test for fetal genetic abnormalities. For example, amniocentesis is used to test for Down's syndrome (see table 4.3), although the procedure is not without risk and can lead to pregnancy

Table 4.3 Types of genetic testing

Type of test	What is it?	Examples
Pre-natal testing	Obtaining genetic information about a fetus to determine whether fetus has a genetic condition	Amniocentesis to test for Down's syndrome. This procedure involves inserting a needle through the women's abdomen into the amniotic sac to obtain amniotic fluid, which can then be tested
		Chorionic villus sampling involves taking a tiny tissue sample from outside the sac where the fetus develops to detect chromosomal or genetic birth defects. Can be undertaken earlier than amniocentesis, at ten to twelve weeks gestation
Carrier testing	Identifying gene mutations which are inherited in autosomal recessive fashion. Couples take the test to see if they are carriers of the gene, and if both are then their offspring may develop the disease	Tay-Sachs disease Cystic fibrosis Sickle-cell disease Fragile X syndrome
Predictive testing	Identifying a person's risk of developing a particular disease later in life. Information obtained (i.e. person's likelihood of getting the disease) varies across the different diseases tested for	Huntingdon's disease Breast cancer, ovarian cancer Childhood polyposis leading to colon cancer Lung cancer

loss (about 1 in 200 women undergoing amniocentesis lose the fetus; Chescheir & Hansen, 1999). Pre-natal testing is recommended for women over 35, women with a family history of genetic defect or inborn metabolic error, women with abnormal ultrasounds and those with elevated levels of maternal serum alpha feto-protein (which may indicate chromosomal or neural tube defects).

The decision to undergo pre-natal testing is difficult, given the potential risks and benefits (Lerman *et al.*, 2002). Surprisingly, research examining factors that influence the decision to undergo pre-natal testing has found that perceived risk, rather than actual risk, is important, while amount of knowledge is not strongly predictive (Marteau *et al.*, 1991). Women undergoing pre-natal testing do not show sustained or clinically significant psychological distress (Lerman *et al.*, 2002), although most women in studies do not receive results indicating abnormalities (such results are relatively rare).

Carrier testing

Carrier testing involves testing couples to examine whether they are carriers of a particular gene which is inherited in an autosomal recessive fashion. It is recommended for couples who are planning to have children and are at risk of a particular disease because of their ethnic origin, or because they have known relatives with the disease (see table 4.3). Couples may choose to undergo the testing to determine their carrier status or to avoid having a child with the disease. Knowing that both partners carry a particular gene may lead to pre-natal diagnosis, and subsequent abortion of affected fetuses (Richards, 1993).

While some evidence suggests that carriers and non-carriers of a particular genetic disease may hold different attitudes and have different levels of anxiety, other evidence suggests that these differences are relatively small and do not persist over time (see Lerman et al., 2002, for a review). Clearly the cultural and social context in which the test is undertaken (e.g. are all members of the family interested in the result?) would influence how genetic carrier testing affects the family, as would knowing that there is available treatment for the disease should couples have an affected child.

Predictive testing

Predictive testing is recommended for individuals who have relatives (especially parents) with a particular disease, to determine their own risk of developing the disease (see table 4.3). The information provided varies according to the disease being tested. For example, testing positively for the Huntingdon's disease gene means the individual is almost certain to go on to develop this disease later in life, while testing negatively means the individual will not develop the disease. This is not the case for genetic tests for breast, ovarian and colon cancer, where testing positively means there may be between a 55 per cent and 85 per cent chance of getting the cancer, as other genetic and environmental factors also play a role in these diseases (see Lerman et al., 2002). Conversely, testing negative for particular cancer genes does not mean that the individual will not develop that cancer later in life. One of the primary reasons put forward for predictive genetic testing for cancer is that individuals who are at 'high risk' based on the genetic test outcome can then engage in risk reduction strategies and be monitored closely via other screening techniques for the early detection of disease. There is much interest in predictive genetic testing among individuals who have a family history of breast or colon cancer, although actual uptake is not as high as interest (Lerman et al., 2002).

Reviews of the research seem to be consistent in showing no adverse, long-term effects of predictive psychological testing (Lerman et al., 2002). However, there may be subsets of people who are more vulnerable to experiencing psychological distress than others, such as people who underestimate the emotional impact of the test (Dorval *et al.*, 2000). Butow and colleagues (2003) report psychological benefits in women who have had genetic testing for breast cancer. In their sample, non-carriers experienced relief, and carriers did not demonstrate any significant increase in depression or anxiety following the test. Furthermore, genetic counselling tended to improve the accuracy of women's risk perception.

Similar findings were obtained in a study investigating the psychological effects of genetic testing in children who carry a gene mutation for familial adenomatous polyposis. Carriers of this gene are almost certain to develop colorectal cancer later in life if they do not have regular endoscopic screening and a colorectomy (complete removal of the colon) when polyps appear (Codori *et al.*, 2003). Forty-eight children were tested for the gene, and twenty-two tested positive. Over the following 38 months psychological well-being did not decrease significantly in the children who were non-carriers or in the children who were carriers. The children's parents in both groups also did not show a significant decrease in psychological well-being. Overall, the researchers concluded that most children do not experience increased psychological distress from genetic testing for hereditary colorectal cancer (Codori *et al.*, 2003).

Little research has investigated whether predictive genetic testing does actually have an influence on whether people engage in risk-reduction behaviour and intensive monitoring for early detection of the disease. One study with women who had learnt that they were carriers of the breast cancer gene found that two years afterwards none of them had undergone a prophylactic **mastectomy** (11 per cent thought they might), whereas 46 per cent of women over 25 years of age had undergone an **oophorectomy** (Botkin *et al.*, 2003). Further, knowledge of carrier status made no difference to the use of mammography services in women over 40 years, although in women aged 25–39 carriers were more likely to have had a mammogram in the previous year than non-carriers. The few studies conducted suggest that predictive genetic testing does not have a large impact on cancer screening behaviour (Lerman *et al.*, 2002).

Research has found that generally women tend to overestimate the role of genetics in the development of breast cancer (Henderson & Kitzinger, 1999). This is partially due to the extent of media coverage of genetic risk and breast cancer: '[genetic risk] must be high because such a big deal is made of it', said one research participant (p. 572). The breast-ovarian cancer susceptibility gene (BRCA 1) was identified in 1994, and much coverage was given to this discovery in national and international media.

In summary, a number of different kinds of genetic tests are currently available, with more and more likely to be so in coming years. Some research has examined the negative and positive psychological effects of such testing, which is where we turn next.

The surgical removal of the entire breast.

The surgical removal of one ovary (a bilateral oophorectomy is the surgical removal of both ovaries). It is also called ovariectomy.

The psychological effects of genetic testing

Overall, taking up genetic tests and receiving the results of these tests does not appear to have adverse psychological consequences (Broadstock *et al.*, 2000; Lerman *et al.*, 2002). Increased anxiety tends 'to be transient and not clinically significant' (Lerman *et al.*, 2002, p. 793). However, as Lerman and colleagues point out, findings showing that people do not demonstrate increased distress following pre-natal, carrier and predictive testing may be the result of a variety of methodological and analytical issues, such as:

- Participants in the research are in settings where good genetic counselling services are offered, therefore their outcomes may be better than those of individuals who have more minimal services available.
- The measures that are employed to assess 'psychological distress' may not be sensitive enough to detect subtle changes in well-being that may be specific to genetic testing.
- Analyses are undertaken at the aggregate level, thus individual information is summarised across groups. This obscures within-group variation in distress and, as mentioned above, there may be subgroups of individuals who may be more psychologically vulnerable to genetic testing.
- The focus has been primarily on responses in individuals, and little research has examined the possible negative effect that the testing has on family members.
- Research samples are self-selected, participants have agreed to participate and response bias may occur with selective drop-out over time (Broadstock *et al.*, 2000).

Broadstock and colleagues (2000) also make the point that protective psychological mechanisms may be operating to reduce distress following genetic testing. Such mechanisms may include denial and relief from uncertainty (Tibben *et al.*, 1997). There are several ways in which potential adverse effects of screening can be minimised, including how screening is presented, how the results of the test are communicated and how risk is communicated and also perceived (Marteau, 1994).

However, as Solomon *et al.* have pointed out (2002), complex issues are involved in genetic testing in terms of its psychological impact, which is why any offer of a genetic test must have heavily fortified guidelines and recommendations. Much of the psychological and behavioural impact is unknown, although it is expected that psychologists will be called on to assist in many aspects of predictive genetic testing. Patenaude and colleagues (2002) have argued that psychologists have an important role to play in researching the emotional implications of tests for individuals, how knowledge of risk affects attitudes and quality of life, what the best interventions are to help people cope with knowledge about their own risk, and the acceptance of prophylactic or chemopreventive techniques (outlined in more detail below) to help 'manage' risk.

Broader implications of genetic testing

By assessing the potential adverse reactions that individuals may have following genetic testing, health psychologists have contributed to traditional biomedical research, where the focus is on the individual, measurement and aggregation. However, the availability of genetic tests raises a number of ethical concerns. In terms of breast cancer susceptibility, it may lead to adverse consequences for women more generally (Press *et al.*, 2000). As there is no known cure for breast cancer, knowledge of 'risk' status and recommendations for comprehensive surveillance heighten women's fears of breast cancer and general anxiety. This has ethical and social implications, some of which are described in table 4.4. The focus on individual factors for breast cancer prevention means that little attention is paid to external factors which may be effective in preventing this disease, such as environmental clean-up, pesticide reduction and reducing amounts of hormone additives in meat and poultry (Press *et al.*, 2000).

There are also traditional bio-ethical concerns about genetic testing, including insurance and workplace discrimination, stigmatisation and loss of privacy (Press *et al.*, 2000). As Willis (1998) points out, **geneism** is starting to take its place alongside racism, sexism and other forms of discrimination. Another potential problem with genetic technologies (and their increase) is **genetic reductionism**. As we have seen, many predictive genetic tests do not provide certainties about developing the disease, but rather risk information. The problem here is that focusing on the gene locates the problem within the individual, and shifts the focus away from the other factors that may also influence the development of the disease.

Discrimination on the basis of genetic make-up.

Assuming that individuals are simply the sum of their genes. Thus causes of diseases are reduced to individual genes rather than broader social, environmental and cultural factors.

There is much research to be done in the area of genetic testing. Richards (1993) posits a number of important questions about 'the new genetics', including:

- How does growing up in a family with an inherited genetic disorder influence an individual's identity?
- How does the knowledge obtained from genetic testing affect sense of identity for the individual tested, as well as for his/her family members?
- How do families communicate about genetic conditions and inherited characteristics?
- Are women expected to be the 'genetic housekeepers' of families?
- What are the lay beliefs held about inheritance? How do these relate to the use of genetic services?
- How has 'the new genetics', and media coverage of genetics, influenced lay beliefs?

Table 4.4 Some ethical and social implications of genetic testing for breast cancer

Ethical implications
- Women's autonomy is threatened by emphasising knowledge of risk and importance of testing, and recommending consequent intensive surveillance
- Neglect of the social and cultural aspects of women's lives while much greater attention and emphasis given to biological, sexual and reproductive aspects
- Women may feel blame if they receive a breast cancer diagnosis as responsibility is placed on them to attend to the 'risk', use screening and genetic testing techniques
- Women's bodies are repressed, disciplined and controlled through strategies based on the rhetoric of risk and fear (see below)

Social and behavioural implications: some suggested strategies to 'save' women from breast cancer
- Teenage girls should engage in a large amount of physical exercise, to delay the start of their periods, which may reduce breast cancer risk later in life
- Women should take a permanent birth control pill (currently being developed) from puberty to menopause to reduce amount of oestrogen in their bodies, except for when they wish to have a child
- Women should delay their education and have babies during their late teens to decrease later risk of breast cancer

Adapted from Press *et al.* (2000).

In addition to these kinds of question, we also need to ask specific questions about risk perception and its consequences. For example, what does it mean for a woman to live with the knowledge that she has a one-in-seven chance of developing breast cancer? Does this lead to a life of living with a personal 'time-bomb'? At the moment, with the advent of more diagnostic and screening technologies, we know little about how such probabilities affect the use of further biotechnologies or, at an individual level, how they are transformed by the adoption of different kinds of lifestyles (Robertson, 2001).

Disease prevention by surgery

Following predictive genetic testing, individuals may choose prophylactic surgery in order to reduce their risk of getting a particular disease. For example, on learning that she carries the breast and/or ovarian cancer gene, and has a 'high' risk for developing one of these cancers, a woman may choose to have her breasts (mastectomy) and/or her ovaries surgically removed (bilateral oophorectomy). Indeed, one of the rationales for predictive genetic testing is for management of risk, through intensive surveillance techniques (for example, annual mammography screening) or through prophylactic surgery.

However, such surgery poses its own risks. There is no guarantee that all of the breast and ovarian tissue is removed, and there are risks associated with anaesthesia, post-operative complications and problems with hormone replacement therapy (HRT) or breast implants (see Hallowell, 1998). Little research has examined the psychological implications of prophylactic surgery, and only a few studies have explored the ways in which women make decisions about such surgery. Hallowell (1998) conducted a qualitative study with women who were at high risk of breast or ovarian cancer to explore their perceptions of prophylactic surgery, and the potential costs and benefits it offers. All of the forty-one women in this study were considered to be at high risk of breast and/or ovarian cancer based on genetic test results. The women were interviewed six to eight weeks following genetic counselling, as well as twelve months later. Twenty-four women said they would consider having prophylactic surgery, while sixteen would not consider it. Three main perceived benefits and seven costs of prophylactic surgery were identified in the women's accounts, and these are summarised in table 4.5.

While genetic testing implicates the entire family, results from this study show that perceptions of prophylactic surgery as a risk management option also implicate family members. The women discussed the surgery in terms of its consequences for other people and balanced their own needs with the needs of others (Hallowell, 1998). Further, some women perceived their body as healthy and working as a balanced system, while other women perceived their health as already compromised. Finally, Hallowell points out that genetic counsellors discuss and frame options of prophylactic surgery quite differently depending on whether the breasts or ovaries are to be potentially removed. Recommendations were given for oophorectomies, but no recommendations were given for mastectomies, even when women asked the counsellor their opinion. Oophorectomy was presented as a simple and straightforward procedure, and HRT as an effective way of dealing with menopausal side-effects.

There is a cultural fascination and horror associated with mastectomy, and consideration of mastectomy as a cancer risk management procedure has been covered in great detail in the media (Henderson & Kitzinger, 1999). Media accounts often focus on one woman's dilemma, using a personal experience story, as these stories have 'soft value appeal' and put genetic testing and genetic risk information into one person's life context. As the health editor of a daily broadsheet newspaper stated, 'it is such a dramatic thing for a woman to do but that makes it quite newsworthy' (Henderson & Kitzinger, 1999, p. 570).

In summary, preventing disease through surgery is a complex decision which has many implications for the individual. There is a lack of psychological research in this area. Knowledge is clearly required, not only in terms of the effectiveness of such surgery, but also in terms of psychological processes of decision making, risk management understandings, information that may be helpful, how information is presented and discussed in counselling sessions and so on.

Table 4.5 Perceived benefits and costs of prophylactic surgery for breast/ovarian cancer

Perceived benefits of prophylactic surgery

Fulfilling social obligations	Surgery seen as only option for some women to enable them to continue to care for and bring up their children
Risk reduction/fear containment	Surgery was seen as a way of removing the fear of cancer, and giving the women a chance. As one woman said: 'it is radical but if it takes away that fear, then that can only be a good thing. Because otherwise the fear will get you in the end'
Incidental benefits	Additional benefits were commented on, such as having larger breasts, or the relief of current gynaecological problems

Perceived costs of prophylactic surgery

Upsetting natural balance	Many women thought removing healthy tissue was not acceptable, or tempting fate, and would upset the natural balance of the body. One woman commented that 'it's like cutting your legs off in case you're going to get run over by a train, which is crazy'
Defeating the object	Some women questioned how effective the surgery would be in avoiding later cancer. They viewed cancer as uncontrollable, and therefore prophylactic surgery would only mean the cancer would develop elsewhere in the body
Social obligations	Some of the women saw the surgery as compromising their social obligations, having to take time off work or interfering with their social role as mother, breadwinner, wife, etc. as a result of time in hospital and convalescence period
Complications	Women mentioned fears concerning operative and post-operative complications, such as anaesthesia and breast reconstruction
Menopause	For oophorectomy, the main cost was the immediate onset of menopause, which was particularly important for women who wanted to have children in the future. There was also a fear of menopause, in that it might result in madness or personality change
Issues of identity	Many women saw surgery as threatening their femininity, and hence their gender identity. One woman said 'you don't want to lose your ovaries because you think, I might become a man'. The breasts were viewed as a public display of femininity, and mastectomy as a threat to that public identity
Sexual relationships	Some women were concerned about the impact a mastectomy would have in terms of how attractive they were for their sexual partners

Hallowell (1998).

Disease prevention with drugs

In recent years another form of managing 'at risk' populations for particular diseases has developed. In this technique, healthy individuals are given medication to reduce their chances of getting a disease (Hogle, 2001). The use of drugs for prophylactic treatment of cancer is known as **chemoprevention**.

For example, chemoprevention is being used in an effort to prevent colorectal cancer. Here, individuals use medications to prevent the development of particular kinds of polyps in the bowel (Jänne & Mayer, 2000). Early research suggests that aspirin, and other non-steroidal anti-inflammatory drugs (NSAIDS), supplemental folate and calcium, as well as HRT (oestrogen), may be beneficial. However, Jänne and Mayer (2000) point out that the value of chemoprevention for colorectal cancer has not been rigorously tested and therefore cannot yet be accepted as standard medical practice. As noted previously, there are also screening programmes for colorectal cancer, which currently involve periodic examination of stools for occult blood, and sometimes include intermittent examination of the bowel.

> **The technique in which healthy individuals take prescribed medication to reduce their risk of getting a disease.**

A chemopreventive medicine (finasteride) for prostate cancer was posited in the early 1990s. This led to the prostate cancer prevention trial, a major chemopreventive programme which involved more than 18,000 men who were randomly assigned to receive either finasteride or a placebo for seven years. Results of this trial showed that there was a major effect of taking the preventive drug on the rate of cancer detection (Thompson *et al.*, 2003). However, other disturbing findings in the trial led to an editorial in the *New England Journal of Medicine* cautioning against using finasteride as a chemopreventive drug for prostate cancer (Scardino, 2003). Specifically, Scardino (2003) noted that:

1 Cancer was detected in the placebo group at a rate of 24.4 per cent, or four times as often as expected (6 per cent). Therefore Scardino questioned whether the cancers being detected during the trial were clinically significant (perhaps they were low-grade cancers that did not actually pose any risk to the men).

2 Increased rates of high-grade cancers were detected in the drug condition: 6.4 per cent of men in this group had a high-grade cancer, compared to 5.1 per cent of men in the placebo condition, cautioning against finasteride as a chemopreventive medicine.

3 The drug had adverse effects on sexual function (but beneficial effects on urinary function), meaning that it may be seen as an unattractive prevention technique to men.

A number of issues arise from chemopreventive medicine. First and perhaps most apparent are the side-effects that long-term use of pharmacological drugs can have. Such side-effects can affect not only individuals' quality of life, but also their physical health – perhaps it will come down to choosing your disease? Furthermore, in countries where it is legal to advertise drugs directly to consumers (such as the USA and New Zealand), drug companies are making the most of being able to do so. For example, large marketing campaigns have been undertaken in the USA by AstraZeneca to advertise the largest selling breast cancer therapeutic drug as a breast cancer preventive medicine (Nolvadex®, the brand name for tamoxifen; Hogle, 2001). Such direct-to-consumer advertising of medication, particularly preventive medication, increases people's awareness of disease and reinforces concerns about risks of developing disease later in life. The concept of risk is rife in Western cultures, and is pervasive in the media, which have become a primary source of health information. As Hogle (2001) points out, 'the concept of chemoprevention would not work without considerable public concern about the risk of becoming ill and a desire to do something to mitigate the risk' (p. 15).

HRT

HRT has been marketed and prescribed as an effective medication that can be used to prevent osteoporosis, heart disease and Alzheimer's disease (Genazzani & Gambaccuani, 1999). Yet much controversy and debate continues regarding the effectiveness of HRT as a preventive medicine (Gannon, 1999). Further, the protective effects that HRT may afford women will not actually continue into old age unless women take HRT for life (Foster, 1995).

Controversies regarding HRT also stem from its association with increased risks of breast and endometrial cancer, and developing thrombosis. The HRT– breast cancer link has been supported by considerable empirical evidence (Gannon, 1999), which indicates a significant increased risk of breast cancer following long-term (five years or more) HRT use. These findings led Worchester and Whatley (1992) to suggest that, in attempting to reduce the risk of coronary heart disease or osteoporosis with HRT, women may be replacing one disease with another. Indeed, a recent randomised controlled trial of HRT found that women receiving oestrogen plus progesterone showed significant increases in coronary disease, stroke and pulmonary embolism – the kinds of diseases such therapy is supposedly protective against (Writing Group for the Women's Health Initiative Investigators, 2002). This led to one arm of this large randomised controlled trial into the effects of HRT being stopped in the USA. There are currently no definitive answers about the long-term preventive effects of HRT (Hunter et al., 1997).

General practitioners in both the UK and Australia have been found to emphasise the value of HRT as a preventive medicine, and indeed view HRT as effective only for preventing long-term disease (Lyons & Leach, 2004; Murtagh & Hepworth, 2003). For example, a study with GPs in the UK (Lyons & Leach, 2004) found comments such as:

> We've had lots of discussions in the practice with the partners and one of my partners put it beautifully – he said, well you can choose your disease.
> I personally think it should be in the drinking water.

While women's primary motivation to take HRT is for symptom relief (Green *et al.*, 2002), many GPs see this view as an example of women being misinformed or ignorant (Green *et al.*, 2002; Lyons & Leach, 2004). As one GP has commented:

> It seems to me to be very symptom driven, the whole HRT approach from the patient's point of view not from my point of view. Women appear to be primarily motivated by suppressing, or a wish to suppress vaso-motor instability and other symptoms of the menopause, rather than the long term benefits of regular HRT use over the years.   (Lyons & Leach, 2004)

Thus, women who do not take HRT for many years, or who choose not to take it at all during midlife, are viewed as ignorant or irresponsible (Guillemin, 1999), which makes women's health choices at midlife constrained and complex. However, with recent negative results from studies examining the longer-term effects of HRT on diseases, such as those from the Women's Health Initiative study, there is much more reticence about its use as a preventive drug.

In summary, there is much controversy about the use of pharmacological drugs to prevent development of disease. At present, there is also little evidence to suggest such drugs are effective. However, there is often tension between the views and approaches employed by health professionals and those of individuals. Again, further research is required to explore what the general public think (and want) with regard to such prevention.

Implications of secondary prevention approaches

Only a handful of secondary prevention approaches have been discussed in this chapter, and there are many others. We have considered self-examination techniques, population screening for different cancers, genetic screening, prevention through surgery and prevention with pharmacological drugs. For each, we have reviewed current understandings of their effectiveness, and factors which influence whether individuals actually engage in the screening. We have also considered some of the implications of these specific forms of secondary prevention. In the following section we take a broader view and discuss the implications of such secondary preventive efforts for people living in Western society today. A number of issues concerning secondary prevention have been identified by sociologists and health psychologists, including risk, medicalisation, self-surveillance and consequences for subjectivity. Each of these concepts is outlined briefly below.

Risk

Although people in the Western world enjoy higher life expectancies than ever before, there has never before been a time when people were so occupied with identifying and fighting the risks that threaten our health. Risk has become an important and pervasive cultural concept (Lupton, 1995); indeed, it is said to be one of the defining cultural characteristics of contemporary Western society (Robertson, 2001). Risk is also a central concept for individual health (Robertson, 2001). By using the concept of 'risk', people no longer look to a symptom or a sign for illness. Rather, risk connotes the idea that there is future illness potential, a potential which may or may not ever be even realised (Armstrong, 1995). The pervasiveness of notions of risk provides a context that encourages and necessitates particular diagnostic and screening technologies (Robertson, 2001). Indeed, medical screening has been called an 'institutionalisation of risk' (Thornton & Dixon Woods, 2002).

The 'risk epidemic' is apparent in the media (Henderson & Kitzinger, 1999), as well as in professional medical journals, where the use of such terms as risk, danger, hazard and uncertainty have increased rapidly since 1967 (Skolbekken, 1995). Our beliefs about what or who is responsible for health risk have shifted from those which were outside our control to those which are individual and well inside our control (Skolbekken, 1995). Health promotion is based on the notion that science can give us ultimate and objective truths about risk, and also provide bases from which to make ethical decisions about personal conduct. However, as we have seen in this chapter, even the expert scientists and medical professionals often cannot agree on the 'facts' about risk (Petersen, 1996). Reading conflicting and changing advice about screening programmes and levels of risk means that as individuals we cannot get security by following a particular set of advice (Petersen, 1996).

Breast cancer provides a good example: there is no cure or foolproof prevention for breast cancer, so instead science has offered 'an elaboration of breast cancer risk factors and programmes of vigilant surveillance via mammography, breast examination and genetic testing' (Press et al., 2000, p. 241). Further, while risk used to be a term applied to populations, it has shifted to being seen as residing within individuals. Women are now able to get their 'relative risk' number telling them their probability of contracting breast cancer at some point in life. They then become responsible for abating their 'risk', through engaging in vigilant self-surveillance and screening programmes. The low number of women performing BSE, and engaging in screening programmes, may be seen as a resistance to vigilant surveillance of their own bodies (Press et al., 2000).

Medicalisation and self-surveillance

We think about the risks of particular behaviours for our health, such as whether we should be eating butter on our toast every morning, given the risks of heart

disease. This is what researchers have called the **medicalisation** of everyday life. Medical discourse about epidemiology and the probabilities of getting
particular diseases is now part of our lives (Richmond, 1998). The new preventive techniques of health promotion, such as those outlined in this chapter, 'target the individual-as-enterprise who is expected to manage his or her
own relationship to risk' (Petersen, 1996, p. 45). Through self-surveillance,
medicine seeks to remove the unpredictable and uncertain from everyday life
(Armstrong, 1995). The upshot of this is the continued and anxious surveillance
of our bodies (Richmond, 1998). Individuals are now expected to take responsibility for their own health and well-being by carrying out self-examinations
and presenting themselves to doctors for other kinds of screening, such as for
cervical and prostate cancer. Furthermore, the disease prevention techniques
outlined in this chapter, along with the health surveillance strategies, have
tended to target women (Howson, 2001) and discourses of risk are particularly
associated with the female body (Oakley, 1998).

> The process by which non-medical problems become defined and treated as medical issues, usually in terms of illnesses, disorders or syndromes (Richmond, 1998).

Surveillance medicine dissolves the categories of healthy and ill, and brings
everyone within the realm of medicine's visibility. It is most effective when
people internalise all these ideas about how to behave and act (seeing themselves from a clinical perspective) (Armstrong, 1995). Sociologists have noted
that there are now new social roles for people, namely health roles, in which
people are given more and more responsibility to maintain and improve their
own health by using various measures based on expert advice (Bunton & Burrows, 1995). This can be viewed as part of a move towards greater reflexivity
in subjectivity and the development of a new form of governance (Bunton &
Burrows, 1995).

Consequences for identity and subjectivity

Medicalisation processes affect the way in which people think about their own
health and their bodies (Hogle, 2001). Lupton has argued that the expectations for individuals to engage in this high degree of personal surveillance
over their bodies means that the body is now regarded as a 'site of toxicity'
(Lupton, 1995). Surveillance medicine provides a new form of identity, which
includes not only the dimensions of a three-dimensional body which may have
illness but, as Armstrong (1995) argues, a four-dimensional body in which
time becomes a crucial aspect. This gives us a new risk identity, where we
end up balanced between being healthy but always with the threat of future
illness. Being 'at risk' of a particular disease is experienced as a state of being
(Gifford, 1986).

Thus, the self becomes a site for concern about future health, a site which
needs to be continually and actively assessed and monitored for the future possibility of disease (Robertson, 2001). The individual is called on to self-govern
through endless self-examination, self-care and self-improvement (Petersen,
1996). There has been a clear ideological shift so that today's individuals should

take responsibility to protect themselves from risk, while the terms 'healthy' and 'unhealthy' have become signifiers of normal and abnormal identity and of moral worth (Petersen, 1996).

In short, 'co-operating with screening, testing, and interventions is a normalized way of staying normal' (Hogle, 2001, p. 329). By taking part in screening programmes such as for cholesterol screening, PSA testing and mammography, individuals enter 'at risk' states where they are not quite sick, but also not quite well (Press et al., 2000). Screening has been called the business of changing identities and producing patients (Thornton & Dixon-Woods, 2002). Becoming a patient has profound health, social, psychological and economic consequences.

Conclusions

Secondary prevention is an example of linear, mechanistic thinking that predominates health care, and Kaplan (2000) has argued that the benefits obtained from this approach to public health have been limited. For example, while identifying and treating cancer early may increase average life expectancy, this may also be achieved in other ways, such as investing to reduce cigarette smoking, building safer roads and strengthening legislation about firearms possession. With the advent of more and newer technology, it is likely that even more cases of various diseases will be identified: the more one looks for a disease, the more one finds, which may create the false appearance of epidemics (Kaplan, 2000). Given that many traditional population screening programmes have produced few measurable benefits, Kaplan argues that more resources should be devoted to primary prevention, changing behaviours and changing lifestyles.

Throughout the field of secondary prevention there is a need for further work by health psychologists. The technology is moving rapidly and yet the impacts of various forms of screening on individuals' psychological and physical well-being is not known. These procedures, which people are asked to undertake regularly (in order to be responsible and moral individuals), do have significant effects on subjectivities. This is where health psychologists can apply critical lenses and examine where the individual fits into secondary health promotion efforts, what such efforts mean to individuals (and for them), why they are hesitant about such efforts and how individuals make difficult decisions about preventive options. Finally, there are tensions between today's risk-conscious citizens who demand tests or screening programmes, and authorities who are becoming more cautious about the provisions of such tests and programmes. As Thornton and Dixon-Woods (2002) point out, resolving the tensions will come about not through 'authoritarian insistence on the "rightness" of the science', but through 'initiatives that engage with the public' (p. 725).

RECOMMENDED READING

Armstrong, D. (1995). The rise of surveillance medicine. *Sociology of Health and Medicine, 17,* 393–404. In this paper Armstrong argues that the surveillance of healthy populations is a new form of medicine that has emerged in recent decades. It is very useful in highlighting how the concept of risk is inherent in such an approach, and how this has consequences for individual identity.

Hogle, L. F. (2001). Chemoprevention for healthy women: harbinger of things to come? *Health: an Interdisciplinary Journal for the Social Study of Health, Illness and Medicine, 5,* 311–33. This paper provides a very good introduction to the whole area of chemoprevention. It examines how even the mere concept of chemoprevention would not work unless people are concerned about their risk of becoming ill. Excellent examples are employed to show how companies are advertising chemopreventive products to the public in the USA, and the implications of such advertising are discussed.

Kaplan, R. M. (2000). Two pathways to prevention. *American Psychologist, 55(4),* 382–96. In this paper Kaplan provides a very clear introduction to primary and secondary prevention approaches employed to enhance the health of the population. He argues strongly that although current health policy emphasises secondary prevention, this approach is problematic. He ends with a list of very clear messages to health psychologists about the effectiveness of primary prevention.

Lerman, C., Croyle, R. T., Tercyak, K. P. & Hamann, H. (2002). Genetic testing: psychological aspects and implications. *Journal of Consulting and Clinical Psychology, 70(3),* 784–97. This review provides a good account of what we currently know about the psychological effects of genetic testing. It considers and critiques the research in the field as a whole, and gives suggestions for where research should be heading.

Special issue on 'Screening for disease'. *Clinica Chimica Acta, 315* (2002). This special issue provides a range of papers which examines screening from different perspectives, including statistical, economic and ethical. All authors consider the evidence that screening is effective, and what may help to improve the effectiveness of screening processes.

5   Becoming ill

[M]ost people, doctors and scientists included, find it inherently easier to believe in the reality of apparently simple physical causes of disease (such as cholesterol, salt, bacteria or viruses) than to accept that mere thoughts or emotions can affect our health   (Martin, 1997, p. 11)

We must now turn our attention toward describing the biological and cultural mechanisms through which psychological processes contribute to disease onset and progression.   (Revenson, 1990, p. 86)

Learning objectives

This chapter reviews factors that influence people becoming ill. We examine research investigating whether psychological factors, such as stress and personality, play any role in disease causation. The chapter also provides a review of social and environmental factors that influence becoming ill, such as social support, gender and SES. Some physiological pathways through which psychosocial factors could influence physical health are described. Finally, we present examples of research which attempt to integrate this somewhat disjointed field through meta-level theorising. By the end of this chapter you should be able to:

- identify key psychological factors which influence people becoming ill;
- explain how sociocultural factors, such as gender, ethnicity and SES, need to be accounted for in any account of illness causation;
- provide an outline of how environments affect disease causation;
- discuss the implications of traditional health psychology research on psychological factors and disease processes;
- highlight the necessity for effective and integrative 'biopsychosocial' theorising in disease etiology.

A scientific discipline devoted to studying interrelationships between the physiological and psychological aspects of brain and behaviour. It is truly interdisciplinary, and includes researchers from a large number of disciplines like psychology, medicine, engineering, anatomy and neuroscience.

The cause or origin of a disease.

Does stress influence health? Are people who repress their emotions more likely to develop cancer? Is there a disease-prone personality? Is disclosing information about yourself good for your health? In this chapter we tackle the large area of **psychophysiology**, and examine the psychological and social factors that have been implicated in disease **etiology**. Whole volumes, numerous journals, hundreds of thousands of journal articles and countless textbooks have been devoted to this topic, not to mention the lucrative industry of self-help books that has developed out of this research (see sidebar 5.1). Needless to say, it is only possible to provide a general overview of this area of health psychology. The review we provide should enable you to critically evaluate the current state of play regarding whether psychological and social factors do directly influence physical health, by what pathways they may work and what health psychologists can contribute to this field.

At the turn of the twentieth century, viruses and other **pathogens** were seen to cause illness and disease (a perspective which remains predominant in biomedicine). When infectious agents were discovered, a great deal of attention was paid to the environment in order to eliminate such agents in Western societies. For example, water treatments were set up and vast improvements were made in food storage, sewage control, sanitation and waste disposal, as we noted in ch. 1. Thus, there was a reduction of infectious disease in the Western world. People became ill and died from slower developing chronic diseases such as heart disease, cancer and diabetes. Behavioural risk factors are involved in the etiology of these diseases, and hence attention has turned from focusing on environmental causes of disease to focusing on the individual and individual behaviour (Taylor *et al.*, 1997). This focus has included not only behaviour, but also psychological states, emotions, personalities and support networks, to name a few.

A disease-causing agent, such as a virus or bacterium, or other micro-organism.

> ## 5.1 Popular self-help books on how psychological factors influence physical health
>
> *Your body speaks your mind: understand how your emotions affect your health* Debbie Shapiro (1996), Piatkus Books
>
> *Heal your body A–Z: the mental causes for physical illness and the way to overcome them* Louise L. Hay (2001), Hay House
>
> *Deadly emotions: understand the mind–body–spirit connection that can heal or destroy you* Don Colbert (2003), Thomas Nelson Publishers
>
> *The mind–body connection: using the power of the brain for health, self-healing, and stress relief* Andrew Goliszek, PhD (2003), Healthnet Pr.
>
> *Journey to health: writing your way to physical, emotional and spiritual well-being* Lori J. Batcheller (2001), iUniverse.com

In the first part of this chapter we will examine some of the specific psychological factors that have been proposed as playing a direct role in causing illness and disease. Stress is the largest (and messiest) construct in this area and we will devote some of our attention to critically examining how it developed, how it has been used and what research says about it. We will then outline other psychological factors that may be involved in disease causation, including dispositional factors (optimism/pessimism, emotional inhibition, hostility), the well-documented type A behaviour pattern and negative emotions.

The next section of the chapter examines broader social and environmental factors which have been shown to play a role in disease. The major factor here is social support, but we will also examine gender, SES and ethnicity. Next we will turn our attention to the physiological pathways which may link pychosocial factors and disease. Any conclusions about whether psychosocial factors directly influence becoming ill must depend in large part on whether we can specify how they work physiologically. Therefore we will briefly review two areas that have generated a wealth of data, namely psychoneuroimmunology and cardiovascular reactivity. There are other physiological pathways but these are less developed and understood, and it is the former two areas which have received the most attention from health psychologists. Finally, we will critically consider the area as a whole and comment on the implications of the research to date, and ways to move our understandings forward.

Psychological influences on becoming ill

Stress

Stress has dominated research on the psychology–disease relationship. However, stress is a highly disputed concept and much debate has been generated about how stress should be defined (and indeed whether the concept is useful at all). In this section we will therefore briefly review the origins of the concept of stress, describe how it has been employed in research and summarise some of the critiques of stress research.

Confusion about what 'stress' actually refers to can be seen in the different ways people use the term in everyday language and in how it has been used in research. In research, stress has been conceptualised in three main ways:

- As a response, stress can be viewed as a person's physiological and psychological reactions to an event or situation ('I feel a lot of stress when I have to talk to an audience'). Here stress is internal to individuals, in that they may feel tension, distress, have a dry mouth, pounding heart and perspiration.
- As a stimulus, stress is viewed as something in the environment that leads to these reactions ('I am under a lot of stress'; 'I have a high-stress job'). Here stress is external to the individual. To help clarify these differences, external stress factors have been termed 'stressors', and researchers have examined the impact of a wide range of stressors on health, including natural disasters (earthquakes, tornadoes), major life events (getting divorced, losing one's job), minor events (daily hassles) and chronic circumstances (living in crowded conditions).
- As a process, stress is seen as a transaction between people and their environment. Here, stress involves interactions and adjustments between the person and the environment, and both are affected by each other.

Despite these confusions and debates about its value as a research construct, stress remains embedded in the field, and appears useful, if only as a shorthand way of defining an area of 'valid human experience and clinical importance' (Steptoe, 1998, p. 41).

Stress as a response

Early models viewed stress as a physiological response. In 1929 Cannon used the term stress to explain the body's response to an emergency. Perceiving danger leads to a physiological response which prepares the person (or animal) to attack the threat or run away from it. This response is known as the fight-or-flight response, and involves increased activity rate and arousal. It has both positive and negative consequences: positive because it mobilises the person (or animal) to react quickly, but negative because there are adverse health effects if the state of high arousal is prolonged.

Hans Selye is credited as being one of the earliest researchers to coherently link stress to illness directly, with his General Adaptation Syndrome (GAS) (Selye, 1956), developed through experimental studies with animals. The animals were subjected to a variety of intense negative experiences, such as being exposed to extremely hot and cold temperatures, X-rays, insulin injections and non-stop exercise over long periods of time. Through this work, Selye noted that the fight-or-flight response was only the first response when the body was subjected to long-lasting stress, and that two further physiological reactions occurred. Together the three reaction phases made up the GAS:

- alarm phase: the body activates systems to respond to the stressor, including nervous system arousal and changes in specific hormone levels;
- resistance phase: nervous, hormone and immune systems all remain in an elevated state as the body tries to adapt to the stressor;
- exhaustion phase: body fails to adapt, the immune system is weakened, there is limited resistance and physical damage can occur.

The GAS served as a paradigm for later conceptions of stress and has been hugely influential in stress research. Yet it is problematic for a number of reasons. First, it is based on a series of studies in which animals were taken out of their social context and subjected to painful, unavoidable and uncontrollable stimuli, making their relevance to everyday experiences questionable (Steptoe, 1998). Second, the GAS does not allow a role for psychological factors. Third, this model suggests that all stressors elicit the same response, but different stressors may lead to different physiological responses. Finally, generalising the results to humans fails to take into account the notion that people's responses to stress are influenced by factors such as their personalities, perceptions and previous experiences.

Stress as a stimulus

Major life events as stressors

The major life events paradigm focuses on stress as an environmental factor that is external to the individual, and assumes that adapting to major events leads to the same physiological responses as described in Selye's GAS. Therefore, experiencing such events may contribute to the initiation of disease and illness.

Research examining the effects of experiencing major life changes on disease has proceeded in a fairly logical manner. Specific measures of life events, and conceptualisations of stressors, have been refined and changed over the years. On the other hand, outcome measures have expanded from self-reports of illness, to clinical ratings of infectious disease, to immune system function.

This work began in the early 1960s, when two psychiatrists (Holmes and Rahe) were intrigued to observe that many of their clients who had experienced a number of major life events often became ill. They decided to test this idea empirically and developed a systematic way of measuring life events: the well-known Social Readjustment Rating Scale (SRRS, Holmes & Rahe, 1967). This measure was widely employed in the early life events research. It consisted of forty-three life events, ranging from those that are quite stressful (divorce, death of a spouse) to those that are not so stressful (vacations, minor violations of the law). Further, both positive and negative items were included, as positive events were also viewed as requiring adaptation. Typical studies with the SRRS asked participants to tick the items they had experienced in the previous twelve or twenty-four months. Studies generally show a relationship between increased life change as measured by the SRRS and more illness. However, although a consistent finding, the relationship between people's scores on the SRRS and illness are usually relatively weak (Chamberlain & Zika, 1990). The SRRS was later modified to include ratings of the severity of events, as well as their frequency.

Much of this early research employed self-report outcome measures of illness. This was problematic, given the overlap between predictor and outcome measures. Life events measures may assess the same thing as outcome measures (e.g. illness can be a major life event, and symptom checklists would measure symptoms of this illness), producing contamination between measures. Later work employed more objective outcome measures (such as visits to medical centres) and focused more on specific disease outcomes, particularly infectious disease, as well as immune system functioning. For example, job strain, unemployment, living near a nuclear reactor, imprisonment in a prisoner of war camp and burn-out at work have all been related to immune functioning (see Kiecolt-Glaser *et al.*, 2002a, for a review). Chronic and ongoing stressors, such as providing care for a spouse or parent with Alzheimer's disease, have also been consistently related to prolonged poor endocrine and immune functioning (e.g. Mills *et al.*, 1999; Vedhara *et al.*, 1999). One impressive study conducted an experiment to examine the relationship between life events and illness. In this study participants were required to stay at the Common Cold Unit in the UK, and objective measures of cold symptoms and immune responses were measured, as described in research in focus box 5.1 (Cohen *et al.*, 1991).

A number of criticisms have been made of the major life events paradigm (see, for example, Bartlett, 1998), some of which are outlined below:

5.1 The effect of psychological stress on infectious illness

Cohen, S., Tyrrell, D. A. J. & Smith, A. P. (1991). Psychological stress and susceptibility to the common cold. *New England Journal of Medicine*, *325*, 606–12.

A prospective study which examined whether psychological stress suppresses resistance to infection. Four hundred and twenty subjects stayed at the Medical Council's Common Cold Unit in Salisbury, UK. During the first two days they completed questionnaires assessing their psychological stress over the past year, including the number of events perceived as having a negative impact, the degree to which demands exceeded their ability to cope and their current negative affect. They also underwent blood tests for immune assessments. Participants were quarantined, either alone, or with one or two others. This quarantine took place two days prior to being given a viral challenge, and remained in place for two days afterwards. Specifically, participants were:

- given nasal drops infected with either one of five respiratory viruses (394 participants), or saline drops (26 participants);
- examined by a physician every day starting from two days before and every day for six days after the challenge;
- the number of cold symptoms each participant exhibited was recorded (e.g. sneezing, nasal stuffiness, postnasal discharge, sore throat, sinus pain). The number of tissues used by each participant each day was also counted (and weighed!);
- tests were conducted to examine whether the specific virus was isolated, or if there was an increase in antibodies designed to attack the virus.

Rates of infection

Of participants who were challenged with the virus 82 per cent caught a cold, while 19 per cent of those given saline also caught a cold.

Effects of psychological stress

The rates of both respiratory infection and clinical colds increased with increases in degree of psychological stress in a dose–response manner. Results for colds are displayed below.

These effects remained even when factors such as age, sex, education, allergic status, weight, number of subjects housed together and the season were statistically controlled. The researchers examined possible

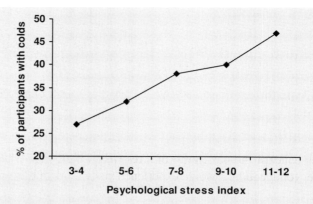

mediators of this observed stress–illness relationship, and found that smoking, alcohol consumption, exercise, diet, quality of sleep, white cell counts and total immunoglobulin levels did not explain the association between psychological stress and illness. Nor did personality factors, self-esteem or personal control introversion–extraversion.

Reflection

This study provided a stringent experimental test of the psychological stress–illness relationship, and found that stress was related to increased risk of infectious respiratory illness in a dose–response manner. These results are surprising given that they were obtained even when psychological stress was assessed with a questionnaire using somewhat crude standard measures, retrospectively, and summed over the previous twelve months.

- No consideration is given to the meaning the event has for the individual, which may be positive, negative or neutral. The individual does not passively respond to stressors.
- The amount of time that has elapsed since the event occurred may change an individual's perception of it, or its impact.
- How successfully the person dealt with the event might also change how it was recalled at a later stage.
- Events in the individual's life at the present time might affect how they retrospectively respond to a life-events measure for the previous year. For example, if a person has developed cancer and is asked to rate his or her experiences of particular events over the last year, the person's present state of mind is likely to influence recollection of that year. The person may be searching for events that might have caused the illness, and thus over-report negative events.

- Interactions between events are not taken into consideration in self-report life-events measures. For example, a divorce, change of job and a marriage would be seen as contributing to a stressful period of time, but the positive effects of one of these might cancel out the stressful effects of the others (Thoits, 1995).
- Life experiences have been conceptualised as one-off, short-term experiences. However, some may be ongoing and chronic, and thus may be different in their nature and have long-term ramifications (Aneshensel, 1992).

Other issues concern the patterning of stressors in particular social groups. For example, younger adults would experience many more of the major events that are given in rating scales of stress (e.g. employment, marriage, pregnancy) given their stage of life. Adverse events experienced by some of the elderly population, such as loss of independence and infirmities, are not included in such measures (Turner *et al.*, 1995). In addition, research suggests that it is not just the combination of events that may have health consequences, but also the sequence in which they occur (Thoits, 1995). Losing a social role that has been difficult for a long time may offset the consequences of other negative events. The patterning or configuration of specific events may also be important in predicting disease onset or susceptibility to infection, as Thoits (1995) has argued.

In summary, there is evidence to support a link between experiencing life events and subsequent illness. The research in this area is consistent and links continue to be found across varying illness outcomes. However, there is a need for further theory development concerning the nature of these stressors and how they relate to physical effects. Considering major events in terms of life stage, the positive effects of some events or pattern of events, the individual's reaction to events, the meanings individuals give to different events, how events may change individuals and how events change social situations and relationships are all possible avenues for future research. Furthermore, integrating this work with other potential influences on illness, as well as exploring pathways through which events operate to affect illness, also requires consideration and investigation.

Minor life events as stressors

Following research into major life events and illness, attention turned to the impact of more minor events, such as daily negative **hassles** (not being able to find a car park, being stuck in traffic) on physical health (Kanner *et al.*, 1981). The effects of experiencing positive minor events (**uplifts**) on health were also examined. Researchers proposed that the cumulative effect of minor daily events may have an impact on health and illness.

In 1987 Stone and colleagues published a prospective study which examined the relationship between undesirable events (hassles), desirable events (uplifts)

Relatively minor negative events.

Relatively minor positive events.

and experiencing symptoms of the common cold (Stone *et al.*, 1987). Seventy-nine participants filled in a questionnaire every day for twelve weeks, answering questions about the hassles, uplifts and symptoms they had experienced on that particular day, especially symptoms which indicated a respiratory illness such as a cold. Of the seventy-nine participants, thirty reported experiencing a cold episode during the twelve weeks. The researchers then examined the daily frequency of hassles and uplifts from one to ten days before each specific cold episode, and compared this with a set of control days for each participant which did not precede a cold episode (control days were matched for day of the week). There were significant decreases in uplifts three to four days before cold onset, and significant increases for hassles four to five days before cold onset. This lag between changes in uplifts and hassles and the onset of cold symptoms is consistent with the incubation period of a rhinovirus infection (the principal cause of the common cold): it usually takes two to five days between encountering an infection and experiencing symptoms. This was the first prospective, daily study to show a relationship between minor events and health, although the 'desirability dip' prior to cold onset has not been consistently replicated (e.g. Stone *et al.*, 1993).

Numerous studies have since shown an effect of hassles and uplifts on self-reported physical health (e.g. Lyons & Chamberlain, 1994), as well as on immune function (e.g. Stone *et al.*, 1994). Generally, hassles have been found to predict health outcomes better than major life events, and hassles that are more central to the person have a bigger impact on health (see Bartlett, 1998, for a review). Further, although the evidence for infectious illness is inconsistent, hassles have been found to be related to health outcomes whereas uplifts have been found to have no relationship. Other work has demonstrated that short-term, commonplace stressors such as the stress students experience prior to sitting an academic exam can affect immune system functioning (Kiecolt-Glaser *et al.*, 2002a). Exam stress has also been found to slow the rate of wound healing (Marucha *et al.*, 1998).

The same general criticisms made of the major life events research have been applied to research examining minor events. Dohrenwend and colleagues (1984) argued there was contamination between measures of daily hassles and outcome measures, with hassles scales containing many items which may reflect psychological symptoms (which are related to physical symptom reports). Modifications were made to minor event measurements (e.g. DeLongis *et al.*, 1988), although Watson and Pennebaker (1989) argued that any relationship between hassles and physical health reports may be due to **negative affect**, which is related both to reporting hassles and uplifts, and reporting physical symptoms.

In summary, the evidence clearly demonstrates an association between both major and minor life events and illness. However, whether this relationship is causal remains to be seen. Methodological issues such as contamination and

Undifferentiated subjective distress, including many negative mood states such as anxiety, depression, hostility.

reporting bias continue to be problematic. Further, a number of questionable assumptions about the nature of stress are made in this research. For example, individuals may not experience the particular major or minor life events that are measured as stressful. It is highly likely that stress is idiosyncratic and some inductive research supports this view (see research in focus box 5.2). Stress is also implicitly assumed to be external to the individual; yet how events are perceived by the individual is crucial in their interpretation. This brings us to the view of stress as a process between both the person and the environment.

Stress as a process

Lazarus proposed that stress involved a transaction between individuals and their external world. According to the transactional theory of stress, a stress response only came about if the individual saw a potential stressor as being stressful. Thus, stress is no longer internal or external to the individual, but rather is a relational concept which combines both person and environment at a higher level of analysis (Lazarus & Launier, 1978). Individuals are seen not as passive reactors to stressful events, but as psychological beings who respond actively to the outside world.

> **5.2**
>
> What would you do if you were stuck in a traffic jam on your way to an important appointment? Would you honk your horn, keep checking your watch and get angry? Or would you realise the uncontrollability of the situation, stay calm, turn on the radio, chill out and listen to music? People differ in their responses to events such as traffic jams (I hate them).

The important concepts employed in the transactional approach are **appraisal** and **coping**. According to this approach, two forms of appraisal occur when responding to a stressor, namely primary and secondary appraisal. In primary appraisal, the individual appraises the event itself, asking herself what it means to her. The event can be appraised in three ways:

A cognitive process which involves classifying or categorising information.

The cognitive and behavioural efforts that a person uses to manage demands that they perceive as exceeding their resources.

- irrelevant (is it relevant for me or not?);
- benign and positive (is it good?);
- harmful and negative (is it stressful?).

Once the stressor is viewed as potentially stressful, an individual engages in secondary appraisal. At this stage the individual evaluates the resources she has for coping, and whether these will be enough to meet the harm, threat or challenge of the stressor. For example, secondary appraisal judgements might be 'I can't do it, I'll fail' or 'I can do it if I work hard'. If people view an event as relevant to them and demanding, and simultaneously view their resources for coping with this event as insufficient, then they are likely to experience stress. Thus, whether a situation is defined as stressful depends on perceptions of coping resources. (Bartlett (1998) has cautioned against seeing appraisal as 'the' most significant psychological process involved in stress research, noting

5.2 The idiosyncratic construction of stress

Kirkcaldy, B. D., Athanasou, J. A. & Trimpop, R. (2000). The idiosyncratic construction of stress: examples from medical work settings. *Stress Medicine, 16*, 315–26.

This study investigated work stress among five individuals working in medical settings (theatre nurse, neurologist, psychiatrist, ophthalmology assistant, paediatrician). The researchers were interested in how individuals viewed stress in their work settings, what factors made them feel stressed and the meanings they gave to such stress. The study is ideographic in that it focuses on specific individuals, compared to nomothetic approaches which focus on groups and categories or levels of stress. An ideographic approach attempts to 'encapsulate the perspective of the persons being studied and leads to an interpretive praxis-based approach that promotes the contextual description of responses' (p. 316).

Repertory grid analysis

In this method there is an assumption that commonly named experiences, such as stress, may not necessarily involve any shared meanings. Kirkcaldy and colleagues asked their participants to identify factors or elements that led to stress in their jobs. Participants were then asked to compare and contrast stressful aspects of their working situation. Next, each element causing stress, and each stressful aspect of the work situation, were put into a matrix grid for each individual (aspects along the rows, and elements in the columns; see matrix below). Participants then were asked to rate each element on a ten-point scale for how much it related to each aspect of their work situation.

General stressful aspects of work (generated by participant)	Specific elements that caused stress at work (generated by participant)			
	Bad mood of boss	Co-worker problems	Holiday arrangements	Low salaries
Medicine vs low income	10	4	5	1
Poor vs rich	6	5	7	1
Impatient vs patient	6	6	6	10
Poor working climate vs understanding	2	1	5	6

The matrix displayed above is a part of the repertory grid for the ophthalmology assistant. It shows the elements she saw as causing stress in her job (in the columns), and which aspects of her working situation were most relevant to each of these. Themes can be identified by looking at the pattern of ratings, and statistical analyses can also be undertaken to calculate the degree of relationship within the ratings for elements and aspects.

Idiosyncratic perceptions of stress

Results are presented in the paper for each of the five individuals separately. They demonstrate convincingly that people working in different roles in medical settings have very individual ideas about what causes stress in their working context, as shown below.

Participant	Most stressful aspects of work
Theatre nurse	Cleanliness, tidiness, time pressures and the infection-oriented aspects of work, including blood sample infection
Neurological consultant	Insufficient personnel, inadequate resources, paperwork, monotonous tasks, patient overload and time pressures
Psychiatrist	Family pressures, phone interruptions, co-worker and office factors
Ophthalmology assistant	Critical of medical care, poor pay and financial situation, tangible aspects of job such as holidays, hours, pay
Paediatrician	Full waiting room, poor working climate, family aspects

Reflection

The study demonstrates that work stress is subjectively constructed, and that this is more important than any common meaning of the phenomenon. The repertory grid gives us an insight into personal meaning at a case level, rather than using pre-structured questionnaires (as employed by most previous research). However, they are a snapshot of an individual at one particular moment in time, and therefore are temporally fragile. Nevertheless, alternative methodologies such as this technique help give us insight into what stress means for individuals themselves.

that this is only one psychological process involved in stress and that others may also be important.)

The strategies people actually use to respond to stressful situations are termed their **coping processes**. Coping has been defined as the cognitive and behavioural efforts a person engages in to manage the internal and external demands of a situation that is appraised as taxing or exceeding the resources of the person (Folkman, *et al.*, 1986). This definition highlights the fact that coping efforts do not necessarily lead to a solution of the problem. So while

All of the efforts a person engages in when attempting to deal with a problem.

efforts can be aimed at correcting or solving the problem, they might also help people to change how they see the problem or help them to escape or avoid the situation. People vary in how they deal with stressful situations. For example, telling students they are about to fail a course if their grades do not improve may stimulate one student to do more work, yet stimulate another to initiate a long night of drinking so as not to have to think about it.

5.3

Examples of problem-focused coping: pulling out of the course you're about to fail, learning new skills, getting an extension on the bills you were supposed to pay last week.

Examples of emotion-focused coping: drinking alcohol or taking drugs, obtaining social support from friends, going out and exercising, watching television to distract attention from the problem.

Lazarus and Folkman (1984) distinguished two particular ways of coping. In problem-focused coping people try to reduce the demands of the stressful situation or increase their resources to deal with it. People tend to use problem-focused coping when they believe it is possible to change the resources or the demands of a situation. In emotion-focused coping, people aim to control their emotional responses to a stressful situation through behaviour and/or changing cognitions (how the situation is thought about and the meaning it has). People tend to use emotion-focused approaches when they believe there is nothing they can do to change the situation. However, both approaches may work together in managing stressful situations.

Reflections on stress and coping research

As we have already noted, stress is a multifaceted and highly disputed concept which continues to generate debates about definition and conceptualisation. Yet it remains an influential and embedded concept in academic research, and it seems difficult for researchers to let it go. Many aspects of daily life may have adverse effects on physiological functioning yet may not qualify as stress (McEwen, 1998). If we remain exclusively focused on conceptualising our work within a stress framework, we will not be able to investigate and explore other ways in which daily life and psychosocial factors affect our physiology and longer-term disease processes.

More ideographic approaches to the study of stress highlight that the meanings of stress are unique to the individual, challenging current thinking about stress. Kirkcaldy *et al.* (2000) conducted a study examining work stress in medical settings. They demonstrated that meanings of stress and perceptions of the situational determinants of stress differed considerably across different medical personnel. This study is described in research in focus box 5.2.

As we have noted, the concept of stress is not confined to the academic realm, and is used widely in public discourse on health and well-being (Lewig

& Dollard, 2001). Pollock (1988) has argued that the notion of 'stress' was picked up and employed in everyday life only once it began to be employed in academic theorising. People hold strong lay theories about what causes stress and what its consequences are, and these ideas can determine what people expect in terms of stress for themselves and others (Furnham, 1997). Pollock, developing arguments put forward by Young (1980), argues that stress is ideological. Meanings and ideas about stress (based on scientific discourse) support the dominant ideology, in that they are consistent with views about the social order and where the individual is located within that order (and what his or her responsibilities are) (Lewig & Dollard, 2001). In such discourse stress is primarily an individual phenomenon and individuals can 'appraise' their situations differently so that stress does not arise. Furthermore, stress is 'bad' as it causes illness, and the individual has a responsibility to avoid stress. This may in turn feed into a culture of blame, where individuals are held responsible for their illnesses because they did not heed warning signs about being stressed. Such a situation is ironic given that people in today's Western societies are working longer hours and finding less of a work–home balance than previously (Reich, 2002). These kinds of arguments highlight that stress is not simply an individual issue but a social and political one as well.

The literature on coping, as with the area of stress more generally, is confusing. Coping is used in different ways to mean different things (Bartlett, 1998), and there is concern about the ways in which coping is measured and employed in research. Steed (1998) highlights particular problems with coping scales, such as content confounding, the specific content of items, response formats and the time period for assessing coping. A recent review noted that there were over four hundred different ways of coping currently being assessed in the research (Skinner *et al.*, 2003). This review, as well as one conducted on coping research in childhood and adolescence (Compas *et al.*, 2001), concluded that given the inconsistency of coping conceptualisation and measurement and the use of diverse stressors and domains, it was extremely difficult to develop any kind of cohesive picture of the structure of coping. Skinner *et al.* (2003, p. 248) comment on what is required for such a structure:

> for the field to fulfil its potential, the structure of coping must span the conceptual space between individual instances of coping, which are the countless changing real-time responses people use in dealing with stressful transactions, and meaningfully link them to coping as an adaptive process, which mediate between stress and its long-term effects on mental and physical health and functioning.

Similarly, an earlier review also concluded that refinement of coping measures is required (Oakland & Ostell, 1996). Qualitative data highlight primary areas of coping that are ignored in coping scales, a point also noted by feminist researchers (see below). For example, in their qualitative study Oakland and Ostell (1996) found that 'efficacy of coping actions' and 'adequacy of external resources' were significant dimensions of coping that were not included in standardised scales, leading them to argue that the use of qualitative methodologies was essential to gain a better understanding of coping and its relationship to stress and health.

Traditional coping research has been also criticised because the coping construct is employed as though it was independent of gender, race and class (Banyard & Graham-Bermann, 1993; Greenglass, 1995). It is assumed that people have equal access to numerous resources, such as money, social support and so on. Feminist critiques highlight how coping paradigms do not provide us with information about experiences of diverse groups of women. As Banyard and Graham-Bermann (1993) have argued, much of the traditional research has examined women's coping only in relation to men's, and where it is different has interpreted it as inferior or lacking. They also highlight how coping paradigms pay insufficient attention to issues of power, and how power might act as a mediator between stress and coping. Clearly, having access to money, a strong social network and education all influence how an individual copes. Yet power is not discussed explicitly in this area of research.

Focusing solely on the individual limits how we understand coping processes. Collective coping occurs when people work together to overcome difficult events or experiences, and this form of coping may be particularly important for people from non-Western cultures (Singh & Pandy, 1985). Coping also involves thinking about how coping choices affect other people who are important (Fine, 1985). Thus, further theorising and qualitative research is required to provide more complete understandings of coping processes in different groups of people.

How might stress affect health?

How might stress, however defined, have an impact on physical health? There are three main ways through which stress might influence our health. First, feeling stressed affects our behaviour and our lifestyle: people who are more stressed engage in more unhealthy behaviours, such as smoking cigarettes, drinking more caffeine, eating poorly, drinking more alcohol, not taking regular exercise and so on (e.g. see Armeli *et al.*, 2001; Steptoe *et al.*, 1998). Second, as we will see in ch. 6, feeling stressed also affects how we perceive possible symptoms, whether we interpret them as symptoms and whether or not we take up the sick role. Finally, feeling stressed may have a direct effect on physiological functioning. Stress leads to a number of changes in the body's physical systems which can affect health, including the neuroendocrine, autonomic and immune systems (see Steptoe, 1998, for a review). Neuroendocrine systems are involved in many of the physiological changes associated with stress, and two of these systems in particular release hormones that may affect illness. High levels of catecholamines and corticos- teroids released during stress can affect the cardiovascular system, which can lead to **atherosclerosis, sudden death** and changes in immune functioning. The potential mechanisms through which stress might affect physical health will be reviewed later in the chapter.

The growth of plaques, or fatty patches, on the walls of the arteries. As the plaques build up, they narrow and harden the arteries, and this causes blood pressure to go up and increases the likelihood of a heart attack or stroke.

First, however, we will review some of the evidence for other psychological and social factors which have been found to relate to becoming ill. The stress model has strongly influenced how psychological and social factors have been conceptualised in this area. These factors are viewed as relating to physical health primarily because they protect a person from stress, or put a person at risk of stress. Most stress models now state that stress leads to illness where there is an existing vulnerability. This vulnerability may occur at a biological level (e.g. some individuals may be predisposed to show a much greater physiological reaction to stress than others), or it may occur at a social level (e.g. some individuals may be vulnerable because they are materially disadvantaged). Vulnerability may also occur at a psychological level, so that people vary in how they cope with stress as a result of their dispositions, or some people may be more likely to see positive outcomes in the future and experience more positive emotions.

Death which results from a cardiac arrest, with the heart ceasing to function as it should. The death is unexpected and occurs within minutes of symptoms appearing. The most common reason for sudden death is coronary heart disease.

Dispositional influences

A great deal of research has focused on the role of personality and dispositional influences in the stress process. Different personality characteristics have been investigated to see whether certain characteristics lead a person to be more vulnerable (or resistant) to different stressors (Lok & Bishop, 1999).

Optimism and pessimism

People who are pessimistic have a tendency to view future outcomes negatively. Such a pessimistic outlook on life has been related to a number of health outcomes, particularly disease progression (Scheier & Bridges, 1995). A 'pessimistic explanatory style' is viewed as a cognitive personality variable reflecting how people tend to attribute causes to life events (Peterson & Seligman, 1984), and consists of three dimensions:

* internality (it's all my fault) versus externality (it's not me);
* stability (it will last forever) versus instability (this will soon pass);
* globality (everything will be affected) versus specificity (everything else will be okay).

People who habitually explain events pessimistically have been found to have poorer physical health over thirty-five years (Peterson *et al.*, 1988) and higher rates of mortality over thirty years than more optimistic people (Maruta *et al.*, 2000). Optimists have been found to adjust better to life transitions than pessimists, partially because they perceive greater social support and reinterpret events or issues in a positive manner, and therefore experience less stress (Brissette *et al.*, 2002). Over the longer term experiencing less stress may influence physical health.

Type A behaviour pattern

The Type A behaviour pattern (TABP) was developed in an attempt to find psychological risk factors for coronary heart disease (CHD). Two cardiologists, Friedman and Rosenman, developed the TABP based on their clinical experience with patients. They noticed that their heart patients had similar characteristics, such as competitiveness, achievement orientation, a strong sense of time urgency, impatience and easily aroused hostility. All of these attributes became part of the TABP. The construct is typified by the view of the high achieving business man who is aggressively struggling to achieve more and more in less time.

The Western Collaborative Group Study was the first large, long-term study investigating TABP and CHD (Rosenman *et al.*, 1975). It involved 3,154 men, mostly white, non-manual workers, aged between 39 and 59 years. At the start of the study each participant took part in a structured interview to assess Type A behaviour. None of the men had CHD at the beginning of the study. In the following eight and a half years, men with TABP had an increased incidence of CHD compared to their more laid back counterparts (type Bs). These results were astonishing and impressive. Even when other risk factors were controlled for (e.g. parental history of heart disease, high blood pressure, lipids, high cholesterol, diabetes, cigarette smoking, lack of education, lack of exercise), Type As were twice as likely to have developed CHD and to have died from CHD than Type Bs. Yet relative risk tells us nothing about causality: the risk of developing CHD in this study was twice as high for Type As as Type Bs, but not all Type As developed heart disease.

Following the Western Collaborative Group Study numerous other large, prospective studies were carried out. Their findings have been inconsistent, and have led to questions about the value of the TABP as a construct. For example, in the Multiple Risk Factor Intervention Trial (MRFIT; Shekelle *et al.*, 1985), 13,000 men were followed (aged 35–57) for seven years and Type A did not predict mortality or myocardial infarction (MI or heart attack). This early research into the TABP was criticised for its focus on men, and men in high-status positions. It is interesting to note with hindsight that the men making decisions about funding large-scale projects such as these were exactly those who had traditional risk factors for CHD. Later research conducted with both male and female participants showed similarly inconsistent results.

So what might be the reasons for these inconsistent results with the TABP? One major limitation of many studies has been the way in which the construct was assessed. Not all studies employed the Type A structured interview, but rather used questionnaire measures of Type A (Siegman, 1994) which did not pick up specific aspects of TABP, such as behavioural style. Further, the relationship between Type A and CHD may be limited to a certain group of people and/or a certain subset of Type A behaviour. Also, it appears that not all components of Type A are important in increasing the likelihood of CHD. Negative emotions (Booth-Kewley & Friedman, 1987), especially hostility (Smith & Ruiz, 2002), have been posited as key aspects of the TABP that may lead to disease. The inconsistent results, and the inconsistency between findings that rates of CHD are actually higher in people of lower SES (than in the middle-class, ambitious and striving businessman), led Carroll (1992) to conclude that it may be more beneficial to talk about Type A environments rather than Type A individuals.

Hostility and anger

Hostility has been defined as a general trait involving 'a devaluation of the worth and motives of others, an expectation that others are likely sources of wrongdoing, a relational view of being in opposition toward others, and a desire to inflict harm or see others harmed' (Smith, 1994, p. 26). Anger refers to an unpleasant emotion which varies in intensity from mild irritation to rage (Miller *et al.*, 1996). There is now a large body of prospective evidence which links anger and hostility to coronary heart disease (CHD), including incidence of CHD, clinical events such as heart attacks and angina and mortality rates from CHD (Smith & Ruiz, 2002). Evidence for the effects of anger and hostility on other diseases, such as cancer, is not so well established (Garssen, 2004; Scheier & Bridges, 1995). A meta-analysis examining the findings of forty-five studies investigating the relationship between hostility and physical health drew much the same conclusion: that hostility is an independent risk factor for CHD (Miller *et al.*, 1996). Further, the effects of anger and hostility are similar to the size of other risk factors, such as smoking and hypertension (Booth-Kewley & Friedman, 1987; Miller *et al.*, 1996).

The pathways through which hostility and anger affect CHD are not fully understood, although large cardiovascular system responses to stress, particularly interpersonal stress, may be important (see Smith & Ruiz, 2002). Compared to people low in hostility, people who are high in hostility have also been found to display poorer immune function following an episode during which they disclosed personal information about themselves. This may be because they find such disclosure more threatening (Christensen *et al.*, 1996).

Consedine and colleagues argue that we need to be cautious about the hostility–disease findings for a number of reasons (Consedine *et al.*, 2004). First, there are a substantial number of null findings. Second, we do not yet know if the findings occur across different genders, ethnicities and ages. Again, the research continues to concentrate on white, middle- and upper-class men, therefore we know little about the effects of hostility on health among people from different SES backgrounds and people of different ethnicities. As for gender, some studies have demonstrated that hostility affects health outcomes in women as well as men, while some show a relationship in men but not women. Some studies show inverse relationships between hostility and disease in women (see Consedine *et al.*, 2004, for a review; also Kivimaki *et al.*, 2003). Third, there is a lack of theoretical frameworks to account for inconsistent findings. Consedine and colleagues have suggested that gender differences in emotional experience and expression may account for the inconsistent findings. Specifically, they provide initial and exciting findings showing that anxiety may play a key role for women in the development of coronary diseases, while hostility plays a key role for men.

Negative mood

Negative affect has been related to both subjective and objective health outcomes. Negative affect is the tendency to experience negative moods, and this has been related to symptoms of respiratory illness (e.g. Cohen *et al.*, 1995). Depression and depressed mood have been associated with recovery from and mortality rates after a MI, as well as with the onset of new cardiac events. Some evidence also exists showing that depression is related to how quickly the HIV virus progresses (see Scheier & Bridges, 1995, for a review). Experiencing negative mood has been related to poorer immune function compared to experiencing positive mood, and across a number of studies psychological distress is associated with the down-regulation of immunity (see Kiecolt-Glaser *et al.*, 2002a, for a review).

The many findings showing that negative moods and emotions are associated with poorer health outcomes have been integrated conceptually by Scheier and Bridges (1995). They begin with the assumption that people's behaviour is usually goal directed and that goals give meaning to what we do in our behaviour and our lives. However, when people are thwarted in achieving their goals, they can either disengage and give up or may feel depressed, which may lead to a more generally negative outlook. Becoming ill can disrupt attainment of goals, and may lead to negative emotions, which in turn may have an adverse effect on progression or recovery from the illness (see ch. 9).

Emotional inhibition

Suppressing your emotions is popularly believed to be damaging for your health. The idea of a cancer-prone personality developed in the 1970s; it was believed that people who repress their emotions and are not forthcoming in any emotional sense were more likely to get cancer. Sontag (1991) argued that such labelling had no basis in fact, and that the victim blaming actually did more harm than good to people who became ill. Some evidence shows that emotional suppression is associated with increased incidence of cancer (see Scheier & Bridges, 1995, for a review). However, in an extensive meta-analytic review, Garssen (2004) recently examined whether psychological factors were involved in cancer development. He concluded that 'there is not any psychological factor for which an influence on cancer development has been convincingly demonstrated in a series of studies' (p. 315), although the 'most promising' constructs were helplessness and repression. Researchers have also been investigating whether suppressing emotions is bad for health more generally.

The largest body of evidence on this matter has come from Pennebaker and colleagues (Francis & Pennebaker, 1992; Pennebaker, 1992; Pennebaker *et al.*, 1987). In a number of studies, these researchers investigated whether disclosing traumatic experiences had any health benefit. The idea behind this work is that inhibiting one's emotions is hard work: it impairs information processing through holding back major thoughts and feelings, and therefore means that the individual cannot assimilate events (Lok & Bishop, 1999). A typical study would involve university students who were asked to come to a psychology laboratory and to sit on their own for about an hour and write about a particular topic. In the experimental group, participants were asked to write about a traumatic experience that they had not discussed with anybody previously. In the control group, participants were asked to write about mundane topics, such as what they had done that morning or the previous day. Participants had to attend and write on three consecutive days. Following this, self-report health measures were taken at various points during the next three to six months, and visits to the university medical centre were recorded (with the informed consent of the participants).

Results generally show that participants who wrote about a traumatic experience showed fewer physical health problems and fewer visits to the medical centre over the following months than the control group. Researchers have also found differences in immune functioning between participants who disclosed traumatic events and those who did not (e.g. Esterling *et al.*, 1994), suggesting that inhibiting strong emotions may influence disease via immune processes (Petrie *et al.*, 1995). The important component of disclosure for physiological and health outcomes may be how much the disclosure enables people to give meaning to the event, make sense of it, cognitively reorganise it and stop avoiding it (Esterling *et al.*, 1994).

A recent **Cochrane review** of sixty-one studies in this field concluded that the impact of interventions involving emotional disclosure on physical health was not conclusive (Meads *et al.*, 2003). No evidence was found for the influence of emotional disclosure on objectively assessed health centre visits. The review also highlighted a number of problems with this field, including small sample sizes, poor reporting and little evidence of a mechanism through which physical health benefits could be achieved. In sum, the report suggests that 'the current evidence available has not demonstrated the effectiveness of this brief emotional disclosure intervention' (p. 38).

A rigorous, well-developed method of reviewing a number of studies (usually in the medical field) on a particular topic.

Religious belief/spirituality

In recent decades there has been a resurgence of interest in examining whether spiritual or religious factors influence physical health outcomes. Associations have been documented between religious and spiritual factors, such

Table 5.1 How might religion affect physical health?

Through psychosocial pathways, such as having stronger social support, positive relationships, and good coping mechanisms

Through psychobiological pathways, such as the direct effects of positive psychological states derived from religion (e.g. faith, hope, inner peace) on immune and endocrine functioning

Through psychobehavioural pathways, such as changing person characteristics (character, willpower, self-efficacy, focused attention, enhanced motivation) which influence taking up and maintaining healthy behaviour

Through 'superempirical' pathways, such as prayer or distant healing, that may operate in a way that is beyond current scientific understanding

Derived from Oman & Thoresen (2002).

as religious beliefs and church attendance, and better physical health and mortality rates (see Matthews *et al.*, 1998, for a review). Seeman and colleagues have recently reviewed studies examining the physiological processes which may mediate the relationship between religious belief and health (Seeman *et al.*, 2003). They note that with recent advances in study designs and methodologies, firmer conclusions can be drawn about this association. Their review concluded that the evidence does support a positive link between religious belief/spirituality and physiological processes that are related to health and disease, particularly cardiovascular system functioning, but also neuroendocrine and immune functioning. Seeman and colleagues also highlighted the need for further strengthening of methodologies in this area, and for a focus on aspects of spirituality other than meditation. Oman and Thoresen (2002) provide some conceptual overview and clarification of this field, reviewing four main (and different) pathways through which religion may influence physical health, as shown in table 5.1.

Summarising psychological factors involved in illness

There is a vast literature examining the effects of psychological factors on physical health, and we have only touched on some of the key issues here. While the evidence is promising, and justifies further work in this area, much of the research has been atheoretical and has proceeded in a largely haphazard fashion (Scheier & Bridges, 1995). The disjointed nature of the field has made it difficult to theorise broadly across findings, and the attention devoted to CHD has limited the study of other illnesses and disease. It is also worth keeping in mind that certain individual psychological factors may be involved in more than one disease, leading to a 'disease-prone personality'. This question was examined by Booth-Kewley and Friedman (1987) a number of years ago, and they concluded that evidence for such a personality is weak. The evidence suggests that it is not so much a disease-prone personality but a way of being in the world that is negative, pessimistic, gloomy and with depressed and hostile mood that is pathogenic for physical health. As we will see in the next section, negative personal relationships and interpersonal conflict also seem to be associated with poor health outcomes.

Individual factors do not exist in isolation, nor are they independent of one another. They develop and exist within a social and cultural world, and a broader perspective is required to develop theories and models which may significantly advance research in this field. For example, employing a perspective that covers the lifespan of a person from birth through childhood, teenage years, adulthood and older age may be one useful way to account for the effect of dispositional factors on health and disease, although such a perspective has been relatively absent in the literature (see Smith & Spiro, 2002).

Social and environmental factors that influence becoming ill

In this section we review some of the social and environmental factors that may play a role in disease etiology. Many studies in this area are from the field of epidemiology, where large community-based samples are employed and followed over a number of years to establish predictors of mortality and ill health. Researchers seek to document which sections of the population have greater incidence of disease and mortality rates, and what specific factors may put them at risk.

Social support

Large epidemiological studies have demonstrated an association between what is called 'social integration' and physical health, including mortality rates (Berkman, 1995). Despite the variations in how social integration or social support have been measured, evidence consistently demonstrates that people with a high quantity and sometimes a high quality of social relationships have lower mortality rates. On the other hand, social isolation seems to be a major risk factor for death from a number of causes in animals and humans (Berkman, 1995).

One of the influential studies in this field was conducted in Alameda County, California (Berkman & Syme, 1979). Over 4,500 people, aged between 30 and 69, were asked about four aspects of their social and community ties: whether or not they were married, their contacts with extended family and friends, their church membership and their formal and informal group associations. They were then followed for over nine years. Results demonstrated that people who

Table 5.2 Some types of functional social support

Emotional support	Receiving expressions of empathy, caring and concern. These provide a sense of comfort, reassurance, belongingness, and of being loved
Esteem support	Receiving expressions of positive regard, including encouragement, agreement with feelings and so on. This builds feelings of self-worth, competence and feelings of being valued
Instrumental support	Receiving direct assistance, such as being lent money, having help with work or childcare
Informational support	Receiving advice, suggestions, directions and feedback
Appraisal support	Receiving information which helps with self-evaluation and appraising an event or situation. It also might help with learning what resources might be used to cope with the situation, or how the situation could be dealt with

Based on Stroebe (2000).

The existence and quantity of social relationships the individual has with others. Measures of structural support are relatively objective and include such matters as whether the individual is married or not, the number of close friends, the number of organisations s/he belongs to, whether s/he attends church regularly, etc.

The quality of social relationships, and the functions they serve for the individual. There are many different types of functional support, including emotional, instrumental, informational and appraisal. Measures of functional support generally ask individuals to rate their perception of whether they have people available who could give different forms of support in times of need, and also whether they actually receive particular forms of support.

had fewer social ties were more likely to die during the nine years than people with more social ties. More specifically, people with fewest social ties died at rates that were approximately twice as high as people with the highest social ties. These effects were not due to SES, health status at the beginning of the study or the practice of health behaviours.

The observed relationships between social integration and mortality and health are impressive, but are primarily correlational – cause and effect cannot be concluded. It may be that the relationship operates in reverse, so that illness affects one's social support. Becoming ill, especially with a chronic disease, affects how people relate to members of the family and other possible sources of support. However, many of the major epidemiological studies began with samples who were healthy (although they may have had subclinical levels of disease). Further, the observed relationship between social support and health could be explained by a third factor, such as social class or personality, which may cause both low social support and ill health. However, many of these factors have been statistically controlled for and the association between social integration and health remains (Berkman, 1995).

Psychologists have focused particularly on social support, and have attempted to tease out the many different forms of social support that exist. A distinction is made between **structural social support** (the existence, quantity and form of social ties), and **functional social support** (the functions that support provides to the individual). Some of the types of functional support employed in research are provided in table 5.2. Different components of social support have been related to a number of different health outcomes, including the experience of physical symptoms and adjustment to illness (see Cohen & Wills, 1985; Matud et al., 2003; Schwarzer & Leppin, 1989). Simply perceiving that one has social support seems to be particularly important. In terms of predicting health outcomes, perceiving that you have support is better than actually receiving that support (Matud et al., 2003).

The literature on both social integration and social support assumes that the population is homogeneous, and the single term 'support' might be too broad to include all of the different ways that people seek help and receive advice from others. Social support might work differently among different sections of the population. Women generally mobilise more varied social support in times of stress, have more emotionally intimate relationships than men and also provide more effective and frequent social support than men. Women seem to have a larger number of close relationships, although men have larger social networks, and women tend to perceive social support globally, whereas men tend to perceive emotional support and instrumental support separately (Matud *et al.*, 2003). Questions concerning why men and women differ in social support, how these differences arise and whether they have differential effects on health have not yet been adequately studied (Matud *et al.*, 2003). Gender differences in social support may well arise from socialisation experiences and social and occupational roles (Eagly, 1987). Finally, studies show that social strain and social isolation are distinct concepts, and may have effects which are independent of social support (Smith & Ruiz, 2002).

How does social support affect health?

It is currently unclear how the existence of close relationships affects health. Two theories have been proposed about the nature of this relationship, as outlined below:

1 The main effects model: stress is seen to influence health directly, and stress is only one of several factors that impact on health. Thus social support and social relationships enhance health and well-being independently of stress, and social support is beneficial to health during non-stressful times as well as stressful times.
2 The stress-buffering model: psychological stress is seen to have a pathogenic effect on health, and social support is beneficial because it limits this effect. Having good functional social support might make a difference at such times because it helps reinterpret the stressful event so that it is no longer viewed as stressful, or through provision of resources such as money, which helps coping with the stressor.

Cohen and Wills (1985) reviewed evidence to demonstrate that structural measures of social support tended to have main effects on health outcomes, whereas functional measures of social support were more likely to show buffering effects.

There are a number of pathways by which social support may have an impact on physical health, including:

- via behaviour: through promoting healthy behaviours, through encouragement, modelling and peer influence. Positive relationships are related to
  healthy behaviours (see Cohen, 1988, for a review);
- via psychological well-being: social support improves self-esteem and low-
  ers distress, which in turn affects physical health (Berkman *et al.*, 2000);
- via self-identity: being part of a social network may also help towards identity
  and defining oneself in relation to others. Totman (1987) argues that not
  engaging in social activities, including those activities that occur in isolation
  but are socially validated, can be detrimental for health. Being part of a
  group also provides a shared sense of reality and often provides a strong set
  of social rules by which people live their lives.

There is accumulating evidence that social support also has direct effects on
physiological processes. People with fewer social ties and/or poorer levels of
social support have been found to be more susceptible to respiratory viruses
(Cohen, 1995; Cohen *et al.*, 1997) and have lower natural killer cell activity
while experiencing chronic stress (see Uchino *et al.*, 1996). Interestingly, many
studies have found that people with hostile or abrasive marital relationships
(including new couples and couples who had been together many years) show
pervasive differences in endocrine and immune function compared to people
with more positive marital relationships (see Kiecolt-Glaser *et al.*, 2002a, for a
review). Supportive, close relationships are related to better immune function
(Uchino *et al.*, 1996), although as Kiecolt-Glaser and colleagues (2002a) note,
'close personal relationships that are chronically abrasive or stressful may
provoke persistent immune dysregulation' (p. 539).

Social support also affects cardiovascular reactions to stress. A growing
body of evidence highlights that social support is beneficially related to the
cardiovascular system (Uchino *et al.*, 1996). Individuals with higher perceived
social support, as well as those who have social support enhanced through
manipulation in a laboratory setting, generally show lower cardiovascular
responses to stress (Smith & Ruiz, 2002). Emotional support seems to be particularly important here compared to instrumental or other forms of support
(Berkman, 1995; Uchino *et al.*, 1996).

While the social integration and health results remain consistent and con-
vincing, relatively little theoretical work has been posited for integrating and
conceptualising the findings. Furthermore, little serious consideration has been
given to the social, environmental and cultural contexts in which social networks form and have their physical and psychological effects (Berkman *et al.*,
2000). Berkman and colleagues provide an overview of some of the theoretical
orientations from different academic disciplines that may assist in moving the
field forward. Their work is impressive in attempting to locate social integration into a broader societal perspective, using a cascading causal process that
includes the 'macro-social to the psychobiological processes that are dynami-
cally linked together to form the processes by which social integration affects

health' (p. 181). Some of these ideas are provided in fig. 5.1. It seems that provision of social support is only one way through which social integration may influence health, and more work is required to examine alternative pathways and explanations for the association (Berkman *et al.*, 2000).

Gender

There is a saying in epidemiology that 'women get sicker but men die quicker'. While women live longer than men, by an average of about seven years, they have higher morbidity. Women report more illness than men, have more days off work due to illness than men, take more medication than men and see doctors and other health care workers more often (Verbrugge, 1985). Women also have higher rates of acute illnesses and most nonfatal chronic conditions, including obesity, diabetes, anaemia, respiratory and gastrointestinal problems.

There has been a great deal of speculation as to why women become ill more than men do. It has been suggested that these differences are more to do with the social positions that men and women occupy than biological sex *per se*. For example, it has been argued that women's lives and the roles they occupy give rise to more stress than men's lives do (and that this stress leads to illness). Women tend to have more non-life-threatening illnesses as a result of the stresses of routinised jobs, childcare, caring for elderly parents and the 'double shift' of being in paid work as well as doing the majority of housework (see Lorber, 1997). When both partners work, women carry out more childcare and housework, in all social classes. A number of surveys from a range of countries show that women do more domestic work than men, and that the division is made on sex-based lines (see Lee, 1998, for a good review of this area). Taken together, findings show that women are engaged in more social roles, do more unpaid work, and when paid do a 'double shift' of work and housework, all of which can have a negative effect on women's physical health (Lee, 1998).

There may be social structural reasons for women experiencing more illness than men. Women are socially disadvantaged in terms of education, income and political influence. Even though gender-equality laws have been passed in most developed countries, these have had little effect on women's status or quality of life (Lee, 1998). Extensive research demonstrates that, compared with men, women are disadvantaged when it comes to type of occupation, pay and work hours (Annandale & Hunt, 2000). In the USA disparities continue to exist between men and women, particularly women from minority groups, in terms of illness rates, educational attainment, employment and income (Strobino *et al.*, 2002). As we discuss later in the chapter, the social and economic standing of individuals in society has profound influences on physical health in a variety of ways (Cooper, 2002). Any attempt to influence the status of women's health must address these fundamental disparities (Strobino *et al.*, 2002).

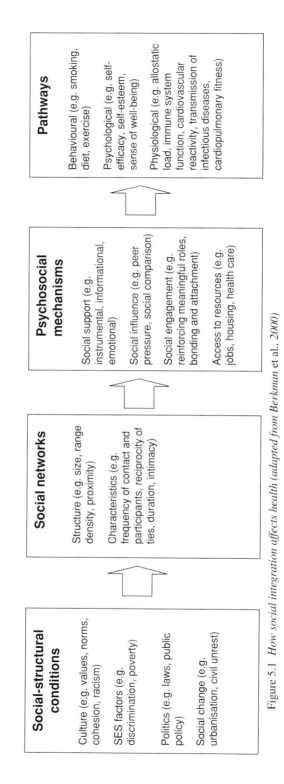

Figure 5.1 *How social integration affects health (adapted from Berkman et al., 2000)*

Social-structural conditions

Culture (e.g. values, norms, cohesion, racism)

SES factors (e.g. discrimination, poverty)

Politics (e.g. laws, public policy)

Social change (e.g. urbanisation, civil unrest)

Social networks

Structure (e.g. size, range density, proximity)

Characteristics (e.g. frequency of contact and participants, reciprocity of ties, duration, intimacy)

Psychosocial mechanisms

Social support (e.g. instrumental, informational, emotional)

Social influence (e.g. peer pressure, social comparison)

Social engagement (e.g. reinforcing meaningful roles, bonding and attachment)

Access to resources (e.g. jobs, housing, health care)

Pathways

Behavioural (e.g. smoking, diet, exercise)

Psychological (e.g. self-efficacy, self-esteem, sense of well-being)

Physiological (e.g. allostatic load, immune system function, cardiovascular reactivity, transmission of infectious diseases, cardiopulmonary fitness)

Ethnicity

As we noted in ch. 1, rates of disease and mortality differ by ethnicity, and in Western societies people from minority groups often show higher incidence of disease and higher mortality rates. In the USA, on virtually whatever health index you choose to look at, African Americans have worse outcomes (see Hayward *et al.*, 2000). Differences in SES and poverty levels account for some of the observed health differences in ethnicity, but not all (see Williams & Collins, 1995). These differences in health outcomes are not due to genetics or biology, or to health risk behaviours, or to the ability to transform socioeconomic resources into good health (Hayward *et al.*, 2000).

Ethnicity has been a neglected dimension in studies comparing men's and women's health (Cooper, 2002). Unequal social relations (including discrimination, exclusion and exploitation) have consequences for well-being and physical health, and women from ethnic minority groups may experience 'multiple discrimination' (Cooper, 2002). SES and ethnicity both strongly determine where and how people live, in which environments, and in which social contexts. Ethnicity, SES and gender do not operate in isolation but interact to affect health. In their review of these factors in child health, McCarthy and colleagues (2000) conclude that these factors are often assumed to affect disease through genetics or biology. Yet evidence demonstrates that they all have strong social dimensions which clearly affect physical health and well-being. Therefore, they recommend that studies which examine the effects of ethnicity, gender and SES on health also include information on the underlying social mechanisms which might explain the associations.

SES

Again, as we discussed in ch. 1, it does not matter how SES is measured (as education, income, occupation or a combination of these factors); results with physical health outcomes remain robust and consistent. The research is extensive and documents that health outcomes are poorer for people in lower SES groups than others. Health outcomes include acute and chronic conditions, as well as morbidity and mortality. Furthermore, this relationship is linear, showing that it is not simply the difference between the healthy rich and the unhealthy poor: health outcomes improve as one moves higher along the SES gradient (see Adler & Snibbe, 2003; Carroll & Sheffield, 1998; Kelly *et al.*, 1997).

Why is SES so strongly related to health? Clearly people who live in poorer environments have more chronic stress than others, including exposure to crime, poorer public transport, poorer recreational facilities, more exposure to physical toxins such as pollutants, hazardous wastes, pesticides, greater crowding and noise, and greater risks due to substandard housing (see Taylor *et al.*, 1997, for a review). However, the gradient between social class and health status tells us that health improves as social class increases. This undermines the proposition that the relationship with health is primarily the result of material deprivation and stressful living conditions. SES affects the health of middle classes (their health is poorer than the health of the upper classes), so rather than deprivation *per se* it seems to be the more general conditions under which people live that are important.

The mechanisms through which SES affects physical health are not well understood (Adler & Snibbe, 2003). Psychological factors are clearly involved in mediating this relationship and, as Carroll and Sheffield (1998) point out, some of the key pathways must be physiological. Conceptualisations of potential physiological pathways to explain the relationship between SES and health have been dominated by notions of stress, and we have noted problems with this construct earlier in the chapter. Researchers have argued that the stress encountered in low SES environments leads to the development of certain behavioural, cognitive and affective tendencies which over time may lead to disease. Kelly and colleagues (1997) describe a more general physiological process: 'there must exist a process of "biological embedding" wherein life experiences condition individual biological responses' (p. 438), with life experiences including those in early childhood, those in daily life and those that arise from one's place in the social environment. Others also emphasise that a focus on the lifecourse is critical, alongside an examination of patternings of adverse physical and psychosocial factors (Carroll *et al.*, 1996). One recent study has examined lifecourse predictors of SES differences in mortality in men at midlife. Findings demonstrated that differences in mortality were only partially predicted by parental home, with educational, marital and employment paths in youth having a much greater effect (Pensola & Martikainen, 2004).

Environments

Social support, gender, ethnicity and SES all contribute to the environments in which we live. These environments have direct effects on health and disease. As Taylor *et al.* (1997) note, the poor and African Americans living in the USA have a higher rate of developing certain kinds of cancers as a result of differential exposure to toxins within their work or home environments. The important point to note here is that although research attention and funds have focused heavily on individual factors which may influence illness and disease, individuals live within a social context which includes family, peers, work, community, society, and culture. Figure 5.2 shows the relationships between the social environments in which people live that are important for physical health.

Environments are influential in many of the factors already discussed in this chapter. Taylor and colleagues (1997) have reviewed a number of ways in which environments can lead to illness and disease. Environments influence:

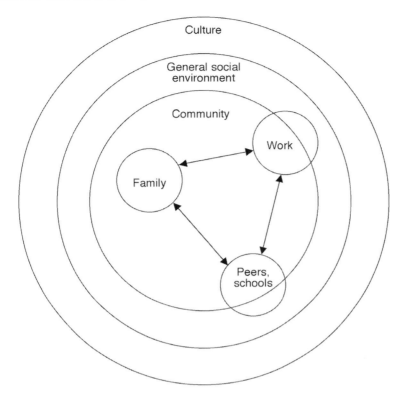

Figure 5.2 *Environments that have health implications. Family, work and peer groups are nested within community, larger social (including SES and race) and cultural environments (adapted from Taylor et al., 1997)*

- mental health and negative emotions, which play a role in disease etiology;
- the development of coping strategies through families and peers;
- choices of coping strategies. Coping with stressful events or experiences in a positive manner (through finding meaning in them, for example) influences health;
- health habits, which are learned, encouraged, developed in social contexts;
- availability of resources to engage in healthy behaviour, such as obtaining a good diet and being able to get regular exercise (which is difficult if you live in areas with high crime and low income).

In concluding their review of unhealthy environments, Taylor *et al.* (1997) comment that negative health outcomes are related to social and cultural contexts which threaten personal safety, limit the ability to develop social ties, and which are characterised by violent, abusive or conflictual relationships. They also make the important point that the effects of such environments work across the lifespan, from before birth to old age.

In summary, the evidence reinforces the importance of our social world for staying healthy and becoming ill. This section shows that disease and mortality rates vary by social relationships, social position, gender and ethnicity. These factors do not operate in isolation, but jointly influence how, where and with whom people live. While these broad social factors are often assumed to affect health and illness directly through biological or genetic pathways, evidence strongly suggests that it is their social dimensions which have the greatest impact on physical health and disease. How might they work together to affect health and illness? Are there certain subgroups of people who are most at risk for disease, based on their social position? Evidence suggests women who are in lower SES groups, and who come from an ethnic minority, may be most at risk. Which aspects of these women's lives might be especially crucial in determining disease? How might we consider their lives from a lifespan perspective? Do we have any understanding of possible physiological mechanisms that mediate between social life and disease? Future research needs to conceptualise and examine how the social dimensions discussed in this section work together to affect health and illness.

Physiological mechanisms

How can psychological factors such as Type A personalities influence physiological diseases such as heart disease or cancer? Two psychophysiological processes in particular have been proposed to act as physiological mediators between psychosocial factors and disease processes. These have both received a great deal of attention from health psychologists, and each is described below.

Cardiovascular reactivity

Cardiovascular reactivity (CVR) refers to specific changes in cardiovascular functioning which occur in response to a stimulus (Lyons *et al.*, 2000). Researchers investigating CVR hypothesise that heart rate, blood pressure and other cardiovascular responses to short-term, physical, cognitive and emotional challenges may tell us something about both psychological and physiological processes involved in the development of disease (Linden *et al.*, 2003). A large body of evidence has accumulated which suggests that exaggerated and consistent cardiovascular responses to challenge play a role in the development of essential hypertension and CHD (although not all findings have been consistent with this proposition; see Manuck, 1994, for a review). Cardiovascular responses include heart rate and blood pressure changes, increased sympathetic stimulation of the heart, reduced parasympathetic dampening, increased cardiac output and peripheral resistance (Smith & Ruiz, 2002). However, it is still not clear whether 'hyper' cardiovascular reactions play a causal role in disease etiology (mediating psychosocial risk factors such as hostility) or whether they are a marker of future risk without being involved causally (Linden *et al.*, 2003).

An overwhelming amount of work documents the influence of psychological challenges, including public speaking, playing video games and reaction time tasks, on heightened blood pressure and heart rate responses. People's cardiovascular reactions to these tasks vary markedly, even when the sample is fairly homogeneous (Sherwood & Turner, 1992). The extent of the reaction has been found to depend upon a variety of psychosocial factors, including social support, disclosure, interactional style, active coping, engagement, level of hostility, presence of an animal, status of people interacting and so on (Lyons *et al.*, 2000). As with other research areas reviewed in this chapter, the literature on CVR is vast but disjointed, and there has been little broad theorisation of CVR findings, although social processes seem to be particularly important in influencing CVR (Cacioppo, 1994). A novel and inherently social way of conceptualising CVR is provided in the research in focus box 5.3. Note that this approach avoids using stress as an explanatory construct.

The majority of CVR studies are conducted in a laboratory, raising questions about their ecological validity. How far can such findings generalise beyond the lab? Are responses in everyday life the same as those captured in the constructed and asocial laboratory environment? This question continues to be investigated. However, there remains little consensus about how CVR should be defined and measured (Kamarck & Lovallo, 2003). We also know little about the actual pathways through which exaggerated CVR may arise within individuals, and how different sources of reactivity may lead to disease (Lovallo & Gerin, 2003). Finally, in examining the causal role of CVR in disease outcome, there is a need to focus on interactions occurring between genetic, environmental and social factors alongside the psychophysiological response (Schwartz *et al.*, 2003). Experimental research with animals (usually non-human primates) provides strong evidence that CVR mediates the effects of psychosocial stress on coronary artery disease (Smith & Ruiz, 2002). Despite the methodological and conceptual problems with the CVR construct, it continues to be of major interest because of its consistently documented relationships with so many psychosocial factors.

Psychoneuroimmunology

In the previous three decades, researchers have been looking at the immune system and its potential for mediating the effects of psychosocial factors on illness and disease. Termed 'psychoneuroimmunology' (or the easier PNI), this relatively new field of study arose after researchers recognised that interactions occurred between behaviour, the brain and the immune system (Maier *et al.*, 1994). Researchers working with animals demonstrated that the relationship between the central nervous system and the immune system is bidirectional (Cohen & Herbert, 1996). Ader and Cohen (1993) showed that it was possible to

5.3 Constructing the self and cardiovascular reactivity

Lyons, A. C., & Farquhar, C. (2002). Past disclosure and conversational experience: effects on cardiovascular functioning while women talk. *Journal of Applied Social Psychology, 32(10)*, 2043–66.

Lyons and colleagues (2000) put forward a theoretical framework to try and account for many of the diverse findings on CVR and engaging in talk and communication. Talking raises blood pressure and heart rate significantly, and this is not because of producing speech sounds. Many psychosocial factors have been shown to influence the extent of CVR during talk and communication. Drawing on ideas from social constructionism, they argued that a sense of self arises primarily through social interaction and social relatedness, and that this process of self-construction may have physiological correlates at the cardiovascular level. Ideas from this framework were drawn on and empirically tested in the present study. It was proposed that the context of a conversation (who is involved), the amount of disclosure that occurs during a conversation, and participants' conversational histories would affect CVR in particular ways. Specifically, talking to a stranger, disclosing more and tending to engage in fewer conversations and feeling less comfortable doing so, were all expected to lead to heightened CVR.

The study

Forty-four undergraduate women were randomly assigned to a friend or stranger condition. Those in the friend condition were asked to bring a close female friend with them to the laboratory. Once in the lab, participants talked to their friend, or a stranger, about a personal experience they had not discussed a great deal previously. The talk was audiotaped. During this talk, participants had their heart rate and blood pressure monitored. The amount of disclosure that occurred during the talk was rated later by independent judges.

For all participants, heart rate and blood pressure increased significantly over resting levels while they were talking. CVR was calculated as the difference between initial resting levels of heart rate, systolic and diastolic blood pressure (averaged) and levels while talking (averaged). Thus, each participant had three reactivity scores: one each for heart rate, systolic blood pressure and diastolic blood pressure.

There were no differences in CVR between participants who were talking to a stranger compared to those talking to a friend. Similarly, how much the women disclosed information about themselves during the talk did not affect CVR. However, women who normally felt very comfortable talking showed higher CVR than women who did not usually feel so comfortable (contrary to predictions). Furthermore, the highest reactivity was found in a group who normally felt quite comfortable talking, but also tended not to disclose much. While explaining these unexpected findings using ideas about 'mismatch', the authors highlight some of the problems that arise with using ideas about the constructionist nature of language within a staged, non-natural situation. The results also indicate that certain conversational histories may be particularly relevant to specific physiological process.

Reflection

This study is novel in that it draws on ideas from one paradigm (social constructionism) yet tests them in another (positivist experimentalism). Yet this also leads to tensions and difficulties: the constructionist paradigm has questioned the nature of empirical scientific methodology and highlights how facts and truths are themselves constructed. Perhaps a focus on the functionality of language would be useful in CVR research in this area. Despite the grapplings with unexpected findings and inconsistent paradigms, the key message to be taken from this paper is that the individual is an embodied social being, and this must be at the forefront of any theorising in the area.

alter immune system functioning through classically conditioned stimuli. Since these early results, research has also examined and demonstrated classical conditioning of the immune response in humans (e.g. Buske-Kirschbaum *et al.*, 1992). Human research also expanded to explore the effects of behaviour and psychological traits and states on immune system functioning (Cohen & Herbert, 1996). The idea that psychological states and processes might influence our immune system and change our susceptibility to infectious illness and disease is an appealing one, and the amount of PNI research published exploded during the 1990s.

It is impossible to provide a succinct overview of the immune system and how it operates here, and this is not the aim of this section (see Cohen & Herbert, 1996; Maier *et al.*, 1994, for good overviews of immune system functioning). While

---

5.4

In the respected journal *Psychosomatic Medicine*, the percentage of PNI articles, commentaries and short reports published rose from approximately 3 per cent during the 1980s to 11 per cent during the 1990s. In terms of all PNI articles published since 1939 in this journal, 66 per cent of them were published in the 1990s. (Kiecolt-Glaser *et al.*, 2002b)

interactions between the central nervous system, the endocrine system and the immune system are well established (see Yang & Glaser, 2002, for a review), the mechanisms through which these interactions occur are not well understood. In this section we will examine some of the conclusions reached by recent reviews of the PNI field, to see whether psychosocial factors influence immune functioning to a sufficient extent to have health consequences. This distinction between transient changes in immune function and physical health outcomes, including actual initiation of disease, is important (Coe & Lubach, 2003). Broadly, three areas of study have examined the impact of psychosocial factors on immune function and health outcomes:

1 General studies: a range of psychosocial factors have been related to alterations in immune function, including interpersonal relationships, social support, acute or short-term stressors, chronic stress and negative emotions (Kiecolt-Glaser *et al.*, 2002a, 2002b). Health outcomes that have been investigated include infectious disease, wound healing, autoimmune disease, cancer and HIV. The strongest evidence that psychosocial stressors or interventions alter immune function sufficiently to produce actual health changes comes from studies on infectious disease and wound healing (Kiecolt-Glaser *et al.*, 2002b).

2 Intervention studies: a number of studies have examined how psychological interventions affect immune responses. These studies provide an opportunity to test causal relationships more rigorously. A meta-analysis of eighty-five such studies concluded that there is 'only modest' evidence for interventions altering immune function (Miller & Cohen, 2001). Hypnosis and conditioning trials provide the most consistent evidence, whereas the effects of disclosure and stress management interventions show inconsistent evidence. Miller and Cohen highlight some of the many conceptual and methodological issues that require further work in this area, including the choice of population studied, the timing of the intervention, the immune system measures employed, and conceptualising and testing appropriate mediational pathways.

Antibodies are produced by the immune system in response to foreign substances that may be a threat to the body (e.g. chemicals, virus particles, bacterial toxins). These foreign substances are called antigens. Each type of antibody is unique and defends the body against one specific type of antigen.

3 Antibody response studies: researchers have also explored whether psychological stress has any impact on the **antibody** response that occurs following immunisation with a foreign substance, including infectious agents. A review of this research concludes that stress does suppress the immune (antibody) response to immunisation (Cohen *et al.*, 2001). Evidence is strong for a relationship with secondary response (the activation of antigen-specific T and B lymphocytes) but weak for primary response (the immune response that occurs immediately on encountering the pathogen). This suggests that stress does influence immune response to a vaccine and, by implication, to pathogens (Kiecolt-Glaser *et al.*, 2002a). The stress–antibody response was not found to be mediated by health behaviours. Cohen *et al.* (2001) raise particular methodological issues that need to be considered in future

research in this area, including study design (cross-sectional versus prospective), and point out that only one of the studies they reviewed employed an experimental design, allowing causal inferences to be drawn.

The majority of PNI studies in humans have been correlational, making it difficult to say anything about causality (Kiecolt-Glaser *et al.*, 2002a). Furthermore, prospective studies are required to clarify the direction of causation between psychosocial stress and immune response (Cohen *et al.*, 2001). While intervention studies provide stronger evidence for causality, these are inconclusive at present (Miller & Cohen, 2001). There is also a need to refine the ways in which psychological constructs and processes are conceptualised and measured (Kiecolt-Glaser *et al.*, 2002b). The majority of studies have been conducted with young or middle-aged adults (almost 70 per cent of studies in *Psychosomatic Medicine* have employed participants being between 19 and 40 years of age (Kiecolt-Glaser *et al.*, 2002b)). Clearly future work needs to carry out PNI research with different age groups. Animal research findings suggest that there are two particular life stages which may be particularly important here, namely infancy and old age (Coe & Lubach, 2003). Some recent evidence suggests that psychosocial factors do influence immune function in children and adolescents (Kiecolt-Glaser *et al.*, 2002b).

In summary, there is now a vast amount of PNI findings, yet further work is required to establish causal relationships between psychosocial factors, immune function and physical health outcomes. Kiecolt-Glaser and colleagues (2002b) conclude their review by stating that 'there are now sufficient data to conclude that immune modulation by psychosocial stressors or interventions can lead to actual health changes' (p. 15). However, the immune pathways responsible for the links are not well known (Kiecolt-Glaser *et al.*, 2002a). As methodologies become more advanced, it is expected that such pathways will be better understood. However, theoretical and conceptual work concerning persons and their characteristics, individual as well as social, is also required if our knowledge is to advance in this field.

Becoming ill: critical reflections

It has been argued that much of the work in health psychology separates the phenomena of interest into small decontextualised pieces and that the 'social' aspect of the biopsychosocial model has yet to be fully integrated into theories and research (Spicer & Chamberlain, 1996). This criticism clearly applies to research examining whether psychosocial factors are involved in illness and disease. There is certainly a great deal of evidence that psychosocial factors may play a role in disease etiology, and potential physiological mechanisms are being identified. However, the field has developed in a piecemeal fashion and compared to the thousands of empirical studies, relatively little attention has been devoted to developing broad theories which integrate psychological, social and cultural factors. A daunting (and messy (Revenson, 1990)) task indeed, especially when temporal and physiological processes also need to be considered. A further problem with research in this field is the reliance on, and dominance of, stress as a construct. The notion of stress is so entrenched in how we think about disease and disease processes in our every-day lives, as well as in our academic research, that it seems difficult for us to let go and think outside the stress–response–illness framework. To advance the field, psychologists need to engage with theorising at broader levels to suggest ways forward. A vast body of empirical results tell us little without theories to guide their interpretation.

Some authors have provided meta-level theories to integrate the diverse and complex literatures on psychosocial factors involved in disease, yet these have generally failed to have a great impact on research. Some examples of meta-level theories are provided below:

- Totman (1987) has posited a structural theory concerning social behaviour (or 'purposeful activity') and consistency with social rules. In this account, all actions (those which are observable to others, and those which are not) derive their meaning and are understood on the basis of their social significance. People select actions based on rules (rules within a peer group, within communities, within cultures). Totman argues that failing to be purposefully 'involved' with social rules and activity can be a risk factor for disease. Thus people who act in ways that are consistent with social rules are at less risk of disease than those who act in ways that are inconsistent with such rules and are therefore not engaged in 'purposeful activity'.

- Revenson (1990) proposed an 'ecological' approach to personality and disease relationships. This perspective emphasises personality and disease processes within their naturally occurring settings. Revenson argues that socio-cultural, interpersonal, situational and temporal contexts are important, for they have all been found to be related to personality and/or health and interact with one another.

Automatic physiological processes which help physical systems fluctuate to adapt to external demands.

The wear and tear on the body and brain which results from chronic overactivity or inactivity of physiological systems normally involved in adaptating to external demands. Over long time periods, allostatic load can lead to disease.

- Berkman and colleagues (2000) have provided a framework which integrates the social, environmental and cultural contexts through which social networks may influence health (displayed in fig. 5.1). They draw on theoretical orientations from different academic disciplines to show how conceptualisations at different levels can be integrated into an overarching framework. Such a framework is beneficial because it provides insight into processes and highlights how different pieces of research, from different backgrounds and employing diverse methodologies, may fit together. It is also beneficial because it can potentially stimulate further conceptualisation, both within and between levels.

- McEwen (1998) has characterised psychophysiological processes over time using the powerful concepts of **allostasis** and **allostatic load**. This approach moves away from static views and the more basic idea of homeostasis. Allostasis refers to the processes involved as physiological systems fluctuate to adapt to external demands. Such adaptation, however, has a price, and when physiological systems are overworked, fail to shut off when appropriate or fail to respond adequately to challenges, allostatic load builds up. Allostatic load is 'the wear and tear on the body and brain resulting from chronic overactivity or inactivity of physiological systems that are normally involved in adaptation to environmental challenge' (McEwen, 1998, p. 37). Over long time periods, allostatic load can lead to disease. From this perspective, people who are born into and grow up in demanding and stressful environments will have repeated and chronic exposure to challenges, which can lead to cumulative physical damage. Furthermore, such environmental factors interact with genetic predispositions, which lead to large differences in susceptibility to stress between individuals (McEwen & Stellar, 1993).

Integration of findings, and broader theories, may occur when specific disease endpoints are examined. In the field of CHD, possible etiological factors that span the psychological, social, environmental and cultural realms are examined. In a recent review, Smith and Ruiz (2002) conclude that 'over the past 10 years, evidence has expanded indicating that psychosocial characteristics predict the development and course of CHD'. A growing body of research suggests that psychosocial factors may affect CHD development through stress and negative emotions. In terms of theorising more broadly, relatively little work has been conducted. Smith and Ruiz (2002) note that, rather than a core dimension of psychological risk, the factors outlined could be seen as transactional processes, whereby individuals both influence and are influenced by their social networks. These processes may increase or decrease cardiovascular risk. There is also a need to pay more attention to gender differences and gender specificity in CHD, and provide theoretical frameworks that account for such differences (Abbey & Stewart, 2000; Consedine et al., 2004).

In terms of the physiological mechanisms involved in CHD development, again little integration or convergence of research has occurred, and PNI research is often conducted independently of cardiovascular reactivity research. Kop (2003) provides an overview of how these two fields could be integrated and applied to coronary artery disease, an account which is represented diagrammatically in figure 5.3. Kop argues that psychological risk factors for coronary artery disease can be classified into three categories, based on how long they last and how close they are to coronary syndromes, such as MI and sudden cardiac death. The closest in terms of proximity to coronary syndromes are acute stressors and short-term experiences or emotions. The second set of factors are 'episodic' and last between a few weeks to up to two years, while the third set are chronic and develop over long time periods. Kop convincingly argues that each of these sets of psychological risk

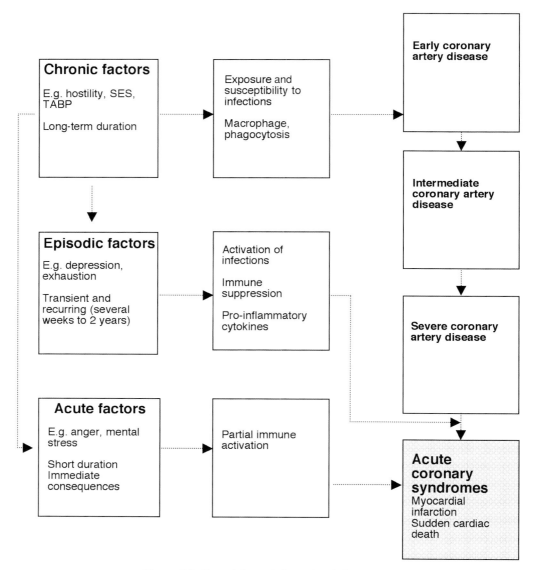

Figure 5.3 *Potential psychological risk factors and immune system pathways involved in coronary artery disease (adapted from Kop, 2003)*

factors plays different roles in the development and onset of coronary artery syndromes, through both cardiovascular and immune system pathways.

In summary, theory which is integrative and innovative is necessary to help make sense of the large and diverse findings in this area, and points to ways to move forward with research programmes. A valuable way of thinking about this task is to try and construct a 'psychosocial epidemiology of everyday life', as Kaplan has put it (Smith & Ruiz, 2002). Health psychologists are well placed to tackle such broader conceptualisations, given that psychology spans a number of levels of knowledge across physiological, psychological and social domains (including neuropsychology, cognitive, social and cultural psychology).

Conclusions

Social, contextual, environmental and cultural factors that may be important in disease etiology have been given relatively little attention in health psychology compared to individual factors. There are implications of focusing on individual-level factors (or intra-individual factors). For example, programmes are developed to diagnose and treat individuals, rather than examining their position in society and trying to increase availability of resources (Banyard & Graham-Bermann, 1993). Explicit considerations of issues such as power and opportunity are crucial, as they affect all contexts of an individual's life (and lifespan). Furthermore, as reflects the research in this area, this chapter has barely touched on issues of culture. Culture affects most of the psychosocial factors reported on here. For example, people from different cultures have very different concepts of emotional inhibition and expression (Markus & Kitiyama, 1991).

In commenting on the state of the field examining psychosocial factors in CHD, Smith and Ruiz (2002) observed that 'the traditional research agenda in CHD is rather full' (p. 559). As in other areas, we know little about how psychosocial risk factors develop, because most of the research has been conducted on adult samples. Furthermore, there has been little conceptualisation and investigation of how sociodemographic factors, such as gender, ethnicity and SES, work together with psychological factors to affect disease. Revenson (1990) noted well over a decade ago that contextual factors were not usually included in the planning or design of research exploring personality–disease relationships, and evidence for their involvement has evolved in a haphazard and non-programmatic way. The situation has improved somewhat since then, particularly concerning SES, but by all accounts there is a long way to go yet.

Harré (1989) argued that 'the task of psychology is to lay bare our systems of representation . . . the rest is physiology' (p. 34). The distinction between psychology as representation, and the rest of the world as physiology, is worth considering. As physiological methodologies continue to improve, psychologists need to devote attention to theorising and speculating about how we represent and understand psychosocial phenomena, and what they might mean for disease processes.

RECOMMENDED READING

Bartlett, D. (1998). *Stress: perspectives and processes*. Buckingham, UK: Open University Press. In ch. 2 of this book, Bartlett provides an insightful discussion of contemporary stress theories, and describes the dominant approach to stress and coping developed by Lazarus and colleagues over the last thirty years. He also highlights both theoretical and methodological problems with stress conceptualisations.

Martin, P. (1997). *The sickening mind: brain, behaviour, immunity and disease.* London: Flamingo. This book provides an engaging and well-informed account of how psychosocial factors might be related to disease. The author is a respected behavioural biologist and health psychologist, and he provides interesting examples of psychosomatic phenomena using well-known literature classics.

Special section on reactivity. *Psychosomatic Medicine, 65 (1)* (2003): This issue of the journal contains a special section on cardiovascular reactivity. It includes five articles which are both a reflection on where the research has got us to date, and what is required in the future. This section provides a very good account of reactivity research and its problems.

Smith, T. W., & Ruiz, J. M. (2002). Psychosocial influences on the development and course of coronary heart disease: current status and implications for research and practice. *Journal of Consulting and Clinical Psychology, 70,* 548–68. In this paper Smith and Ruiz provide a concise and accessible review of some of the physiological mechanisms linking psychosocial factors and CHD. The paper covers cardiovascular psychophysiology, particularly 'cardiovascular reactivity'. It also reviews research linking psychosocial factors to disease, as well as findings from intervention studies.

Taylor, S. E., Repetti, R. L. & Seeman, T. (1997). Health psychology: what is an unhealthy environment and how does it get under the skin? *Annual Review of Psychology, 48,* 411–47. This paper provides a good overview of how environments and psychosocial factors work together to affect health. It explicitly includes race and SES as contextual factors, and also considers health outcomes across the lifespan.

6   Comprehending bodily experience

The symptom itself is rarely questioned. But is the symptom so unproblematic? Why does one person experience headaches and sore throats whereas another has migraines and tonsillitis? Why does retirement exacerbate symptoms but a busy job make them disappear? . . . An understanding of how symptoms arise and how only some are given the status of a problem can create a broader psychological perspective in which to understand patients' health and illness.   (Ogden, 2003a, p. 409)

An essential characteristic of physical sensations [are that] they are as often socially influenced *interpretations* as they are the direct output of a biological system. In matters of health and illness, it is difficult to imagine a more fundamental process than that by which we perceive, interpret, and act on the information from our own bodies.   (Cioffi, 1991, p. 25)

Learning objectives

The aim of this chapter is to review the literature on how people interpret and respond to bodily sensations which have implications for physical health. By the end of this chapter you should be able to:

- provide an overview of psychological research on recognising symptoms;
- offer a critique of the biomedical model of symptom recognition;
- distinguish between a 'bodily sign' and a 'physical symptom';
- argue why cognitive factors involved in perceiving changes in bodily states need to be understood within a social and cultural framework;
- describe and critique the main theories of pain;
- discuss the implications of constructing factors that influence bodily experience as located within the individual;
- compare and contrast differing accounts of the body and bodily experience.

The ways in which we make sense of physical sensations and interpret them as **symptoms** depend on a variety of factors. Interpreting a particular change in bodily experience as a symptom, such as a sore throat, is not as straightforward as we might think. People might interpret a sore throat as a possible symptom of an illness if they had been exposed to other people with similar symptoms (belief in a virus), or if they had been out in cold weather without a hat and scarf

> A sensation or physical feeling that is recognised and interpreted as different to normal bodily feeling, and which may indicate disease to the person.

181

(folk beliefs of how illness begins) or if they had recurring bouts of tonsillitis (prior experience). On the other hand, it is unlikely this sore throat would be interpreted as a symptom if the previous night had been spent smoking heavily or screaming out lyrics at a rock concert. These examples are reasonably individualistic in that they focus solely on the person, and there are broader factors that influence how we interpret physical sensations in our bodies, including those that are social and cultural. There is a distinction to be made

A change in a somatic feeling.

between **bodily signs** or sensations, or the awareness of something different in one's bodily state, and physical symptoms, which imply that interpretation of the bodily feeling has taken place (Radley, 1994). To start we will examine the main psychological research on factors influencing symptom perception. First, however, we need to understand why this research is important.

Why bother researching how people interpret physical sensations in their own bodies?

Whether or not we seek treatment for symptoms depends on how we interpret physical sensations. This can affect the outcome of a disease in various ways, for example:

- How we interpret physical sensations affects adherence to treatment for illness (see ch. 8). This is particularly so for certain types of treatment and certain types of illnesses.
- How we respond to our own bodies also influences how we respond to other people with obvious symptoms or other people with particular diseases. This will be more apparent towards the end of this chapter.
- How we perceive and interpret physical changes in our bodies influences our subjectivities – how we view ourselves – and this is particularly apparent when looking at the medicalisation and segmentation of women's bodies.
- How we interpret and respond to somatic symptoms can be functional in the social world. In other words, particular interpretations and responses can be an act of social positioning or a form of social commentary or protest, either intentionally or unintentionally (Kirmayer & Young, 1998).

Interpretation of physical symptoms is not as straightforward as we might initially think, and whether people interpret their symptoms as serious enough to seek medical attention can affect their survival. For example, studies have found that when people have the symptoms of a heart attack or cancer they often do not seek help for long periods of time (Neale *et al.*, 1986; Goldberg *et al.*, 2002). The longer a person takes to decide whether or not he or she is actually having a heart attack, the longer the delay, and one predictor of survival from a heart attack is time taken to receive medical attention (Gibler *et al.*, 2002). Studies show that most people who delay seeking help for a heart attack say it was because they were not sure if it actually was a heart attack – they wait until they are sure (see research in focus box 6.1).

The biomedical view of symptom recognition

The traditional view in biomedicine regarding symptom perception is straightforward and simple: there is some kind of pathology in the body and the individual notices, feels and responds to this pathology in an appropriate manner. This view sees symptoms as directly caused by pathological processes in the body. Thus, there is a very close correspondence between how individuals perceive physical sensations and their actual biological state. It is further assumed that as pathology increases, the more obvious it is for the individual, who goes on to seek medical care (Schwartz, 1982). These biomedical views of how we comprehend our bodily experiences and physical sensations are simplistic at best. Research by psychologists in the 1970s and 1980s suggested that how a physical sensation is interpreted and responded to depends a great deal on perceptual and cognitive factors. In fact, whether the sensation is interpreted as a symptom at all depends on a whole range of psychological processes. Psychologists have argued that physical symptoms are phenomena derived from our cognitions and perceptions which are subject to complex psychosocial processes (Cioffi, 1991; Pennebaker, 1982). Some of these are outlined in the following section. However, there is also evidence that social and cultural factors are important in influencing how people comprehend their bodily experience, both directly and indirectly. These will be outlined later in the chapter.

Individual influences on recognising and interpreting symptoms

Psychologists have examined how people differ in their responses to interpreting physical sensations. Research shows that some people simply perceive and report more symptoms than others. But is this because they actually have more symptoms? According to Pennebaker (1982), bodily experience is often ambiguous and the ways in which people perceive their symptoms depend upon a number of individual factors.

Stable factors: self-awareness, neuroticism, negative affectivity, somatisation

Research suggests that people differ in how much they attend to their internal states or in their self-awareness (Duval & Wicklund, 1972). Some people are more internally focused and therefore more sensitive to changes in physical

Research in focus

6.1 Is it indigestion or is it a heart attack?

Ruston, A., Clayton J., & Calnan, M. (1998). Patients' action during their cardiac event: qualitative study exploring differences and modifiable factors. *British Medical Journal, 316*, 1060–5.

This study aimed to explore factors which might influence how long a person takes to seek help when they are experiencing a heart attack, and to identify factors that might be potentially modifiable. The researchers used semi-structured interviews with forty-three patients who had been admitted to hospital following a cardiac event, as well as with twenty-one people (relatives and bystanders) who were present at the time the patient was experiencing the heart attack. The patients were divided into three groups: those who took less than four hours to seek medical help once their symptoms began (non-delayers), those who sought help between four and twelve hours following symptom onset (delayers), and those who took longer than twelve hours to seek help (extended delayers). The researchers identified several stages that patients went through once they began to experience symptoms, including warning, interpretation, preliminary action, re-evaluation and final action. How long each stage lasted varied across the participants, and depended on the extent to which they mobilised and integrated their resources to get their symptoms under control. Most of the participants said that what they experienced was quite different from their preconceived notions about what a heart attack was like. Non-delayers had a wider range of symptoms before their heart attack and many more of them thought they were potentially at risk of a heart attack than did the delayers and extended delayers. Other differences across the groups are summarised below.

Non-delayers: once symptoms began these people tended to isolate themselves and evaluate what was happening. They distracted themselves with, for example, cups of tea, did not take medication and used their experience, medical knowledge and intuition to reinterpret their symptoms as evidence of a cardiac event.

'I can't really explain how I felt, but I didn't feel well and I thought it was time to sit down and think about things.'

'Well I'm not an expert, I just have what I have read in the newspapers, but I asked my husband if it could be a heart attack because he had a feeling like . . . a belt around [his] chest and down the left arm' [wife of non-delayer].

Delayers: these patients talked to lots of people, and obtained lots of information, and compared their experience with that of others.

Reassurance, and readjustment to the symptoms, meant these people delayed the realisation that the symptoms were serious.

'Yes I said: "Oh you know, I've got this indigestion" and of course my missus says: "well take some of your Zantac". So I did like, you know, but it made no difference and they [mother-in-law and wife] said "try some lemonade". Then her mum gave me some mints. I tried everything'.

Extended delayers: These people sought both lay and medical help, and tried different treatments and movement. Some contacted health professionals who discounted their risk of heart attack, attributing the symptoms to other causes. This considerably influenced decision making and added to the delay. One patient was told by her GP she had a viral infection, and another that he had a hiatus hernia. These people did not tend to see themselves at risk of having a heart attack.

'My opinion is that it is the guy that's on the dole, sits in front of the TV all day, drinking pints of beer and lager and eating fish and chips. Of course, that's not me!'

Reflection

This study is an example of qualitative research being used in a post-positivist way. Interviews are conducted and the aim is to compare differences between groups of people (cf. more constructionist approaches to qualitative research). This approach offers much more insight into why people might not seek help when they are experiencing cardiac symptoms, and pays more attention to the patients' views than traditional questionnaire-based research.

sensations than others (Pennebaker, 1983). Further, teenagers who are more introspective than others have been found to report more physical symptoms (Hansell & Mechanic, 1985). Somewhat surprisingly, however, research by Pennebaker (1983) highlights that being more internally focused does not necessarily mean being more accurate in symptom perception. People who were more internally focused tended to overestimate changes in their heart rate compared to people who were externally focused.

Individual differences have also been observed in **neuroticism**, defined as the tendency to experience negative, distressing emotions, including anger, anxiety and depression (Costa & McCrae, 1987). People who score highly on measures of neuroticism also report experiencing higher levels of symptoms and health complaints (Costa & McCrae, 1987; Watson & Pennebaker, 1989). As Holroyd and Coyne (1987) point out, people high in neuroticism have a biased perception of physiological experiences, in that they over-report physical symptoms.

A construct that is extremely similar to neuroticism is **negative affectivity**. Negative affectivity is a general dimension of subjective distress and includes

> An individual difference in the tendency to experience negative, distressing emotions.

> A predisposition to experience negative emotions and negative self-concept.

a range of aversive mood states (e.g. anger, distrust, guilt, fearfulness). Trait negative affectivity (usually simply called negative affectivity or NA) is a predisposition to experience negative mood states and negative self-concept (Watson & Clark, 1984; Watson & Pennebaker, 1989). People high in negative affectivity consistently report experiencing more somatic symptoms than others (Watson & Pennebaker, 1989). It has been argued that although there are no observable health differences between people who are high and low in negative affectivity, those high in this trait are more likely to notice and attend to normal physical sensations (Watson & Pennebaker, 1989). Further, it has been hypothesised that negative affectivity may influence reporting physical symptoms through its effect on selective attention or, in other words, that people high in negative affectivity are more likely to selectively attend to bodily cues and somatic sensations. However, a recent study found no evidence for this suggestion (Kolk *et al.*, 2002). Gijsbers van Wijk and Kolk (1997), in commenting on the research generated around the construct of negative affectivity, point out that its similarity to the construct of neuroticism 'gives one the uneasy feeling of old ideas parading as new ones' (p. 240).

Transient factors: mood, attention, expectations

Internal states also influence how physical sensations are interpreted. Experiencing negative mood has been consistently related to increased reports of somatic symptoms (Gijsbers van Wijk, *et al.*, 1999; Watson & Pennebaker, 1989). Interestingly, one study suggests that negative mood may mediate the consistently observed gender differences in physical symptom reporting (Gijsbers van Wijk *et al.*, 1999).

Attentional state is also related to symptom perception. Boredom is related to over-reporting of physical symptoms, while distraction and attention diversion is related to under-reporting of symptoms (Pennebaker, 1983). Described within a cognitive-perceptual framework, the amount of external information vying for attention affects what (and how much) individuals will notice and attend to (Cioffi, 1991). As we have a limited capacity for information processing, an abundance of external cues will limit the amount of attention paid to internal, somatic sensations and consequently fewer symptoms will be perceived. On the other hand, if there is little external information available, there is an increased tendency to focus on somatic information (Pennebaker, 1982). For these reasons distraction has often been employed as an intervention for managing pain.

Expectations also affect perceptions of internal states. In a study by Anderson and Pennebaker (1980) participants touched a vibrating board and what they said they felt as they did this depended on what they were led to expect. Those told they would experience some pleasure interpreted the sensation in this way, while those who were told they would experience some pain reported feeling pain. Further evidence for the influence of expectations on perceiving and interpreting physical symptoms comes from research into **placebos**. These are substances that are inert, or sham treatments. Research shows that people who are given placebos to reduce their pain often report a lessening in their pain symptoms (Roberts, 1995). The effects of placebos are discussed in more detail in ch. 8.

A substance or procedure that has no inherent power to produce an effect that is sought or predicted (Stewart-Williams & Podd, 2004).

Stress

Recent life stress has been found to affect both symptom perception and seeking medical care in a sample of older adults. When a life stressor had begun within the previous three weeks, adults attributed ambiguous symptoms to stress (but not unambiguous symptoms) and were less likely to seek professional health care for their symptoms (Cameron *et al.*, 1995). It has been proposed that the increased physiological arousal induced by stress increases how much attention we pay to the body, and because in Western society there is a general belief that stress causes illness, we are more likely to label physical sensations as symptoms (Cohen & Williamson, 1991).

Furthermore, research has demonstrated that stress interacts with gender to influence whether people are likely to label symptoms as serious or as needing medical care (see sidebar 6.1).

People have been found to recommend that men seek medical help for cardiac and other symptoms, whether the men are described as stressed or not. However, people are less likely to recommend that women seek help for the same symptoms if they are described as stressed (Martin *et al.*, 1998; Martin & Lemos, 2002). This suggests that people have stereotypes about women, men and stress, notably that women are more likely to experience physical symptoms (with no underlying pathology) when they are stressed than men. These beliefs, in turn, influence what people advise men and women experiencing symptoms to do, and also affect how men

6.1

Consider the following two scenarios.

John is a 62-year-old man whose son recently returned home to live with him after going through a difficult and distressing divorce. John has been worried about his son, who is feeling depressed and concerned about his future. John has also been worried about his own financial situation. He tells you that today he is feeling out of breath, is sweating and has chest pain. What do you tell him to do about these symptoms?

Ruth is a 62-year-old woman who has recently retired, and who has been worrying about her long-term financial situation. She has also been dealing with caring for her elderly mother, who has just recently come to live with her after suffering a fall and experiencing severe depression. Ruth worries about her mother, and how she will manage to cope with everything. Today, Ruth tells you she has a pain in her chest, and that she has been sweating and feeling out of breath. What do you tell her to do about these symptoms?

Do you consider the symptoms serious in each case? Would you recommend that each person telephone emergency services, ring a doctor or make an urgent appointment to see a medical professional? Would you give different advice to John and Ruth? Why or why not? Research suggests that people would advise John to seek medical help, but not Ruth. (Martin *et al.*, 1998) and women interpret their own physical symptoms (e.g. Martin *et al.*, 1998; Martin *et al.*, 2004).

Cognitions about illness and disease

According to psychologists who investigate cognitions and symptom perception, how we interpret symptoms depends on the cognitive representations we have of different diseases. Bishop (1991) argues that we hold cognitive **disease prototypes**, in which certain symptoms cluster together and represent specific illnesses. For example, if your friend says he has been sneezing a lot, has inflamed sinuses, an itchy nose, nasal congestion and teary eyes, taken together these symptoms are consistent with the disease prototype of hayfever. Studies show that people are more likely to say that particular symptoms indicate a disease when presented with a high-prototype symptom set, and also to identify illnesses more correctly, than when presented with medium- or low-prototype sets (Bishop, 1991). Examples of high-, medium- and low-prototype sets are shown in sidebar 6.2.

An organised set of ideas about specific diseases which include causes, duration, symptoms and other disease attributes.

6.2

Some examples of varying illness prototype sets ($\sqrt{}$ = consistent with illness; x = inconsistent with illness)

High prototype for hayfever

$\sqrt{}$ sneezing frequently
$\sqrt{}$ inflamed sinuses
$\sqrt{}$ itchy nose
$\sqrt{}$ runny nose
$\sqrt{}$ teary eyes

Medium prototype for stroke

$\sqrt{}$ feelings of numbness
$\sqrt{}$ dizziness
x swollen ankle
x sore throat
$\sqrt{}$ blurred vision
$\sqrt{}$ slurred speech

Low prototype for strep throat

x trouble remembering things
$\sqrt{}$ sore throat
$\sqrt{}$ difficulty swallowing
x pain near heart
x swollen wrist
x burning in eyes
(Adapted from Bishop, 1991)

The research on disease prototypes also suggests that people will engage in self-diagnosis more when medical categories have clear-cut symptom sets. For example, abdominal pain could indicate a number of things, but a lump in the breast is fairly clearly defined in relation to a disease entity. The personal context in which symptoms occur also works in with illness prototypes. For example, mumps are associated with children, typhoid with people who have been backpacking around the world (see Bishop, 1991). Indeed, in making lay diagnoses, adults have been found to employ information about the typical person who gets the disease and typical environmental causes as least as much as they employ information about actual physical symptoms (Lalljee *et al.*, 1993). Overall

Table 6.1 Dimensions of illness cognitions

Dimension	Description	Example questions to oneself
Identity	The label given to an illness (medical diagnosis) and the symptoms experienced. Groups of symptoms are often linked together into an explanatory label	What symptoms might I expect with this illness?
Cause	The perceived cause of illness. This may be biological (e.g. virus) or psychosocial (e.g. stress, behaviour)	How did I get to be like this?
Time line	Ideas about how long the illness will last, short term or long term	How long might the recovery take?
Consequences	Perceptions of the possible effects of the illness on one's life. Could be physical (can't go to work), social (can't get out to visit friends) or emotional (loneliness, depression). These can interact. Could be serious (e.g. AIDS) or not (e.g. a cold)	How much will this illness affect me?
Curability/ controllability	Beliefs about whether the illness can be treated, cured or controlled (by the self or others)	Can I control my symptoms?

this research shows that the lay person understands illness in terms of symptoms and the personal contexts in which symptoms are thought to arise.

Disease prototypes have been found to influence behaviour. People who hold disease prototypes to a strong degree are more likely to visit a doctor when feeling ill, and to go for routine check-ups, than people who hold them to a lesser degree (Lau *et al.*, 1989). Disease prototypes have also been found to influence how people present their symptoms to a health care provider. People may bias their reports for a number of reasons, including self-enhancement and to make them consistent with their selected disease prototype (Croyle & Williams, 1991).

Researchers have also examined more general **illness cognitions**, or the beliefs a person holds about illness (see Petrie & Weinman, 1997). The underlying premise of this work is that people differ in the beliefs and **cognitive representations** (or schemas) they have about illness. Thus, how we think about illness depends on our own experiences and shared understandings. We have beliefs about its causes, the context, and the types of illness we know about. These beliefs provide a framework for perceiving symptoms, as well as understanding and coping with illness. Studies show that there appear to be five main dimensions of people's illness cognitions (Leventhal *et al.*, 1980; Lau & Hartman, 1983; Lau *et al.*, 1989) which they use to integrate and organise information, as described in table 6.1.

illness cognitions General beliefs about illness.

cognitive representations An organised set of beliefs about a particular topic, such as illness.

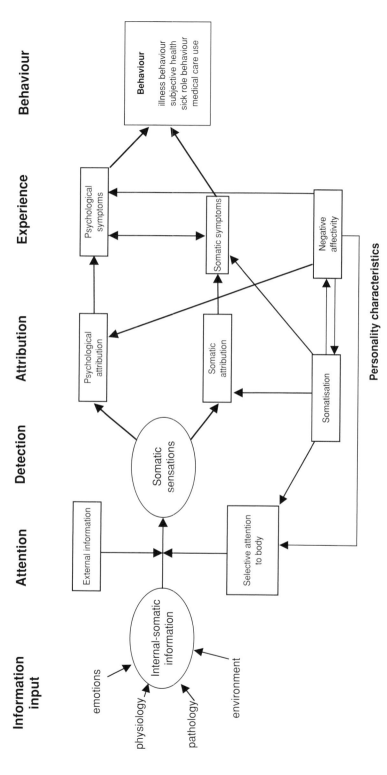

Figure 6.1 *A symptom perception model (from Gijsbers van Wijk & Kolk, 1997)*

According to research examining cognitive representations about illness, beliefs regarding these five dimensions inform the way individuals perceive and interpret physical changes, as well as how they respond to these interpretations. Illness representations appear to develop very early in life. In one study children aged between 4 and 6 were interviewed about health and illness, and their talk showed that they employed the same five dimensions when discussing particular illnesses (Goldman *et al.*, 1991).

In this section we have outlined some of the individual factors that influence the sensation and interpretation of physical symptoms. Much of this work is based within a cognitive-perceptual framework, which has been given a lot of attention within health psychology. Kolk and colleagues (among others) have argued that the cognitive-perceptual approach highlights how the interpretation of physical sensations is not as straightforward as we might initially imagine (see Gijsbers van Wijk & Kolk, 1997; Kolk *et al.*, 2003). Figure 6.1 provides an overview of this approach to symptom perception, which can be conceptualised as having six different temporal steps (Gijsbers van Wijk & Kolk, 1997). First, there is some kind of somatic information input, and this may come from physiology, emotions, etc. Second, specific kinds of information are selected for attention, based on attentional processes (e.g. how much external information is vying for attention). Third, somatic sensations are actually detected by the person. Fourth, the person attributes these sensations to either somatic or psychological causes (e.g. 'I'm feeling this just because I've been stressed'). Cognitive representations of illness are also influential in this process. Fifth, personality characteristics (such as negative affectivity) influence how the sensations are experienced. Finally, all of these cumulatively affect people's behaviour, such as whether to seek medical help or take up the sick role.

Social influences on recognising and interpreting symptoms

The social context within which individuals live influences their interpretation of bodily sensations. As with many aspects of health and illness that have been discussed previously in this book, people's interpretations of bodily sensations are inextricably bound up in their gender, age and social class.

Gender

A social factor that must be considered here is gender. Almost all studies that have examined symptom reporting show that women report experiencing more physical symptoms than men and they also engage in more illness behaviour (Gijsbers van Wijk & Kolk, 1997; Verbrugge, 1985; 1989). A number of reasons have been posited for the gender differences that have been observed in perceiving physical sensations. Some of these focus on gender roles and what it means to be a woman. Health and the body are traditionally the realm of the 'feminine world', which means that noticing the body and being sensitive to physical changes in the body is part of the feminine gender role (Nathanson, 1975). In a similar manner, socially it is easier for women to report experiencing symptoms than it is for men. In this way, ill health and sickness have been positioned traditionally as aligned with the 'feminine world', while health and being healthy have been aligned with the 'masculine world' (Herzlich, 1973). Studies which have examined gender role and symptom reporting are inconclusive. Some have found that gender role (i.e. femininity or masculinity) does influence symptom reporting (e.g. Annandale & Hunt, 1990) whereas others have not (e.g. Gijsbers van Wijk & Kolk, 1996; Williams & Wiebe, 2000).

Sociologists have argued that women perceive more symptoms because they experience more symptoms, arising out of the stresses of their everyday lives. Women occupy multiple social roles, experience more 'inter-role' conflict than men, and often have to do the '**double shift**' (Lorber, 1997). Stress may influence women's bodily experience directly by affecting physiological functioning. On the other hand, women may label sensations as symptoms because of a belief that stress causes illness.

Working in paid employment as well as doing the majority of unpaid domestic work and childcare.

Clearly, the processes of gender socialisation for men also influence how they perceive bodily changes. For example, traditional versions of masculinity teach men not to attend to their bodies and to resist labelling sensations as symptoms (Addis & Mahalik, 2003). However, researchers examining the current state of men's health point out that men's possible under-reporting of illness and failure to perceive or act on changes in somatic sensations is not fully understood by traditional psychological and sociological research (Hodgetts & Chamberlain, 2002). To gain a more complete understanding 'we need to explore the intertwined character of biological processes, individual agency and social restraints' (p. 271).

Psychologists have argued that women and men differ in how they perceive information, which in turn may lead to differences in symptom perception (Pennebaker & Roberts, 1992). Further, it may be that women's and men's social roles affect symptom perception, but that this is mediated by psychological factors such as mood and attention (e.g. Gijsbers van Wijk *et al.*, 1999). In their study of gender differences in physical symptoms, Gijsbers van Wijk and colleagues asked their adult sample to record their mood and physical symptoms in a diary every day for four weeks. As expected, women reported more physical symptoms than men and rated these as more severe (female symptoms such as those concerning menstruation, or swollen breasts, were not included). However, these differences in symptoms disappeared when positive and negative mood were considered, suggesting that differences between women and men in symptom reporting were more to do with psychological and social factors than biology.

It is interesting to note, however, that in studies which have focused on specific illness conditions, and in which there were 'objective' as well as 'subjective' symptom measures, no differences in symptom reporting between men and women occurred (or men had higher reports than women). For example, symptoms among men and women with osteoarthritis were found to be related to X-ray evidence of osteoarthritis, and not the sex of the patient. Further, in this sample men were more likely to report pain than women, independent of disease severity and treatment (Davis, 1981). Similarly, in a study with people who had cancer of the colon or rectum, results showed that women were not more likely to recognise or respond to symptoms than men (Marshall & Funch, 1986); rather, women actually delayed seeking care longer than men. Further evidence comes from research carried out at the Common Cold Unit in England (MacIntyre, 1993). Participants stayed at the unit for ten days, where they were inoculated with a cold virus or a placebo. Trained clinical observers assessed the presence and severity of cold symptoms and signs, and participants rated their own perceptions of their cold using the same categories. Results based on 1,700 individuals collected over five years showed that clinical observers were more likely to rate women as having a cold, although women were not more likely than men to rate themselves as having a cold. More interestingly, men were significantly more likely than women to 'over-rate' their symptoms than a clinical observer. These results suggest that women do not have lower thresholds for perceiving and reporting symptoms than men (MacIntyre, 1993).

The overwhelming majority of studies examining gender differences in symptom perception have been carried out with Western adult samples, and their findings cannot be generalised to other groups in society. For example, in one of the few studies carried out with children, no difference was observed in symptom reporting between girls and boys, and the results suggested that the difference may even be reversed (van den Bosch et al., 1992). This supports explanations for observed adult sex differences based on socialisation and adult roles.

Age

Among elderly individuals, some research indicates that views about ageing affect the ways in which somatic sensations are interpreted (Leventhal & Prohaska, 1986). Prohaska and colleagues (Prohaska et al., 1987) found that physical sensations such as tiredness and weakness among elderly adults were attributed to old age rather than illness, even when the sensations were quite severe. While these attributions might be viewed as 'incorrect' if they did indicate illness, mild symptoms such as tiredness and weakness could also quite legitimately indicate ageing to this population. Further, as with any group, the social context in which elderly people live, who they talk to and how they regularly feel will all have an influence on recognising and interpreting particular bodily experiences as symptoms.

Social class

There has been a large amount of psychological research into how we comprehend somatic sensations, but very little of it has examined how this might vary by social class. While we know that social class influences morbidity and mortality, we know little about differences in perceptions of bodily sensations among people from different socioeconomic backgrounds. However, different social groups have different reactions to bodily disturbances. Zola (1966) notes how back pain is dismissed among working-class women as part of everyday life and is certainly not viewed and interpreted as a symptom of illness. Kolk *et al.* (2002) examined social class within a symptom perception approach, and found that SES did not influence any symptom perception variable (such as somatic attribution, selective attention, negative affectivity), but directly affected frequency of symptoms experienced during the previous year. People from lower SES groups had more symptoms as recorded by general practitioners over a one-year period (Kolk *et al.*, 2002).

Cultural influences on recognising and interpreting symptoms

Our ideas about health and illness generally, as well as what particular bodily signs might mean, are grounded in the understandings we have in the wider world (Radley, 1994). Therefore our knowledge regarding somatic sensations, symptoms and disease owes much to the culture in which we live. As Radley (1994) succinctly notes, 'culture – in the sense of meanings placed upon symptoms – does not just arise once illness is present, but is there in the apprehension of bodily signs themselves' (p. 63). For example, Mexican Indians in the United States understand their diarrhoea, sweating and coughing as part of everyday life, and not as symptoms that require medical treatment (Zola, 1966).

Cultural orientation

Obviously, the cognitions and representations we have of illness and disease come in large part from our social world, and this includes not just our family, friends and wider social group, but also the culture in which we live. For example, a study that was carried out with Singaporean Chinese living in Singapore examined the extent to which people were embedded in and oriented towards their Chinese culture (indexed by several measures including endorsing Chinese values, use of Chinese language, espousing a Chinese religion, and age (as a measure of cohort differences)) and how this affected their illness cognitions. Findings showed that the higher people's Chinese culture orientation, the more likely they were to employ Chinese illness concepts. On the other hand, people lower in Chinese culture orientation were more likely to emphasise the physical causation of disease model and to seek help from a physician practising Western medicine (Quah & Bishop, 1996).

Dominant representations

Dominant social and cultural representations of health and illness influence how we perceive and interpret bodily sensations. Critical researchers have argued that the ways in which health information is constructed in media and popular accounts can influence and mediate individuals' lived experience of physical sensations (e.g. Lyons, 2000). Representations of particular physical experiences can highlight how issues are constructed and the meanings that they have in a certain sociocultural time and place. For example, the ways in which menopause has been represented have varied considerably across different times and places.

During the Victorian era a menopausal woman was constructed as having a decaying body and a sinful mind, and as suffering from dizziness, stupidity and vulnerability to insanity (McCrea, 1983 and Formanek 1990, cited in Gannon & Ekstrom, 1993). Today's dominant perspective on menopause is a biomedical view that it is a disease caused by oestrogen deficiency (Gannon, 1999) which requires medical treatment. Although very different, both of these representations of menopause are negative. Such representations have been contrasted with the more positive construction of menopause in Asian cultures, where this time of life is viewed with a sense of liberation and freedom from pregnancy (Moaz et al., 1970). The view of menopause as a deficiency disease is dominant in popular Western media accounts. Studies have examined newspapers, magazines and self-help texts, and overwhelmingly conclude that menopause is portrayed as a negative experience or disease, which reinforces ideas of ill health, psychological disturbance and disease management for women at midlife (e.g. Gannon & Stevens, 1998; Lyons & Griffin, 2003; Shoebridge & Steed, 1999). Examples of the different ways in which menopause is constructed in medical discourse, self-help literature and GPs' accounts are shown in table 6.2.

These dominant representations of menopause provide a framework within which women can interpret their own experiences. A woman might ask herself whether the joint aches she feels are associated with menopause, or if two missed menstrual cycles mean it is time to see a general practitioner, or if her depression can be attributed to hormonal changes. How menopause is characterised in cultural accounts also creates a dominant 'normative' reality of women at midlife, providing women with contextual information about how to comprehend their bodily experiences.

Table 6.2 Quotes from textbooks, self-help books and interviews with GPs showing differing constructions of the menopause

The construction of menopause	In medical textbooks (from Lyons & Griffin, 2000)	In self-help books (from Lyons & Griffin, 2003)	In GPs' accounts (from Lyons & Leach, forthcoming)
As a deficiency disease	Menopause can be considered as a state of hormone deficiency; HRT is, in effect, merely bringing women back up to the baseline from which they *descended* as a result of the deficiency	What is surprising is the length of time that replacing hormones has been available to help women *suffering* from the effects of *oestrogen deficiency* (Smith & Smith, 1996)	Menopause is basically *deterioration* of your ovarian function
The menopause is essentially the time around the *failing* ovary basically
Focuses on symptoms, failure, deterioration, suffering	[Menopause] is the most obvious manifestation of a gradual *decline* in ovarian function . . . The ovaries *fail* because they run out of primordial follicles . . . hormone production progressively *declines* (Smith & Studd, 1993)	The vagina, uterus and cervix are areas where oestrogen is readily taken up and which consequently *suffer* when *deficiency* occurs: their lining, or surface tissue, then tends to *atrophy*. The vagina shortens, the skin surface *weakens* and *thins* and blood supply *diminishes* . . . Shrinkage of the uterus and cervix . . . (Wilson, 1996)	The menopause is when the ovaries basically stop producing oestrogen, and you *suffer* a variety of physical effects as a result
As a natural event
Focuses on menopause as a natural physiological event in women's lives	Not apparent	The word 'menopause' literally means the time when your periods cease permanently. It is a natural process for all women (Sundquist, 1992)	[HRT is] an attempt to return to normal physiology. But there is an argument actually that I agree with which is that the menopause is part of normal physiology . . . So it could be considered to be normal physiology in which case HRT isn't a return to normal physiology because the menopause is normal
And sometimes [patients] say . . . this is nature taking its course and I'm happy with that, that's fine
		The menopause, as we've said, is a natural stage in a woman's life. It's not a disease or an illness. It's not something bad which makes female bodies fall apart and minds fall to pieces (Smith & Smith, 1996)	
As complex and confusing	Not apparent	Some experts, usually doctors, view menopause as a disease that must be treated; others see it as a more natural process. If even the experts can't agree, no wonder we women are confused! (Sundquist, 1992)	The menopause is confusing for women and doctors

Somatisation and culture

Somatisation refers to the experience of somatic symptoms in the absence of any underlying physical pathology. These are often called 'medically unexplained' symptoms and much of the research in this area assumes that different cultural groups vary in the extent to which they somatise. For example, the idea that somatisation is more common among people in non-Western cultures, particularly Asians and Africans, has become entrenched. However, recent ethnographic and anthropological research highlights that somatisation is universal and that people in all cultures experience somatic symptoms that cannot be medically explained (Kirmayer & Young, 1998).

The process by which physical symptoms arise from psychological distress rather than organic pathology.

Ethnographic research on somatisation examines the ways in which people from diverse ethnocultural groups interpret and understand physical sensations. Kirmayer and Young (1998) reviewed much of this work and concluded that 'somatic symptoms are located in multiple systems of meaning that serve diverse psychological and social functions' (p. 420). This is highlighted by the fact that there are culture-specific somatic symptoms and physical syndromes (MacLachlan, 1997). For example, Kirmayer and Young (1998) describe a common syndrome in Nigeria called 'brain fag', which involves sensations of heaviness or heat in the head from the effort of studying. Further, within Korean culture, experiencing feelings of heaviness, burning, headaches, muscular aches and indigestion (as well as others) may lead people to conclude they are suffering from *hwa-byung*, a syndrome which comes about because of suppressed anger and resentment. These syndromes show how cultural views about the body can lead to the experience of culture-specific somatic symptoms.

Kirmayer and Young (1998) have outlined seven different ways in which somatic sensations may be comprehended and interpreted, based on psychological, sociological and anthropological research. Although this interpretive framework was developed from research on somatisation, it can be related to physical symptoms more generally. This framework is shown in table 6.3, and demonstrates clearly how social and cultural meanings pervade the recognition and interpretation of and response to physical sensations.

Brown (2004) has recently proposed an integrative model to help to explain and understand 'medically unexplained' symptoms. This model draws on the psychological concepts of dissociation and conversion, as well as somatisation, and is based on cognitive psychological principles. As part of this explanatory framework, Brown suggests that unexplained symptoms stem from alterations of information in an individual's cognitive system, rather than in physical pathology. He uses the term 'rogue representation' to refer to inappropriate information in the cognitive system, and outlines some of the sources which might lead to such representations (e.g. memory of previous physical states, physical states in others, verbal suggestion). One such source is our

Table 6.3 Seven potential meanings of somatic symptoms

As indices of disease: the biomedical view that symptoms are an index of physical disease which follow automatically from disturbed physiology

As expressions of psychological conflict: the psychological/psychiatric view that emotional distress can lead to physiological disturbances with a wide range of symptoms

As manifestations of specific psychopathology: the psychological/psychiatric view that symptoms may indicate some kind of psychopathology within the person (such as neuroticism or alexithymia)

As cultural idioms of disease: the anthropological view that symptoms can be understood as encoding cultural models of disease and sickness. Thus within one's own social milieu these symptoms are intelligible, but may not be so to outsiders. Culture-related syndromes often have somatic, emotional and social meanings

As metaphors for experience: the more sociologically oriented view that symptoms can be 'idioms of distress' but, further, that the specific meanings symptoms may have change and develop within different social contexts. Thus the meaning of any particular symptom is embedded within the local social world, and we can understand its meaning in terms of how it is presented (rather than represented)

As social positioning: the view that symptoms can be functional; they can serve to reposition social roles or relationships (although the individual may not be consciously aware of this)

As social commentary or contestation: symptoms that are attributed to oppressive circumstances can be seen as protest or contestation (although this does not mean that the symptoms are wilful or intentional)

Adapted from Kirmayer & Young (1998).

sociocultural ideas about symptoms and illness, including 'family, the medical profession, the media, the Internet and society more generally' (p. 803).

However, sociocultural ideas do not only influence 'rogue representations'. We understand all biological changes in our own bodies within a cultural and social framework. This framework is historically contingent. Duden (1991, cited in Nettleton, 1995) analysed accounts of the body and experiences of symptoms in people living in the eighteenth century. Duden noted the very different way in which people experienced bodily signs compared to how we experience our bodies today. She convincingly argued that how the body is understood, and more importantly how it is experienced, is related to the historical context in which people reside. Thus our experiences and interpretations of bodily changes, or physical sensations, are embedded within the historical sociocultural framework in which we live (Lyons, 2000; Yardley, 1997). Such a framework can also function to provide a 'normative' reality for a subgroup of people at a particular time of life. In these ways meanings that are embedded within representations of health and illness can have a strong influence both on how individuals perceive themselves, and on how others view them.

Understanding the experience of pain

The experience of pain is elemental: it is one of the most basic human experiences that we can have (Morris, 1991). However, its interpretation depends heavily on biological, psychological, social and cultural factors. For this reason it is presented here as a case study which highlights how a particular 'sensation' is much more than this: it is a perception and an experience. Research which has examined the experience of pain highlights that although early accounts of pain were relatively simple, the experience of pain is much more complex than this, and comprehending this particular bodily sensation is inherently context bound. This section gives a brief history on how the experience of pain has been understood in the Western world, and how this understanding has changed dramatically over the course of the twentieth century.

Dominant understandings: mechanistic nature of pain

The dominant view of the experience of pain has remained reasonably consistent over the past three hundred years, and can be traced back to Descartes. Descartes gave a mechanistic and behaviourist account of the pain response. He proposed that there was a specific biological pain system which carried messages from pain receptors to the brain, and that pain was observable through behavioural responses to noxious stimuli. These ideas were dominant in conceptions of pain in Western science and medicine until the mid-1960s. Such conceptions of pain are known as **specificity theories** (Horn & Munafò, 1997). Essentially these theories propose that some kind of injury leads to an activation of specific pain channels in the body: receptors and transmitters project messages along a unique spinal pathway to a pain centre isolated in the brain (Horn & Munafò, 1997). This understanding of pain is causal and linear, reinforces the dualistic nature of the body, allows no role for psychological or social factors and emphasises the idea of 'body as machine'. Specificity theories could not account for cases in which there was no observable organic pathology for the pain, such as **phantom limb pain**.

Pain arises from one specific linear biological system. In sum, injury leads to an activation of specific pain receptors which project messages to a pain centre via a spinal pain pathway.

A person experiencing pain in a limb that has been amputated.

To try and account for non-organic pain, more comprehensive theories of pain were put forward and were together known as **pattern theories**. Essentially, these theories were based on the idea that sensory information is transmitted along more than one pathway to specific spinal cord regions where it is summed and, depending on the output, may or may not be transmitted on to the brain. Horn and Munafò (1997) note that the advantage of pattern theories was that they acknowledged that a simple linear model of pain was inadequate, but their disadvantages stemmed from the fact that the brain was conceptualised as passive (receptive) rather than active, and thus failed to give any active role to psychological processes.

Pain arises from the summation of sensory pain information transmitted to the brain. In sum, sensory information is transmitted along more than one pathway to the dorsal horns, where it is summed (or balanced) and depending on the output, may or may not be transmitted on to the brain.

These models of pain are simplistic and are unable to account for various pain phenomena. For example, they have difficulty accounting for the experience of chronic back pain in patients who have no organic pathology for their pain, the positive effects of placebos on the experience of pain, and individual and cultural differences in pain responses (see below). It was not until the 1960s that Melzack and Wall (1965), building on pattern theories, produced a new theory of pain, **gate-control theory**, which incorporated psychological and cognitive factors, and which essentially redefined pain as a process and provided a new epistemology of pain (Kugelmann, 1997).

Pain arises from an aggregation of pain fibre transmission to the brain which is influenced by the opening or closing of a 'gate' located at the base of the spinal column. This gate can be opened or closed by signals from ascending (e.g. from pain fibres) and descending (e.g. from emotions) pathways.

Gate-control theory: individual and social factors

At its most basic, gate-control theory suggests that psychological and cognitive factors, which are influenced by sociocultural learning and experience, affect the physiological processes involved in the experience of pain perception and response (Bendelow, 1993). Gate-control theory remains a basic stimulus–response model, but its complexity stems from the inclusion of mediating and moderating factors. Its central feature is the notion that there is a 'gate' at the base of the spinal column, which influences pain fibre transmission (Horn & Munafò, 1997). Horn and Munafò succinctly describe the operation of the gate: 'The extent to which this gate is open or closed determines the degree to which pain fibre transmissions pass to the brain stem and cerebral cortex, and consequently the degree to which pain is felt' (p. 3). The gate can be opened or closed by both ascending signals (e.g. from pain fibres) or from descending signals (e.g. from anxiety). In this way gate-control theory integrates psychological, behavioural and physiological elements, and its main value has stemmed from the conceptual shift from a linear to an integrative way of thinking about pain (Horn & Munafò, 1997).

There are clear differences between individuals in their experience of and response to pain. These can stem from a variety of sources. Emotional well-being, anxiety, depression, coping style, memory, locus of control and attention have all been related to pain perception (see Horn & Munafò, 1997, for a review). These factors are often interrelated, raising the query that there may

---

6.3   Lovemaking as a metaphor for pain?

Kugelmann (1999) suggests lovemaking can be considered a metaphor for pain: 'just as people make love, they also make pain' (p. 1663). Both love and pain are manufactured and natural. People fall into love, they also (sometimes quite literally) fall into pain. How we express, alleviate and suffer from pain is a performance. For example, one chronic pain sufferer's boyfriend said 'I could feel when she was hurting real bad because her whole body sent signals to me when I was touching her, and you could feel – and then there were certain points in her body like, right at the base of her spine where there was a big knot' (p. 1668). The performance of pain is cultural, in that the meanings we associate with it are culturally derived, but at the same time it is inherently personal. The same things can be said about the making of love.

be underlying factors having an influence on the relationship. Further, the direction of causality is not always clear (Horn & Munafò, 1997). Differences in pain experience have been found between women and men, in that women are more willing to report pain than men (Robinson *et al.*, 2001). Both men and women report that women are more able to cope with pain than men, and people view this as the result of both biological differences and cultural expectations of gender roles (Bendelow, 1993). A recent review of the literature on age, sex and experience of chronic pain concluded that the evidence was inconsistent: neither age nor sex correlated with chronic pain (Hunter, 2001). SES has also been linked to the reporting of pain in both men and women, in that people of lower SES report experiencing more pain (Hemingway *et al.*, 1997). Cultural differences in pain also exist, as outlined in the next section.

While the gate-control theory does incorporate cognitive and emotional factors, its explanation for the various differences observed between individuals in their experiences of pain is limited. Its major weakness is that it is still mainly a physiological model, with reference to some psychological factors (Horn & Munafò, 1997). Further, the gate-control theory also remains inherently dualistic, with little real integration between physical and psychological systems (Crossley, 2000). The body remains central and primary, with psychological factors playing their role by means of cause and effect relationships upon this physiological system (see Radley, 1997). As Crossley (2000) has argued, gate-control theory is an example of a theory which throws together physical, emotional and behavioural factors with 'little theoretical understanding of how they connect together' (p. 70) (a criticism she also makes of other biopsychosocial models).

Research into pain perception based on the gate-control model has also been criticised. As Bendelow (1993) argues, 'the so-called objective measures such as pain scales are unable to transcend the mind-body dualism and limit how pain is defined' (p. 288). Much of the research has used experimental methods, in which pain is induced in participants at a laboratory while confounding factors are held constant. Psychological factors are varied to examine and quantify their effects on pain perception (Horn & Munafò, 1997). While this provides a controlled environment, these methods isolate participants from the contexts in which they live (Bendelow, 1993). Using alternative methods, Bendelow has highlighted that the meanings and definitions of pain given by participants were not only focused on physical sensations (as experimental paradigms have traditionally assumed), but included feelings and emotions, as well as spiritual and existential notions.

Further, Kugelmann (1997) has argued that a substantive effect of the gate-control theory has been to legitimate new treatment possibilities for pain. Redefining pain as a perception (or experience) rather than a sensation opened all aspects of a patient's life to professional management. Self-management techniques, behaviourist manipulation and cognitive-behavioural therapy all became legitimate treatments for pain (Kugelmann, 1997). Simultaneously, there was a shift in responsibility for pain management from the practitioner to the patient and the practitioner jointly. Kugelmann argues that 'since pain is a multifaceted, essentially subjective experience, the patient-as-person is required to participate "as a person" in the health care system that seeks to comprehend and help him or her' (p. 61). Thus there are no limits to intervention in the person's life, and greater technical management of human suffering (Kugelmann, 1997).

The majority of the research into pain has examined people's chronic pain experiences. Little research in health psychology has examined experiences of specific painful episodes, particularly childbirth. This is surprising given that childbirth is a painful event, but one which has a beginning and an end, and is therefore ideal for examining perceptions and experiences. Two studies in the USA demonstrated that women found childbirth more painful than they had anticipated (see DiMatteo & Kahn, 1997), although one study in the UK found that women's expectations of pain corresponded quite closely with their experiences (Greene, 1993). If the experience of intense pain is perceived as abnormal, this is likely to heighten a woman's anxiety and increase her perceptions of pain (DiMatteo & Kahn, 1997). The more we learn about the psychology of pain in childbirth, the more health professionals may be able to assist women in coping with pain during labour and childbirth. This research would be welcome in health psychology, and may also provide us with further insight into the experience of pain more generally.

Contextualising the pain experience: cultural influences

The extent to which a person responds to or articulates experiencing pain is heavily shaped and modified by specific human cultures. In our Western, industrial culture, we have been persuaded that pain is a medical problem, but as Morris (1991) has argued, pain is much more than complex signals over nerves and neurotransmitters. The scientific Western worldview of pain strips it of human meaning, and it is the individual, social and cultural meaning that will assist with furthering our understanding of pain.

For example, a well-known study by Zborowski (1952) investigated reactions to pain in hospitalised men who came from four different cultural groups: Jewish Americans, Italian Americans, Irish Americans and Old Americans (largely Protestant). Both Jewish American men and Italian American men readily expressed their pain, but in different ways. Jewish American men were mainly concerned about their pain in relation to their health, what it meant, how significant it was, how it might affect their welfare and future, while Italian American men emphasised experiencing the pain itself and forgot it once it had passed. Old Americans did not discuss their pain or display their feelings, but reported them in a matter-of-fact manner. These differences were explained in terms of the different cultural attitudes that we are socialised into (Zborowski, 1952). However, while there were similarities within these ethnic groups, there were also similarities across them. People of lower social class from all groups were concerned about their pain in terms of unemployment and financial worry. The study occurred in a particular social milieu: New York in the early 1950s. If the study were to be repeated today, in a society of mass culture and consumerism, results would be different but still meaningful: interpretations of pain would arise from today's culture, imbuing it with meanings of which we are, in most cases, unaware (Morris, 1991).

In a further study of ethnic differences and pain experience, Lipton and Marbach (1984) investigated the reported pain experience of fifty black, Irish, Italian, Jewish and Puerto Rican patients attending a clinic for facial pain. These patients completed a thirty-five-item questionnaire of their pain experiences and the results showed that the groups did not actually differ in their pain responses for two-thirds of these items. Where differences were found, these concerned emotionality (stoicism versus expressiveness) and how much the pain interfered with daily functioning. Black, Italian and Jewish patients were more likely to be expressive about their pain and report it as affecting their daily functioning than were Irish and Puerto Rican patients. Once again, we see how the cultural world infuses the experience of pain.

In addition to examining pain responses, the study also examined factors that influenced the pain experience. There were clear differences in 'triggers' of the pain experience across the five ethnic groups. Among black patients, increased dependency on social and cultural group members related to greater expressive responses to pain and disrupted daily functioning. For Irish patients, belonging to a close long-standing friendship group of people from an Irish background was related to non-emotional responses to pain and disruptions in usual functioning. Among Italian patients, how long the pain had persisted was most important; pain that had persisted for more than six months was related to expressive pain response and disrupted daily functioning. Psychological distress predicted expressive pain responses in Jewish patients, while psychological distress, social assimilation, medical acculturation and duration of pain were important for pain responses among Puerto Rican patients. In summary, while cultural groups may be quite similar in how they respond to pain, the things that influence these responses are quite different (Lipton & Marbach, 1984).

In different cultures, various settings and conditions are available for the expression of pain (MacLachlan, 1997). Culture shapes our ideas about how much pain we can bear and how we can express our experiences of pain (Radley, 1994). To achieve more of an understanding of pain, we need to look beyond the dominant views of medicine and realise that pain emerges 'at the intersection of bodies, minds and cultures' (Morris, 1991, p. 3).

Summary and implications: the meaning of pain

Despite the emergence of the gate-control theory and the biopsychosocial model in medicine, there remains in clinical practice a clear distinction between 'real' and not-real, or 'psychological', pain. New technologies provide 'objective' measures for determining organic pathology, identifying 'real' and therefore justifiable pain. There is a practical usefulness in legitimising pain through organic pathology, because this fits both with patients' understandings of pain and medical discourses about the body (May *et al.*, 1999). Pain for which there is no observable organic cause is interpreted within a psychosocial model, which, from patients' point of view, casts doubt upon the reality of their embodied experience (see May *et al.*, 1999).

Such a distinction between 'real' and 'unreal' pain has been observed in interviews with patients undertaking a pain management programme in the United States (Kugelmann, 1999). These patients associated 'real' pain with the body, and 'unreal' pain with the mind. Further, the discourses drawn on in these interviews indicated that as we can only know the pain of other people through their expression of it, pain must be produced, brought forth to provide legitimation of it (Kugelmann, 1999). In terms of living in the world with chronic pain, participants described themselves as restless; they were not able to stay in one position for a great length of time, and having to continually move was the primary way of showing pain. Thus chronic pain is not simply a sensation, perception or experience: it is also a way of being and living in the world.

If we want to comprehend the human experience of pain, we need to examine the ways in which the pain has meaning for the individual (Crossley, 2000). Morris (1991) has argued that part of the torment experienced by people in pain today arises from the lack of a cultural understanding of pain, and that this is what we desperately need. We do not just suffer pain: we need to make sense of it, on several levels. It not only invites explanation, it requires one (Morris, 1991). In this way it is an encounter with meaning.

Implications of traditional psychological research for our knowledge concerning symptom perception

The traditional psychological research approach into the ways in which people comprehend and understand somatic sensations is based on the Western dualistic ideology of the person, and its epistemological and ontological assumptions are those of biomedicine. In other words, there is a sharp distinction between objective evidence of disease and individuals' subjective reports of symptoms, and a corresponding discourse about the 'correctness' or 'incorrectness' of how individuals interpret symptoms (biomedicine gives us the 'correct' view). Thus, 'real' symptoms have an underlying, identifiable physical cause, and 'unexplained' symptoms are the result of emotional distress or psychopathology. Such a view has serious implications for the individual. Patients who 'correctly' recognise and interpret 'real' symptoms are not held responsible for them, have the right to occupy the sick role and its associated behaviour, and are viewed as 'rational' because their experience fits with the dominant medical worldview of the body. On the other hand, patients who recognise and interpret 'unexplained' symptoms are positioned as neurotic, malingering, hypochondriac, irrational and so on (Kirmayer & Young, 1998). Thus, there is an underlying assumption that people ought to think in medical terms (Radley, 1994).

When we examine findings from more socially and culturally based research, we find that people employ various systems of meaning when comprehending their bodily experience, both within and between cultures. Somatic symptom recognition and interpretation is not straightforward and is not primarily due to cognitive-perceptual factors, which operate within social and cultural contexts. Traditional psychological research into symptom perception reinforces the dominant status of Western medicine by uncritically accepting that it provides an ultimate truth, rather than viewing it as just one of many sociocultural explanatory frameworks.

If as psychologists we focus on the individual to the exclusion of the social and cultural, we fail to see a huge array of factors that influence our lives as individuals who perceive, experience, explain and interpret bodily sensations and physical changes. We reinforce both the notion that there is only one system of meaning, and also the inequities in status that exist between individuals and medical doctors. We also tend to ignore the meanings that individuals actually give to their somatic sensations, and how these meanings work, what they do and where they come from.

This is important for health professionals, who see, listen to and treat people with physical symptoms. A broader perspective and understanding of the meanings particular symptoms have for individuals from various social and ethnocultural backgrounds, and how these come about, may assist health professionals in understanding their significance and treating them appropriately.

Conclusion

How we interpret bodily sensations depends upon a range of factors, from the cognitive to the cultural. Interpreting sensations as 'symptoms' is not straightforward and has as much to do with the culture in which we live as it does with the mechanics of attention-processing that go on in our minds. Recognising bodily sensations and interpreting them as symptoms is not a solely individual judgement: the work we have reviewed in this chapter shows that this process occurs in a social context, with others and employing ideas from others. However, most importantly we must realise that how we comprehend our bodily experience itself is embedded within social contexts and cultures (Radley, 1994). In trying to further understand how we recognise, perceive and interpret bodily sensations, the reductionism of much mainstream psychology neglects (or fails to even observe) the importance of social and cultural factors.

RECOMMENDED READING

Kirmayer, L. J., & Young, A. (1998). Culture and somatization: clinical, epidemiological and ethnographic perspectives. *Psychosomatic Medicine, 60,* 420–30. This paper provides a solid review of the research on somatisation across cultures. In doing so, it highlights how somatic symptoms have many potential meanings, and how these meanings serve diverse psychological and social functions.

Kolk, A. M. M., Hanewald, G. J. F. P., Schagen, S. & Gijsbers van Wijk, C. M. (2003). A symptom perception approach to common physical symptoms. *Social Science and Medicine, 57,* 2343–54. In this paper Kolk and colleagues provide an introduction to their symptom perception model, which is based on the theoretical work of Pennebaker, Kirmayer and Cioffi. It provides an accessible review of findings on the cognitive-perceptual processes involved in interpreting symptoms.

Kugelmann, R. (1997). The psychology and management of pain. *Theory and Psychology, 7,* 43–65. In this paper Kugelmann outlines how pain has been conceptualised since the 1950s, and how it has been dealt with in the biomedical model. He shows how the gate-control theory of pain, by redefining pain as a process, opened up new possibilities for patients with pain, and also new possibilities for health professionals. The outcome, as Kugelmann argues critically and coherently, is that professionals now have authority over much greater realms of people's lives, and there is more technical management of people's suffering.

7 Interacting with health professionals

There is ample evidence that communication should be considered as a power-ful tool in medicine, not only in establishing a workable relationship with the patient, but also in both the diagnosis and therapeutic process.   (Bensing *et al.*, 2003, p. 27)

Effective delivery of health care depends to a great extent on the quality of the interaction between health care providers (doctors, nurses, allied health care professionals, informal caregivers) and consumers of health care (those seeking care and their loved ones).   (Kreps *et al.*, 2003, p. 3)

Learning objectives

The aim of this chapter is to review research on what influences people to seek health care, and what factors influence the quality of the interaction they have with health professionals. By the end of this chapter, you should be able to:

- identify factors that influence when and why people seek health care;
- discuss some of the functions of patient–health professional interaction;
- describe influences on the quality of patient–health professional interactions, including those at the individual, social and cultural level;
- offer an analysis of the ways in which power operates within interactions with health professionals;
- critique the current state of research into patient–health professional interaction;
- outline some of the implications of traditional patient–health professional interaction research;
- offer suggestions for future research in this area.

Why is it that some people are notoriously bad at going to see a doctor? They may be lying in their sick bed, feeling terrible and yet refuse to contact their GP to make an appointment and be extremely reluctant to get any medical help. Men tend to do this more than women. And why is it that we can often feel so ill at ease when we do have an appointment with a doctor? Is it simply because we are not feeling very well, or because we have fears: fearing the potential of bodily probing, fearing that we may really be quite ill, or alternatively fearing that there may be nothing wrong with us at all and that the doctor may privately think that we are malingering? Or is it because, once in the consultation room, our status and personhood is suddenly gone, and we are forced to take up the submissive position of 'patient'? Do we fear being judged as 'sick' (or not) by the expert, the person to whom we trust our physical (and sometimes psychological) well-being? The relationship between an individual and a health professional is unique, and this is partly to do with the power imbalance and the roles imposed on each party. In this chapter we explore the research on the relationships people have with health professionals, including aspects of the consultation, communication and broader contexts in which these interactions occur.

Who are 'health professionals'?

In Western societies, health professionals are people who have been trained and licensed (usually by governments) to work within a medical system of health care. This system is one which derives its knowledge from modern science, and which is based on the biomedical model of health and illness (see ch. 1). Health professionals work in various settings and deliver various kinds of health care. Pharmacists, nurses, occupational therapists, physiotherapists, consultant surgeons, GPs, district nurses, midwives and clinical psychologists are all examples of health professionals.

Within this group of trained professionals there is a status hierarchy, with physicians (doctors) located at the top. Since the first developments in biomedicine, doctors have held a dominant position in health care. During the twentieth century this dominance has been bolstered by the use of new technologies and new medicines and drugs, such as insulin and antibiotics. The effectiveness of these drugs in treating common illnesses has reinforced the power of the doctor (the only person able to prescribe drugs) and sustained people's beliefs that they are better off seeing a doctor rather than other types of healer or practitioner, such as homeopaths. However, this appears to be

The degree to which patients adhere to, rather than comply with, medical recommendations for treatment.

changing (see ch. 8). State legislation ensures that only doctors are allowed to prescribe drugs and carry out most surgical procedures. This means that doctors hold the greatest authority and control within the Western system of medicine (Lorber, 1997). However, recently there have been some developments to allow other health professionals, such as nurses and psychologists, prescribing rights.

The degree to which a patient complies with or follows explicitly the expert treatment recommendations of a health professional.

Perhaps this is why most psychological research examining interactions between people seeking health care and health professionals has focused almost exclusively on the doctor–patient relationship. In addition, the majority of this research has been undertaken to examine patients' **adherence** to (or **compliance** with) medical advice, whether this is in the form of taking medication, making lifestyle changes or keeping follow-up appointments. Often patients do not adhere to what their doctor tells them to do, and psychologists have explored why this is the case. Again, this research has largely focused on the doctor–patient consultation (see ch. 8 for more on adherence to treatment regimes). Although people in industrialised societies increasingly seek health care and advice from complementary and alternative practitioners (Eisenberg *et al.*, 2001), relatively little health psychology research has been conducted in this area. Chapter 8 provides an overview of complementary and alternative medicine and its uptake. In this chapter we focus on the processes involved in seeking medical health care, as well as on the nature of the interactions people have with medical professionals once they have sought care.

Terminology employed in this area varies greatly. Some researchers talk about patients and doctors, others about patients and medical personnel or health professionals. Kreps (2001) points out that his use of the terms 'provider' and 'consumer' is strategic, to encourage a broadening of research. Specifically, 'provider' implies less of a focus on the doctor and more on a variety of health professionals, while 'consumer' implies less of a focus on the individual patient and more on family members and other concerned parties. In this chapter we will primarily discuss 'patients', 'doctors' and 'health professionals' as relevant, because these have been the focus of the majority of the studies reviewed here.

What influences people to seek care from a health professional?

Commonsense tells us that people see a doctor because they are ill or are experiencing symptoms. Indeed, the number of chronic health problems, the number of symptoms and the extent of disability from symptoms are all strongly influential in whether a person seeks care (see Edelmann, 2000). The more symptoms individuals have, the more health problems they experience and the more disability they feel, the more likely they will be to seek professional care. Further, if physical symptoms are recurrent, then it is more likely that a person will seek help for them from a medical professional (Zola, 1973). Thus, individuals' physical health status is a strong predictor of their seeking medical attention. Yet people visit their GP for a variety of reasons, including psychosocial problems, legitimation, explanations, support and advice (Salmon & Quine, 1989).

There are factors other than physical ones that influence help seeking. A number of factors have been studied, from the individual to the cultural. Psychologists have employed models, such as the health belief model (see fig. 7.1), to examine care-seeking behaviour. As we saw in ch. 6, the culture within which we live influences the ways in which we interpret and make sense

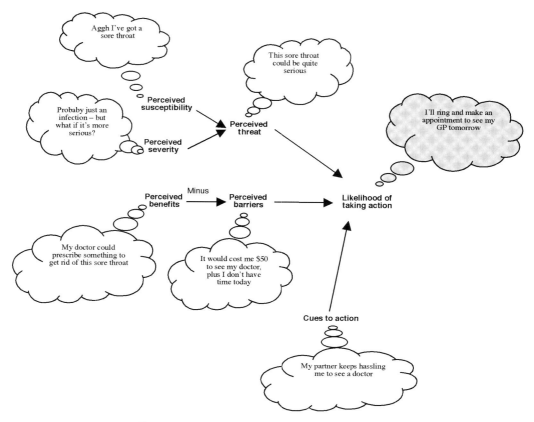

Figure 7.1 *Do I go to see a doctor for my sore throat? The Health Belief Model decision process*

of physical symptoms, and consequently influences seeking health care. Other factors that have been shown to influence care seeking behaviour are discussed below.

Social factors

The group of people (friends, relatives, colleagues) we talk to and seek advice from.

Social factors, such as our **lay referral network**, influence decisions about going to the doctor. When we are not sure about our physical symptoms and whether they are serious enough to seek professional help, we often talk to other people about them to get advice and reassurance. Other people's advice to go and see a doctor is a significant predictor of whether or not a doctor is seen, especially if the person with symptoms was thinking about seeking professional care initially (Berkanovic *et al.*, 1981). Impact on social activities is also important: people are more likely to seek medical care if their physical symptoms are disrupting their routine activity, or if they interfere with enjoyable social activity (Zola, 1973).

Age

Age is another factor that influences how people make decisions to visit health professionals. For example, Ginsburg *et al.* (1997) found that teenagers in the USA worry a lot about disease transmission when they enter a health care setting, and that this can deter them from seeking care. They are also concerned about the competence and interpersonal style of the doctor. Ginsburg *et al.* point out that some simple steps could be taken by health professionals to alleviate teenagers' main concerns about seeking help, such as washing their hands in front of the patient before using sterile equipment, displaying diplomas and certificates and explaining why patients are sometimes seen in the order in which they arrive at the clinic.

Stress

Research evidence indicates that stress is positively related to seeking health care. The more 'stressed' people feel, the more likely they are to visit a doctor (e.g. Cockerham *et al.*, 1988). Stress may affect susceptibility to infectious diseases directly through immune pathways (see ch. 5), or indirectly through changes in health behaviours (drinking more alcohol, eating less well), leading to more illness and therefore to more health centre visits (see Cohen & Williamson, 1991). Alternatively, stress may affect the way in which we perceive our bodily sensations (see ch. 6). According to Zola (1973), one potential trigger for seeking health care is an interpersonal crisis, such as relationship or work difficulties. In these cases a doctor may be seen for emotional support as much as medical advice.

Gender

Research evidence consistently demonstrates that women see doctors and health care professionals more often than men, a difference which remains even when visits for reproductive issues such as menstruation and pregnancy are not included (Verbrugge, 1985). This may appear to contradict the consistent finding that women live longer than men. As epidemiologists note, 'women get sicker, but men die quicker' (Lorber, 1997). So why is it that women seek more care from health practitioners than men? As shown in table 7.1, explanations range from the biological through to the psychological and social (Nettleton, 1995). Women appear to experience more non-serious **acute illness** and **chronic illness** than men (Rodin & Ickovics, 1990), suggesting biological reasons for the difference. Other researchers have argued that there are social psychological explanations for why women see health professionals more than men do. Radley (1994) discusses data from Great Britain which show that in 1991, women did see their GP more than men did, but that this difference depended upon the economic situation of men – those

Illness that lasts only a relatively short time and has an end

Illness that is ongoing and is usually irreversible.

Table 7.1 Why do women see health professionals more than men?

Level	Explanation
Biological	Women have higher rates of acute illnesses and most nonfatal chronic conditions, including obesity, diabetes, anaemia, respiratory and gastrointestinal problems (Verbrugge, 1985)
Social psychological employment	Men who are economically inactive (defined as not seeking or not wanting work) report just as high levels of illness as women
sick role	Due to social roles, it is easier for women to take up the 'sick role' than men. Many women are in a domestic situation, while many men are in full-time employment and are less able to take time off sick (Nathanson, 1975)
stress	Women's lives are more stressful than men's, which leads to illness. The stress arises from occupying multiple roles, routinised jobs, childcare, caring for elderly parents and the 'double shift' of work and housework (Lorber, 1997)
gender roles	Culturally it is more acceptable for women to say they are ill than it is for men. Traditionally, femininity has been aligned with health and caring while masculinity is aligned with work and the public sphere
Social / structural	Women are more likely to suffer poverty, earn less and be in the lower SES groups, all of which are major determinants of ill health (Lee, 1998; Nettleton, 1995)

who were economically inactive (defined as not seeking or not wanting work) reported similar rates of visiting a GP as did women. Nathanson (1975) has argued that the ease of taking up a 'sick role' might explain these differences. As many women are in a domestic situation, it is easier for them to take up the sick role.

It has also been argued that women's lives and the roles they occupy give rise to more stress than men's, which in turn leads to illness (Lorber, 1997). When both partners work, women carry out more childcare and housework, and this is observed in all social classes. Some evidence shows that juggling combinations of roles can have a negative effect on women's physical health (e.g. Lee, 1998). Gender roles may also help to explain differences in men's and women's care-seeking behaviour. The feminine sphere is defined in terms of care, nurturance and attending to physical well-being and symptoms, while the masculine sphere is defined in terms of work, rationality and goals. Men are encouraged to be strong and healthy, and not to see a doctor for anything but a serious illness. Differences in masculinity and femininity mean that there are differences in sensitivity to illness and in the ability to report it (Annandale & Hunt, 1990). Further, as discussed in ch. 3, recent research evidence shows that health care for all members of the family, including male partners, continues to be constructed as women's responsibility (Lyons & Willott, 1999).

At the wider social and political level, researchers have argued that women's poorer health can be explained by the fact that women are socially disadvantaged in terms of education, income and political influence. Even though gender-equality laws have been passed in most developed countries, these have had little effect on women's status or quality of life (Lee, 1998). Other researchers argue that current sociopolitical structures are not only disadvantageous to women, but also to some groups of men (e.g. those in lower socioeconomic groups, those marginalised by ethnicity or disability), which may help to explain men's under-reported illness and higher rates of mortality at all ages (Hodgetts & Chamberlain, 2002).

In summary, we can see that whether or not we seek professional care depends on many more factors than simply physical symptoms, biological changes or perceived need. Psychological factors, social roles, daily activities and culture all affect the decision to seek medical attention. While much research has examined factors that influence the decision to seek medical care, more recently the focus has also been on exploring factors that influence how long it takes people to seek medical care. This has arisen partly out of findings that show the longer a person delays seeking help for some illnesses, the worse their outcome (see sidebar 7.1).

> **7.1 Taking one's time to seek medical care for a lump in the breast affects life expectancy**
>
> The longer women delay after finding a lump in their breast, the worse their long-term outcome appears to be. In one study, 50 per cent of women who sought help within three months of detecting a lump in their breast were alive eight years later. Of the women who took more than six months to seek help, only 31 per cent were alive eight years later. (Neale *et al.*, 1986)

Doctor–patient interactions: why is a successful interaction so important?

Despite advances in science and medicine over the past hundred and fifty years, 'a large proportion of patient illness and disease remains undiagnosable, in practice unpreventable, and increasingly in Western societies, incurable' (Winefield, 1992, p. 171). Often, whether patients receive effective help depends on their interaction with doctors, and the help is often psychological rather than physiological in nature. The following examples (adapted from Winefield, 1992) illustrate this point:

- Many patients see their doctor for chronic conditions that cannot be effectively treated or cured (e.g. arthritis, heart disease), and medical care mainly consists of providing emotional and practical support.
- Interpersonal stress can influence and aggravate existing physical symptoms and problems, so interactions focus on dealing with patients' stresses to alleviate symptoms.

- In a similar manner, psychological problems such as anxiety and depression can exacerbate physical conditions.
- GPs are the first point of contact for individuals with psychological symptoms, and non-psychiatrist GPs provide most medical care for patients with psychological symptoms, including anxiety disorders, behavioural disorders, bereavement, stress and chronic mental illness.
- Some patients present physical symptoms for psychological problems and interpersonal inadequacies. It is easier to get help for physical symptoms than for other problems, and there is no stigma attached to seeking care for physical symptoms. Winefield quotes Foss and Rothenberg (1987) who make the point that 'the biomedical model is pathology-inducing in its own right by virtue of its systematic exclusion of extra-somatic etiological factors'. Essentially, these authors are saying that the biomedical model focuses only on physical causes of illness and excludes a consideration of other causes of illness (e.g. psychological, environmental, social, cultural – see ch. 5), and this in itself may have negative consequences for health.

7.2 Some of the functions of a medical encounter

eliciting information
giving advice
giving explanations
giving reassurance
finding and communicating a diagnostic label
weighing diagnostic and/or risk information
discussing therapeutic options and alternative solutions
checking on health progress
giving referrals
strengthening self-efficacy in maintaining difficult
  therapeutic regimes
reaching a medical decision (shared or not)
acknowledging, fighting or relieving anxiety and
  depression
providing moral support, comfort and strength
(Adapted from Bensing *et al.*, 2003)

Over a decade ago, Winefield (1992) pointed out that within the Western biomedical system interactions between patients and health professionals were viewed as an adjunct to care. Doctors did not spend much of their training learning about the importance of interaction and communication with the patient. From the medical viewpoint, effective interactions between patients and health professionals are important, not because they are an essential part of the care package but for other, more basic, reasons. For example, depending on the stage of treatment and the needs of the patient, medical encounters serve a variety of purposes (see sidebar 7.2). The importance of the quality of the interaction between patients (and their loved ones) and health professionals for effective health care is now widely acknowledged (Kreps *et al.*, 2003) and has a direct influence on many important health outcomes (Kreps, 2001).

What makes a good doctor–patient consultation? How do we measure success in this area? On the whole there is a lack of theoretical frameworks. The research has been piecemeal, with separate and specific factors selected and examined across a number of different disciplines, including psychology, communication, medicine, sociology, public health, nursing, pharmacy and anthropology (Kreps *et al.*, 2003). The ultimate outcome for any medical encounter should be improved health (Winefield, 1992). However, as you can imagine, this can be a difficult concept to measure within one research study. Health psychologists have tended to examine the success of the doctor–patient interaction in terms of adherence, communication recall, and satisfaction:

* Adherence: many studies in health psychology have used adherence as the main outcome measure to assess the quality of the doctor–patient encounter. However, there are other influences on adherence besides the medical interaction, and the ways in which adherence is assessed are diverse, making it difficult to make comparisons across studies (see ch. 8).
* Retaining information: the ability of patients to retain and recall information they have been told in a medical encounter is one outcome measure that has been used to assess the encounter, especially in comparisons of how information is best delivered (e.g. verbally, verbally and with a letter, by videotape, etc.).
* Satisfaction: how satisfied the patient is with the interaction is another factor that has been employed to assess outcome. As Winefield (1992) also notes, patient loyalty and failure to sue could also be considered here! The research on doctor–patient interaction tends to show that patients are often dissatisfied with aspects of the communication in the encounter (Ong *et al.*, 1995). Patient satisfaction, in turn, is related to a number of positive health outcomes (Bensing *et al.*, 2003). How satisfied the doctor is with the interaction has also been employed as an outcome in this area of research.

Influences on the quality of doctor–patient interactions

Interactions that take place between a health professional and a patient are dynamic exchanges of information and communication. Much research has examined social factors, such as age and gender, in medical encounters to see whether these impact on the outcome. In this section, we review evidence concerning aspects of the patient, the doctor, the communication, the context of the interaction and specific patient populations that influence the quality of interaction.

The patient in doctor–patient interaction

Research indicates that patients who have more education, and those from higher SES groups, are given more information in their interactions with health professionals, and that their consultations last longer than those with less education and those from lower SES groups. Women patients tend to be given more information, while older patients tend to be more satisfied with their interactions with health professionals than younger patients, although not all studies support this (Roter & Hall, 1992). Sicker patients are less satisfied with their doctors than are healthier patients. Why is this the case? As Hall (2003) states:

> Because physicians like their sicker patients less than their healthier ones, one hypothesis is that physicians behave toward sicker patients in ways that hurt their satisfaction. On the other hand, a more direct path would be that sicker patients are dissatisfied with life in general (including their physicians), so that their physician's negative attitudes are not what produces dissatisfaction ...   (p. 10)

Research supports this latter path, although also shows that doctors engage in less social conversation with sicker patients, which in turn affects satisfaction (Hall *et al.*, 1998).

Children

The asymmetry that occurs in interactions with adult patients and health professionals is doubled in children's interactions: the doctor has not just institutional but also adult authority (Tates & Meeuwesen, 2001). Little research has actually examined the experiences of children in studies on interactions with health professionals (Carter, 2002). The research that has been carried out shows that children are usually not given the opportunity to discuss their experiences in doctor–patient interactions and are often not actively involved in the encounter (Carter, 2002; Tates & Meeuwesen, 2001; van Dulmen, 1998). This is highlighted in a recent qualitative study, which is described in research in focus box 7.1. Parents speak for children and doctors focus their attention on parents rather than children. Carter identified the process of professional ventriloquism, whereby doctors effectively bypass the children's experience and articulate what they believe the child's experience to be.

In a review of research examining doctor–parent–child interaction, Tates and Meeuwesen (2001) concluded that, first, this topic has been insufficiently studied, and second, the studies which have been conducted focus on the dyad interaction between parent and doctor. Research methodologies in the studies were also primarily based on dyads (despite the presence of three individuals) and outcome measures surprisingly do not include children's satisfaction with the interactions.

Culture

Individuals' cultural identities (their understanding of their cultural background, not simply their race or ethnicity) influence how they interact with both health professionals and the health system more generally (Prideaux, 2001). Ethnic minorities living within a Western society often have different information needs and preferences for particular ways of communicating from those of the dominant culture, and this can lead to problematic and dissatisfying

7.1 Children with chronic pain interacting with doctors

Carter, B. (2002). Chronic pain in childhood and the medical encounter: professional ventriloquism and hidden voices. *Qualitative Health Research, 12*, 28–41.

Very little research has examined children's experiences of chronic pain or their experiences of interacting with health professionals. The original aim of this study was to explore the impact of living with chronic pain among children experiencing the pain and their families. Only as the research progressed did the importance of medical encounters emerge as an issue. Three children with chronic pain and their families took part in the study (two girls aged 13, one boy aged 12). There were two phases to the data collection. The children and their parents wrote a journal for six weeks about their own experiences and feelings of 'living with chronic pain' before family interviews were conducted. The diaries were briefly analysed before the interviews, to help with an interview guide and to follow up particular concerns. Each family was interviewed at least twice. Data were thematically analysed. Transcripts of each interview with some preliminary analysis notes were sent back to each family so that they could comment, delete or add data. The final themes derived from the analysis were interrelated and highlighted the importance of the medical encounter as an issue in all the data sets.

The quest for a diagnosis and referral fatigue

Families were frustrated and distressed that it was so difficult to get a diagnosis for the child's pain. Although they felt let down, parents tried to be fair in talking about what they viewed as unsuccessful medical encounters. Nurses were seen as peripheral. Children also felt frustrated by seeing different doctors and having the same questions asked of them:

> Same pain, different doctor. Similar checks, then started on the 'how are things going at school?' routine. [she] rolled her eyes in desperation at me – knew she wasn't going to get any help. (Mother in interview)

Professional judgement and disbelief

Children and families felt that they were being judged and disbelieved in their interactions with medical professionals, which was clearly distressing and undermined confidence. Children said they felt angry about this:

> One doctor told me that what she was seeing on examination and what she was being told were two different things. I was 11, and I knew that I was being accused of lying. This made me really angry, because it didn't help the pain (it actually got worse) and it really hurt me to be called a liar when the pain was very real. (Child in diary entry)

Communication or ventriloquism?

Children felt they had a lot to say but were rarely asked and were rarely involved in the 'important stuff' in any medical encounter. Any interaction between the doctor and the child was restricted to providing answers to specific medical-diagnostic questions. Often parents were used as a conduit for their child's experiences, a form of adult–child ventriloquism. Children were acutely aware of this and wanted to be dealt with as individuals:

> [doctors should] . . . explain everything a bit more widely . . . tell me what they'd decided and why . . . and talk to me more, not just my mum. (Child in interview)

Professionals who believe the family

Children viewed successful medical encounters as those in which they were listened to and believed, even when no diagnosis was given. The 'pain team' (a multidisciplinary group of professionals caring for children with chronic pain) were helpful here since their starting assumption was that the child's pain was real. Children and adults felt that encounters with this team were also helpful because they listened and were effective communicators.

Overall, families felt that doctors misinterpreted and reinterpreted what was said about the child's pain through their own paradigmatic understanding. Children felt they were not listened to, taken seriously or given any opportunity to voice their concerns or experiences in a medical encounter.

Reflection

These findings demonstrate clearly how there are two parties (or more) to any medical encounter, each with their own perspectives, understandings and interpretations. This study is a good example of qualitative research drawing on a constructivist approach. The aim is to obtain insights into other people's experiences (similar to phenomenological approaches) but its starting assumption is that these children's and families' experiences are one (or even two) version(s) of reality, which is just as valid as any other version of reality (for example, just as important as the medical professionals' view of the world). Findings from studies such as these highlight the importance of taking into account the lived experiences of the patient in any medical encounter, whether that patient is 10 or 70 years of age.

interactions with health professionals. For example, Australian researchers used focus groups and individual interviews to explore the information needs and communication preferences in a group of Chinese cancer patients and their relatives (Huang *et al.*, 1999). Their results showed the need for interpreters, and psychological and spiritual support. Overall this group preferred a poor prognosis not to be disclosed, and they emphasised the importance of family members liaising with health professionals. The researchers concluded that good quality care would be improved if doctors were aware of the needs of people from ethnic minorities within a country, and were able to provide information in a culturally appropriate and sensitive manner.

The doctor in the doctor–patient interaction

In any interaction between health professionals and patients, health professionals are seen as holding the responsibility for ensuring optimal communication (Winefield, 1992). This is partly because it is their professional role to ensure the interaction goes well and because they have more power and status within the interaction. Winefield also points out that doctors (or other health professionals) occupy a role that is central to their identity: this is what they do and who they are. On the other hand, the patient role is often unwelcome and is (usually) a part-time role. It is interesting to note what happens when doctors themselves become patients (see research in focus box 7.2).

Placing responsibility for the interaction with the professional may heighten his or her view of its importance, although it also reinforces the view of the patient as a passive player in the encounter. Despite the professional role of the doctor in the interaction, very little research has actually examined health professional attributes and characteristics to see how they influence the quality of the encounter.

How a doctor communicates with a patient depends on a variety of factors. These include training and education, informal learning through modelling, peer reinforcement, cultural expectations of the doctor's role, finance and fees (which encourage keeping interactions as brief as possible) (Winefield, 1992). As part of their professional role, doctors are required and expected to show care and respect for all patients, even those whom they find intensely dislikeable or difficult (Winefield, 1992). However, if feelings of hostility or dislike are aroused in the doctor during a medical encounter, this will show in the way in which the interaction proceeds. Patients can detect how much doctors like or dislike them, and personal liking by the doctor has been found to predict patients' satisfaction one year later; patients who perceived that the doctor disliked them felt less satisfied (see Hall, 2003).

The most studied characteristic of health professionals in patient–doctor interaction research is gender (Hall, 2003). A recent meta-analysis of this field concluded that, compared with male doctors, female doctors spend more time with patients, discuss more emotional and psychosocial topics, and demonstrate more partnership building and positive verbal and non-verbal behaviour

7.2 **When general practitioners become patients**

Jaye, C., & Wilson, H. (2003). When general practitioners become patients. *Health: an Interdisciplinary Journal for the Social Study of Health, Illness and Medicine, 7*, 201–25.

There has been limited research into what it means for a doctor to become ill, seek treatment and become a patient. This study reports an analysis of interviews with twenty-six doctors (seventeen male and nine female) who had experienced an illness for which they had sought treatment from another doctor. Participants reported difficulties around selecting a doctor in whom they had confidence, and often delayed seeking help. Having an illness was seen as a source of weakness and, sometimes, of shame, and made it difficult to be a 'good' patient. Having their own medical expertise meant that they felt pressure to remain in control of the situation and they sometimes engaged in self-treatment. Their position as medical experts also warranted ongoing surveillance of their doctor's competence. This in turn frequently made the negotiation of the patient role problematic. These issues are reflected in the following quotations:

> I try to be a good patient . . . I try not to go in and pre-diagnose. I go in with symptoms and try very hard to give a free history, and then sit down and listen to an interrogation and go through the proper process . . . it's sort of stupid to pretend that you're not another doctor but you've got to be honest about it. (p. 209)

> You have to be much clearer and more explicit about your relationship [than with lay patients]. It's got to be spelt out each time you see that person, that; 'Right now, you are the patient, I am the doctor.' And you as doctor need to also make sure that you concentrate on this patient as a patient, and not as a doctor. (p. 213)

> It's almost like sitting an exam . . . The person that you're dealing with has knowledge and will compare your knowledge with their knowledge and you're very aware of that . . . So when you're sitting there as a patient you're aware that this is stressful for the other doctor and therefore you try to make it easy for them. (p. 213)

The authors argue that three intersecting discourses, of patienthood, professionalism and competence, were used to negotiate the complex positioning which arises in doctor-to-doctor consultation and treatment. Although doctors do become ill, they cannot cease being doctors when they are being patients.

Reflection

Doctors, like other people, become ill, yet research like this into doctors' illness suggests that they feel it is inappropriate for them to become ill. When they do become patients, they feel that they should be 'good' patients and demonstrate a rapid recovery, but at the same time that they should avoid giving up control and critically evaluate their treatment and care in the light of their professional experience. Doctors as patients thus problematise both the doctor and patient role in treatment, and acutely expose the issues involved for people seeking and receiving treatment. This research highlights the dilemmas that exist for patients who are expected to be informed and to take charge of their treatment yet be compliant with the expertise of the treatment provider, and how much more complicated that is when the patient is also a doctor.

(Roter *et al.*, 2002). Compared to male doctors, female doctors also like their patients more. In addition, patients like female doctors more than male doctors (Hall, 2003). Patients also speak differently to female doctors than to male doctors, talking in a more positive manner (Hall & Roter, 2002). This may reflect what patients expect women doctors to speak like and be interested in, based on stereotypes of gender (e.g. women are more interpersonally oriented than men) (Hall, 2003). The sensitivity of the doctor to the patient also influences patient satisfaction, with doctors who show more sensitivity having patients who are more satisfied with the interaction (DiMatteo *et al.*, 1986).

The difference in views that health professionals hold of men's and women's visits to GPs was demonstrated in a qualitative study conducted in the UK (Seymour-Smith *et al.*, 2002). These researchers interviewed doctors, a consultant and two nurses to discuss men's health and men's visits to see their GP. Generally, male patients were viewed as passive, irresponsible and childlike when it came to health matters but also as stoical (women were viewed as both responsible and health conscious). These health professionals discussed women forcing their male partners to go and see a doctor, with men being 'brought kicking and screaming by partners' (p. 257). Men were also viewed as 'bad' at discussing emotional issues, as one male doctor described it: 'once she's [woman partner] provided the sort of, the initial sort of idea, of the problem I can now turn to him . . . it's almost like pulling toenails' (p. 258). This view of men was presented as something we all know, a taken-for-granted fact. What was particularly interesting, however, was that in addition to these views of men, male patients were also seen as the serious users of the health service. As Seymour-Smith *et al.* note, 'this normalizes women's presence at health services but as a consequence women are also seen as the less significant patients and this works rhetorically to construct men as the more serious users of the health service' (p. 259). The study also highlighted how gay men are invisible in health professionals' talk about male patients.

Communication in the doctor–patient interaction

Providing information (by both patients and doctors) is one of the main processes of communication that occurs during interaction between a patient and a health professional. Different aspects of the communication itself have been studied, including the use of technical language, types of communication patterns used within interactions, and topics of communication, such as discussing uncertainty and unconventional therapies and breaking bad news to patients.

Technical language

The use of technical language by health professionals has been identified as limiting effective communication with patients. Employing technical language in a consultation contributes to the power imbalance between the patient and the health professional. This technical language, the possible time pressures involved in a consultation, and the status differences between patient and health professional may mean that patients do not ask questions or seek explanations. For example, Lyons *et al.* (2002) carried out interviews with patients who had undergone **coronary catheterisation**, and found that the doctor's technical language was an obstacle to patients' understandings of what the procedure involved, as shown by the following quote:

A procedure performed to see the presence and degree of narrowing or blockages in the coronary arteries. It involves directing a tube into these arteries (via groin or arm) and injecting an x-ray dye.

> with all due respect, doctors tend to speak in doctor language. They don't realize that they are talking to laymen, or laypeople . . . they tend to speak to you, you know, as though you know all the lingo and you don't. So you . . . you might nod your head and say yes, yes, but when you go away you think, 'what the heck was that about?'   (p. 464)

Communication patterns

Two decades ago, Mishler (1984) argued that communication patterns between doctors and patients were distorted because doctors used the rational, scientific voice of medicine, which was incompatible with the natural, everyday 'voice of the lifeworld' employed by patients. The result of this incompatibility was that patients' coherent and meaningful accounts were suppressed in the interaction (Barry *et al.*, 2001). Barry and colleagues recently investigated whether the same distorted patterns of communication occur between patients and GPs in the UK today. After gaining consent from both patients and GPs, the researchers audiotaped actual consultations between patients and GPs. They also undertook individual interviews with patients prior to and following the consultation, and they interviewed the doctors following each consultation. Their results showed that four different patterns of communication took place during the medical encounter. Table 7.2 provides a description of these patterns and identifies the major outcome resulting from each. Doctors used different voices in different consultations, sometimes drawing on the voice of medicine and sometimes on the voice of the lifeworld.

Table 7.2 Giving voice to the lifeworld: four doctor–patient communication patterns

Pattern	Description	Outcome
Strictly medicine	Both doctors and patients spoke exclusively in the voice of medicine; the consultation was typically focused on single acute problems	Successful for simple consultations
Mutual lifeworld	Both doctors and patients spoke predominantly in the voice of the lifeworld; consultations were typically focused on psychological problems	Most favourable: achieves empathy, equality and is holistic
Lifeworld blocked	Patients talk in voice of lifeworld but this is silenced by doctors' use of voice of medicine; typically associated with consultations involving chronic physical problems	Most dysfunctional consultation
Lifeworld ignored	Patients talk extensively in voice of the lifeworld but this is completely ignored by doctors, who remain speaking in the voice of medicine; also associated with chronic physical problems	Most problematic and difficult consultation

Barry *et al.* (2001).

Discussing uncertainty

There is an increasing move for doctors to be more open and honest with patients. Uncertainty is a central part of medicine, and is frequently a factor in many interactions between patients and doctors. Is it beneficial for doctors to tell patients when they are not sure about something? One study suggests that some expressions of uncertainty are actually detrimental and damage patients' confidence in their doctor (e.g. asking a nurse for advice), whereas other expressions of uncertainty are seen as having no influence or a positive influence on patient's confidence (e.g. using a book or computer to find information) (Ogden *et al.*, 2002). Expressions of uncertainty were most detrimental to patients who were younger, of a lower SES group and who had known their doctor for less time than other patients.

Discussing unconventional therapies

Communication about complementary and alternative therapies also influences both patients' and doctors' perceptions of the general success of the interaction. For example, patients with cancer who wished to discuss their interest in unconventional therapies with their doctors found their interactions disappointing (Gray *et al.*, 1998). This study showed that, from the patients'

7.3   What undermines patients' confidence? What patients and GPs think about doctors' uncertain statements and behaviour

Patients' views on what undermines their confidence in GPs in consultations

1 'Let's see what happens.'
2 'I don't know.'
3 Asking a nurse for advice.
4 'I think this might be . . .'
5 'I haven't come across this before . . .'
6 'I'm not sure about this.'
7 'I need time to find out more.'
8 Used a book to find out about a condition.
9 Used a computer to find out about a condition.
10 Asked another GP for advice.

GPs' views on what undermines patients' confidence

1 'I haven't come across this before.'
2 'I don't know.'
3 Asking a nurse for advice.
4 'Let's see what happens.'
5 'I'm not sure about this.'
6 Used a book to find out about a condition.
7 Asked another GP for advice.
8 'I think this might be. . .'
9 'I need time to find out more.'
10 Used a computer to find out about a drug. (Adapted from Dobson, 2002, and Ogden *et al.*, 2002)

perspective, doctors who would talk to them about unconventional therapies openly (whether positively or negatively) were more helpful than doctors who remained neutral and disengaged. Overall, patients wanted their doctors to be responsive, less dismissive and less rooted in an inflexible medical orthodoxy. On the other hand, doctors viewed patients as responsible for communication about unconventional therapies, and viewed problematic encounters as arising from aspects relating to patients, such as their denial or hostility, unrealistic expectations of their doctor, disorganisation in seeking information and inability to tolerate reality. As we will see in ch. 8, the joint use of conventional and alternative therapies is rising (Eisenberg *et al.*, 2001), and doctors are increasingly referring patients to alternative therapists (Zollman & Vickers, 1999a). Conversely, however, most patients do not disclose their use of alternative therapies to their doctors. Eisenberg *et al.* (2001) reported that over 60 per cent of patients did not reveal such use. Common reasons given for this were 'It wasn't important for the doctor to know', 'The doctor never asked', 'It was none of the doctor's business' and 'The doctor would not understand' (Eisenberg *et al.*, 2001, p. 349).

Breaking bad news

Some research has examined how health professionals break bad news to patients. According to this research, there are many problems with ensuring effective communication with patients when the communication is negative. Dosanjh *et al.* (2001) report that medical and surgical residents in Canada identified their own fears, a lack of supervisory support and time constraints as hindering their communication and delivery of bad news to patients. They comment that no delivery of bad news can be read off a script, and that it must include an emotional connection or response for it to be effective. To improve the way in which health professionals communicate bad news to patients, increased skills training, the provision of a stronger support network of peers and supervisors and fewer time constraints were suggested (Dosanjh *et al.*, 2001). Indeed, specific education initiatives have been developed to prepare health professionals for the task of communicating bad news to patients, and these seem to be beneficial (Farrell *et al.*, 2001). Other researchers have interviewed both cancer patients and health professionals about delivering prognostic information. Results demonstrate the importance of several factors, including a long-term and caring relationship with the health professional, consistency of communication within the multidisciplinary team, and communicating the prognosis in a clear and straightforward manner if the patients wish it (Butow *et al.*, 2002). To ensure successful delivery of bad news, there needs to be social engagement between the patient and the doctor, some kind of relationship history and adequate time available for doctors to spend in consultation with patients.

The context of the doctor–patient interaction

Interactions between patients and health professionals do not exist in a vacuum, but are influenced by the context in which they take place (Bensing *et al.*, 2003). Situational influences such as amount of time available, patient load and previous history in the relationship all affect the success of the communication between patients and health professionals (Roter & Hall, 1992). Bensing and colleagues (2003) have argued that it is now time for research to examine some of the contextual features of doctor–patient interaction. They outline four particular contexts which have largely been ignored but deserve attention in this field:

- the context of goals or targets of both parties: a focus on addressing the goals of both the patient and the health professional during interactions, and using relevant communication strategies to achieve this;
- the context of time: a focus on the influence of previous encounters, the patient's medical history, the continuity of care that has been received (or not);
- the context of the organisation: a focus on time constraints, priorities (both implicit and explicit) of health professionals, policies regarding working conditions and teamwork;
- the context of multifaceted parties: a focus on all parties present in an interaction, including partners, child, caregiver, nurse, other care providers, and their needs, expectations, knowledge, skills, experience, etc. The dynamics of an interaction change even with the mere presence of another person.

Other, broader contextual features are also important for any consideration of interactions between patients and health professionals.

Society

Consideration of context must include a consideration of the position of medicine in society. In Western medicine the encounter between the health professional and the patient is imbalanced, because the patient has less status, knowledge and power than the health professional. The interaction is political in that it can legitimise the patient's suffering and distress, and allow individuals to enter the 'sick role', within which there are considerable social benefits (Parsons, 1951). For example, by taking up the sick role a people are able to stay off work, rest in bed, have others take care of them, and receive attention and concern. Further, participants in a medical encounter come to the situation with different expectations, ideas and worldviews. As we saw previously with interactions between children and doctors, the patient's worldview and experience are often reinterpreted into the doctor's own paradigms of understanding. The differences in social status and power between doctor and patient influences what can be said in any encounter, particularly by the patient but also by the doctor (for example, in the role of doctor one cannot tell patients that they smell and should leave the room).

Culture and the health care system

The doctor–patient interaction in Western medicine reflects the ethos of a patient as an independent individual seeing an autonomous doctor. However, in different cultures there is less emphasis on individuality and autonomy. For example, the individual in Mexico is not isolated but embedded within a family and a moral order, and this is reflected in health care (see Finkler, 1991). However, as noted previously, often the form of help provided in doctor–patient interactions in Western medicine is psychological, rather than biological, to a much greater extent than we acknowledge (Winefield, 1992). Finkler (1991, p. 226) argues that the nature of the medical encounter in Western medicine is extremely important, and views it as part of the therapy of healing:

> Biomedical practice relies greatly upon patient management during the therapeutic encounter because its healing techniques lack means to resolve the contradictions by which the patient is encompassed, to deal with the patient's subjective experience, or to reorder the patient's life. For this reason treatment hinges not only on healing techniques and underlying etiological understandings but on the encounter itself and the physician's personality.

Finkler (1991) has undertaken research in Mexico examining the differences in relationships and interactions that patients have with doctors (trained in Western medicine) and with complementary health care workers, namely spiritualists. These two types of healer are very dissimilar on the face of it, with disparate epistemologies, practices and methods. Doctors work within a biomedical context in a professionalised system which is legitimised by the state. Spiritualists work within a sacred context without state legitimation and are usually denigrated by the medical establishment (Finkler, 1991). However, there are also strong similarities in the healing relationship each offers, as shown in sidebar 7.4.

Interactions with specific populations

As populations become more diverse, understanding doctor–patient interactions with specific populations becomes particularly important (Ramirez, 2003). This includes a consideration of interactions between people from different minority ethnic and cultural backgrounds (whether doctor or patient). Despite the large body of research on doctor–patient interactions, very little of it has specifically addressed minority groups or other populations. The research that has been conducted has involved African Americans and Hispanics/Latinos in the USA (Ramirez, 2003), and some work has also been conducted with minority groups (particularly Pakistani and Indian) in the UK. Even less research has examined interactions between doctors and people with disabilities.

7.4 Similarities between Western doctors and Mexican spiritualists

Both types of healers:

have a dualist view of the body;
focus primarily on bodily disturbances;
wear white robes (symbolically separating them from their patients);
try and look inside the patient's body; spiritualists are assisted by the gaze of spirits, doctors by technological apparatus;
have similar lengths of consultation.

Patients of both types of healers:

seek help for physical symptoms;
present their symptoms in a similar way;
take a largely passive role in interactions.
(Adapted from Finkler, 1991)

Ethnicity

Concordance between doctor's and patient's ethnicity has been found to be important in studies examining ethnicity. When doctors and patients are of the same ethnicity, there is more patient satisfaction (Saha *et al.*, 1999). African Americans who see black doctors report that they are treated with more respect, and receive more medical and preventive care, than African Americans who see other doctors (Saha *et al.*, 1999).

There are very few places in the world in which health care operates in a monocultural context (Prideaux, 2001). The importance of teaching cultural awareness and diversity in medical training has become a priority over recent decades, although this is only now beginning to be achieved (for example, the inclusion and study of Aboriginal culture in medical training in Australia; Prideaux, 2001). However, there are still likely to be problems of communication across cultural understandings where illness can have very different meanings, as we noted in ch. 6. Increasing the cultural competence of health professionals, by training in cultural education (e.g. the cultural values, practices and beliefs of patients) and language as appropriate can make a large difference to interactions between doctors and patients (Ramirez, 2003).

Language barriers

Problems with doctor–patient interaction arise when one of the participants does not speak the dominant language. While the use of translators may appear to solve this problem, this is not necessarily the case. A study examining the experiences of Somali women living in the UK found that these women did not receive the maternity information they needed when they were pregnant, and that the usefulness of interpreters was limited by patient fears about misinterpretation and confidentiality (Davies & Bath, 2001). A number of women in this study who used interpreters said they did not seek information from health professionals because they were worried about the information being misinterpreted. Moreover, McCourt and Pierce (2000) found that pregnant women who come from ethnic minorities viewed effective communication with their midwives as a dialogue, in which the midwives sought and attended to the women's views. However, they were also worried that the racial stereotypes held by these health professionals were a barrier to effective communication. These examples demonstrate how parties in any interaction come with their own worldviews and understandings, and consequently how these affect communications and subsequent interpretations.

A qualitative study carried out in a deprived area in the UK showed that even when patients have English as their first language, there are difficulties with communication in medical consultations with GPs (Gardner & Chapple, 1999). Patients viewed the doctors as busy, did not want to be a bother and had low expectations of treatment. These researchers concluded that cultural gaps existed between patients and their GPs and that this could lead to diagnostic confusion, especially when there were other psychological and physical symptoms.

People with disabilities

Health professionals have been found to hold similar prejudices towards people with disabilities as those found more widely (French, 1994). A recent study carried out in Britain examined consultations between people with congenital disabilities and their GP (Muir & Ogden, 2001). Three main themes emerged as helping or hindering giving care:

- aspects of the patient, such as their appearance or mental or speech impairments. Doctors may feel that they (and their consultations with the patient) are affected by these aspects, in terms of feelings of blame and lack of trust. The nature and relationship of the carer may also influence doctors' views and interactions with patients (for example, caregivers who are very protective);
- Aspects of the doctor, such as level of knowledge, emotional reactions (frustration, guilt, pity, respect, aversion), perception of their role as a GP, time

pressure, perceptions of the patient (for example, as normal or tragic), distinguishing between GP roles and hospital roles;

- sociohistorical context, such as prior experiences of both the doctor and the patient, as well as the carer, and prior hospital involvement.

Particular patient or doctor factors were not related to the quality of the consultation in a straightforward manner. Rather, patient or doctor factors were found to either help or to hinder the care that was provided across different encounters. Part of the reason for this variation, according to the researchers, had to do with historical aspects, such as previous experience. The more experience GPs had with people with congenital disabilities generally, or as patients, the more positive perceptions they held. Conversely, doctors who had little experience dealing with people with disabilities had more feelings of anxiety and failure. Muir and Ogden conclude by noting the importance of communication skills training, not just generally but in specific situations, such as when a patient has a speech impairment, to increase a doctor's confidence. Further, they argue that professional structures could develop and promote formal work and training in the area of interacting with people with disabilities.

Some reflections on doctor–patient interaction research

According to Drew (2001), much of the research on doctor–patient interaction has focused on the doctor's position of power and control, and has sidelined patient perspectives. He describes a paradox in the research in this area: while researchers are censuring medical practice for the silencing of patients' voices, they themselves have ignored the role of the patients in the interaction. However, the situation is changing and there is an increasing focus on the patient's perspective. Reviewing a collection of papers on patient–GP consultations, Drew summarises and highlights some themes which show the patient as an active and decisive participant. These themes are outlined in table 7.3.

A shift to patient-centredness

Changes have been occurring in health care systems which have major implications for research examining the relationships between doctors and patients. As Welch Cline (2003, pp. 13–14) states:

> an array of literature concurs that the physician-patient relationship model is changing from a paternalistic to a more participatory and, ultimately, consumerism model . . . Consumers actively participate in interaction and take greater charge of their health care by getting informed, independently researching diagnosis and treatment information and alternatives, suggesting and sometimes demanding particular regimens, implementing self-treatments, and, if not satisfied, seeking another physician.

Table 7.3 Patient practices that constitute the 'active patient' in GP consultations

Practice	Description
Patient initiatives	Patients have objectives in consultations, including conveying information and achieving specific treatment outcomes
Patient concerns, breaking free of the medical agenda	Patients have their own agendas and manage to break free from doctor's interactional moves, and are not bound by answering doctor's questions
Delicacy	Patients are aware of the doctors' sceptical or uncertain view of their concerns, and therefore proceed in a manner able to ascertain their own initiatives, for example, more cautiously and delicately
Lay theories and self-diagnoses	Patients' accounts in consultations reflect and embody their own views of cause and possible diagnosis, and patients are aware of the non-medical nature of such theories

Drew (2001).

There has been a shift to a patient-centred approach and shared decision making in medical care (Tates & Meeuwesen, 2001). **Patient-centred care** involves the doctor responding to the patient in a manner which allows patients to express all of their reasons for seeing the doctor, including symptoms, thoughts, feelings and expectations (van Dulmen & Bensing, 2002). A number of studies have found that the more patient-centred doctors are in their interactions with patients, the better the patients' health outcomes (see Michie *et al.*, 2003; van Dulmen & Bensing, 2002).

> Doctor responding to the patient in a manner which allows the patient to express all of their reasons for seeing the doctor, including symptoms, thoughts, feelings and expectations.

In studies of chronic illness, the evidence for the beneficial effects of a patient-centred approach has been inconsistent. This may be because a variety of definitions of patient-centredness have been employed, as a review by Michie and colleagues recently found (Michie *et al.*, 2003). Definitions included:

- the patients' perspective of how understood they felt, how 'at ease' the health professional appeared and their willingness to accept the advice of health professionals;
- the health professional's and the patient's perceptions of their relationship, particularly mutual regard and agreement on goals;
- Patients committing themselves to perform a certain behaviour voluntarily and initiating it themselves, believing that their treatment plan was good for them and would lead to an improvement of health;
- patients being equipped to make informed choices for themselves with sufficient skills and support from the health services.

Michie and colleagues concluded that two particular approaches to patient-centredness can be identified:

- the doctor's ability to elicit and discuss patients' beliefs;
- the doctor's ability to activate patients to take control of the consultation and the management of their illness.

Their review concluded that the latter approach to patient-centredness was related to positive physical health outcomes more than the former. Thus, 'activating' patients appears to be more beneficial in chronic illness than simply taking on the patient's perspective. This review highlights that the concept of 'patient-centredness' is not unitary and may consist of specific components that are beneficial in different ways.

> Interactions between patients and health professionals are interactions between equals which aim for therapeutic alliance.

A related concept is that of **concordance**. Concordance has been defined by a working party in the UK as:

> Concordance is based on the notion that the work of the prescriber and patient in the consultation is a negotiation between equals and the aim is therefore a therapeutic alliance between them. This alliance, may, in the end, include an agreement to differ. Its strength lies in a new assumption of respect for the patient's agenda and the creation of openness in the relationship, so that both doctor and patient together can proceed on the basis of reality and not of misunderstanding, distrust and concealment.   (Working Party, 1997, p. 8, cited in Bissell *et al.*, 2004)

This concept can also be contrasted with the more paternalistic approach to patient–doctor interaction. However, Bissell and colleagues examined how well the concept of concordance was being applied in health care interactions between doctors and Pakistani patients living with Type II diabetes in the UK. Their results showed that 'not even a loose approximation of the idea of concordance (at least in terms of the idea of promoting discussion and dialogue) figured in [the participants'] depictions of encounters with health professionals' (p. 858). Patients also found it difficult to understand what negotiation, discussion and partnership might mean in their interactions with doctors. Futhermore, Bissell and colleagues point out that using concepts such as concordance may actually result in diverting attention from the material circumstances of people's lives (see ch. 8 for further discussion of concordance).

The Internet and health communication

The Internet has grown exponentially in the past ten years, and people increasingly use it to gain information and communicate with others. Both professionals and lay people use the Internet as an 'interactive health communication' tool more and more frequently (Cline & Haynes, 2001). People like to use the Internet for health information because it is convenient, anonymous, provides diversity of information and is not time limited (Hardey, 1998b). Over 50 million people seek health information on line, and at least 70,000 websites disseminate such information (Grandinetti, 2000).

The Internet is also being used more and more as a way to communicate with health professionals. Many doctors e-mail patients, and people can use e-mail to interact with 'cyberdocs', which are interactive virtual doctor's offices (Cline & Haynes, 2001). However, as an everyday tool, many doctors (especially GPs) who are already facing shorter appointment times and higher patient numbers may not welcome the additional responsibility of e-mailing as well as seeing patients.

Access to diverse health information may also increase conflict and challenge health professionals, and can lead to diminished trust. Hardey (1998b) has argued that the amount and diversity of health information on the Internet, and the fact that Internet users decide what material is accessed and used, enables lay people to access, evaluate and challenge expert knowledge. In this way it 'forms the site of a new struggle over expertise in health' (p. 820). This struggle, according to Hardey, has the potential to transform the nature of the patient–health professional relationship. All information is treated equally on the Internet; therefore alternative treatments and non-orthodox views come up in any Internet search alongside conventional medical views. In this sense the Internet can be seen as encouraging pluralist approaches to health (Hardey, 1998b). In Hardey's qualitative study on Internet use for health information, one respondent explicitly compared interaction with his/her GP and using the Internet:

> My GP is very busy and does not have time to answer questions fully. Actually it is much easier to think about what you want to ask when you look things up on the Net. I don't get that nagging feeling that I'm needlessly taking up his time.   (p. 828)

What are the implications for such interactive health communication for the relationship between patients and health professionals? Optimistically we might say that people are better informed, making face-to-face interaction more balanced and efficient. Further, as Cline and Haynes (2001) have noted, as people 'increasingly use the Internet to more actively and independently manage their health care, they are likely to take this active role into encounters with providers' (p. 675). A consequence of this is that 'patients' will increasingly become proactive 'health consumers' in their interactions with health professionals. Indeed, the research in this area describes Internet users who seek health information as 'consumers' in articles and reports.

The Internet is also a useful tool for health professionals in their clinical work. In an article outlining the value of the Internet for endocrinologists, Blonde *et al.* (1999) provided a number of ways in which the Internet could be used:

- current awareness of developments in the area;
- provision of information to answer clinical questions;

- provision of information to support practice guidelines, which are updated and modified;
- provision of information to support diagnostic and therapeutic decisions, such as pharmaceutical decisions;
- information on clinically relevant patient care;
- communication with patients via e-mail.

While potentially very valuable, the use of the Internet by health professionals also raises a number of other issues, particularly legal and ethical ones (Blonde *et al.*, 1999). This is certainly an area requiring more research and investigation.

For all the potentially positive aspects of the Internet, we must remember that there are important limitations as well. First and foremost, access to the Internet is unequal. (People in greatest need, such as those living in poor inner city areas, those in lower socioeconomic groups and the elderly, are least likely to have Internet access (Eng *et al.*, 1998).) Globally the picture is even worse. For example, figures from the late 1990s indicate that one person in six used the Internet in the USA, while one person in five thousand used the Internet in Africa (excluding South Africa) (Lown *et al.*, 1998). In developing countries the cost of Internet access is prohibitively expensive and little is being done to change this. As English is the dominant on-line language, people who do not read or understand English are disadvantaged (Pereira & Bruera, 1998). Further limitations of the Internet concern the quality of information that is provided, with some information being dubious or outright incorrect. Also, design features, such as disorganisation, technical language and constantly changing web pages and links can make access and navigation around the information difficult. Additionally, recent research shows that accessibility to Internet information for visually impaired people who rely on automated screen readers is low. Davis (2002) examined health information on the Internet and found that, of 500 websites displaying information on common illnesses and conditions, only 19 per cent were accessible to people using automated screen readers. Hence, increasing use and availability of the Internet brings a mixed bag of opportunities, benefits, limitations and problems.

Where to go from here? Agendas for research examining interactions with health professionals

A number of suggestions have been made for future research in this area. These range from the development of theoretical frameworks, as well as the use of relevant theories that exist in other subdisciplines (Bensing *et al.*, 2003), through to topics of study and specific methodological issues. Hall (2003) points out the importance of examining whether the values of patients and the values of health professionals are in accord, and what effect this has on interaction outcomes. Furthermore, research has examined effects of interactions on patients, but very little work has looked at the effect that patients have on health professionals (Hall, 2003). Health professionals also have emotions, attitudes, personal characteristics, likes and dislikes, just as patients do, and these will affect their communication with patients. Consideration of the influence of technology (and using multiple forms of technology) on interactions are also important in this field.

In terms of methodology, researchers have highlighted the importance of:

- ecological validity – in other words, studying real interactions that patients have with health professionals in a variety of different contexts and settings (Kreps *et al.*, 2003);
- the inclusion of specific populations in studies, including caregivers, people with disabilities, and patients from different ethnic and cultural backgrounds (Kreps *et al.*, 2003);
- not employing methodologies based on dyad communication when there are more than two people involved in the interaction;
- using multiple research methods, including ethnographic, survey, discourse-analytic techniques and so on (Barry, 2002; Kreps *et al.*, 2003). Barry cogently argues that it is only through the use of multiple methods that we can pay attention to the 'central tensions, the gaps and white spaces, and the discrepancies and misunderstandings that are so important in understanding human interaction' (p. 1093).

Perhaps one of the greatest weaknesses of the research in the area of patient–health professional interaction is a lack of attention to the social, historical and environmental contexts in which it takes place (Kreps, 2001). We feel and act differently in different settings. How differently might you feel talking to a doctor privately in their office and sitting on the other side of their desk, from when you are talking to a doctor, partially clothed, in an examination room about to have a rectal examination? The context is of crucial importance and must be considered in all research conducted in this field.

Some implications of doctor–patient relationship research

The patient as consumer

There have been recent changes to the ways in which patients are positioned in the medical system. Increasingly patients are viewed as active decision makers who have their own experiences and views that are worthy of hearing. For example, in a recent paper a US physician, Delbanco (2001), argued that the medical establishment has shown a collective arrogance for too long in not asking patients about their hopes and experiences and about what matters to them. He makes the point that doctors assume that they understand patients' priorities, and summarises research showing that this is not the case. He also highlights the beneficial use of cases and anecdotes (medical school teaches students to avoid anecdotes) as well as patient focus groups.

The push for a more patient-centred approach in medical encounters comes not so much from the insistence of psychologists and psychiatrists (which is unlikely given their marginal status within the medical system (Winefield, 1992)), but from the increased business orientation of health care systems. In these systems patients are seen as 'consumers' who are 'served' by the medical profession. This is apparent in Delbanco's (2001) concluding paragraph, where the language of business-speak is overt:

> the simple strategies I propose have in them the seeds of a system of care based on a principle of *production, governance*, and *accountability* shared and created by patients working closely with health professionals . . . The first step is to listen very carefully to those we *serve* . . . (p. 4S, emphases added).

Focusing on what the patient wants, and using business rhetoric in health care systems, masks the power and authority of medicine in society and also obscures processes of **medicalisation**.

> The process by which non-medical problems become defined and treated as medical issues, usually in terms of illnesses, disorders or syndromes (Richmond, 1998).

The medicalisation critique

Sociologists in the late 1960s and 1970s began to question the role of medicine within Western society. In particular, Illich (1976) identified problems with the practice of Western medicine. He argued that the power and authority of medicine actually undermined people's health because it encouraged them to depend upon the medical system rather than taking responsibility for their own health and well-being, and it diminished their capacity for autonomy in dealing with health care issues. In addition, he argued that the side-effects of medical treatments also undermined health. Other critics argued that, due to its status and authority, medicine performs a social regulation function in society, similar to the roles previously occupied by religion and the law (e.g. Zola, 1972; Friedson, 1970: see Lupton, 1997). In other words, medicine tells us what we should and should not do, and in this way regulates how we live our lives. For example, we know that we should not smoke or eat an unhealthy diet, that we should get regular exercise, practise safe sex and so on (see ch. 3). In this way, problems in social life become medicalised, or viewed through the lens of scientific medicine as diseases (Crossley, 2000). For example, being overweight or feeling depressed may lead to individuals being labelled as ill when the problem may actually be the way medicine defines illness (Senior & Viveash, 1998).

The medicalisation critique contends that the powerful role of medicine is particularly detrimental for traditionally disempowered or disadvantaged groups in society (Lupton, 1997). Questions about social inequality are

Table 7.4 Some effects of viewing female physiology as a deviation from the norm

Effect	Description
Women's differences defined as illness	Medical norms, based on white, middle-class able-bodied male bodies, view women who menstruate, become pregnant and go through menopause as ill (Lorber, 1997)
Women's reproductive function as the major focus of women's health research	Most research into women's health has focused on issues around reproductive function (Lee, 1998), leading to the exclusion of other aspects of health, and fragmenting women's health care. This also operates to sustain professional medical specialisms such as obstetrics and gynaecology
Problems of special concern to women are not taken seriously	Research priorities tend to ignore conditions that present differently (AIDS), exclusively (fibroids, dysmenorrhoea) or with greater frequency (migraine headaches, cystitis, osteoporosis) in women (see Doyal, 1995)
Women have been excluded in much major health research	More than anything else, women's exclusion as research participants has limited progress in the area of women's health. This is most apparent in clinical trials, especially on CHD, which is the single most important cause of death in post-menopausal women. For example, the Physical Health study, which demonstrated the effectiveness of daily aspirin consumption in preventing cardiovascular disease, involved 22,071 men and no women, while the sample used in the 'MR FIT' study of the relationship between heart disease, cholesterol and lifestyle involved 15,000 men and no women (Doyal, 1995)

rendered invisible as illness and disease become the focus. Feminist critics of medicine point out that medicine is a patriarchal institution, and that the biomedical model of illness and disease propounded in the medical profession focuses on individual pathology measured against universal norms (Lorber, 1997). For a long time these universal norms were the male, middle-class, young, white body and its functioning. Any physiological or other difference in other bodies was viewed as a deviation from this norm. Thus, menstruation, pregnancy and menopause became viewed as pathology and became medicalised. There have been a number of effects of the medicalisation of female physiology, some of which are outlined in table 7.4.

Although traditional research into doctor–patient interaction does include some examination of power relations and the submissive role of the patient within any medical encounter, it does not extend far beyond this. The focus tends to be on adherence, communication and satisfaction, and on identifying isolated factors that may influence these three outcomes. By taking such a narrow focus and accepting the medical view uncritically, medicalisation continues (Crossley, 2000).

Technological reductionism

Over the past fifteen years there has been a great increase in the use of multiple technologies to diagnose and compare conditions. Technologies such as x-rays, ultrasound, computer tomography, magnetic resonance imaging, angiography and positive emission tomography provide information about the physical state of the body that was never before obtainable. However, reliance and over-use of such technology in Western medicine has been criticised because it raises the cost of health care, while simultaneously favouring machine output over human judgement (Simon, 1999). Increasing technology also facilitates the objectification of the patient and, as Crossley (2000) has noted, the doctor as well.

In his ethnographic work on the use of technology in a North American hospital, Simon (1999) shows that using multiple technologies and images to diagnose patients is both beneficial and problematic. His findings highlight that diagnosing patients with multiple technologies is not as straightforward as we might imagine, and involves much negotiating, debate, rhetoric and, surprisingly, impression management by physicians on the medical team. He concludes (p. 158) that

> blanket autonomy and private decision-making still find sanctuary in biomedicine. And life-changing decisions continue to be made behind closed doors, without the full participation of those whose lives will be most profoundly affected.

In this way, diagnosing with images from technology may distance doctors from their patients, providing 'objective' information which is contrasted with the ever decreasing importance of 'subjective' information.

The working lives of health professionals

Research looking at health professionals' views on the Western system of medicine indicates that they have concerns about this system of offering health care. For example, an ethnographic study carried out in two small communities in Northern Ireland found that health professionals saw little coherence in the delivery of health care, very little collaboration and minimal interaction between different professional groups (Mason et al., 1999). Further, GPs in particular were exhausted, demoralised and suspicious of the business-oriented health service. Taking part in a working life in which they feel demoralised, demotivated and let down by the system of health care provision offered by the National Health Service, GPs may well have different (and more negative) interactions with their patients than they would do if they felt more satisfied and considered that their work was valued. This also may affect the sorts of treatments that GPs working in such contexts offer patients.

The obsessive concern with doctor–patient encounters in much research and teaching has left many facets of social action in medicine invisible (Atkinson, 1994), such as rhetoric and impression management, as in Simon's (1999) study described above. It is important that we start to focus on other aspects of communication and social processes in the medical practitioner's working life. As Atkinson (1994) has pointed out, medical work and medical life are enacted with talk, as well as with written words (e.g. in patient files). Knowledge is generated and grounded in talk between colleagues, teachers and students, and Atkinson argues that researchers need to pay more attention to this talk. In addition, Radley and Chamberlain (2001) argue that researchers also need to pay attention to how health professionals construct a 'case' (or a case study) out of the clinical situation of their patients. The case forms an important facet of communication between health professionals, and is central to patient management and control. The case is constructed and arises from the social context and talk in which doctors take part. Therefore, the social aspects of health professionals' working lives, particularly their interactions with one another, is an important but under-researched topic in health psychology.

Conclusion

Despite the large body of research which has accumulated examining the interactions people have with health professionals, this work has been limited in a number of ways. There has been a myopic focus on doctors' communication to the exclusion of other health professionals and others involved in health care (Kreps, 2001). Similarly, research has focused heavily on the patient–doctor dyad, even when others are present (family members, children, carers, other health professionals). This myopic dyadic perspective has meant there has been little exploration of the role and influence of other people's presence in the process, content and outcome of the interaction (Bensing *et al.*, 2003). Research has also tended to treat interactions between patients and health professionals as discrete, one-off occurrences. However, these interactions are usually ongoing and contain developmental processes; past interactions inevitably influence future interactions (with the same and with different health professionals) (Kreps, 2001). There has also been a heavy focus on verbal communication (and written transcripts) to the exclusion of non-verbal communication (Kreps, 2001). Other absences include a lack of consideration of contextual features (both specific and more general), and little research has been conducted with ethnic minority groups, people with disabilities and people with different sexual orientations (it is assumed in almost all of the studies that the people involved are heterosexual). Clearly, there is plenty that health psychologists can continue to contribute to this field.

While decades of research have adequately described associations between specific factors and the quality of patient–health professional communication (e.g. the more information provided, the more satisfied the patient), it is now time to start trying to explain such relationships (Hall, 2003). Kreps and colleagues (2003) recently stated that 'this is a young and vibrant area of research that will benefit from conceptual integration, methodological development, and careful translation of research findings into health care delivery innovations' (p. 4). This final point is particularly pertinent: if the research findings are not communicated to, taken up or used by health professionals and patients, few advances in the delivery of care will be made. Researchers need to ensure that their findings are used in medical education (Hall, 2003).

While the field may be relatively young, a more critical perspective is required to address our current lack of knowledge of how associations might work, and our current lack of understanding of many aspects of patient–health professional interactions. We need to take account of broader contextual factors and consider how our research might reinforce the status quo. As professionals working in biomedicine are encouraged to shift their focus from individual bodies to the person as a social being, it is likely that biological, psychological and social benefits will occur.

RECOMMENDED READING

Special issue on consumer–provider research. *Patient Education and Counseling*, *50* (2003). This special issue gives a good account of the state of the research in this field at present. A number of papers highlight the importance of considering contextual factors in research on interactions between patients and health professionals, as well as the importance of developing theory and moving beyond descriptive accounts. It is a good starting point to the field (even though many papers focus primarily on communication with cancer patients).

Kreps, G. L. (2001). Consumer/provider communication research: a personal plea to address issues of ecological validity, relational development, message diversity and situational constraints. *Journal of Health Psychology, 6*, 597–601. This paper provides a critical commentary on the research in this area. Kreps highlights the importance of terminology, and uses the terms 'consumer' and 'provider' to make the research field more inclusive of a variety of relationships between health care professionals and their patients and other relevant people. He also reviews some of the areas in this field that require further consideration and thought, and a higher level of sophistication.

Michie, S., Miles, J. & Weinman, J. (2003). Patient-centredness in chronic illness: what is it and does it matter? *Patient Education and Counseling, 51*, 197–206. Michie and colleagues provide a solid examination of the patient-centredness concept in this paper, and explore how it has been employed in research on chronic illness. One of the key messages here is that 'patient-centredness' is not a unitary construct, and the importance of defining key constructs adequately in research. Furthermore, what patient-centredness may mean in one population (e.g. people with chronic illness) may not be the same in another population (e.g. children with acute conditions).

Crossley, M. L. (2000). 'Managing' illness: relationships between doctors and patients. In M. L. Crossley, *Rethinking health psychology* (pp. 130–57). Buckingham, UK: Open University Press. In this chapter Crossley casts a critical eye over the doctor–patient interaction field. She provides a good overview of some of the critiques made of this field of research, and highlights some of the assumptions and implications of the traditional approach to the topic and the traditional research methods employed.

8   Treating illness

World travellers who have had to see a doctor in a foreign country have usually discovered that medicine is not quite the international science that medicine would like us to believe. Not only do ways of delivering medical care differ from country to country; so does the medicine that is delivered. The differences are so great that one country's treatment of choice may be considered malpractice across the border . . . Often, all one must do to acquire a disease is to enter a country where that disease is recognised – leaving the country will either cure the malady or turn it into something else.   (Payer, 1989, pp. 24–5)

Learning objectives

The aim of this chapter is to consider research relating to various forms of treatment for illness, and issues which are important in treating illness. By the end of this chapter you should be able to:

- provide an overview of the different forms of treatment for illness;
- outline the different sectors of health care and their approaches to treatment;
- discuss the research on self-treatment for minor illnesses;
- describe the reasons that people give for seeking treatment from health professionals;
- review the psychological issues in treatment for serious acute illness in hospital;
- discuss the psychological factors involved in self-care for chronic illness;
- discuss the issues involved in non-conventional treatment;
- explain the different approaches to and meanings of adherence;
- discuss the nature of the placebo effect;
- comment critically on who receives treatment and structural issues affecting access to treatment;
- outline the changing nature of treatment.

The treatment of illness is complex and variable. When we think of treatment for illness, our first thoughts are likely to turn to visiting a doctor and seeking advice and assistance for a health problem. Or we might think of visiting an emergency medical centre to seek help with sudden and severe symptoms such as unexplained vomiting, severe and persistent headache or persistent diarrhoea. We might also think about more serious and complex treatments, such as those delivered through surgical procedures or other forms of medical technology, such as radiotherapy or chemotherapy. All these situations are likely to involve an ongoing interaction between a person who has a health problem and one or more health professionals who are considered to have the skills and training to deal with the problem. However, for a good many problems – sore throats, mild headaches, minor cuts and sprains – people may choose not to interact with specially trained professionals at all. Rather, they may treat themselves, acting on their own understandings of what is wrong, or drawing on advice from friends and relatives.

Many people also seek treatment outside the area of 'conventional' medicine entirely, and many others seek their care from both conventional and 'alternative' sources simultaneously. Even when a health professional is consulted, in many situations the treatment will remain substantially in the hands of the ill person, who is obliged to comply with the treatment in order to improve. More serious and severe treatments, delivered through the application of specialist technology – the most recent drug combinations, the latest surgical procedures, the transplantation of organs – leave the treatment firmly in the hands of the health professionals.

What is considered as appropriate treatment may differ from person to person, and may also differ between 'patients' and health professionals. Health problems may be constituted quite differently between people, with one person seeking help to deal with some particular symptoms and another not seeking help for the same symptoms (see ch. 6). Many people do not seek treatment when it is considered they should (for example, for testicular cancer), which prompts health promotion campaigns aimed at increasing self-referral for treatment (see chs. 3 and 4). Others do not adhere to the treatment proposed for them, and others again refuse treatment. The definition of an appropriate treatment provider is also variable, with some people seeking help from providers that others would regard as inappropriate or even incompetent. The age, gender, class and situation of a person also affects both access to treatment and the problems considered as needing treatment. Events thought to require medical intervention in some parts of the world, such as pregnancy and childbirth, are considered natural events in other places. The nature of illness and the need for specific types of treatment also varies considerably around the world. Radley (1994) makes some relevant and important distinctions here – between disease (pathological changes in the body), illness (the experience of disease and malaise) and sickness (the social implications of being ill). These are not the same thing, although they may overlap in various ways. As Radley notes, one may be ill, but not be considered to have a disease or to be sick; conversely, one may have a disease without feeling ill. Although we will mention various diseases throughout the chapter, our primary focus here is on treatment in the context of illness, considered as 'a way of being for the individual' (Radley, 1994, p. 3).

Health psychologists have examined how psychological issues relate to treatment in a variety of ways, but have focused mainly on treatments for serious illnesses, both acute and chronic. This chapter deals with treatment more broadly. First, it describes the different sectors of health care: the lay or popular sector, the professional biomedical sector and the folk or alternative sector (Kleinman, 1980). The chapter then discusses five different modes of treatment in turn: self-treatment of minor illnesses, treatment in consultation with health professionals, treatment in hospital, self-care in the context of chronic illness and treatment through alternative or non-conventional means. The next section of the chapter considers two important issues in treatment, adherence and placebo effects. The chapter closes with a discussion of who can access and receive treatment and the changing face of contemporary treatment.

Sectors of health care and contemporary practice

As we have indicated, treatment and health care are complex and may be obtained in many different ways. Over twenty years ago, Kleinman (1980) presented a model of health care systems which proposed that there were three major overlapping sectors of care operating in conjunction with one another. As shown in fig. 8.1, these were:

- the popular sector (also referred to as lay, commonsense, or informal): this sector refers to the non-professional arena of popular culture and under-standings where illness is first detected and where self-medication and self-treatment is the norm;
- the professional sector (also referred to as biomedicine, allopathic, modern scientific or orthodox medicine): this sector refers to the activities of people who are recognised and licensed to practise, such as doctors, nurses and pharmacists;
- the folk sector (also referred to as alternative, complementary, traditional and non-orthodox, or CAM – complementary and alternative medicine): this sector contains those practitioners working outside mainstream Western biomedical practice, and includes a wide mix of practices and treatments, delivered by people with a variety of specialist training.

People may react in a variety of ways to symptoms, such as the experience of a headache. They may discuss the symptoms with family, and attempt some treatment through self-care (relax and try to sleep) or self-medication (take paracetamol), thereby operating in the popular sector. If the headache persists, a person may move into the professional sector, and consult a pharmacist (for stronger medication) or a doctor (for reassurance or further exploration),

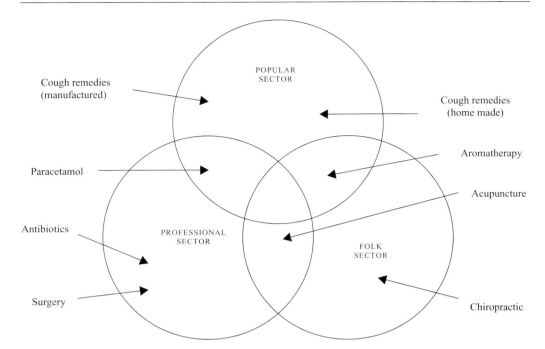

Figure 8.1   *The three sectors of health care (adapted from Kleinman (1980, p. 50) and Stevenson* et al. *(2003, p. 518))*

resulting in additional medication or some tests being prescribed. At the same time, or subsequently, the person may seek help for the headache from an acupuncturist or a herbal healer, thereby operating in the folk sector. These three sectors have been characterised by Scambler (2002) as concerned with caring, fixing and restoring respectively.

Recently, Stevenson *et al.* (2003) investigated self-care in relation to this model. They suggest that Kleinman's original model is still useful but is too simplistic to deal with contemporary practice as health care has become more plural and complex and the boundaries between the three sectors have blurred. In support of this, they point to a number of aspects of health care that have changed. First, many of the remedies that exist in the popular sector have become commodified and commercialised, as has happened with a large variety of cough and cold mixtures. Similarly, many popular remedies are now marketed as commercial herbal and 'natural' remedies by manufacturers operating in the folk sector. These developments have leaked into the professional sector, with most pharmacies stocking these products and providing professional advice on their use. Second, there is more acceptance of the folk sector by the professional sector. Referrals go in both directions across sectors, and an increasing number of doctors offer folk treatments (e.g. Zollman & Vickers, 1999a). Doctors in the UK, for example, can prescribe homeopathic remedies

Table 8.1 Medical doctors and inpatient care for selected countries

Country	Medical doctors per 1,000 population		Hospital beds per 1,000 population		Average length of hospital stay (days)	
	1990	1999	1990	1999	1990	1999
Austria	2.2	3.0	10.2	8.7	13.0	8.9
Finland	2.4	3.1	12.5	7.5	18.2	10.6
Germany	3.1	3.5	10.4	9.2	17.2	12.0
Hungary	2.9	3.2	10.1	8.3	12.6	10.0
Ireland	1.6	2.3	10.5	–	7.9	7.6
Italy	4.7	5.9	7.2	–	11.7	–
Japan	1.7	–	16.0	16.4	50.5	39.8
Mexico	1.1	1.7	0.8	1.1	4.4	4.2
Netherlands	2.5	3.1	11.5	11.3	34.1	–
New Zealand	1.9	2.3	8.5	–	9.6	8.5
Poland	2.1	2.3	5.7	5.1	12.5	9.3
Sweden	2.9	3.1	12.4	3.7	18.0	–
Turkey	0.9	1.2	2.1	2.6	6.9	6.0
United Kingdom	1.4	1.8	5.9	4.1	15.6	–
United States	2.4	–	5.9	4.1	15.6	–

Note: – = not available.
United States Census Bureau (2002).

alongside more traditional pharmaceuticals. However, this does not mean that resistance to CAM has ceased to exist within the professional sector, and most professional use of CAM regards it as an addition to conventional treatment (Stevenson *et al*., 2003). As Stevenson *et al*. point out, people perceive the professional sector as offering stronger legitimation of treatments and remedies, although there is increasing recognition of professionalisation for practitioners in the folk sector. People therefore retain preferences for remedies which are endorsed through professional expertise, although, especially in the popular and folk sectors, people also stress their perceived effectiveness as legitimating their use.

This discussion reflects the complexity that can be involved in seeking and obtaining appropriate treatment for the consumer of health services, although we need to be careful not to view the professional sector as more consistent and standardised than is actually the case. Even in 'developed' countries, medical care can vary substantially. Table 8.1 presents the numbers of doctors, hospital beds and average length of hospital stay for several developed countries. As we see, the number of doctors per 1,000 people in 1999 varied between 1.2 (Turkey) and 5.9 (Italy), with most countries having between 2 and 3. Similarly, the average length of a stay in hospital in 1990 varied from 4.4 (Mexico) to 50.5 (Japan). Although the average stay decreased across the decade in almost all countries, large disparities between countries remain. This reflects the differing arrangements for health care that exist across countries, even for those with westernised allopathic health care systems.

However, even if we consider countries that could be expected to be highly similar, substantial treatment differences are apparent. Some years ago Payer (1989) discussed differences in health care provision and treatment between four countries that might be regarded as relatively similar – Britain, France, West Germany and the USA. She documents how such aspects as rates and types of surgical procedures, content of prescriptions and dosage of medications all vary substantially between these countries:

> Some of the most commonly prescribed drugs in France, drugs to dilate the cerebral blood vessels, are considered ineffective in England and America; an obligatory immunisation against tuberculosis in France, BGG, is almost impossible to obtain in the United States. German doctors prescribe from six to seven times the amount of digitalis-like drugs as their colleagues in France and England, but they prescribe fewer antibiotics, with some German doctors maintaining antibiotics shouldn't be used unless the patient is sick enough to be in the hospital. Doses of the same drug may vary drastically, with some nationalities getting ten to twenty times what other nationals get. French people have seven times the chance of getting drugs in suppository form as do Americans. In the late 1960s American surgery rates were twice those of England; and the intervening years have seen this surgery gap widen, not close. Rates for individual operations vary even more. One study found three times as many mastectomies in New England as in England or Sweden, even though the rate of breast cancer was similar; another found that German-speaking countries had three times the rate of appendectomies of other countries; there are six times the number of coronary bypasses per capita in America when compared to England . . . Blood pressure considered treatably high in the United States might be considered normal in England; and the low blood pressure treated with eighty-five drugs as well as hydrotherapy and spa treatments in Germany would entitle its sufferer to lower life insurance rates in the United States.   (Payer, 1989, pp. 24–5)

How is this to be explained? As Payer comments, 'while medicine benefits from a certain amount of scientific input, culture intervenes at every step of the way' (p. 26). The same idea was proposed a decade earlier by Illich (1976): 'Each civilisation defines its own diseases. What is sickness in one might be chromosomal abnormality, crime, holiness or sin in another.'

Modes of treatment

Self-treatment

A considerable amount of treatment involves self-treatment – people treating their own symptoms in some way. Exactly how much self-treatment occurs is difficult to document as very little research has explored this issue directly.

When Verbrugge and Ascione (1987) asked a general population sample of 589 adults to keep health diaries for six weeks, they found that almost their entire sample – 95 per cent of women and 89 per cent of men – reported having some symptoms over the six-week period. However, contact with a health professional of any type was noted on only 5 per cent of all days when symptoms were reported. Even older people, who have more health problems, engage in considerable self-treatment. For example, Musil *et al.* (1998) asked older adults (mean age 75 years) to keep health diaries for four weeks, reporting all health problems experienced and the actions taken to alleviate them. Self-care activities were reported for about three-quarters (72 per cent) of all problems, and non-prescription medication use was widely used (for 83 per cent of problems). Prescription medication was used for about half (53 per cent) of the problems, and professionals were consulted for only 43 per cent of problems. In a study examining factors that relate to preference for self-treating over care-seeking, Ganther *et al.* (2001) report that self-treatment is preferred by younger people, women, people in better health and people from rural areas. They also found that individuals who preferred care-seeking reported using nearly twice as many prescription medications and making one-and-a-half times more visits to doctors in the previous month. Presumably, such preferences for seeking or not seeking health care are reported in the light of current illness experience and the accessibility of doctors.

Curiously enough, although the experience of everyday minor illness and its treatment through self-care is so prevalent, only limited research has focused specifically on this area. One exception is the work of Olesen and her colleagues (1990). They interviewed a range of adults in California about their experience and management of everyday aches and pains – headaches, colds, sore throats, constipation, back aches, etc. – or mundane ailments, as Olesen *et al.* termed these. Their research documented how these people know and understand their bodily function and malfunction, and how they manage and adjust to everyday mundane ailments. As one participant reported:

> I know all my weak spots pretty much and my ankles are another one [he had mentioned his back earlier]. Not that they are bad . . . I can sometimes feel my ankle caving in and instead of just going ahead on a full sprain I can shift my weight just enough without thinking about it and keep from really hurting myself from my ankles.   (cited in Olesen *et al.*, 1990, p. 452)

Mundane ailments were self-treated in a variety of ways: asked if he trusted his body, one of the participants in Olesen *et al.*'s study responded:

> I think so. That may be one reason I don't go or am not inclined to go to a doctor right away. I guess I figure it will take care of itself and the headaches. If I do get a headache, it's telling me I'm tense about something, so then I review things, trying to pinpoint where the tenseness is coming from.   (cited in Olesen *et al.*, 1990, p. 452)

Olesen *et al.* also document how the experience of mundane ailments is drawn on and incorporated into a person's 'health biography' and operates to establish a sense of a 'physical self' (these issues are discussed further in ch. 9).

In a British study examining self-treatment by young adults, Gray *et al.* (2002) proposed that these young people had a 'health repertory' of information for treating minor illness, which influenced how and when they engaged in treatment routines. From their analyses they suggested that repertories contained a description and labelling of the symptoms, strategies for self-medication and contingency plans if these failed. This is exemplified by one of their participants:

> I have also heard that you can get prescribed drugs for acne, but I would feel stupid going to the doctor, asking for that, because I don't consider I've got a bad case of acne, and I feel it would be like going to the doctor for a broken toe nail, 'would be silly. But I think I might do actually if this doesn't work, because I've heard good things about that – a friend of mine used it and he had a very bad acne problem and it cleared him up quite well.   (cited in Gray *et al.*, 2002, p. 242)

A good deal of self-treatment is achieved with the use of non-prescription, or over-the-counter medicines which are available through pharmacies and other retail outlets. Bissell *et al.* (2001) conducted a number of interviews and focus groups with people who were buying non-prescription medicines in a British pharmacy. For these people, like those in Olesen *et al.*'s study, taking non-prescription medicines to relieve symptoms and to get better was a routine and ingrained activity. It was also associated with achieving personal control over symptoms and autonomy over bodily malfunction, and the participants reported having considerable expertise in self-treatment, as illustrated by the following comment:

> I don't have a problem with it because I've been using it (Canestan cream) for years, and I know how it works and what it does to my body. I might not know the chemistry of it or what not but I know where to put it and how to use it. It works.   (cited in Bissell *et al.*, 2001, p. 16)

Of course, self-treatment for one condition does not prevent people seeking treatment from health professionals for another condition, or even for the same condition. Sleath *et al.* (2001) interviewed patients attending a medical centre in the USA and asked them about self-treatment with over-the-counter medications. Over half (57 per cent) of these medical centre patients reported using one or more over-the-counter medications in the previous month, with analgesics, cold and allergy products, and antacid products being the most common self-medications. More interestingly, of those patients who had used such medications, most (58 per cent) did not tell their doctor about this use, even though 86 per cent believed that it was important for their doctor to know this.

Stevenson *et al.* (2003) explored these issues in a study with both doctors and patients in the UK. As with Bissell *et al.*'s study, patients preferred to use remedies which were obtained from legitimated and professionalised sources, such as over-the-counter medications or recognised alternative therapies like homeopathy. Over-the-counter medications in particular were regarded as safe and convenient ways of initial self-treatment, and consultations with the doctor were expected to add to that. In spite of this, patients did not readily disclose the use of self-treatments to doctors, particularly if they had concerns about their value or appropriateness or, especially in the case of alternative remedies, if they perceived the doctor as opposed to or critical of the treatment. Although doctors were not proactive in discussing self-treatment, when this did arise in the consultation they were generally supportive of it. Stevenson *et al.* report that doctors use three different strategies to manage this, by:

- suggesting that patients continue with the treatment (as in the use of paracetamol for colds);
- suggesting that patients continue the treatment but supplement it with a prescription medication (usually the addition of antibiotic medication);
- suggesting that patients replace the treatment with an alternative treatment (usually presented as the substitution of a more effective remedy).

What this reveals is that self-treatment and professional treatment are often interlinked. Even when actively engaged in self-treatment, people continually monitor their symptoms and make decisions about whether to continue, stop or change treatment. This frequently leads them to seek treatment in multiple ways.

In summary, self-treatment for illness is extensive, and is not restricted to minor ailments or conditions. People use self-treatments for a range of illnesses, and are likely to engage in self-treatment even when seeking professional help for the same condition. People continually attempt to manage their symptoms, and they have a range of strategies for understanding and treating symptoms, some of which, like minor pain relief, are routine. When people do engage in self-treatment, they prefer to use treatments that have professional recognition, such as over-the-counter medications from pharmacies. Health psychologists have so far given very little attention to self-treatment or to the treatment of mundane, everyday ailments, preferring to focus on treatment for more severe chronic and acute illnesses. However, everyday mundane ailments can be quite disruptive, and the processes involved in their treatment, and especially their self-treatment, deserve increased research attention.

Treatment by health professionals

In spite of the fact that self-treatment for everyday illness is so common, people do consult health professionals at a substantial rate, at least in Western societies, where the organisation of health care systems facilitates professional care and

Table 8.2 Visits to the doctor in the USA

Of the estimated 880,487 ambulatory care visits made to physician offices in the United
States during 2001

Frequency of visits
- About 1 in every 10 visits (11.8%) was by a new patient
- For established patients, about 1 in 20 (7.5%) made no visits in the year, almost one-third (30.0%)
  made 1–2 visits, almost one-third (29.3%) made 3–5 visits, and one quarter (26.4%) made 6 or
  more visits
- Only one half of visits (50.3%) were to the patient's primary physician

Purpose of visit
- Just under one-third (29.3%) were an initial visit for a problem and almost one-half (44.3%) were
  a follow-up visit for a problem
- Over one-third (37.2%) were for chronic conditions
- Over one-third (35.3%) were for acute problems
- About 1 in 6 (16.8%) were for preventive care
- Just over 1 in 10 (11.3%) were for injuries
- About 1 in 20 (5.6%) were for pre- or post-surgical consultations

Services provided at visit
- Diagnostic and screening services were ordered or provided at 82.8% of visits
- Therapeutic and preventive services were ordered or provided at 41.4% of visits
- Medications were prescribed or provided at 61.9% of visits, with an average of 2.4 medications
  prescribed or provided at a visit where medication was involved
- Blood pressure checks occurred at 47.8% of all visits

Demographic variation of visitors
- After the youngest ages, visit rates increased by age, with rates per 100 persons of 242.7 for under
  15 years, 168.7 for 15–24 years, 241.9 for 25–44 years, 373.3 for 45–64 years, 624.9 for 64–74
  years, and 738.5 for 75 years and over
- Visits were made at a higher rate by females (362.3 visits per 100 females) than by males (264.0
  visits per 100 males)
- Preventive care visits were made at a higher rate by females (67.1 visits per 100 females) than by
  males (37.7 visits per 100 males), and this is sustained (at 54.5 versus 37.7) when visits for normal
  pregnancy are excluded
- Visits were made at a higher rate by white people (342.6 visits per 100 white persons) than by
  black people (189.4 visits per 100 black persons) or Asian people (263.9 visits per 100 Asian
  persons)
- The preventive care visit rate for white persons (56.5 visits per 100 white persons) is close to
  double that for black persons (31.7 visits per 100 black persons)
- The visit rate was higher in metropolitan areas than in non-metropolitan areas (338.3 visits versus
  218.0 visits per 100 persons)

The average doctor's week
- During an average week, the average physician in office-based practice received 80 office visits,
  16 telephone consultations, 0.5 e-mail consultations and made 13 hospital visits and 0.9 house
  calls

Cherry *et al.* (2003).

Table 8.3A The twenty principal reasons for a visit to a doctor in the USA

Principal reason for visit	No.	%
All visits	880,487	100.0
General medical examination	68,844	7.8
Progress visit	39,783	4.5
Cough	27,062	3.1
Post-operative visit	23,995	2.7
Routine pre-natal examination	19,848	2.3
Medication, other and unspecified	16,457	1.9
Symptoms referable to throat	15,082	1.7
Back symptoms	13,707	1.6
Stomach pain, cramps and spasms	13,594	1.5
Vision dysfunctions	13,555	1.5
Knee symptoms	12,743	1.4
Diabetes mellitus	12,502	1.4
Well-baby examination	12,361	1.4
Skin rash	12,088	1.4
Fever	10,910	1.2
Gynaecological examination	10,782	1.2
Hypertension	10,467	1.2
Headache, pain in head	9,876	1.1
Nasal congestion	9,592	1.1
Earache or ear infection	9,449	1.1
All other reasons	517,791	58.8

Note: percentages are of visits, as the table lists the principal reason for each visit.
Cherry *et al.* (2003, table 9).

health professionals are generally readily available. In a study of care-seeking visits to physician offices in the USA using a national probability sample survey, Cherry *et al.* (2003) estimated that 880.5 million such visits were made during 2001, giving an overall visit rate of 314.4 visits per 100 persons. Table 8.2 documents details of these visits. The types of visits were quite varied, with about one-third being for acute problems, another third for chronic conditions, about 20 per cent for preventive care, 10 per cent for injuries and 5 per cent relating to pre- or post-surgical consultations (see 'Purpose of visit').

This is a medical classification of visits, but Cherry *et al.* (2003) also document the principal reason that people (the patients) reported for consulting the doctor. These focus more specifically on the symptomatic grounds for the consultation, as we see in table 8.3A, which lists the twenty most common principal reasons given by patients in the USA for consultation. Table 8.3B lists the findings from an Australian study which provides the twenty most

Table 8.3B The twenty principal reasons for visits to doctors in Australia

Reason for encounter	No.	%
Total reasons for the encounter	144,654	100.0
Check-up – all	12,945	9.0
Prescription – all	9,450	6.5
Cough	6,280	4.3
Test results	4,565	3.2
Immunisation/vaccination – all	4,452	3.1
Back complaint	3,716	2.6
Throat complaint	3,642	2.5
Rash	2,724	1.9
Upper respiratory tract infection	2,234	1.5
Abdominal pain	2,041	1.4
Hypertension/high blood pressure	2,004	1.4
Headache	1,972	1.4
Fever	1,926	1.3
Depression	1,836	1.3
Ear pain	1,679	1.2
Sneeze/nasal congestion	1,479	1.0
Weakness/tiredness	1,471	1.0
Knee complaint	1,374	1.0
Diarrhoea	1,358	0.9
Skin complaint	1,276	0.9
All other reasons	76,233	52.7

Note: more than one reason could be specified for a visit and percentages are of all reasons listed for a visit.
Britt *et al.* (2002, table 6.5).

common reasons for visiting a doctor in that country. Although these countries have different health systems, and the databases and procedures of the studies differed, the reasons listed from each country are reasonably similar. As we see, a significant number of visits are not actually made for illness, but rather for routine check-ups, tests and preventive consultations.

Some groups of people make more visits to the doctor than others (see table 8.2). In the USA women visit more than men, both in total and for preventive care, white people visit more than black people, again in total and for preventive care, and urban people visit more than rural people. However, some individuals make many more visits than others. Table 8.2 also documents that a small percentage of established patients make no visits in a year and about one-third make one or two visits per year, but around one-quarter are 'frequent attenders', making six or more visits per year. Such frequent attending has been regarded as problematic, leading to investigations into its nature. The most obvious reason for high attendance is that these people have more symptoms or a higher severity of ill health, and this is borne out in research (Kersnik *et al.*, 2001; Little *et al.*, 2001a). However Kersnik *et al.* (2001) also found that, controlling for factors such as ill health, number of symptoms and SES, frequent attending was more likely where people had medically unexplained symptoms, high anxiety about their health and poorer perceived health. Frequent attenders were also found to be less likely to engage in self-treatment (Kersnik *et al.*, 2001; Little *et al.*, 2001a).

In a review of 283,842 consultations in the UK, and with a definition of frequent attending as twelve or more consultations per year, Scaife *et al.* (2000) found that women were more likely than men to be frequent attenders but that this difference lessened with age. Frequent attenders were also higher on factors signifying isolation or poverty, and Scaife *et al.* concluded that frequent attending 'is a complex process associated with many factors outside the control of the GP' (p. 298). Neal *et al.* (2000) conducted interviews with twenty-eight frequent attenders sampled from three general practices. These people exhibited two different patterns of consultation, either 'regular' frequent attending or a 'burst and gap' pattern of consultation, and Neal *et al.* argued that the reasons underlying each decision to consult were complex. In contrast to Scaife *et al.* (2000), they found that frequent attenders perceived GPs to have control over the consultation, prescribing and further care. Therefore Neal *et al.* proposed that interventions to produce more functional consultations would be better made with GPs than through targeting frequent attenders.

Some research has also investigated the opposite phenomenon – failure to attend or delay in attending for treatment (see e.g. Burgess *et al.*, 2001; also see ch. 6). However, health psychologists have largely focused their attention on doctor–patient interactions and the process of the consultation, rather than on treatment issues directly. Consequently, there are many other opportunities for research around treatment by health professionals beyond this, such as resistance to treatment options or refusal to accept treatment. One interesting issue is what happens when doctors themselves become patients (see ch. 7, research in focus box 7.2).

Treatment in hospital

Many people are hospitalised for treatment, especially when the treatment requires technology, such as for surgery, chemotherapy, radiotherapy or magnetic resonance imaging (MRI) and computerised axial tomography (CAT) scans. However, the hospital is not only a source of treatment but also a place for observation, diagnosis and recovery. In the UK it is estimated that around 12 per cent of women and 8 per cent of men are currently admitted to hospital each year (Morgan, 2003). The average length of stay in hospital for acute care is not long, averaging 6.9 days across all OECD countries in 2000 (OECD, 2003). However, this varies considerably according to the reason for

Table 8.4 Average length of stay in hospital (days) for acute care by specific conditions for selected countries in 2000

Country	Myocardial infarction	Cerebrovascular	Pneumonia/ influenza	Normal childbirth
Australia	6.8	12.3	7.0	2.9
Austria	15.0	15.5	16.3	5.7
Belgium	9.7	15.8	12.6	5.3
Canada	8.4	14.8	7.8	2.0
Finland	14.4	35.1	29.6	3.7
France	7.5	11.6	9.8	4.9
Hungary	11.6	11.9	10.4	6.6
Italy	9.4	10.2	10.5	3.9
Netherlands	–	21.1	13.3	2.7
New Zealand	6.5	38.2	9.8	2.0
Norway	7.4	10.0	8.1	4.0
Spain	11.0	13.6	10.5	3.0
Sweden	6.6	12.9	6.8	2.8
Turkey	–	6.3	6.0	1.7
United States	5.7	5.4	5.8	2.0
Average[a]	**9.5**	**15.9**	**10.5**	**3.7**
Median[a]	**9.3**	**13.6**	**10.1**	**3.7**

Notes: – = not available.
[a] Average and median figures are OECD estimates for all OECD countries where data for both 1990 and 2000 was available, and do not apply to the figures in this table. Data from the UK are not available.
Source: OECD (2003, table 2.11).

hospitalisation (see table 8.4), with acute myocardial infarction, cerebrovascular episodes, pneumonia or influenza, and a normal childbirth requiring an average of 9.5, 15.9, 10.5 and 3.7 days in hospital respectively across OECD countries. Also (and as we saw earlier, table 8.1), the length of hospitalisation varies considerably between countries, reflecting different 'cultures' of health care, with the time spent in hospital for a myocardial infarction ranging from 5.7 days in the USA to 15.0 days in Austria, and hospitalisation for pneumonia or influenza ranging from 5.8 days in the United States to 29.6 days in Finland.

Admission to hospital can be a stressful experience. Not only does it involve some degree of giving over control for care and treatment to professionals, it also involves restrictions and loss of privacy. Patients are required to give up their personal belongings, including their clothes, and to adapt to the regimen of the ward, remaining in bed as required and receiving visitors only when authorised to do so by the institution. They are likely to lack familiarity with ward routines, and with the different categories of hospital staff, leaving them unclear about who they can ask about their situation and how they should behave. At the same time, they are likely to have substantial concerns about forthcoming treatment, and uncertainty about how they will cope, whether treatment will be successful and whether they will be cured, left with some level of disability or even possibly die. Although becoming hospitalised can require considerable adjustment, it has not been a major focus of research for health psychologists, who have preferred to concentrate their research on treatment issues, and especially on examining stressful medical procedures of various kinds.

Surgery has been a particular focus of interest in this regard. Patients awaiting surgery certainly view it as a stressful procedure, and a good deal of research has examined procedures designed to prepare patients for surgery and to reduce pre-operative anxiety. This is often achieved by providing various types of information (see sidebar 8.1) to the patient, either person-ally, or in written or audiovisual form. For example, Doering *et al.*

> ### 8.1 Types of information provided to prepare patients for surgery
>
> Procedural: information about medical and technical aspects of the operation, such as the procedure, anaesthesia and post-surgery therapy.
> Behavioural: information about behaviour expected or to be avoided after the operation, such as care with coughing, therapeutic movements and how soon expected to get out of bed.
> Sensory: information about sensations and emotions likely to be felt during and after the operation, such as pain levels, nausea and anxiousness.

(2000) presented patients undergoing hip replacement surgery with a video-tape of the entire procedure from the patient's perspective, from admission to discharge. Compared to a control group, patients shown this 12-minute video before surgery reported less anxiety about their forthcoming surgery.

Procedures aimed at preparing patients for surgery, and at reducing stress and anxiety before surgery, are also expected to lead to better outcomes from surgery. This has been the focus of considerable research, and reviews of the field (e.g. Duits *et al.*, 1997; Munafò & Stevenson, 2001; Shuldham, 1999a; Whelan & Kirkby, 1998) generally identify positive effects on a variety of surgical outcomes. For example, Doering *et al.* (2000) found that, compared to control patients, patients who were prepared for surgery reported lower levels of anxiety and lower cortisol levels (a marker of stress) for the first two post-operative days. Although there were no differences in pain between the two groups, prepared patients required less analgesic relief after surgery. Longer-term effects are also reported. For example, Schelling *et al.* (2003) reported that exposure to high levels of stress in the cardiovascular intensive care unit was associated with reduced quality of life six months after surgery. In a review of seventeen prospective studies examining recovery after coro-nary artery bypass surgery, Duits *et al.* (1997) found that all studies reported psychological factors to predict post-operative adjustment. More recently, Munafò and Stevenson (2001) reviewed studies on surgical recovery that had assessed anxiety, either state or trait, pre-operatively using a specific measure, the State–trait Anxiety Inventory. They concluded that findings consistently

8.2 A personal pharmacy for self-care in treatment

John Diamond was a well-known British journalist who developed cancer of the tongue and underwent a lengthy programme of treatments, which included surgery, radiotherapy and having a tracheotomy. In his popular book, *C Because cowards get cancer too . . .* , he recounts his experience of the illness. Throughout the illness he was involved in a range of self-care activities, which is marked at one point in the book where, in his own humorous style, he lists the contents of his 'small pharmacy' collected along the way:

- four boxes co-proxamol (paracetamol and codeine painkillers);
- four boxes co-codamol (ditto, more or less);
- two large cartons co-codamol dispersible (or soluble to you and me);
- two bottles Voltarol (heavy-duty painkiller);
- three boxes dispersible Voltarol (raspberry flavoured);
- one bottle diclofenac (the generic name for Voltarol);
- one bottle Zantac (used to mollify potential stomach problems caused by Voltarol);
- three bottles temazepam (sedative masquerading as sleeping pill);
- one bottle temazepam elixir (drinkable sleeping pills);
- one bottle lactulose (laxative);
- one bottle cyclizine hydrochloride (anti-emetic to stop sickness during radiotherapy);
- two bottles metoclopramide (as above, but effective);
- one bottle metoclopramide hydrochloride solution (as above but for non-pill-swallows);
- one box co-danthramer capsules (laxative to overcome constipation caused by morphine);
- one bottle amitriptyline hypochloride (normally prescribed as an antidepressant, but also has painkilling function);
- two bottles Corsodyl Mint (for swabbing round mouth and tongue in act of oral hygiene);
- four syringes of Instillagel antiseptic lignocaine (ulcer-numbing gel);
- four antibiotics, various (all now empty and so only in my pharmacy in spirit);
- six Durogesic 25 (the morphine equivalent of the nicotine patch);
- six Durogesic 50 (as above, but double strength).

showed relationships between pre-operative anxiety and post-operative mood and pain, but associations with other recovery outcomes were less consistent.

Not all studies return positive results. For example, Shuldham *et al.* (2002) in a carefully planned randomised control trial found no effects of a one-day multidisciplinary pre-operative educational intervention on psychological functioning either three days or six months after coronary artery surgery. Nevertheless, the overall conclusions from reviews of this research are generally in support of positive effects of preparation and pre-operative psychological state on psychological outcomes following surgery. However, most reviews state reservations about the generalisability of these conclusions, citing methodological limitations and variations which restrict the comparability of studies (e.g. see Munafò & Stevenson, 2001; Shuldham, 1999b). Studies vary substantially in how they assess psychological states and post-surgery outcomes, the type of surgery investigated, the gender and age range of participants and the nature of interventions, and are limited by the lack of theory, relevant controls and the inappropriate use of statistics.

Although we have concentrated here on surgery as a stressful procedure, health psychologists have researched a variety of other stressful treatment procedures. One significant area of research activity has been into treatments for cancer using chemotherapy (e.g. Larsen *et al.*, 2003) and radiotherapy (e.g. Haeggmark *et al.*, 2001), and particularly into the fatigue (e.g. Stone *et al.*, 2001) and nausea (e.g. Montgomery & Bovjerg, 2003) associated with such treatments. There has also been considerable

> This list does not include the extensive range of non-drug items listed, such as tracheotomy tubes, cleaning brushes, swabs, foam pads, disposable forceps, plastic syringes, cotton buds, etc., mostly involved in self-care associated with the tracheotomy. (Adapted from Diamond, 1998, pp. 187–9)

research on psychological factors in organ transplantation, examining transplantation of a variety of organs including heart (e.g. Zipfel *et al.*, 2002), heart and lung (e.g. Trumper & Appleby, 2001), kidney (e.g. Franke *et al.*, 2000), liver (e.g. Forsberg *et al.*, 2002) and bone marrow (e.g. Ho *et al.*, 2002). Several reviews of psychological issues in transplantation have appeared (e.g. Engle, 2001; Olbrisch *et al.*, 2002; Rodrigue, 2001) and generally conclude that several aspects of psychological functioning, such as self-esteem, self-efficacy, anxiety and depression, coping strategies and social support, are important for successful transplantation. However, here again, studies involve wide variation in measures, procedures and outcomes assessed, making specific conclusions difficult to establish in this area.

In summary, the hospital is a major setting for providing treatment, especially for serious and life-threatening illnesses. The process of adjustment to the hospital as a setting is itself stressful for patients, but the focus of most research in this area has been on stressful medical procedures, such as surgery, chemotherapy and transplantation. It is clear that psychological factors, such as preparation and anxiety, play an important role in adjustment to and recovery from such procedures, but the specific findings from this research are mixed. Although there has been substantial research into treatment in the hospital setting, more research needs to be undertaken if we are to develop a full understanding of the involvement of psychosocial variables in this arena. So far, much of the existing research has focused on individual factors, and it is only more recently that social and environmental factors have begun to receive attention (Keefe *et al.*, 2002). We also need to consider whether it is reasonable to expect generalised findings across this area, or whether it is more likely that variation in the specific group, defined by age, gender, social status, ethnicity and the specific illness involved, will shape the particular factors involved in successful progress through, and adjustment following, stressful medical treatments. Issues around access to treatment are also an issue of concern, and these are considered later in the chapter.

Self-care in the treatment of chronic illness

The treatment of many chronic illnesses today requires the person with the illness to manage many facets of their treatment for themselves (see sidebar 8.2). This is different from self-treatment discussed above, because it will be undertaken under the general guidance of health professionals.

Perhaps the clearest example of this is diabetes. People with insulin-dependent, or Type I, diabetes need to follow a complex daily regime to maintain their blood glucose levels as close to a normal range as possible. This involves regular blood glucose testing, administering injections of insulin two to four times daily, and carefully monitoring food intake and activity levels. People with Type I diabetes will receive regular assessments by specialist health professionals (GPs, endocrinologists, dieticians and diabetes nurses), will have insulin medication prescribed and will have been given an education programme in self-management. Such programmes stress the need for close adherence to the recommended regime in order to avoid the long-term complications of the disorder – loss of vision, failure of kidney function, loss of peripheral body parts and cardiovascular disease. However, failure to maintain blood glucose levels as close to normal as possible has immediate consequences as well, leading to impaired cognitive function, loss of consciousness and even death in extreme situations. In the case of non-insulin-dependent, or Type II, diabetes, initial treatment will involve blood glucose control through testing, diet and exercise, but for most this is supplemented by oral medication or the use of insulin therapy. The same long-term complications face people with this form of diabetes, making adherence equally important. Gonder-Frederick *et al.* (2002, p. 613) note that

> patients with diabetes must perform multiple self-treatment behaviors on a daily basis for the remainder of their life spans after diagnosis. From a psychobehavioral perspective, it is difficult to imagine any other illness that places the same level of demand on patients to self-monitor and self-regulate their own health status.

Given this, the management of self-care in diabetes has been a major focus of psychological research, particularly in relation to enhancing adherence and providing appropriate self-care interventions. Gonder-Frederick *et al.* (2002) review recent developments in the field and document the wide range of psychosocial factors found to be influential in self-management and outcomes, ranging from individual (e.g. self-efficacy, control, coping, distress, anxiety) through social (e.g. support, family characteristics, interactions with health professionals, impact of diabetes on significant others) to environmental variables (e.g. access to health care, constraints on exercise and diet, and cultural factors).

There are several other illnesses that place considerable responsibility on the person for self-care. Asthma, for example, also requires complex self-care processes. It involves daily avoidance of many common environmental triggers, such as pollen, insects, household pets, foods and air pollutants, alertness to and recognition of symptoms, self-testing of breathing capacity, as well as a complex medication regime involving different types of drugs for the control of chronic inflammation and acute episodes, taken on different schedules and with different potential side-effects. Again, considerable research has examined the psychological factors that have been implicated in the exacerbation of asthma, the recognition of symptoms, adherence to self-care and treatment (see Lehrer *et al.*, 2002, for a review). Although asthma is not caused by psychological factors, Lehrer *et al.* (2002, p. 703) comment that:

> It is well established that behavioral factors play an important role in exacerbation and treatment of asthma. Behavioral factors such as exposure to asthma triggers, accurate perception and evaluation of asthma symptoms, seeking proper medical care, and adherence to medical regimen strongly predict the frequency and severity of asthma exacerbations. Mediators of these behaviors, including psychopathology and family disorganisation, can exacerbate asthma, decrease asthma quality of life, and increase asthma-related medical care costs. Under some circumstances these factors may increase threat to life from asthma.

Asthma also provides an example of the involvement of psychological treatments alongside medical treatments to control illness. Many studies have demonstrated the effects of relaxation training in enhancing pulmonary function, although clinically significant outcomes appear to be limited to reducing exacerbation rather than prevention of asthma, and similar findings are reported for **biofeedback training** (Lehrer *et al.*, 2002). Some preliminary findings suggest that both training in yoga techniques (Lehrer *et al.*, 2002) and treatment with hypnosis (Hackman *et al.*, 2000) may also be beneficial.

Training which utilises procedures for providing feedback about a physiological system or response in order for an individual to develop a learned process of self-regulation of the system or response.

The management of recurrent headache is another example of a disorder where psychological treatments have relevance in conjunction with medical treatments. Holroyd (2002) reviewed the research on psychological management of recurrent headaches, concluding that relaxation training, some forms of biofeedback and cognitive-behavioural therapy have value as treatments for the prevention of migraine and chronic tension type headache. Hypertension, or elevated blood pressure, is another disorder where psychologically based treatments have been investigated as important supplements to pharmacological treatment. Hypertension is a symptomless disorder considered to place individuals at increased risk of stroke, myocardial infarction, heart and kidney failure and peripheral vascular disease. In a review of this area, Blumenthal *et al.* (2002) note that most adjunct treatments, such as aerobic exercise therapy, dietary modifications, biofeedback and cognitive-behavioural therapy, exhibit quite limited effects in reducing blood pressure, although they also remark on the considerable limitations of much of the research, and suggest that combination treatments may have better outcomes than single behavioural treatments.

There are a range of other illnesses, such as epilepsy, arthritis, chronic pain, end-stage renal disease and gastrointestinal disorders, where psychological treatments and interventions, either alone or in combination with medical treatments, have been explored. Extensive research has been conducted across all these fields and the conclusions are generally similar to those reported for the illnesses discussed above. In general, the benefits of psychological treatments appear to be promising but their clinical effectiveness is often found to be relatively limited, although this is frequently ascribed to the limitations of the research evaluating them. Psychosocial factors have, however, been demonstrated to influence adherence to medical and behavioural treatments and to have associations with treatment outcomes in a variety of self-care contexts.

Non-conventional treatment

Alongside 'conventional', 'orthodox' or allopathic medicine as a system of treatment, there is a whole complex system of 'alternative' or 'complementary' therapies with their own providers and regimens of treatment. This area has been variously labelled as 'holistic', 'natural', 'fringe' or 'mind–body', but today is commonly referred to as complementary and alternative medicine (CAM). Although such treatments are considered 'alternative' in the West, it should be noted that these are the sort of treatments that the majority of the world's people use and rely on (World Health Organisation, 2002). CAM covers a range of philosophies and a variety of therapeutic practices and treatments, including acupuncture, chiropractic, homeopathy, naturopathy, energy therapies such as therapeutic touch and reiki, mind–body therapies such as tai chi, yoga and chi gong, as well as meditation, herbal remedies of various sorts and special diets. Tataryn (2002) has proposed a classification of CAM (and allopathic) treatments under four different paradigms according to the assumptions each makes about health and illness (see table 8.5). Such a classification

Table 8.5 A framework for classifying CAM treatments

Body paradigm
- Assumes disease is caused through biological mechanisms
- Interventions involve use of physical substances, such as herbs and vitamins, or physical manipulations, such as massage and chiropractic

Body–mind paradigm
- Assumes the mind plays a crucial role in disease and illness, either directly (causing illness) or indirectly (affecting experience of illness)
- Interventions include suggestion, affirmations, meditation, hypnosis

Body–energy paradigm
- Assumes health and disease are a function of the flows and balances of life energies
- Interventions include reflexology, therapeutic touch, acupuncture, homeopathy

Body–spirit paradigm
- Assumes that transcendental aspects beyond the material influence health and disease
- Interventions include exorcism, faith healing, prayer, rites and rituals

---

Tataryn (2002).

scheme has value in revealing similarities and differences between treatments, but it has yet to be adopted for use in research on CAM.

It has been suggested that there is a significant and increasing uptake of CAM by people in the general population in industrialised societies today, although the figures vary widely, depending on the groups sampled, the range of CAM therapies involved and the time period covered. Eisenberg *et al.* (1998) compared CAM use in the United States between 1990 and 1997, reporting that the percentage of the general population who had used at least one alternative therapy in the last year had increased from 34 per cent in 1991 to 42 per cent in 1997. Therapies which increased the most across the decade included herbal medicine, massage, megavitamin doses, self-help groups, folk remedies, energy healing and homeopathy. Eisenberg *et al.* also found that the percentage of people visiting an alternative medical practitioner increased across the decade from 36 per cent to 46 per cent. Extrapolating to the general population, they concluded that total visits to alternative medicine practitioners in 1997 exceeded total visits to all primary care physicians in the country. Kessler *et al.* (2001) surveyed a US population sample on lifetime and recent use of twenty different CAM therapies, finding that 67 per cent of respondents had used at least one CAM therapy in their lifetime, and that usage had increased consistently since the 1950s. They concluded that the use of CAM therapies was not a passing fad associated with particular therapies, a particular generation or a specific segment of the population.

CAM usage in the UK shows broadly similar patterns. Thomas *et al.* (2001) surveyed the general population in England on their lifetime use and last twelve months' use for six more established CAM therapies (acupuncture, chiropractic, homeopathy, hypnotherapy, medical herbalism and osteopathy), as well as two additional therapies (reflexology and aromatherapy), and for homeopathic or herbal remedies purchased over the counter. They estimated, using data adjusted for age and sex, that 10.6 per cent of English adults had visited at least one therapist providing one of the six more established therapies in the last year, and this increased to 13.6 per cent for use of any of the eight therapies. The proportion rose to 28.3 per cent if the eight therapies plus self-care using over-the-counter remedies were included, and the lifetime use of any of these therapies was estimated to be 47 per cent. These estimates are supported by other research showing consultation for any of four major alternative therapies (acupuncture, chiropractic, homeopathy/naturopathy and massage therapy) in Canada and the USA to be 16 per cent and 5 per cent respectively (McFarland *et al.*, 2002), and full consultation with any of five CAM practitioners (osteopath or chiropractic, homeopathic, herbalist, acupuncturist or other alternative therapist) in a region of the UK in the preceding three months to be 8 per cent (Ong *et al.*, 2002).

CAM usage rates among people with specific illnesses tend to be higher than those for general population samples. Estimates range from 85 per cent for headaches (von Peter *et al.*, 2002), 67 per cent for prostate cancer

Disorders relating to the temporomandibular joint in the jaw, which may involve one or more of: discomfort or pain in the muscles that control jaw function and the neck and shoulder muscles; a dislocated jaw, displaced disc, or injury to the bones in the jaw; or degenerative osteoarthritis or rheumatoid arthritis in the jaw joint.

(Diefenbach *et al.*, 2003), 63 per cent for **temporomandibular disorders** (DeBar *et al.*, 2003), 57 per cent for diabetes (Yeh *et al.*, 2002), 53 per cent for HIV (Hsiao *et al.*, 2003), 39 per cent for cancer (van der Weg & Streuli, 2003) and 27 per cent for allergies (Schafer *et al.*, 2002). Again these variations in rates of use reflect not only the type of illness involved but also the range of CAM treatments included and the timeframe for the estimates. Further, not all of this CAM use is related specifically to the illness; although people may be using CAM to treat their illness, those with illness may also use CAM therapies to prevent other illnesses, improve their overall health and well-being, or any combination of these (see e.g. Rafferty *et al.*, 2002). There are also variations in CAM usage by ethnicity. For example, Verna *et al.* (2005) report that, in a US general population sample of adults aged 18 to 64 years, African Americans and Hispanics were less likely than whites to use CAM, and Asian Americans did not differ from whites in usage.

The high usage of CAM raises the question as to why people use such therapies. It is frequently argued that the use of CAM reflects dissatisfaction with conventional medical treatment and care (e.g. Paterson & Britten, 1999). This is certainly reported commonly by people (e.g. Kroesen *et al.*, 2002), but is only one reason among many. Other reasons for using CAM relate to the fear of side-effects from conventional treatments, the assumption that CAM is free from side-effects, a desire to try anything that might help with an illness or symptoms, the holistic approach taken in CAM therapies and, more generally, using CAM to promote overall health and well-being (e.g. Patterson *et al.*, 2002). Foote-Ardah (2003) argues that three different perspectives explain CAM use; patients are 'pushed' towards CAM use by dissatisfaction with conventional medical care, they are 'pulled' towards CAM when treatments are congruent with their own worldview and personal health beliefs, and they use CAM as a meaningful way of achieving and managing personal treatment objectives in daily living (see research in focus box 8.1). Many recent studies (e.g. Eisenberg *et al.*, 2001) suggest that the push away from conventional medicine is less likely to motivate CAM use today, and this is supported by research demonstrating high rates of conjoint use of conventional treatments and CAM therapies. For example, Eisenberg *et al.* (2001) estimate that, of those who have consulted a medical doctor in the previous year, 45 per cent had used CAM therapies and 23 per cent had consulted a CAM practitioner.

All of this indicates that CAM is becoming more recognised and accepted as a legitimate treatment today, particularly in the USA. This legitimisation reflects the increasing institutionalisation of alternative medicine (Schneirov & Geczik, 2002) and can be identified in a number of related developments. Courses on CAM treatments are increasingly incorporated into the medical training curriculum. For example, some years ago Wetzel *et al.* (1998) reported that 64 per cent of US medical schools had a least one course on alternative medicine and this number is increasing (Bhattacharya, 2000). The proportion

8.1 The meaning of complementary and alternative therapies for people with HIV

Foote-Ardah, C. E. (2003). The meaning of complementary and alternative medicine practices among people with HIV in the United States: strategies for managing everyday life. *Sociology of Health and Illness, 25*, 481–500.

Foote-Ardah describes and discusses the ways in which people with HIV used CAM practices as a component of their treatment for HIV, and the meanings that CAM had for them. An analysis of in-depth interviews with forty people with HIV who reported using CAM to manage their HIV or its complications revealed four major strategies for the use of CAM. These were:

- Managing symptoms, medications and emotions: CAM was used for the physical relief of symptoms, to alleviate the emotional effects of living with HIV, and to mitigate the side-effects of conventional medications. This allowed people to manage stress, maintain a positive state of mind and cope with normal social roles in everyday life.
- Self-experimentation: CAM was used to allow respite from conventional medications, to check whether conventional therapy was working or needed, to determine the progress of infection and to gain some control over the medication regime. The medication regime could be suspended to check how well it was working and symptoms could be controlled by CAM therapies which were regarded as less 'toxic' and more 'natural'.
- Freedom from medical constraints: CAM was used as a way of resisting a life that was felt to be bounded and constrained by doctors' appointments, laboratory tests and medication regimes. Conventional drugs do not cure HIV, only control it, and require adjustments to daily life such as time and food restrictions, and have mild to severe side-effects. CAM provided a means to obtain some freedom from these constraints. CAM treatment itself was understood as more flexible and freeing than the strict regime associated with conventional medications. It was also regarded as being of lower risk, with fewer side-effects, and having no cost if doses were missed.
- Stigma management: usage of CAM was a strategy for avoiding disclosure of HIV status to family, friends or employees. CAM usage allowed people to avoid contact with medical professionals and the daily regime of medication, practices which could allow others to view them, and react to them, as HIV infected. Also, practitioners were viewed differently; CAM practitioners were considered to regard HIV as a chronic illness, whereas conventional practitioners regarded it as a terminal illness, providing an incentive to avoid conventional treatments and to utilise CAM treatments.

Reflection

This paper provides an excellent illustration of self-treatment, the complex nature of treatments, the diverse ways in which adherence to treatment is managed, the integration and relationship of CAM with conventional treatment and the management of illness in everyday life – in fact, it illustrates almost all the major issues of concern in this chapter.

of medical schools in the UK offering such courses increased from 10 per cent to 40 per cent between 1995 and 1997 (Zollman & Vickers, 1999b). Recently the US National Institutes of Health established the National Center for Complementary and Alternative Medicine to research the effectiveness of CAM treatments, and a large number of other centres are undertaking research into CAM (Vickers, 2000). US health insurance companies are increasing coverage of CAM treatments (Sturm & Unutzer, 2000/2001), and complementary health centres are increasingly located within conventional medical facilities such as hospitals (Schneirov & Geczik, 2002). Zollman and Vickers (1999a) reported that 40 per cent of general practices in the UK offered access to complementary medicine.

These changes indicate that CAM is becoming accepted and established as a treatment modality and is likely to be offered in conjunction with conventional treatment rather than in opposition to it. Vickers (2000) has suggested that acceptance of CAM is due in part to the rise of evidence-based medicine and the accumulating research evidence supporting CAM therapies. He argues that both parties have changed their views; conventional practitioners have accepted the value of CAM because of the research evidence, and complementary practitioners have demonstrated increased acceptance of the value of research. However, the integration of CAM into conventional medicine has not been entirely comfortable, as might be expected for a field which includes such diversity of treatment. Schneirov and Geczik (2002) document how conventional practitioners feel threatened by the incursion of CAM into the medical arena, and how alternative practitioners are keenly aware that their position is precarious and ambiguous. This ambiguity is related to beliefs that conventional research on the effectiveness of CAM treatments cannot adequately address the holistic processes held to underlie the treatments, and that integration is likely to result in restriction of treatment to those that fit easily into the requirements of conventional practice, such as giving limited time per patient. Shuval *et al.* (2002) interviewed conventional and alternative practitioners who were working alongside each other in hospital settings in Israel. They found that dual processes of acceptance and marginalisation were simultaneously operative for alternative practitioners. They were not accepted as regular staff members and their marginal status was made clear in a variety of ways: although they were accepted as having technical skills, they were regarded as another type of paramedic rather than professionals. Their marginality was reinforced by informal appointment processes, lower pay, lack of permanent status, location within the setting and 'exclusion from one of the critical and central rituals of medical practice: hospital rounds' (p. 1752). As Shuval *et al*. argue, this allowed conventional practitioners to reduce any threat from alternative practitioners and to locate them in familiar, lower-status, instrumental roles, while maintaining the dominance of biomedicine. The alternative practitioners were tolerant of these processes because practising in a biomedical setting provided legitimation for their practices and was also considered to broaden their knowledge base and improve their practice.

In summary, CAM covers a wide range of therapies and treatments, and its use is both extensive and increasing. It is also increasingly used alongside rather than instead of conventional treatment. The increasing acceptance and use of CAM by lay people is paralleled by a developing professionalisation of CAM, and more recently by the initial stages of integration of CAM with allopathic medicine. Thus, the involvement of CAM therapies in treatment is increasing and changing the nature of treatment. There is limited psychological research in this area and it provides many opportunities for health psychologists to conduct further research. Such research could examine who uses CAM and how its use relates to their understandings of health and illness, reasons for CAM use, how CAM is used and understood across different illnesses, how different CAM therapies are understood and used, and the meaning of CAM to patients, doctors and CAM practitioners, as well as more critical questions around who benefits from CAM use and how it is promoted and legitimated.

Issues in treatment

Compliance, adherence or concordance?

When treatment is specified for a patient, a treatment programme or regimen is established and expected to be followed. This can involve taking a series of doses of cough medication to ease a sore throat, following a course of antibiotics, changing dietary practices to eat more healthily or returning for a regular series of check-ups. For a number of chronic illnesses, the treatment regime can be much more demanding and may involve taking medication daily or receiving treatment over the course of the person's life. For example, people with AIDS are often required to take complex daily doses of multiple medications, sometimes as many as ten to fifteen different drugs per day. People with Type I diabetes must follow a daily regimen of insulin injections, frequently with different types of insulin required at different times of the day. People with epilepsy are commonly required to take daily medication as a preventive measure in the absence of symptoms. In order for people to manage or recover from illness, it is usually considered important that they follow the treatment regime carefully and completely.

How we label this activity of following treatment recommendations and regimens has changed over time and is fundamentally bound up in the assumptions that we make about the relationship between health professionals and those undergoing treatment, essentially between patients and their doctors (Kyngäs *et al.*, 2000). As Trostle (1988) has argued, this is related to the ideology of health care provision. When doctors were considered as professional experts and patients assumed to be passive recipients of treatment, patients could be assessed for their degree of **compliance** with medical directives for treatment. Compliance therefore reflects the degree to which the patient complies with or follows explicitly the treatment recommendations of the health professional as expert, and reinforces the role of health professionals as central to treatment. However, understandings of the patient–doctor relationship have been changing; patients today are more likely to be viewed as taking responsibility for their own care, and consequently constructed as active partners in treatment decision making, making informed choices about treatments. The concept of compliance has changed to reflect this, and conforming to mutually planned treatment regimens has come to be termed **adherence** – the degree to which patients adhere to, rather than comply with, medical recommendations for treatment. However, this term still carries implicit assumptions of professional power and frequently becomes only a synonym for compliance (Playle & Keeley, 1998). More recently, new understandings have emerged which view the patient–doctor relationship as a partnership and recognise the patient as a person involved in his or her own treatment. Consequently, concerns about how treatment regimens are managed have been framed within the notion of **concordance** – how well the treatment recommendations of the health professional and the treatment practices of the person match one another (see ch. 7). Essentially this view recognises that patients are more than their illnesses, and that the demands of illness are threaded into everyday lives.

The topic of adherence has been an important focus of research for health psychologists and has given rise to a considerable body of research. Adherence is considered important because research documents that good management of illness leads to fewer symptoms, better monitoring of the condition, enhanced functioning and lower use of health care services (Clark, 2003). Adherence is also a focus of attention because generally people adhere to treatment recommendations quite poorly. It has been estimated that at least 50 per cent of people do not adhere to their recommended medication regimes (e.g. Haynes *et al.*, 1996; Wright, 1993). Obviously this varies by group, illness and the type of adherence investigated, with rates averaging around 50 per cent, but ranging from 10 per cent to 85 per cent (Donovan & Blake, 1992). For example, Zeppetella (1999) examined prescribed medication use in terminally ill patients living at home, and found that 60 per cent did not adhere to the recommended regimen. Almost half of this group (44 per cent) took less medication than prescribed, with most of these omitting medications and a smaller

---

The degree to which a patient complies with or follows explicitly the expert treatment recommendations of a health professional.

The degree to which patients adhere to, rather than comply with, medical recommendations for treatment.

Interactions between patients and health professionals are considered as interactions between equals which aim for a therapeutic alliance.

number reducing the amount taken. Over one-quarter took additional medication, mostly by adding over-the-counter medications to the mix. This was a heavily medicated group: the 106 patients were prescribed a total of 597 drugs, with 20 per cent prescribed 8 or more drugs; they had an average of four health professionals engaged in their care, and all but two of them had two or more prescribers. In a different study, Mitchell *et al.* (2001) also assessed the management of prescription medications, interviewing a group of rural community-dwelling adults over 65 years of age. They concluded that mismanagement of prescribed medication regimens was common in this group, and was predicted in those who were younger, having poorer mental health, having more acute care visits to a doctor and finding the costs of medications difficult to meet.

Failure to adhere to recommended treatments is not restricted to prescribed medication use, however, but is a broader concern for such matters as attending for a medical check-up or a further consultation. Hardy *et al.* (2001) report that 15 per cent of diabetes patients in a UK setting failed to meet their appointments for an out-patient clinic review of their condition. Hardy *et al.* invoked a simple informational procedure (mailing out information about where to come, what to bring, where to park, who they would see and what to expect) and reduced non-adherence to appointments to 7 per cent. Following up the mailing with a supplementary reminder phone call reduced this to almost 1 per cent. Bakry *et al.* (1999) examined non-adherence in referrals from one sector of the health system to another in Morocco. They followed up referrals from general practitioners in rural and urban health centres to hospitals, finding that only 43 per cent of patients overall visited the hospital. Adherence was lower for referrals from rural than urban health centres and for referrals with a longer delay for the appointment. However, the best uptake of hospital appointments, for urban health centres and immediate appointments, was still only 77 per cent of the total. Bakry *et al.* concluded that the organisation of the health care system can influence adherence. Clearly, the level of adherence is a function of what is being adhered to, and obviously it is easier to increase attendance at an appointment for a check of a chronic condition than it is to ensure that a complex regimen of daily medications is taken as prescribed.

In a review of interventions designed to enhance management of chronic conditions by patients, Clark (2003, p. 298) suggests:

> Two or three observations are reasonably clear from decades of studies of adherence to medical regimes: there are no observable characteristics to alert the health care provider that the patient is a complier or non-complier; similarly, physicians cannot predict better than chance alone which patients will actually follow their clinical recommendations. Therefore, all patients should be assumed to need assistance to follow medical regimens. The situation regarding effective deployment of management strategies beyond the use of medicines appears to be similar.

Although many successful interventions have been documented, Clark laments that many are 'home grown, created from the personal experience of well-intentioned health care providers and devoid of a theoretical perspective' (p. 304). She advocates the need for a more theorised approach to such interventions, more care in addressing the outcomes sought and a recognition that successfully planned interventions can work across multiple chronic conditions. She also identifies a range of processes whereby clinicians can improve disease management by their patients, such as using accepted treatments, communicating effectively with patients, and providing information that connects with patients' understandings.

Assessing adherence can be a major problem, complicated by a number of considerations such as the nature of the illness and its treatment, the complexity of the treatment regimen, and the need to assess different components of a regimen in appropriate ways (Kyngäs *et al.*, 2000). Medication use can be assessed by assays of blood or urine, although such methods can be labour-intensive and expensive. Medication use may also be assessed through behavioural observation or residual pill counts, or more covertly through technological monitoring. Devices have been developed to register the date and time a pill box is opened and to record the outcome of blood glucose testing, either with or without the patient's knowledge. Most research has used some form of self-report through questionnaires or daily diaries, methods that are cheap and convenient although potentially open to reporting errors of various kinds. Interviews are becoming more widely used, and have considerable utility to provide insight into the processes underlying adherence.

A fundamental question in this area is why people do not adhere to treatment, especially because following treatment fully appears to be in their best interests. A substantial amount of research has addressed this issue and the findings reveal a diversity of explanations. As Annandale and Hunt (1998) demonstrate, patients may disagree with their doctors about the value of treatments, about their diagnosis and prognosis and other clinical decisions. These disagreements may not be expressed during the consultation, but may affect adherence to treatment. Mehta *et al.* (1997) reviewed the literature on adherence for three groups, patients with HIV infection, chronic illness and mental illness, and documented a wide range of factors associated with adherence. They divided these into four categories:

- demographic characteristics, such as age, gender, SES and ethnicity;
- psychosocial or behavioural characteristics, such as stress, attitudes and beliefs, and social relationships and activities;
- medication characteristics, such as the form of medication, side-effects and complexity of regimen;
- health care administration and delivery characteristics, such as patient knowledge, patient–practitioner communication and extrinsic barriers to treatment.

Research using questionnaires which present researcher-determined barriers to adherence reveal only one aspect of the picture behind non-adherence. Approaches which engage more directly with people and examine the ill person's own explanations for non-adherence can provide more depth and insight into the processes involved. For example, Conrad (1985) interviewed eighty people with epilepsy to explore the meaning of medication in their lives. He found that non-compliance went beyond difficulties with drug efficacy and side-effects. Epilepsy medication had a range of meanings – taking such medication served to mark the person as having the disorder and the condition as under control. Varying the medication was engaged in for a number of reasons: to test and evaluate whether the condition was progressing; to attempt to limit dependency on the drug and regain control over the disorder; to vacate the stigmatised status of epileptic; and to safeguard performance in important social settings. Conrad concluded that 'From the perspective of the person with epilepsy, the issue is more clearly one of responding to the meaning of medications in everyday life than 'compliance' with physicians' orders and medical regimes' (p. 36). Wilson *et al.* (2002) conducted interviews with sixty-six HIV-infected people, in part to examine their adherence to the complicated medication regimens that these people are expected to follow over long periods of time. They found that adherence was variable, with adherence choices to comply with, not comply with, or self-adjust the medication regime being influenced by a number of contextual factors. More importantly, they found that choices were variable from day to day and from dose to dose, and argued that adherence is better considered as a fluctuating rather than a static or fixed phenomenon. They concluded 'perhaps the most startling finding in this qualitative work is the discovery that we might need to conceptualise adherence on a dose-to-dose basis. The decision to adhere is made each day, dose by dose' (p. 1319).

Here again we have an area of research where the highly rational cognitive models widely used by health psychologists do not engage satisfactorily with the complexity of the issues. Nor do they account adequately for the social context or the daily lifeworlds of people undergoing treatment. When we begin to explore adherence from the perspective of people managing their treatment, we obtain more complete understandings of the complexities that surround efforts to comply with treatment and why it is not always taken up fully or eagerly by the ill person. As we have argued throughout the text, illness is not merely a biological 'fact', but is always a part of living for the ill person. Therefore issues involved in following treatment are necessarily woven into people's daily lives, and adherence becomes only a part of what needs to be accomplished within the context of many other daily tasks. This is not to say that findings about beliefs and understandings around adherence are not useful, but that they only constitute one part of the total picture. As health psychologists, we need to engage more fully with the complexities involved in achieving satisfactory concordance in treatment.

The problematic placebo

Many treatment effects are produced by substances, procedures or interventions that are not expected to have any causal effects. These have been labelled **placebo effects**, and researchers have suggested that such effects demonstrate support for the influence of the mind on the body. Papakostos and Daras (2001) document the history of the **placebo**, showing how it has changed from use as a powerful therapy to a methodological tool designed to distinguish specific from non-specific effects in treatment. In 1955 Beecher published an influential paper, 'The powerful placebo', promoting wide acceptance of the view that there was a causal effect between receiving a placebo treatment, such as a dummy pill, and clinical improvement. Many studies have reported such effects. For example, Eccles (2002) reviewed eight placebo-controlled clinical trials for cough medications, showing that the reduction in cough frequency achieved for the medication was almost exactly matched in magnitude and time course to the placebo condition. Eccles concluded that only 15 per cent of the effect on cough was directly attributable to the active medication (see also research in focus box 8.2).

A genuine psychological or physiological effect, in a human or another animal, which is attributable to receiving a substance or undergoing a procedure, but is not due to the inherent powers of that substance or procedure (Stewart-Williams & Podd, 2004).

A substance or procedure that has no inherent power to produce an effect that is sought or predicted (Stewart-Williams & Podd, 2004).

The study by Eccles (2002) also noted the difficulty in defining exactly what a placebo effect involves. As Hróbjartsson and Gøtzsche (2001a, p. 312) have noted:

> The phrase has been used to describe phenomena as different as patients' improvement after a placebo intervention, the effect of a placebo intervention, psychologically mediated effects in general, the effect of the patient–provider interaction, the effect of suggestion, the effect of expectancies, and the effect of patients' experience of meaning, etc. We think that the notion is associated with too different (though overlapping) phenomena to serve as a conceptual tool for clear analysis.

Similarly, Kaptchuk (2002) proposes that an examination of placebo effects needs to consider effects beyond the specific effect of a dummy intervention, and take account of at least five different non-specific components that may be involved – patient characteristics, practitioner characteristics, the relation between the patient and practitioner, the nature of the illness involved and the treatment and setting in question.

Much research on placebo effects has compared the efficacy of placebo with an 'active' treatment in randomised controlled trials, using the placebo condition as a control for the effects of 'genuine' treatments. This has led placebo effects frequently to be considered as artifactual, extraneous or sham, and to considerable debate around the question of whether placebo effects are 'real'. In a recent example, Hróbjartsson and Gøtzsche (2001b) asked the question 'Is the placebo powerless?' They suggested that studies which compared the effects of placebo with an active treatment were inadequate

8.2 Placebo effects in surgical analgesia

Pollo, A. *et al.* (2001). Response expectancies in placebo analgesia and their clinical relevance. *Pain, 93*, 77–84.

Response expectancies have been suggested to be a major determinant of placebo effects, and this study examined their function in pain relief after thoracic surgery. After the operation, all patients were placed on buprenorphine analgesia for three days on demand; patients made a verbal request for the analgesia when they felt they required it. Over the same period, they were also administered a basal intravenous infusion of saline solution, but three different groups were told quite different things about this infusion:

- Group 1 were told the infusion was a rehydration solution and nothing was said about analgesic effects.
- Group 2 were told that it might contain a painkiller or a placebo (the classic double-blind procedure). Only patients who were not administered additional buprenorphine this way (placebo only) were included in the data analysis.
- Group 3 were told that the infusion was a powerful painkiller (deceptive administration), although they received either painkiller or placebo just as for group 2. Again, only those not receiving additional buprenorphine (placebo only) were included in the data analysis.

All groups were equivalent in terms of age, gender, weight and type of surgery, and all groups reported equal levels of pain over the three days and also all requested analgesia when pain was at equivalent levels. There were quite significant differences in the number of doses and also in the total amount of analgesia requested between the three groups. Compared to group 1, who received 11.55 mg over the three days, group 2 received 21 per cent less (9.15 mg) and group 3 received 34 per cent less (7.65 mg). Yet all three groups achieved the same analgesia despite the dosage differences. The researchers concluded that this indicated strong placebo effects with deceptive administration producing larger effects than the usual double-blind procedure.

Reflection

This paper is one of several with appropriate controls that demonstrate the existence of placebo effects. However, as Stewart-Williams and Podd (2004) argue, the mechanisms behind placebo effects can be difficult to unravel. Expectancy effects, manipulated through verbal instructions as here, provide one way of inducing placebo effects, but how they operate remains open to question. Nevertheless, this research does document an important clinical benefit for patients experiencing pain – a means to produce a considerable reduction in the amount of analgesic drug required for pain relief after surgery. More difficult for treatment application is the fact that the optimal effects are produced under conditions of deception.

because this approach fails to control for such things as natural history effects, such as remission or regression to the mean. Hróbjartsson and Gøtzsche proposed that it would be more appropriate to compare trials where the control for placebo was a no-treatment condition. They located 114 relevant studies which met this criterion and conducted a meta-analysis on these, concluding that there was 'little evidence that placebos in general have powerful clinical effects' (p. 1599). This paper challenged current understandings and was consequently subject to substantial challenge itself (for example, see the set of responses in *Advances in Mind–Body Medicine*, vol. XVII). These challenges centred largely on the problems of combining effects across different outcomes and different diseases, the narrow definition of placebo effects involved and the limitations of randomised controlled trials. In their recent review of the field, Stewart-Williams and Podd (2004) ask 'The placebo effect: fact or fiction?', and argue that 'despite claims to the contrary, the placebo effect is a genuine and potentially important phenomenon' (p. 326).

8.3   Revisiting treatment a century later

In vol. 2 of the *Lancet* a well-known French neurologist and physiologist, Charles Brown-Séquard (1889), reported on the effects obtained by administering himself extracts made from dog and guinea pig testes. He reported that these injections produced a 'radical change' in him, including a 'decided gain of strength' and a renewal of intellectual facility. In the same paper, he reported that similar effects had been observed in three other men, but that injections of water in two further men had produced no effects. These findings were widely discussed and contributed to a method of treatment, organotherapy, that promoted the use of extracts of animal testes, adrenal and pituitary glands, spinal cord, spleen and liver to treat various diseases.

One hundred and thirteen years later, a group of Australian medical researchers (Cussons *et al.*, 2002),

Accepting that placebos can have effects in treatment raises questions about their mechanism of operation. The most common explanations have been concerned with expectancy and conditioned learning. Expectancy involves induced expectations that a particular agent or treatment will have effects. For example, Beneddetti *et al.* (1999) demonstrated that inducing expectations of analgesic effects in particular areas of the body produced specific analgesia only in those areas. Alternatively, placebo effects have been produced through classical conditioning processes, largely in non-human animals. For example, conditioned immunosuppression in rats has been well documented (e.g. Ader & Cohen, 1991). Stewart-Williams and Podd (2004) discuss the evidence for each of these explanations. They argue, contrary to most previous understandings that have pitted one against the other, that the two mechanisms are not incompatible. Rather, they suggest that some placebo effects are mediated by conscious learning from both expectancy and conditioning, and other effects are attributable to nonconscious learning through conditioning processes.

The evidence for placebo effects suggests that various components of regular treatments have the potential to be 'placebogenic' (Kaptchuk, 2002). This can make effective treatment problematic, particularly in relation to the ethics of treatment (see sidebar 8.3).

As Stewart-Williams and Podd (2004) comment, expectancies around treatment may produce undesirable as well as desirable effects. For example, listing the possible side-effects of a drug may enhance

followed Brown-Séquard's procedures to produce testicular extracts from dogs, and tested them for the presence of testosterone. (They obtained testes from five healthy dogs of different breeds undergoing routine castration at a veterinary surgery.) They found that the extracts contained extremely small amounts of testosterone, and concluded that the effects reported by Brown-Séquard were almost certainly placebo effects, noting that his experience 'demonstrates that the placebo effect can be powerful, even in a highly educated physician who was well aware of its existence' (p. 679).

However, Cussons *et al.* were also concerned to comment on the present-day use of testosterone treatment for men who are considered to be suffering from androgen deficiency or the 'andropause'. This is a situation where it is considered that the ageing process in men arises from testicular insufficiency, and can be corrected by testosterone supplementation applied through skin patches or subcutaneous implants. They were concerned that such androgen treatment can evoke a strong placebo effect, and noted that randomised controlled trials in healthy elderly men have shown no clear benefit of testosterone therapy on such factors as muscle strength, well-being or sexual function. They cautioned that their results serve 'as a warning against the empirical use of testosterone in older males with non-specific symptoms unless hypogonadism has been clearly demonstrated, as a placebo response can easily be confused with therapeutic efficiency, resulting in inappropriate, long-term treatment' (p. 679).

the likelihood that patients will experience them. Providing prognoses may influence the course of disease negatively. It has been suggested that placebo effects could be taken up and used positively in treatment provision, provided non-deceptive processes and adequate practitioner training in their use could be established (Papakostos & Daras, 2001). More fundamental, as Kaptchuk (2002) comments, is the question of what constitutes legitimate healing and what can and should be offered by practitioners:

> Besides clinical and scientific value, the question of enhanced placebo effects raises complex ethical questions concerning what is 'legitimate' healing. What should determine appropriate healing, a patient's improvement from his or her own baseline (clinical significance) or relative improvement compared with the placebo (fastidious efficacy)? As one philosopher of medicine has asked, are results less important than method? Both performative and fastidious efficacy can be measured. Which measurement represents universal

science? Which measurement embodies cultural judgement on what is 'correct' healing? Are the concerns of the physician identical to those of the patient? Is denying patients with nonspecific back pain treatment with a sham machine an ethical judgement or a scientific judgement? Should a patient with chronic neck pain who cannot take diazepam because of unacceptable side effects be denied acupuncture that may have an 'enhanced placebo effect' because such an effect is 'bogus'? Who should decide?   (Kaptchuk, 2002, p. 821)

As Kaptchuk's comment demonstrates, this area of treatment raises difficult questions around ethical practice, patient autonomy and the power of science and medicine. Hence, placebo effects continue to be contentious, and research into their extent, mechanisms of action and role in treatment continues. This is an appealing area for health psychologists because of its promise to reveal mind–body interactions.

Who gets treatment?

In ch. 6 we documented disparities in treatment seeking by gender, SES and ethnicity. We find that precisely the same factors influence who receives treatment, and a considerable body of research documents such disparities in treatment. For example, Ladwig et al. (2000) reported higher usage of medical services by women in a large German community study. Green and Pope (1999), in a longitudinal analysis of medical service use, found that after controlling for factors such as symptoms, self-reported health status and health knowledge, female gender was an independent predictor of the use of health services over the twenty-two-year period of the study. Altman and Lillie-Blanton (2003, p. 300), in summarising a recent report (Smedley et al., 2002) which reviewed research on racial and ethnic disparities in the USA, commented:

> racial and ethnic disparities in patient care occur among similarly insured groups. One study of Medicare beneficiaries, for example, found that black patients with early stage lung cancer were nearly half as likely as whites to undergo surgery and had lower five-year survival rates. Another study found that Latino patients who had undergone diagnostic angiography were 40% less likely than whites to undergo coronary bypass surgery. A study that identified patients considered appropriate candidates for renal transplantation found that the procedure occurred among 17% of black patients and 52% of white patients. While the evidence varies for specific conditions and racial/ethnic minority groups, the data sufficiently compel us to begin undertaking actions to systematically and aggressively eliminate disparities in needed medical care.

Why should this be so? In an interesting recent study, Adamson et al. (2003) suggest that this arises from difficulties in accessing health care rather than the desire to seek health care. They obtained questionnaire responses from a stratified sample of 1,350 UK general practice patients who were asked to identify their care seeking behaviour in response to symptom scenarios. Their findings showed no differences between women and men in their likelihood of seeking immediate help in response to these scenarios, but blacks and people of lower SES were more likely to report an intention to seek immediate help than were whites or people of upper SES respectively. However, this difference was reduced if attitudes to health and health care and anxiety about the symptoms were controlled for. More interestingly, controlling for access to services (assessed by questions such as the time taken to reach the surgery and patterns of care seeking over the last year) made no difference to the likelihood of seeking care. Adamson *et al.* concluded that inequalities in access to care are not the result of differing intentions to seek care, but rather to barriers in the provision of care to these groups. However, we need to remember in interpreting these findings that they are based on questionnaire responses to scenarios rather than on actual care-seeking behaviour.

In researching treatment issues, health psychologists have focused most attention on psychosocial factors affecting treatment and generally have not attended to structural factors, such as poverty, financial ability or rural location, which provide barriers to care and affect access to treatment. However, there is potential for psychologists to contribute to this field, and to include structural factors in their research agendas. Some recent research taking a community health psychology approach illustrates the contribution that can be made in this field (see Campbell & Murray, 2004).

Disparities in health care also serve to remind us that all health systems are not equal. The material in this chapter has focused almost exclusively on health care and treatment within the 'developed' world but, as we noted in ch. 2, the patterning of disease, and consequently requirements for treatment, are quite different in other areas of the world. For example, over 2 million children die each year from diarrhoeal diseases (Kosek *et al.*, 2003), a cause of death almost unknown in the richer countries of the world. The organisation Medicins sans Frontières notes that infectious and parasitic diseases, many of which are readily treatable, kill more than 12 million people a year in poor countries (Orbinski & Pecoul, 2002). These countries have insufficient resources to develop or sustain health care systems that can provide adequate treatment. As one illustration of this, table 8.1 documented the variation in medical doctors per 1,000 population in a range of developed countries, but in poorer countries these rates are substantially lower. For example, Canada's rate of 2.29 doctors per 1,000 population compares to rates of 0.3 in Cambodia, 0.07 in Cameroon, 0.03 in Chad, 0.25 in the Congo, 0.9 in the Cook Islands and 0.09 in Côte d'Ivoire (World Health Organisation, n.d.). Rates for other health professionals, such as nurses, midwives, dentists and pharmacists, are equally low.

The situation of poorer countries is compounded by their economic inability to pay for medication and a consequent lack of interest by pharmaceutical companies in research and development for treatments for the diseases that afflict poor countries. Orbinski and Pecoul (2002) argue:

Effectively the health needs of a large part of the world's population are ignored. Over the last 25 years, less than 1% of all medicines developed globally were for tropical diseases and tuberculosis – diseases that account for more than one tenth of the world's illness and death. Purchasing power, not need, is defining drug research priorities. Only 10% of global health research money is devoted to conditions that account for 90% of the global disease burden. Last year, the total global expenditure on health research was estimated at US$60–70 billion. Of this less than US$70 million was spent on developing new and badly needed treatments for malaria, tuberculosis, African sleeping sickness, and kala-azar [a parasitic disease that kills many thousands of people in Africa and Asia each year.]   (paras. 11–12)

We should note that this spending occurs in a context where US$3.1 billion was spent on cancer research alone.

This seems a long way away from health psychology, but it is important for us to consider where our research is directed and who benefits from it. As long as we continue to focus our research largely on treatment for stressful medical procedures or interventions to enhance adherence to self-care regimens, we are effectively supporting the hegemony of biomedicine. Although our research is unlikely to influence the practices of large international pharmaceutical companies, research into treatment and health care issues in poorer countries can be accomplished and can make an important contribution (see e.g. de-Graft Aikins, 2004).

The changing face of treatment

We have discussed treatment from a number of different perspectives in this chapter, but it is salient to consider that treatment is not a fixed or static entity: new forms and types of treatment are constantly being introduced in a variety of ways. Self-treatment is transformed as a greater variety of over-the-counter drugs are made available, leading to increased concern about risks for consumers (see Bissell *et al.*, 2001). Prescription medicines are marketed directly to consumers in the USA and New Zealand, and this process is under discussion in the European Union. Some argue that the direct marketing of medicines creates professional and consumer demand for specific medications, increases patient pressure on health professionals for specific treatments, and promotes the medicalisation of society and the positioning of people as health consumers (e.g. Cohen *et al.*, 2001; Lyles, 2002). As the costs of health care systems escalate, treatments are prioritised and restricted, and interventions aimed at increasing self-treatment are developed (e.g. Little *et al.*, 2001b). The increased turn to CAM, and the ongoing integration of CAM with allopathic medicine, is also opening up new treatment scenarios (e.g. Vickers, 2000). The development of new technologies, such as MRI and CAT scanning, have changed treatments, and have also led to their use for whole-body rather than disease-specific scans. Genetic screening has transformed understandings of risk and led to forms of prophylactic treatment, such as surgical removal of healthy ovaries to prevent possible future occurrence of ovarian cancer (Hallowell & Lawton, 2002) or prophylactic chemotherapy to reduce the risk of healthy women getting breast cancer in the future (Hogle, 2001). New, less invasive surgical techniques are changing the way surgery is conducted (see e.g. Garry *et al.*, 2004, comparing abdominal, vaginal and laparoscopic surgical procedures for hysterectomy). Developing technologies, such as better forms of insulin and the development of insulin pumps, have allowed people with diabetes more freedom from the intensive self-care previously required for their condition. Not all developments in treatment have been completely positive, and concerns have been expressed about over-treatment and unnecessary treatment (e.g. Deyo, 2002) and the adverse effects of medical errors in the use of medications (e.g. Phillips & Bredder, 2002). Computer technology has also affected health care, with the Internet providing major sites of information about medical issues, enhancing the knowledge of the informed health consumer and potentially increasing demands on treatment providers (Powell *et al.*, 2003). However, debate continues as to whether the Internet is a positive source of information for improving consultation and care seeking (e.g. Skinner *et al.*, 2003), and questions have also been raised about the accuracy of Internet information (e.g. Mathews *et al.*, 2003). These changes are all linked strongly to an ongoing medicalisation of society, and in many ways medicine has come to permeate people's lifeworlds. For example, issues of health, illness and medicine pervade television documentaries, docudramas and reality programmes, and are prominent topics of news and features in all media.

All these changes in medicine and society have operated to transform treatment, and at the same time have transformed the nature of the patient receiving treatment and the relationship between the health professional and the patient. Patients are now expected to be informed and actively involved in determining choices for their health care and treatment. Consequently, people have effectively become consumers in relation to their health, purchasing and consuming health care as a commodity. However, this raises its own problems and ambiguities. As Bissell *et al.* (2001) note, medical knowledge is always contingent and uncertain, and lay people are often placed in circumstances where they recognise this. One of their participants, who had searched extensively for detailed information about the risks and benefits of a prescription medication that she was taking, comments explicitly on the ambiguities that often surround treatment for the new health consumer:

> I mean surely you are taking it into your own hands by enquiring and getting as much information as possible, that is a way of controlling it, so you aren't at the will of whoever is prescribing the drugs. But the problem comes when the information is not certain itself. I mean, when I looked, no one was sure about whether it might cause rectal cancer or not. It was all about probability, it might be linked with cancer, it might not. So, I didn't know what to do. So, educating yourself isn't the answer, is it?   (cited in Bissell *et al.*, 2001, p. 19)

Conclusion

So what does all this mean for health psychology? For the most part, and as we have noted at various points throughout this chapter, health psychologists have limited their attention to research on treatment for major medical procedures, like surgery, or to interventions designed to ensure that self-care practices adhere to medical recommendations. A more critical examination of health psychology practice would ask who benefits from our research and practice. For the most part health psychology research on treatment operates to support medicine, and to enhance the medicalisation of everyday life. However, as this chapter identifies, there are a substantial number of alternatives and openings for different directions in our research. The changing nature of treatment provides a significant arena for expanding health psychology research. Taking a wider perspective on treatment provides openings to develop research areas that have been largely neglected, such as self-treatment and non-conventional treatment, in more depth. Also, extending the focus of our questions about treatment to examine such issues as people's understandings of medications, medical technologies and treatments will allow us to obtain a more complete picture of the diverse field that treating illness constitutes.

RECOMMENDED READING

Edelmann, R. J. (2000). *Psychosocial aspects of the health care process*. Harlow, UK: Prentice Hall. This book contains several chapters on seeking and receiving care and adhering to treatment, and develops many of the issues covered in this chapter in more detail.

Journal of Consulting and Clinical Psychology, vol. 70, issue 3. This special issue of the journal provides a review of the field of behavioural medicine and clinical health psychology across the previous decade. The articles review developments and research findings in relation to several specific diseases, and cover treatment issues for many.

Ogden, J. (2004). *Health psychology: a textbook* (3rd edn). Maidenhead, UK: Open University Press. A chapter in this text provides a detailed treatment of placebos and their role in health and illness.

Payer, L. (1989). *Medicine and culture*. London: Victor Gollancz. Although an older book, this provides an excellent account of the way in which allopathic treatment is culturally located, even with the focus limited to four countries, Britain, the USA, France and Germany. Written as a popular text, it is highly recommended.

9 Being ill

[B]ecoming ill (especially chronically, or seriously ill) *colours* people's lives. The use of the word 'colours' refers to the way that everyday life is reflected through either the knowledge that one is ill, or the way that ordinary actions are affected by bodily limitations . . . Illness, once given form by the social realm that it metaphorically colours, can then inflect other domains of experience with new meaning. In turn, they provide another reflection upon the illness situation, so that it, too, is once more re-figured . . . Because it is always reflected through social realms, and because the reflection of these realms, one against the other, is the way in which individuals display their worth and competence, then being ill is not a specific state, but an inflection of the whole of the person's being. (Radley, 1999a, pp. 19–22)

Learning objectives

The aim of this chapter is to consider the experience of illness, including factors that are important in adjusting to and recovering from illness, approaches taken to researching and theorising being ill, ways in which illness is presented, and issues involved in caring for ill people. By the end of this chapter you should be able to:

- describe the extent of illness in contemporary Western society;
- critically evaluate research on coping with illness;
- outline the various ways in which people with illness find support;
- discuss how illness can have positive as well as negative effects;
- outline arguments for and against considering illness as a crisis requiring adjustment;
- explain what is meant by quality of life and discuss its value in research on illness;
- discuss how people find meaning in illness;
- review the ways through which people with illness regain normalcy;
- discuss the value of a narrative approach to illness;
- comment critically on caregiving in chronic illness.

As we have argued consistently throughout this text, illness is much more than disease, and this chapter illustrates a range of ways in which this is so. We consider the scope of illness in society today, and discuss a range of issues that influence the processes involved in being ill and recovering from illness. We also argue that being ill and recovering from illness are complex processes that extend well beyond the illness itself. We discuss how illness can disrupt life, and how ill people must recreate meaning and coherence in life, rethink their identities and restructure their lives in the face of illness. This raises concerns about how illness can be presented and represented to others, invoking concerns about stigma and worth. We also discuss how illness has consequences that extend beyond the ill person, affecting families and social relationships, and we conclude the chapter with a discussion of caregiving and the effects of illness on those who care for the ill person.

Illness as morbidity: the scope of illness

How much illness is there in Western society today? A considerable amount, according to official statistics. If people are asked to assess their own state of health, considerable numbers report experiencing limited health. In Great Britain, the 2002 General Household Survey found that, for people aged 16 and over, only 56 per cent reported good health, 30 per cent said they had fairly good health and 14 per cent said their health was not good. In contrast, only 4 per cent of people under 16 years were reported to have health that was not good (Office for National Statistics, 2004). In the USA 9.2 per cent of people reported poor or fair health in a national survey (National Center for Health Statistics, 2003). As expected, this percentage increased systematically with age, ranging from 1.8 per cent for those under 18 years, 5.4 per cent for 18–44-year-olds, 11.7 per cent for 45–54-year-olds, 19.2 per cent for 55–64-year-olds and 26.6 per cent for those 65 years and over. Disparities in the proportions of people with poorer health are more marked when level of poverty is considered, with overall rates of people reporting poor or fair health being 6.2 per cent for the non-poor, 15.5 per cent for the near poor and 21.0 per cent for the poor. As these surveys only include households and not people who are institutionalised, these estimates under-represent the full impact of illness.

Another way to examine this issue is to consider how many people have their activities limited by chronic conditions. In the USA, 12.1 per cent of all non-institutionalised people had some activity limitation of this sort. Again, reported limitations increased with age, from 6.7 per cent for those under 18 years, 6.1 per cent for 18–44-year-olds, 13.1 per cent for 45–54-year-olds, 20.7 per cent for 55–64-year-olds and 34.5 per cent for those 65 years and over. People in poverty were more likely to experience limitations resulting from chronic conditions, with the reported rates increasing from 9.9 per cent for the non-poor to 18.8 per cent for the near poor and 24.1 per cent for the poor. Rates for men and women were not different (National Center for Health Statistics, 2003). The amount of reported illness in Great Britain in 2002 is presented in table 9.1. This shows the rates of acute illness through the percentages of people reporting restricted activity due to illness in the previous 14 days, and the average number of restricted activity days per person in a year. The table also shows the amount of chronic illness through the percentage of people reporting longstanding illnesses. There is little difference in any of these rates between men and women, but they do vary systematically by age and SES: as age increases, all of these illness rates increase; as SES declines, all of these illness rates increase.

These findings all attest to the considerable amount of illness experienced by people in contemporary Western societies. The remainder of this chapter examines how people deal with and react to illness experience.

Illness as crisis: adjusting to illness

Traditionally, health psychology has viewed chronic illness as a crisis requiring adjustment and adaptation. When people experience a severe chronic illness, they often need to make substantial adjustments in their lives. Moos and Tsu (1977) argued that the experience of chronic illness could be understood and investigated as a life crisis, and suggested a framework for adjustment to such illness. They proposed a set of seven 'adaptive tasks' that were implicated in chronic illness, distinguishing between those that were specific to the illness and those that were more general. The illness-related tasks involved:

- ensuring adequate communication with the health care professionals involved in treatment and management of the illness (see ch. 7);
- dealing with the requirements of the hospital regime and medical treatment procedures (see ch. 8);
- dealing with the pain, discomfort and physical incapacity occasioned by the illness.

The more general adaptive tasks proposed by Moos and Tsu (1977) extend beyond the immediacy of the specific illness to issues that are implicated in people's psychological responses to the illness, and their social situation and context, namely:

- maintaining an emotional balance in the face of illness;
- preserving an appropriate self-image through illness;
- maintaining social relationships with family and friends;
- preparing for an uncertain future.

As we argued earlier, these tasks recognise that illness has a wider context than simply being ill and engaging in activities to ensure recovery and a return to normalcy. As King *et al.* (2003) have shown, the person experiencing illness and chronic disability engages in a range of psychologically protective

Table 9.1 Amount of reported illness in Great Britain in 2002, by gender, age and SES

	Males					Females				
	Age					Age				
Occupational classification	0–15	16–44	45–64	64+	Total	0–15	16–44	45–64	64+	Total
Acute sickness: percentage reporting restricted activity in last 14 days										
Managerial and professional	9	11	14	20	12	8	13	17	21	14
Intermediate	9	10	17	19	13	7	11	17	23	14
Routine and manual	9	13	21	22	16	10	14	21	25	17
Never worked / unemployed	9	9	[27]	–	13	11	21	[54]	34	24
All persons	9	11	17	21	14	9	13	19	24	16
Acute sickness: average number of restricted activity days per person per year										
Managerial and professional	12	20	32	51	25	8	23	33	54	27
Intermediate	11	21	42	62	30	10	21	40	68	32
Routine and manual	15	27	53	68	38	17	28	52	69	41
Never worked / unemployed	13	20	[78]	–	30	11	49	[128]	111	58
All persons	13	23	43	62	31	12	26	43	67	34
Chronic sickness: percentage reporting longstanding illnesses										
Managerial and professional	18	20	40	63	30	13	22	39	65	30
Intermediate	20	22	40	68	32	14	26	37	63	34
Routine and manual	22	25	54	70	40	21	28	51	69	41
Never worked / unemployed	21	38	[71]	–	37	22	30	[69]	57	37
All persons	20	23	46	68	34	17	25	44	66	35

Notes: – = Insufficient data; [ ] approximate estimate only.
Office for National Statistics (2004): *Living in Britain* General Household Survey 2002, tables 7.4 and 7.6.

processes, such as replacing a loss with a gain to transcend the experience, making decisions about relinquishing something in life and accommodating to the changed circumstances, and recognising new things about the self.

The notion of chronic illness as disruptive has been a common theme in research on illness. Charmaz (2000) proposed that people who contract chronic illnesses 'lose their previously taken-for-granted continuity of life' (p. 280). Earlier, in a qualitative study of people with a range of chronic illnesses, Charmaz (1983) identified the loss of self that accompanies chronic illness, and the ways in which this was brought about (see sidebar 9.1). Bury (1982, p. 169) also discussed illness as disruptive, contending that:

9.1 Threats of illness to the self

Through having to lead a more restricted life: illness, when it limits people from being able to go about their usual daily lives and tasks, or in more extreme cases, from caring adequately for themselves, affects self-competence, individuality, and independence, qualities which have high cultural regard in modern society.

Through being discredited: lack of confidence and loss of independence felt by chronically ill individuals can lead to them being discredited, by themselves and others, especially if their illness is marked externally in some way and they also face stigmatisation as a result.

Through becoming more socially isolated: illness often renders the ill person less able to reciprocate adequately in social relations and social life generally, leading to social isolation and consequent distress.

Through becoming a burden to others: illness presents a threat of dependency on others and a loss of autonomy, and becoming useless is a major concern of ill people when illness places limits on the contribution they can make. (Charmaz, 1983)

---

illness, and especially chronic illness, is precisely that kind of experience where the structures of everyday life and the forms of knowledge which underpin them are disrupted. Chronic illness involves our recognition of the worlds of pain and suffering, possibly even of death, which are normally only seen as distant possibilities or the plight of others. In addition, it brings individuals, their families, and wider social networks face to face with the character of their relationships in stark form, disrupting normal rules of reciprocity and mutual support. The growing dependency involved in chronic illness is a major issue here. Further, the expectations and plans that individuals hold for the future have to be re-examined.

Bury considered the onset of chronic illness to be a 'biographical disruption', involving at least three different aspects:

- the disruption of taken-for-granted assumptions and commonsense boundaries, raising questions of 'what is going on here?', and requiring ill individuals to attend to bodily states that they are not usually aware of, and to make decisions about their state and where and how to seek help;
- the disruption of explanatory frameworks and meaning, giving rise to questions of 'why me?', 'why now?', and requiring a rethinking of the person's biography and self-concept;
- the need to respond and mobilise resources in the face of the altered situation.

For an alternative look at illness as biographical disruption, see research in focus box 9.1.

9.1 Chronic illness as biographical disruption or biographical flow

Faircloth, C. A., Boylstein, C., Rittman, M., Young, M. E., & Gubrium, J. (2004). Sudden illness and biographical flow in narratives of stroke recovery. *Sociology of Health and Illness, 26,* 242–61.

It has been argued that the effects of a sudden illness are disruptive, presenting the ill person with a crisis in everyday living, and requiring a negotiation of new understandings of how to live, how to relate to others and how to represent the self. The authors of the present study argue that this notion has come to dominate research into the everyday experience of chronic illness. However, this study challenges these notions and queries whether this framing of sudden onset chronic illness is inevitable. It uses stroke as a serious sudden-onset condition that could produce biological disruption. The researchers analysed in-depth interviews conducted with eighteen Puerto Rican Hispanic, sixteen African American and twenty-three non-Hispanic white stroke survivors at one, six and twelve months after discharge from hospital following an episode of acute stroke. Participants were aged between 46 and 88, with a median age of 67, and included only two women.

The findings expose how these survivors resisted the connotation of stroke as disruptive in several ways:

Seeing stroke as a normal component of old age: stroke was seen as fitting 'into the social clock of the individual' and to be expected at an older age, allowing the experience to be normalised as 'part-and-parcel of the old age experience' (p. 248). As well, a discourse of ageing allows limitations to be credited to 'normal' ageing and not attributed specifically to the stroke.

Seeing stroke in relation to comorbidity: only two participants did not have any comorbidity, and most had two or more coexisting conditions alongside the stroke. Stroke was viewed within this context and the serious effects of other conditions, such as diabetes, were regarded as more disruptive than stroke. In giving their accounts of everyday living, stroke was often ignored and other conditions given prominence. Rather than reflecting the stroke experience as disruption, it was 'simply expressed as one event in an ongoing life' (p. 252).

Minimising stroke through knowledge of stroke: for some, previous experience of a stroke offered a context for understanding the latest episode. For others, this was given through relationships and encounters with other stroke survivors. Knowledge gained in these ways provide her with an awareness 'of what one can expect as a stroke survivor and how to cope with the illness', 'mitigating its disruptive impact', and serving as 'a resource for the survivor in describing his recent stroke as part of the flow of his everyday life' (p. 253).

The authors conclude that the concept of illness as biographical disruption can often be inadequate for explaining the experience of illness and the influence of illness on people's lives. Rather, they propose that the significance of illness will depend upon the life context in which it occurs and how illness is incorporated into the person's biography. They propose a concept of 'biographical flow' as a better means to understand sudden serious illness in ongoing everyday life.

Reflection

This paper illustrates an important point for us – that illness is always part of life. Illness always occurs in context and, as these authors note, ways of making sense of illness experience are a function of the social location of the person. This means that these findings would be different, and perhaps reveal biographical disruption as more prominent, if conducted with a younger cohort of stroke survivors, with less comorbidity and experience of illness. Further, this paper alerts us to the dangers of reifying any particular conception of how illness affects everyday life, and taking any specific ideas for granted in seeking interpretations of our research data. While biographical disruption is a powerful and engaging concept for analysing illness experience, we need always to regard our findings critically, and seek the best interpretation for the data at hand.

The crisis and disruption that people face through illness leads them to take stock of their lives and to react to their illness. In the following section we focus on issues that relate particularly to adapting and adjusting to chronic illness – coping with illness, the role of social support in illness, finding meaning and purpose in illness and finding benefits from the experience of illness.

Coping with illness

The idea that illness presents a crisis or a disruption naturally turns attention to how this can be managed. The need to adapt to illness has led health psychologists to draw heavily on notions of coping – ways of managing and reacting to the threats and challenges posed by chronic illness. Substantial research has addressed these issues, using a variety of coping assessments, outcome measures and different illnesses.

For example, Penedo *et al.* (2003) report that greater use of approach-oriented coping styles and lower use of avoidant-oriented coping styles were associated with lower levels of psychological distress in symptomatic

HIV-positive gay men. McCabe *et al.* (2004) compared coping and psychological adjustment in people with multiple sclerosis with healthy people from the general population. They found that people with multiple sclerosis, particularly if they were men, were less likely to adopt problem-solving coping and support-seeking coping strategies, and were more likely to have poorer levels of psychological adjustment. Hack and Degner (2004) examined coping responses in a three-year follow-up of women with breast cancer, and concluded that women who respond to breast cancer diagnosis with passive acceptance and resignation are at risk of poor long-term psychological adjustment. Similarly, Bishop and Warr (2003) found, for women experiencing chronic pain due to cancer or cancer treatment, that active coping was associated with less disability, whereas passive coping was associated with greater disability. Anagnostopoulos *et al.* (2004) compared coping strategies used by women with breast cancer with women facing benign breast disease and healthy women. Women with breast cancer were less likely than other women to attribute blame to themselves, but they did not differ from the other women on other forms of coping, including passive acceptance, seeking social support, problem-focused coping, positive reappraisal, distancing and wishful thinking. Anagnostopoulos *et al.* suggested that the differences in self-blame were a function of the need for women with breast cancer to avoid guilt and low self-esteem, and enabled them to maintain their potential to engage successfully in the adjustment process.

However, as we discussed earlier (see ch. 5), it is difficult to draw clear conclusions in this field because of the wide variety of methods used to assess coping. For example, although it is commonly supposed that problem-focused coping strategies are more adaptive than emotion-focused coping, this finding can be variable. Stanton *et al.* (2000) suggested that this was because the assessment of emotion-focused coping covered a range of different types of coping, combining items that indicated acceptance and avoidance of emotional issues, and also confounded coping with outcomes assessing distress. In a study of adjustment to breast cancer, Stanton *et al.* (2000) restricted their focus to coping which involved actively processing and expressing emotion, and found that women who coped through expressing emotion surrounding cancer in the aftermath of medical treatment had fewer medical appointments for cancer-related concerns, increased physical health and vigour and decreased distress over the next three months. In a chronic pain context, McCracken and Eccleston (2003) compared a coping approach to pain with an approach that promoted acceptance of pain, and concluded that acceptance of pain was more appropriate for managing chronic pain than more commonly suggested coping strategies. However, many researchers would consider acceptance to be a coping strategy, highlighting the conceptual difficulties in this field.

The context within which coping is examined is also important. For example, Banthia *et al.* (2003) examined coping and distress in couples faced with prostate cancer, and found that the strength of the couple's relationship moderated the effects of avoidance coping and intrusive thinking on mood disturbance, with members of stronger dyads reporting less distress than those in less strong relationships. In a study with HIV-positive Latino gay men, Bianchi *et al.* (2004) found that active coping was important in mediating between the experience of social discrimination and engagement in positive health-promoting behaviour. Other research has examined the relation between the types of coping strategy used and the context in which they are deployed. Particular emphasis here has been given to relating the type of coping to the controllability of the situation, referred to as the goodness-of-fit approach (e.g. Park *et al.*, 2001). This approach proposes that problem-focused efforts will be more effective when the situation is controllable, and emotion-focused efforts more effective in less controllable situations. Park *et al.* (2001) examined the goodness-of-fit hypothesis in a study of coping comparing three groups of gay men, those who were HIV-positive or HIV-negative and involved in caregiving, and HIV-positive men not involved in caregiving. They found support for the fit between problem-focused coping and controllability, but only limited support for the fit between emotion-focused coping and lack of controllability.

Once again we find that, although there is an extensive body of research relating to coping and adjustment from illness, the variation in theories, conceptualisations and assessments of coping makes it difficult to draw any clear conclusions from this research. These variations, coupled with substantial variation in the ways in which illness outcomes are conceptualised and measured, make a summary of this field very difficult (see Somerfield & McRae, 2000 for a methodological critique). Research into coping also reveals that many other factors are implicated, including personality, dispositions and attributions, as influences on the choices of coping practices and the pathways to outcomes. Folkman and Moskowitz (2004, p. 748) state in a recent review:

> Despite the substantial gains that have been made in understanding coping per se, we seem only to have scratched the surface of understanding the ways in which coping actually effects (outcomes) . . . Coping is not a standalone phenomenon. It is embedded in a complex, dynamic stress process that involves the person, the environment, and the relationship between them.

In a related argument, Bury (1991) proposed that adaptation to illness involved three overlapping but conceptually different mechanisms:

- coping process, referring to the cognitive processes that an individual uses to learn 'how to tolerate or put up with the effects of illness' (p. 461), whereby ill people work to maintain a sense of value and meaning in the face of illness and its effects;
- coping strategy, referring to what people do, the actions or behaviour that they engage in when faced with the demands of illness, and the means they use to mobilise resources and engage support;
- coping style, referring to 'the way people respond to and present, important features of their illnesses' (p. 462).

Although these terms are similar to those used by psychologists, the approach suggested by Bury promotes a rather different, more inclusive understanding of what is involved in adjusting to illness. Rather than disconnecting coping from the person's lifeworld and treating it as a separable and measurable process occurring outside experience, this approach regards the ill person as actively engaged day to day in managing and adapting, not just to illness, but to living. As Radley (1994, p. 150) has argued,

> [b]eing ill, in the long-term, is not a sphere of experience separate from the remainder of life. It often has considerable effects upon other things that people do and think. Therefore, the idea that coping can be defined as a response to an *external* life-strain becomes questionable in the context of chronic illness. Sometimes such an illness appears as an external threat, sometimes it is part of oneself, and sometimes it appears as a problem concerning other people. Indeed, the sick person's way of responding can itself become part of the problem that he or she then has to deal with.

As Radley goes on to argue, once we approach illness in this way, the traditional health psychology approach to adjustment and coping becomes problematic. As Radley puts it:

> This calls into question the idea of coping as bringing to bear a specifiable psychological mechanism upon a definite external difficulty. This view assumes that these mechanisms have a stable form, like tools in a toolbox. It also assumes that problems appear the same to all individuals, when it is arguably true that a given hindrance might be a challenge to one person, and a major problem for another. It seems more useful . . . to look beyond the individual to what researchers into chronic disease have repeatedly observed: that is the entire lifestyle of the person – physical, social and medical – which is brought into play in the adaptation to longstanding illness.   (p. 150)

Using social support

Support from others is a major issue for people experiencing illness. People seek support in many forms and find it helpful in a variety of ways. Psychologists have classified several different types of social support (see ch. 5, table 5.2). Those with particular relevance to chronic illness include:

- emotional support, providing evidence that the person is cared for and esteemed (e.g. warmth and nurturance provided by a friend in times of despair during illness);
- tangible support, involving assistance with such things as material resources, or physical help (e.g. food delivered to a family with an ill caregiver);
- appraisal or informational support, involving advice or help to understand stressful events and circumstances (e.g. providing information on sources of help for managing illness);
- affiliation support, involving companionship and participation in activities with others (e.g. attending a self-help group meeting with people who have experienced a similar illness).

There has been extensive research on social support and its relation to health and illness (see ch. 5). Various forms of social support have been found to relate to better adjustment to and recovery from a wide range of chronic illnesses, including cancer, rheumatoid arthritis, diabetes, multiple sclerosis, coronary artery disease and stroke (Edelmann, 2000; Taylor *et al.*, 2003). This research identifies the many forms that support can take and demonstrates that some forms of support are more appropriate at different stages of chronic illness – emotional support, for example, may be more relevant at early stages of diagnosis, whereas informational support may be more appropriate during later stages of an illness.

Support for chronically ill people is often provided through the family. In many cases this is a spouse, who is heavily involved with the illness, sharing in the experience and supporting and caring for the ill person. For example, Banthia *et al.* (2003) found that the quality and strength of the dyadic relationship in couples where one member had prostate cancer moderated the relationship between coping efforts and distress, with members of stronger dyads reporting less distress. Trief *et al.* (2003) asked couples who lived with diabetes to define support in the context of their illness. Their analysis showed that supportive behaviour was particularly helpful for dietary control and the management of treatment regimes, as well as providing general support with the illness. However, not all behaviours were considered helpful, particularly nagging, poor communication and raising problems with diet management (see below). DiMatteo (2004) reports that being married or living with another person increased adherence to treatment for illness, and that adherence was better for people with cohesive families than it was for those with families in conflict.

For some illnesses, such as HIV, people who have the illness may be shunned and stigmatised. Where stigma is associated with illness, support from family members and friends is complicated, especially as it raises issues of disclosure; who can be told and who cannot? In a study examining support and disclosure among HIV-positive men and women, Kalichman *et al.* (2003) found patterns of selective disclosure, with participants disclosing their HIV status to some people and not to others. Disclosure was associated with social support, and interestingly, friends were disclosed to and perceived as more supportive than family members, and female family members were disclosed to and perceived as more supportive than male family members. Similarly, Chapple *et al.* (2004) found that people with lung cancer experienced stigmatisation and felt shame, and that this limited them from both receiving and seeking support. Such research documents how support, and its function, is always contextual.

Difficulties in obtaining social support can involve more than the experience of stigmatisation. For example, Schrimshaw and Siegel (2003) investigated barriers to obtaining emotional and practical social support from friends and family among older adults living with HIV/AIDS. Many of these people, aged 50 or more, reported a lack of support and assistance. Although non-disclosure of their status and other people's fear about HIV/AIDS were identified as important issues contributing to this, several other factors, including a desire to be self-reliant and independent, not to be a burden, the loss of supportive friends through AIDS-related death and ageist reactions to illness, were also identified as barriers to locating support by this group.

Barriers such as these may be overcome through involvement in self-help and support groups for specific illnesses. Such groups are a growing phenomenon, and Davison *et al.* (2000) estimated that the participation rate in self-help groups in the USA was around 3–4 per cent over a one-year period. The experience of physical illness has been identified as the predominant reason for participation in support groups (Lieberman & Snowdon, 1993), accounting for over 40 per cent of the total memberships in such groups. Groups appear to exist in proportion to the severity of the illness and the costs of treatment (Yaskowitch & Stam, 2003) so it is not surprising to find that cancer groups are the most prevalent (Davison *et al.*, 2000). The supportive function of these groups is reflected in their operating principles, which involve valuing reciprocity, the belief that people facing a similar issue can help one another by coming together, and collective wisdom, drawing on participant experience rather than involving professional help or invoking organised forms of management, as well as providing a free service (Adamson, 2002; Davison *et al.*, 2000). Adamson (2002) found that self-help group participants suffering from cancer or HIV/AIDS reported positive benefits from group participation with regard to contact with other people, forming friendships and new networks, increased self-competence and the ability to cope with the psychological and social consequences of living with a life-threatening disease. Yaskowitch and Stam (2003) examined the way in which support groups for people with cancer functioned, interviewing participants from four different support groups. Their analysis identified that these groups provided a place for people to talk safely, to demystify the unknown, to explore new ideas and make decisions, and to find hope. Groups were particularly important in finding a unique and separate social space where members did not feel isolated or marginalised, and could engage in biographical work to reconceptualise their identities. As one participant stated:

> There's almost like a support fatigue . . . there's a tendency for people to say or to think, 'okay, well it's over . . . just put it behind you and get on with your life'. What they don't understand is that it is never really over and at some point, at some level, it's always there because you live in the 'remission society' . . . you never know that you are truly well . . . there's a change that comes about, just in terms of the way you think about yourself and your own life . . . you can't forget it . . . sometimes you need to talk about it longer, just to put it in place in your life.   (from Yaskowitch & Stam, 2003, p. 732)

For a consideration of support from a different perspective, see research in focus box 9.2.

Modern technology provides another avenue of support, with many people using the Internet to access information and check experience with others who

Research in focus

9.2 Social well-being in the context of illness

Ferrell, B., Smith, S., Ervin, K., Itano, J. & Melancon, C. (2003). A qualitative analysis of social concerns of women with ovarian cancer.
Psycho-Oncology, 12, 647–63.

Much research on chronic illness focuses on the illness itself and medical markers of outcome and recovery. This study examined the effects of a specific illness, ovarian cancer, on the lives and social well-being of the sufferers. It presents a detailed content analysis of all the correspondence received by *Conversations! The newsletter for those fighting ovarian cancer* over a period of seven years, consisting of 21,806 letters, cards and e-mails. The analysis of this very large database focused on issues of social well-being, defined to include roles and relationships at work or at home, including aspects such as isolation, support, family distress, sexuality and employment issues. The paper includes extensive quotations from this correspondence, examples of which are given below.

Social support, present and needed

I have a wonderful support group of co-workers, friends, family and a fiancé who has remained loving and steadfast through this whole ordeal. I feel truly blessed as a day hardly goes by when I don't receive phone calls or visitation, gifts, flowers, kind acts from some caring person. At times it has been overwhelming.

In spite of all the supportive people I have around me and all the love, I do feel somewhat alienated from all the folks around me who are not fighting cancer.

Sisterhood

Although this is a journey I never would have chosen, along the way I have met some remarkable and courageous women. We have cried and laughed together and have a special bond. I am thankful for one extraordinary friendship that I never would have had if it had not been for my OVCA. I'm so very proud to know all these cancer warriors!

Need for peer support

While I was able to communicate with my wonderful physician just fine, I still felt the need to just talk with someone else that 'had walked or was walking in my shoes'. It was extremely difficult to convey my feelings to my husband, even though he truly tried to understand how I felt inside about this unexpected turn of events in my life.

A legacy of cancer

My family has a terrible history of breast cancer (maternal grandmother, mother, and two aunts – my brother recently had a benign tumour removed from his breast) and colon cancer (my paternal grandfather) – I was the lucky one to get ovarian cancer. I never knew until my diagnosis, about the link between the breast, colon, and ovarian cancer and was shocked when I found it out. All those years I had worried myself sick over getting breast cancer with not a thought given to ovarian cancer. Live and learn!!!

Family distress

Everyone in my family is terrified. I have two sisters. Many of them seem to think that if they come around me somehow they might catch cancer.

I must give credit to my husband who was routed out as the world's greatest 'keeper'. So often they are the forgotten one. All concern is directed toward the patient. I heard my husband say 'we were diagnosed with ovarian cancer last December'. What a great expression of love and concern that was.

Sexuality

Sexuality? No one seems to want to talk about this topic because I don't feel that many doctors feel comfortable or have the necessary information. Women in my post-treatment support group didn't seem to have the same concerns I did. A sex therapist was suggested to me and I knew my problem was physiological and not psychological, so I said I wasn't interested in seeing that doctor. I just wanted the passion back in my life again. I knew somehow I would find my way, and I did.

Employment – returning to 'normal'

With my surgeon's approval (but not my husband's), I have returned to work the third week after surgery. I am recovering quickly, and wanted to get back to 'normal' as soon as possible, although what is 'normal' will be different now. My work schedule undoubtedly will be erratic during the summer as I continue with chemotherapy, but my partners and clients have been wonderful and supportive, and I will take each day as it comes . . .

Reflection

This paper provides detailed information, in the words of the women themselves, as to how their illness pervades and influences their lives. It vividly demonstrates how illness affects almost every aspect of life. Biomedicine, issues of treatment and care, of interaction with health professionals, and engagement with health care systems, are peripheral here, relegated to the background as these women express their needs, hopes, fears and experiences.

have had similar illnesses. Wright and Bell (2003) reviewed the research on health-related computer-mediated support groups, suggesting that these are best conceptualised as groups with weak ties (as distinct from close personal ties, such as with family members). As such, these groups provide a forum where individuals with health-related problems can gain access to people with similar concerns and through this foster a sense of control as well as a sense of community. By their nature, Internet support groups provide safe places to discuss potentially offensive aspects of illness conditions or to disclose information that may stigmatise or produce judgemental reactions from close others. Wright and Bell also note the limitations of these forums, where people may engage in optimal self-presentation and offer idealised understandings, as well as the possibility that this medium provides for disseminating deceptive information. Also, as they point out, there is limited information on how people integrate support gained from these groups with support from more traditional sources. In a different approach, Hardey (2002) analysed the variety of personal pages placed on the Internet by people with illness, and suggested that these may be classified into four types, serving mixed functions but all open to offering support at some level (see sidebar 9.2). Ziebland *et al.* (2004) investigated uses of the Internet by patients with cancer, and showed that their use served a variety of functions, including accessing support. As one of their participants stated:

9.2   A classification of personal illness accounts on the Internet

1   My story and explanation: accounts where the authors set out to explain their personal illness and its effects on themselves to others.

> It is a little embarrassing to keep explaining why I am ill. My page makes it easy to tell people about me and MS and they can understand why sometimes I may be a bit off or down without me feeling a constant pressure to explain myself.

2   My story and advice: accounts where the author is cast as an 'expert', offering advice derived from their experience of illness and treatment to others with similar conditions.

> This page has been designed to provide information to people who want to learn more about paraplegics. On this page I will tell you about my life as a paraplegic and provide links to other information sources, as well as, links to pages of other paraplegics. It wasn't long ago that my girlfriend was doing searches on the Internet for information about paraplegics and disabilities. After much time and effort she found very little information. Hopefully this page can be a starting point of information for those people in situations like hers and mine.

3   My story and my solution: accounts promoting a particular health regime or approach to illness.

> We wanted to help people who had MS. I know a lot about MS and medicine is too much in the hands of pharmaceutical companies to be able to recognise [the role of] simple natural treatments. Our web page helps sufferers choose what is right for them and escape from medicine into alternative healing.

4   My story and my products and services: accounts where the authors draw on their experience of illness and recovery to recommend particular treatments and to provide health care products and treatments.

> . . . through the Web . . . I tell people about the treatments I have been given and explain what works and the effects you should watch out for. I know more than most doctors now and I hope that my website will answer people's questions and get them to buy things I recommend. It is a full-time job for me and I make a living out of dispatching orders to people around the world. (Hardey, 2002)

> I think that the worst thing about getting a diagnosis like this is a feeling of isolation, because you feel that your world has suddenly shrunk and all you can think about is yourself and you feel very frustrated because nobody has maybe experienced this. And when you're able to talk to other patients it's just very good to know that other people have been through this and to kind of share the experience with other people, and you feel much less isolated . . . It's not just the medical information aspect, it's just the kind of support, moral support, which is very, very important when you've had a diagnosis of cancer.   (51-year-old man with prostate cancer)

However, not all support has positive effects for the ill person. It has been noted, especially in relation to pain, that support of certain types may exacerbate the distress and disability experienced by some ill people. For example, Itkowitz *et al.* (2003) found that solicitous responding, such as expressing sympathy, to coronary heart disease symptoms was associated with increased symptom severity, disability and depressed mood. These findings support previous research (e.g. Kerns *et al.*, 2002) showing that overprotective responses from others, particularly from family members, served to perpetuate declines in independent behaviour and functional capacity. Similarly, Krause (2003) found that a support group for people with inflammatory bowel disease led members to represent the disease as a serious handicap, leading to exaggerated attention to the illness and unnecessary restrictions on their daily living. However, she conducted a participatory intervention with the support group, which led to the development of increased competence in living with the illness for group members.

Finding meaning

As we saw earlier, illness brings disruption, not only to future plans and directions, but also to personal identities and relations. This promotes a need for people to find meaning in relation to illness, both in the situation and personally. Meaning, however, is a complex term with many connotations. Bury (1988), for example, has argued that two different forms of meaning are engaged by illness:

• meaning as consequence, relating to the effects that chronic illness has on the everyday lives of sufferers, living with pain and discomfort, bodily disruption and a loss of roles and resources;
• meaning as significance, referring to the connotations that illness has for sufferers, the cultural significance of the particular illness, its potential to stigmatise and its threat to competence and personal worth.

These connotations have considerable significance for how ill people see themselves and how they consider others see them. Kleinman (1988) stated this somewhat differently, proposing that cultural meanings give significance to illness, while illness meaning gives significance to living. This distinction between the meaning *of* illness and meaning *in* illness is important, and needs to be clarified in research discussing illness meaning. For example, Degner *et al.* (2003) asked women with breast cancer to categorise the meaning *of* the illness they experienced. Most of the women regarded their illness as a 'challenge' or a 'value', with small numbers regarding the illness as being an 'enemy', an 'irreparable loss' or a 'punishment'. In this section, we focus on meaning *in* illness, and we discuss the cultural meanings of illness later when we consider narratives of illness.

King (2004) proposes a general framework for ways in which people find meaning during their lives that has application to the experience of illness. She proposes that people find meaning in three fundamental ways: through their relationships with others, through meaningful engagement in activities and through understandings of themselves and the world. All of these are engaged by illness, but the last is of particular interest here. Considerable research has documented that people who have high levels of meaning are better off in terms of their health. For example, Krause and Shaw (2003) report that elderly people who develop a deep sense of personal meaning in life enjoy better overall health than those who are unable to find meaning. Farber *et al.* (2003) found, in a sample of people with HIV/AIDS, that higher levels of meaning were predictive of better outcomes in relation to well-being and depression, and that meaning predicted such outcomes over and above the effects of problem-focused coping and social support. Lyon and Younger (2001) report that purpose in life is lower and depression higher in people with HIV/AIDS than in normative samples of people without illness. Further, they document that the level of life purpose predicts depression more strongly than markers of disease severity and progression, such as viral load, lymphocyte counts or number of symptoms.

Coward (2000) reviewed research on meaning in the context of life-threatening illness. Treating such illness as a crisis, she suggested there were three potential crisis points – at the time of diagnosis, on completion of active treatment, and at recurrence or on marked progression of the disease – when meaning-making was especially salient. Coward focuses on notions of identity and the self as especially important in relation to meaning in illness, through mechanisms of self-transcendence – 'reaching beyond a present conceptualisation of self through an extension of one's self-boundaries' (Coward, 2000, p. 161). Self-transcendence may be achieved in three ways: personally, through increased introspection and self-awareness; socially, through investing oneself in relationships with others; and temporally, through integrating understandings of one's past experiences and future expectations to enhance present living. Coward reports a range of research illustrating the processes of transcendence and meaning-making in people suffering from AIDS and cancer.

A related way of considering meaning is proposed by Janoff-Bulman and Frantz (1997). They suggest that one process of finding meaning in a trauma or loss event involves making sense of how the event and its consequences fit with understandings of the world as fair, just and predictable. They refer to this type of meaning-making as meaning-as-comprehensibility. In contrast, they propose an alternative process, meaning-as-significance, where meaning is achieved by understanding how the event and its consequences may produce some value or benefit. Finding benefit in the event can alleviate feelings of loss and helplessness, and promote a sense of purpose, value and worth in life. Janoff-Bulman and Frantz (1997) argue that successful adaptation to events like illness involves making sense of the experiences by finding some value or benefit in them.

Finding benefit

Although illness is traumatic and has considerable negative outcomes and effects, it would be a mistake to assume that this is the whole story. Many people report finding significant positive benefits from the experience of chronic illness. Recently, positive outcomes from illness experience have received specific attention, and a benefit finding scale has even been developed (Antoni *et al.*, 2001). In a study comparing breast cancer and myocardial infarction patients, Petrie *et al.* (1999) sought reports of positive change approximately three months after treatment. They found that substantial numbers of patients in both groups reported positive change, which they grouped into seven themes, of healthy lifestyle change, improved close relationships, greater appreciation of life and health, change in personal priorities, greater knowledge of health, feeling fortunate to be given a second chance and improved empathy towards others. The type of change was related to the type of illness (the most common themes were healthy lifestyle change for myocardial infarction patients, at 68 per cent, and improved close relationships for breast cancer patients, at 33 per cent), although the reporting of positive change was unrelated to illness severity. Schulz and Mohamed (2004) used benefit finding as a major outcome in a study examining the aftermath of tumour surgery for cancer. Benefits were reported one year after surgery, and were found to be directly related to social support and to coping strategies of acceptance and social comparison, but not to negative concerns such as worry and depression. Sears *et al.* (2003) provide a brief review of studies reporting positive benefits across a wide range of illnesses. In a longitudinal study of women with early-stage breast cancer, these authors found that almost all (83 per cent) of their participants reported at least one benefit from their experience. Benefits covered categories such as health behaviour change, improved relations with others, greater appreciation of life, enhanced personal strength and growth, and new possibilities for living. However, it should be noted that these authors found no relationship between identifying benefits or the number of benefits and the outcomes of positive mood, perceived health or **post-traumatic growth**. They also caution against suggesting to patients that they must engage in benefit finding, because this could be offensive, minimise personal experience and limit grief processes.

The experience of positive change and growth arising out of the struggle with a major trauma or life crisis, such as serious or life-threatening illness.

Reflections on adjusting to illness

In summary, adjustment to illness involves many different processes and issues, all of which have important implications for the ill person. The recently emerging focus on the more positive aspects of being ill – finding meaning and purpose in illness, making sense of the experience, finding benefit in the experience – should not allow us to lose sight of the fact that being ill, particularly when the illness is serious, chronic, incurable or life threatening, is very difficult and unpleasant. As we discuss above, being ill means that people can face substantial disruption to their lives, their futures and their relationships. They may face being discredited, marginalised and stigmatised as a result of their illness. While they struggle to 'put on a good face', and to find meaning and benefit in the experience, they must also come to terms with loss and deterioration, frustration with their condition, becoming a burden to others and a reworking of who they are, where they belong and how they can face the future. Although health psychology research has produced considerable information about adjustment to illness, much of this research suffers from the same critiques we have highlighted in other chapters – the ill person is often decontextualised, illness is separated from the person and from daily life, and findings have limited utility for helping to improve conditions for ill people. We also need to be careful that the recent focus on potentially positive aspects of illness is not used to develop further standards of 'better adjustment', thereby alienating ill people further from their experience, and rendering being ill even more difficult.

Illness overcome: recovering and surviving illness

Recovery from illness is also a complex process and cannot readily be separated from the specific issue we have covered above; people with illness are engaged in recovery from the time of diagnosis and this should not be considered a specific and separate phase of illness. In this section, we consider two specific issues that relate somewhat more appropriately to recovery than to adjustment – the quality of life experienced, and the struggle to be normal.

Maintaining quality in life

The levels of increasing morbidity and chronic illness in Western populations have led to an emphasis on quality of life; as medicine has moved from cure to care, questions about how well people are doing have come more sharply into focus. Such questions can be answered by reference to the quality of life experienced by people with chronic illness and disability. Although quality of life is a very general concept that can be, and has been, applied as easily to environmental conditions as to living circumstances, our interest here is in

9.3 Example scales for assessing quality of life

SF-36: A 36-item scale developed out of the Medical Outcomes Study to assess generic health concepts that are not specific to any age, disease or treatment group. It provides scores for eight domains, physical functioning, role limitations arising from physical health problems, bodily pain, general health, vitality, social functioning, role limitations due to emotional problems and mental health, as well as an overall score, and physical and mental component summary scores. It may be self-administered or interview-administered, and may be used in standard (four-week recall) or acute (one-week recall) form. It is available in a wide range of languages. A short twelve-item form is also available. (Turner-Bowker *et al.*, 2002)

WHOQOL: A 100-item scale developed by a specialist group for the World Health Organisation to assess adults' perception of the quality of their lives. It covers six domains – physical, psychological, independence, social relationships, environment and spiritual well-being. The scale has translations into a wide range of languages and can be self-administered or interview-administered. There is also a brief version of twenty-six items. (WHOQOL Group, 1998)

SEIQoL: A thirty-item measure assessing quality of life in health and illness from an individual idiographic perspective. The procedure determines overall scores for a range of domains which are individually elicited, using a complex scoring process which combines ratings of these domains weighted by current satisfaction and relative importance. It may be self-administered or interview-administered. There is also a shorter direct-weighted version. (Joyce *et al.*, 2003)

EORTC QLQ-C30: A thirty-item scale developed by the European Organisation for Research and Treatment of Cancer designed to assess general quality of life in adult cancer patient populations. It covers physical functioning, role functioning, emotional functioning, cognitive functioning, social functioning, general quality of life, pain, fatigue, nausea and vomiting, and specific symptoms. It is self-administered and has translations into a wide range of languages. There are also a range of specific modules which can be added to address issues relevant to different forms of cancer. (Aaronson *et al.*, 1993)

health-related quality of life. This has received substantial attention from health researchers in the past three decades, and quality of life measures have been used as indicators of a whole range of health-related issues, from outcomes in new drug trials to recovery from treatments to progression through illness to adaptation to illness.

Definitions of quality of life are variable, leading Fayers and Machin (2000) to conclude that 'in the absence of any universally accepted definition, some investigators argue that most people, in the western world at least, are familiar with the expression "quality of life" and have an intuitive understanding of what it comprises' (p. 3). Even if we restrict the focus to health-related quality of life, the definition and coverage of the construct remains quite variable. Fayers and Machin (2000) comment that the aspects considered under this heading may include any or all of 'general health, physical functioning, physical symptoms and toxicity, emotional functioning, cognitive functioning, role functioning, social well-being and functioning, sexual functioning, and existential issues' (p. 3). Some examples of different approaches to assessing quality of life are presented in sidebar 9.3.

Quality of life has been used as an outcome to assess changes over time following treatment, to track changes during the progression of illness, to compare life quality across different illnesses, and to compare life quality across different settings. In this section we consider studies that consider quality of life in adaptation and recovery from illness. A good deal of this research has focused on cancer. Botteman *et al.* (2003), for example, provide a narrative review of the literature relating to quality of life with bladder cancer. As might be expected, the greatest concerns for these patients were in

> FACT-G: A twenty-seven-item scale for the functional assessment of cancer therapy in adult populations. It assesses four components of well-being, physical, social and family, emotional and functional well-being, in relation to cancer. It may be self-administered or administered by interview or telephone. Supplementary modules are available for specific types of cancer and treatment, as well as for other diseases. (Holzner *et al.*, 2004)

the domains of sexuality and urinary function. Botteman *et al.* were critical of the wide variety of measures used, and the limited relevance of some measures to assessing quality of life in this area adequately. Vacek *et al.* (2003) explored changes in quality of life for women over a four-year period following treatment for breast cancer. They found that life quality declined over time, with the rate of decline being higher for older women. The presence of comorbidity was also associated with lower life quality but did not affect the rate of decline. Neither overall levels of life quality nor rate of decline were influenced by factors such as having a family history of breast cancer, the type of treatment or the stage of cancer. Vacek *et al.* concluded that breast cancer produces a significant reduction in quality of life that persists for years after diagnosis and treatment. In contrast to this, Bloom *et al.* (2004) assessed quality of life in young women who were cancer free five years after initial diagnosis, and found that these survivors reported improved quality of life at the five-year follow-up than that reported at the time of initial diagnosis. They also distinguished between physical and mental components of quality of life (using the SF-36 subscales), and reported different influences on each; increased physical quality of life was predicted by having received chemotherapy treatment, being employed and reporting fewer symptoms, whereas increased mental quality of life was predicted by levels of emotional support and reporting fewer symptoms. Discrepancies between the findings of studies such as Vacek *et al.* (2003) and Bloom *et al.* (2004) reflect the problems in this field, where different assessments of quality of life are widespread, as well as a focus on different populations with different ages, disease stages and disease characteristics. For example, Elliott *et al.* (2004) examined quality of life for a combined group of cancer patients with either breast or colorectal cancer diagnosis, and demonstrated substantial effects of comorbidity on quality of life (assessed differently from either Vacek *et al.* or Bloom *et al.*). They reported different effects of specific comorbid conditions on particular domains of life quality, and noted the importance of assessing comorbidity in health-related quality of life research.

Although there has been a strong focus on cancer in quality of life research, the construct has been examined in relation to many other illnesses. Hart *et al.* (2003) examined quality of life for people with Type I diabetes. Interestingly, they found that these people did not report lower life quality than members of the general population on most dimensions assessed by the SF-36 measure, except for bodily pain (which was higher) and general health (which was lower). However, quality of life assessed with another measure (EuroQol) involving some different life quality domains did identify lower quality of life for people with diabetes. Relationships between the various domains of the two measures in this group ranged from moderate to low, highlighting again the difficulties of measurement agreement in this field. Hesselink *et al.* (2004) examined the relationships between coping and quality of life for groups of patients suffering from asthma and chronic obstructive pulmonary disease. They report differences between diseases in the coping styles and coping resources associated with poorer quality of life, concluding that interventions to enhance coping would improve quality of life for both conditions. In a more general study, Arnold *et al.* (2004) examined quality of life for eight chronic conditions – lung disorder, heart condition, hypertension, diabetes mellitus, back problems, rheumatoid arthritis, migraine and dermatological disorders – and compared physical, social and psychological functioning domains of quality of life for these conditions with a group of healthy participants. They found that psychological functioning contributed to overall quality of life for all disorders but the other domains, physical and social functioning, contributed to overall quality of life only for some disorders. Further, most disorders differed from the healthy group with regard to physical functioning, but only some disorders differed from the healthy group in relation to social and psychological functioning. These findings reflect the importance of the specific disorder and the domain of life quality investigated in research on health-related quality of life. For a similar study comparing quality of life across conditions and countries see research in focus box 9.3.

Quality of life instruments assess the domains of life that may be expected to be affected by illness. As we see in the research above, these domains vary from instrument to instrument and are not always strongly associated or necessarily relevant to the illness under consideration. These issues were highlighted in a study by Hansel *et al.* (2004) who were interested to investigate the impact of tuberculosis on functioning and quality of life. They conducted focus groups with patients receiving treatment for tuberculosis and with doctors and nurses caring for tuberculosis patients. Their findings identified a wide range of domains relevant to life quality for this illness, including the expected domains of general health, psychological health, and physical, social and role functioning that are common in quality of life instruments. However, they also identified a range of other issues, such as social stigmatisation, isolation, the burden of pills, sexual dysfunction, loss of income and fear as additional specific problems related to tuberculosis. Although patients and health professionals both identified many of these domains, only patients mentioned the impact on sexual function, spirituality and improved life perspectives. This study documents the difficulties in identifying relevant quality of life domains

9.3 Chronic illness and health-related quality of life across eight countries

Alonso, J. *et al.* and the IQOLA Project Group (2004). Health-related quality of life associated with chronic conditions in eight countries: results from the International Quality of Life Assessment (IQOLA) project. *Quality of Life Research, 13*, 283–98.

This ambitious project assessed the self-reported prevalence of chronic conditions (allergies, arthritis, chronic lung disease, hypertension, ischaemic heart disease, congestive heart failure and diabetes, as well as back problems, dermatitis, and vision and hearing problems) in large representative population samples obtained from eight countries (Denmark, France, Germany, Italy, Japan, the Netherlands, Norway and the United States), and examined the impact of these conditions on health-related quality of life assessed with the SF-36.

Chronic conditions were commonly reported in all eight countries with 55 per cent of the pooled sample reporting at least one chronic condition, and 30 per cent reporting more than one. In the pooled sample the most common conditions reported were hypertension (17.1 per cent), arthritis (15.7 per cent) and allergies (15.5 per cent). The prevalence of self-reported chronic conditions was highest in the USA and Italy (67 per cent) and lowest in Denmark and Japan (42 per cent). The most common chronic condition varied by country, with hypertension being the most commonly reported condition in Germany, Japan, the Netherlands and Norway, arthritis in France and Italy, and allergies in Denmark and the USA.

Despite the variation in prevalence, the impact of these chronic conditions was roughly similar across countries. However, the impact of different chronic conditions on quality of life components, assessed by comparison with those people who reported no conditions, was varied. The greatest impact was on the physical health components, and was strongest for arthritis, chronic lung disease and congestive heart failure, with allergies and hypertension being closest to those with no chronic conditions. Certain conditions had large effects on specific components of quality of life, as follows:

- ischaemic heart disease on physical role limitations and general health;
- arthritis on bodily pain and physical role limitations;
- diabetes on general health;
- congestive heart failure on physical role limitations, physical functioning and bodily pain;

- chronic lung disease on general health, physical role limitations and physical functioning.

The effects on mental health components were smaller in size but similar in overall effects, with arthritis, chronic lung disease, ischaemic heart disease and congestive heart failure having the strongest impacts.

Reflection

This paper reflects many of the issues covered in the chapter. It provides evidence of the extent of chronic illness and disability in contemporary Western societies. It provides a detailed illustration of the effects of illness in reducing the reported quality of life experienced by people with chronic conditions. It also reveals how different illnesses have different overall impacts, both in terms of the size of the effects and the specific domains of life quality affected. The findings were similar across a varied set of countries, although we need to remember that they are relevant only to Western societies, a point the authors do acknowledge. This study demonstrates the value of having a general measure of life quality that allows comparison across different populations and chronic conditions, while allowing differences between conditions to be identified. However, although the study is based on self-report, it does not provide detail of the experience of people with chronic conditions as they go about living with illness. This is not a limitation of the study, but a reflection that there are different kinds of questions to be asked about illness and different ways of answering them.

to assess for a particular disease, and identifies the differences in the perceived relevance of domains that can occur between sufferers and health care providers.

One of the important issues in examining adaptation to and recovery from illness is to identify change over time and understand how it occurs. Research into quality of life has produced some surprising and counterintuitive findings, as when ill people report similar (Hart *et al.*, 2003) or higher (Groenvold *et al.*, 1999) levels of life quality than healthy comparison people. This may be a result of the change actually occurring (e.g. the level of depression has reduced) or it may be artifactual and due to some form of **response shift**. Response shifts refer to a change in the meaning of the construct being evaluated. This may result from a change in internal standards (depression is no longer assessed from the same baseline), a change in values and priorities (depression is no longer so important in the overall scheme of things) or a change in conceptualisation of the construct (depression means something different at a later point in time) (see

Mechanisms that lead to potential error in assessing change, relating to a change in the meaning of the assessed construct through a shift in internal standards (recalibration), a shift in values or priorities (reprioritisation) or a shift in definition (reconceptualisation).

Schwartz *et al.*, 2004). Recent work in quality of life research has recognised the dynamic nature of quality of life assessments and is developing methods of assessment which take factors such as response shift into account (e.g. Schwartz *et al.*, 2004; Schwartz & Sprangers, 2000).

This brief treatment of quality of life research hardly does justice to the vast range of research on health-related quality of life that exists. For example, there is a considerable body of research relating specifically to children (e.g. Eiser, 2004). However, it does provide some indication of the variation in findings and the difficulties in measurement and assessment of the quality of life construct. These differences in the meaning of quality of life for different illnesses, for different people and at different times, mean that it is extremely difficult to draw generalised conclusions. In fact, Rapley (2003) has asked the question 'Should we hang up quality of life as a hopeless term?' He concludes that the concept of quality of life can be useful, but only if we consider it as a 'sensitising concept' (p. 212) for approaching issues around service provision and the question of how well ill people live, rather than as a 'formalised, psychometric, conceptual framework' (p. 212).

This argument raises more fundamental critiques of quality of life as a concept. Instead of taking for granted the notion that individuals have a certain level and type of quality of life that can be unproblematically assessed, Rapley (2003) suggests that asking about quality of life amounts to an aesthetic judgement, not a scientific one. He proposes that requests to interrogate a person's standing on quality of life may be better thought of as a request for a qualitative appreciation of how things stand. Similarly, Little *et al.* (1998) have suggested that 'measures of health outcome and quality of life . . . currently do little to capture the main preoccupations of those suffering from serious chronic illness' (p. 1485), and argue that patients' accounts or narratives would provide a means of engaging more adequately with these preoccupations. Rapley (2003, p. 216) makes a similar, and more critical, observation:

> Paradoxically, then, given their avowed purpose of furnishing an explanation of the quality of life which people experience, while current theories may (or may not) offer compelling accounts of depersonalised (and entirely hypothetical) homeostatically controlled cognitive componentry, they cannot tell us anything about the meaning of the quality of life, as a state of being-in-the-world, of *persons*. Such a state of affairs, it would seem, requires both that we suspend our habitual, a priori, beliefs about the nature of ourselves, and also that we theorise not only the object of our inquiry (persons, and the quality of their lives), but also the procedures whereby we investigate ourselves.

Getting back to normal

People with chronic illnesses continually struggle to return to normal. For example, in a study by Drew (2003) on survival following cancer in childhood, one participant stated:

> Heather: I read this article in [a newspaper] – I don't know if you read it – and she was saying sort of like that her recovery was probably perhaps harder than having cancer itself. That was like the first time – what I read this year, and it was kind of the first time I felt the sense that maybe I am normal, you know? 'Cause I honestly thought of this whole depression thing, I honestly thought I was the only one that – and people would always say, 'Look at you, you're so lucky, you survived this,' and me not feeling lucky, me feeling miserable. And this article it just came up – just how she felt. How people would say this to her and she didn't feel that way. And reading this article was just really inspirational, because I did feel like – yeah, I'm normal.   (Drew, 2003, p. 196)

Of course, this person knows that she is not 'normal', as Drew demonstrates, but she is seeking 'successful survival' (Frank, 1997) and attempting to limit the effects of her illness and the possibilities of its recurrence.

The notion of striving for normalcy is a frequent issue within people's accounts of illness. For example, Dabbs *et al.* (2004) report 'striving for normalcy' as the key process in their qualitative study of people adjusting to lung transplantation. However, regaining a position as a 'normal' person is not easy and is fraught with difficulty and paradox. Dabbs *et al.* note the paradoxical nature of seeking normalcy: to be 'normal', illness has to be relegated to the background, but for ill people it is constantly being foregrounded. A related dilemma is that, by ignoring symptoms and illness-related changes in order to background illness, the ill person may contribute to more serious or more rapid disease progression. Hence, the ill person can try, but can rarely successfully accomplish, the minimisation or backgrounding of illness. Thus, attempts to be 'normal' are fraught with contradictions for people with serious chronic illnesses.

Also, as Radley (1994) notes, the ill person must come to terms with 'living with illness in a world of health' (p. 157), involving concerns about how to manage oneself with illness, and how to present to others although ill. This is, as Radley notes, unarguably bound up in issues about what the healthy think of the ill. McKenzie and Crouch (2004) illustrate this in their discussion of how, for people with cancer, the uncertainties and fears of recurrence mean that everyday practices and relationships with others are always underpinned by emotional states that disrupt taken-for-granted routines. They demonstrate how cancer patients are often at odds with those around them, and how the boundaries between themselves and the 'ordinary other' are always marked by the presence of the illness. This can make it uncomfortable, and sometimes impossible, for ill people to lead a 'normal' life, even though this may be exactly what they strive for. Radley (1994) cites an example where town officials acted on neighbours' complaints and requested that a man draw his curtains while undergoing dialysis. The neighbours were not unsympathetic to the man's situation but considered that they should not have to watch the 'unpleasant' procedure. This illustrates the way in which ill people have to be always concerned about their presentation to others and how they will be reminded, and can be brought to task, if they transgress. Radley (1994, p. 158) comments:

> What this shows . . . is that the price of the healthy person's compassion is the concealment of things by the afflicted, things that could be considered abhorrent. The chronically ill must bear their illness in ways that do not imply either that this burden is too heavy for them, or that bearing it makes them markedly different from the healthy . . . On the other hand, should they, like the man dialysing in view of his neighbours, act as if they are 'really normal', then sanctions will be applied to remind them of their 'true' status. This means that the 'good adjustment' of the handicapped is actually a quality granted to them by others. Then people say things about them like, 'he's very brave', or 'she's always so cheerful'.

For the ill person, her presentation must sustain and warrant herself as worthy, and as meeting the same standards as 'normal' others. By doing the wrong thing, by exposing the illness in the wrong way, the ill person may become discreditable (Radley, 1994).

Galvin (2002) discusses the links that connect chronic illness and individual responsibility in contemporary Western societies, arguing that it is becoming less acceptable to be ill and incapacitated as this clashes with notions of good citizenship, with conceptions of persons who are self-reliant, independent and responsible. Consequently, this requires ill people to warrant themselves as worthy, responsible and moral, as can be seen in the quotation from one of Bury's (1982) rheumatoid arthritis participants, discussing how she deals with her ability to work as hard as her colleagues in spite of being ill:

> At the moment I'm treated as an equal, which I am, I do the same amount of work as them. I get more or less the same money, so I think, well at least I'm keeping my part up.   (p. 177)

Bury (2001) argues that normalisation may proceed in two directions. On one hand, ill people may seek to hold their pre-illness identities and lifestyles intact, and therefore attempt to maintain as many pre-illness activities as possible, along with disguising or minimising the display of illness to others (holding the past as normal). On the other hand, ill people may attempt normalisation through openly adopting a changed lifestyle that is accommodated to the illness (making the present normal). The stories they tell will reflect the pattern of normalisation, with the former seeking to retain prior identities and the latter presenting changed identities. Further, it must be acknowledged again that not all illnesses are equal, and the possibilities for normalisation will depend on the nature of the illness, how it is regarded socially and the degree of stigma associated with it. Although seeking normalcy is an important issue in illness, very little research has been conducted into this area by health psychologists and much remains to be done.

Reflections on surviving illness

For the purposes of the text we have separated out our discussions of adjusting to illness and recovering from illness, but we must always be aware that these cannot be partitioned; each implicates the other. The two issues on which we have focused in this section – maintaining quality in life and returning to normal – raise a number of different issues. Quality of life is an important construct for illness research, and it certainly forces us to go beyond the illness and consider a wide range of issues surrounding it. However, the critiques of how quality of life is utilised as a construct in research remain familiar – failure to conceptualise and theorise the construct adequately, disagreement between assessment procedures, and a consequent problem of identifying and understanding key findings in the area. Although the construct does have potential to implicate daily living into illness in research, the measurement and research practices of health psychologists constrain this substantially, as Rapley (2003) cogently argues above. This does not mean that we should abandon quality of life, as it has considerable potential to provide an epidemiological account of life quality around illness experience if we can agree on theoretical and assessment issues. However, if we seek to use this notion in research on how illness is implicated in peoples' lives, then we need to conceptualise it more appropriately for use in that way. The other issue discussed here, returning to normality, is also complexly linked to living, and may be accomplished in many different ways. As we have seen, the attempt to regain normalcy raises issues of how we can represent ourselves as normal in spite of illness, and how we are likely to be constantly reminded by others that we are ill, and therefore not really 'normal'. These issues are closely allied to concerns about identity, moral worth and stigmatisation in illness that lie behind the issues discussed in these sections. As we continue to point out, health psychologists have much to offer these areas of research but so far have contributed little to them.

Illness as story: telling about illness

We considered earlier the notion that illness can be construed as biographical disruption (Bury, 1982) and how illness may be a particularly salient event in people's lives. Consequently, illness becomes part of an individual's health biography and an important aspect of daily life that will be told and retold to others. This has led many researchers to examine the storied nature of illness as a means of understanding it (e.g. Bury, 2001; Frank, 1995; Hydén, 1997; Kelly & Dickinson, 1997). As Kleinman (1988, p. 49) has argued:

> patients order their experience of illness – what it means to them and to significant others – as personal narratives. The illness narrative is a story the patient tells, and significant others retell, to give coherence to the distinctive

events and long-term course of suffering. The plot lines, core metaphors, and rhetorical devices that structure the illness narrative are drawn from cultural and personal models for arranging experiences in meaningful ways and for effectively communicating those meanings. Over the long course of chronic disorder, these model texts shape and even create experience. The personal narrative does not merely reflect illness experience, but rather it contributes to the experience of symptoms and suffering.

Here we see the core arguments for the value of narrative in understanding the experience of illness. Storying illness allows ill people to voice their concerns, to find coherence in unpredictable and unusual events, to make sense of and find meaning in those events, to construct and reconstruct themselves and retain or rework their identities, and to present and represent themselves to others. Perhaps more fundamentally, narratives of illness (as Kleinman argues here) produce stories that both create and contribute to the experience of illness. See sidebar 9.4 for a related account of what can be accomplished through narrative for people with illness.

Bury (2001) suggests that the recent rise in importance of illness narratives reflects the increasing dissemination of information about disease and illness, the changing nature of morbidity in modern society, and ongoing debates about the effectiveness of medicine. A recent phenomenon is the development

9.4 What can narratives accomplish?

Five uses that can be made of the illness narrative:

- to transform illness events and construct a world of illness – a means to transform and unify the symptoms and events of illness into a coherent account within a biography, giving form to the illness and so creating a world of illness;
- to reconstruct one's life history in the event of a chronic illness – a means to create continuity in our life histories, to reorient and to repair disruption created by illness, to reestablish the relationship between ourselves, our worlds and our bodies, and to reconstruct identity and personal life in the face of illness;
- to explain and understand the illness – a means to establish a relationship with illness, to engage with possible explanations for the illness, and to relate the illness to our moral values and how we live;
- as a form of strategic interaction in order to assert or protect one's identity – a means to justify, explain and excuse the illness itself and actions following the illness, to assert and ensure moral worth and value as a person with illness;
- to transform illness from an individual into a collective phenomenon – a means to call attention to the political and social implications of illness, and to extend illness accounts beyond the individual level to become collective experience. (Hydén, 1997)

of 'narrative-based medicine' (Greenhalgh & Hurwitz, 1998), and arguments for why narratives should be involved in medical practice are outlined in sidebar 9.5.

Presenting personal accounts of illness has become a popular activity in recent times. Aronson (2000) identifies, and analyses, about 270 book-length 'patient's tales', or 'autopathographies', noting that the vast majority of these have been published within the last twenty years. Many other versions exist in essay or photographic form, and are readily located through the Internet (e.g. the illness narrative/pathography section of the Literature, Arts and Medicine

9.5   Narrative-based medicine: why study narrative?

In the diagnostic encounter, narratives:

- are the phenomenal form in which patients experience ill health;
- encourage empathy and promote understanding between clinician and patient;
- allow for the construction of meaning;
- may supply useful analytical clues and categories.

In the therapeutic process, narratives:

- encourage a holistic approach to management;
- are intrinsically therapeutic or palliative;
- may suggest or precipitate additional therapeutic options.

In the education of patients and health professionals, narratives:

- are often memorable;
- are grounded in experience;
- encourage reflection.

In research, narratives:

- help to set a patient-centred agenda;
- may challenge received wisdom;
- may generate new hypotheses. (Greenhalgh & Hurwitz, 1999)

database). All of these sources can provide texts for analysis. For example, Murray (1997) analysed a set of popular books written by women who had experienced breast cancer, showing how they used narrative form to account for and explain their illness, to take control of it and to transform it into a life-enhancing event. Such public texts also promote the circulation of shared understandings of illness and contribute to 'cultural narratives' or 'ideological narratives' (see Murray, 2000), transforming illness from an individual to a collective phenomenon (Hydén, 1997). Also, as Hydén (1997) has noted, narratives have progressed over the last few decades from being a way to examine the experience of doctors to a way to examine the experiences of patients: patient stories are frequently considered as a means through which ill people give voice to their experience (Frank, 1995), articulate their suffering (Kleinman, 1988) and demonstrate their worth and morality (Bury, 2001; Radley, 1999b). Importantly, such articulations allow illness experience to be presented and set apart from the biomedical framing of illness (Hydén, 1997).

Several classifications of narrative forms have been suggested and used in research on chronic illness. For example, Robinson (1990) drew on a typology of narratives proposed earlier by Gergen and Gergen (1986) to examine how these different forms of narrative could be identified in the stories of people suffering from multiple sclerosis. These narrative types were defined by the relationship between the narrator and his or her personal goals:

- progressive narratives, where there was movement towards personally valued goals, with the person describing illness as a challenge for personal advancement and growth, and as something to be overcome;
- stable narratives, where the person remained effectively in the same position in relation to valued goals, and illness was described as ongoing and effectively stable;

- regressive narratives, with an increasing discrepancy between valued goals and the possibility of their attainment, where the account was one of decline involving an illness that could not be overcome.

Robinson found progressive narratives to be the most common form used by his participants, with only a few that could be classified as regressive. However, not all participants' accounts could be allocated uniquely to one or other of these types, demonstrating the limitation of the classification and the complexity of narrative accounts.

Frank (1995) describes a similar framework involving three 'narrative types', or storylines, ways of talking about illness that are culturally available, and may be drawn on by people in telling their story. The most commonly occurring of these is the 'restitution narrative', providing a sequenced account of the loss of health in the encounter with illness, the experience of the illness and the (anticipation of the) return to health. Although aspects of this storyline may be helpful to sufferers, Frank notes that it broadly reflects biomedical thinking, privileging treatment and cure, and sustaining medical control of illness with a social imperative to return to health. A contrasting type is the 'chaos narrative', where the chaos of illness leads to a disorderly account of the vulnerability, futility and impotence associated with illness and the 'wreckage' it causes (Frank, 1995, p. 110). The third storyline is the 'quest narrative', where illness is considered as transformative and a challenge and impetus to change. This type, Frank suggests, although therapeutic and inspirational, is often overly idealised and heroic, and can lead to deprecation of those who fail to overcome illness or transform themselves through it. Thomas-MacLean (2004) examined how these narrative types were drawn on by women in accounting for breast cancer. She found that all three forms of storytelling were used, but their narratives were not simply attributable to a particular type; rather, their stories were told in complex formats shifting between and combining types. Similarly, Jackson (1994), in a compelling analysis of one man's story of pain, discusses how her narrator adopted five different positions in telling his story, keeping 'all the important factors in play simultaneously, somewhat like a juggler's pins moving through the air' (p. 830). These positions were not always consistent and moved between contradictory stances as the person sought for understanding and meaning in his condition.

Other researchers have proposed alternative frameworks for classifying narrative. Bury (2001), for example, suggested a framework which involved 'three types or levels of narrative formation in the face of illness' (p. 265), namely:

- contingent narratives, that involve explanations of illness causation and the effects of symptoms on daily life;
- moral narratives, that involve evaluative accounts of the relationship between the person, the illness and their social identity; and
- core narratives, that involve the connections between the ill person's experience and the deeper cultural levels associated with illness and suffering.

These classifications reveal that narratives are not all at the same level. Most narrative analysis in health psychology tends to examine the story told at the personal level, where the accounts reveal components such as those identified in Bury's first two levels. For example, C. S. Lee (2001) reports a narrative analysis of one person's experience of cancer, showing how her account involved three interrelated stories – how others have reacted to her illness, how she struggled to understand her illness, and how the illness changed her priorities. This analysis remains on the level of the personal story, in contrast to analyses such as those reported by Thomas-MacLean (2004) or Robinson (1990) above, which identify more generic cultural narratives, or core narratives in Bury's terms, that are used to frame the stories told. As a further example of this, Kelly and Dickinson (1997) report a case of a person suffering from ulcerative colitis, and document the heroic nature of the account, which draws on a core theme of the courageous fighter against the adversity of illness. However narratives are classified, they reveal the ways in which people construct accounts to make sense of what is happening to them and to represent themselves to others. Through the analysis of narratives we can gain understanding of these processes, and the functions of storying illness.

However, narratives also have their limitations. Although people may draw on core narratives in telling their stories, these may not be located in a single story. As we saw above (Jackson, 1994; C. Lee, 2001; Thomas-MacLean, 2004), narratives can have complex formats and intertwine several different positions, stories or story types, and we need to be careful not to reify a particular narrative that is told. Further, as Hydén (1997) and others have noted, the narrative told is always contextual and changing – new narratives are produced in new contexts, so that the narrative told to one listener (e.g. the spouse) will be recounted for different purposes and in different ways to another listener (e.g. the doctor); the narrative told during an illness may well be different from the narrative told after recovery from the illness. Also, important aspects of illness may exist outside the narrative. For example, Radley (2004) has commented on how suffering may not always be able to be told, even though it may be shown, and that the researcher, in requesting stories of illness, may be forcing (a version of) suffering to be told, but on the terms of the researcher rather than of the sufferer. Similarly, most narrative research relies upon interviews with the ill and this can lead to the omission of some voices. For example, Rier (2000) notes how critically ill patients in the intensive care unit cannot be accessed in this way, but presents an interesting account of his own illness experience, an 'inadvertent ethnography', which was derived from a notebook kept while he was a patient in the unit.

In summary, illness narratives and their analysis, in spite of the limitations identified here, have considerable potential to provide insight into the experiences and meanings of illness, and they deserve wider attention in health psychology research. However, in taking this up, we need to be aware of the epistemological stance involved (generally some form of social constructionsm), and what narrative analysis is able to accomplish. However, if we are interested in stories of illness, and the associated concerns around illness involving meaning, identity and personal (re)construction, then narrative provides a powerful way to investigate this. Also, as Hydén (1997) and others have argued, narratives provide a means for transforming illness from an individual account into a collective entity, through which we can come to know and understand the nature of contemporary illness.

Illness in context: illness and the 'other'

Illness always involves more than the ill person; illness pervades everyday life and affects the lives and practices of the people who are connected in any way to the afflicted person. We noted one aspect of this above, when we considered spousal support as an important component of social support implicated in adjustment to and recovery from illness. We encounter it again in the next chapter when we examine caring for the dying. Here, we examine the effects of illness specifically in relation to those who serve as caregivers for the ill. This is an important and growing issue for health psychology because of the changing nature of care and the changing demographics of the population. Sales (2003) identifies five major reasons for the increasing concern with caregiving:

- increased life expectancies are likely to increase the time-span over which care is needed and must be provided by family members;
- the trend to smaller family sizes and increased geographical separation between family members exacerbate problems in providing necessary care;
- de-institutionalisation and managed-care practices have resulted in more chronically ill people being located in the community and consequently in need of care;
- technological advances in medical care, which can be delivered as outpatient care, require ill people and their families to engage in increasingly complex tasks of care;
- increasing complexities of changing health care systems render it more difficult to negotiate these systems, obtain adequate information and negotiate access.

All of these changes have the potential to complicate caregiving, and render caregivers more vulnerable to adverse effects from caregiving. They also function to increasingly locate the family as an important agent in providing help and assistance in the care and treatment of the chronically ill.

The demands of caregiving can be seen clearly in the following account by Rose, a 72-year-old woman caring for her 79-year-old husband who has Alzheimer's disease. He began having problems with memory thirteen years ago, and Rose spends an average of 150 hours a week caring for him. When asked 'What is it like being a caregiver for your husband?' part of her response was:

> *Exasperating* sometimes. It is almost like having a small child again because I've had to just gradually pick up doing things for him that he had normally done for himself – dressing him, first of all taking him down to shower, telling him you have to take off your shirt, you have to take off this, get down to be bare skin . . . I have just had to do almost everything . . . Brushing his teeth, I have to make sure that he has a toothbrush in his mouth before I leave the room, and he scrubs and scrubs and scrubs. Then I come in and he is scrubbing the sink with the toothbrush. I guess the hard thing was for me to realise that what he was doing was not him. There is no reason to get upset or angry. At night I have had to get up with him to go to the bathroom to show him where the bathroom is, to get him in the right position . . . It just seems like you have to be with him every minute and to anticipate what is going to happen. He gets agitated, starts prancing around and moving things. The rug will be on the table. Shoes could be in the refrigerator, and the dishes wherever. Some things we have never found. Some things have been lost for four months. Some things that are found it was not him that put them in a bad place, it was me. He is the first one blamed, anyway. It just seems strange to me sometimes that this grown-up big hulk of a man is acting like a three-year-old. You have to respond with care in that way. Put his coat on him, zip it up, put his mittens on.   (from Butcher & Buckwalter, 2002, p. 120)

A considerable body of research has focused on the role of family members as caregivers for the chronically ill and disabled, and has examined the consequences of caring for their health and well-being. A good deal of this research has focused on the negative impacts of caregiving, often labelled as **caregiver burden**, caregiver stress or caregiver strain (see Hunt, 2003). In one study that followed participants over four years, Schultz and Beach (1999) found that caregivers under strain had a death rate that was 63 per cent higher than non-caregivers. Vitaliano *et al.* (2003) conducted a meta-analysis of twenty-three studies on caregiving for persons with dementia, which allowed a comparison between 1,594 caregivers and 1,478 non-caregivers of comparable age and gender. They examined effects on a wide range of health measures, including self-reported health, health care use, reports of symptoms, use of medication and physiological measures of health, including cellular and functional immunity, levels of stress hormones and cardiovascular and metabolic measures. They found that caregivers exhibited a slightly greater risk of health problems than non-caregivers, with caregivers reporting poorer overall health and greater medication use for physical problems than non-caregivers. Caregivers also had higher levels of stress hormones and poorer immune function than non-caregivers.

The negative psychological and social costs and consequences to the caregiver of providing care for an ill person.

It is in this context that Vitaliano *et al.* (2004) pose the question: is caregiving a risk factor for illness? They point to a range of studies that suggest caregiving to be a risk factor for health, including their own meta-analysis, but conclude that it is not possible to reach a 'definitive inference that caregiving is a risk factor for illness' (p. 16). Some studies find mixed evidence of health differences between caregivers and others. For example, the Women's Health Australia project (C. Lee, 2001) looked at family caregiving in a cohort of 11,939 women aged 70 to 75 years. About 10 per cent of these women (1,235) identified themselves as engaged in caregiving for frail, ill or disabled family members. However, these women did not differ from non-caregivers on physical health measures, such as self-rated health, the physical component of the SF-36 scale, and the number of symptoms reported. They were actually less likely to have visited a general practitioner, a specialist or to have been admitted to hospital in the previous year. However, they did score lower on the SF-36 mental health component, and reported higher levels of stress and time pressure than non-caregivers. The Women's Health Australia project also reported on caregiving in middle-aged women (Lee & Porteous, 2002). This research located 1,775 women who reported involvement in caregiving from the total cohort of 13,888 women aged 45 to 50 years. In marked contrast to older caregivers, caregivers in this group did report poorer physical and psychological health, higher levels of stress and higher use of health services than non-caregivers. This identifies the contextual nature of caregiving and suggests that the effects of caregiving are quite complex.

In one of the few studies to examine the transition into caregiving longitudinally, and explore the effects of changing from a non-caregiver to a caregiver, Marks *et al.* (2002) found that the effects depended upon the nature of the caring relationship and the context in which it occurred. Their results showed that the transition into caregiving for primary kin (a child, spouse or biological parent) was associated with an increase in depressive symptoms and negative effects on psychological well-being. However, if care for parents was delivered outside the household, results were mixed, with some negative and some positive changes in well-being. Further, when care was for non-kin (friends, ex-spouses and neighbours), it was associated with positive effects, including increased autonomy, personal growth and purpose in life. Obviously, when caregiving is for a close relative living in the same household, the obligation to care and the penetration of caring into family members' lives are stronger, and there is greater potential for caregiving to be a burden.

The impact of caregiving is also gendered, with most evidence concluding that women experience a greater burden and more psychological distress from the caregiving role than men (Yee & Schultz, 2000). However, effects are mixed and, as Marks *et al.* (2002, p. 665) suggest:

> it is important to consider gender differences in the context of particular role relationship types of caregiving. For example, spousal care and co-residential care appeared more problematic for women than men; non-residential care for a biological parent appeared more problematic for men than women; non-kin care was more beneficial for women than men; but no clear pattern of gender differences existed for other types of care.

This research on caregiving may be critiqued for its focus on the carer for the ill person. Just as when we focus on the ill person, this focus on the carer promotes a separation of carers, those around the ill person providing care and support, from the ill, as the recipients of care and support. In taking on that focus, we lose the interconnectedness of the ill person and those that care for him or her. Some research has focused more directly on the ways in which illness pervades the daily interactions of those around the ill person. For example, Öhman and Söderberg (2004) documented the experience of close relatives (thirteen spouses and a daughter) who were caring for chronically ill family members. They suggested that the experience consisted of three components: living a life with a reduced sense of personal freedom, an increased sense of responsibility for and duty to the ill person, and a struggle with the demands to find the strength to manage this duty. These prominent themes were:

- A shrinking life: where carers were forced to alter their daily living, felt imprisoned and lonely, and struggled to keep their home as a home.

> Yes, [sigh] this lack of freedom is really a feeling I had . . . I could have greater freedom, but then X would have to have gone into institutional care. And she shouldn't be there. So, those two things weighed against each other. I accepted this lack of freedom, so she could stay at home . . . Yes, I did it.

- Forced to take responsibility: where carers had to come to terms with feeling like a mother or a nurse, with the ill person's decline, with becoming more dependent on others for help, and struggle to be stronger than they were.

> I see how he is suffering. And it affects me too; psychologically . . . that he is probably scared [whispering] at the same time . . . He is always saying that he wants to die. I really understand that it is . . . ebbing now. So I'm conscious of that, obviously.

- Struggling to keep going: where carers had to come to terms with the situation, learn to live in the present, find joy in being together and consider being together until the end.

> You can't wish that he would be healthy again; I know that he can't be. I know that. It doesn't work . . . But in that case I only wish that I will have strength enough – that I'll remain healthy above all.

These themes were interrelated and connected, and allow us to see the complexities of the engagement between the carer and the cared for, and the ways in which carers had to struggle to make sense of their own and the ill person's constantly changing situations of caring.

As we discussed above, illness can have positive as well as detrimental effects for the ill person. Similarly, it can be an error to consider caregiving solely as a burden; caring can also involve positive effects for the carer, bringing joy, personal growth and new meaning. For instance, the longitudinal research by Marks *et al.* (2002) discussed above found that for women the transition into parental care delivered outside the household was associated with increased depression, but also with higher levels of purpose in life. Kramer (1997) has proposed the notion of caregiver gain to recognise the ways in which caregiving may enhance and enrich a carer's life. For example, Kinney *et al.* (1995) found that the satisfactions obtained from caregiving limited the amount of distress experienced. Rapp and Chao (2000) showed that caregiver gain reduced the effects of stress on negative affect outcomes for caregivers. Ayers (2000) demonstrated how caregivers interpreted their experiences to make sense and meaning of them. Farran (2001) reviewed caregiver intervention studies and noted the need for more work on positive interventions, and particularly the importance of meaning-making in the experience. Perhaps, as Cheung and Hocking (2004) propose, the experience of caregiving may be best considered as paradoxical, involving gains and losses, positives and negatives, which are intertwined and must be negotiated. From their interviews with ten people involved in caring for a spouse with the unpredictable disease, multiple sclerosis, Cheung and Hocking (2004) proposed that carers needed to continually work through three important paradoxes constituted through caring: evaluating losses and gains in roles, relationships and responsibilities; countering the limitations of caring with enabling aspects of the role; and balancing vulnerabilities exposed with strengths gained in the experience. Their interpretation makes it clear how losses and gains are constantly changing and being reworked, and how carers find personal meaning that gives them 'the courage to weather illness and adversity in life' (p. 164). Alongside this is the ethic of care and the responsibility to take on caring. While this can be a paradoxical source of pleasure and pain for many carers, it is not taken on without substantial personal cost:

> After spending more than three-quarters of your life raising kids – looking after a husband – friends – relatives – other people's kids – full-time care of your elderly mother – divorcing – selling – moving house – building – kids leaving home – sudden death of your parents and mother – who you've looked after full-time for years – bad relationships – when the partner can't stand you speaking to your kids, etc. One morning you wake up completely exhausted – everything's gone. And you wonder – 'Who the hell are you?' And where am I supposed to go from here? And why do women – mostly – give so much time of themselves doing for others – and never taking some time out for themselves – or even given some thought to – one day it might all disappear – everyone else gets on with their lives and you're left wonder[ing] where to start again – or . . . if you've even got or care to have the strength to do so.   (from Lee & Porteous, 2002, p. 91)

Although there is a considerable body of research examining the impacts of caregiving, there are still many opportunities for further research activity in this area. Vitaliano *et al.* (2004) point out the need for further studies which are doubly prospective, following a cohort from the time before either caregiving or illness develop. Also, most research in this field has been focused on dementias and mental health conditions, and there is a need for more research on physical health conditions, and on the differences for caregiving between different illnesses, along with research that examines and controls for comorbidity in caregivers. Vitaliano *et al.* (2004) also note the need to develop theoretical models in the field, and the need to utilise better measurements, such as health service records rather than retrospective self-reports. Sales (2003) has also argued for the assessment of caregiving to involve the family as a system rather than continue the current common focus on the primary caregiver. Further, she argues for longitudinal studies that can follow the trajectory of caregiving over time. As we have seen above, caregiving entails a complex set of processes and social relationships, set in an ever-changing context, and there is a clear need for more interpretative research which can uncover the processes of caregiving in illness. One important issue that needs to be addressed more fully is the obligation and ethic of care. This obligation falls most heavily on women, especially daughters, and the gendered nature and consequences of care need further attention. Also, the focus on positive outcomes arising from care need to be understood in the context of caring, which has mostly negative effects for carers, and should not be taken up as a means for perpetuating the gendered world of caring. In particular, a more critical view that limits the current focus on the individual carer and makes her responsible for care would address developing concerns about structural issues in providing appropriate systems of care, and support for the growing group of people with chronic illness and disability in our societies.

Conclusion

This chapter has been organised largely around the notion of illness, particularly chronic and life-threatening illness, as a major crisis and disruption requiring adaptation and adjustment. This is a predominant view in health psychology and frames a great deal of the health psychology research conducted on illness. However, as we see in the discussions of these issues within this chapter, the experience of illness is much more than simply how we adapt to or cope with illness. As Radley (1999a) states in the quote at the head of this chapter, illness pervades and colours all aspects of life. Consequently, it is limiting to examine aspects of illness, such as coping processes, independently of other concerns, such as moral worth.

The model of illness as crisis, or more specifically as biographical disruption, has been discussed critically by Williams (2000). His critiques have considerable relevance for health psychology and the approach it takes to researching chronic illness. Although broadly supportive of the model, Williams raises several major concerns with this approach. First, it privileges an adult-centred notion of illness, and omits consideration of a wide range of conditions existing from early childhood, where continuity rather than disruption is likely to be salient. Secondly, the approach has specific relevance only to some sectors of society. Williams points out that much illness is accepted by the elderly and less affluent people as a 'normal' part of life, and may actually be biographically anticipated rather than disruptive. As such, illness may even operate to confirm and sustain personal identities and biographies, rather than produce a reworking of them. Thirdly, rather than illness producing a disruption, Williams argues that in some cases disruption in daily life is attributed as the cause of illness, thus providing an explanatory account of illness and meaning in the event for the person afflicted. As Williams suggests, there is a need 'to *extend* the biographical focus of studies . . . to *both ends of the lifecourse*' and to give 'greater attention to the *timing, context and circumstances* within which illnesses are "normalised" or "problematised", and the manner in which identities are threatened or affirmed' (2000, pp. 61–2, italics in original).

These critiques may be generally applied to much of the research on chronic illness within health psychology. In this chapter we have considered some of the key areas that have been extensively investigated within traditional health psychology research. But we have also opened up a range of issues to which health psychology has so far given limited attention – suffering, stigma, authenticity, storying illness, contextualising illness – and yet these are fundamental to a full understanding of illness. By taking a more critical approach to the field, reconsidering how we approach it, conceptualise it and research it, we have potential to increase our understandings and to make a difference for those who experience, and those who live and work amongst, chronic illness.

RECOMMENDED READING

Bury, M. (2001). Illness narratives: Fact or fiction? *Sociology of Health and Illness*, 23, 263–85. A good general article that provides a detailed discussion of narratives in relation to illness, outlining a framework for narrative accounts, a discussion of the value of each, methodological issues in narrative analysis and critiques of the approach.

Radley, A. (1994). *Making sense of illness: the social psychology of health and disease*. London: Sage. Although older, this book has certainly not dated and it provides an excellent chapter on chronic illness. It is one of the very few health psychology texts to address illness from a similar perspective to the present chapter.

Rapley, M. (2003). *Quality of life research: a critical introduction*. London: Sage. A review of the field that offers a good overview and a strong critical perspective, examining what quality of life means and how it is assessed, with a specific chapter exploring quality of life as a psychological object. This book raises many issues and problems relevant to quality of life as a concept and its use in research.

Suls, J., & Wallston, K. (eds.) (2003). *Social psychological foundations of health and illness*. Malden, MA: Blackwell. An edited book containing a number of chapters that provide an up-to-date review of theory and research on adaptation to illness from a traditional health psychology perspective.

10 Dying

[D]ying is not simply a biological fact, but a social process, and death not a moment in time, but a social phenomenon.   (McNamara, 2001, p. 5)

Learning objectives

By the end of this chapter you should be able to:

- discuss variations in mortality and influences on rates of death;
- describe different types of death and the changing constructions of death over time;
- comment on the ways in which a 'good death' is constructed;
- review research on how people face death and adjust to dying;
- discuss bereavement and the relation of the bereaved to the deceased;
- comment on the role of medical technology in death and dying;
- outline the effects of dying on health professionals and caregivers;
- argue why death and dying are essentially social processes.

In health research, particularly in epidemiology, death is often taken as a 'hard' data point, a status that cannot be disputed – a person is either dead or alive. However, dying is much more complex than this. There is substantial variation in rates of death around the world; the pace of death varies by country, by ethnicity, by gender, by age and by SES. Further, the process of dying can be highly variable. A person dying slowly from emphysema goes through a very different experience from a person who dies suddenly from a heart attack; a person dying peacefully in his or her sleep at home aged 85 is understood quite differently from an 18-year-old dying in agony in a car accident. Some people want to die and others resist dying. As the quote above contends, death is essentially a social phenomenon, and the meaning of death is constructed out of the circumstances of dying. People may meet a 'good' death or a 'not-so-good' death, depending on the conditions surrounding the death and the processes involved in dying. Dying has obvious implications for the dying person, but also affects those around the person dying, including the health professionals who provide care. These are some of the issues we examine in this chapter.

Mortality

As we saw earlier (see ch. 1), the causes of death have changed across the last century, so that people in Western societies today are dying from quite different diseases than they were 100 years ago. Death in Western societies today is predominantly caused by chronic degenerative diseases like cancer and heart disease rather than by infectious diseases like influenza and gastroenteritis. Over the same period, life expectancy has increased or, to put it another way, the pace of dying has slowed. For example, life expectancy at birth across the world was 48 years in 1955 but had increased to 65 years by 1995 (World Health Organisation, 1998). These changes in life expectancy appear to be mostly the result of changes in perinatal and infant mortality, with infant mortality worldwide reducing from 148 per 1,000 live births in 1955 to 59 per 1,000 live births in 1995 (World Health Organisation, 1998). However, worldwide life expectancy refers only to the average and there is substantial variation in life expectancy across different countries, ranging from 26 years in Sierra Leone to 75 years in Japan (Mathers *et al.*, 2001).

10.1   How long have I got?

Should you book a lunch date for 24 January 2055? Thanks to the Internet you can estimate whether you are likely to be around to make the engagement. There are a wide choice of life expectancy counters and 'death clocks' available that will tell you the date of your death.
(http://www.findyourfate.com/deathmeter/), how old you will be when you die
(http://www.livingto100.com), or how many seconds of life you have remaining
(http://www.deathclock.com/ The Internet's friendly reminder that life is slipping away . . .)
These all use combinations of questions which ask about standard risk factors for disease, such as your family and medical history, your lifestyle in relation to diet, exercise, smoking and whether you have an optimistic personality style. Of course these are not meant to be taken seriously, as you can easily discover from the widely fluctuating answers given by different sites. One website gave my day of death as 22 July 2036 and another as 14 October 2057. I think I'll just have to wait and see whether I get to the lunch or not.

Increased life expectancy in Western countries has meant that death has become generally associated with the health and illness experiences of older age. This has led to the development of alternative measures of life expectancy that attempt to capture the years of healthy life rather than years of total life. One such measure is disability-adjusted life expectancy (DALE) or the number of years expected to be lived in full health. This measure has been used by the World Health Organisation to compare member countries, and their data provide a vivid account of the marked differentials in healthy life expectancy around the world, as we see in table 10.1. Healthy life expectancy in the highest countries, which are all Western 'developed' countries, is the traditional three score and ten (seventy) years. In contrast, life expectancy in the lowest countries is only around thirty years. These countries are all located on the African continent and, while it may be tempting to explain this effect

Table 10.1 Healthy life expectancy around the world (DALE scores[a] in years)

Highest ten countries		Middle ten countries		Lowest ten countries	
Country	DALE	Country	DALE	Country	DALE
Japan	74.5	Russian Fed.	61.3	Ethiopia	33.5
Australia	73.2	Honduras	61.1	Mali	33.1
France	73.1	Ecuador	61.0	Zimbabwe	32.9
Sweden	73.0	Belize	60.9	Rwanda	32.8
Spain	72.8	Lebanon	60.6	Uganda	32.7
Italy	72.7	Iran	60.5	Botswana	32.3
Greece	72.5	Guyana	60.2	Zambia	30.3
Switzerland	72.5	Thailand	60.2	Malawi	29.4
Monaco	72.4	Uzbekistan	60.2	Niger	29.1
Andorra	72.3	Jordan	60.0	Sierra Leone	25.9

Note: [a]DALE scores are disability-adjusted life expectancy scores, calculated as the number of years of life expected to be lived in full health.
Mathers *et al.* (2001).

as the result of limited medical systems, it is certainly contributed to by a range of other factors such as warfare, AIDS, poverty, starvation and poor water supplies. What these figures document is that the pace of death is quite unequal throughout the world.

The pace of death varies by other important factors as well as country of location. We saw in ch. 1 how SES is implicated in mortality differences. In other sections of the book, we have referred to gendered differences in patterns and experience of disease and illness. In most societies, but particularly in Western societies, women outlive men. For example, in the USA, women have a consistently higher life expectancy than men, regardless of their age, ethnicity or level of education (Crimmins & Saito, 2001). Figure 10.1 presents this data by gender, and also shows variation by ethnicity, age and education. There are complicated interrelationships between these factors and life expectancy. Life expectancy in the USA is longer for people with higher levels of education, regardless of age, gender or ethnicity. The patterns for ethnicity are more complicated, with ethnic differences apparent at lower levels of education but not as obvious at higher levels. For example, at age 30, African American females with higher levels of education have the longest life expectancy, but in stark contrast African American males of the same age with low levels of education have a life expectancy that is almost twenty years less than this group. This pattern is also evident at age 65, but the discrepancy there is narrowed to around ten years. Crimmins and Saito (2001) document how these variations are even more marked if alternative estimates of life expectancy, such as healthy life expectancy or proportion of healthy life, are used instead. Such analyses reveal that considering only overall estimates of all-cause mortality can mask

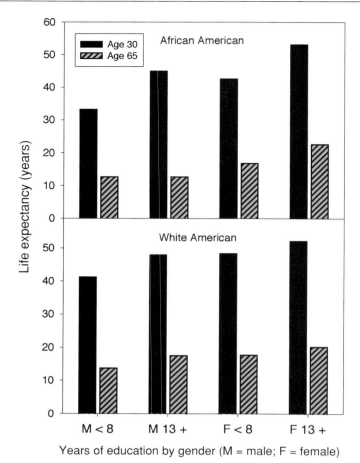

Figure 10.1 *Life expectancy by ethnicity, gender and education at ages 30 and 65 in the USA*
Crimmins & Saito (2001).

a range of factors that affect the pattern and pace of death. Another example from a different part of the world is documented in research in focus box 10.1.

In spite of the recent worldwide trend towards increasing life expectancy, not all countries have shown a consistent increase in life expectancy. Some, particularly in the newly independent states of the former USSR, have shown periods of marked decline. In Russia, for example, life expectancy has fluctuated markedly over the past thirty-five years, with a substantial decline in the early 1990s and a recovery by the end of the decade (see table 10.2). The pattern of change is complicated (see Shkolnikov *et al.*, 2001) and differs by disease, gender and age. For instance, within this decade, the changes were more marked for people between the ages of 25 and 60, and little change was shown for children and the elderly. In contrast, the mortality rates for young adults aged 15–24 showed an increase between 1991 and 1994 but this did

Table 10.2 Age-standardised mortality rates[a] for Russia 1990–8

	Males			Females		
1991	1994	1998		1991	1994	1998
1463.1	2181.1	1716.7		587.1	791.8	656.1

Note: [a]Age-standardised rates per 100,000 at age 15–74 years for all causes of death.
Shkolnikov *et al.* (2001).

not decline again and remained high right across the decade. As table 10.2 shows, men had consistently higher rates of mortality than women across this period, although the patterns of change were generally similar for men and women. These differences in mortality rates raise questions about the diversity of factors that underlie death, which we now consider.

What causes death?

On the surface, this may seem like an obvious question, but there is no easy answer, and the picture is far from clear. We all die of something, be it the result of an accident, a disease, or merely from 'old age'. In the West, the major causes of death are well known – cancer (of various types) and coronary heart disease (also of various types). However, as indicated above, these major causes of death are not necessarily relevant to the world at large or even to many segments of the population within a specific country. This is illustrated in table 10.3, which lists some culturally and socially specific causes of death.

These findings demonstrate that the causes of death are socially and materially located, and they problematise the discussion of general patterns of mortality and the use of all-cause mortality as indicators of death and dying. These are statistical and epidemiological findings that have utility in documenting trends and changes. However, health psychologists are not epidemiologists and so we might ask how this information is relevant to us. Consideration of these patterns of death does not provide much room for the involvement of traditional health psychology research, with its emphasis on individualised psychosocial constructs. What these patterns do reveal is the social, material and structural factors behind death that are too often ignored in health psychology research and theorising about health and illness. Knowing about these factors, considering their implications and taking a more critical approach to our research means that we should attempt to include such factors in our theorising, to ask questions about why they occur, how they may be altered and how appropriate interventions may be developed. If we believe that psychology has something to offer with regard to changing the patterns of dying, then these are important issues. Wilkinson's theory, discussed in ch. 1, invoking psychological factors such as social exclusion to explain the effects of socioeconomic differentials in

10.1 Dying down under

O'Donoghue, B., Howden-Chapman, P. & Woodward, A. (2000). Why do Australians live longer than New Zealanders? *Health Education & Behavior, 27*, 307–16.

This paper argues that Australia and New Zealand are very similar countries: both are located at the southern edge of South-east Asia; both have heritages, social systems and cultures largely shaped by British colonisation; both have predominantly European populations, alongside indigenous minorities; both have substantial migrant populations from Europe, although from different regions; and both have significant migrant communities from Asia and Polynesia. Before 1970 life expectancy was higher in New Zealand than in Australia, but after that the pattern was reversed. This paper considers 1996, when male life expectancy at birth was 74.3 years in New Zealand and 75.4 years in Australia (a difference of 1.1 years) and female life expectancy at birth was 79.6 years in New Zealand and 81.1 years in Australia (a difference of 1.5 years). Having about one extra year of life may not seem much, but, as the authors point out, this is a substantial gain at the population level. They suggest that it would be equivalent to removing all deaths due to injury in New Zealand – a major source of premature death and the loss of many years of potential life – which would raise life expectancy by 1.3 years overall. The authors consider several potential reasons for this difference and conclude:

> Possible explanations for the emergence of the gap in life expectancies include slower economic growth in New Zealand, more marked economic inequalities that have particularly affected Māori (the New Zealand indigenous people), modest differentials in the effectiveness of health care, and different patterns of immigration after the Second World War. (p. 315)

Reflection

This paper considers a range of possible differences between two very similar populations that may lead to life expectancy differences. Interestingly, the conclusions offered do not relate to biomedical explanations but implicate differences in structural factors between these countries. One prominent explanation is that economic disparities between the best and worst off in these two societies have altered since the 1970s to produce stronger differentials in New Zealand than in Australia, particularly for indigenous populations, with consequent effects on mortality. Also, policies on assisted immigration, which have resulted in quite different migrant compositions in each country, are suggested as a partial explanation. In New Zealand, migration has been predominantly from northern Europe and the Pacific Islands, whereas Australia has received a substantial influx of people from southern Europe and Asia, and this is considered to have altered the pattern of deaths, particularly in relation to the decline of circulatory disease in Australia. It is notable that even small population differences in mortality have complex explanations that have more to do with how society is structured than to how often people are exposed to pathogens.

Table 10.3 Varying influences on death around the world

- Infant mortality around the turn of the 21st century was highly variable around the world, being more than seven times higher in Africa (85.6 per 1000 live births) than in Europe (11.6 per 1000 live births) (Seale, 2000). This effect is likely to be due to a range of factors including access to health care, nutrition and safe water, as well as natural disasters and warfare.
- The effect of AIDS has a serious effect on life expectancy in some countries, especially in Africa. There, in countries with more than 10% HIV/AIDS prevalence rates, it is estimated that average life expectancy will be reduced to 47 years by 2015 rather than reach the 64 years that could be expected if AIDS was not present (UNAIDS, 1998).
- Although there was a noticeable increase in mortality in Russia between 1991 and 1994 (see table 10.2), this did not hold for motor vehicle accidents, which showed a decline (Shkolnikov *et al.*, 2001). This was attributed to the considerable increase in fuel costs in the period combined with a decline in economic activity and reduced disposable income for individuals.
- Suicide is often found to be associated with a prior decline in personal resources but a Finnish study documented the opposite effect (Hintikka *et al.*, 1999), showing that suicide increased during a period of economic improvement and was not associated with factors such as unemployment or divorce. In this case, it was associated with increased alcohol consumption.
- The major causes of death for males aged 18–24 in New Zealand are accidents and suicides; cancer and heart disease are rare in this group (Ministry of Health, 1999). Accidents are most likely to be related to motor vehicle use and this reflects the high levels of risk-taking by this group.
- Deaths due to stomach cancer have declined in industrialised countries throughout the world. This is not thought to be due to an advance in medical cure, but rather to a reduction in exposure to a particular infection in childhood as a result of improvements in the socioeconomic conditions in those countries (Eslick *et al.*, 1999).
- Increases in the incidence of some types of cancer that have been documented in Eastern Europe have been attributed to changes in patterns of childbearing (for breast cancer), and levels of nutrition in childhood (for prostate cancer) (Davey Smith *et al.*, 2000).

health, provides one example of an attempt to achieve this (Wilkinson, 1996). At present few health psychologists concern themselves with these issues.

The changing context of dying

Until about the end of the nineteenth century, death was a public affair. People commonly died at home surrounded by their family and among their local community; their bodies were 'laid out' in their homes and were viewed, touched and mourned in the company of others. Death was thus a normal part of everyday existence, and an integral part of life; people lived with dying (Kellehear, 1998; Lawton, 2000; McNamara, 2001). During the twentieth century, the context of dying changed; people were much more likely to die in medical settings such as hospitals and nursing homes. For example, Field and James (1993) note that in the UK by the mid-1960s almost two-thirds of all deaths occurred in a medical setting and by the late 1980s this had increased to almost three-quarters of all deaths. Seale (2000) notes that in 1996 two-thirds of all deaths in the UK occurred in hospitals rather than in other medical settings, and that this figure was representative of other industrialised countries. Seale also notes that this appears to be an upper limit because there are always a residual number of sudden deaths, and an increasing move to hospice and nursing home use, coupled with a more recent encouragement to return home to die. However, most people in industrialised societies today do not die at home.

The historical change over the last century in the place of dying, from the person's home to a medical setting, such as a hospital or nursing home.

The change in the place of death over the last century, moving death from homes to medical settings, has been labelled the **hospitalisation of death** (Lawton, 2000). A number of interrelated factors have been suggested to account for this. The decreasing size and increasing mobility of families has made it more difficult for people to care for dying family members and relatives (Field & James, 1993). Changing occupational status, and especially the increased involvement of women in the labour force, has limited possibilities for unpaid caring (Field & James, 1993). The rise in life expectancy has led to an increasing number of chronically ill older people requiring substantial care (Seale, 1998), and increases in medical and drug technologies have motivated the move to institutions where these are readily available (Moller, 1996). Increasing secularisation and acceptance of medicalisation in society has also transferred the oversight of dying from the priest to the doctor (Walter, 1994). The hospitalisation of dying results in some paradoxical tensions. Sequestering death in a hospital can be problematic as hospitals, and the health professionals who work in them, are primarily oriented to saving life rather than supporting death. Tensions can also emerge around medical technologies designed to be life enhancing when these are used to prolong life in the face of inevitable death. Research into hospital care of the dying around the middle of last century (e.g. Glaser & Strauss, 1966) documents the problematic nature of the person dying in hospital. Dying patients were generally not informed of their state, were frequently isolated from other patients and often heavily sedated. They were deprived of control and effectively disempowered. At another level, the hospitalisation of death removes it from everyday experience and renders it socially invisible. This has led to the proposition that modern society denies death and treats it as a taboo topic (e.g. Ariès, 1981; Illich, 1976), although as Seale (1998) has argued, this proposition has been overstated and there is considerable evidence of the acceptance and incorporation of death into modern social practices. He suggests that death, rather than being denied, is hidden away in late modern society, drawing on Ariès's (1981) discussion of 'hidden death'.

Although death and the dying are largely removed from everyday life in Western societies, leaving the living free to manage their own affairs, there have been substantial changes in the way that death is managed since the 1960s. Around that time Kubler-Ross (1969) published her seminal work on the stages of dying (discussed later) and successfully promoted attention to the needs of the dying person. Simultaneously, arguments were made in the UK for the development of the hospice as a special place of care for the dying. These quickly developed and proliferated, predominantly throughout the English-speaking world (see Clark & Seymour, 1999; Seale, 1998). Hospices were founded on a premise of restoring control and empowerment to patients, and they prioritised control over symptoms, particularly pain, incontinence and breathing difficulties. They operated on a dual notion of medical care and volunteer support, and came to adopt a premise of helping the patient to die peacefully at home. In this way they were essentially bound up in the construction of the 'good' or 'natural' death (see below). Although their promise was to empower patients and provide more humane care at the end of life, the hospice movement has been criticised for becoming institutionalised, for placing an emphasis on physical rather than psychosocial care, and for being drawn back into a biomedical model which operates to reduce dying to matters of professional management (see Crossley, 2000; McNamara, 1988; Seale, 1998). In doing so, the movement has influenced the nature of medical understandings of dying and has been influential in the production of palliative care as a medical specialisation (Seale, 1998).

As we can see from this brief account, the context of dying has changed quite radically in the last fifty years, and it continues to change in accordance with an increasing medicalisation of everyday life and the possibilities of new medical and genetic technologies to prolong life and resist death. As Wass (2001) has noted, these have created increased expectations for treatment and survival, and consequently make it more difficult for people to acknowledge their mortality. Yet in the face of this how we die remains important in contemporary society.

Living with dying

The ways we die: classifying deaths

Clearly there are different forms of death and several commentators have attempted to classify types of death or to discuss the trajectory of dying. For example, Clark and Seymour (1999) suggest that three types of death may be distinguished:

- gradual death – death in modern industrial societies with ageing populations appearing as a slow wasting process at the end of a long life. This is the predominant way in which most people think about death, and how most people expect to die, in Western societies today;
- catastrophic death – death as a sudden and unexpected event, arising out of war, famine, genocide and disaster. This is similar to the notion of horrendous death (Wass, 2001) and is rarely experienced in Western societies, except through media representations;
- premature death – these involve 'early' deaths through the everyday disasters of modern life, such as accidents and homicides, and other forms of early death from preventable illnesses such as AIDS, cancer and heart attacks. These deaths are particularly noticeable when they occur in children and young adults.

Looking more broadly, Walter (1994) proposed three sorts of death that can be anchored in particular social practices and historical contexts:

- traditional death – deaths that occur in societies where there is low life expectancy and where death is continually a threat. Here, death is likely to be due to infectious disease and to occur relatively rapidly;
- modern death – deaths that occur in Western societies, associated strongly with old age, hidden from view, and regarded as events to be managed by medical experts;
- neo-modern (or post-modern) death – deaths that have much in common with modern deaths, but with a greater emphasis on living-while-dying and on 'dying well' in the company of family and friends. Medical care is regarded ambiguously, drawn on as necessary, but with the individual asserting control and seeking meaning in the process.

Walter's account is more developed than this and considers notions of subjectivity and social practices such as funeral rites. While this analysis does provide recognition of the historical and cultural diversity that surrounds death, it has been criticised for the underlying assumption that these types form a historical progression. To some degree these forms continue to appear in present-day social practices around death.

Alternatively, we could ask people directly for their personal understandings of death. Williams (1990) used interviews and questionnaires with older people in the UK and found they held at least four different types conceptions of death:

- ritual dying – valuing readiness or preparedness for death, including reunion with those closest to the dying person;
- disregarded dying – the expectation and moral valuing of death late in life, which ideally would be quick and unaware;
- transitional dying – a combination of the notions of ritual and disregarded dying, involving preparedness and ease of death;
- controlled dying – valuing putting one's affairs in order, avoiding pain and dependency at death, and consideration of suicide or euthanasia as a means to ensure this.

These typologies of dying vary in their frameworks and orientations, but they all make the point that death cannot be comprehended in any simple manner and is always a product of historical, social and cultural understandings. They also promote the notion that death can be categorised, and so obscure the fact that dying is a process, usually occurring over a period of time.

The ways we die: the process of dying

In contemporary Western societies most deaths occur later in life and, to a considerable degree, are anticipated and prepared for. However, this can often result in the dying person experiencing a social death before reaching a biological one. This occurs as the person becomes increasingly unable to manage daily routines and bodily functions, often leading to institutionalisation. Seale (1998) discusses the process of dying as a 'falling from culture', whereby the dying person becomes increasingly limited and isolated as death draws nearer. This process also applies to control over the projects of self-identity – maintaining oneself as a functional being – and Lawton (2000) details the 'falling from personhood' that occurs as death approaches. As Walter (1994) has argued, much of the modern attempt to achieve a good death is aimed at ensuring that social and biological death coincide, with

10.2 Dying from cancer in Scotland and Kenya

Patients' experience with having a life-threatening disease, cancer, is quite different between 'developed' and 'developing' countries.

Scotland

- Major issue is the prospect of death
- Pain is unusual
- Reaction is often one of anger
- Diagnosis bought active treatment
- Concern about how carers will cope in the future
- Support available from hospital and primary care team
- Specialist palliative care available
- Cancer seen as a national priority

'You're wondering if you are going to see tomorrow. When I first was told, that was the first thing that went through my head. How long? When . . .? It's been like going to hell and back.'

Kenya

- Major issue is physical suffering, and pain
- Analgesia is unaffordable
- Reaction is often acceptance
- Diagnosis signalled waiting for death
- Concern about being a physical and financial burden to carers
- Lack of medical support, treatment options, equipment and basic necessities
- Specialist palliative care not available
- Cancer not given a national priority

'I want to go to sleep and wake up dead because the disease may take a long time, and I will have to suffer a long time.' (Adapted from Murray *et al.*, 2003)

people retaining their personhood and their social relations intact as close to the time of death as possible.

The process of dying also encompasses the transition from 'subject', as a living person, to 'object', as a corpse (Lawton, 2000). Considered from this perspective, dying raises issues of embodiment and the deterioration and loss of bodily function that accompanies dying. These losses can be particularly difficult, both for the person dying and those around him or her, with the consequence that this type of 'dirty death' (Lawton, 2000) is frequently hidden from view. Failing, leaking bodies challenge our notions of individual personhood and self-containment. We have already noted that the removal of death from view in modern society renders real deaths invisible, and 'dirty dying' is a major pressure for this 'sequestration of the unbounded body' (Lawton, 2000). Other current social practices in Western societies also work to sustain this: the management of death by medical professionals, the location of dying in hospitals and nursing homes, removal of the body to a funeral parlour, ritual viewing and rapid burial or cremation, all operate to distance us from the reality of death, and the dead body, in contemporary Western society. However, we should not forget that death and dying may be understood and managed quite differently in other cultures (see Parkes *et al.*, 1997; Shin *et al.*, 2005), or within cultures by people with different religious beliefs.

Is there such a thing as a good death?

Most of us want to die a 'good' death, and much of the work around end-of-life care is directed towards ensuring a good death. However, an examination of this issue reveals, not surprisingly, that a good death is no simple affair. For example, Bradbury (1993, 1999), in discussing different representations of death, argues that there are at least three important ways that death can be represented as 'good':

- the sacred good death, where the person is held to be reborn into a new life beyond death;
- the medical good death, where the person dies free of pain and suffering and has received all necessary care to do so;
- the natural good death, where the person's death is expected, and where the individuality and personality of the dying person are respected.

As Bradbury notes, echoing Walter's (1994) concept of neo-modern death above, these are not tidy, or even very separate, categories today. The medicalisation of death and dying means that medicine is likely to be involved in all types of death, even those considered to be predominantly natural or spiritual. Further, these categories are themselves multidimensional. For example, a death can be represented as 'natural' if it is an 'easy' death following an illness, if it is free from trauma and intrusive medical control, if the dying person retains dignity and a sense of personhood, or if it is quick, sudden and unexpected. Hence, we can see how the representation or understanding of any death is a construction of the circumstances surrounding it, and is particularly related to how control surrounding the death is accounted for. For example, the medical good death allocates control to medicine, giving control over both the location and timing of the death, and also over the process of dying, which is orchestrated by medical personnel, who prevent pain, control physical symptoms and interpret the process to others involved.

As Bradbury (1999) observes, these constructions of a good death can also work to shift the focus from the dying person to those around him or her. What makes a good death may be very different for the person dying than for others surrounding the death. Williams (1990) has drawn a similar distinction between these two types of good death. In one sense, a good death is to die quickly, easily and probably unconsciously. This construction works for the person dying, but is in conflict with the understanding that the dying should be cared for. An alternative type of good death is constructed more in the interests of the living. In this case, well-cared for death means the death should occur in a context that allows the next of kin to be present, to care for and support the dying person, and to farewell him or her appropriately. However, even this category of death is not clear cut, and is dependent on the nature of the death. A sudden unexpected death may be 'good', in the sense of being fast and easy, but also 'bad', in that the person did not have the time or opportunity to put his or her affairs in order, to plan for the death and to farewell the next of kin. Sudden unexpected deaths may also be far from easy, and may involve intense medical intervention along with very difficult decision making about provision and withdrawal of treatment. These issues are illustrated for one death in research in focus box 10.2.

Bradbury (1999) notes how the sacred death today tends to be displaced by the medical death, which in turn is being challenged and displaced by a more recent representation of natural death. However, any particular death may be constructed in a variety of ways and aspects of all three types of death may be invoked. As Long (2004) documents in a study contrasting death in the USA and Japan, there are also cultural variations in the scripts for a good death, and such scripts are interpreted within the sociocultural context of any particular death. Thus the notion of a good death is complex and open to contested representation. The construction of a specific death will be a combined function of the cause of death, how the death was experienced,

Research in focus

10.2 Being there: The reflexive researcher present at the death

Weitz, R. (1999). Watching Brian die: the rhetoric and reality of informed consent. *Health: An Interdisciplinary Journal for the Social Study of Health, Illness and Medicine, 3*, 209–27.

This is a very unusual paper because the author is also caught up in the action. Weitz is an academic medical sociologist, but is also a family member present at the death of her brother-in-law. In this paper she grapples with both positions as she discusses the ethical concerns surrounding this traumatic crisis – involving family conflicts, medical decision making, the right to die, and the debate about how such decisions should be made. She comments:

> Since Brian's death, I have had the chance to reflect more on our experiences, and have come to see them as an example both of the difficulties of implementing informed consent in the complex, murky terrain of clinical practice and of the consequences for families when informed consent is not obtained. This article is my attempt to make something useful from this tragedy. Writing, then, both as a family member and as a sociologist, I first describe how the doctors, whether intentionally or not, arrogated decision-making authority, and compare the actions of Brian's doctors to those observed in other studies of intensive care units. I then describe the impact of this on the family, explore why the doctors arrogated decision-making, and discuss what this suggests about the continuing power and clinical autonomy of US doctors. (p. 211)

This paper is essentially a case study – an in-depth investigation into some issues surrounding a particular death. Unlike most research studies in psychology, the methods of this research are clear but not separated from the account. The primary focus of the paper is ostensibly on the ethics of decision making about the right to die and the prolongation of end-of-life care, but in fact its main work is to document how such decisions are complex, social and negotiated. In reading this paper, we are present at a particular death. We learn about the competing wishes of different family members involved in the death, and we see how the decision making is contested by a variety of parties to the death. We see how the medical decision making processes privileged some family members over others. The account of the process is very moving, and also very informative. Weitz invokes her account through a critical engagement with relevant literature, informed by her position as an academic who is both knowledgeable about medical practice and who has access to resources for making sense of the events at hand. She engages with most, but not all, of the participants, and relates the processes to the situation in which the actors are enmeshed.

Reflection

This paper is remarkable because of the researcher's position and for the way in which this is made explicit in the account. Weitz cannot avoid discussing her involvement in the process of this death from the perspective of an involved family member, but she also comments on her position as the researcher and author of this text. In doing so, the paper offers a reflexive commentary on the research and opens the interpretation of the researcher to scrutiny. Many questions arise from this. Is it possible for a family member to also be a researcher in this situation, and what are the implications for the interpretations offered? Are the multiple positions that Weitz occupies in this research advantageous or disadvantageous? Although we may concede that the notion of a detached researcher is inappropriate in interpretative research practice, is some level of detachment necessary for ensuring sound research practice? What are the ethical implications of acting as an analyst of a family member's death? Perhaps most problematically, this paper raises serious issues around the question of who has the right to give informed consent to allow another to die. Weitz offers a position on many of these issues, but they remain open to debate.

   Once you have read and considered this paper, you may also like to read the two commentaries, one by Ellis and Bochner and the other by Frank, which follow in the same issue of the journal. Each offers some interesting reactions and alternative perspectives on this piece of research.

current cultural values about death, the social value of the person who died, and the needs of the survivors. In the light of these social and contextual influences, McNamara (1998, 2001) suggests that those involved may have to settle for a 'good enough' death, one that makes allowance for the disruption caused by death.

   Although we are focusing here on the person dying, we should not lose sight of the fact that deaths are also constructed by the survivors, in the service of accepting and managing the death that has occurred. We return to these issues later in the chapter.

Fearing death

Although health psychologists have conducted very little research into types of death and the process of dying, fear and anxiety about dying have been a particular focus of psychological research, generating many hundreds of studies. In a review of this research with elderly people, Fortner and Neimeyer

Essentially anxiety surrounding all aspects of death; a multidimensional concept relating to fear and anxiety about one's own and other people's death and dying and concerns about the objects of death, especially corpses; synonymous with fear of death and death fear.

People in the oldest stage of life, usually defined as those aged over 75 years and contrasted with the young-old, people aged over 60 and under 75 years.

(1999) report that fear of death is stronger for those experiencing psychological problems, such as depression or anxiety. Stronger fear of death is also reported for people who report poorer overall physical health, and for those reporting lower levels of life satisfaction and purpose in life. Religiosity has also been linked to **death anxiety**, although it appears to be related to religious belief (e.g. belief in a God, belief in an afterlife) rather than to religious behaviour (e.g. frequency of reading the Bible) (Neimeyer & Van Brunt, 1995). Contrary to expectation perhaps, fear of death is reported to be higher for middle-aged people than for older people, and to decline as people reach their later years (Fortner & Neimeyer, 1999). This result is supported by a later meta-analysis (Fortner *et al.*, 2000) and in research by Cicirelli (2001) with the **old-old**. However, Cicirelli found that, while fear of death declined with age, fear of the dying process continued to increase with age. This suggests that as people of advanced age come closer to death, they may accept death and not fear it, but continue to fear the processes that they may go through to die.

These findings suggest that fear of death can take many different forms, and it has been argued that fear of death, fear of dying and anxiety about death are all different aspects of the same construct (e.g. see Wittkowski, 2001). Others have argued that measures of personal orientation to dying need not focus only on negative aspects, but should also focus on positive aspects, such as acceptance of death (e.g. Gesser *et al.*, 1987–8). Certainly numerous measures of death anxiety and fear of death are available, many having a multidimensional structure and covering a variety of different aspects which are subsumed under this general heading (see Neimeyer, 1997–8; Wittkowski, 2001). An example of a recently developed multidimensional measure is given in table 10.4 and demonstrates the variety of dimensions that may be assessed in research under the heading of death anxiety.

10.3   Worrying about death

A *New Scientist* poll in 2002 found that almost 70 per cent of people in Britain were very concerned about dying, with up to one in five people worrying so much that they thought about death more than ten times a day. While 33 per cent of people said they would like to live past 100, only 10 per cent thought they would live that long, and 4 per cent thought that they would not reach 50 years old.

As we have pointed out previously in this book, measures of this type are researcher driven and assume that such experience can be standardised and accessed by questionnaire. Some researchers have taken different approaches to assessing death anxiety, including the use of open-ended and free form questions, open-ended rating and sorting techniques, and the use of death personifications. The last of these aims to locate a person's view of death in human form. Kastenbaum and Herman (1997) reported that death in the 1970s could be viewed as a macabre figure (disfigured and decaying), a gentle comforter (powerful yet kindly), a seductive deceiver (attractive and sophisticated, promising a good time but leading people to their doom) or as an automaton (impersonal,

Table 10.4 The multidimensional orientation towards dying and death inventory

Subscale	Example item
Fear of one's own dying	I feel fear at the very idea of dying slowly and in agony some day
Fear of one's own death	The idea that I will never be able to think and experience anything after my death disturbs me
Fear of another person's dying	I am afraid of having to support another person in his/her last hours
Fear of another person's death	The possibility of losing another person forever through death disturbs me
Fear of corpses	When I think of how pale a corpse is, I feel panic
Acceptance of one's own dying and death	The fact that I will die someday is something absolutely natural for me
Acceptance of another person's death	Ultimately, I am at peace with the fact that even people who are close to me have to die
Rejection of one's own death	Inwardly, I rebel against the fact that my life on earth is limited

Wittkowski (2001).

unfeeling and robotic). However, by the 1990s the automaton figure was not apparent and, although death continued to be viewed predominantly as a male figure, there was a shift towards more frequent representation as female. There were also gender differences, with females reporting more gentle comforter personifications and males reporting death as a cold and remote person (Kastenbaum & Herman, 1997).

However, this research is also based on forced choice and does not avoid the criticisms of questionnaire-based research noted above. Alternative approaches using qualitative methods to research in the field of **thanatology** have been promoted recently by Owens and Payne (1999) and Carverhill (2002). These have been used to address questions about the experience of death anxiety in more detail and from the perspective of the person approaching death. For example, Johnson and Barer (1997) conducted a longitudinal study over six years with people who were aged 85 years or more at the start of their research, using predominantly unstructured interviews for data collection. They found that these very elderly people had minimal fear of death, regarding it more as something to be anticipated, accepted and planned for. In this way, death had essentially become part of living and could be approached with equanimity. However, as mentioned earlier, these people were apprehensive about the process of dying, and feared becoming a burden, experiencing a long period of illness and dying alone. Some were bored with living and wished for an assisted death (see below).

> The study of death and dying.

Adjusting to dying

Another major focus in thanatology research has been on the ways in which people adjust to and accept their own impending death. Kubler-Ross (1969) proposed that dying people go through a sequence of emotional responses, involving denial, anger, bargaining, depression and acceptance. This research was influential in directing attention to the dying person, who at that time was often isolated, ignored and regarded as socially dead. Although Kubler-Ross premised her research on hearing the voice of the dying person, the stages she proposed were widely adopted and quickly reified in writing on dying and bereavement. However, her work has also been criticised, largely for the staged process invoked (e.g. Corr, 1993). As we have seen, the process of dying is highly variable, and rather than reactions being sequenced in stages, terminally ill people are found to fluctuate considerably in their reactions to impending death. This is even more relevant if cultural and religious background and beliefs are taken into account (e.g. see Firth, 1993).

As with chronic illness (see ch. 9), people who learn that they are suffering from a terminal illness experience disruption of their expected lifecourse (Coward, 2000). This can lead them to initiate the negotiation of a new identity and to attempt to find or create meaning in the experience (e.g. Neimeyer, 1997). Bolmsjo (2000) has documented how existential concerns – concerns about the nature and meaning of existence – are particularly important for people approaching death. Resolving these can provide an acceptance of dying, as illustrated by the following comment:

> I'm learning and it's just nourishing . . . It's wonderful. I'm learning to die. It seems that, under certain circumstances, there's room for growth, which I never expected. You know, I used to think dying was going downhill and into the bottom of a cone. It's not that at all. I feel a new dimension in me, which I will tell you, serves me. I'm very curious to know for myself how I'll respond to a worsening condition. If tomorrow the metastases do something, I think I would take it with equanimity . . . This voyage is just expanding onto horizons that I've not quite made out. It's all very affirmative, very freeing. I'm almost enjoying studying it. Who would think that a dying person is capable of making it worthwhile for others to nurture him? What is a dying person capable of? There is something worthwhile in this. It means that not so much will have been lost. It will have made life a success. Not only my life, but it confirms that human life can be very good, even in very dire circumstances. (Robert, 82-year-old terminal cancer patient, cited in Yedidia & MacGregor, 2001, p. 815).

A process of looking back over and reviewing what has been gained and learned from life as death approaches; a therapeutic technique for finding meaning and purpose in life.

As Yedidia and MacGregor (2001) document, there can be considerable variation around the meaning attributed to life, living and dying by terminally ill people; meaning can be found in different ways, including finding a new balance in life and triumphing over adversity (Yedidia & MacGregor, 2001). Although not all people resolve such concerns successfully at the end of life, the value of reminiscence and **life review** has been widely held to be important at the end of life, a process recognised by hospice and palliative care services that provide opportunities for people approaching death to prepare personal biographies (e.g. Lichter *et al.*, 1993).

Producing a personal biography not only allows the person facing death to engage in life review and reformulate an identity as a dying person, but it also remains after death for survivors to read and keep. This process of negotiating an identity beyond death is important for people facing death. Exley (1999) documents how terminally ill people negotiate a revised living identity, but importantly also work at establishing an after-death identity as well. Her cancer patients, all under 65 years of age and expecting death within six months, reported engaging in a range of activities to construct an after-death identity, including planning funerals and memorials, writing wills and testaments, distributing possessions, making tapes, videos and photographs, writing letters and generally working to manage their 'social life after death' (Exley, 1999). As Howarth (2000) notes, recent technology such as videos allow the dead to 'reconstitute themselves, bringing us animated images, representations which can convey their thoughts and messages transported to a future time: a time which they will not experience' (p. 134).

After-death identity negotiation is more likely to be achieved successfully by people dying from illnesses such as cancer and AIDS than for people who die suddenly or who are institutionalised in old age. The person with a chronic terminal illness has more opportunity to reach awareness and acceptance of death, to accomplish a 'heroic death' (Seale, 1995), and therefore to be regarded as dying with dignity. In contrast, the institutionalised are more likely to be regarded as socially dead and to experience a 'dirty death' (Lawton, 2000). However, for the chronically ill elderly who are not institutionalised, similar processes around planning for the future have been reported. For example, Carrese *et al.* (2002) found that these people view the future in three different but interrelated ways: as an uncertain immediate future in relation to serious chronic illness, which they are largely unwilling to contemplate directly; as a time when death is near, for which they engage in planning and discussion; and as a time after death, for which they are likely to have made arrangements. Two of these three views of the future thus contribute to an after-death identity. In the case of sudden death, after-death identity work is not possible for the dead person and must be left up to the survivors. Once again, we find that death and dying are complex and raise issues that are not amenable to ready generalisations.

Caring for and about the dying

In discussing the ways we die and how we live with dying we have concentrated on the person facing death. However, death rarely or never occurs in isolation, but always involves and affects other people: spouses, children, siblings, friends, acquaintances, neighbours and others. Contemporary dying almost always involves health professionals as well: nurses, doctors, intensive care specialists and hospice physicians, alongside other caregivers who may relieve spouses, bring meals and provide advice and support. It is important to consider how death and dying affect the carers and survivors as well.

Being bereaved

The loss of a person close to us can be a devastating experience:

> The pain has eased off. It's not as bad as it was. You know, this pain – no one understands it if they haven't been through it. There are no words. It's not pain like you cut your arm. It's a terrible pain – no one knows. You have to feel it yourself to know. It's here [hand on heart]. (65-year-old man who lost his wife thirteen months previously, cited in Nolen-Hoeksma & Larson, 1999, p. 24)

Being bereaved can have substantial effects on the health of the bereaved person. In summarising this research, Stroebe *et al.* (2001, p. 8) conclude:

> Although it is still debateable which subgroups of bereaved individuals are most vulnerable, that the health of bereaved people in general is at risk (compared to their nonbereaved counterparts) has by now been well established. There is no longer any doubt that the costs of bereavement in terms of health can be extreme. Bereaved individuals suffer elevated rates of depression, anxiety and other psychiatric disorders, somatic complaints and infections, and a variety of other physical illnesses. They have higher consultation rates with doctors, use more medication, are hospitalised more often, and have more days of disability. The risk of mortality is associated with many different causes, including, particularly, suicide.

This research has been carried out predominantly on partners of people who have died and has most frequently assessed mortality effects, with recent research suggesting a gendered effect, widowers being more likely to die following bereavement than widows, at all ages and all social class levels (e.g. Mineau *et al.*, 2002).

Many different theoretical models of loss and grieving have been proposed. Kubler-Ross (1969) proposed one such model, outlining stages of grieving, that was developed out of grief theory and applied to dying. Subsequently this model has been widely applied back to grieving, as have a variety of other time-based phase or stage models. Payne *et al.* (1999) propose that these models can be summarised as constructing grieving to occur in four sequential stages, involving numbness, yearning, despair and recovery respectively. An alternative approach (Worden, 1991) considers grieving as a series of overlapping tasks that people suffering loss need to work through and solve – facilitating the widespread therapeutic notion of **grief work** around bereavement. These models, as we saw previously, may all be criticised for an overemphasis on fixed stages, for pathologising grief and for ignoring the complexity and

A cognitive process of facing loss through bereavement, going over events around the death, working towards detachment from the deceased person, and coming to terms with the loss.

variability of grieving. Grief work has also been criticised for assuming that confrontation with loss is essential and that there should be an end point where 'recovery' from grief is reached. As we see below, many people sustain a positive ongoing connection with the deceased person, and current conceptions of 'healthy grieving' involve maintaining bonds with the deceased person (Fisher, 2001).

A more recent and elaborated model of grieving, outlined by Stroebe and Schut (2001), suggests that adaptation to bereavement involves two interrelated orientations:

- a loss orientation, focusing on issues such as breaking ties with the deceased person, relocating that person, and the intrusion of grief into everyday living;
- a restoration orientation, focusing on attending to life changes, doing new things, distraction from and avoidance of grief, and the development of new roles, identities and relationships.

The grieving person is considered to oscillate between these orientations, coping with the stresses and demands of each in an interwoven way. Although this model is more flexible than previous stage models, and it attempts to invoke everyday life experience, it remains very cognitively oriented, with a primary focus on the individualised bereaved person who is coping rationally with loss. As Attig (2001) has argued, it is misleading to consider these processes as primarily cognitive and readily accessible. Rather, they are better thought of as 'deeply embedded and obscured in habitual life and operative automatically in all dimensions of our being, not merely in belief or cognition' (p. 41).

Bradbury (1999) also makes some salient observations on these psychological models of grieving, documenting how they reflect current social representations and are therefore subject to change and renegotiation. She points out that grief occurs in a social context and is therefore 'a social phenomenon, dependent on other people' (p. 181). More importantly, she argues that the loss of a person always involves more than their loss – it also involves a loss of self for the survivors. In recognising this, we can see how the survivors must attempt to renegotiate their own identities after the death that take account of their loss and also incorporate and retain a relationship with the dead person (see below). Because the loss of a loved person involves, in this real sense, the loss of self, then making sense of and finding meaning in the loss is as important for survivors as it is for people dying. As Attig (2001, p. 43) writes:

> We often find and make meaning in the ways that may not have occurred had we not suffered loss. We have no choice about what happened, but we can, and often do, grow positively through the experience. We find new strength of character. We grow in self-understanding and self-esteem. We become more sensitive and responsive to others. We learn how much others mean to us and learn new ways to show appreciation and love. We gain new critical perspectives on our relationships, on reality, and on the human condition.

This demonstrates that loss is not always negative, and many people report positive consequences of loss, such as having more relevant priorities, becoming more self-reliant and more involved with others. However, this does not apply to everyone and a small number of people report being worse off after bereavement (Frantz *et al.*, 2001). This may be more applicable to difficult deaths, involving a death that could not be construed as 'good', a sudden death, or the death of a child (see Wheeler, 2001). It can be even more complicated when the dead person has ambiguous status, as happens with very premature stillborn children who are not officially regarded as 'persons'. The difficulties experienced in this situation, involving the 'death of a nobody', have been documented by Littlewood (1999).

As we saw earlier, the nature, location and process of dying are highly variable, and the constructions that are made of a death can be variable, inconsistent and contested (see research in focus box 10.2). Understanding and constructing the death is as important for the survivors as for the dying person, although we have noted previously how this may serve quite different purposes for the people surrounding the death than for the person dying (Williams, 1990). Also, the reconstruction of death continues beyond the death itself for the survivors, as 'resurrective practices' (Seale, 1998) are invoked.

Life after death

As we have seen, death transforms the survivors. One way in which this operates is to sustain the dead person in life beyond death. Survivors frequently report experiencing the dead person for some time after the death. For example:

> No, I can't accept it. I mean, I know he has gone. But you know? But it's like, when I go out I still expect him to be there when I get back. I just can't . . .
> (Christine, cited in Bradbury, 1999, p. 178)

These reports of experiencing the dead are very common. For example, Davies (1997) reported that one-third of his respondents reported some sense of the presence of the dead. Bennett and Bennett (2000) document how this covers quite diverse events such as hearing a voice, smelling a particular smell, having feelings of being observed, seeing the dead person and holding conversations. Howarth (2000) notes how the dead are kept alive by various strategies. These involve talking about the dead and constructing their biographies, particularly focusing on anniversaries, special achievements and personal characteristics. They also involve memorial rituals, such as visiting the grave. The marking of graves with headstones and other, more immediately visible mementos, such as photographs and display of the dead person's prized possessions, also work to sustain life after death.

However, as we saw in Exley's (1999) research earlier, the invocation of the dead person is not solely the province of survivors as, in many instances, dying people will have left 'cues' to how they should be remembered. The use of such memorabilia serves to relocate and reintegrate the dead person into the lives of survivors (Walter, 1996). As Rosenblatt (2001) notes, continuing relationships with the dead are very common across cultures, although their meaning and social expression may take many different forms. For example, Vitebsky (1993) reports how the tribal Sora in eastern India do not regard the dead person as gone forever, but regard death as a separate part of existence and a phase in the totality of a person's conscious existence across time. All aspects of daily life are interpreted through ongoing relationships with the living and the dead, and dialogue with dead people continues in this culture. As noted above, the loss of a loved person involves, in some real sense, the loss of self (Bradbury, 1999). Memorials, remembering and the resurrection of the dead serve important survival requirements for those left behind. As Seale (1998) observes, 'resurrective practices' restore security for the living about their place in the world in spite of death occurring around them. They also serve to warrant the living person's moral status as a caring individual who is maintaining a social bond with the loved one.

Death and the health professional

Earlier, we considered how dying, in contemporary Western society at least, has become increasingly medicalised, and noted how the location and timing of death are frequently subject to medical surveillance and control. Understandings of medicine as the proper source for the treatment and cure of illness raise dilemmas for health professionals around dying. Is the person to be treated and cured, and when can he or she be considered to be dying and assisted in the process? More importantly, what does assistance mean in this context? At some stage in the process of dying, the person must undergo an important transition in the eyes of the medical carers – from a patient, consequently deserving and requiring treatment to sustain life, to a person who is dying, who may require palliation, and allowed (or helped) to die. Knowing how and when to make this transition can pose a dilemma for medical staff, as can conveying it to the dying person and family members (see Norton & Bowers, 2001).

Because dying today is medically situated, most dying people are involved in some way with health professionals: general practitioners, palliative care specialists, intensive care nurses, palliative nurses and others are all involved in care for the dying. These professionals are affected by dying and must learn to manage this in their practice. As MacLeod (2001) notes, medical training may not prepare them well for the experience as it typically defines care as the professional behaviour of attending to the patient's medical needs. However, MacLeod suggests that care requires commitment on a more holistic level, or as he puts it 'To care is to be receptive and responsible for others. This is care motivated by true empathy: a concern for the patient's wellbeing that comes from a sensitive identification with the patient's situation' (p. 1719). From interviews with doctors he identified 'turning points' when they first experienced caring for a dying person. For example, one doctor stated:

> Dr R: 'I realise now that one of the early influences for me was a man called Roy. I was a GP and visited him daily for weeks. I could still describe the room, the medications, the dog, the care, even his clothes! He and his wife had been married for decades but they also worked with each other daily. He taught me about symptoms and he taught me the importance of making accurate assessments, because I got it wrong sometimes. They taught me the importance of broadening the medical model to include an acknowledgment that in many ways I was powerless and vulnerable myself. Towards the end of his life there were no truly "medical" things to do . . . I was their companion; there was no curative or "medical" role in the accepted sense. Despite knowing that he was dying, when it came, I was devastated.'   (MacLeod, 2001, p. 1723)

Similarly, Saunderson and Ridsdale (1999) found that general practitioners felt under-prepared for dealing with bereavement in their practice and developed strategies from their personal experience for managing the death of patients. They also reported feelings of loss and grieving on the death of patients they knew well.

In contrast, nurses, and especially intensive care and palliative care nurses, are more heavily involved in the process of care for dying patients, and this can mean that they may be more affected by death and dying. Marquis (1993) documents the different effects that the setting and the type of death can have for nurses. Caring for the dying child is particularly problematic, and Kaplan (2001) reports on the struggle to balance emotional tensions with competent caring that is experienced by nurses working with dying children. Palliative care nurses are reminded daily of the fragility of life (McNamara, 2001), and nurses working in palliative care settings report the sadness of clients as a major source of stress (Newton & Waters, 2001). Seymour (2001) analyses the complexity of caring that faces the intensive care nurse, and demonstrates how 'good nursing' in this setting is 'entwined with notions of respect for personhood, bodily care and emotional investment' (p. 126). She elaborates how the ideological premises of 'caring' and 'knowing the person', fundamental to nursing practice, are challenged and excluded by medical and technological imperatives around dying that are largely beyond the nurse's control. Such tensions must be worked through and integrated into these nurses' daily practice.

Further tensions, among health professionals themselves and also between health professionals, dying patients and family members, arise around requests to die, decisions to withhold treatment, and decisions to not resuscitate patients. Given that the understandings of death may differ considerably between these groups (e.g. Flacker *et al.*, 2001), this may not be surprising, and reflects the contradictions that exist around end-of-life medical decision making. For example, do-not-resuscitate (DNR) decisions are made ideally in joint consultation between the dying patient, family members and the involved health professionals. However, critical care nurses report that, in practice, the status of a DNR decision frequently remains ambiguous for many patients, and that DNR decisions are most often made by physicians rather than the wider group (Thibault-Prevost *et al.*, 2000). Also, the use of technology in medicine has led to a blurring of the boundaries between life and death. Technological intervention, introduced as a necessary part of treatment for the patient, may be extremely difficult to withdraw from the dying person. Withdrawal of treatment can create a tension between the need to avoid prolonging life 'artificially' and the suggestion of promoting death. As Seymour (2001) notes, withdrawing treatment can elide with active euthanasia, and must be managed with great care by physicians, as they attempt to align 'technical' dying with 'bodily' dying in order to ensure that death occurs at the 'right' time.

Requests for assisted death also pose very difficult ethical and moral issues for medical staff, particularly when they judge suffering to be involved (Oberle & Hughes, 2001). Requested death can allow social and biological death to coincide (see Seale, 1998) and may be requested for that reason by people who feel they have become a burden or face a difficult death. Requests are more likely to come from people who are more educated, have less religious affiliation and are more politically liberal (Caddell & Newton, 1995), the very people who are most likely to resist and challenge medical control over dying. Requests to die are as problematic for patients and family members as they are for health professionals, and this remains a highly debated arena, as can be seen in sidebar 10.4.

The increasing medicalisation of death and use of technology around death in contemporary Western societies means that health professionals are faced with substantial ambiguities and conflicts around end-of-life care. These work to complicate their roles as carers of (and for) the dying. As with every other facet of dying we have discussed, the involvement of health professionals in death is subject to change and contestation, and the construction of related issues, such as medical technology, are always open to debate.

Technology as care?

The use of medical technology is often considered to be inappropriate at the time of dying and to contribute to the indignity of death (Timmermans, 1998). Constructions of a 'good' death are generally resistant to the use of medical technology, as this can imply overt medical control and potential denial of the dying person's wishes about the process of dying. Use of technology can also raise problematic issues for the relatives and next of kin. As we saw earlier, there can be an array of competing demands that are complicated by technological intervention. The medical professionals see themselves as helping to prolong or sustain life, avoid pain, palliate symptoms and possibly hold out hope for recovery in the future. The dying person may or may not wish for any of these things to happen, but his or her ability to consent or to withhold consent may

10.4   Contested views on end-of-life care: two letters to the Editor of the British Medical Journal

Why physician-assisted suicide should not be legalised

I have several severe disabling conditions that make my life difficult and, at times, extremely painful. My spine is collapsing, causing extreme pain that is not always controlled, even with morphine. When my pain is at its worst I cannot move or speak. The pain can go on for hours, and at times I am afraid that it will never stop. In addition, I am a full-time wheelchair user because I have spina bifida, and I have emphysema and osteoporosis.

Some years ago, I did want to die. It was a 'settled wish' lasting many years, and had euthanasia or physician-assisted suicide been legal then, I would have requested it. Under the criteria of the Dutch law, often cited as a model to be followed, I would qualify for this legal killing. I am alive now only because my friends refused to go along with my sincere belief that my life had no value. Over time, they enabled me to re-establish a sense of my own inherent dignity and worth.

Alison Davis *patient*

Help me end my life if it becomes intolerable

I am a 70-year-old woman who nursed both a husband and a mother who ended their days in indignity and ill health. I would like to have the reassurance of knowing that, if I reached the state where my life was no longer of value to me, there would be a caring and kindly doctor who would not put his career and reputation on the line to help me leave this world with dignity.

When my mother started developing Alzheimer's and understanding what was happening, she begged me 'to get some tablets so I do not live to be a stupid old woman'. She survived for five years – an incontinent, shambling wreck of the strong and intelligent person she had been. My husband, following a physically disabling stroke at the age of 53, repeatedly stated that should he become more disabled, he would not wish to live. Twelve years later having, for seven years, been unable to communicate or understand language, he died in a psychiatric unit

be considered to be compromised. The relatives may be required to take over this consent, either willingly or against their best judgement. They may be empowered in this by having knowledge of the dying person's wishes, or by advice from medical professionals, or they may be disempowered by lacking these, or by seeking to countermand the doctor's opinions as to what should happen for the best. Support for using life-sustaining technology can differ by cultural background and, not surprisingly, may be complicated further when the family and the health professionals have different cultural understandings (see Blackhall *et al.*, 1999). There are also gender differences in preference for life-sustaining treatments, with men preferring to receive it more than women (Bookwala *et al.*, 2001).

However, there is another construction of technological intervention around the time of death. As McNamara (2001) notes, the use of technology can offer a kind of clinical assurance that the death, albeit 'chaotically social and personal' (p. 73), is being managed well. In the case of sudden death Timmermans (1998) has shown that the use of resuscitation technology can provide a positive benefit for family and friends. He argues that the opposition to technology stems from 'naïve romanticised notions of dignified dying in technologically impoverished eras and cultures' (p. 162). Rather, he suggests the use of resuscitation turns sudden death from a meaningless event into 'a period of liminality which allows the relatives and friends to prepare for the transition to death if the reviving attempt fails to restore life' (p. 162). Similarly, Seymour (1999) found that it was the meaning of technology rather than its use that determined the representation of death in an intensive care setting. If the technology was seen as

> exhibiting such bizarre behaviour that I could no longer care for him at home.
>
> Others may decide that they wish their lives to be sustained in these sorts of circumstances. I know I would rather die with some dignity remaining at a time of my choosing.
>
> Diane Mundy *retired*
>
> (Rapid responses from BMJ.com, *British Medical Journal USA*, 2, 20)

amenable to human manipulation, if it helped to deliver expected outcomes, or if its use was comprehensible and fitted within the context of dying, then the death could be constructed as 'natural'. In this sense, the use of technology can promote a more dignified death. In an interesting recent variant on the use of technology at death, the rise of right-to-die activism has seen the development and promotion of several technological devices for assisting terminally ill people to die, providing 'assisted suicide' (see Ogden, 2001). These devices leave negligible evidence of their use, thereby avoiding post-mortem difficulties, and offering a challenge to medical control of end-of-life decision-making. However, preferences about the use of end-of-life technology and who should be involved in assisting death are hotly contested (see sidebar 10.4).

Research such as this reveals clearly how generalised reactions to factors such as technology at death are too simple. Rather than being simply undesirable, technology can be important for the transition from life to death, but once again, this will depend on the specific circumstances of the dying and how it is constructed and negotiated. However, medical technology can symbolise care for the dying, although this cannot be pressed too far, and we should note McNamara's (2001) comment that 'technology offers no real answers to the pain of leaving others behind' (p. 73).

Conclusions

The field of death and dying is extensive and we have only been able to touch on some limited aspects of it in this chapter. The main conclusion that can be drawn here is that death (the event) and dying (the process) are both complex social phenomena. Both are multiply constructed and open to competing interpretations. Any particular death usually involves several different parties – besides the dying person there are likely to be family members, friends, relatives, colleagues and health care professionals. Each of these parties comes to the event with agendas and understandings that may be in potential conflict. Any single death, and the process of dying that accompanies it, requires a reworking of understandings, negotiation and possibly conciliation. As with all the other topics in this book, we find that death and dying are essentially social activities and, as such, are not fully amenable to satisfactory investigation by the methods of mainstream psychology. Curiously, health psychology has had very little to say about this field, yet, as we have seen throughout this chapter, it is replete with issues that could be productively investigated by critical health psychologists. Perhaps we will see more of this in the future.

RECOMMENDED READING

Bradbury, M. (1999). *Representations of death: a social psychological perspective.* London: Routledge. This book takes a social representations approach to death and dying, and provides a detailed account of an ethnographic study carried out in the UK. It discusses and develops many of the issues covered in this chapter in more detail. It also includes material on the rituals of death and burial.

Lawton, J. (2000). *The dying process: patients' experiences of palliative care.* London: Routledge. This book is focused on the dying process for cancer patients in palliative care. It takes up and elaborates a number of the issues discussed in the chapter, particularly in relation to how we die.

McNamara, B. (2001). *Fragile lives: death, dying and care.* Buckingham, UK: Open University Press. This book provides an informed account of death and dying based in the stories and accounts of people dying and those providing care for them. It overlaps with many of the issues in this chapter, but provides a more elaborated account of this material.

Seale, C. (1998). *Constructing death: the sociology of dying and bereavement.* Cambridge: Cambridge University Press. This text provides a thorough coverage of the field of dying and bereavement, documenting the social nature of death and dying and giving a very good account of the complexity and contestation that surrounds death and dying as a social process.

Seymour, J. E. (2001). *Critical moments: death and dying in intensive care.* Buckingham, UK: Open University Press. This book reports an ethnographic study that focuses on the processes surrounding dying in intensive care units. It provides a very good overview of these processes, and is particularly useful for the detailed treatment of the ways in which health professionals are involved in the negotiation of care for dying people in this setting.

Stroebe, M. S., Hannson, R. O., Stroebe, W. & Schut, H. (eds.) (2001). *Handbook of bereavement research: consequences, coping and care.* Washington, DC: American Psychological Association. This text gives an up-to-date overview and detailed coverage of mainstream psychological research on bereavement and caring in the context of death.

11 Relocating the field: critical health psychology

We live in a world in which poverty and inequalities in wealth and access to resources are the major causes of ill-health. (Campbell & Murray, 2004, p. 194)

[T]he most powerful corporations are more powerful than many elected governments, able to influence legislation, especially in relation to health, education and welfare and to ensure massive public expenditures in support of the medical model, including pharmacological consumption. (Albee & Fryer, 2003, p. 74)

[H]ealth psychologists are seriously reflecting on their discipline and attempting to articulate theories and methods so that they can participate in the broader movement for social justice and health. (Murray & Campbell, 2003, p. 235)

Learning objectives

The aim of this chapter is to reflect on health psychology as a field, and to consider the approach taken to health psychology in this text. We consider the critical perspective taken, and how this influences conceptualisations of, and research on, health and illness. By the end of this chapter you should be able to:

- show an understanding of the traditional approaches to health research and their limitations;
- discuss social influences on health and illness;
- reflect on alternative possibilities for research into health and illness;
- outline challenges and opportunities for improving health from a global international perspective;
- explain what is meant by a 'critical' perspective on health and illness research;
- compare and contrast 'critical health psychology' with 'mainstream health psychology';
- describe the requirements for enabling health psychology to enhance its contributions to the health and well-being of individuals, communities and societies.

As we approach the close of this text we need to consider what we have attempted and what we have accomplished. What do we understand health and illness to be today? How are they changing? How do they vary and affect people in different locations? How should we approach the study of health and illness today? To what extent are the approaches taken by health psychology useful and to what extent are they limited and constrained? How could health psychology do better? In what ways should we work as health psychologists if we are to be more effective in improving the human condition? Where should we look for inspiration? Where should our partnerships lie – with medicine, with health sciences, with other social sciences, with people in the community, or perhaps with all of these in different ways for different purposes? What does a critical health psychology mean and how can it be achieved?

These are the kinds of questions and issues that we examine in this chapter. Initially, we reflect on the content of the book and the degree to which we have successfully contextualised the issues covered. We follow this with a more general consideration of health in a global context, and how health psychology could be more engaged in that way. We then consider how a critical health psychology can be constituted, and conclude the chapter with a discussion of ways to go forward, a consideration of opportunities and possibilities for the ongoing development of a critical health psychology.

Locating individuals within their lived social worlds

A great deal of health psychology research and practice, as we have continually commented throughout this book, separates people from their experience and the conditions in which they live; it fails to take their experiential and social worlds sufficiently into account. Mainstream health psychology tends to function quite comfortably under a biomedical model, and although it claims to take a biopsychosocial approach, this is more often rhetoric than reality, as we saw in ch. 1. One of the contingent effects of this is a ready acceptance of medical **ideology**, and an uncritical adoption of medical concepts and medicalised views of health and illness. This involves regarding both diseases and bodies as objects: diseases as discrete, identifiable 'things' that are amenable to diagnosis and treatment and can be separated from the person experiencing them; the body as an object to be examined and treated, separate from the person who inhabits it (Freund *et al.*, 2003). A significant consequence of this is an emphasis on individualistic, rather than on social, cultural and political meanings of, and responses to, health and illness. Although psychology has an agreed disciplinary focus on the individual, this should not lead to the wider social meanings and the settings within which individuals function being excluded from view or examination.

> A system of ideas, beliefs and values that relates to the way that society should be organised, and that explains and legitimises the interests and actions of particular groups within societies.

Throughout this text, one of our objectives has been to present the theoretical framings and empirical findings from mainstream health psychology alongside some alternative, and more critical, understandings and ways of working. This has sometimes been difficult given the tensions that exist between these orientations, especially with regard to the epistemological assumptions under-lying the different approaches (see ch. 1 and later this chapter). Throughout the book we have also tried to present alternatives – different ways of looking at and understanding health phenomena. To achieve this we have frequently drawn on research and theory from other social science disciplines, in par-ticular from sociology and anthropology. We have also tried, as far as space has allowed, to consider health research findings within different contexts. To this end we have aimed to reflect on research findings and discuss their impli-cations for groups who are often marginalised or overlooked in much health psychology research – groups such as women, children, the aged, the disabled and ethnic minorities. Reflecting back on this, how have we fared?

Gender issues have figured prominently throughout the preceding chapters, and the gendered nature of issues relating to health and illness has been a consistent theme. We have considered differences between men and women in relation to various health issues, such as being embodied, experiencing illness, seeking care and receiving treatment, throughout the text. We have commented on a range of factors, including medicalisation, caregiving and poverty, that have a greater impact on women than men. The gendering of health and illness is pervasive, and readily documented by a considerable body of research. For example, Shaw et al. (2004) demonstrate that women received fewer needed surgical procedures for coronary heart disease than men in England in the 1990s. They calculated that, after allowing for gender differences in need, it would require more than 12,000 extra coronary artery bypass graft procedures and more than 5,000 extra coronary angioplasty procedures for women to achieve equity with men. They note that this amounts to 19 per cent and 10 per cent increases in the total volume of each procedure respectively. As they comment, 'heart problems, and heart treatment, are perceived in a gendered way, by both the lay and medical worlds' (p. 2505).

The relation of age to health and illness has been addressed in several places throughout the text. Changes in health understandings, health behaviours and care-seeking across the lifespan were considered, as well as issues such as the increasing burden of illness and the changing interpretation of symptoms in older age. It should be noted that older people, like women, can also be marginalised in relation to treatment and care. The research by Shaw et al. (2004), discussed above, also documents how age discrimination occurs for coronary revascularisation procedures. In this context, they calculated that, to gain equity for people up to 75 years old, more than 26,000 additional proce-dures would be required for men and more than 24,000 for women. Turning to the other end of the lifespan, the coverage of issues relating to children throughout the text has not been extensive, reflecting the limited attention given to children in current health psychology research. There are notable exceptions, such as Eiser's work on quality of life for children with cancer (Eiser, 2004), but children's health is an area where health psychologists could be engaged much more substantially.

Ethnicity and cultural concerns have been an important focus of attention throughout the text. Ethnic and cultural differences have been examined in relation to a range of health concerns, including health understandings and behaviour, rates of illness, interpretation and somatisation of symptoms and doctor–patient communication. The influences of ethnic and cultural factors in health are as pervasive as gender issues, but they are taken up less frequently as a topic of research by health psychologists. Hence, much of the research in this area cited in the text has been drawn from disciplines other than health psychology, and led us to comment on the need for more health psychology engagement in this field. Also, this research largely contrasts different ethnic groups sampled from within Western industrialised countries, and very little health psychology research takes up a cross-cultural perspective on health issues.

In regard to other minority group issues, the coverage has been less extensive. The effects of disability have been considered only to a limited extent. Once again, this reflects the restricted research attention that health psychologists have given to disability and health concerns. Although we have drawn on some research with gay men and women, we have also not given any major consideration to sexual orientation and its relation to health. Although there is a reasonable body of research in this area, particularly in relation to illness experience, we can only plead a lack of space that precluded coverage of some issues, and restricted coverage of many others. Among these we could note issues around the consumerisation and technologisation of health – issues that are usually considered beyond the ambit of health psychology but are important contextual influences on contemporary health and illness.

As we note throughout the text, many of these issues deserve more consideration by health psychologists. The relative lack of attention to these issues in health psychology research does not mean that we should continue to marginalise them. Our failure to include people from these segments of our communities marks the degree to which our research findings and practical applications are limited and constrained. Mainstream health psychology tends to avoid this concern, adopting the standard, taken-for-granted view of science that knowledge is absolute and, once known, can be generalised readily. We hope we have demonstrated in numerous places throughout the text how findings established for adult white men with a specific illness do not hold in the same way for adult women, young people, children, older people, ethnically different people, or more generally, for people from other social contexts. Recognising this provides a start to acknowledging the contextual and provisional nature of the findings from our research and the applications that they may be put to. There does appear to be recognition within mainstream health psychology that findings do not generalise readily across illnesses, but somewhat less recognition of the fact that they do not generalise as readily across people in different settings. An obvious example of this is provided by Dutta-Bergman (2004), who explored the meanings of health and illness among the Santali people of rural Bengal. For these people, food was a central issue for health, as hunger is one of the greatest causes of illness. Further, poverty and related structural barriers (lack of work, education and health care) were also central to their health meanings. Such findings would not emerge from research into health understandings conducted with well-off participants within an industrialised country. Although this seems self-evident when stated directly, it is the converse that needs emphasis here – that our research findings from the industrialised world are limited in their focus and potential applications.

One further aim for the text was to contextualise the research discussed into an international perspective as far as possible, by providing examples and commenting on different understandings from around the world. This aim was also constrained somewhat by the scope of coverage possible within the text. To this end we have deliberately drawn on findings from a variety of countries and different cultures throughout the chapters. Again, this has not been as extensive as we would have liked, but it serves the same purpose – to locate our research and, more importantly, to show up the limits to the scope and extent of our research quite clearly. In the following section, we take up this issue directly and discuss the global context of health research.

Health in a global context

Health can be considered, not just within the local context, but much more broadly within an international, global context. However, generally speaking, health psychology has tended to ignore this perspective. Throughout the text we have concentrated substantially on research and findings obtained from developed industrialised countries because this is predominantly where health psychologists have focused their attention and undertaken their work. Their efforts to understand health and illness have also largely concentrated on chronic diseases in those countries where health psychology practices are most established – North America, Europe and Australasia. However, there are exceptions – see, for example, the work of Campbell on AIDS prevention in South Africa (Campbell, 2003) or Cornish's research with sex workers in Calcutta (Cornish, 2004).

Although there have been substantial improvements in health around the world, the World Health Organisation's policy goal of health for all is far from realised. Major differences can be found throughout the world in health services (see table 8.1), treatment options (see table 8.4) and mortality (see table 10.1). Nevertheless, we can recognise that many aspects of health are improving on average around the world. For example, worldwide life expectancy at birth has increased by seven years over the last thirty years, from 56 to 63 (UNICEF, 2005). The under-5 mortality rate per 1,000 live births for children has dropped from 198 in 1960 to 80 in 2003, a reduction of 1.3 per cent per year over the period (UNICEF, 2005). However, consideration of the average state of affairs can mask major discrepancies in health that are significant and persistent. For instance, worldwide life expectancy at birth is 63 years, but it is only 46 years across sub-Saharan Africa and is 78 years in industrialised countries (UNICEF, 2005). Further illustrations of health inequalities are given in table 11.1, which lists a wide range of inequalities found around the world. Although many of these provide comparisons between countries, others document significant inequalities within countries. Essentially, these issues of inequality in health, covering mortality, morbidity, access to care, and the provision of care, reflect disparities between people in their access to resources, and are linked strongly to their SES.

As Sen and Bonita (2000) note, 'all major causes of death are strongly and increasingly inversely associated with social class, irrespective of the degree of wealth of the country' (p. 579). This is the socioeconomic health differential which is consistently found in countries where relevant data are collected (Kawachi & Kennedy, 2002). Woolf et al. (2004) take a different look at this issue, and document an interesting within-country differential. They note how, in the USA, there is substantial emphasis on developing better medical technologies – better drugs, medical devices and procedures. Providing equity in health care commands much less attention. Woolf et al. estimated and contrasted the numbers of deaths that could be averted by improving the technology of health care with those that could be averted by enhancing equity in health care. Their findings suggest that in the USA between 1991 and 2000 medical advances averted more than 176,000 deaths. However, equalising the mortality rates of whites and African Americans would have averted more than 886,000 deaths. As they note, if attention was focused on equity in health care 'five deaths could have been averted for every life saved by medical advances' (p. 2079). They suggest that this effect may be increased if other ethnic groups, such as Native Americans, were included. They also noted that socioeconomic conditions are a more relevant cause of health disparity and reflect on 'whether more lives are saved by medical advances or by resolving social inequities in education and income' (p. 2080).

As we can see in table 11.1, poverty and deprivation are directly associated with health outcomes. To illustrate this we can consider the global situation for child mortality. The overall rates of child mortality (for children under 5) have fallen noticeably in recent years, reducing from 93 per 1,000 live births in 1990 to 80 per 1,000 live births in 2003 (UNICEF, 2005). However, there are still more than 10 million children dying each year (Black et al., 2003), or stated more pointedly, each day 29,158 children around the world die before they reach their fifth birthday (UNICEF, 2005). Almost all of these deaths (around 90 per cent) occur in low-income countries or in poor areas of middle-income countries (Jones et al., 2003), and are almost all from preventable causes – diarrhoea, pneumonia, measles, malaria, HIV/AIDS, the underlying cause of undernutrition, and some causes leading to neo-natal deaths (Black

Table 11.1 Health inequalities around the world

- About 90 per cent of the global burden of disease is carried by the developing world, which has access to only 10 per cent of the world's resources for health (Lee, 2003).
- Of the 56 million deaths throughout the world each year, 80 per cent occur in the poorer regions of the world (Lee, 2003).
- Although life expectancy has increased worldwide (from 56 to 63 years) over the last thirty years, life expectancy has actually declined in eighteen countries in Africa since 1970 (UNICEF, 2005).
- While communicable diseases account for 34.2 per cent of all deaths in the world, the world's poorest people (lowest 20 per cent) experience much higher mortality than the richest people (highest 20 per cent) from such diseases (58.6 per cent versus 7.7 per cent) (Heuveline *et al.*, 2002).
- One-tenth of deaths in the developing world (about 1.6 million) are caused by conditions such as measles, diphtheria, and tetanus, which are routinely vaccinated for in the developed world (Jha & Mills, 2002).
- If all countries had the rate of child mortality for children under 5 years achieved by Japan (the lowest in the world), then only 1 million children under 5 would die each year instead of the 11 million currently dying (Sen & Bonita, 2000).
- Of the 38 million blind people in the world, about 6 million are thought to be blind from trachoma, the world's leading preventable cause of blindness. This was a common disease in Europe and North America in the early twentieth century, but disappeared from these regions as economic conditions, water quality and sanitation improved (Cook, 2002).
- About 10 per cent of the world's population lives in Africa, but they suffer more than 90 per cent of the world's malarial infections. Between 500,000 and 2 million people die of malaria each year, and it is estimated that around 1 million children under 5 each year die from malaria alone or malaria in combination with other diseases (Cook, 2002).
- While the Western world experiences an 'obesity epidemic', it is estimated that 30 per cent to 50 per cent of adults in South Asia and 15 per cent to 30 per cent of adults in Africa are underweight. This undernourishment affects women and children more than men, and increases susceptibility to illness, including chronic illness in later life (Underwood, 2002).
- Women in Africa and South Asia are up to 200 times more likely than women in the USA to die from causes related to pregnancy (Germain, 2002).
- The probability at birth of *not* surviving to age 40 is about 1.8 per cent in Hong Kong and 1.9 per cent in Singapore, but is 70.1 per cent in Zambia and 74.8 per cent in Zimbabwe (United Nations Development Programme, 2004).
- In India the prevalence of tuberculosis and childhood mortality is three times higher amongst the lowest income groups than among the highest (Jha & Mills, 2002).
- In Peru rates of underweight and stunting among the poorest 20 per cent of people is about five times that of the richest 20 per cent of people (Wagstaff & Watanabe, 2000).
- In the Ukraine, about twice as many women (43 per cent) as men (25 per cent) rate their health as poor (Gilmore *et al.*, 2002).
- In Ecuador, childhood stunting through malnutrition affects 26 per cent of all children under 5 years of age, with the effects being more pronounced for children living in poverty (Larrea & Kawachi, 2005).

et al., 2003). Jones *et al.* (2003) reviewed the availability of intervention for these diseases, such as effective immunisation, provision of antibiotics, clean birth facilities and clean water. They concluded that feasible interventions that could be effectively delivered with high coverage in low-income settings exist for virtually all these causes of childhood death. Further, they estimated that, had these interventions been made available, 63 per cent of these 10 million childhood deaths could have been prevented. For another view on the effects of poverty in relation to maternal health see sidebar 11.1.

Poverty does not just encompass economic and material deprivation, but has wide-ranging effects on people through restricted access to educational opportunities and health care, restricted quality of housing and property, insecurity of food, hunger and undernutrition, vulnerability and exposure to environmental toxins and occupational risks, as well as rendering them powerless and without voice. Hence the relation between poverty and ill health is often regarded as a vicious circle (World Health Organisation, 2001a), with good health being a prerequisite for development, and a lack of good health preventing development in poor communities and sustaining poverty. Poverty affects health in a variety of ways:

> living in poverty is associated with lower life expectancy, high infant mortality, poor reproductive health, higher rates of infectious diseases, notably tuberculosis and HIV infection, higher rates of substance use (tobacco, alcohol and illegal drugs), higher rates of noncommunicable diseases, depression and suicide, and increased exposure to environmental risks.   (World Health Organisation, 2001a, p. 3)

Poverty also has differential impacts, with women making up 70 per cent of the world's population living in absolute poverty (on less than the equivalent of about US$2 per day) (United Nations Development Programme, 2000). Also, people living in urban areas can be more affected by poverty as they may be exposed to higher risks (through poor housing, lack of housing, poor diet, lack of sanitation, etc.) and lack the resources and social networks that are available to poor people living in rural areas. Further, we should not consider poverty as solely an issue for the developing world. If measures of relative poverty are used (such as the percentage of people living on less than half of the median household disposable income), then we find significant rates of disadvantage in developed countries. For example, 14.3 per cent, 17.0 per cent, 12.5 per cent and 8.3 per cent of the population in Australia, the USA, the UK and Germany respectively live on less than 50 per cent of the median household disposable income for those countries (United Nations Development Programme, 2004), a significant factor in determining the state of health for those people.

Another factor widely considered to effect global health is the process of globalisation. **Globalisation** refers to the increasing interdependence and interconnectedness between people, communities, regions and countries, and is used to describe social as well as economic relationships. The effects of

The increasing interdependence and interconnectedness between peoples, communities, regions and countries involving social as well as economic relationships.

globalisation on health are contested (McClean, 2003). Globalisation has the potential to enhance health through processes of sharing information and technology; advances in health care and treatment, such as proposals for the successful treatment of tuberculosis, the effective control of tobacco or the proficient organisation of community clinics, can be transferred rapidly from one setting or country to another. However, globalisation is also seen to have detrimental effects on global health. The economic development, market and trade policies that are currently promoted under globalisation are seen by many as promoting inequality and poverty in many regions of the world, with substantially negative effects on health. Lee (2003), for example, has argued that the processes of globalisation are bound up in the production of inequalities and have effects on human health, which in turn can serve as an indicator of the health of the planet at large:

> Changing patterns of health and disease provide vital evidence of the trajectory we are currently following, and can serve as a touchstone for the sustainability of current globalisation practices. The damage to the ozone layer so far has coincided with a marked rise in the incidence of skin cancers ... Extreme weather patterns have increased in intensity, resulting in such threats to health as floods, increased disease vectors (for example mosquitos, rodents) and reduced food protection ... The pollution of clean water supplies is accompanied by growing rates of waterborne diseases. Intense farming methods by an increasingly globalised agro-industrial complex are creating transborder foodborne risks, as well as dietary shifts towards the overconsumption of fats, salt and sugar. The loss of biodiversity is closing down possible avenues for new treatments and therapies from animal species and natural compounds. In short, the status of human health is a key indicator of the health of the planet as a whole. The two are inextricably intertwined, with environmental sustainability a critical prerequisite to the long-term survival of the human species.   (Lee, 2003, p. 199)

What has all this to do with health psychology? Clearly, there is a lot of research and application to be achieved in the field of global healthcare, and health psychologists have considerable potential to contribute to this work. So far, their contribution has been relatively small. Aboud (1998), in her text *Health psychology in global perspective*, asks 'How many hats can you wear?' (p. 6). She suggests that, to work in the field of international health, one needs to be familiar with a range of issues and perspectives. Two of these, the 'psychosocial hat' and the 'biomedical hat' are relatively familiar to health psychologists, although the latter may require them to gain some knowledge about diseases that may be unfamiliar or uncommon in the West (leprosy, malaria, dengue fever, Chagas' disease) or of the ways that health care is organised in different countries. In addition, Aboud argues, health psychologists need the 'epidemiologist's hat' – an ability to understand health statistics used to assess mortality (age-specific mortality rates, DALY scores, DALE scores, etc.), morbidity (prevalence, incidence of disease) and health service usage and coverage (access to services, effectiveness of services, coverage of

11.1   A global perspective on maternal health

Adrian Germain, President of the International Women's Health Coalition, points out that, despite having the necessary knowledge and technologies to prevent the deaths of women during childbirth, during every minute of every day, at least one woman dies somewhere in the world through a lack of maternal health care.

> Who was the woman who died in the minute just passed, and why did she die? It could have been Hanatu, a girl of twelve in northern Nigeria, the second wife of a much older and very conservative man who denied her permission to go to a health centre. It could have been Salma, a 28-year-old rural Bangladeshi woman in her fourth pregnancy who did not have the bus fare to get to a nearby clinic. It could have been Betania, a middle-class teenager in Recife, Brazil, pregnant by rape, refused an abortion by the municipal hospital. She died terrified and alone after a desperate attempt to abort herself.(Germain, 2002, p. 222)

As Germain points out, in addition to the almost 600,000 woman who die every year in these sorts of circumstances, a further 15 million women are left disabled or chronically ill, and maternal mortality represents the largest gap in health between rich and poor countries (see also table 11.1). One reason that so little attention is given to this issue, Germain suggests, is that these deaths

> are largely invisible and undervalued. They attract no headlines, and the women die one by one, many at home or on the journey to a distant or poorly equipped health facility. Most of the woman who die are poor and young, with no political power or representation. Legislators and policymakers often think their deaths are a low priority, given the nearly twelve million deaths of children under age five every year. In fact, these deaths of women and children are intimately linked. For example, we cannot reduce the eight million stillbirths and newborn deaths and the twenty million low-birthweight babies born annually without taking better care of women before, during, and after they give birth. A mother's death also dramatically affects the health and survival of her living children: in Bangladesh, for example, children up to age ten whose mothers die are three to ten times more likely to die within two years then those with both parents living. (Germain, 2002, pp. 222–3)

services such as immunisation rates). Again, most health psychologists have at least some of the understandings required by this 'hat'. Finally, they need to be able to don the 'international organiser's hat', requiring knowledge about the countries of the world (where is Papua New Guinea?) and international health organisations (what is WHO, UNICEF, the G8 or Médicins sans Frontières?).

Related to this, Brundtland (2002) offers four challenges for improving global health. First, we need to reduce the burden of excess mortality and morbidity suffered by the poor. This requires both a focus on alleviating poverty *per se*, as a significant factor in health, and also giving increased attention to diseases like tuberculosis and malaria which disproportionately affect poorer people around the world (see sidebar 11.2). Brundtland also notes how poverty has a greater impact on women and children than on men. Second, Brundtland argues, we need to be active in countering threats to health that result from economic crises, unhealthy environments and risky behaviours. Smoking provides an illustration of this issue. Although a lot of attention has been paid to reducing smoking in the West, little has been done in developing countries, where 80 per cent of the world's smokers reside. As Brundtland notes, 'a global commitment to tobacco control can potentially avert scores of millions of premature deaths in the next half-century, and its success can point the way for

effective control of other threats'
(p. 7). While tobacco control provides one example, broad global
strategies established within specific
contexts for the provision of clear
air and water, adequate sanitation,
healthy diets, safe transportation and
safe cities, all of which can be facili-
tated by stable economic conditions,
can make an enormous difference to
health, as can ensuring that women
have adequate educational opportunities.

The third challenge for improving health, Brundtland argues, is
the development of more effective
health systems throughout the world.
We have documented some aspects
of the disparities in health care
resources in parts of the world previously (see table 8.1). Brundtland
notes how the unregulated growth
of the private sector, and we could
add the increasing commodifica-
tion of health, is one of the potential threats to health care development, especially in developing
countries. Recently we have seen
a major debate and political argument around the provision of adequate antiretroviral medication for
HIV/AIDS in Africa (see Thomas,
2003, for a detailed account; see also
sidebar 11.3). Even within developed industrialised countries, governments have struggled with health
care reforms. In fact, many of the
recent reforms of health care systems in the West are arguably not in
the best interests of some segments
of the population, as governments
struggle to rationalise waiting lists
for treatments and ration expensive

11.2 Priorities for funding the fight against infectious disease

In 2001 the G7 countries (now the G8 – France, Great
Britain, the USA, Germany, Italy, Japan, Canada and
Russia), who dominate the world political and
economic order, established the Global Fund to Fight
AIDS, Tuberculosis and Malaria (the GFATM) to fight
'against infectious diseases and to break the vicious
cycle between disease and poverty' (G8, 2001, p. 15).
So far financial commitments from these governments
and other bodies total US$5.71 billion phased over
several years, with US$3.24 billion contributed to date
(GFATM, 2004). However, it is estimated that GFATM
will require US$8 billion *per year* by 2007, and US$12
billion *per year* by 2015 to support adequate
prevention and treatment efforts for these diseases. To
put these figures into some perspective, US$8 billion is
roughly what people in the USA spend on cosmetics
or bathroom renovations annually, and about
one-sixth of what Europeans spend on cigarettes
annually (Labonte & Schrecker, 2004).

11.3 Changing the face of AIDS: an urgent international challenge

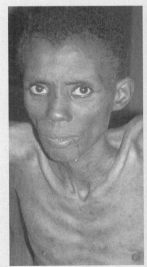

These two photographs show how the history of
HIV/AIDS can be changed. They are of Joseph Jeune, a
26-year-old peasant farmer in Lascahobas, a small

town in central Haiti. When the first picture was taken in March 2003, his parents had already bought his coffin. Suffering from the advanced stages of AIDS, Joseph probably had only weeks to live. The second picture, taken six months later, shows him 20 kg heavier and transformed after receiving treatment for HIV/AIDS and tuberculosis (TB) co-infection at the small clinic in his home town.

There are millions of people like Joseph Jeune around the world. For most of them, HIV/AIDS treatment is still beyond reach, but Joseph shows what can be achieved. HIV/AIDS is the world's most urgent public health challenge. The disease has already killed more than 20 million people. Today, an estimated 34–46 million others are living with HIV/AIDS. In 2003, 3 million people died and 5 million others became infected. HIV/AIDS was unknown a quarter of a century ago, but is now the leading cause of death and lost years of productive life for adults aged 15–59 years worldwide.

Until now, treatment has been the most neglected element in most developing countries. Yet among all possible HIV-related interventions it is treatment that can most effectively drive the strengthening of health systems, enabling poor countries to protect their people from a wide range of health threats. Almost 6 million people in developing countries will die in the near future if they do not receive treatment – but only about 400,000 of them were receiving it in 2003.

In September 2003, WHO, the Joint United Nations Programme on HIV/AIDS (UNAIDS) and the Global Fund declared the lack of access to AIDS treatment with antiretroviral medicines a global health emergency. In response, these organisations and their partners launched the **3 by 5 initiative**, a programme to provide 3 million people in developing countries with antiretroviral therapy by the end of 2005 – one of the most ambitious international public health projects ever developed.

(Adapted from *The World Health Report 2004* Copyright 2002 © Partners in Health. All rights reserved.)

new medical technologies. Brundtland argues that reforms, while necessary, need to be underpinned by specific values and a sense of direction – she proposes that the broad goal of 'better health for all' should guide reforms. There is no reason why health psychologists should not take part in this debate, and attempt to influence the development and direction of health care policies, health care reforms and health care systems.

Fourth, Brundtland suggests that there is a need to expand, promote and utilise the knowledge we have about health more effectively around the globe. Although high-income countries and international pharmaceutical companies invest heavily in research and development on health (involving products, treatments and services), these cater predominantly to the affluent peoples of the world. While these have the potential to benefit all, Brundtland highlights two major gaps that emerge here. One is the lack of attention to infectious diseases that afflict the poor of the world (see ch. 8). The other is the need for the systematic generation of an information base that can assist in health care system development by poorer countries. One recent development here is the initiative between the World Health Organisation and six leading medical publishers to bridge the information gap between the 'information-rich' and the 'poor'. This allows about a hundred low- and middle-income countries to have electronic access to almost 1,000 leading medical and scientific journals (World Health Organisation, 2001b).

Mercer (2004) suggests that there are two key principles that should underlie the promotion of global health. In her words:

Table 11.2 Seven actions to improve global health

- Promote equity in the global economic system; develop and promote initiatives to restrict the power of transnational corporations and multilateral lending institutions; restructure trade policies to promote fair trade, cancel debts of poorest countries, tax international transactions.
- Restrict or ban international trade in industries whose products are designed or destined to kill – military hardware, including land mines, and tobacco.
- Promote national responsibility for the provision of health to all; resist privatisation of health care and support national health care systems.
- Assure that basic needs, including food and clean water, are seen as basic human rights and protected from profit-oriented exploitation.
- Redesign and enforce an international essential drug policy that will regulate prices for the supply of and research on drugs, so that essential medicines can be provided to all who need them.
- Involve worker health and well-being issues whenever industrial protection and trade are discussed; promote international pressure to ban sweatshop labour and promote fair trade practices.
- Demand environmental protection for the planet; require control of toxic wastes, clean and reduced energy use, and other similar measures.

Adapted from Mercer (2004).

> The first is to *promote equity* as the central focus of efforts, going beyond health services to recognise that it is mostly broader conditions of life that provide more or less opportunity for achieving health – water, land, housing, health care, food security, work, dignity.
>   The second is to press for the provision of *health care as a fundamental universal human right*, as agreed by all countries that signed the 1948 Universal Declaration of Human Rights. Such a movement would seek to revive the concept of comprehensive primary health care as it was proposed in 1978 at Alma-Ata. Both principles demand that health care not be a commercial product, to be bought and sold in the marketplace. Both will require, in the longer run, deep changes in the basic economic and political systems that currently define our lives.   (p. 170, italics in original)

Mercer also outlines seven key actions that could be taken to improve global health, which are outlined in table 11.2. It is interesting to consider how few of these involve health *per se*, reinforcing the point Mercer makes above about the achievement of health being largely through 'the broader conditions of life'.

   All of this takes a more global approach to health than health psychology has considered previously. So, how can health psychologists become involved in these issues? Essentially, this requires political engagement at some level, and a need to rethink the roles available to health psychologists – recreating health psychology as a discipline that is concerned with making a difference internationally, and promoting global change. As Brundtland (2002) notes, there is a strong case for 'negotiating realistic national and international targets as a means of mobilising resources, concentrating international attention on the most important problems, and ensuring proper monitoring of progress and achievement' (p. 7). If health psychologists are to become engaged in this way, they will need to adopt a more critical approach to their involvement in health, and move beyond a biomedically influenced model of individual treatment and management to broader concerns that relate to local action for international goals, strategies and achievements. As Campbell and Murray (2004) argue 'this requires that as health psychologists we transform ourselves from scientist-practitioners to scholar-activists' (p. 194). If health psychologists are seriously concerned with changing health for the better, then they cannot ignore the pressures of globalisation, poverty, deprivation – the wider conditions of life – and their effects on health. Next, we develop the case for a critical health psychology, one which could open the door to such an engagement.

A critical health psychology

There are many ways of being critical, and in many senses of the word, all of health psychology should have being critical as a major objective (Owens, 2001). For example, the objects which we study as health psychologists, such as pain, health behaviours, experiences of disease and suffering, and so on, 'must be open to question and critical examination' (Owens, 2001, p. 263). Also, all health psychologists should be reflexive, and take into account the experiences of their participants in a respectful and ethical manner (Nicolson, 2001). Ideally, health psychologists should also recognise and consider how social and cultural factors determine their choices of study, as well as the political implications of choosing to study certain topics and not study others (Owens, 2001). As evidence continues to grow showing how cultural and socioeconomic factors play a large role in health and illness, health psychologists also need to be attending to broader and more macro levels of analysis, such as organisational, cultural and economic levels (Smith & Suls, 2004).

However, it is possible to distinguish mainstream health psychology from a critical health psychology. As Crossley (2001) has noted, mainstream health psychology is 'portrayed as a science, with objective researchers and practitioners who "uncover the truth" about health and illness-related behaviour and help individuals adjust to the demands of health and illness in contemporary society' (p. 244). This alignment with positivist science and objectivity has been beneficial for health psychology. It has meant that it has been taken seriously by medical disciplines and medical practitioners and researchers (Yardley, 1997). On the other hand, by focusing on objectivity and scientific methods, it has been argued that health psychology has failed to capture those unique issues that individuals are often engaged with when it comes to matters of health and illness, issues involving values, morality and reflexivity

(Crossley, 2001). On the whole, it has been argued that mainstream health psychology has 'focused neither on the subjective experience and meaning of illness, nor on the macrosocial determinants of health illness' (Murray *et al.*, 2004, p. 324).

A 'critical health psychology' does more than simply fill these gaps. It not only situates issues within their social and cultural contexts, but explores how these contexts operate in terms of power, resistance, struggle and so on. Thus, it explicitly examines power, and is concerned with social justice and health. Indeed, power is said to be 'cardinal' to the enterprise of critical health psychology (Prilleltensky & Prilleltensky, 2003). Rather than accepting and working within existing economic and political power relations, critical psychologists are more likely to focus on social inequalities and injustices, and challenge dominant economic and political relationships. Injustice and oppression are all around us, not just in remote corners of the globe (Sloan, 2000). Similarly, rather than accepting dominant forms of knowledge production (such as post-positivist ways of 'doing' science), critical psychologists are more likely to challenge these forms and argue for alternative ways of producing knowledge that, again, challenge social inequalities (Campbell & Murray, 2004). Consequently, critical psychologists deny that biomedicine holds the one and only 'true' knowledge. Clearly, biomedical knowledge has been immensely beneficial in alleviating pain and saving lives, but its claim to having superior knowledge, as well as ethical and ideological neutrality, is challenged by critical psychologists (Stainton Rogers, 1996).

What does this actually mean? If we employ mainstream theories and methods to explore why people in marginalised communities engage in unhealthy behaviours, we locate responsibility for these behaviours (and consequent health problems) within individuals (as we saw in ch. 3). This research serves as a smoke screen by drawing attention away from social structures and social inequalities and their influences on health (Campbell & Murray, 2004), instead focusing on individual 'voluntary' behavioural changes. The distinction between voluntary and mandatory illness prevention efforts can be blurred, as shown in sidebar 11.4.

As critical health psychology is concerned with the broader issues of

---

11.4 Challenging 'voluntary' health behaviour change

What is sometimes called 'voluntary' behaviour change can be subject to overwhelming multilevel coercion. Albee and Fryer (2003, p. 72) make this point in relation to smoking cigarettes:

> There is widespread understanding that smoking cigarettes increases the likelihood of physical ill health. Although nicotine addiction is widely recognized as a consequence of cigarette smoking, 'stopping smoking' is popularly positioned as a 'voluntary' way to prevent or reduce the likelihood of lung cancer and other physical illnesses and individual smokers are subject to exhortation to quit smoking by health education lobbies. However, smokers are also subjected to massive advertising by the tobacco industries and are immersed in a popular culture that actually promotes smoking. Ultimately government action against those who create, market and profit from cigarettes, rather than against their victims who smoke cigarettes, is necessary to prevent or reduce smoking related physical ill health.

social structures and social justice, it can usefully draw upon research, theorising and writing outside the discipline of psychology (such as anthropology and sociology) and employ it in ways to make sense of individuals' experiences, understandings and ways of being in their worlds. Critical psychologists 'identify and challenge explicit and implicit power structures that shape respondents' experiences' (Nicolson, 2001, p. 258). Critical psychologists argue for structural change, and perhaps reconceptualisations of problems, based on research data (Nicolson, 2001) – behaviour not always welcomed by those operating within the status quo.

In discussing critical psychology more generally, Sampson (2000) argues that critical psychology is critical in two main ways, as outlined below:

- Critical psychology is critical of the whole field of psychology, including its methods, choice of research problems, and the way it evaluates and uses its findings. More generally, critical psychology considers that the paradigm of inquiry adopted by mainstream psychology is 'ill-suited to understanding human behaviour and experience' (Sampson, 2000, p. 1).
- Critical psychology is committed to specific values, involving concerns for human betterment, achieving social transformations and change that lead to such betterment, providing a voice for marginalised people and so on. These values mean that critical psychology is more likely to be aligned with the causes of minority peoples, of the poor and disadvantaged, with feminism, and with developing cultures than with dominant Western worldviews.

Obviously, these issues are directly applicable to critical health psychology as well.

There are also other issues that are central to a critical health psychology. Despite many views to the contrary, critical health psychology is not linked to particular methods (e.g. those using qualitative approaches) but to particular research questions and particular views on knowledge production. The link between critical health psychology and qualitative methods has been made because many of the research questions asked can be best answered using particular qualitative methodologies. Indeed, some qualitative methodologies (such as discourse analysis) have been particularly valuable in answering some of the questions posed by critical health psychologists (e.g. how is testicular cancer represented in the media?). Further, although many qualitative approaches have a general promise that they will be *critical*, when it comes to how they are actually used and written up in research papers, many simply use these methods to provide a backdrop, illustrating the ecological context (Nicolson, 2001). As Nicolson (2001) rightly states, this is not critical psychology.

The nature and form of reality; ontological questions ask what there is that can be known.

How reality can be known; epistemological questions ask about how reality can be known, and what the relationship is between the knower and the knowable.

Many kinds of qualitative methodologies have underlying **ontologies** (assumptions about the nature and form of reality) and **epistemologies** (assumptions about how reality can be known) that differ from positivist methods (see Chamberlain *et al.*, 1997). For example, many qualitative approaches begin with the view that there are many realities out there, and these realities are socially and experientially based (Denzin & Lincoln, 1994). Thus, realities are seen to be constructed in and through social and cultural life. As we noted in ch. 1, these views are part of **social constructionism**. The point to make here, though, is that qualitative research is not all the same, and can be based within positivist or other paradigms. A further point to note is that how qualitative research is evaluated depends entirely on the paradigm in which it is based (see Lyons, 1999, for an overview of evaluation issues with qualitative research).

> The notion that the world we experience, and our understandings of reality and people, come from social life. Thus, our reality is a product of social life and does not exist in a straightforward, taken-for-granted manner.

Ways forward: opportunities and possibilities

Despite a growing accumulation of critical research on health issues, a coherent critical research and intervention strategy integrating this health psychology work with similar social science developments does not exist (Murray et al., 2004). However, there are currently many opportunities and possibilities for critical health psychology, particularly in relation to possibilities for theory, method and practice. These are all highly interrelated concerns, as will become clear when we discuss the implications for each in turn.

Moving forward with theory

Moving forward in health psychology requires moving forward with theory first and foremost. As Murray and Campbell (2003) point out, 'health, illness and suffering have been defined as something that belongs to the individual. Our theories are designed to define our very subjectivity as an asocial experience' (p. 232). Critical health psychology aims to examine and explore power structures inherent in people's lives, as well as the systems and institutions within which they operate, and how these issues are important for health and illness. Prilleltensky and Prilleltensky (2003, p. 198) put it in the following terms:

> Health can be promoted, maintained and restored in micro (e.g. close personal relations, family), meso (e.g. school, work) and macro spheres (e.g. community, society). From a critical psychology perspective, each one of these contexts is suffused with power differentials that privilege the powerful and discriminate against the weak.

While it is essential to explore the power differentials within each of these contexts, it is also important to examine how these contexts work together and interact. Very few theories or models explicitly link individual health with broader community or societal contexts (Cornish, 2004). The implications of failing to focus on process, and failing to theorise the linkages across contexts, has been aptly summarised by McLaren (1998, p. 91):

gathering biological, psychological and sociological data about people will only yield scattered lumps of information that do not relate to each other in any coherent sense. Without an overarching theory to integrate the fields from which the data derive, associations between differing classes of information are meaningless.

Cornish (2004) classifies models that involve individual, community and social levels into two types, those that are aggregative and those that are integrative. She views the biopsychosocial model as aggregative, focusing on biological, psychological and social phenomena as different levels of a system, with no explication of potential processes linking them. As Suls and Rothman (2004) have noted, specifying processes that connect biological, psychological and social systems is one of the daunting challenges facing all health psychologists. We have noted problems with the biopsychosocial model earlier (see ch. 1). On the other hand, integrative models (such as Bronfenbrenner's (1979) ecological model) distinguish different levels of a system, but emphasise how the systems relate to one another. Indeed, Cornish argues that one of the main benefits of Bronfenbrenner's approach is 'that each of the systems is defined relative to the concrete, experienced setting of the person's microsystem' (p. 283). Theorising relationships between and across different levels of systems, and theorising and focusing on processes that occur between these levels, will be one way that helps to move health psychology forward.

Stam (2000) argues that mainstream health psychology draws on a particular kind of theory, namely functionalism. From such a perspective, individuals are seen as machines, and their actions make sense in larger control systems (e.g. systems theory, biopsychosocial theory, self-regulatory theories). However, the self, or the individual as a thinking and embodied being, is absent in these conceptualisations. Such theorising works to construct health and illness as a set of variables which can be measured and analysed using statistics, and to exclude a consideration of their embeddedness in social and political communities (Stam, 2004). Furthermore, Stam points out that theorising 'is never done in a vacuum but reflects the interests of those so engaged' (p. 29), and theorising is an important part of our positions as professionals in the social order – an order that we need to reflect on and consider in our theorising. In other words, we need to be reflexive about our roles as health psychologists, in our theorising, researching and practice. This includes explicit consideration of the moral and ethical aspects of our work and knowledge production.

Moving forward with method

Many critical psychologists have turned to the study of language and discourse as a way 'out of the blind alley of measurement and objectivity' (Murray & Campbell, 2003, p. 232). Thus, researchers have drawn on social constructionist ideas concerning the functional and organising nature of language, and studied language as a primary topic in its own right through various methods of discourse analysis (e.g. Potter & Wetherell, 1987; Parker, 1992). This has included studies of what people say in various contexts (e.g. individual interviews, consultations, group discussions, etc.) as well as written language (e.g. newspaper and magazine articles, self-help books, government reports, etc.). However, discourse analysis has been criticised for its primary focus on language, as this fails to take materiality into account, both in terms of bodily materiality and the materiality of the worlds in which people live (Hook, 2001; Murray & Campbell, 2003). Therefore, more work is required to theorise relationships between discourse, practice, experience and subjectivity (Willig, 2000), as well as to connect the focus on language 'with the possibility of concrete social action in the interests of reducing poverty and health inequalities, and increasing social justice' (Murray & Campbell, 2003, p. 233).

Materiality, including bodies and embodiment, needs to become a primary focus in health psychology, and this will necessitate the creation of original, distinctive and diverse methods. Being embodied is more than simply being able to do things; certain postures, gestures, ways of being in the world signify meaning within that social world (Radley, 2000). Thus, theorising embodiment is an essential part of enabling the development of appropriate methods to study embodiment. Similarly, methods are required that anchor research in culture and context (Yali & Revenson, 2004), again a difficult task and one that will require methodological innovation (Keefe & Blumenthal, 2004). However, as Murray and Campbell (2003) note, we need to be careful that debates about methodology do not detract from the broader issues about how our research can potentially impact on improving the quality of life of the many.

A further concern about the use of qualitative methods is their uncritical acceptance and reification – what has been termed '**methodolatry**' (see Chamberlain, 2000). This occurs when methodological concerns are privileged over other qualitative health research concerns. For example, emphasising methodology issues may occur at the expense of critically reflecting on the research itself and its underlying assumptions. As people who employed qualitative approaches fought hard to have these methods accepted by the mainstream, there has been 'an overemphasis on describing and defending the methodology within and outside of health psychology' (Nicolson, 2001, p. 257). Struggling for acceptance has also meant that results are often written up in a bland and somewhat 'distanced' manner (perhaps to claim some kind of objectivity), which is 'diametrically opposed to a critical stance' (Nicolson, 2001, p. 257). We need to beware of reifying qualitative health research methods (Chamberlain, 2000).

Privileging methodological concerns over other considerations in research.

Moving forward with practice

In addition to theorising the complex interactions between individuals, communities, societies and nations, critical health psychologists need to be able to employ such theorisations in an actionable way (Murray & Campbell, 2003).

Table 11.3 Strategies for combating poverty and promoting health

WHO strategy	Role of health psychology
Act on the determinants of health by influencing development policy	Use research to expose negative impact of widening health inequalities throughout the world. Translate these findings into action through participation in social movements
Reduce risks through a broader approach to public health	Use research and action to promote healthy cities, workplaces, homes and schools. Work with communities to expose inadequate living conditions
Focus on the health problems of the poor	Develop theories and methods that can help to enable oppressed and marginalised groups to change their living and working conditions
	Explore how to connect community efforts to improve health with broader national and international movements
Ensure that health systems serve the poor more effectively	Resist attempts to dismantle health care systems which are universally accessible
	Campaign for health facilities which are widely available and accessible

Adapted from Murray & Campbell (2003).

Clearly, this is no small task! However, in making this a broad objective, health psychologists may find ways to challenge and reshape 'mutually reinforcing subjectivities and structures that are damaging to the health and well-being of people' (Murray & Campbell, 2003, p. 235). One way of doing this is by becoming politically engaged. For example, health psychology can contribute to the broad strategies for health that were identified by the World Health Organisation in 1999. These descriptions, and health psychology's potential contributions, are shown in table 11.3.

The largest employers of health psychologists are health and medical settings (Stam, 2000). Despite this, there is very little debate or discussion within health psychology concerning the political, social and contested issues that create and exist within health care systems. This absence, as Stam (2000) has noted, is strange, if not suspicious. Psychologists working and researching in health and illness tend to ignore the political debates around health care systems, and suppress how these wider social issues affect their own research and practice (Stam, 2000). This is why it is important for psychologists to theorise health and illness within their social and political context, and use methods which allow for an explicit examination of the role of the researcher, the researched and the contexts involved. An additional problem is that often the findings and implications of research do not have any impact on actual practice (Suls & Rothman, 2004). Therefore, one of the ways to move forward in terms of practice is to find more and alternative ways of translating findings into

Table 11.4 Examples of critical psychology interventions in health settings.

	Ecological levels and associated values		
Type of intervention	Personal wellness values: *self-determination, protection of health, caring and compassion*	Relational wellness values: *collaboration, democratic participation, respect for diversity*	Collective wellness values: *support for community structures, social justice*
Reactive	Power sharing in developing treatment plans for pain management	Communication training for professionals dealing with vulnerable patients	Securing access of minorities, refugees and the poor to all health services
Proactive high risk	Smoking cessation with emphasis on exploitation of community by tobacco companies	Organisational interventions to reduce stress in hospital staff	Self-help/mutual aid and support groups for people caring for disabled family members
Proactive universal	Self-instruction guide on HIV prevention	Bill of rights and responsibilities for patients and staff in hospitals	Critique and boycotts of media and corporations making profits at expense of population health

Adapted from Prilleltensky & Prilleltensky (2003).

implications, recommendations and action for health psychologists as well as health practitioners.

As we have seen throughout the text, health psychologists can be involved in a range of services, from clinical services to health promotion programmes within community settings (Prilleltensky & Prilleltensky, 2003). Critical psychologists can contribute to practice in many ways. Some examples of interventions critical health psychologists might employ, based on the values discussed earlier, are provided in table 11.4. This shows that potential interventions can occur at the individual, community and societal levels. For example, we can examine power structures within interactions and institutions, and ensure that clients' voices are heard and decision making power is shared. We can also do our best to ensure adequate access to healthcare for all members of society, alongside highlighting the importance of broader social and economic structures on health (Prilleltensky & Prilleltensky, 2003).

Concluding comments

In conclusion, the biomedical model, with its emphasis on individualism, a seemingly 'objective' stance and an overarching reductionist framework, can be seen to conveniently mask the effects that economic and political factors have had in producing patterns of ill health (Campbell & Jovchelovitch, 2000). Indeed, it is much easier and safer to 'seek grants for teaching job-search skills to the unemployed or for studying the brain chemistry of those labelled deviant than to tackle the oppressive structural labour market and poverty related factors that are the underlying causes of the problems' (Albee & Fryer, 2003, p. 73). Health psychology is an enterprise that is profoundly value laden. It is an ideological endeavour, and therefore we need to ask such questions as whose interests are at stake and, crucially, questions about power. In terms of research and practice, we must examine who 'has the power to construct, distribute and legitimate knowledge' (Stainton Rogers, 1996, p. 75).

We can also consider how health psychology contributes to the ideology of psychology more generally. Rose (1989) has argued that increasingly in the twentieth century, 'psychology has participated in the development of regulatory practices which operate not by crushing subjectivity but by producing it, shaping it, modelling it, seeking to construct citizens committed to a personal identity, a moral responsibility and a social solidarity' (p. 130). Thus, psychology itself, by virtue of the knowledge and practices it creates, can be seen to be constructing and producing certain kinds of individuals, certain kinds of subjectivities. As a knowledge producer it is powerful; those of us working as psychologists need to be committed to being aware of this power and its implications for the health and well-being of individuals, communities, societies and cultures.

RECOMMENDED READING

Aboud, F. E. (1998). *Health psychology in global perspective*. Thousand Oaks, CA: Sage. A valuable text that explores and discusses an international role for health psychology. This text is unique in taking up global issues in health from a psychological perspective.

Crossley, M. L. (2000). *Rethinking health psychology*. Buckingham, UK: Open University Press. A book that raises many concerns that are critical of mainstream health psychology and proposes alternatives. It is important reading for developing an understanding of critical health psychology.

Health Psychology, 2004, vol. 23. Special section on the future of health psychology. This special section contains eight articles reflecting on different aspects of the progress in health psychology over the last twenty-five years. Although largely from a mainstream health psychology perspective, it raises interesting concerns and calls for increased attention to a number of areas.

Lee, K. (2003). *Globalisation and health: an introduction*. Basingstoke, UK: Palgrave Macmillan. This book provides an excellent overview and discussion of the complex relationships between globalisation and health.

Murray, M. (ed.) (2004). *Critical health psychology*. Basingstoke: Palgrave Macmillan. This edited book contains a range of chapters which elaborate many of the issues discussed here. It covers theory, context, methods and practice, and provides a further background to many aspects of critical health psychology.

Prilleltensky, I. & Prilleltensky, O. (2003). Towards a critical health psychology practice. *Journal of Health Psychology, 8,* 197–210. An important article which focuses on critical health psychology, and discusses it in terms of values, assumptions and practices. The paper is followed in this issue of the journal by several commentaries, which react to the discussion and develop the arguments in different ways, and make interesting reading.

Glossary

Action research Research which endeavours to gain understanding and also make change at the same time. It uses different research methodologies, and is usually participative (includes participants in the process of the research as much as possible) and qualitative.

Acute illness Illness that lasts only a relatively short time and has an end.

Adherence The degree to which patients adhere to, rather than comply with, medical recommendations for treatment (see **compliance** and **concordance**).

Allostasis Automatic physiological processes which help physical systems fluctuate to adapt to external demands.

Allostatic load The wear and tear on the body and brain which results from chronic overactivity or inactivity of physiological systems normally involved in adapting to external demands. Over long time periods, allostatic load can lead to disease.

Antibodies Antibodies are produced by the immune system in response to foreign substances that may be a threat to the body (e.g. chemicals, virus particles, bacterial toxins). These foreign substances are called antigens. Each type of antibody is unique and defends the body against one specific type of antigen.

Appraisal A cognitive process which involves classifying or categorising information.

Atherosclerosis The growth of plaques, or fatty patches, on the walls of the arteries. As the plaques build up, they narrow and harden the arteries, and this causes blood pressure to go up and increases the likelihood of a heart attack or stroke.

Behavioural health A multidisciplinary area of study concerned with enhancing health and preventing illness in healthy individuals.

Behavioural medicine A multidisciplinary area of study concerned with applying behavioural principles and techniques to the prevention, diagnosis and treatment of illness and rehabilitation.

Biofeedback training Training which utilises procedures for providing feedback about a physiological system or response in order for an individual to develop a learned process of self-regulation of the system or response.

Bodily sign A change in a somatic feeling.

Caregiver burden The negative psychological and social costs and consequences to the caregiver of providing care for an ill person.

Caregiving The activities and experiences involved in caring, generally on an voluntary, unpaid basis, for friends, family and relatives suffering from severe or chronic illness who cannot care for themselves.

Chemoprevention The technique in which healthy individuals take prescribed medication to reduce their risk of getting a disease.

Chronic illness Illness that is ongoing and is usually irreversible.

Clinical gaze The direct and unquestioned access a doctor has to a patient's body (which tends to ignore the patient's emotions or psychological state) (from Foucault, 1975).

Cochrane review A rigorous, well-developed method of reviewing a number of studies (usually in the medical field) on a particular topic.

Cognitive representations An organised set of beliefs about a particular topic, such as illness.

Compliance The degree to which a patient complies with or follows explicitly the expert treatment recommendations of a health professional.

Concordance Interactions between patients and health professionals are considered as interactions between equals which aim for a therapeutic alliance.

Conversion hysteria A condition in which patients have physiological symptoms, such as paralysis or blindness, without any apparent physiological cause.

Coping The cognitive and behavioural efforts that a person uses to manage demands that they perceive as exceeding their resources.

Coping processes All of the efforts a person engages in when attempting to deal with a problem.

Coronary catheterisation A procedure performed to see the presence and degree of narrowing or blockages in the coronary arteries. It involves directing a tube into these arteries (via groin or arm) and injecting an x-ray dye.

Death anxiety Essentially anxiety surrounding all aspects of death; a multidimensional concept relating to fear and anxiety about one's own and other people's death and dying and concerns about the objects of death, especially corpses; synonymous with fear of death and death fear.

Disease prototypes An organised set of ideas about specific diseases which include causes, duration, symptoms and other disease attributes.

Double shift Working in paid employment as well as doing the majority of unpaid domestic work and childcare.

Dualism The philosophical view that the body and the mind (or soul, or mental processes) are fundamentally different substances.

Embodiment The experience of both *being* and *having* a body.

Empowerment A process in which people are helped to assert control over factors which affect their health. This can occur at the individual, group, or community level.

Epidemiology A discipline of study which examines and documents the frequency, distribution and causes of disease in a population.

Epistemology How reality can be known; epistemological questions ask about how reality can be known, and what the relationship is between the knower and the knowable.

Essential hypertension Consistently elevated blood pressure with no identifiable cause.

Ethnic minority An ethnic group which is not the dominant ethnic group in a country or society. The term highlights power differences between different ethnic groups.

Ethnicity A term used widely in sociology, referring to a shared cultural background.

Etiology The cause or origin of a disease.

Functional social support The quality of social relationships, and the functions they serve for the individual. There are many different types of functional support, including emotional, instrumental, informational and appraisal. Measures of functional support generally ask individuals to rate their perception of whether they have people available who could give different forms of support in times of need, and also whether they actually receive particular forms of support.

Gate-control theory of pain Pain arises from an aggregation of pain fibre transmission to the brain which is influenced by the opening or closing of a 'gate' located at the base of the spinal column. This gate can be opened or closed by signals from ascending (e.g. from pain fibres) and descending (e.g. from emotions) pathways.

Gender roles Masculinity and femininity are behaviour sets into which members of each sex are socialised. Distinct from biological sex.

Geneism Discrimination on the basis of genetic make-up.

Genetic reductionism Assuming that individuals are simply the sum of their genes. Thus causes of diseases are reduced to individual genes rather than broader social, environmental and cultural factors.

Globalisation The increasing interdependence and interconnectedness between peoples, communities, regions and countries, and involving social as well as economic relationships.

Grief work A cognitive process of facing loss through bereavement, going over events around the death, working towards detachment from the deceased person and coming to terms with the loss.

Hassles Relatively minor negative events.

Health behaviour Any activity that is undertaken by people to enhance or maintain their health.

Health education Planned activity to promote learning about health and illness. Such learning aims to effect positive change in an individual's health-related behaviour.

Health locus of control The extent to which people believe their health is due to their own actions, to the actions of powerful others, or to chance or fate.

Health promotion Interventions designed to promote changes to improve good health in individuals, communities or populations. These interventions can range from the governmental, environmental and legislative through to the behavioural and individual.

Hospitalisation of death The historical change over the last century in the place of dying, from the person's home to a medical setting, such as a hospital or nursing home.

Hypertension High blood pressure (at rest).

Iatrogenesis Illness caused by doctors and medicine.

Ideology A system of ideas, beliefs and values that relates to the way that society should be organised, and that explains and legitimises the interests and actions of particular groups within societies.

Illness cognitions General beliefs about illness.

Incidence The number of new cases (people) with a particular illness, injury or disability reported during a particular time (e.g. over the previous year).

Lay referral network The group of people (friends, relatives, colleagues) we talk to and seek advice from.

Life review A process of looking back over and reviewing what has been gained and learned from life as death approaches; a therapeutic technique for finding meaning and purpose in life.

Lifestyle The ways in which an individual lives his/her life, including specific behaviours s/he engages in.

Lifestyle diseases Diseases in which a person's everyday behaviours (e.g. diet, exercise, smoking) play roles in their development, such as coronary heart disease, lung cancer, Type II diabetes.

Mammogram X-ray pictures of the breast, used to detect tumours and cysts. One breast at a time is rested on a flat surface that contains the x-ray plate, and a compressor is pressed firmly against the breast to help flatten out the breast tissue. The X-ray pictures are taken from several angles (from http://www.nlm.nih.gov/medlineplus/ency/article/003380.htm#Definition).

Mastectomy The surgical removal of the entire breast.

Medicalisation The process by which non-medical problems become defined and treated as medical issues, usually in terms of illnesses, disorders or syndromes (Richmond, 1998).

Methodolatry Privileging methodological concerns over other considerations in research.

Monism The philosophical view that the body and the mind (or soul, or mental processes) are essentially one substance, and are part of one underlying reality.

Morbidity Illness, injury or disability; morbidity rates are the number of people with a particular illness, injury or disability.

Mortality Death; mortality rates are the number of deaths that are due to a particular cause.

Negative affect Undifferentiated subjective distress, including many negative mood states such as anxiety, depression, hostility.

Negative affectivity A predisposition to experience negative emotions and negative self-concept.

Negative health behaviour Behaviour that is detrimental to a person's health.

Neuroticism An individual difference in the tendency to experience negative, distressing emotions.

Old-old People in the oldest stage of life, usually defined as those aged over 75 years and contrasted with the young-old, people aged over 60 and under 75 years.

Ontology The nature and form of reality; ontological questions ask what there is that can be known.

Oophorectomy The surgical removal of one ovary (a bilateral oophorectomy is the surgical removal of both ovaries). It is also called ovariectomy.

Pathogen A disease-causing agent, such as a virus or bacterium, or other micro-organism.

Patient-centred care Doctor responding to the patient in a manner which allows the patient to express all of their reasons for seeing the doctor, including symptoms, thoughts, feelings and expectations.

Pattern theories of pain Pain arises from the summation of sensory pain information transmitted to the brain. In sum, sensory information is transmitted along more than one pathway to the dorsal horns, where it is summed (or balanced) and depending on the output, may or may not be transmitted on to the brain.

Phantom limb pain A person experiencing pain in a limb that has been amputated.

Placebo effect A genuine psychological or physiological effect, in a human or another animal, which is attributable to receiving a substance or undergoing a procedure, but is not due to the inherent powers of that substance or procedure (Stewart-Williams & Podd, 2004).

Placebo A substance or procedure that has no inherent power to produce an effect that is sought or predicted (Stewart-Williams & Podd, 2004).

Positive health behaviour Behaviour that is beneficial for a person's health.

Post-traumatic growth The experience of positive change and growth arising out of the struggle with a major trauma or life crisis, such as serious or life-threatening illness.

Prevalence The number of cases (people) with a particular illness, injury or disability. Refers to the total number of cases, including previously reported and current cases.

Primary prevention The promotion of healthy lifestyles to prevent the development of disease.

Psychophysiology A scientific discipline devoted to studying interrelationships between the physiological and psychological aspects of brain and behaviour. It is truly interdisciplinary, and includes researchers from a large number of disciplines like psychology, medicine, engineering, anatomy and neuroscience.

Psychosomatic medicine A multidisciplinary area of study concerned with treating physical symptoms and disease using a holistic approach.

Response shift Mechanisms that lead to potential error in assessing change, relating to a change in the meaning of the assessed construct through a shift in internal standards (recalibration), a shift in values or priorities (reprioritisation) or a shift in definition (reconceptualisation).

Risk society The way in which risk and risk calculations are a dominant part of people's lives in Western society today.

Secondary prevention Medical-based prevention aiming to identify disease at an early stage and treat it.

Self-awareness An individual difference in the tendency to pay attention to internal states.

Self-efficacy The extent to which people believe they are competent to deal with challenges and events in their lives.

Social constructionism The notion that the world we experience, and our understandings of reality and people, come from social life. Thus, our reality is a product of social life and does not exist in a straightforward, taken-for-granted manner.

Social representations The idea that the knowledge individuals hold about the world is a part of broader 'systems of knowledge' that are shared in society.

Somatisation The process by which physical symptoms arise from psychological distress rather than organic pathology.

Specificity theories of pain Pain arises from one specific linear biological system. In sum, injury leads to an activation of specific pain receptors which project messages to a pain centre via a spinal pain pathway.

Structural social support The existence and quantity of social relationships the individual has with others. Measures of structural support are relatively objective and include such matters as whether the individual is married or not, the number of close friends, the number of organisations s/he belongs to, whether s/he attends church regularly, etc.

Sudden death Death which results from a cardiac arrest, with the heart ceasing to function as it should. The death is unexpected and occurs within minutes of symptoms appearing. The most common reason for sudden death is coronary heart disease.

Symptoms A sensation or physical feeling that is recognised and interpreted as different to normal bodily feeling, and which may indicate disease to the person.

Technological reductionism Reducing a complex whole down to individual parts via the use of technology.

Temporomandibular disorders Disorders relating to the temporomandibular joint in the jaw, which may involve one or more of: discomfort or pain in the muscles that control jaw function and the neck and shoulder muscles; a dislocated jaw, displaced disc, or injury to the bones in the jaw; or degenerative osteoarthritis or rheumatoid arthritis in the jaw joint.

Thanatology The study of death and dying.

Uplifts Relatively minor positive events.

References

Aaronson, N., Ahmedzai, S., Bergman, B., Bollinger, N., Cull, A., Duez, N. *et al.* (1993). The European Organisation for Research and Treatment of Cancer QLQ-C30: a quality-of-life instrument for use in international clinical trials in oncology. *Journal of the National Cancer Institute*, *85*, 365–76.

Abbey, S. E., & Stewart, D. E. (2000). Gender and psychosomatic aspects of ischaemic heart disease. *Journal of Psychosomatic Research*, *48*, 417–23.

Aboud, F. E. (1998). *Health psychology in global perspective*. Thousand Oaks, CA: Sage.

Abraham, C., & Sheeran, P. (1994). Modelling and modifying young heterosexuals' HIV-preventive behaviour: a review of theories, findings and educational implications. *Patient Education and Counseling*, *23*, 173–86.

Adamson, J., Ben-Shlomo, Y., Chaturvedi, N. & Donovan, J. (2003). Ethnicity, socio-economic position and gender: do they affect reported health-care seeking behaviour? *Social Science & Medicine*, *57*, 895–904.

Adamson, L. (2002). 'From victim to agent': the clinical and social significance of self-help group participation for people with life-threatening diseases. *Scandinavian Journal of Caring Sciences*, *16*, 224–31.

Addis, M. E., & Mahalik, J. R. (2003). Men, masculinity and the contexts of help-seeking. *American Psychologist*, *58*, 5–14.

Ader, R., & Cohen, N. (1991). The influence of conditioning on immune responses. In R. Ader, D. L. Felton & N. Cohen (eds.), *Psychoneuroimmunology* (2nd edn, pp. 611–46). San Diego, CA: Academic Press.

   (1993). Psychoneuroimmunology: conditioning and stress. *Annual Review of Psychology*, *44*, 53–85.

Adler, N. E., & Snibbe, A. C. (2003). The role of psychological processes in explaining the gradient between socioeconomic status and health. *Current Directions in Psychological Science*, *12*, 119–23.

Airhihenbuwa, C. O. (1994). Health promotion and the discourse on culture: implications for empowerment. *Health Education Quarterly*, *21*, 345–53.

Airhihenbuwa, C. O., & Obregon, R. (2000). A critical assessment of theories/models used in health communication for HIV/AIDS. *Journal of Health Communication*, *5*, S5–15.

Ajzen, I. (1991). The theory of planned behavior. *Organizational Behavior and Human Decision Processes*, *50*, 179–211.

Ajzen, I., & Fishbein, M. (1980). *Understanding attitudes and predicting social behavior*. Englewood Cliffs, NJ: Prentice-Hall.

(2004). Questions raised by a reasoned action approach: comment on Ogden (2003). *Health Psychology*, *23*, 431–34.

Albee, G. W., & Fryer, D. M. (2003). Praxis: towards a public health psychology. *Journal of Community and Applied Social Psychology*, *13*, 71–5.

Albee, G. W., & Gullotta, T. P. (1997). *Primary prevention works*. Thousand Oaks, CA: Sage.

Allison, K. R. (1991). Theoretical issues concerning the relationship between perceived control and preventive health behavior. *Health Education Research*, *6*, 141–51.

Alonso, J. *et al.* and the IQOLA Project Group. (2004). Health-related quality of life associated with chronic conditions in eight countries: results from the International Quality of Life Assessment (IQOLA) project. *Quality of Life Research*, *13*, 283–98.

Altman, D., & Lillie-Blanton, M. (2003). Racial/ethnic disparities in medical care. *British Medical Journal USA*, *3*, 300–1.

Anagnostopoulos, F., Vaslamatzis, G. & Markidis, M. (2004). Coping strategies of women with breast cancer: a comparison of patients with healthy and benign controls. *Psychotherapy and Psychosomatics*, *73*, 43–52.

Anderson, D., & Pennebaker, J. W. (1980). Pain and pleasure: alternative interpretations of identical stimulation. *European Journal of Social Psychology*, *10*, 207–12.

Anderson, J. (2000). Clinical practice guidelines: review of the recommendations for colorectal cancer screening. *Geriatrics*, *55*, 67–73.

Aneshensel, C. S. (1992). Social stress: theory and research. *Annual Review of Sociology*, *18*, 15–38.

Annandale, E. (1998). Health, illness and the politics of gender. In D. Field & S. Taylor (eds.), *Sociological perspectives on health, illness and health care* (pp. 115–33). Oxford: Blackwell.

Annandale, E., & Hunt, K. (1990). Masculinity, femininity and sex: an exploration of their relative contribution to explaining gender differences in health. *Sociology of Health and Illness*, *12*, 24–46.

(1998). Accounts of disagreements with doctors. *Social Science & Medicine*, *46*, 119–29.

(2000). Gender inequalities in health: research at the crossroads. In E. Annandale & K. Hunt (eds.), *Gender inequalities in health* (pp. 1–35). Buckingham, UK: Open University Press.

Antoni, M., Lehman, J., Kilbourn, K., Boyers, A., Culver, J., Alferi, S. *et al.* (2001). Cognitive-behavioral stress management intervention decreases the prevalence of depression and enhances benefit finding among women under treatment for early stage breast cancer. *Health Psychology*, *20*, 20–32.

Arber, S., & Ginn, J. (1993). Gender and inequalities in health in later life. *Social Science & Medicine*, *36*, 33–46.

(1998). Health and illness in later life. In D. Field & S. Taylor (eds.), *Sociological perspectives on health, illness and health care* (pp. 134–52). Oxford: Blackwell.

Ariès, P. (1981). *The hour of our death*. London: Allen Lane.

Armeli, S., Carney, M. A., Tennen, H., Affleck, G. & O'Neil, T. P. (2001). Stress and alcohol use: a daily process examination of the stressor-vulnerability model. *Journal of Personality and Social Psychology*, *78*, 979–94.

Armitage, C. J., & Conner, M. (2001). Efficacy of the theory of planned behaviour: a meta-analytic review. *British Journal of Social Psychology*, *40*, 471–99.

Armstrong, D. (1983). *Political anatomy of the body: medical knowledge in Britain in the twentieth century*. Cambridge: Cambridge University Press.

  (1987). Theoretical tensions in biopsychosocial medicine. *Social Science & Medicine*, *25*, 1213–18.

  (1995). The rise of surveillance medicine. *Sociology of Health and Medicine*, *17*, 393–404.

Arnold, R., Ranchor, A., Sanderman, R., Kempen, G., Ormel, J. & Suurmeijer, T. (2004). The relative contribution of domains of quality of life to overall quality of life for different chronic diseases. *Quality of Life Research*, *13*, 883–96.

Aronson, J. K. (2000). Autopathography: the patient's tale. *British Medical Journal*, *321*, 1599–602.

Ashing-Giwa, K. (1999). Health behaviour change models and their socio-cultural relevance for breast cancer screening in African American women. *Women and Health*, *28*, 53–71.

Atkinson, P. (1994). Rhetoric as skill in a medical setting. In M. Bloor & P. Taraborrelli (eds.), *Qualitative studies in health and medicine* (pp. 110–30). Aldershot: Avebury.

Attig, T. (2001). Relearning the world: making and finding meanings. In R. A. Neimeyer (ed.), *Meaning reconstruction and the experience of loss* (pp. 33–53). Washington, DC: American Psychological Association.

Austin, L. T., Ahmad, F., McNally, M. J. & Stewart, D. E. (2002). Breast and cervical cancer screening in Hispanic women: a literature review using the health belief model. *Women's Health Issues*, *12*, 122–8.

Ayers, L. (2000). Narrative of family caregiving: the process of making meaning. *Research in Nursing and Health*, *23*, 424–34.

Backett, K. C., & Davison, C. (1992). Rational or reasonable: perceptions of health at different stages of life. *Health Education Journal*, *51/2*, 55–9.

  (1995). Lifecourse and lifestyle: the social and cultural location of health behaviours. *Social Science and Medicine*, *40*, 629–38.

Backett, K., Davison, C. & Mullen, K. (1994). Lay evaluation of health and healthy lifestyles: evidence from three studies. *British Journal of General Practice*, *44*, 277–80.

Bagozzi, R. P. (1992). The self-regulation of attitudes, intentions and behavior. *Social Psychology Quarterly*, *55*, 178–204.

Bakry, N., Laabid, A., De Brouwere, V. & Dujardin, B. (1999). Why don't patients comply with referral decisions made by general practitioners? *Revue d'Epidemiologie et de Santé Publique*, *47*, 65–74.

Ballantyne, P. J. (1999). The social determinants of health: a contribution to the analysis of gender differences in health and illness. *Scandinavian Journal of Public Health*, *27*, 290–5.

Bandura, A. (1977). Self-efficacy: toward a unifying theory of behavioral change. *Psychological Review*, *84*, 191–215.

Banthia, R., Malcarne, V. & Varni, J. (2003). The effects of dyadic strength and coping styles on psychological distress in couples faced with prostate cancer. *Journal of Behavioral Medicine*, *26*, 31–52.

Banyard, V. L., & Graham-Bermann, S. A. (1993). Can women cope? A gender analysis of theories of coping with stress. *Psychology of Women Quarterly*, *17*, 303–18.

Baranowski, T., Anderson, C. & Carmack, C. (1998). Mediating variable framework in physical activity interventions. How are we doing? How might we do better? *American Journal of Preventive Medicine*, *15*, 266–97.

Barnard, S. (2000). Construction and corporeality: theoretical psychology and biomedical technologies of the self. *Theory and Psychology*, *10*, 669–88.

Barry, C. A. (2002). Multiple realities in a study of medical consultations. *Qualitative Health Research*, *12*, 1093–1111.

Barry, C. A., Stevenson, F. A., Britten, N., Barber, N. & Bradley, C. P. (2001). Giving voice to the lifeworld: more humane, more effective medical care? A qualitative study of doctor-patient communication in general practice. *Social Science & Medicine*, *53*, 487–505.

Bartlett, D. (1998). *Stress: perspectives and processes*. Buckingham, UK: Open University Press.

Batcheller, L. J. (2001). *Journey to health: writing your way to physical, emotional and spiritual well-being*. Lincoln, NE: iUniverse.com.

Baum, A., & Posluszny, D. M. (1999). Health psychology: mapping biobehavioral contributions to health and illness. *Annual Review of Psychology*, *50*, 137–63.

Bayer, B. M., & Malone, K. R. (1996). Feminism, psychology and matters of the body. *Theory and Psychology*, *6*, 667–92.

Beck, U. (1992). *Risk society: towards a new modernity*. London: Sage.

Beck, U., & Beck-Gernsheim, E. (2001). *Individualization: institutionalized individualism and its social and political consequences*. London: Sage.

Beecher, H. K. (1955). The powerful placebo. *Journal of the American Medical Association*, *159*, 1602–6.

Bekker, M. H. (2000). The gendered body: body and gender and the inter-relationships with health. In L. Sherr & J. St. Lawrence (eds.), *Women, health and the mind* (pp. 17–32). Chichester, UK: John Wiley & Sons.

Bell, S. E. (2002). Photo images: Jo Spence's narratives of living with illness. *Health: An Interdisciplinary Journal for the Social Study of Health, Illness and Medicine*, *6*, 5–30.

Belloc, N. B., & Breslow, L. (1972). Relationship of physical health status and health practices. *Preventive Medicine*, *1*, 409–21.

Bendelow, G. (1993). Pain perceptions, emotion and gender. *Sociology of Health and Illness*, *15*, 3.

Bendelow, G., & Pridmore, P. (1998). Children's images of health. In A. Petersen & C. Waddell (eds.), *Health matters: a sociology of illness, prevention and care* (pp. 128–40). Buckingham, UK: Open University Press.

Beneddetti, F., Arduino, C. & Amanzio, M. (1999). Somatotopic activation of opiod systems by target-directed expectations of analgesia. *Journal of Neuroscience*, *19*, 3639–48.

Bennett, G., & Bennett, K. M. (2000). The presence of the dead: an empirical study. *Mortality*, *5*, 139–57.

Bennett, P., & Murphy, S. (1997). *Psychology and health promotion*. Buckingham, UK: Open University Press.

Bennett, P., Norman, P., Murphy, S., Moore, L. & Tudor-Smith, C. (1997). Health locus of control and value for health in smokers and non-smokers. *Health Psychology*, *16*, 179–82.

Bensing, J., van Dulmen, S. & Tates, K. (2003). Communication in context: new directions in communication research. *Patient Education and Counseling*, *50*, 27–32.

Berkanovic, E., Telesky, C. & Reeder, S. (1981). Structural and social psychological factors in the decision to seek medical care for symptoms. *Medical Care*, *19*, 693–709.

Berkman, L. F. (1995). The role of social relations in health promotion. *Psychosomatic Medicine*, *57*, 245–54.

Berkman, L. F., & Syme, S. L. (1979). Social networks, host resistance and mortality: a nine-year follow-up of Alameda County residents. *American Journal of Epidemiology*, *109*, 186–204.

Berkman, L. F., Glass, T., Brissette, I. & Seeman, T. E. (2000). From social integration to health: Durkheim in the new millennium. *Social Science & Medicine*, *51*, 843–57.

Bernard, L. C., & Krupat, E. (1994). *Health psychology: biopsychosocial factors in health and illness*. Fort Worth, TX: Harcourt Brace.

Bhattacharya, B. (2000). M.D. programmes in the United States with complementary and alternative medicine education opportunities: an ongoing listing. *Journal of Alternative and Complementary Medicine*, *6*, 77–90.

Bianchi, F., Zea, M., Poppen, P., Reisen, C. & Echeverry, J. (2004). Coping as a mediator of the impact of sociocultural factors on health behaviour among HIV-positive Latino gay men. *Psychology and Health*, *19*, 89–101.

Bishop, G. D. (1991). Understanding the understanding of illness: lay disease representations. In J. A. Skelton & R. T. Croyle (eds.), *Mental representation in health and illness* (pp. 32–59). New York: Springer.

Bishop S., & Warr, D. (2003). Coping, catastrophising and chronic pain in breast cancer. *Journal of Behavioral Medicine*, *26*, 265–81.

Bissell, P., May, C. R. & Noyce, P. R. (2004). From compliance to concordance: barriers to accomplishing a re-framed model of health care interactions. *Social Science & Medicine*, *58*, 851–62.

Bissell, P., Ward, P. R. & Noyce, P. R. (2001). The dependent consumer: reflections on accounts of the risks of non-prescription medicines. *Health: An Interdisciplinary Journal for the Social Study of Health, Illness and Medicine*, *5*, 5–30.

Black, R., Morris, S. & Bryce, J. (2003). Where and why are 10 million children dying each year? *Lancet*, *361*, 2226–34.

Blackhall, L., Frank, G., Murphy, S. Michel, V., Palmer, J. & Azen, S. (1999). Ethnicity and attitudes towards life sustaining technology. *Social Science and Medicine*, *48*, 1779–89.

Blane, D., Bartley, M. & Davey Smith, G. (1998). Making sense of socio-economic health inequalities. In D. Field & S. Taylor (eds.), *Sociological perspectives on health, illness and health care* (pp. 78–95). Oxford: Blackwell.

Blaxter, M. (1990). *Health and lifestyles.* London: Tavistock/Routledge.

Blonde, L., Cook, J. L. & Dey, J. (1999). Internet use by endocrinologists. *Recent Progress in Hormone Research, 54,* 1–29.

Bloom, J., Stewart, S., Chang, S. & Banks, P. (2004). Then and now: quality of life of young breast cancer survivors. *Psycho-Oncology, 13,* 147–60.

Blumenthal, J., Sherwood, A., Gulette, E., Georgiades, A. & Tweedy, D. (2002). Bio-behavioral approaches to the treatment of essential hypertension. *Journal of Consulting and Clinical Psychology, 70,* 569–89.

Bolmsjo I. (2000). Existential issues in palliative care: interviews with cancer patients. *Journal of Palliative Care, 16,* 20–4.

Bookwala, J., Coppola, K., Fagerlin, A., Ditto, P., Danks, J. & Smucker, W. (2001). Gender differences in older adults' preferences for life-sustaining medical treatments and end-of-life values. *Death Studies, 25,* 127–49.

Booth-Kewley, S., & Friedman, H. S. (1987). Psychological predictors of heart disease: a quantitative review. *Psychological Bulletin, 101,* 343–62.

Bordo, S. (1997). The body and the reproduction of femininity. In K. Conboy, N. Medina & S. Stanbury (eds.), *Writing on the body: female embodiment and feminist theory* (pp. 90–110). New York: Columbia University Press.

Borg, Jr., M. (2002). The Avalon Gardens Men's Association: a community health psychology case study. *Journal of Health Psychology, 7,* 345–57.

Boruchovitch, E., & Mednick, B. R. (1997). Cross-cultural differences in children's concepts of health and illness. *Revista de Saúde Pública, 31,* 448–56.

Botkin, J. R., Smith, K. R., Croyle, R. T., Baty, B. J., Wylie, J. E., Dutson, D. *et al.* (2003). Genetic testing for a BRCA1 mutation: prophylactic surgery and screening behaviour in women two years post testing. *American Journal of Medical Genetics, 118A,* 201–9.

Botteman, M., Pashos, C., Hauser, R., Laskin, B. & Redaelli, A. (2003). Quality of life aspects of bladder cancer: a review of the literature. *Quality of Life Research, 12,* 675–88.

Bourdieu, P. (1984). *Distinction: a social critique of the judgement of taste.* London: Routledge & Kegan Paul.

Bradbury, M. (1993). Contemporary representations of 'good' and 'bad' death. In D. Dickenson & M. Johnson (eds.), *Death, dying and bereavement* (pp. 68–71). London: Sage.

   (1999). *Representations of death: a social psychological perspective.* London: Routledge.

Braun, V. (2000). Conceptualizing the body. *Feminism and Psychology, 10,* 511–18.

Breckenridge, C. A., & Vogler, C. (2001). The critical limits of embodiment: disability's criticism. *Public Culture, 13,* 349–57.

Breen, N., Kessler, L. G. & Brown, M. L. (1996). Breast cancer control among the undeserved: an overview. *Breast Cancer Research and Treatment, 40,* 105–15.

Brehm, J. W. (1966). *A theory of psychological reactance.* New York: Academic Press.

Breslow, L. (1983). The potential of health promotion. In D. Mechanic (ed.), *Handbook of health, health care, and the health profession.* (pp. 50–66). New York: The Free Press.

Breslow, L., & Enstrom, J. E. (1980). Persistence of health habits and their relationship to mortality. *Preventive Medicine, 9,* 469–83.

Brissette, I., Scheier, M. F. & Carver, C. S. (2002). The role of optimism in social network development, coping, and psychological adjustment during a life transition. *Journal of Personality and Social Psychology, 82,* 102–11.

Britt, H., Miller, G., Knox, S., Charles, J., Valenti, L., Henderson, J. *et al.* (2002). *General practice activity in Australia 2001–02.* Canberra: Australian Institute of Health and Welfare (General Practice series no. 10).

Broadstock, M., Michie, S. & Marteau, T. (2000). Psychological consequences of predictive genetic testing: a systematic review. *European Journal of Human Genetics, 8,* 731–8.

Brock, B. M., Haefner, D. P. & Noble, D. S. (1988). Alameda County Redux: replication in Michigan. *Preventive Medicine, 17,* 483–95.

Bronfenbrenner, U. (1979). *The ecology of human development: experiments by nature and design.* London: Harvard University Press.

Broom, D. (1998). Gender and health. In J. Germov (ed.), *Second opinion: an introduction to health sociology* (pp. 39–56). Oxford: Oxford University Press.

Brown Parlee, M. (1998). Situated knowledges of personal embodiment: transgender activists' and psychological theorists' perspectives on 'sex' and 'gender'. In H. J. Stam (ed.), *The body and psychology* (pp. 120–40). London: Sage.

Brown, P. (1995). Naming and framing: the social construction of diagnosis and illness. *Journal of Health and Social Behavior,* (extra issue), 34–52.

Brown, R. J. (2004). Psychological mechanisms of medically unexplained symptoms: an integrative conceptual model. *Psychological Bulletin, 130,* 793–812.

Brown-Séquard, C. (1889). Note on the effects produced on man by subcutaneous injections of a liquid obtained from the testicles of animals. *Lancet, 2,* 105–7.

Brundtland, G. H. (2002). The future of the world's health. In C. Koop, C. Pearson & M. Schwarz (eds.), *Critical issues in global health* (pp. 3–11). San Francisco: Jossey-Bass.

Buchbinder, D. (1994). *Masculinities and identities.* Melbourne: Melbourne University Press.

Bunton, R., & Burrows, R. (1995). Consumption and health in the 'epidemiological' clinic of late modern medicine. In R. Bunton, S. Nettleton & R. Burrows (eds.), *The sociology of health promotion* (pp. 206–22). London: Routledge.

Burgess, C., Hunter, M. & Ramirez, A. (2001). A qualitative study of delay among women reporting symptoms of breast cancer. *British Journal of General Practice, 51,* 967–71.

Burrows, R., Nettleton, S. & Bunton, R. (1995). Sociology and health promotion: health, risk and consumption under late modernism. In R. Bunton, S. Nettleton & R. Burrows (eds.), *The sociology of health promotion* (pp. 1–9). London: Routledge.

Bury, M. (1982). Chronic illness as biographical disruption. *Sociology of Health and Illness, 4*, 167–82.

(1988). Meanings at risk: the experience of arthritis. In R. Anderson & N. Bury (eds.), *Living with chronic illness: the experience of patients and their families.* London: Unwin Hyman.

(1991). The sociology of chronic illness: a review of research and prospects. *Sociology of Health and Illness, 13*, 451–68.

(2001). Illness narratives: Fact or fiction? *Sociology of Health and Illness, 23*, 263–85.

Bush, J. (2000). 'It's just part of being a woman': cervical screening, the body and femininity. *Social Science & Medicine, 50*, 429–44.

Buske-Kirschbaum, A., Kirschbaum, C., Stierle, H., Lehnert, H. & Hellhammer, D. (1992). Conditioned increase of natural killer cell activity (NKCA) in humans. *Psychosomatic Medicine, 54*, 123–32.

Butcher, H., & Buckwalter, K. (2002). Exasperations as blessings: meaning-making and caregiving experience. *Journal of Aging and Identity, 7*, 113–32.

Butler, J. (1990). *Gender trouble: feminism and the subversion of identity.* London: Routledge.

Butow, P. N., Dowsett, S., Hagerty, R. & Tattersall, M. H. (2002). Communicating prognosis to patients with metastatic disease: what do they really want to know? *Supportive Care in Cancer, 10*, 161–8.

Butow, P. N., Lobb, E. A., Meiser, B., Barratt, A. & Tucker K. M. (2003). Psychological outcomes and risk perception after genetic testing and counselling in breast cancer: a systematic review. *Medical Journal of Australia, 178*, 77–81.

Cacioppo, J. T. (1994). Social neuroscience: autonomic neuroendocrine and immune responses to stress. *Psychophysiology, 31*, 113–28.

Caddell, D. P., & Newton, R. R. (1995). Euthanasia: American attitudes toward the physician role. *Social Science & Medicine, 40*, 1671–81.

Calnan, M. (1984). The Health Belief Model and participation in programmes for the early detection of breast cancer: a comparative analysis. *Social Science & Medicine, 19*, 823–30.

Cameron, L. D., Leventhal, E. A. & Leventhal, H. (1995). Seeking medical care in response to symptoms and life stress. *Psychosomatic Medicine, 57*, 37–47.

Campbell, C. (2003). *Letting them die: why HIV prevention programmes often fail.* Bloomington, IN: Indiana University Press.

Campbell, C., & Jovchelovitch, S. (2000). Health, community and development: towards a social psychology of participation. *Journal of Community and Applied Social Psychology, 10*, 255–70.

Campbell, C., & Murray, M. (2004). Community health psychology: promoting analysis and action for social change. *Journal of Health Psychology, 9*, 187–95.

Campbell, C., & Williams, B. (1999). Beyond the biomedical and behavioural: towards an integrated approach to HIV prevention in the Southern African mining industry. *Social Science & Medicine, 48*, 1625–39.

Canales, M. K. (2004). Taking care of self: health care decision making of American Indian women. *Health Care for Women International, 25*, 411–35.

Cannon, W. B. (1929). *Bodily changes in pain, hunger, fear and rage* (2nd edn). New York: Appleton.

Carrese, J., Mullaney, J., Faden, R. & Finucane, T. (2002). Planning for death but not serious future illness: qualitative study of household elderly patients. *British Medical Journal*, *325*, 125–9.

Carroll, D. (1992). *Health psychology: stress, behaviour and disease.* London: Falmer Press.

Carroll, D., & Davey Smith, G. (1997). Health and socio-economic position: a commentary. *Journal of Health Psychology*, *2*, 275–82.

Carroll, D., & Sheffield, D. (1998). Social psychophysiology, social circumstances and health. *Annals of Behavioral Medicine*, *20*, 333–7.

Carroll, D., Davey Smith, G. & Bennett, P. (1996). Some observations on health and socioeconomic status. *Journal of Health Psychology*, *1*, 23–39.

Carter, B. (2002). Chronic pain in childhood and the medical encounter: professional ventriloquism and hidden voices. *Qualitative Health Research*, *12*, 28–41.

Carverhill, P. A. (2002). Qualitative research in thanatology. *Death Studies*, *26*, 195–207.

Castel, R. (1991). From dangerousness to risk. In G. Burchell, C. Gordon & P. Miller (eds.), *The Foucault effect: studies in governmentality* (pp. 281–98). Chicago: University of Chicago Press.

Chamberlain, K. (1997). Socio-economic health differentials: from structure to experience. *Journal of Health Psychology*, *2*, 399–411.

    (2000). Methodolatry and qualitative health research. *Journal of Health Psychology*, *5*, 285–96.

Chamberlain, K., & O'Neill, D. (1998). Understanding social class differences in health: a qualitative analysis of smokers' health beliefs. *Psychology and Health, 13,* 1105–19.

Chamberlain, K., & Zika, S. (1990). The minor events approach to stress: support for the use of daily hassles. *British Journal of Psychology*, *81*, 469–81.

Chamberlain, K., Stephens, C. & Lyons, A. C. (1997). Encompassing experience: meanings and methods in health psychology. *Psychology and Health*, *12*, 691–709.

Chan, P. P., Morley, D. S., Hong, W. & Mostofsky, D. I. (2002). Health psychology and behavioural medicine in China. *Asian Psychologist*, *3*, 3–10.

Chapple, A., Campbell, S., Rogers, A. & Roland, M. (2002). Users' understanding of medical knowledge in general practice. *Social Science and Medicine*, *54*, 1215–24.

Chapple, A., Ziebland, S. & McPherson, A. (2004). Stigma, shame, and blame experienced by patients with lung cancer: qualitative study. *British Medical Journal*, *328*, 1470–4.

Chapple, A., Ziebland, S., Shepperd, S., Miller, R., Herxheimer, A. & McPherson, A. (2002). Why men with prostate cancer want wider access to prostate specific antigen testing: qualitative study. *British Medical Journal*, *325*, 737–8.

Charmaz, K. (1983). Loss of self: a fundamental form of suffering in the chronically ill. *Sociology of Health and Illness*, *5*, 168–95.

(2000). Experiencing chronic illness. In G. Albrecht, R. Fitzpatrick & S. Scrimshaw (eds.), *The handbook of social studies in health and medicine.* London: Sage.

Chen, Y. (2001). Chinese values, health and nursing. *Journal of Advanced Nursing, 36,* 270–3.

Cherry, D. K., Burt, C. W. & Woodwell, D. A. (2003). National ambulatory medical care survey: 2001 summary. *Advance Data from Vital and Health Statistics, No. 337.* Hyattsville, MD: National Center for Health Statistics.

Chescheir, N. C., & Hansen, W. F. (1999). What's new in perinatalogy. *Pediatrics in Review, 20,* 57–63.

Cheung, J., & Hocking, P. (2004). The experience of spousal carers of people with multiple sclerosis. *Qualitative Health Research, 14,* 153–66.

Christensen, A. J., Edwards, D. L., Wiebe, J. S., Benotsch, E. G., McKelvey, L., Andrews, M. *et al.* (1996). Effect of verbal self-disclosure on natural killer cell activity: moderating influence of cynical hostility. *Psychosomatic Medicine, 58,* 150–5.

Cicirelli, V. G. (2001). Personal meanings of death in older adults and young adults in relation to their fears of death. *Death Studies, 25,* 663–83.

Cioffi, D. (1991). Beyond attentional strategies: a cognitive-perceptual model of somatic interpretation. *Psychological Bulletin, 109,* 25–41.

Clark, D., & Seymour, J. (1999). *Reflections on palliative care.* Buckingham, UK: Open University Press.

Clark, N. M. (2003). Management of chronic disease by patients. *Annual Review of Public Health, 24,* 289–313.

Clarke, J., & Robinson, J. (1999). Testicular cancer: medicine and machismo in the media (1980–94). *Health: An Interdisciplinary Journal for the Social Study of Health, Illness and Medicine, 3,* 263–82.

Cline, R. J., & Haynes, K. M. (2001). Consumer health information seeking on the Internet: the state of the art. *Health Education Research, 16,* 671–92.

Coburn, D. (2004). Beyond the income inequality hypothesis: class, neo-liberalism and health inequalities. *Social Science & Medicine, 58,* 41–56.

Cockerham, W. C., Kunz, G. & Lueschen, G. (1988). Psychological distress, perceived health status and physician utilisation in America and West Germany. *Social Science & Medicine, 26,* 829–38.

Codori, A., Zawacki, K. L., Petersen, G. M., Miglioretti, D. L., Bacon, J. A., Trimbath, J. D. *et al.* (2003). Genetic testing for hereditary colorectal cancer in children: long-term psychological effects. *American Journal of Medical Genetics, 116A,* 117–28.

Coe, C. L., & Lubach, G. R. (2003). Critical periods of special health relevance for psychoneuroimmunology. *Brain, Behavior and Immunity, 17,* 3–12.

Cohen, D., McCubbin, M., Collin, J. & Pérodeau, G. (2001). Medications as social phenomena. *Health: an Interdisciplinary Journal for the Social Study of Health, Illness and Medicine, 5,* 441–69.

Cohen, S. (1988). Psychosocial models of the role of social support in etiology of physical disease. *Health Psychology, 7,* 269–97.

(1995). Psychological stress and susceptibility to upper respiratory infections. *American Journal of Critical Care Medicine, 152,* 553–8.

Cohen, S., & Herbert, T. B. (1996). Health psychology: psychological factors and physical disease from the perspective of human psychoneuroimmunology. *Annual Review of Psychology*, *47*, 113–42.

Cohen, S., & Williamson, G. M. (1991). Stress and infectious disease in humans. *Psychological Bulletin*, *109*, 5–24.

Cohen, S., & Wills, T. A. (1985). Stress, social support and the buffering hypothesis. *Psychological Bulletin*, *98*, 5–24.

Cohen, S., Doyle, W. J., Skoner, D. P., Fireman, P., Gwaltney, J. M. & Newsom, J. T. (1995). State and trait negative affect as predictors of objective and subjective symptoms of respiratory viral infections. *Journal of Personality and Social Psychology*, *68*, 159–69.

Cohen, S., Doyle, W. J., Skoner, D. P., Rabin, B. S. & Gwaltney, J. M. (1997). Social ties and susceptibility to the common cold. *Journal of the American Medical Association*, *277*, 1940–4.

Cohen, S., Miller, G. E. & Rabin, B. S. (2001). Psychological stress and antibody response to immunization: a critical review of the human literature. *Psychosomatic Medicine*, *63*, 7–18.

Cohen, S., Tyrrell, D. A. & Smith, A. P. (1991). Psychological stress and susceptibility to the common cold. *New England Journal of Medicine*, *325*, 606–12.

Colbert, D. (2003). *Deadly emotions: understand the mind–body–spirit connection that can heal or destroy you*. Nashville, TN: Thomas Nelson Publishers.

Compas, B. E., Connor-Smith, J. K., Saltzman, H., Thomsen, A. H. & Wadsworth, M. E. (2001). Coping with stress during childhood and adolescence: problems, progress and potential in theory and research. *Psychological Bulletin*, *127*, 87–127.

Connell, R. W. (1993). The big picture: masculinities in recent world history. *Theory and Society*, *22*, 507–623.

Conner, M., & Norman, P. (1995). The role of social cognition in health behaviours. In M. Conner & P. Norman (eds.), *Predicting health behaviour* (pp. 1–22). Buckingham, UK: Open University Press.

Conrad, P. (1985). The meaning of medications: another look at compliance. *Social Science and Medicine*, *20*, 29–37.

Consedine, N. S., Magai, C. & Chin, S. (2004). Hostility and anxiety differentially predict cardiovascular disease in men and women. *Sex Roles*, *50*, 63–75.

Cook, J. (2002). Tropical diseases. In C. Koop, C. Pearson & M. Schwarz (eds.), *Critical issues in global health* (pp. 135–43). San Francisco: Jossey-Bass.

Cooper, H. (2002). Investigating socio-economic explanations for gender and ethnic inequalities in health. *Social Science and Medicine*, *54*, 693–706.

Cooper, R. (1993). Health and the social status of blacks in the United States. *Annals of Epidemiology*, *3*, 137–44.

Cornish, F. (2004). Making 'context' concrete: a dialogical approach to the society–health relation. *Journal of Health Psychology*, *9*, 281–94.

Corr, C. A. (1993). Coping with dying: lessons that we should and should not learn from the work of Elizabeth Kubler-Ross. *Death Studies*, *17*, 69–83.

Costa Jr, P. T., & McCrae, R. R. (1987). Neuroticism, somatic complaints and disease: is the bark worse than the bite? *Journal of Personality*, *55*, 316.

Coward, D. (2000). Making meaning within the experience of life-threatening illness. In G. Reker & K. Chamberlain (eds.), *Exploring existential meaning: optimizing human development across the life span* (pp. 157–70). Thousand Oaks, CA: Sage.

Crawford, R. (1980). Healthism and the medicalization of everyday life. *International Journal of Health Services, 10*, 365–88

(1994). The boundaries of the self and the unhealthy other: Reflections on health, culture and AIDS. *Social Science and Medicine, 38*, 1347–65.

Crichton, M. (1990). Greater expectations: the future of medicine lies not in treating illness but in preventing it. *Newsweek*, 24 September.

Crimmins, E. M., & Saito, Y. (2001). Trends in healthy life expectancy in the United States, 1970–1990: gender, racial, and educational differences. *Social Science and Medicine, 52*, 1629–41.

Crossley, M. L. (2000). *Rethinking health psychology*. Buckingham, UK: Open University Press.

(2001). Do we need to rethink health psychology? *Psychology, Health and Medicine, 6*, 243–65.

(2003). 'Would you consider yourself a healthy person?': Using focus groups to explore health as a moral phenomenon. *Journal of Health Psychology, 8*, 501–14.

Croyle, R. T., & Williams, K. D. (1991). Reactions to medical diagnosis: the role of illness stereotypes. *Basic and Applied Social Psychology, 12*, 227–41.

Cunningham-Burley, S., & Backett-Milburn, K. (2001). Introduction. In S. Cunningham-Burley & K. Backett-Milburn (eds.), *Exploring the body* (pp. xii–xxi). Houndmills, UK: Palgrave.

Cussons, A., Bhagat, C., Fletcher, S. & Walsh, J. (2002). Brown-Séquard revisited: a lesson from history on the placebo effect of androgen treatment. *Medical Journal of Australia, 177*, 678–9.

d'Houtard, A., & Field, M. G. (1984). The image of health: variations in perception by social class in a French population. *Sociology of Health and Illness, 6*, 30–60.

Dabbs, A., Hoffman, L., Swigart, V., Happ, M., Dauber, J., McCurry, K. *et al.* (2004). Striving for normalcy: symptoms and the threat of rejection after lung transplantation. *Social Science and Medicine, 59*, 1473–84.

Davey Smith, G., Bartley, M. & Blane, D. (1990). The Black Report on socioeconomic inequalities in health: 10 years on. *British Medical Journal, 301*, 373–7.

Davey Smith, G., Gunnell, D. J. & Ben-Shlomo, Y. (2000). Life course approaches to socio-economic differentials in case-specific adult mortality. In D. A. Leon & G. Walt (eds.), *Poverty, inequality and health*. Oxford: Oxford University Press.

David, R. J., & Collins, J. W. (1997). Differing birth weights among infants of US-born blacks, African-born blacks, and US-born whites. *New England Journal of Medicine, 337*, 1209–14.

Davies, D. J. (1997). *Death, ritual and belief: the rhetoric of funerary rites*. London: Cassell.

Davies, M. M., & Bath, P. A. (2001). The maternity information concerns of Somali women in the United Kingdom. *Journal of Advanced Nursing, 36*, 237–45.

Davis, J. (2002). Disenfranchising the disabled: the inaccessibility of Internet-based health information. *Journal of Health Communication, 7,* 355–68.

Davis, L. (1995). *Enforcing normalcy: disability, deafness and the body.* London: Verso.

Davis, M. (1981). Sex differences in reporting osteoarthritic symptoms: a sociomedical approach. *Journal of Health and Social Behavior, 22,* 298–310.

Davison, C., & Davey Smith, G. (1995). The baby and the bathwater: examining socio-cultural and free-market critiques of health promotion. In R. Bunton, S. Nettleton & R. Burrows (eds.), *The sociology of health promotion* (pp. 91–9). London: Routledge.

Davison, C., Davey Smith, G. & Frankel, S. (1991). Lay epidemiology and the prevention paradox: the implication of coronary candidacy for health education. *Sociology of Health and Illness, 13,* 1–19.

Davison, K., Pennebaker, J. & Dickerson, S. (2000). Who talks? The social psychology of illness support groups. *American Psychologist, 55,* 205–17.

Davison, S., Frankel, S. & Davey Smith, G. (1992). The limits of lifestyle: re-assessing 'fatalism' in the popular culture of illness prevention. *Social Science & Medicine, 34,* 675–85.

Daykin, N., & Naidoo, J. (1995). Feminist critiques of health promotion. In R. Bunton, S. Nettleton & R. Burrows (eds.), *The sociology of health promotion* (pp. 59–69). London: Routledge.

de la Cancela, V., Chin, J. L. & Jenkins, Y. M. (1998). *Community health psychology: empowerment for diverse communities.* New York: Routledge.

DeBar, L., Vuckovic, N., Schneider, J. & Ritenbaugh, C. (2003). Use of complementary and alternative medicine for temperomandibular disorders. *Journal of Orofacial Pain, 17,* 224–36.

Degner, L., Hack, T., O'Neil, J. & Kristjanson, L. (2003). A new approach to eliciting meaning in the context of breast cancer. *Cancer Nursing, 26,* 169–78.

de-Graft Aikins, A. (2004). Strengthening quality and continuity of diabetes care in rural Ghana: a critical social psychological approach. *Journal of Health Psychology, 9,* 295–309.

Delbanco, T. (2001). Hospital medicine: understanding and drawing on the patient's perspective. *The American Journal of Medicine, 111(9B),* 2S–4S.

DeLongis, A., Folkman, S. & Lazarus, R. S. (1988). The impact of daily stress on health and mood: psychological and social resources as mediators. *Journal of Personality and Social Psychology, 54,* 486–95.

Denzin, N. K., & Lincoln, Y. S. (1994). Introduction: entering the field of qualitative research. In N. K. Denzin & Y. S. Lincoln (eds.), *Handbook of qualitative research* (pp. 1–17). Thousand Oaks, CA: Sage.

Deyo, R. A. (2002). Cascade effects of medical technology. *Annual Review of Public Health, 23,* 23–44.

Diamond, J. (1998). *C Because cowards get cancer too . . .* London: Random House.

Diefenbach, N., Hamrick, N., Uzzo, R., Pollack, A., Horwitz, E., Greenberg, R. *et al.* (2003). Clinical, demographic and psychosocial correlates of complementary and alternative medicine use by men diagnosed with localised prostate cancer. *Journal of Urology, 170,* 166–9.

DiMatteo, M. (2004). Social support and patient adherence to medical treatment: a meta-analysis. *Health Psychology, 23,* 207–18.

DiMatteo, M. R., & Kahn, K. L. (1997). Psychosocial aspects of childbirth. In S. J. Gallant, G. P. Keita & R. Royak-Schaler (eds.), *Health care for women: psychological, social and behavioral influences* (pp. 175–86). Washington, DC: American Psychological Association.

DiMatteo, M. R., Hays, R. D. & Prince, L. M. (1986). Relationships of physicians' nonverbal communication skills to patient satisfaction, appointment non-compliance, and physician workload. *Health Psychology, 5,* 581–94.

Dobson, R. (2002). Sharing of uncertainty can unnerve patients. *British Medical Journal, 325,* 1319.

Doering, S., Katzlberger, F., Rumpold, G., Roessler, S., Hofstoetter, B., Schatz, D. *et al.* (2000). Videotape preparation of patients before hip replacement surgery reduces stress. *Psychosomatic Medicine, 62,* 365–73.

Dohrenwend, B. S., Dohrenwend, B. P., Dodson, M. & Shrout, P. E. (1984). Symptoms, hassles, social supports, and life events: problem of confounded measures. *Journal of Abnormal Psychology, 93,* 222–30.

Donaldson, L. (2000). Disease emergence and health transitions in the last millennium. *Journal of the Royal College of Physicians of London, 34,* 543–8.

Donovan, J., & Blake, D. (1992). Patient non-compliance, deviance or reasoned decision making? *Social Science & Medicine, 34,* 507–13.

Dorval, M., Patenaude, A. F., Schneider, K. A., Kieffer, S. A., DiGianni, L., Kalkbrenner, K. J. *et al.* (2000). Anticipated versus actual emotional reactions to disclosure of results of genetic tests for cancer susceptibility: findings from p53 and BRCA1 testing programs. *Journal of Clinical Oncology, 18,* 2135–42.

Dosanjh, S., Barnes, J. & Bhandari, M. (2001). Barriers to breaking bad news among medical and surgical residents. *Medical Education, 35,* 197–205.

Doyal, L. (1995). *What makes women sick: gender and the political economy of health.* Basingstoke, UK: Macmillan.

   (2000). Gender equity in health: debates and dilemmas. *Social Science & Medicine, 51,* 931–9.

   (2001). Sex, gender and health: the need for a new approach. *British Medical Journal, 323,* 1061–3.

Drew, P. (2001). Spotlight on the patient. *Text, 21,* 261–8.

Drew, S. (2003). Self-reconstruction and biographical revisioning: survival following cancer in childhood or adolescence. *Health: an Interdisciplinary Journal for the Social Study of Health, Illness and Medicine, 7,* 181–99.

Dubbert, P. M. (2002). Physical activity and exercise: recent advances and current challenges. *Journal of Consulting and Clinical Psychology, 70,* 526–36.

Duden, B. (1991) *The woman beneath the skin: a doctor's patients in eighteenth-century Germany.* Cambridge, MA: Harvard University Press.

Duffy, M. (1997). You say words that I find frightening. In *Vital signs: crip culture talks back.* Directed by S. L. Snyder & D. T. Mitchell. Chicago: Brace Yourselves Productions.

Duits, A., Boeke, S., Taams, M., Passchier, J. & Erdman, R. (1997). Prediction of quality of life after coronary artery bypass surgery: a review and evaluation of multiple, recent studies. *Psychosomatic Medicine, 59,* 257–68.

Durie, M. (1998). *Whaiora: Maori health development* (2nd edn). Auckland, New Zealand: Oxford.

Dutta-Bergman, M. J. (2004). Poverty, structural barriers, and health: a Santali narrative of health communication. *Qualitative Health Research*, *14*, 1107–22.

Duval, S., & Wicklund, R. A. (1972). *A theory of objective self-awareness*. New York: Academic Press.

Eagly, A. H. (1987). Gender and social influence: a social psychological analysis. *American Psychologist*, *38*, 971–81.

Eccles, R. (2002). The powerful placebo in cough studies? *Pulmonary Pharmacology & Therapeutics*, *15*, 303–8.

Edelmann, R. J. (2000). *Psychosocial aspects of the health care process*. Harlow, UK: Prentice Hall.

Edley, N. (2001). Unravelling social constructionism. *Theory and Psychology*, *11*, 433–41.

Eisenberg, D., Davis, R., Ettner, S., Appel, S., Wilkey, S., Van Rompay, M. *et al.* (1998). Trends in alternative medicine use in the United States, 1990–1997: results of a follow-up national survey. *Journal of the American Medical Association*, *280*, 1569–75.

Eisenberg, D., Kessler, R., Van Rompay, M., Kaptchuk, T., Wilkey, S., Appel, S. *et al.* (2001). Perceptions about complementary therapies relative to conventional therapies among adults who use both: results from a national survey. *Annals of Internal Medicine*, *135*, 344–51.

Eiser, C. (2004). *Children with cancer: the quality of life*. London: Lawrence Erlbaum.

Eiser, C., Patterson, D. & Eiser, J. R. (1983). Children's knowledge of health and illness: implications for health education. *Child: Care, Health and Development*, *9*, 285–92.

Elliott, B., Renier, C., Haller, I. & Elliott, T. (2004). Health-related quality of life (HRQoL) in patients with cancer and other concurrent illnesses. *Quality of Life Research*, *13*, 457–62.

Eng, T. R., Maxfield, A., Patrick, K., Deering, M. J., Ratzan, S. C. & Gustafson, D. H. (1998). Access to health information and support: a public highway or a private road? *Journal of the American Medical Association*, *280*, 1371–5.

Engel, G. L. (1977). The need for a new medical model: a challenge for biomedicine. *Science*, *196*, 129–36.

Engle, D. (2001). Psychosocial aspects of the organ transplantation experience: what has been established and what we need for the future. *Journal of Clinical Psychology*, *57*, 521–49.

Eslick, G. D., Lim, L. L., Byles, J. E., Xia, H. H. & Talley, N.J. (1999). Association of *Helicobacter pylori* infection with gastric carcinoma: a meta-analysis. *American Journal of Gastroenterology*, *94*, 2373–9.

Esterling, B. A., Antoni, M. H., Fletcher, M. A., Margulies, S. & Schneiderman, N. (1994). Emotional disclosure through writing or speaking modulates latent Epstein-Barr virus antibody titers. *Journal of Consulting and Clinical Psychology*, *62*, 130–40.

Esteva, G. (1992). Development. In W. Sachs (ed.), *The development dictionary* (pp. 6–25). London: Zed Books.

Evans, G. W., & Kantrowitz, E. (2002). Socioeconomic status and health: the potential role of environmental risk exposure. *Annual Review of Public Health*, *23*, 303–31.

Ewart, C. K. (1991). Social action theory for a public health psychology. *American Psychologist, 9*, 931–46.

Exley, C. (1999). Testaments and memories: negotiating after-death identities. *Mortality, 4*, 249–67.

Faircloth, C. A., Boylstein, C., Rittman, M., Young, M. E. & Gubrium, J. (2004). Sudden illness and biographical flow in narratives of stroke recovery. *Sociology of Health and Illness, 26*, 242–61.

Farber, E., Mirsalimi, H. & Williams, K. (2003). Meaning of illness and psychological adjustment to HIV/AIDS. *Psychosomatics, 44*, 485–91.

Farran, C. (2001). Family caregiving intervention research: where have we been? Where are we going? *Journal of Gerontological Nursing, 27*, 38–45.

Farrell, M., Ryan, S. & Langrick, B. (2001). 'Breaking bad news' within a paediatric setting: an evaluation of a collaborative education workshop to support health professionals. *Journal of Advanced Nursing, 36*, 765–75.

Fayers, P., & Machin, D. (2000). *Quality of life: assessment, analysis and interpretation*. Chichester, UK: Wiley.

Fernández-Esquer, M. E., Espinoza, P., Ramirez, A. G. & McAlister, A. L. (2003). Repeated Pap smear among Mexican-American women. *Health Education Research, 18*, 477–87.

Ferrell, B., Smith, S., Ervin, K., Itano, J. & Melancon, C. (2003). A qualitative analysis of social concerns of women with ovarian cancer. *Psycho-Oncology, 12*, 647–63.

Field, D., & James, N. (1993). Where and how people die. In D. Clark (ed.), *The future for palliative care: issues of policy and practice* (pp. 6–29). Buckingham, UK: Open University Press.

Fine, M. (1985). Coping with rape: critical perspectives on consciousness. *Imagination, Cognition, and Personality, 3*, 249–67.

Finkler, K. (1991). *Physicians at work, patients in pain: biomedical practice and patient response in Mexico*. Boulder, CO: Westview Press.

Finn, M., & Dell, P. (1999). Practices of body management: transgenderism and embodiment. *Journal of Community and Applied Social Psychology, 9*, 463–76.

Firth, S. (1993). Approaches to death in Hindu and Sikh communities in Britain. In D. Dickenson & M. Johnson (eds.), *Death, dying and bereavement* (pp. 26–32). London: Sage.

Fisher, J. (2001). Harming and benefiting the dead. *Death Studies, 25*, 557–68.

Flacker, J. M., Won, A., Kiely, D. K. & Iloputaife, I. (2001). Differing perceptions of end-of-life care in long-term care. *Journal of Palliative Medicine, 4*, 9–13.

Flick, U., Fischer, C., Neuber, A., Schwartz, F. W. & Walter, U. (2003). Health in the context of growing old: social representations of health. *Journal of Health Psychology, 8*, 539–56.

Fogarty, J. S. (1997). Reactance theory and patient noncompliance. *Social Science & Medicine, 45*, 1277–88.

Folkman, S., & Moskowitz, J. (2004). Coping: pitfalls and promise. *Annual Review of Psychology, 55*, 745–74.

Folkman, S., Lazarus, R. S., Dunkel-Schetter, C., DeLongis, A. & Gruen, R. J. (1986). The dynamics of a stressful encounter: cognitive appraisal, coping and encounter outcomes. *Journal of Personality and Social Psychology*, *50*, 992–1003.

Foote-Ardah, C. E. (2003). The meaning of complementary and alternative medicine practices among people with HIV in the United States: strategies for managing everyday life. *Sociology of Health and Illness*, *25*, 481–500.

Forsberg, A., Baeckman, L. & Svensson, E. (2002). Liver transplant recipients' ability to cope during the first 12 months after transplantation: a prospective study. *Scandinavian Journal of Caring Sciences*, *16*, 345–52.

Fortner, B. V., & Neimeyer, R. A. (1999). Death anxiety in older adults: a quantitative review. *Death Studies*, *23*, 387–411.

Fortner, B. V., Neimeyer, R. A. & Rybarczyk, B. (2000). Correlates of death anxiety in older adults: a comprehensive review. In A. Tomer (ed.), *Death attitudes and the older adult: theories, concepts and applications* (pp. 95–108). Philadelphia, PA: Taylor & Francis.

Foster, P. (1995). *Women and the health care industry: an unhealthy relationship?* Buckingham, UK: Open University Press.

Foss, L., & Rothenberg, K. (1987). *The second medical revolution: from biomedicine to infomedicine*. Boston: Shambhala.

Foucault, M. (1975). *The birth of the clinic: an archaeology of medical perception* (trans. A. M. Sheridan). New York: Vintage Books.

Francis, M. E., & Pennebaker, J. W. (1992). Putting stress into words: the impact of writing on physiological, absentee, and self-reported emotional well-being measures. *American Journal of Health Promotion*, *6*, 280–7.

Frank, A. (1995). *The wounded storyteller*. Chicago: University of Chicago Press.
    (1997) Illness as moral occasion: restoring agency to ill people. *Health: an Interdisciplinary Journal for the Social Study of Health, Illness and Medicine*, *1*, 131–48.

Franke, G., Heemann, U., Kohnle, M., Luetkes, P., Maehner, N. & Reimer, J. (2000). Quality of life in patients before and after kidney transplantation. *Psychology and Health*, *14*, 1037–49.

Frankel, S., Davison, C. & Davey Smith, G. (1991). Lay epidemiology and the rationality of responses to health education. *British Journal of General Practice*, *41*, 428–30.

Frantz, T., Farrell, M. & Trolley, B. (2001). Positive outcomes of losing a loved one. In R. A. Neimeyer (ed.), *Meaning reconstruction and the experience of loss* (pp. 191–209). Washington, DC: American Psychological Association.

French, S. (1994). Attitudes of health professionals towards disabled people: a discussion and review of the literature. *Physiotherapy*, *80*, 687–93.

Freund, P., McGuire, M. & Podhurst, L. (eds.) (2003). *Health, illness, and the social body: a critical sociology*. Upper Saddle River, NJ: Prentice Hall.

Friedson, E. (1970). *Professional dominance: the social structure of medical care*. Chicago: Aldine

Friis, R. H., Nomura, W. L., Ma, C. X. & Swan, J. H. (2003). Socioepidemiologic and health-related correlates of walking for exercise among the elderly: results from the longitudinal study of aging. *Journal of Aging and Physical Activity*, *11*, 54–65.

Furnham, A. (1997). Lay theories of work stress. *Work and Stress*, *11*, 68–78.

G8 (Group of 8 Nations). (2001). *Communiqué*. Genoa, July 22. Retrieved 31 December 2004 from the G8 website: http://www.g8.utoronto.ca/summit/2001genoa/finalcommunique.html.

Galvin, R. (2002). Disturbing notions of chronic illness and individual responsibility: towards a genealogy of morals. *Health: An Interdisciplinary Journal for the Social Study of Health, Illness and Medicine, 6,* 107–37.

Gannon, L., & Ekstrom, B. (1993). Attitudes towards the menopause: the influence of sociocultural paradigms. *Psychology of Women Quarterly, 17,* 275–88.

Gannon, L., & Stevens, J. (1998). Portraits of menopause in the mass media. *Women and Health, 27,* 1–15.

Gannon, L. R. (1999). *Women and ageing: transcending the myths.* London: Routledge.

Ganther, J. M., Weiderholt, J. B. & Kreling, D. H. (2001). Measuring patients' medical care preferences: care-seeking versus self-treating. *Medical Decision Making, 21,* 133–40.

Gardner, K., & Chapple, A. (1999). Barriers to referral in patients with angina: qualitative study. *British Medical Journal, 319,* 418–21.

Garry, R., Fountain, J., Mason, S., Napp, V., Brown, J., Hawe, J. *et al.* (2004). The eVALuate study: two parallel randomized trials, one comparing laparoscopic with abdominal hysterectomy, the other comparing laparoscopic with vaginal hysterectomy. *British Medical Journal, 328,* 129–33.

Garssen, B. (2004). Psychological factors and cancer development: evidence after 30 years of research. *Clinical Psychology Review, 24,* 315–38.

Geczi, L., Gomez, F., Horvath, Z., Bak, M., Kisbenedek, L. & Bodrogi, I. (2001). Three-year results of the first educational and early detection program for testicular cancer in Hungary. *Oncology, 60,* 228–34.

Genazzani, A. R., & Gambaccuani, M. (1999). Hormone replacement therapy: the perspectives for the 21st century. *Maturitas, 32,* 11–17.

Gergen, K. (1985). The social constructionist movement in modern psychology. *American Psychologist, 40,* 266–75.

Gergen, K., & Gergen, M. (1986). Narrative form and the construction of psychological science. In T. R. Sarbin (ed.), *Narrative psychology* (pp. 22–44). New York: Praeger.

Germain, A. (2002). Women's health. In C. Koop, C. Pearson & M. Schwarz (eds.), *Critical issues in global health* (pp. 221–8). San Francisco: Jossey-Bass.

Gesser, G. P., Wong, P. & Reker, G. T. (1987–8). Death attitudes across the life-span: the development and validation of the Death Attitude Profile (DAP). *Omega: Journal of Death and Dying, 16,* 113–28.

GFATM (Global Fund to Fight AIDS, Tuberculosis and Malaria). (2004). *Pledges.* Retrieved 31 December 2004 from the GFATM website: http://www.globalfundatm.org.

Gibler, W. B., Armstrong, P. W., Ohman, E. M., Weaver, W. D., Stebbins, A. L., Gore, J. M. *et al.* (2002). Persistence of delays in presentation and treatment for patients with acute myocardial infarction: the GUSTO-I and GUSTO-III experience. *Annals of Emergency Medicine, 39,* 123–30.

Giddens, A. (1991). *Modernity and self-identity: self and society in the late modern age.* Stanford, CA: Stanford University Press.

Gifford, S. M. (1986). The meaning of lumps: a case study of the ambiguities of risk. In C. R. Janes, R. Stall & S. M. Gifford (eds.), *Anthropology and epidemiology: interdisciplinary approaches to the study of health and disease* (pp. 213–48). New York: D. Reidel.

Gijsbers van Wijk, C. M. & Kolk, A. M. (1996). Psychometric evaluation of symptom perception related measures. *Personality and Individual Differences*, *20*, 55–70.

  (1997). Sex differences in physical symptoms: the contribution of symptom perception theory. *Social Science & Medicine*, *45*, 231–46.

Gijsbers van Wijk, C. M., Huisman, H. & Kolk, A. M. (1999). Gender differences in physical symptoms and illness behaviour: a health diary study. *Social Science & Medicine*, *49*, 1061–74.

Gill, J. S., & Donaghy, M. (2004). Variation in the alcohol content of a 'drink' of wine and spirit poured by a sample of the Scottish population. *Health Education Research*, *19*, 485–91.

Gilmore, A., McKee, M. & Rose, R. (2002). Determinants of and inequalities in self-perceived health in the Ukraine. *Social Science & Medicine*, *55*, 2177–88.

Ginsburg, K. R., Menapace, A. S. & Slap, G. B. (1997). Factors affecting the decision to seek health care: the voice of adolescents. *Pediatrics*, *100*, 922–30.

Glaser, B., & Strauss, A. (1966). *Awareness of dying*. Chicago: Aldine.

Goldberg, R. J., Steg, P. G., Sadiq, I., Granger, C. B., Jackson, E. A., Budaj, A. *et al.* (2002). Extent of, and factors associated with, delay to hospital presentation in patients with acute coronary disease (the GRACE registry). *American Journal of Cardiology*, *89*, 791–6.

Goldman, S. L., Whitneysaltiel, D., Granger, J. & Rodin, J. (1991). Children's representations of everyday aspects of health and illness. *Journal of Pediatric Psychology*, *16*, 747–66.

Goliszek, A. (2003). *The mind–body connection: using the power of the brain for health, self-healing and stress relief*. Winston-Salem, NC: Healthnet Press.

Gonder-Frederick, L., Cox, D. & Ritterband, L. (2002). Diabetes and behavioral medicine: the second decade. *Journal of Consulting and Clinical Psychology*, *70*, 611–25.

Gøtzsche, P. C., & Olsen, O. (2000). Is screening for breast cancer with mammography justifiable? *The Lancet*, *355*, 129–34.

Graham, H. (1987). Women's smoking and family health. *Social Science & Medicine*, *25*, 47–56.

Grandinetti, D. A. (2000). Doctors and the Web: help your patients surf the Net safely. *Medical Economics*, April, 28–34.

Gray, D., & Saggers, S. (1998). Indigenous health: the perpetuation of inequality. In J. Germov (ed.), *Second opinion: an introduction to health sociology* (pp. 57–74). Oxford: Oxford University Press.

Gray, N., Cantrill, J. & Noyce, P. (2002). 'Health repertories': an understanding of lay management of minor ailments. *Patient Education and Counselling*, *47*, 237–44.

Gray, R. E., Fitch, M. & Greenberg, M. (1998). A comparison of physician and patient perspectives on unconventional cancer therapies. *Psycho-Oncology*, *7*, 445–52.

Green, B. B., & Taplin, S. H. (2003). Breast cancer screening controversies. *Journal of the American Board of Family Practice*, *16*, 233–41.

Green, C., & Pope, C. (1999). Gender, psychosocial factors and the use of medical services: a longitudinal analysis. *Social Science & Medicine*, *48*, 1363–72.

Green, E. E., Thompson, D. & Griffiths, F. (2002). Narratives of risk: women at midlife, medical 'experts' and health technologies. *Health, Risk and Society*, *4*, 273–87.

Greene, J. M. (1993). Expectations and experiences of pain in labor: findings from a large, prospective study. *Birth*, *17*, 15–24.

Greenglass, E. R. (1995). Gender, work stress and coping: theoretical implications. *Journal of Social Behavior and Personality*, *10*, 121–34.

Greenhalgh, T., & Hurwitz, B. (1999). Narrative based medicine: why study narrative? *British Medical Journal*, *318*, 48–50.

Greenhalgh, T., & Hurwitz, B. (eds.) (1998). *Narrative based medicine: dalogue and discourse in clinical practice*. London: BMJ Books.

Gregory, S., & McKie, L. (1991). The smear test: women's views. *Nursing Standard*, *5*, 32–6.

Groenvold, M., Fayers, P., Sprangers, M., Bjørner, J., Klee, M., Aaronson, N. *et al.* (1999). Anxiety and depression in breast cancer patients at low risk of recurrence compared with the general population: a valid comparison? *Journal of Clinical Epidemiology*, *52*, 523–30.

Guillemin, M. N. (1999). Managing menopause: a critical feminist engagement. *Scandinavian Journal of Public Health*, *27*, 273–8.

Guttman, N. (1997). Ethical dilemmas in health campaigns. *Health Communication*, *9*, 155–90.

Hack, T., & Degner, L. (2004). Coping responses following breast cancer diagnosis predict psychological adjustment three years later. *Psycho-Oncology*, *13*, 235–47.

Hackman, R., Stern, J. & Gershwin, M. (2000). Hypnosis and asthma: a critical review. *Journal of Asthma*, *37*, 1–15.

Haeggmark, C., Bohman, L., Ilmoni-Brandt, K., Naeslund, I., Sjoeden, P-O. & Nilsson, B. (2001). Effects of information supply on satisfaction with information and quality of life in cancer patients receiving curative radiation therapy. *Patient Education & Counseling*, *45*, 173–9.

Hall, J. A. (2003). Some observations on provider–patient communication research. *Patient Education and Counseling*, *50*, 9–12.

Hall, J. A., & Roter, D. L. (2002). Do patients talk differently to male and female physicians? A meta-analytic review. *Patient Education and Counseling*, *48*, 217–24.

Hall, J. A., Milburn, M. A., Roter, D. L. & Daltroy, L. H. (1998). Why are sicker patients less satisfied with their health? Tests of two explanatory models. *Health Psychology*, *17*, 70–5.

Hallowell, N. (1998). 'You don't want to lose your ovaries because you think "I might become a man"': women's perceptions of prophylactic surgery as a cancer risk management option. *Psycho-Oncology*, *7*, 263–75.

Hallowell, N., & Lawton, J. (2002). Negotiating present and future selves: managing the risk of hereditary ovarian cancer by prophylactic surgery. *Health: an*

Interdisciplinary Journal for the Social Study of Health, Illness and Medicine, *6*, 423–43.

Hamilton, E. L., Wallis, M. G., Barlow, J., Cullen, L. & Wright, C. (2003). Women's views of a breast screening service. *Health Care for Women International*, *24*, 40–8.

Hansel, N., Wu, A., Chang, B. & Diette, G. (2004). Quality of life and tuberculosis: patient and provider perspectives. *Quality of Life Research*, *13*, 639–52.

Hansell, S., & Mechanic, D. (1985). Introspectiveness and adolescent symptom reporting. *Journal of Human Stress*, *11*, 165–76.

Hardey, M. (1998a). *The social context of health*. Buckingham, UK: Open University Press.

   (1998b). Doctor in the house: the Internet as a source of lay health knowledge and the challenge to expertise. *Sociology of Health and Illness*, *21*, 820–35.

   (2002). 'The story of my illness': personal accounts of illness on the Internet. *Health: an Interdisciplinary Journal for the Social Study of Health, Illness and Medicine*, *6*, 31–46.

Hardy, K., O'Brien, S. & Furlong, N. (2001). Information given to patients before appointments and its effect on non-attendance rate. *British Medical Journal*, *323*, 1298–1300.

Harkness, S., & Keefer, C. H. (2000). Contributions of cross-cultural psychology to research and interventions in education and health. *Journal of Cross-Cultural Psychology*, *31*, 92–109.

Haron, Y., Eisikovits, R. & Linn, S. (2004). Traditional beliefs concerning health and illness among members of the Circassian community in Israel. *Journal of Religion and Health*, *43*, 59–72.

Harré, R. (1989). Language games and texts of identity. In J. Shotter & K. J. Gergen (eds.), *Texts of identity* (pp. 20–35). London: Sage.

Harrison, J. A., Mullen, P. D. & Green, L. W. (1992). A meta-analysis of studies of the health belief model with adults. *Health Education Research, Theory and Practice*, *7*, 107–16.

Hart, H., Bilo, H., Redekop, W., Stolk, R., Assink, J. & Meyboom-de Jong, B. (2003). Quality of life in patients with type I diabetes mellitus. *Quality of Life Research*, *12*, 1089–97.

Haveman-Nies, A., de Groot, L., Burema, J., Amorin Cruz, J. A., Osler, M. & van Staveren, W. A. (2002). Dietary quality and lifestyle factors in relation to 10-year mortality in older Europeans. *American Journal of Epidemiology*, *156*, 962–8.

Hay, L. L. (2001). *Heal your body A-Z: the mental causes for physical illness and the way to overcome them*. London: Hay House.

Haynes, R. B., McKibbon, A. & Kanani, R. (1996). Systematic review of randomized trials of interventions to assist patients to follow prescriptions of medications. *Lancet*, *348*, 383–6.

Hayward, M. D., Crimmins, E. M. Miles, T. P. & Yang, Y. (2000). The significance of socioeconomic status in explaining the racial gap in chronic health conditions. *American Sociological Review*, *65*, 910–30.

Hemingway, H., Nicholson, A., Stafford, M., Roberts, R. & Marmot, M. (1997). The impact of socioeconomic status on health functioning as assessed by the

SF-36 questionnaire: the Whitehall II Study. *American Journal of Public Health*, *87*, 1484–90.

Henderson, L., & Kitzinger, J. (1999). The human drama of genetics: 'hard' and 'soft' media representations of inherited breast cancer. *Sociology of Health and Illness*, *21*, 560–78.

Hepburn, S. J. (1988). W. H. R. Rivers Prize Essay (1986): Western minds, foreign bodies. *Medical Anthropology Quarterly*, *2*, 59–74.

Herzlich, C. (1973). *Health and illness: a social psychological analysis*. London: Academic Press.

(1995). Modern medicine and the quest for meaning: illness as a social signifier. In M. Augé & C. Herzlich (eds.), *The meaning of illness: anthropology, history and sociology* (pp. 151–73). Paris: Harwood Academic.

Herzlich, C., & Pierret, J. (1985). The social construction of the patient: patients and illnesses in other ages. *Social Science and Medicine*, *20*, 145–51.

Hesselink, A. E., Penninx, B., Schlosser, M., Wijnhoven, H., van der Windt, D., Kriegs-man, D. & van Eijk, J. (2004). The role of coping resources and coping style in quality of life of patients with asthma or COPD. *Quality of Life Research*, *13*, 509–18.

Heuveline, P., Guillot, M. & Gwatkin, D. (2002). The uneven tides of the health tran-sition. *Social Science and Medicine*, *55*, 313–22.

Hickman, P. E. (2002). Introduction to 'Screening for disease'. *Clinica Chimica Acta*, *315*, 3–4.

Hintikka, J., Saarinen, P. I. & Vinamaki, H. (1999). Suicide mortality in Finland during an economic cycle, 1985–1995. *Scandinavian Journal of Public Health*, *27*, 85–8.

Hippert, C. (2002). Multinational corporations, the politics of the world economy, and their effects on women's health in the developing world: a review. *Health Care for Women International*, *23*, 861–9.

Ho, S., Horne, D. & Szer, J. (2002). The adaptation of patients during the hospitalization period of bone marrow transplantation. *Journal of Clinical Psychology in Medical Settings*, *9*, 167–75.

Hobfoll, S. E., Jackson, A. P., Lavin, J., Johnson, R. J. & Schroder, K. E. (2002). Effects and generalizability of communally oriented HIV-AIDS preven-tion versus general health promotion groups of single, inner city women in urban clinics. *Journal of Consulting and Clinical Psychology*, *70*, 950–60.

Hodgetts, D., & Chamberlain, K. (2002). 'The problem with men': working-class men making sense of men's health on television. *Journal of Health Psychology*, *7*, 269–83.

Hogle, L. F. (2001). Chemoprevention for healthy women: harbinger of things to come? *Health: an Interdisciplinary Journal for the Social Study of Health, Illness and Medicine*, *5*, 311–33.

Holmes, T. H., & Rahe, R. H. (1967). The social readjustment rating-scale. *Journal of Psychosomatic Research*, *11*, 213–18.

Holroyd, K. A. (2002). Assessment and psychological management of recurrent headache disorders. *Journal of Consulting and Clinical Psychology*, *70*, 656–77.

Holroyd, K. A., & Coyne, J. (1987). Personality and health in the 1980s: psychosomatic medicine revisited. *Journal of Personality*, *55*, 359–75.

Holzner, B., Kemmler, G., Cella, D., De Paoli, C., Meraner, V., Kopp, M. *et al.* (2004). Normative data for functional assessment of cancer therapy: general scale and its use for the interpretation of quality of life scores in cancer survivors. *Acta Oncologica*, *43*, 153–60.

Hook, D. (2001). Discourse, knowledge, materiality, history: Foucault and discourse analysis. *Theory and Psychology*, *11*, 521–47.

Horn, S., & Munafò, M. (1997). *Pain: theory, research and intervention*. Buckingham, UK: Open University Press.

Horrocks, R. (1994). *Masculinity in crisis*. New York: St Martin's Press.

Horton, P. (2001). Commentary: screening mammography – an overview revisited. *The Lancet*, *358*, 1284–5.

Howarth, G. (2000). Dismantling the boundaries between life and death. *Mortality*, *5*, 127–38.

Howson, A. (1999). Cervical screening, compliance and moral obligation. *Sociology of Health and Illness*, *21*, 401–25.

  (2001). Locating uncertainties in cervical screening. *Health, Risk and Society*, *3*, 167–79.

Hróbjartsson, A., & Gøtzsche, P. C. (2001a). Core belief in powerful effects of placebo interventions is in conflict with no evidence of important effects in a large systematic review. *Advances in Mind–Body Medicine*, *17*, 312–18.

  (2001b). Is the placebo powerless? An anlysis of clinical trials comparing placebo with no treatment. *New England Journal of Medicine*, *344*, 1594–1602.

Hsiao, A., Wong, M., Kanouse, D., Collins, R., Liu, H., Andersen, R. *et al.* (2003). Complementary and alternative medicine use and substitution for conventional therapy by HIV-infected patients. *Journal of Acquired Immune Deficiency Syndromes*, *33*, 157–65.

Huang, X., Butow, P., Meiser, B. & Goldstein, D. (1999). Attitudes and information needs of Chinese migrant cancer patients and their relatives. *Australian and New Zealand Journal of Medicine*, *29*, 207–13.

Huisman, M., Kunst, A. E. & Mackenbach, J. P. (2003). Socioeconomic inequalities in morbidity among the elderly: a European overview. *Social Science and Medicine*, *57*, 861–73.

Hunt, C. K. (2003). Concepts in caregiver research. *Journal of Nursing Scholarship*, *35*, 27–32.

Hunter, J. (2001). Demographic variables and chronic pain. *Clinical Journal of Pain*, *17*, S14–S19.

Hunter, M. S., O'Dea, I. & Britten, N. (1997). Decision-making and hormone replacement therapy: a qualitative analysis. *Social Science and Medicine*, *45*, 1541–8.

Hydén, L.-C. (1997). Illness and narrative. *Sociology of Health and Illness*, *19*, 48–69.

Ibáñez, T. (1997). Why a critical social psychology? In T. Ibáñez & L. Iñiguez (eds.), *Critical social psychology* (pp. 27–41). London: Sage.

Illich, I. (1976). *Limits to medicine: medical nemesis, the expropriation of health*. London: Boyars.

Ingham, R., & Kirkland, D. (1997). Discourses and sexual health: Providing for young people. In L. Yardley (ed.), *Material discourses of health and illness* (pp. 150–75). London: Routledge.

Itkowitz, N., Kerns, R. & Otis, J. (2003). Support and coronary heart disease: the importance of significant other responses. *Journal of Behavioral Medicine*, *26*, 19–30.

Jackson, J. E. (1994). The Rashomon approach to dealing with chronic pain. *Social Science and Medicine*, *38*, 823–33.

James, A. (1998). Children, health and illness. In D. Field & S. Taylor (eds.), *Sociological perspectives on health, illness and health care* (pp. 97–114). Oxford: Blackwell.

Jamison, J. (1995). Australian dietary targets in 1995: their feasibility and pertinence to dietary goals for 2000. *Australian Journal of Public Health*, *19*, 522–4.

Jänne, P. A., & Mayer, R. J. (2000). Primary care: chemoprevention of colorectal cancer. *The New England Journal of Medicine*, *342*, 1960–8.

Janoff-Bulman, R., & Frantz, C. (1997). The impact of trauma on meaning: from meaningless world to meaningful life. In M. Power & C. R. Brewin (eds.), *The transformation of meaning in psychological therapies* (pp. 91–106). New York: Wiley.

Janz, N., & Becker, M. H. (1984). The health belief model: a decade later. *Health Education Quarterly*, *11*, 1–47.

Jaye, C., & Wilson, H. (2003). When general practitioners become patients. *Health: an Interdisciplinary Journal for the Social Study of Health, Illness and Medicine*, *7*, 201–25.

Jha, P., & Mills, A. (2002). *Improving health outcomes of the poor.* Report of Working Group 5 of the Commission on Macroeconomics and Health. Geneva: World Health Organisation.

Jirojwong, S., & MacLennan, R. (2003). Health beliefs, perceived self-efficacy and breast self-examination among Thai migrants in Brisbane. *Journal of Advanced Nursing*, *41*, 241–9.

Johansson, I., & Berterö, C. M. (2003). Getting no respect: barriers to mammography for a group of Swedish women. *Health Care for Women International*, *24*, 8–17.

Johnson, C. L., & Barer, B. M. (1997). *Life beyond 85 years: the aura of survivorship.* New York: Springer.

Jones, G., Steketee, R., Black, R., Bhutta, Z., Morris, S. & Bellagio Child Survival Study Group. (2003). How many child deaths can we prevent this year? *Lancet*, *362*, 65–71.

Joralemon, D. (1999). *Exploring medical anthropology.* Boston: Allyn & Bacon.

Jordanova, L. (1989). *Sexual visions: images of gender in science and medicine between the eighteenth and twentieth centuries.* New York: Harvester Wheatsheaf.

Jovchelovitch, S., & Gervais, M. (1999). Social representations of health and illness: the case of the Chinese community in England. *Journal of Community and Applied Social Psychology*, *9*, 247–60.

Joyce, C., Hickey, H., McGee, H. & O'Boyle, C. (2003). A theory-based method for the evaluation of individual quality of life: the SEIQoL. *Quality of Life Research*, *12*, 275–80.

Julian, R. (1998). Ethnicity, health and multiculturalism. In J. Germov (ed.), *Second opinion: an introduction to health sociology* (pp. 77–95). Oxford: Oxford University Press.

Kalichman, S., DiMarco, M., Austin, J., Luke, W. & DiFonzo, K. (2003). Stress, social support, and HIV-status disclosure to family and friends among HIV-positive men and women. *Journal of Behavioral Medicine, 26*, 315–32.

Kamarck, T. W., & Lovallo, W. R. (2003). Cardiovascular reactivity to psychological challenge: conceptual and measurement considerations. *Psychosomatic Medicine, 65*, 9–21.

Kangas, I. (2002). 'Lay' and 'expert': illness knowledge constructions in the sociology of health and illness. *Health: an Interdisciplinary Journal for the Social Study of Health, Illness and Medicine, 6*, 301–4.

Kanner, A. D., Coyne, J. C., Schaefer, C. & Lazarus, R. S. (1981). Comparison of two modes of stress measurement: daily hassles and uplifts versus major life events. *Journal of Behavioral Medicine, 4*, 1–39.

Kaplan, L. J. (2001). Toward a model of caregiver grief: nurses' experiences of treating dying children. *Omega: Journal of Death and Dying, 41*, 187–206.

Kaplan, R. M. (2000). Two pathways to prevention. *American Psychologist, 55 (4)*, 382–96.

Kaptchuk, T. J. (2002). The placebo effect in alternative medicine: can the performance of a healing ritual have clinical significance? *Annals of Internal Medicine, 136*, 817–25.

Karlsen, S., Nazroo, J. Y. & Stephenson, R. (2002). Ethnicity, environment and health: putting ethnic inequalities in health in their place. *Social Science and Medicine, 55*, 1647–61.

Kastenbaum, R., & Herman, C. (1997). Death personification in the Kevorkian era. *Death Studies, 21*, 115–30.

Kavanagh, A. M., & Broom, D. H. (1997). Women's understanding of abnormal cervical smear test results: a qualitative interview study. *British Medical Journal, 314*, 1388–91.

Kawachi, I., & Kennedy, B. P. (1999). Income inequality and health: pathways and mechanisms. *Health Services Research, 34*, 215–27.
    (2002). *The health of nations: why inequality is harmful to your health.* New York: New Press.

Keefe, F. J., & Blumenthal, J. A. (2004). Health psychology: what will the future bring? *Health Psychology, 23*, 156–7.

Keefe, F., Buffington, A., Studts, J. & Rumble, M. (2002). Behavioral medicine: 2002 and beyond. *Journal of Consulting and Clinical Psychology, 70*, 852–6.

Kellehear, A. (1998). Health and the dying person. In A. Peterson & C. Waddell (eds.), *Health matters: a sociology of illness, prevention and care* (pp. 287–99). Buckingham, UK: Open University Press.

Kelly, M. P., & Charlton, B. (1995). The modern and the postmodern in health promotion. In R. Bunton, S. Nettleton & R. Burrows (eds.), *The sociology of health promotion* (pp. 78–90). London: Routledge.

Kelly, M., & Dickinson, H. (1997). The narrative self in autobiographical accounts of illness. *The Sociological Review, 45*, 254–78.

Kelly, S., Hertzman, C. & Daniels, M. (1997). Searching for the biological pathways between stress and health. *Annual Review of Public Health, 18,* 437–
62.

Kerns, R., Rosenberg, R. & Otis, J. (2002). Self-appraised problem-solving and pain-
relevant social support as predictors of the experience of chronic pain. *Annals
of Behavioral Medicine, 24,* 100–5.

Kersnik, J., Svab, I. & Vegnuti, M. (2001). Frequent attenders in general practice: quality of life, patient satisfaction, use of medical services and GP characteristics.
Scandinavian Journal of Primary Health Care, 19, 174–7.

Kessler, R., Davis, R., Foster, D., Van Rompay, M., Walters, E., Wilkey, S. *et al.*
(2001). Long-term trends in the use of complimentary and alternative medical
therapies in the United States. *Annals of Internal Medicine, 135,* 262–8.

Khandra, A., & Oakeshott, P. (2002). Pilot study of testicular cancer awareness and
testicular self-examination in men attending two South London general practices. *Family Practice, 19,* 294–6.

Kiecolt-Glaser, J. K., McGuire, L., Robles, T. F. & Glaser, R. (2002a). Psychoneuroimmunology: psychological influences on immune function and health.
Journal of Consulting and Clinical Psychology, 70, 537–47.

(2002b). Psychoneuroimmunology and psychosomatic medicine: back to the future.
Psychosomatic Medicine, 64, 15–28.

Kimmel, M., & Messner, M. (1993). *Men's lives.* New York: Macmillan.

Kinder, P. (2002). Reflexive practice: the relationship between social research and
health promotion in HIV prevention. *Sex Education, 2,* 91–105.

King, G. (2004). The meaning of life experiences: application of a meta-model to
rehabilitation sciences and services. *American Journal of Orthopsychiatry,
74,* 72–88.

King, G., Cathers, T., Brown, E., Specht, J., Willoughby, C., Polgar, J. *et al.* (2003).
Turning points and protective processes in the lives of people with chronic
disabilities. *Qualitative Health Research, 13,* 184–206.

Kinney, J., Stephens, M., Franks, M. & Norris, V. (1995). Stresses and satisfactions of
family caregivers to older stroke patients. *Journal of Applied Gerontology,
14,* 3–21.

Kirkcaldy, B. D., Athanasou, J. A. & Trimpop, R. (2000). The idiosyncratic construction of stress: examples from medical work settings. *Stress Medicine, 16,*
315–26.

Kirmayer, L. J., & Young, A. (1998). Culture and somatization: clinical, epidemiological and ethnographic perspectives. *Psychosomatic Medicine, 60,* 420–30.

Kiss, A., & Meryn, S. (2001). Effect of sex and gender on psychosocial aspects of
prostate and breast cancer. *British Medical Journal, 323,* 1055–8.

Kivimaki, M., Elovainio, M., Kokko, K., Pulkkinen, L., Kortteinen, M. & Tuomikoski,
H. (2003). Hostility, unemployment and health status: Testing three theoretical models. *Social Science and Medicine, 56,* 2139–52.

Kleinman, A. (1980). *Patients and healers in the context of culture: an exploration
of the borderland between anthropology, medicine and psychiatry.* Berkeley,
CA: University of California Press.

(1988). *The illness narratives: suffering, healing and the human condition.* New
York: Basic Books.

Kolk, A. M. M., Hanewald, G. J. F. P., Schagen, S. & Gijsbers van Wijk, C. M. (2002). Predicting medically unexplained physical symptoms and health care utilization: a symptom-perception approach. *Journal of Psychosomatic Research*, *52*, 35–44.

(2003). A symptom perception approach to common physical symptoms. *Social Science and Medicine*, *57*, 2343–54.

Kop, W. J. (2003). The integration of cardiovascular behavioral medicine and psychoneuroimmunology: new developments based on converging research fields. *Brain, Behavior and Immunity*, *17*, 233–7.

Kosek, M., Bern, C. & Guerrant, R. (2003). The magnitude of the global burden of diarrhoeal disease from studies published 1992–2000. *Bulletin of the World Health Organisation*, *81*, 197–204.

Kramer, B. (1997). Gain in the caregiving experience: where are we? What next? *The Gerontologist*, *37*, 218–32.

Krause, M. (2003). The transformation of social representations of chronic disease in a self-help group. *Journal of Health Psychology*, *8*, 599–615.

Krause, N., & Shaw, B. (2003). Role-specific control, personal meaning, and health in late life. *Research on Ageing*, *25*, 559–86.

Kreps, G. L. (2001). Consumer/provider communication research: a personal plea to address issues of ecological validity, relational development, message diversity and situational constraints. *Journal of Health Psychology*, *6*, 597–601.

Kreps, G. L., Arora, N. K. & Nelson, D. E. (2003). Consumer/provider communication research: directions for development. *Patient Education and Counseling*, *50*, 3–4.

Krieger, N. (2000). Discrimination and health. In L. F. Berkman & I. Kawachi (eds.), *Social epidemiology* (pp. 36–75). Oxford: Oxford University Press.

Kroesen, K., Baldwin, C., Brooks, A. & Bell, I. (2002). US military veterans' perceptions of the conventional medical care system and their use of complementary and alternative medicine. *Family Practice*, *19*, 57–64.

Kubler-Ross, E. (1969). *On death and dying*. New York: Macmillan.

Kugelmann, R. (1997). The psychology and management of pain. *Theory and Psychology*, *7*, 43–65.

(1999). Complaining about chronic pain. *Social Science & Medicine*, *49*, 1663–76.

Kyngäs, H., Duffy, M. & Kroll, T. (2000). Conceptual analysis of compliance. *Journal of Clinical Nursing*, *9*, 5–12.

Labonte, R., & Schrecker, T. (2004). Committed to health for all? How the G7/G8 rate. *Social Science and Medicine*, *59*, 1661–76.

LaBotz, D. (1993). Manufacturing poverty: the maquiladorization of Mexico. *Multinational Monitor*, *14*, 18–23.

Ladwig, K., Marten-Mittag, B., Formanek, B. & Dammann, G. (2000). Gender differences of symptom reporting and medical health care utilization in the German population. *European Journal of Epidemiology*, *16*, 511–18.

Lalljee, M., Lamb, R. & Carnibella, G. (1993). Lay prototypes of illness: their content and use. *Psychology and Health*, *8*, 33–49.

Larrea, C., & Kawachi, I. (2005). Does economic inequality affect child malnutrition? The case of Ecuador. *Social Science and Medicine*, *60*, 165–78.

Larsen, J., Nordstrom, G., Bjorkstrand, B., Ljungman, P. & Gardule, A. (2003). Symptom distress, functional status, and health-related quality of life before high-dose chemotherapy with stem-cell transplantation. *European Journal of Cancer Care*, *12*, 71–80.

Lau, R. R., & Hartman, K. A. (1983). Common sense representations of common illnesses. *Health Psychology*, *2*, 167–86.

Lau, R. R., Bernard, T. M. & Hartman, K. A. (1989). Further explorations of common sense representations of common illnesses. *Health Psychology*, *8*, 195–219.

Lawler, J. (ed.) (1997) *The body in nursing*. Melbourne: Churchill Livingstone.

Lawton, J. (2000). *The dying process: patients' experiences of palliative care*. London: Routledge.

(2002). Colonising the future: temporal perceptions and health-relevant behaviours across the adult lifecourse. *Sociology of Health and Illness*, *24*, 714–33.

(2003). Lay experiences of health and illness: past research and future agendas. *Sociology of Health and Illness*, *25*, 23–40.

Lazarus, R. S., & Folkman, S. (1984). *Stress, appraisal and coping*. New York: Springer.

Lazarus, R. S., & Launier, R. (1978). Stress-related transactions between person and environment. In L. A. Pervin & M. Lewis (eds.), *Perspectives in interactional psychology* (pp. 287–327). New York: Plenum Press.

Lechner, L., Oenema, A. & de Nooijer, J. (2002). Testicular self-examination (TSE) among Dutch young men aged 15–19: determinants of the intention to practice TSE. *Health Education Research*, *17*, 73–84.

Lee, C. (1998). *Women's health: Psychological and social perspectives*. London: Sage.

(2001). Experiences of family caregiving among older Australian women. *Journal of Health Psychology*, *6*, 393–404.

Lee, C., & Owens, R. G. (2002). *The psychology of men's health*. Philadelphia: Open University Press.

Lee, C., & Porteous, J. (2002). Experiences of family caregiving among middle-aged Australian women. *Feminism & Psychology*, *12*, 79–96.

Lee, C. S. (2001). The use of narrative in understanding how cancer affects development: The stories of one cancer survivor. *Journal of Health Psychology*, *6*, 283–93.

Lee, K. (2003). *Globalisation and health: an introduction*. Basingstoke, UK: Palgrave Macmillan.

Lehrer, P., Feldman, J., Giardino, N., Song, H-S. & Schmaling, K. (2002). Psychological aspects of asthma. *Journal of Consulting and Clinical Psychology*, *70*, 691–711.

Lerman, C., Croyle, R. T., Tercyak, K. P. & Hamann, H. (2002). Genetic testing: psychological aspects and implications. *Journal of Consulting and Clinical Psychology*, *70 (3)*, 784–97.

Levenson, H. (1974). Multidimensional locus of control in psychiatric patients. *Journal of Consulting and Clinical Psychology*, *41*, 397–404.

Leventhal, E. A., & Prohaska, T. R. (1986). Age, symptom interpretation and health behavior. *Journal of the American Geriatrics Society*, *34*, 185–91.

Leventhal, H., & Hirschman, R. S. (1982). Social psychology and prevention. In G. S. Sanders & J. Suls (eds.), *Social psychology of health and illness* (pp. 183–226). Hillsdale, NJ: Erlbaum.

Leventhal, H., Meyer, D. & Nerenz, D. (1980). The commonsense representation of illness changes. In S. Rachman (ed.), *Contributions to medical psychology* (pp. 7–30). Oxford: Pergamon.

Lewig, K. A., & Dollard, M. F. (2001). Social construction of work stress: Australian newsprint media portrayal of stress at work, 1997–98. *Work and Stress, 15,* 179–90.

Lichter, I., Mooney, J. & Boyd, M. (1993). Biography as therapy. *Palliative Medicine, 7,* 133–7.

Lieberman, M., & Snowdon, L. (1993). Problems in assessing prevalence and membership characteristics of self-help group participants. *Journal of Applied Behavioral Science, 29,* 166–80.

Linden, W., Gerin, W. & Davidson, K. (2003). Cardiovascular reactivity: status quo and a research agenda for the new millennium. *Psychosomatic Medicine, 65,* 5–8.

Lipton, J. A., & Marbach, J. J. (1984). (1984). Ethnicity and the pain experience. *Social Science and Medicine, 19,* 1279–98.

Literature, Arts and Medicine Database. *Illness Narrative/Pathography.* Available at http://endeavor.med.nyu.edu/lit-med/lit-med-db/webdocs/webkeywords/illness. narrative.kw.html.

Little, M., Jordens, C., Paul, K., Montgomery, K. & Philipson, B. (1998). Liminality: a major category of the experience of cancer illness. *Social Science and Medicine, 47,* 1485–94.

Little, P., Somerville, J., Williamson, I., Warner, G., Moore, M., Wiles, R. *et al.* (2001a). Psychosocial, lifestyle, and health status variables in predicting high attendance amongst adults. *British Journal of General Practice, 51,* 987–94.

(2001b). Randomised controlled trial of self management leaflets and booklets for minor illness provided by post. *British Medical Journal, 322,* 1214–17.

Littlewood, J. (1999). From the invisibility of miscarriage to an attribution of life. *Anthropology & Medicine, 6,* 217–30.

Lock. M. (1998). Menopause: lessons from anthropology. *Psychosomatic Medicine, 60,* 410–19.

Lok, C., & Bishop, G. D. (1999). Emotion control, stress and health. *Psychology and Health, 14,* 813–27.

Long, S. O. (2004). Cultural scripts for a good death in Japan and the United States: similarities and differences. *Social Science and Medicine, 58,* 913–28.

Lorber, J. (1997). *Gender and the social construction of illness.* London: Sage.

Lovallo, W. R., & Gerin, W. (2003). Psychophysiological reactivity: mechanisms and pathways to cardiovascular disease. *Psychosomatic Medicine, 65,* 36–45.

Lown, B., Bukachi, F., & Xavier, R. (1998). Health information in the developing world. *Lancet, 352,* SII34–SII38.

Lupton, D. (1995). *The imperative of health: public health and the regulated body.* London: Sage.

(1997). Foucault and the medicalisation critique. In A. Petersen & R. Bunton (eds.), *Foucault, health and medicine* (pp. 94–110). London: Routledge.

(1998). The body, medicine and society. In J. Germov (ed.), *Second opinion: an introduction to health sociology* (2nd edn, pp. 121–35). Oxford: Oxford University Press.

Lyles, A. (2002). Direct marketing of pharmaceuticals to consumers. *Annual Review of Public Health, 23*, 73–91.

Lynch, J. (2000). Income inequality and health: expanding the debate. *Social Science and Medicine, 51*, 1001–5.

Lynch, J. W., Davey Smith, G., Kaplan, G. A. & House, J. S. (2000). Income inequality and mortality: importance to health of individual income, psychosocial environment, or material conditions. *British Medical Journal, 320*, 1200–4.

Lyon, D., & Younger, J. (2001). Purpose in life and depressive symptoms in persons living with HIV disease. *Journal of Nursing Scholarship, 33*, 129–33.

Lyons, A. C. (1999). Shaping health psychology: qualitative research, evaluation and representation. In M. Murray & K. Chamberlain (eds.), *Qualitative health psychology: theories and methods* (pp. 241–55). London: Sage.

(2000). Examining media representations: benefits for health psychology. *Journal of Health Psychology, 5*, 343–52.

Lyons, A. C., & Chamberlain, K. (1994). The effects of minor events, optimism and self-esteem on health. *British Journal of Clinical Psychology, 33*, 559–70.

Lyons, A. C., & Farquhar, C. (2002). Past disclosure and conversational experience: effects on cardiovascular functioning while women talk. *Journal of Applied Social Psychology, 32 (10)*, 2043–66.

Lyons, A. C., & Griffin, C. (2000). Representations of menopause and women at midlife. In J. Ussher (ed.), *A reader in women's health* (pp. 470–76). Leicester: BPS Books.

(2003). An analysis of menopause self-help books: implications for women. *Social Science and Medicine, 56*, 1629–42.

Lyons, A. C., & Leach, J. (forthcoming) 'The woman's choice': general practitioners' views on menopause and HRT.

Lyons, A. C., & Willott, S. (1999). From suet pudding to superhero: representations of men's health for women. *Health: an Interdisciplinary Journal for the Social Study of Health, Illness and Medicine, 3*, 283–302.

Lyons, A. C., Fanshawe, C. & Lip, G. Y. H. (2002). Knowledge, communication and expectancies of cardiac catheterization: the patient's perspective. *Psychology, Health and Medicine, 7*, 461–7.

Lyons, A. C., Spicer, J., Tuffin, K. & Chamberlain, K. (2000). Does cardiovascular reactivity during speech reflect self-construction processes? *Psychology and Health, 14*, 1123–40.

MacIntyre, S. (1993). Gender differences in the perception of common cold symptoms. *Social Science and Medicine, 36*, 15–20.

MacIntyre, S., Hunt, K. & Sweeting, H. (1996). Gender differences in health: are things really as simple as they seem? *Social Science and Medicine, 42*, 617–24.

MacLachlan, M. (1997). *Culture and health*. Chichester, UK: John Wiley.

(2004). *Embodiment: clinical, critical and cultural perspectives on health and illness*. Berkshire, UK: Open University Press.

MacLeod, R. D. (2001). On reflection: doctors learning to care for people who are dying. *Social Science and Medicine, 52*, 1719–27.

Madjar, I. (1997). The body in health, illness and pain. In J. Lawler (ed.), *The body in nursing* (pp. 53–73). Melbourne: Churchill Livingstone.

Maibach, E. W., Maxfield, A., Ladin, K. & Slater, M. (1996). Translating health psychology into effective health communication: the American healthstyles audience segmentation project. *Journal of Health Psychology, 1*, 261–77.

Maier, S. F., Watkins, L. R. & Fleshner, M. (1994). Psychoneuroimmunology: the interface between behavior, brain and immunity. *American Psychologist, 49*, 1004–17.

Manton, K. G., Stallard, E. & Corder, L. (1995). Changes in morbidity and chronic disability in the US elderly population: evidence from the 1982, 1984 and 1989 National Long Term Care Survey. *Journal of Gerontology, 50B*, S104–S204.

Manuck, S. B. (1994). Cardiovascular reactivity in cardiovascular disease: 'Once more into the breach'. *International Journal of Behavioral Medicine, 1*, 4–31.

Maoz, B., Dowty, N., Antonovsky, A. & Wijsenbeck, H. (1970). Female attitudes to menopause. *Social Psychiatry, 5*, 35–40.

Marcus, B. H., Dubbert, P. M., Forsyth, L. H., McKenzie, T. L., Stone, E. J., Dunn, A. L. *et al.* (2000). Physical activity behavior change: issues in adoption and maintenance. *Health Psychology, 19(1) Supp.*, 32–41.

Marks, D. F. (1996). Health psychology in context. *Journal of Health Psychology, 1*, 7–21.

(2002). Freedom, responsibility and power: contrasting approaches to health psychology (editorial essay). *Journal of Health Psychology, 7*, 5–19.

Marks, D. F., Murray, M., Evans, B. & Willig, C. (2000). *Health psychology: theory, research and practice*. London: Sage.

Marks, N., Lambert, J. & Choi, H.-J. (2002). Transitions to caregiving, gender, and psychological well-being: a prospective US national study. *Journal of Marriage and Family, 64*, 657–67.

Markus, H. R., & Kitiyama, S. (1991). Culture and the self: implications for cognition, emotion and motivation. *Psychological Review, 98*, 224–53.

Marmot, M., & Wilkinson, R. G. (2001). Psychosocial and material pathways in the relation between income and health: a response to Lynch *et al. British Medical Journal, 322*, 1233–6.

Marquis, S. (1993). Death of the nursed: burnout of the provider. *Omega: Journal of Death and Dying, 27*, 17–33.

Marshall, J. R., & Funch, D. P. (1986). Gender and illness behaviour among colorectal cancer patients. *Women and Health, 11*, 67–82.

Marteau, T. M. (1994). Psychology and screening: narrowing the gap between efficacy and effectiveness. *British Journal of Clinical Psychology, 33*, 1–10.

Marteau, T. M., Kidd, J., Cook, R., Michie, S., Johnston, M., Slack, J. *et al.* (1991). Perceived risk not actual risk predicts uptake of amniocentesis. *British Journal of Obstetrics and Gynaecology, 98*, 282–6.

Martin, E. (1987). *The woman in the body: a cultural analysis of reproduction*. Milton Keynes, UK: Open University Press.

Martin, P. (1997). *The sickening mind: brain, behaviour, immunity and disease.* London: Flamingo.

Martin, R., & Lemos, K. (2002). From heart attacks to melanoma: do common sense models of somatization influence symptom interpretation for female victims? *Health Psychology, 21,* 25–32.

Martin, R., Gordon, E. & Lounsbury, P. (1998). Gender disparities in the attribution of cardiac-related symptoms: contribution of common sense models of illness. *Health Psychology, 17,* 346–57.

Martin, R., Lemos, K., Rothrock, N., Bellman, B., Russell, D., Tripp-Reimer, T. *et al.* (2004). Gender disparities in common sense models of illness among myocardial infarction victims. *Health Psychology, 23,* 345–53.

Marucha, P. T., Kiecolt-Glaser, J. K. & Favegehi, M. (1998). Mucosal wound healing is impaired by examination stress. *Psychosomatic Medicine, 60,* 362–5.

Maruta, T., Colligan, R. C., Malinchoc, M. & Offord, K. P. (2000). Optimists vs pessimists: survival rate among medical patients over a 30-year period. *Mayo Clinical Proceedings, 75,* 140–3.

Mason, C., Orr, J., Harrison, S. & Moore, R. (1999). Health professionals' perspectives on service delivery in two Northern Ireland communities. *Journal of Advanced Nursing, 30,* 827–34.

Matarazzo, J. D. (1980). Behavioral health and behavioural medicine: frontiers for a new health psychology. *American Psychologist, 35,* 807–17.

(1984). Behavioral health: a 1990 challenge for the health sciences professions. In J. D. Matarazzo, N. E. Miller, S. M. Weiss, J. A. Herd & St M. Weiss (eds.), *Behavioral health: a handbook of health enhancement and disease prevention* (pp. 3–40). New York: Wiley.

Mathers, C. D., Sadana, R., Salomon, J. A., Murray, C. J. L. & Lopez, A. D. (2001). Healthy life expectancy in 191 countries, 1999. *Lancet, 357,* 1685–91.

Mathews, S., Camacho, A., Mills, P. & Dimsdale, J. (2003). The Internet for medical information about cancer: help or hindrance? *Psychosomatics, 44,* 100–3.

Matthews, D. A., McCullough, M. E., Larson, D. B., Koenig, H. G., Swyers, J. P. & Milano, M. G. (1998). Religious commitment and health status: a review of the research and implications for family medicine. *Archives of Family Medicine, 7,* 118–24.

Matud, M. P., Ibáñez, I., Bethencourt, J. M., Marrero, R. & Carballeira, M. (2003). Structural gender differences in perceived social support. *Personality and Individual Differences, 35,* 1919–29.

May, C., Doyle, H. & Chew-Graham, C. (1999). Medical knowledge and the intractable patient: the case of chronic low back pain. *Social Science and Medicine, 48,* 523–34.

McBride, A. B., & McBride, W. L. (1994). Women's health scholarship: From critique to assertion. In A. J. Dan (ed.), *Reframing women's health: multidisciplinary research and practice* (pp. 3–12). London: Sage.

McCabe, M., McKern, S. & McDonald, E. (2004). Coping and psychological adjustment among people with multiple sclerosis. *Journal of Psychosomatic Research, 56,* 355–61.

McCarthy, P. L., Christoffel, K. K., Dungy, C. I., Gillman, M. W., Rivara, F. P. & Takayama, J. I. (2000). Race/ethnicity, gender, socioeconomic status research exploring their effects on child health: a subject review. *Pediatrics, 105,* 1349–51.

McClean, S. (2003). Globalisation and health. In J. Orme, J. Powell, P. Taylor, T. Harrison & M. Grey (eds.), *Public health for the 21st century: new perspectives on policy, participation and practice* (pp. 210–24). Maidenhead, UK: Open University Press.

McCormick, W. (1989). Cervical smears: a questionable practice? *The Lancet, 2* (8656), 207–9.

McCourt, C., & Pierce, A. (2000). Does continuity of carer matter to women from minority ethnic groups? *Midwifery, 16,* 145–54.

McCracken, L., & Eccleston, C. (2003). Coping or acceptance: what to do about chronic pain? *Pain, 105,* 197–204.

McCrea, F. B. (1983). The politics of menopause: the 'discovery' of a deficiency disease. *Social Problems, 31,* 111–23.

McDonough, P., & Walters, V. (2001). Gender and health: reassessing patterns and explanations. *Social Science and Medicine, 52,* 547–59.

McEwen, B. S. (1998). Stress, adaptation, and disease: allostasis and allostatic load. *Annals of the New York Academy of Sciences, 840,* 33–44.

McEwen, B. S., & Stellar, E. (1993). Stress and the individual: mechanisms leading to disease. *Archives of Internal Medicine, 153,* 2093–101.

McFarland, B., Bigelow, D., Zani, B., Newsom, J. & Kaplan, M. (2002). Complementary and alternative medicine use in Canada and the United States. *American Journal of Public Health, 92,* 1616–18.

McKenzie, H., & Crouch, M. (2004). Discordant feelings in the lifeworld of cancer survivors. *Health: an Interdisciplinary Journal for the Social Study of Health, Illness and Medicine, 8,* 139–57.

McKeown, T. (1979). *The role of medicine.* Oxford: Blackwell.

McKie, L. (1995). The art of surveillance or reasonable prevention? The case of cervical screening. *Sociology of Health and Illness, 17,* 441–57.

McKinlay, J. B., & McKinlay, S. M. (1981). Medical measures and the decline of mortality. In P. Conrad and R. Kern (eds.), *The sociology of health and illness* (pp. 12–30). New York: St Martins.

McLaren, N. (1998). A critical review of the biopsychosocial model. *Australian and New Zealand Journal of Psychiatry, 32,* 86–92.

McNamara, B. (1998). A good enough death? In A. Peterson & C. Waddell (eds.), *Health matters: a sociology of illness, prevention and care* (pp. 169–84). Buckingham, UK: Open University Press.

  (2001). *Fragile lives: death, dying and care.* Buckingham, UK: Open University Press.

Meads, C., Lyons, A. C. & Carroll, D. (2003). The impact of the emotional disclosure intervention on physical and psychological health: a systematic review. *A West Midlands Health Technology Assessment Collaboration Report.* Birmingham, UK: West Midlands Health Technology Assessment Collaboration.

Mehta, S., Moore, R. & Graham, N. (1997). Potential factors affecting adherence with HIV therapy. *AIDS, 11,* 1665–70.

Meiller, L. K., Lund, A. B. & Kok, G. (1996). Reactions to health education among men. *Health Education Research, 11,* 107–15.

Melzack, R., & Wall, P. D. (1965). Pain mechanisms: a new theory. *Science, 150,* 971–9.

Mercer, M. A. (2004). Shall we leave it to the experts? In M. Fort, M. A. Mercer & O. Gish (eds.), *Sickness and wealth: the corporate assault on global health* (pp. 167–72). Cambridge, MA: South End Press.

Merleau-Ponty, M. (1962). *Phenomenology of perception* (trans. by C. Smith). New York: Routledge & Kegan Paul.

Michie, S., Miles, J. & Weinman, J. (2003). Patient-centredness in chronic illness: what is it and does it matter? *Patient Education and Counseling, 51,* 197–206.

Miller, G. E., & Cohen, S. (2001). Psychological interventions and the immune system: a meta-analytic review and critique. *Health Psychology, 20,* 47–63.

Miller, T. Q., Smith, T. W., Turner, C. W., Guijarro, M. L. & Hallet, A. J. (1996). A meta-analytic review of research on hostility and physical health. *Psychological Bulletin, 119,* 322–48.

Mills, P. J., Yu, H., Ziegler, M. G., Patterson, T. L. & Grant, I. (1999). Vulnerable caregivers of patients with Alzheimer's disease have a deficit in circulating CD62L-T lymphocytes. *Psychosomatic Medicine, 61,* 168–74.

Mineau, G. P., Smith, K. R. & Bean, L. L. (2002). Historical trends of survival among widows and widowers. *Social Science and Medicine, 54,* 245–54.

Ministry of Health. (1999). *Our health, our future: Hauora pakari, koiora roa: the health of New Zealanders 1999.* Wellington: Ministry of Health.

Mishler, E. G. (1984). *The discourse of medicine: dialectics of medical interviews.* Norwood, NJ: Ablex.

Mitchell, J., Mathews, H., Hunt, L., Cobb, K. & Watson, R. (2001). Mismanaging prescription medications among rural elders: the effects of socioeconomic status, health status, and medication profile indicators. *Gerontologist, 41,* 348–56.

Moaz, B., Dowty, N., Antonovsky, A. & Wijsenbeck, H. (1970). Female attitudes to menopause. *Social Psychiatry, 5, 35–40.*

Mokounkolo, R., & Mullet, E. (1999). Lay beliefs on the nature of health: an English-French comparison. *Social Behavior and Personality, 27,* 439–54.

Moller, D. W. (1996). *Confronting death: values, institutions and human mortality.* New York: Oxford University Press.

Montgomery, G., & Bovjerg, D. (2003). Expectations of chemotherapy-related nausea: emotional and experimental predictors. *Annals of Behavioral Medicine, 25,* 48–54.

Moore, R. A., & Topping, A. (1999). Young men's knowledge of testicular cancer and testicular self-examination: a lost opportunity? *European Journal of Cancer Care, 8,* 137–42.

Moos, R. H., & Tsu, V. D. (1977). The crisis of physical illness: an overview. In R. H. Moos & V. D. Tsu (eds.), *Coping with physical illness* (pp. 3–21). New York: Plenum Medical Book Company.

Morgan, M. (2003). Hospitals and patient care. In G. Scambler (ed.), *Sociology as applied to medicine* (5th edn, pp. 66–78). London: Saunders.

Morris, D. B. (1991). *The culture of pain.* Berkeley: University of California Press.

Morris, J. (1996). The case against TSE. *Nursing Times, 92,* 41.

Morse, J. M. (2004). Editorial: the complexities of health promotion. *Qualitative Health Research*, *14*, 3–4.

Moscovici, S. (1984). The phenomenon of social representations. In R. M. Farr & S. Moscovici (eds.), *Social representations* (pp. 3–69). Cambridge: Cambridge University Press.

Moynihan, R. (2003). The making of a disease: female sexual dysfunction. *British Medical Journal*, *326*, 45–7.

Muir, E. H., & Ogden, J. (2001). Consultations involving people with congenital disabilities: factors that help or hinder giving care. *Family Practice*, *18*, 419–24.

Munafò, M., & Stevenson, J. (2001). Anxiety and surgical recovery: reinterpreting the literature. *Journal of Psychosomatic Research*, *51*, 589–96.

Muncer, S. J., Taylor, S. & Ling, J. (2001). Lay and professional perspectives of the causes of health: a comparative network approach. *Social Behavior and Personality*, *29*, 365–74.

Murray, M. (1997). *Narrative health psychology*. Massey University Visiting Scholar Series No. 11. Palmerston North, NZ: Massey University.

  (2000). Levels of narrative in health psychology. *Journal of Health Psychology*, *5*, 337–347.

Murray, M. (ed.). (2004). *Critical health psychology*. Basingstoke: Palgrave Macmillan.

Murray, M., & Campbell, C. (2003). Living in a material world: reflecting on some assumptions of health psychology. *Journal of Health Psychology*, *8*, 231–6.

Murray, M., Nelson, G., Poland, B., Maticka-Tyndale, E. & Ferris, L. (2004). Assumptions and values of community health psychology. *Journal of Health Psychology*, *9*, 323–33.

Murray, M., Pullman, D. & Heath Rodgers, T. (2003). Social representations of health and illness among 'baby-boomers' in eastern Canada. *Journal of Health Psychology*, *8*, 485–99.

Murray, S., Grant, E., Grant, A. & Kendall, M. (2003). Dying from cancer in developed and developing countries: lessons from two qualitative interview studies of patients and their carers. *British Medical Journal*, *326*, 368–72.

Murtagh, M. J., & Hepworth, J. (2003). Feminist ethics and menopause: autonomy and decision-making in primary medical care. *Social Science and Medicine*, *56*, 1643–52.

Musil, C., Ahn, S., Haug, M., Warner, C., Morris, D. & Duffy, E. (1998). Health problems and health actions among community-dwelling older adults: results of a health diary study. *Applied Nursing Research*, *11*, 138–47.

Nathanson, C. A. (1975). Illness and the feminine role: a theoretical review. *Social Science & Medicine*, *9*, 57–62.

National Center for Health Statistics. (2003). *Health, United States, 2003*. Hyattsville, MD: National Center for Health Statistics.

Neal, R., Heywood, P. & Morley, S. (2000). 'I always seem to be there': a qualitative study of frequent attenders. *British Journal of General Practice*, *50*, 716–23.

Neale, A. V., Tilley, B. C. & Vernon, S. W. (1986). Marital status, delay in seeking treatment and survival from breast cancer. *Social Science and Medicine*, *23*, 305–12.

Neimeyer, R. A. (1997). Meaning reconstruction and the experience of chronic loss. In K. Doka & J. Davidson (eds.), *Living with grief when illness is prolonged* (pp. 159–76). Bristol, PA: Taylor & Francis.

(1997–8). Death anxiety research: the state of the art. *Omega: Journal of Death and Dying*, *36*, 97–120.

Neimeyer, R. A., & Van Brunt, D. (1995). Death anxiety. In H. Wass & R. A. Neimeyer (eds.), *Dying: facing the facts* (3rd edn, pp. 49–58). New York: Taylor & Francis.

Nettleton, S. (1995). *The sociology of health and illness*. Cambridge: Polity Press.

(1997). Governing the risky self: how to become healthy, wealthy and wise. In A. Petersen & R. Bunton (eds.), *Foucault, health and medicine* (pp. 207–22). London: Routledge.

Nettleton, S., & Bunton, R. (1995). Sociological critiques of health promotion. In R. Bunton, S. Nettleton & R. Burrows (eds.), *The sociology of health promotion* (pp. 41–58). London: Routledge.

Newman, S. (1997). Masculinities, men's bodies and nursing. In J. Lawler (ed.), *The body in nursing* (pp. 135–53). Melbourne: Churchill Livingstone.

Newton, J., & Waters, V. (2001). Community palliative care clinical nurse specialists' descriptions of stress in their work. *International Journal of Palliative Nursing*, *7*, 531–40.

Nicolson, P. (2001). Critical health psychology: a radical alternative to the 'mainstream'? Commentary on Crossley. *Psychology, Health and Medicine*, *6*, 256–59.

Nightingale, D. J., & Cromby, J. (2002). Social constructionism as ontology: exposition and examples. *Theory and Psychology*, *12*, 701–13.

Nolen-Hoeksma, S., & Larson, J. (1999). *Coping with loss*. Mahwah, NJ: Lawrence Erlbaum.

Norcross, W. A., Ramirez, C. & Palinkas, L. A. (1996). The influence of women on the health care-seeking behavior of men. *Journal of Family Practice*, *43*, 475–80.

Norman, P., & Bennett, P. (1996). Health locus of control. In M. Conner & P. Norman (eds.), *Predicting health behaviour* (pp. 62–94). Buckingham, UK: Open University Press.

Norton, S. A., & Bowers, B. J. (2001). Working towards consensus: providers' strategies to shift patients from curative to palliative treatment choices. *Research in Nursing and Health*, *24*, 258–69.

Nosek, M. A., Hughes, R. B., Howland, C. A., Young, M. E., Mullen, P. D. & Shelton, M. L. (2004). The meaning of health for women with disabilities: a qualitative analysis. *Family and Community Health*, *27*, 6–21.

O'Brien, M. (1995). Health and lifestyle: a critical mess? Notes on the dedifferentiation of health. In R. Bunton, S. Nettleton & R. Burrows (eds.), *The sociology of health promotion* (pp. 191–205). London: Routledge.

O'Donoghue, B., Howden-Chapman, P. & Woodward, A. (2000). Why do Australians live longer than New Zealanders? *Health Education and Behavior*, *27*, 307–16.

Oakland, O., & Ostell, A. (1996). Measuring coping: a review and critique. *Human Relations*, *49*, 133–55.

Oakley, A. (1998). Science, gender, and women's liberation: an argument against post-modernism. *Women's Studies International Forum*, *21*, 133–46.

Oberle, K., & Hughes, D. (2001). Doctors' and nurses' perceptions of ethical problems in end-of-life decisions. *Journal of Advanced Nursing*, *33*, 707–15.

OECD (2003). *Health at a glance: OECD indicators 2003*. Paris: Organisation for Economic Co-operation and Development.

Office for National Statistics (2004). *Living in Britain*. London: The Stationery Office.

Ogden, J. (1997). The rhetoric and reality of psychosocial theories: a challenge to biomedicine. *Journal of Health Psychology*, *2*, 21–9.

    (2003a). What do symptoms mean? *British Medical Journal*, *327*, 409–10.

    (2003b). Some problems with social cognition models: a pragmatic and conceptual analysis. *Health Psychology*, *22*, 424–8.

    (2004) *Health psychology: a textbook* (3rd edn). Maidenhead, UK: Open University Press.

Ogden, J., Fuks, K., Gardner, M., Johnson, S., McLean, M., Martin, P. *et al.* (2002). Doctors' expressions of uncertainty and patient confidence. *Patient Education and Counseling*, *48*, 171–6.

Ogden, R. D. (2001). Non-physician assisted suicide: the technological imperative of the deathing culture. *Death Studies*, *25*, 387–401.

Öhman, M., & Söderberg, S. (2004). The experience of close relatives living with a person with serious chronic illness. *Qualitative Health Research*, *14*, 396–410.

Olbrisch, M., Benedict, S., Ashe, K. & Levenson, J. (2002). Psychological assessment and care of organ transplant patients. *Journal of Consulting and Clinical Psychology*, *70*, 771–83.

Olesen, V., Schatzman, L., Droes, N., Hatton, D. & Chico, N. (1990). The mundane ailment and the physical self: analysis of the social psychology of health and illness. *Social Science and Medicine*, *30*, 449–55.

Oman, D., & Thoresen, C. E. (2002). 'Does religion cause health?' Differing interpretations and diverse meanings. *Journal of Health Psychology*, *7*, 365–80.

Ong, C-K., Peterson, S., Bodeker, G. & Stewart-Brown, S. (2002). Health status of people using complementary and alternative medical practitioner services in 4 English counties. *American Journal of Public Health*, *92*, 1653–6.

Ong, L. M., de Haes, J. C. & Lammes, F. B. (1995). Doctor–patient communication: a review of the literature. *Social Science and Medicine*, *40*, 903–18.

Orbinski, J., & Pecoul, B. (2002). *G8: drugs for neglected diseases*. Retrieved 20 October 2003 from Access to Essential Medicines Campaign at the Medicins sans Frontières website: http://www.msf.org.

Otto, S. J., Fracheboud, J., Looman, C. W. N., Broeders, M. J. M., Boer, R. *et al.* (2003). Initiation of a population-based mammography screening in Dutch municipalities and effect on breast-cancer mortality: a systematic review. *The Lancet*, *361*, 1411–17.

Owens, R. G. (2001). Is critical health psychology sufficiently self-critical? Commentary on Crossley. *Psychology, Health and Medicine*, *6*, 259–64.

Owens, R. G., & Payne, S. (1999). Qualitative research in the field of death and dying. In M. Murray & K. Chamberlain (eds.), *Qualitative health psychology: theories and methods* (pp. 148–63). London: Sage.

Papadopoulos, I. (1999). Health and illness beliefs of Greek Cypriots living in London. *Journal of Advanced Nursing*, *29*, 1097–1104.

Papakostos, Y., & Daras, M. (2001). Placebos, placebo effect, and the response to the healing situation: the evolution of a concept. *Epilepsia*, *42*, 1614–25.

Parish, R. (1995). Health promotion: rhetoric and reality. In R. Bunton, S. Nettleton & R. Burrows (eds.), *The sociology of health promotion* (pp. 13–23). London: Routledge.

Park, C., Folkman, S. & Bostrom, A. (2001). Appraisals of controllability and coping in caregivers in HIV+ men: testing the goodness-of-fit hypothesis. *Journal of Consulting and Clinical Psychology*, *69*, 481–8.

Parker, I. (1992). *Discourse dynamics: critical analysis for social and individual psychology*. London: Routledge.

Parkes, C. M., Laungani, P. & Young, B. (eds.). (1997). *Death and bereavement across cultures*. London: Routledge.

Parsons, T. (1951). *The social system*. New York: The Free Press.

Patenaude, A. F., Guttmacher, A. E. & Collins, F. S. (2002). Genetic testing and psychology: new roles, new responsibilities. *American Psychologist*, *57*, 271–82.

Paterson, C., & Britten, N. (1999). 'Doctors can't help much': the search for an alternative. *British Journal of General Practice*, *49*, 626–9.

Patterson, R., Neuhouser, M., Hedderson, M., Schwartz, S., Standish, L., Bowen, D. *et al.* (2002). Types of alternative medicine used by patients with breast, colon, or prostate cancer: predictors, motives, and costs. *Journal of Alternative and Complementary Medicine*, *8*, 477–85.

Payer, L. (1989). *Medicine and culture*. London: Victor Gollancz.

Payne, S., Horn, S. & Relf, M. (1999). *Loss and bereavement*. Buckingham, UK: Open University Press.

Penedo, F., Gonzalez, J. & Davis, C. (2003). Coping and psychological distress among symptomatic HIV+ men who have sex with men. *Annals of Behavioral Medicine*, *25*, 203–13.

Pennebaker, J. W. (1982). *The psychology of physical symptoms*. New York: Springer-Verlag.

(1983). Accuracy of symptom perception. In A. Baum, S. E. Taylor & J. Singer (eds.), *Handbook of psychology and health, IV* (pp. 189–218). Hillsdale, NJ: Erlbaum.

(1992). Inhibition as the linchpin of health. In H. S. Friedman (ed.), *Hostility, coping and health* (pp. 127–39). Washington, DC: American Psychological Association.

Pennebaker, J. W., & Roberts, T. A. (1992). Toward a his and hers theory of emotion: gender differences in visceral perception. *Journal of Social and Clinical Psychology*, *11*, 199–212.

Pennebaker, J. W., Hughes, C. F. & O'Heeron, R. C. (1987). The psychophysiology of confession: linking inhibitory and psychosomatic processes. *Journal of Personality and Social Psychology*, *52*, 781–93.

Pensola, T., & Martikainen, P. (2004). Life-course experiences and mortality by adult social class among young men. *Social Science and Medicine*, *58*, 2149–70.

Pereira, J., & Bruera, E. (1998). The Internet as a resource for palliative care and hospice: a review and proposals. *Journal of Pain and Symptom Management, 16*, 59–68.

Petersen, A., & Lupton, D. (1996). *The new public health: health and self in the age of risk*. London: Sage.

Petersen, A. R. (1996). Risk and regulated self: the discourse of health promotion as politics of uncertainty. *Australia and New Zealand Journal of Sociology, 32*, 44–57.

Peterson, C., & Seligman, M. E. (1984). Causal explanations as a risk factor for depression: theory and evidence. *Psychological Review, 91*, 347–74.

Peterson, C., Seligman, M. E. & Vaillant, G. E. (1988). Pessimistic explanatory style is a risk factor for physical illness: a thirty-five year longitudinal study. *Journal of Personality and Social Psychology, 55*, 23–7.

Petrie, K. J., & Weinman, J. A. (eds.) (1997). *Perceptions of health and illness: current research and applications*. Chur: Harwood.

Petrie, K. J., Booth, R. J., Pennebaker, J. W., Davison, K. P. & Thomas, M. G. (1995). Disclosure of trauma and immune response to a hepatitis B vaccination program. *Journal of Consulting and Clinical Psychology, 63*, 787–92.

Petrie, K., Buick, D., Weinman, J. & Booth, R. (1999). Positive effects of illness reported by myocardial infarction and breast cancer patients. *Journal of Psychosomatic Research, 47*, 537–43.

Phillips, D., & Bredder, C. (2002). Morbidity and mortality from medical errors: an increasingly serious public health problem. *Annual Review of Public Health, 23*, 135–50.

Phillips, Z., Johnson, S., Avis, M. & Whynes, D. K. (2003). Human papillomavirus and the value of screening: young women's knowledge of cervical cancer. *Health Education Research, 18*, 318–28.

Pierret, J. (1993). Constructing discourses about health and their social determinants. In A. Radley (ed.), *Worlds of illness: biographical and cultural perspectives on health and disease* (pp. 9–26). London: Routledge.

  (1995). The social meanings of health: Paris, the Essonne, the Herault. In M. Augé & C. Herzlich (eds.), *The meaning of illness: anthropology, history and sociology* (pp. 175–206). Paris: Harwood Academic.

Pignone, M., Saha, S., Hoerger, T. & Mandelblatt, J. (2002). Cost-effectiveness analyses of colorectal cancer screening: a systematic review for the US Preventive Services Task Force. *Annals of Internal Medicine, 137*, 96–104.

Playle, J. F., & Keeley, P. (1998). Non-compliance and professional power. *Journal of Advanced Nursing, 27*, 304–11.

Pollo, A., Amanzio, M., Arslanian, A., Casadio, C., Maggi, G. & Benedetti, F. (2001). Response expectancies in placebo analgesia and their clinical relevance. *Pain, 93*, 77–84.

Pollock, K. (1988). On the nature of social stress: production of a modern mythology. *Social Science and Medicine, 26*, 381–92.

Popay, J., Williams, G., Thomas, C. & Gatrell, T. (1998). Theorising inequalities in health: the place of lay knowledge. *Sociology of Health and Illness, 20*, 619–44.

Potter, J., & Wetherell, M. (1987). *Discourse and social psychology: beyond attitudes and behaviour*. London: Sage.

Pound, P., Gompertz, P. & Ebrahim, S. (1998). Illness in the context of older age: The case of stroke. *Sociology of Health and Illness, 20*, 489–506.

Powell, J., Darvell, M. & Gray, J. (2003). The doctor, the patient and the world-wide web: how the internet is changing healthcare. *Journal of the Royal Society of Medicine, 96*, 74–6.

Press, N., Fishman, J. R. & Koenig, B. A. (2000). Collective fear, individualized risk: the social and cultural context of genetic testing for breast cancer. *Nursing Ethics, 7*, 237–49.

Price, C. P. (2002). Foreword to 'Screening for disease'. *Clinica Chimica Acta, 315*, 1.

Prideaux, D. (2001). Cultural identity and representing culture in medical education: who does it? *Medical Education, 35*, 186–7.

Prilleltensky, I., & Fox, D. (1997). Introducing critical psychology: values, assumptions and the status quo. In D. Fox & I. Prilleltensky (eds.), *Critical psychology: an introduction* (pp. 3–20). London: Sage.

Prilleltensky, I., & Prilleltensky, O. (2003). Towards a critical health psychology practice. *Journal of Health Psychology, 8*, 197–210.

Prior, L. (2003). Belief, knowledge and expertise: the emergence of the lay expert in medical sociology. *Sociology of Health and Illness, 25*, 41–57.

Prior, L., Chun, P. L. & Huat, S. B. (2000). Beliefs and accounts of illness: views from two Cantonese-speaking communities in England. *Sociology of Health and Illness, 22*, 815–39.

Prochaska, R., & DiClemente, C. C. (1984). *The transtheoretical approach: crossing traditional boundaries of change*. Homewood, IL: Irwin.

Prochaska, R., DiClemente, C. C. & Norcross, J. C. (1992). In search of how people change: application to additive behaviours. *American Psychologist, 47*, 1102–14.

Prohaska, T. R., Keller, M. L., Leventhal, E. A. & Leventhal, H. (1987). Impact of symptoms and aging attribution on emotions and coping. *Health Psychology, 6*, 495–514.

Quah, S. H., & Bishop, G. D. (1996). Seeking help for illness. *Journal of Health Psychology, 1*, 209–22.

Radley, A. (1994). *Making sense of illness: the social psychology of health and disease*. London: Sage.

  (1997). What role does the body have in illness? In L. Yardley (ed.), *Material discourses of health and illness* (pp. 50–68). London: Routledge.

  (1999a). Social realms and the qualities of illness experience. In M. Murray & K. Chamberlain (eds.), *Qualitative health psychology* (pp. 16–30). London: Sage.

  (1999b). The aesthetics of illness: narrative, horror and the sublime. *Sociology of Health and Illness, 21*, 778–96.

  (2000). Health psychology, embodiment and the question of vulnerability. *Journal of Health Psychology, 5*, 298–304.

  (2004). Suffering. In M. Murray (ed.), *Critical health psychology* (pp. 31–43). New York: Palgrave.

Radley, A., & Billig, M. (1996). Accounts of health and illness: dilemmas and representations. *Sociology of Health and Illness, 18*, 220–40.

Radley, A., & Chamberlain, K. (2001). Health psychology and the study of the case: from method to analytic concern. *Social Science and Medicine, 53*, 321–32.

Raeburn, J., & Rootman, I. (1998). *People-centred health promotion*. Chichester, UK: John Wiley.

Rafferty, A., McGee, H., Miller, C. & Reyes, M. (2002). Prevalence of complementary and alternative medicine use: state-specific estimates from the 2001 behavioural risk factor surveillance system. *American Journal of Public Health, 92*, 1598–1600.

Raffle, A. E., Alden, B., Quinn, M., Babb, P. J. & Brett, M. T. (2003). Outcomes of screening to prevent cancer: analysis of cumulative incidence of cervical abnormality and modelling of cases and deaths prevented. *British Medical Journal, 326*, 901–4.

Ramirez, A. G. (2003). Consumer-provider research with special populations. *Patient Education and Counseling, 50*, 51–4.

Rapley, M. (2003). *Quality of life research: a critical introduction*. London: Sage.

Rapp, S., & Chao, D. (2000). Appraisals of strain and of gain: effects on psychological well-being of caregivers of dementia patients. *Ageing and Mental Health, 4*, 142–7.

Reich, R. B. (2002). *The future of success: work and life in the new economy*. London: Vintage.

Revenson, T. A. (1990). All other things are not equal: an ecological approach to personality and disease. In H. S. Friedman (ed.), *Personality and disease* (pp. 65–94). New York: John Wiley.

Richards, M. P. M. (1993). The new genetics: some issues for social scientists. *Sociology of Health and Illness, 15*, 567–86.

Richmond, K. (1998). Health promotion dilemmas. In J. Germov (ed.), *Second opinion: an introduction to health sociology* (pp. 156–73). Melbourne: Oxford University Press.

Rier, D. A. (2000). The missing voice of the critically ill: a medical sociologist's first-person account. *Sociology of Health and Illness, 22*, 68–93.

Ritchie, J., Herscovitch, F. & Norfor, J. (1994). Beliefs of blue collar workers regarding coronary risk behaviours. *Health Education Research, 9*, 95–103.

Roberts, A. H. (1995). The powerful placebo revisited: magnitude of nonspecific effects. *Mind/Body Machine, 1*, 35–43.

Robertson, A. (2001). Biotechnology, political rationality and discourses on health risk. *Health: an Interdisciplinary Journal for the Social Study of Health, Illness and Medicine, 5*, 239–309.

Robinson, I. (1990). Personal narratives, social careers and medical courses: analysing life trajectories in autobiographies of people with multiple sclerosis. *Social Science and Medicine, 30*, 1173–86.

Robinson, M. E., Riley, J. L., Myers, C. D., Papas, R. K., Wise, E. A., Waxendberg, L. B. *et al.* (2001). Gender role expectations of pain: relationship to sex differences in pain. *Journal of Pain, 2*, 251–7.

Rodin, J., & Ickovics, J. R. (1990). Women's health: review and research agenda as we approach the 21st century. *American Psychologist, 45*, 1018–34.

Rodrigue, J. R. (ed.) (2001). *Biopsychosocial perspectives on transplantation*. New York: Kluwer.

Rogers, E. (1983). *Diffusion of innovations*. New York: The Free Press.

Root, M. (2000). The problem of race in medicine. *Philosophy of the Social Sciences,* *31,* 20–39.

Rose, G. (1985). Sick individuals and sick populations. *International Journal of Epidemiology, 14,* 32–8.

Rose, N. (1989). Individualizing psychology. In J. Shotter & K. J. Gergen (eds.), *Texts of identity* (pp. 119–32). London: Sage.

  (1990). *Governing the soul: the shaping of the private self.* London: Routledge.

Rosella, J. (1994). Testicular cancer health education: an integrative review. *Journal of Advanced Nursing, 20,* 666–71.

Rosen, C. S. (2000). Is the sequencing of change processes by stage consistent across health problems? A meta-analysis. *Health Psychology, 19,* 593–604.

Rosenblatt, P. C. (2001). A social constructionist perspective on cultural differences in grief. In M. S. Stroebe, R. O. Hansson, W. Stroebe & H. Schut (eds.), *Handbook of bereavement research: consequences, coping and care* (pp. 285–300). Washington, DC: American Psychological Association.

Rosenman, R. H., Brand, R. J., Jenkins, C. D. *et al.* (1975). Coronary heart diseae in the Western Collaborative Group Study: final follow-up experiences of $8\frac{1}{2}$ years. *Journal of the American Medical Association, 223,* 872–7.

Rosenstock, I. M. (1974). Historical origins of the health belief model. *Health Education Monographs, 2,* 1–8.

Roter, D. L., & Hall, J. A. (1992). *Doctors talking with patients/patients talking with doctors.* Westport, CT: Auburn House.

Roter, D. L., Hall, J. A. & Aoki, Y. (2002). Physician gender effects in medical communication: a meta-analytic review. *Journal of the American Medical Association, 288,* 756–64.

Rotter, J. B. (1954). *Social learning and clinical psychology.* Englewood Cliffs, NJ: Prentice Hall.

  (1966). Generalized expectancies for internal and external control of reinformcent. *Psychological Monographs: General and Applied, 80,* 1–28.

Royak-Schaler, R., & Rose, D. P. (2002). Mammography screening and breast cancer biology in African American women: a review. *Cancer Detection and Prevention, 26,* 180–91.

Russell, K. M., Swenson, M. M., Skelton, A. M. & Shedd-Steele, R. (2003). The meaning of health in mammography screening for African American women. *Health Care for Women International, 24,* 27–39.

Ruston, A., Clayton, J. & Calnan, M. (1998). Patients' action during their cardiac event: qualitative study exploring differences and modifiable factors. *British Medical Journal, 316,* 1060–5.

Rutter, D., & Quine, L. (2002). *Changing health behaviour.* Buckingham, UK: Open University Press.

Sabo, D., & Gordon, D. F. (1995). *Men's health and illness: gender, power and the body.* Thousand Oaks, CA: Sage.

Sachs, W. (1992). Introduction. In W. Sachs (ed.), *The development dictionary* (pp. 1–5). London: Zed Books.

Saha, S., Komaromy, M., Koepsell, I. & Bindman, A. (1999). Patient–physician racial concordance and the perceived quality and use of health care. *Archives of Internal Medcine, 159,* 997–1004.

Salazar, M., & Carter, W. B. (1994). A qualitative description of breast self-examination beliefs. *Health Education Research*, *9*, 343–54.

Sales, E. (2003). Family burden and quality of life. *Quality of Life Research*, *12* (Suppl. 1), 33–41.

Salmon, P., & Quine, L. (1989). Patient's intentions in primary care: measurement and preliminary investigation. *Psychology and Health*, *3*, 103–10.

Saltonstall, R. (1993). Healthy bodies, social bodies: men's and women's concepts and practices of health in everyday life. *Social Science and Medicine*, *36*, 7–14.

Sampson, E. (2000). Of rainbows and differences. In T. Sloan (ed.), *Critical psychology: voices for change* (pp. 1–5). Houndmills, UK: Macmillan Press.

Santow, G. (1995). Social roles and physical health: the case of female disadvantage in poor countries. *Social Science and Medicine*, *40*, 147–61.

Sarafino, E. P. (1998). *Health psychology: biopsychosocial interactions*. New York: John Wiley.

Saunderson, E. M., & Ridsdale, L. (1999). General practitioners' beliefs and attitudes about how to respond to death and bereavement: qualitative study. *British Medical Journal*, *319*, 293–6.

Scaife, B., Gill, P., Heywood, P. & Neal, R. (2000). Socio-economic characteristics of adult frequent attenders in general practice: secondary analysis of data. *Family Practice*, *17*, 298–304.

Scambler, G. (2002). *Health and social change: a critical theory*. Buckingham, UK: Open University Press.

Scardino, P. T. (2003). The prevention of prostate cancer: the dilemma continues. *New England Journal of Medicine*, *349*, 295–7.

Schafer, T., Riehle, A., Wichmann, H. & Ring, J. (2002). Alternative medicine in allergies: prevalence, patterns abuse, and costs. *Allergy*, *57*, 694–700.

Scheier, M. F., & Bridges, M. W. (1995). Person variables and health: personality predispositions and acute psychological states as shared determinants for disease. *Psychosomatic Medicine*, *57*, 255–68.

Schelling, G., Richter, M., Roozendaal, B., Rothehausler, H., Krauseneck, T., Stoll, C. *et al.* (2003). Exposure to high stress in the intensive care unit may have negative effects on health-related quality-of-life outcomes after cardiac surgery. *Critical Care Medicine*, *31*, 1971–80.

Schneirov, M., & Geczik, J. (2002). Alternative health and the challenges of institutionalization. *Health: An Interdisciplinary Journal for the Social Study of Health, Illness and Medicine*, *6*, 201–20.

Schofield, P. E., Butow, P. N., Thompson, J. F., Tattersall, M. H. N., Beeney, L. J. & Dunn, S. M. (2003). Psychological responses of patients receiving a diagnosis of cancer. *Annals of Oncology*, *14*, 48–56.

Schrimshaw, E., & Siegel, K. (2003). Perceived barriers to social support from family and friends among older adults with HIV/AIDS. *Journal of Health Psychology*, *8*, 738–52.

Schultz, R., & Beach, S. (1999). Caregiving as a risk factor for mortality: the Caregiver Health Effects study. *Journal of the American Medical Association*, *282*, 2215–60.

Schulz, U., & Mohamed, N. (2004). Turning the tide: benefit finding after cancer surgery. *Social Science and Medicine*, *59*, 653–62.

Schwartz, A. R., Gerin, W., Davidson, K. W., Pickering, T. G., Brosschot, J. F., Thayer, J. F. *et al.* (2003). Toward a causal model of cardiovascular responses to stress and the development of cardiovascular disease. *Psychosomatic Medicine*, *65*, 22–35.

Schwartz, C., & Sprangers, M. (eds.) (2000). *Adaptation to changing health: response shift in quality-of-life research*. Washington, DC: American Psychological Association.

Schwartz, C., Sprangers, M., Carey, A. & Reed, G. (2004). Exploring response shift in longitudinal data. *Psychology and Health*, *19*, 51–69.

Schwartz, G. E. (1982). Testing the biopsychosocial model: the ultimate challenge facing behavioral medicine? *Journal of Consulting and Clinical Psychology*, *50*, 1040–53.

Schwarzer, R. (1992). *Self-efficacy: thought control of action*. London: Hemisphere.
  (1994). Optimism, vulnerability and self-beliefs as health-related cognitions: a systematic overview. *Psychology and Health*, *9*, 161–80.

Schwarzer, R., & Fuchs, R. (1996). Self-efficacy and health behaviours. In M. Conner & P. Norman (eds.), *Predicting health behaviour* (pp. 163–96). Buckingham, UK: Open University Press.

Schwarzer, R., & Leppin, A. (1989). Social support and health: a meta-analysis. *Psychology and Health*, *3*, 1–15.

Seale, C. (1995). Heroic death. *Sociology*, *29*, 597–613.
  (1998). *Constructing death: the sociology of dying and bereavement*. Cambridge: Cambridge University Press.
  (2000). Changing patterns of death and dying. *Social Science and Medicine*, *51*, 917–30.

Sears, S., Stanton, A. & Danoff-Berg, S. (2003). The yellow brick road and the emerald city: benefit finding, positive reappraisal coping and posttraumatic growth in women with early stage breast cancer. *Health Psychology*, *22*, 487–97.

Seedhouse, D. (1986). *Health: the foundations for achievement*. Chichester: John Wiley.

Seeman, T. E., Fagan Dubin, L. & Seeman, M. (2003). Religiosity/spirituality and health: a critical review of the evidence for biological pathways. *American Psychologist*, *58*, 53–63.

Selye, H. (1956). *The stress of life*. New York: McGraw-Hill.

Sen, K., & Bonita, R. (2000). Global health status: two steps forward, one step back. *Lancet*, *356*, 577–82.

Senior, M., & Viveash, B. (1998). *Health and illness*. Basingstoke, UK: Macmillan.

Seymour, J. E. (1999). Revisiting medicalisation and 'natural' death. *Social Science and Medicine*, *49*, 691–704.
  (2001). *Critical moments: death and dying in intensive care*. Buckingham, UK: Open University Press.

Seymour-Smith, S., Wetherell, M. & Phoenix, A. (2002). 'My wife ordered me to come!': a discursive analysis of doctors' and nurses' accounts of men's use of general practitioners. *Journal of Health Psychology*, *7*, 253–67.

Shapiro, D. (1996). *Your body speaks your mind: understand how your emotions affect your health*. London: Piatkus Books.

Shaw, M., Maxwell, R., Rees, K., Ho, D., Oliver, S., Ben-Shlomo, Y. *et al.* (2004). Gender and age inequity in the provision of coronary revascularisation in England in the 1990s: is it getting better? *Social Science and Medicine, 59,* 2499–507.

Shekelle, R. B., Hulley, S. B., Neaton, J. D., Billings, J. H., Borhani, N. O., Gerace, T. A. *et al.* (1985). The MRFIT behaviour pattern study. II: Type A behavior and incidence of coronary heart disease. *American Journal of Epidemiology, 122,* 559–70.

Sheridan, S., Pignone, M. & Donahue, K. (2003). Screening for high blood pressure: a review for the US Preventive Services Task Force. *American Journal of Preventive Medicine, 25,* 151–8.

Sherwood, A., & Turner, J. R. (1992). A conceptual and methodological overview of cardiovascular reactivity research. In J. R. Turner, A. Sherwood & K. C. Light (eds.), *Individual differences in cardiovascular responses to stress* (pp. 3–32). New York: Plenum Press.

Shin, K. R., Cho, M. O. & Kim, J. S. (2005). The meaning of death as experienced by elderly women of a Korean clan. *Qualitative Health Research, 15,* 5–18.

Shkolnikov, V., McKee, M. & Leon, D. A. (2001). Changes in life expectancy in Russia in the mid-1990s. *Lancet, 37,* 917–21.

Shoebridge, A., & Steed, L. (1999). Discourse about menopause in selected print media. *Australian and New Zealand Journal of Public Health, 23,* 475–81.

Shuldham, C. (1999a). A review of the impact of pre-operative education on recovery from surgery. *International Journal of Nursing Studies, 36,* 171–7.

(1999b). Pre-operative education: a review of the research design. *International Journal of Nursing Studies, 36,* 179–87.

Shuldham, C., Fleming, S. & Goodman, H. (2002). The impact of pre-operative education on recovery following coronary artery bypass surgery: a randomised controlled trial. *European Heart Journal, 23,* 666–74.

Shuval, J., Mizrachi, N. & Smetannikov, E. (2002). Entering the well-guarded fortress: alternative practitioners in hospital settings. *Social Science and Medicine, 55,* 1745–55.

Siegel, M. (2002). The effectiveness of state-level tobacco control interventions: a review of program implementation and behavioral outcomes. *Annual Review of Public Health, 23,* 45–71.

Siegman, A. W. (1994). From Type A to hostility to anger: reflections on the history of coronary-prone behaviour. In A. W. Siegman & T. W. Smith (eds.), *Anger, hostility and the heart* (pp. 1–21). Hillsdale, NJ: Erlbaum.

Simon, C. M. (1999). Images and image: technology and the social politics of revealing disorder in a North American hospital. *Medical Anthropology Quarterly, 13,* 141–62.

Singh, A., & Pandy, J. (1985). Dimensions of coping with socioeconomic problems. *Social Change, 15,* 51–4.

Skinner, E. A., Edge, K., Altman, J. & Sherwood, H. (2003). Searching for the structure of coping: a review and critique of category systems for classifying ways of coping. *Psychological Bulletin, 129,* 216–69.

Skinner, H., Biscope, S. & Poland, B. (2003). Quality of internet access: barrier behind internet use statistics. *Social Science and Medicine, 57,* 875–80.

Skolbekken, J. A. (1995). The risk epidemic in medical journals. *Social Science and Medicine, 40,* 291–305.

Sleath, B., Rubin, R. H., Campbell, W., Gwyther, L. & Clark, T. (2001). Physician–patient communication about over-the-counter medications. *Social Science and Medicine, 53,* 357–69.

Sloan, T. (ed.) (2000). *Critical psychology: voices for change.* Houndmills, UK: Macmillan Press.

Smedley, B., Stith, A. & Nelson, A. (eds.) (2002). *Unequal treatment: confronting ethnic and racial disparities in health care.* Washington, DC: National Academies Press.

Smith, A. (1988). Cervical cytology screening. *British Medical Journal, 296,* 1670.

Smith, D. J. (2004). Youth, sin and sex in Nigeria: Christianity and HIV/AIDS-related beliefs and behaviour among rural-urban migrants. *Culture, Health and Sexuality, 6,* 425–37.

Smith, M., & Smith, I. (1996). *Dr Mike Smith's Postbag: HRT.* London: Kyle Cathie Ltd.

Smith, R., & Studd, J. (1993). *The menopause and hormone replacement therapy.* London: Martin Dunitz.

Smith, T. W. (1994). Concepts and methods in the study of anger, hostility and health. In A. W. Siegman & T. W. Smith (eds.), *Anger, hostility and the heart* (pp. 33–48). Hillsdale, NJ: Erlbaum.

Smith, T. W., & Ruiz, J. M. (2002). Psychosocial influences on the development and course of coronary heart disease: current status and implications for research and practice. *Journal of Consulting and Clinical Psychology, 70,* 548–68.

Smith, T. W., & Spiro, A. (2002). Personality, health and aging: prolegomenon for the next generation. *Journal of Research in Personality, 36,* 363–94.

Smith, T. W., & Suls, J. (2004). Introduction to the special section on the future of health psychology. *Health Psychology, 23,* 115–18.

Snyder, S. L., & Mitchell, D. T. (2001). Re-engaging the body: disability studies and the resistance to embodiment. *Public Culture, 13,* 367–89.

Solomon, C. H., Pho, L. N. & Burt, R. W. (2002). Current status of genetic testing for colorectal cancer susceptibility. *Oncology, 16,* 161–71.

Solomon, L. J. (2003). What is postmodernism? Retrieved 12 March 2004 from http://music.research.home.att.net/postmod.htm.

Somerfield, M., & McRae, R. (2000). Stress and coping research: methodological challenges, theoretical advances, and clinical applications. *American Psychologist, 55,* 620–5.

Sontag, S. (1991). *Illness as metaphor: AIDS and its metaphors.* Harmondsworth: Penguin.

Spicer, J., & Chamberlain, K. (1996). Developing psychosocial theory in health psychology: problems and prospects. *Journal of Health Psychology, 1,* 161–71.

Stainton Rogers, W. (1991). *Explaining health and illness: an exploration in diversity.* London: Harvester Wheatsheaf.

(1996). Critical approaches to health psychology. *Journal of Health Psychology, 1,* 65–78.

Stam, H. J. (2000). Theorizing health and illness: functionalism, subjectivity and reflexivity. *Journal of Health Psychology*, *5*, 273–84.

(2004). A sound mind in a sound body: a critical historical analysis of health psychology. In M. Murray (ed.), *Critical health psychology* (pp. 15–30). New York: Palgrave.

Stam, H. J. (ed.) (1998). *The body and psychology*. London: Sage.

Stanton, A., Danoff-Burg, S., Twillman, R., Cameron, C., Bishop, M., Collins, C. *et al.* (2000). Emotionally expressive coping predicts psychological and physical adjustment to breast cancer. *Journal of Consulting and Clinical Psychology*, *68*, 875–82.

Steed, L. G. (1998). A critique of coping scales. *Australian Psychologist*, *33*, 193–202.

Steele, G. D. Jr (1994). The national cancer database report on colorectal cancer. *Cancer*, *74*, 1979–89.

Steptoe, A. (1998). Psychophysiological bases of disease. In D. W. Johnston & M. Johnston (eds.), *Comprehensive clinical psychology. VIII: Health psychology* (pp. 39–78). Oxford: Elsevier.

Steptoe, A., & Wardle, J. (2001). Locus of control and health behaviour revisited: a multivariate analysis of young adults from 18 countries. *British Journal of Psychology*, *92*, 659–72.

Steptoe, A., Lipsey, Z. & Wardle, J. (1998). Stress, hassles and variations in alcohol consumption, food choice and physical exercise: a diary study. *British Journal of Health Psychology*, *3*, 51–63.

Stevenson, F. A., Britten, N., Barry, C. A., Bradley, C. P. & Barber, N. (2003). Self-treatment and its discussion in medical consultations: how is medical pluralism managed in practice? *Social Science and Medicine*, *57*, 513–27.

Stewart-Williams, S., & Podd, J. (2004). The placebo effect: dissolving the expectancy versus conditioning debate. *Psychological Bulletin*, *130*, 24–40.

Stone, A. A., Neale, J. M., Cox, D. S., Napoli, A., Valdimarsdottir, H. & Kennedy-Moore, E. (1994). Daily events are associated with a secretory immune response to an oral antigen in men. *Health Psychology*, *13*, 440–6.

Stone, A. A., Porter, L. S. & Neale, J. M. (1993). Daily events and mood prior to the onset of respiratory illness episodes: a non-replication of the 3–5 day 'desirability dip'. *British Journal of Medical Psychology*, *66*, 383–93.

Stone, A. A., Reed, B. R. & Neale, J. M. (1987). Changes in daily event frequency precede episodes of physical symptoms. *Journal of Human Stress*, *13*, 70–4.

Stone, P., Richards, M., A'Hern, R. & Hardy, J. (2001). Fatigue in patients with cancer of the breast or prostate undergoing radical radiotherapy. *Journal of Pain and Symptom Management*, *22*, 1007–15.

Strobino, D. M., Grason, H. & Minkowitz, C. (2002). Charting a course for the future of women's health in the United States: concepts, findings and recommendations. *Social Science and Medicine*, *54*, 839–48.

Stroebe, M. S., & Schut, H. (2001). Models of coping with bereavement: a review. In M. S. Stroebe, R. O. Hansson, W. Stroebe & H. Schut (eds.), *Handbook of bereavement research: consequences, coping and care* (pp. 375–403). Washington, DC: American Psychological Association.

Stroebe, M. S., Hannson, R. O., Stroebe, W. & Schut, H. (2001). Introduction: concepts and issues in contemporary research on bereavement. In M. S. Stroebe, R. O.

Hansson, W. Stroebe & H. Schut (eds.), *Handbook of bereavement research: consequences, coping and care* (pp. 3–22). Washington, DC: American Psychological Association.

Stroebe, W. (2000). *Social psychology and health* (2nd edn). Buckingham, UK: Open University Press.

Sturm, R., & Unutzer, J. (2000/2001). State legislation and the use of complementary and alternative medicine. *Inquiry, 37*, 423–9.

Subramanian, S. V., Belli, P. & Kawachi, I. (2002). The macroeconomic determinants of health. *Annual Review of Public Health, 23*, 287–302.

Suls, J., & Rothman, A. (2004). Evolution of the biopsychosocial model: prospects and challenges for health psychology. *Health Psychology, 23*, 119–25.

Sundquist, K. (1992). *Menopause made easy: how to turn a change into a change for the better.* London: Robinson.

Tataryn, D. J. (2002). Paradigms of health and disease: a framework for classifying and understanding complementary and alternative medicine. *Journal of Alternative and Complementary Medicine, 8*, 877–92.

Tates, K., & Meeuwesen, L. (2001). Doctor–parent–child communication: a (re)view of the literature. *Social Science and Medicine, 52*, 839–51.

Taylor, S. E. (1999). *Health psychology* (4th edn). Boston: McGraw-Hill.

Taylor, S. E., Klein, L., Gruenewald, T., Gurung, R. & Fernandes-Taylor, S. (2003). Affiliation, social support, and biobehavioural responses to stress. In J. Suls & K. Wallston (eds.), *Social psychological foundations of health and illness* (pp. 314–31). Malden, MA: Blackwell.

Taylor, S. E., Repetti, R. L. & Seeman, T. (1997). Health psychology: what is an unhealthy environment and how does it get under the skin? *Annual Review of Psychology, 48*, 411–47.

Thibault-Prevost, J., Jensen, L. A. & Hodgins, M. (2000). Critical care nurses' perceptions of DNR status. *Journal of Nursing Scholarship, 32*, 259–65.

Thoits, P. A. (1995). Stress, coping and social support processes: where are we? What next? *Journal of Health and Social Behaviour* (Extra Issue), 53–79.

Thomas, C. (2003). Trade policy, the politics of access to drugs and global governance for health. In K. Lee (ed.), *Health impacts of globalization: towards global governance* (pp. 177–91). Basingstoke, UK: Palgrave Macmillan.

Thomas, K., Nicholl, J. & Coleman, P. (2001). Use and expenditure on complementary medicine in England: a population-based survey. *Complimentary Therapies in Medicine, 9*, 2–11.

Thomas-MacLean, R. (2004). Understanding breast cancer stories via Frank's narrative types. *Social Science and Medicine, 58*, 1647–57.

Thompson, I. M., Goodman, P. J., Tangen, C. M. *et al.* (2003). The influence of finasteride on the development of prostate cancer. *New England Journal of Medicine, 349*, 213–22.

Thompson, S. J., & Gifford, S. M. (2000). Trying to keep a balance: the meaning of health and diabetes in an urban Aboriginal community. *Social Science and Medicine, 51*, 1457–72.

Thornton, H., & Dixon-Woods, M. (2002). Prostate specific antigen testing for prostate cancer: engaging with the public may address their concerns and produce workable solutions. *British Medical Journal, 325*, 725–6.

Tibben, A., Timman, R., Bannink, E. C. & Duivenvoorden, H. J. (1997). Three-year follow-up after presymptomatic testing for Huntingdon's disease in tested individuals and partners. *Health Psychology*, *16*, 20–35.

Timmermans, S. (1998). Resuscitation technology in the emergency department: towards a dignified death. *Sociology of Health and Illness*, *20*, 144–67.

Totman, R. (1982). Psychosomatic theories. In J. R. Eiser (ed.), *Social psychology and behavioral medicine* (pp. 143–75). New York: John Wiley.

    (1987). *Social causes of illness* (2nd edn). London: Souvenir Press.

Tourigny, S. C. (1998). Some new dying trick: African American youths 'choosing' HIV/AIDS. *Qualitative Health Research*, *8*, 149–67.

Triandis, H. C. (1994). *Culture and social behavior*. New York: McGraw-Hill.

Trief, P. M., Sandberg, J., Greenberg, R., Graff, K., Castronova, N., Yoon, M. & Weinstock, R. Describing support: a qualitative study of couples living with diabetes. *Families, Systems & Health*, *21*, 57–67.

Trostle, J. A. (1988). Medical compliance as an ideology. *Social Science & Medicine*, *12*, 1299–1308.

Trumper, A., & Appleby, L. (2001). Psychiatric morbidity in patients undergoing heart, heart and lung, or lung transplantation. *Journal of Psychosomatic Research*, *50*, 103–5.

Turner, B. S. (1984). *The body and society: explorations in social theory*. Oxford: Blackwell.

    (1991). Recent developments in the theory of the body. In M. Featherstone, M. Hepworth & B. S. Turner (eds.), *The body: social process and cultural theory* (pp. 1–35). London: Sage.

Turner, R. J., Wheaton, B. & Lloyd, D. A. (1995). The epidemiology of social stress. *American Sociological Review*, *60*, 104–25.

Turner-Bowker, D. M., Bartley, P. J. & Ware, J. E. (2002). *SF-36 Health Survey and 'SF' Bibliography: Third Edition (1988–2000)*. Lincoln, RI: QualityMetric Incorporated.

Uchino, B. N., Cacioppo, J. T. & Kiecolt-Glaser, J. K. (1996). The relationship between social support and physiological processes: a review with emphasis on underlying mechanisms and implications for health. *Psychological Bulletin*, *119*, 488–531.

UNAIDS (1998). *AIDS Epidemic Update: December 1998*. Geneva: UNAIDS / World Health Organisation.

Underwood, B. (2002). Undernutrition. In C. Koop, C. Pearson & M. Schwarz (eds.), *Critical issues in global health* (pp. 229–37). San Francisco: Jossey-Bass.

Unger, R. K., & Crawford, M. (1996). *Women and gender: a feminist psychology*. New York: McGraw-Hill.

UNICEF (2005). *The state of the world's children 2005*. New York: United Nations. Retrieved 31 December 2004 from the UNICEF website: http://www.unicef.org.

United Nations Development Programme (2000). *Human development report 2000*. New York: United Nations Development Programme.

    (2004). *Human development report 2004*. New York: United Nations Development Programme.

United States Census Bureau (2002). *Statistical abstract of the United States: 2002* (122nd edn). Washington, DC: United States Census Bureau.

US Department of Health and Human Services (2000). *Healthy people 2010* Washington, DC US Department of Health and Human Services.

US Preventive Services Task Force (USPSTF) (2002). Update: Breast Cancer Screening. Retrieved 23 November 2003 from http://www.ahrq.gov/clinic/uspstf/uspsbrca.htm.

Vacek, P., Winstead-Fry, P., Secker-Walker, R., Hopper, G. & Plante, D. (2003). Factors influencing quality of life in breast cancer survivors. *Quality of Life Research*, *12*, 527–37.

van den Bosch, W. J., Huygen, F. J., van den Hoogen, H. J. & van Weel, C. (1992). Morbidity in early childhood: Differences between boys and girls. *British Journal of General Practice*, *42*, 366–9.

van der Riet, P. (1997). The body, the person, technologies and nursing. In J. Lawler (ed.), *The body in nursing* (pp. 95–107). Melbourne: Churchill Livingstone.

van der Weg, F., & Streuli, R. (2003). Use of alternative medicine by patients with cancer in a rural area of Switzerland. *Swiss Medical Weekly*, *133*, 233–40.

Van Dulmen, A. M. (1998). Children's contributions to pediatric outpatient encounters. *Pediatrics*, *102*, 563–8.

Van Dulmen, A. M., & Bensing, J. M. (2002). Health promoting effects of the physician–patient encounter. *Psychology, Health and Medicine*, *7*, 289–300.

Vedhara, K., Cox, N. K. M., Wilcock, G. K., Perks, P., Hunt, M., Anderson, S. *et al.* (1999). Chronic stress in elderly carers of dementia patients and antibody response to influenza vaccination. *Lancet*, *353*, 627–31.

Verbrugge, L. M. (1985). Gender and health: an update on hypotheses and evidence. *Journal of Health and Social Behavior*, *26*, 156–82.

    (1989). The twain meet: empirical explanations of sex differences in health and mortality. *Journal of Health and Social Behavior*, *30*, 282–304.

Verbrugge, L. M., & Ascione, F. J. (1987). Exploring the iceberg: common symptoms and how people care for them. *Medical Care*, *25*, 539–69.

Verna, M., Kronenfeld, J., Rivers, P. & Liang, S-Y. (2005). Assessing the effects of race and ethnicity on use of complementary and alternative therapies in the USA. *Ethnicity and Health*, *10*, 19–32.

Vickers, A. (2000). Recent advances: complementary medicine. *British Medical Journal*, *321*, 683–6.

Vitaliano, P., Young, H. & Zhang, J. (2004). Is caregiving a risk factor for illness? *Current Directions in Psychological Science*, *13*, 13–16.

Vitaliano, P., Zhang, J. & Scanlan, J. (2003). Is caregiving hazardous to one's physical health? A meta-analysis. *Psychological Bulletin*, *129*, 946–72.

Vitebsky, P. (1993). *Dialogues with the dead: the discussion of mortality among the Sora of Eastern India*. Cambridge: Cambridge University Press.

von Peter, S., Ting, W., Scrivani, S., Korkin, E., Okvat, H., Gross, M. *et al.* (2002). Survey on the use of complementary and alternative medicine among patients with headache syndromes. *Cephalalgia*, *22*, 395–400.

Wagstaff, A., & Watanabe, N. (2000). *Socioeconomic inequalities and child nutrition in the developing world*. Washington, DC: World Bank.

Waitzkin, H. (1983). *The second sickness: contradictions of capitalist health care*. New York: The Free Press.

Waldo, C. R., & Coates, T. S. (2000). Multiple levels of analysis and intervention in HIV prevention science: exemplars and directions for new research. *AIDS*, *14* (Suppl. 2), 518–26.

Waldron, I. (1995). Contributions of changing gender differentials in behaviour to changing gender differences in mortality. In D. Sabo & G. Gordon (eds.), *Men's health and illness: gender, power and the body* (pp. 22–45). London: Sage.

Wallston, K. A. (1992). Hocus-pocus, the focus isn't strictly on locus: Rotter's social learning theory modified for health. *Cognitive Therapy and Research*, *16*, 183–99.

Wallston, K. A., Wallston, B. S. & DeVellis, R. (1978). Development of multidimensional health locus of control (MHLC) scales. *Health Education Monographs*, *6*, 160–70.

Walsh, J. M. E., & Terdiman, J. P. (2003). Colorectal cancer screening: scientific review. *Journal of the American Medical Association*, *289*, 1288–96.

Walter, T. (1994). *The revival of death*. London: Routledge.

  (1996). A new model of grief: bereavement and biography. *Mortality*, *1*, 7–25.

Wang, C. (1992). Culture, meaning and disability: injury prevention campaigns and the production of stigma. *Social Science and Medicine*, *35*, 1093–1102.

Wardle, J., & Pope, R. (1992). The psychological costs of screening for cancer. *Journal of Psychosomatic Research*, *36*, 609–24.

Wass, H. (2001). Past, present and future of dying. *Illness, Crisis and Loss*, *9*, 90–110.

Watson, D., & Clark, L. A. (1984). Negative affectivity: the disposition to experience aversive emotional states. *Psychological Bulletin*, *96*, 465–90.

Watson, D., & Pennebaker, J. W. (1989). Health complaints, stress, and distress: exploring the central role of negative affectivity. *Psychological Review*, *96*, 234–54.

Weinstein, N. D., Rothman, A. J. & Sutton, S. R. (1998). Stage theories of health behavior: conceptual and methodological issues. *Health Psychology*, *17*, 290–9.

Weitz, R. (1999). Watching Brian die: the rhetoric and reality of informed consent. *Health: an Interdisciplinary Journal for the Social Study of Health, Illness and Medicine*, *3*, 209–27.

Welch Cline, R. J. (2003). At the intersection of micro and macro: opportunities and challenges for physician–patient communication research. *Patient Education and Counseling*, *50*, 13–16.

Wetzel, M., Eisenberg, D. & Kaptchuk, T. (1998). Courses involving complementary and alternative medicine at US medical schools. *Journal of the American Medical Association*, *280*, 784–7.

Wheeler, I. (2001). Parental bereavement: the crisis of meaning. *Death Studies*, *25*, 51–66.

Whelan, T., & Kirkby, R. (1998). Advantages for children and their families of psychological preparation for hospitalisation and surgery. *Journal of Family Studies*, *4*, 35–51.

Whitaker, E. D. (2003). The idea of health: history, medical pluralism, and the management of the body in Emilia-Romagna, Italy. *Medical Anthropology Quarterly*, *17*, 348–75.

WHOQOL Group (1998). The World Health Organisation Quality of Life Assessment (WHOQOL): development and general psychometric properties. *Social Science and Medicine*, *46*, 1569–85.

Wilkinson, R. G. (1996). *Unhealthy societies: the afflictions of inequality*. London: Routledge.

(1997). Comment: income, inequality and social cohesion. *American Journal of Public Health*, *87*, 1504–6.

Williams, D. R., & Collins, C. (1995). US socioeconomic and racial differences in health: patterns and explanations. *Annual Review of Sociology*, *21*, 349–86.

Williams, G. H. (2003). The determinants of health: structure, context and agency. *Social Science & Medicine*, *25*, 131–54.

Williams, P. G., & Wiebe, D. J. (2000). Individual differences in self-assessed health: gender, neuroticism and physical symptom reports. *Personality and Individual Differences*, *28*, 823–35.

Williams, R. (1990). *A Protestant legacy: attitudes towards death and illness among older Aberdonians*. Oxford: Clarendon Press.

Williams, S. J. (2000). Chronic illness as biographical disruption or biographical disruption as chronic illness? Reflections on a core concept. *Sociology of Health and Illness*, *22*, 40–67.

Willig, C. (2000). A discourse-dynamic approach to the study of subjectivity in health psychology. *Theory and Psychology*, *10*, 547–70.

Willis, E. (1998). The Human Genome Project: a sociology of medical technology. In J. Germov (ed.), *Second opinion: an introduction to health sociology* (pp. 174–88). Oxford: Oxford University Press.

Wilson, H., Hutchinson, S. & Holzemer, W. (2002). Reconciling incompatibilities: a grounded theory of HIV medication adherence and symptom management. *Qualitative Health Research*, *12*, 1309–22.

Wilson, R. C. D. (1996). *Understanding HRT and the menopause*. London: Which? Books Consumer's Association.

Winefield, H. R. (1992). Doctor–patient communication: an interpersonal helping process. In S. Maes, H. Leventhal & M. Johnston (eds.), *International review of health psychology, I*. (pp. 167–87). Chichester: John Wiley.

Winett, R. A. (1995). A framework for health promotion and disease prevention programs. *American Psychologist*, *50*, 341–50.

Wittkowski, J. (2001). The construction of the Multidimensional Orientation towards Dying and Death Inventory (MODDI-F). *Death Studies*, *25*, 479–95.

Wohl, R. E., & Kane, W. M. (1997). Teacher's beliefs concerning teaching about testicular cancer and testicular self-examination. *Journal of School Health*, *67*, 106–11.

Wolf, R. L., Zybert, P., Brouse, C. H., Neugut, A. I., Shea, S., Gibson, G. *et al.* (2001). Knowledge, beliefs, and barriers relevant to colorectal cancer screening in an urban population: a pilot study. *Family and Community Health*, *24*, 34–47.

Woolf, S. H. (1996). Immunizations. In S. H. Woolf, S. Jonas & R. S. Lawrence (eds.), *Health promotion and disease prevention in clinical practice* (pp. 388–425). Baltimore: Williams and Wilkins.

(2001). The accuracy and effectiveness of routine population screening with mammography, prostate-specific antigen, and prenatal ultrasound: a review of the published scientific evidence. *International Journal of Technology Assessment in Health Care, 17*, 275–304.

Woolf, S., Johnson, R., Fryer, G., Rust, G. & Satcher, D. (2004). The health impact of resolving racial disparities: an analysis of US mortality data. *American Journal of Public Health, 94*, 2078–81.

Worchester, N., & Whatley, M. H. (1992). The selling of HRT: playing on the fear factor. *Feminist Review, 41*, 1–26.

Worden, J. W. (1991). *Grief counselling and grief therapy: a handbook for the mental health practitioner* (2nd edn). New York: Springer.

Working Party (1997). *From compliance to concordance: achieving shared goals in medicine taking*, Report of the Working Party. London: Royal Pharmaceutical Society of Great Britain/Merck, Sharp and Dohme.

World Health Organisation (1946). *Constitution*. New York: World Health Organisation.

(1998). *World health report*. Geneva: World Health Organisation.

(1999). *Poverty and health: report by the Director-General*. World Health Organisation, Executive Board, RB105/5.

(2001a). *Poverty and health: evidence and action in WHO's European region*. World Health Organisation, Regional Office for Europe, EUR/RC51/8.

(2001b). WHO and top publishers announce breakthrough on developing countries' access to leading biomedical journals. World Health Organisation, Press Release, WHO/32, 9 July, 2001.

(2002). *WHO traditional medicine strategy 2002–2005*. Geneva: World Health Organisation.

(2004). *The World Health Report 2004: changing history*. Geneva: World Health Organisation.

(n.d.). *WHO Estimates of Health Personnel*. Retrieved 15 November 2003 from WHO Statistics at the World Health Organisation website: http://www3. who.int.

Wright, E. C. (1993). Non-compliance: or how many aunts has Matilda? *Lancet, 342*, 909–13.

Wright, K., & Bell, S. (2003). Health-related support groups on the Internet: linking empirical findings to social support and computer-mediated communication theory. *Journal of Health Psychology, 8*, 39–54.

Writing Group for the Women's Health Initiative Investigators (2002). Risks and benefits of estrogen plus progestin in healthy postmenopausal women. *Journal of the American Medical Association, 288*, 321–33.

Wynd, C. A. (2002). Testicular self-examination in young adult men. *Journal of Nursing Scholarship, 34*, 251–5.

Yali, A. M., & Revenson, T. A. (2004). How changes in population demographics will impact health psychology: incorporating a broader notion of cultural competence into the field. *Health Psychology, 23*, 147–55.

Yang, E. V., & Glaser, R. (2002). Stress-induced immunomodulation and the implications for health. *International Immunopharmacology, 2*, 315–24.

Yarbrough, S. S., & Braden, C. J. (2001). Utility of health belief model as a guide for explaining or predicting breast cancer screening behaviours. *Journal of Advanced Nursing, 33*, 677–88.

Yardley, L. (1997). *Material discourses of health and illness*. London: Routledge.

Yaskowitch, K., & Stam, H. (2003). Cancer narratives and the cancer support group. *Journal of Health Psychology*, *8*, 720–37.

Yedidia, M. J., & MacGregor, B. (2001). Confronting the prospect of dying: reports of terminally ill patients. *Journal of Pain and Symptom Management*, *22*, 807–19.

Yee, J., & Schultz, R. (2000). Gender differences in psychiatric morbidity among family caregivers: a review and analysis. *The Gerontologist*, *40*, 147–64.

Yeh, G., Eisenberg, D., Davis, R. & Phillips, R. (2002). Use of complementary and alternative medicine among persons with diabetes mellitus: results of a national survey. *American Journal of Public Health*, *92*, 1648–52.

Yoder, P. S. (1997). Negotiating relevance: belief, knowledge and practice in international health projects. *Medical Anthropology Quarterly*, *11*, 131–46.

Young, A. (1980). The discourse on stress and the reproduction of conventional knowledge. *Social Science and Medicine*, *148*, 133–46.

Zborowski, M. (1952). Cultural components in responses to pain. *Journal of Social Issues*, *8*, 16–30.

Zeppetella, G. (1999). How do terminally ill patients at home take their medication? *Palliative Medicine*, *13*, 469–75.

Ziebland, S., Chapple, A., Dumelow, C., Evans, J., Prinjha, S. & Rozmovits, L. (2004). How the Internet affects patients' experience of cancer: a qualitative study. *British Medical Journal*, *328*, 564-9.

Zipfel, S., Schneider, A., Wild, B., Loewe, B., Juenger, J., Haass, M. *et al.* (2002). Effect of depressive symptoms on survival after heart transplantation. *Psychosomatic Medicine*, *64*, 740–7.

Zola, I. (1966). Culture and symptoms: an analysis of patients presenting complaints. *American Sociological Review*, *31*, 615–30.

    (1972). Medicine as an institution of social control. *Sociological Review, 29,* 487–504.

    (1973). Pathways to the doctor – from person to patient. *Social Science and Medicine, 7,* 677–98.

Zollman, C., & Vickers, A. (1999a). ABC of complementary medicine: complementary medicine in conventional practice. *British Medical Journal*, *319*, 901–4.

    (1999b). ABC of complementary medicine: what is complementary medicine? *British Medical Journal, 319,* 693–6.

Author index

Subject index